Empiricism and the Foundations of Psychology

Advances in Consciousness Research (AiCR)

Provides a forum for scholars from different scientific disciplines and fields of knowledge who study consciousness in its multifaceted aspects. Thus the Series includes (but is not limited to) the various areas of cognitive science, including cognitive psychology, brain science, philosophy and linguistics. The orientation of the series is toward developing new interdisciplinary and integrative approaches for the investigation, description and theory of consciousness, as well as the practical consequences of this research for the individual in society.

From 1999 the Series consists of two subseries that cover the most important types of contributions to consciousness studies:

Series A: Theory and Method. Contributions to the development of theory and method in the study of consciousness; Series B: Research in Progress. Experimental, descriptive and clinical research in consciousness.

This book is a contribution to Series A.

For an overview of all books published in this series, please see
http://benjamins.com/catalog/aicr

Editor

Maxim I. Stamenov
Bulgarian Academy of Sciences

Editorial Board

Volume 87

Empiricism and the Foundations of Psychology
by John-Michael Kuczynski

Empiricism and the Foundations of Psychology

John-Michael Kuczynski
Virginia Commonwealth University

John Benjamins Publishing Company
Amsterdam / Philadelphia

^{TM} The paper used in this publication meets the minimum requirements of
the American National Standard for Information Sciences – Permanence
of Paper for Printed Library Materials, ANSI z39.48-1984.

Library of Congress Cataloging-in-Publication Data

Kuczynski, John-Michael.
    Empiricism and the foundations of psychology / John-Michael Kuczynski.
        p.   cm. (Advances in Consciousness Research, ISSN 1381-589X ; v. 87)
    Includes bibliographical references and index.
    1. Consciousness. 2. Psychology. 3. Empiricism. I. Title.
    BF311.K813   2012
    150.1--dc23   2012009871
    ISBN 978 90 272 1353 2   (Hb ; alk. paper)
    ISBN 978 90 272 7385 7   (Eb)

John Benjamins Publishing Co. · P.O. Box 36224 · 1020 ME Amsterdam · The Netherlands
John Benjamins North America · P.O. Box 27519 · Philadelphia PA 19118-0519 · USA

To my mother, Jane Casey

I couldn't have done it without you, mom!

Table of contents

Part I

Part II

PART I

CHAPTER 1

Introduction
Empiricism and scientism

1.0   The present work consists of two parts. In Part I, it will be argued that a doctrine known as "empiricism" is untenable. Empiricism is the doctrine that all knowledge is either

    (i)   directly derived from observation,

or

    (ii) derived from observation in accordance with inference-rules of whose validity observation has apprised one.[1]

Thus, for the empiricist, a belief isn't justified unless it is directly or *almost* directly justified by observation.

In Part II, it will be shown that attempts to empiricize psychology have had ruinous effects on that discipline.

To say that attempts have been made to "empiricize" psychology is to say that attempts have been made to reconstitute it so that both its methodology and its results are compliant with the strictures of empiricism.

1.1   In attempting to empiricize psychology, or any other scientific discipline, one is on a fool's errand. The external world would be nothing more than a collection of mutually disconnected, *ex nihilo* events if all there were to it was what observation revealed. To the extent that a scientist complies with the empiricist credo that one must "stick to the facts," he cannot embed observable events in otherwise unobservable continuities. Thus forced to hold that such events occur spontaneously, he is *ipso facto* incapable of explaining them and, therefore, of restoring to the external world the integrity of which raw observation has stripped it.

Similar but more extreme points hold of the *internal* world. If completely described by the information borne in his conscious experiences, a given person's mind would consist of spontaneities internal to stretches of consciousness that, flanked by lapses in consciousness, would themselves be spontaneities. Not permitted to embed

---

1.   In this context, the word "observation" refers to *sensory* observation – sight, audition, touch, etc. – and also to non-sensory, but direct experience, such as one has of one's pains, tickles, and conscious mental images.

conscious events within otherwise unconscious psychological continuities, the empiricist is *ipso facto* incapable of explaining them and, therefore, of restoring to the mind the integrity of which conscious introspection has stripped it.

1.2   Of course, the mind is but one small part of a larger reality. Since mental events are obviously mediated by physiological structures, it is widely held that the mere existence of such structures accounts for the discontinuities within conscious experience. According to this viewpoint, absorbing the mental into the physiological eliminates the pockets of nothingness that pervade conscious experience, and there is thus no need to embed unconsciousness-flanked bouts of consciousness, or the events internal to such bouts, in otherwise unconscious psychological continuities: the data is adequately modeled by citing the independently verified fact that consciousness is mediated by continuously existing, explanatorily intact physiological structures.[2]

1.2.1   This line of thought involves four oversights. First, it doesn't distinguish the statement that:

(i)   X's parts are governed by laws $L_n...L_n$

from the non-equivalent statement that:

(ii)   X itself is governed by $L_n...L_n$.

Second, it doesn't distinguish the statement that:

(i*)   X complies with the same laws as Y,

from the non-equivalent statement that:

(ii*)   X-internal events are to be explained in terms of the same principles as Y-internal events.

Third, it doesn't distinguish statement that:

(a)   X is the cause of Y,

from the non-equivalent statement that:

(b)   The occurrence (or existence) of Y is to be explained in terms of that of X.

The third oversight is a consequence of the fourth, namely: This line of reasoning doesn't distinguish the statement:

---

2.   This is what Carnap (1934) says. In that work, Carnap says that all legitimate science is (watered down) physics. In his view, biology, *qua* legitimate science, is merely watered down physics.

(A)   Hypothesis H models observational (or experiential) data $d_1 \ldots d_n$.

From the non-equivalent statement that:

(B)   Hypothesis H identifies the data-transcendent facts in virtue of which $d_1 \ldots d_n$ hold.

Thus, we have just put forth four contentions, namely that the argument in 1.2 fails to distinguish between (i)/(ii)/(a)/(A) and (i*)/(ii*)/(b)/(B). No two of these contentions perfectly coincide, but any given two of them are *near* corollaries of each other.

1.2.2   The term "mediate" occurred in Section 1.2, and it will often occur in the pages to come. Before proceeding, I must say exactly what I mean by that term, and I will take the opportunity to say exactly what I will mean by a few other terms that will frequently occur in this book. Those terms are "proposition," "fact," "thing," "object," "concept," "property," and "universal."

To say that that x "mediates" y is say that y's existence *constitutively* depends on x's. By this it is meant that the things composing y are identical with (a subset of) the things composing x. Your house would cease to exist if the bricks composing it ceased to exist. So your house's existence depends on that of those bricks. But those bricks don't *cause* your house to exist. Your house's existence is therefore not causally, but *constitutively*, dependent on that of those bricks.

A "proposition," as I will be using this word, is what one affirms when one makes a statement. If I say "snow is white," I am affirming the proposition that snow is white. That proposition is not identical with the sentence "snow is white," or with any other sentence. (That is why that proposition can be the meaning of distinct sentences, e.g. "schnee ist weiss" and "snow is white.") Moreover, that proposition is not identical with my usage of that sentence or indeed with anyone's usage of any expression. The *act* of affirming a given proposition is to be distinguished from that proposition itself, and so is the sentence used to carry out that act.

In the context of the present work, "truth" and "falsehood" are synonymous with, respectively, "true proposition" and "false proposition." In everyday life, we often describe sentences, or occurrences of sentences, as "truths" and "falsehoods." But a given sentence is true only by virtue of its association with a true proposition. So to say that a sentence S is true is to say that S has a true proposition for its meaning; it is to say, in other words, that S bears a true meaning. But to describe a proposition as "true" obviously isn't to say that it *bears* a true meaning: propositions *are* meanings; they don't *bear* them. (Later in this chapter, we will make it clear what it means to describe a proposition as "true.") Thus, the terms "true" and "false," as ordinarily used, are ambiguous. But they are not ambiguous, as we will be using them.

When I refer to "facts," I am *not* referring to truths; I am referring to the data-transcendent realities in virtue of which truths hold; I am referring, in other words, to the externalities that make certain propositions true. I am referring to rocks and trees and protons, and also to the changes undergone by such things, and also to changes undergone by object-free energy-fields.

Jim just had a heart attack, let us suppose. This event consisted of a redistribution of mass-energy. The proposition that Jim just had a heart attack holds *in virtue of* that redistribution of mass-energy. So that proposition is a truth and that redistribution of mass-energy is a fact. *That fact is not identical with that truth.* It remains a truth that Jim had a heart attack, but the corresponding fact is no more. Given any truth, a similar argument shows that it is distinct from the fact in virtue of which it holds.

For an object of a certain kind to exist is for mass-energy to be allocated in a certain way. Therefore, changes in objects are *redistributions of mass-energy*. But I will use the term "redistribution of mass-energy" to refer to *any* change, even ones that involve object-free energy-fields.

Some truths (e.g. *the cat is on the mat*) hold in virtue of static situations and, therefore, in virtue of static allocations of mass-energy. Such facts are mere distributions, as opposed to *re*distributions, of mass-energy. I will use the word "fact" to refer to both distributions and redistributions of mass-energy. I will often use the term "(re)distribution of mass-energy," leaving it to the context how it is to be disambiguated.

An event is nothing other than a redistribution of mass-energy. Therefore, we will use the word "fact" to refer to events, as well as to objects, and also to static assemblages thereof.

We will use the word "thing" to refer to rocks, trees, and other similarly "concrete" objects. We will not use the word "thing" to refer to numbers, principles, or other abstract entities. The words "object" and "thing" will be used interchangeably.

A "property" is a characteristic. Anything that has a given property is an "instance" of it. Two is an even number; therefore, it has the property of being an even number; therefore, it is an instance of that property. In the present work, the terms "property" and "universal" are synonyms. Two is an even number; therefore, it has the property of being an even number; therefore, it is an instance of the universal *even number*.

In the present work, "property" and "concept" will be veritable synonyms. (Why "veritable"? See below.) For two to be an even number is for it to fall under they concept *even number*. But in some contexts, a distinction will be made between properties and concepts. The property of being an even prime is identical with the property of being identical with the number two: it is incoherent to suppose that anything should have the one property but lack the other; wherefore, those two properties are one. But the concept *even prime* is distinct from the concept *identical with the number two*. That is why one can have the concept of the number two without having the concept of an even prime.

This way of using the word "concept" is not stipulative. It would be contrary to extant usage of that term to identify the concept of being an even number with the concept of being identical with the number two. That said the words "property" and "concept" can almost always be treated as synonyms, and on the rare occasions when they cannot be so treated, it will be made clear how differ in meaning.

Concepts are not psychological entities. When we say that the Romans didn't have *the* concept of the number zero, we are not saying that there is some part of somebody's mind that the Romans didn't grasp. One's *grasp* of a concept is a psychological entity, but not that concept *per se*. (This is subject to a qualification. We will occasionally will use the word "concept" to refer to a person's grasp of something and, consequently, to something psychological. This is how we will use it in, for example, Section 7.4.1 of the present chapter.) Exactly what concepts are will be stated in Chapter 3, Section 8.2.1. But, as previously stated, in the present work, the terms "concept" and "property" are effectively synonymous; and on the rare occasions when they are not functioning as synonyms in this work, it will be made clear exactly how they are functioning.

Having taken care of these terminological preliminaries, we can now evaluate the claim that the mind is to be understood in physiological terms.

1.2.3   First of all, mentality *is* mediated by physiology.[3] But it doesn't follow that principles in terms of which the physiological are to be understood coincide with those in terms of which the mental is to be understood. A story will make this clear.

My house's micro-constituents are differently arranged from your house's micro-constituents; and because my house isn't built out of the same kind of material as your house, the one's micro-constituents are qualitatively different from the other's. But *within the limits set by those facts*, our houses are qualitatively identical, and the micro-structural differences between them lead to no macrostructural differences. (This is a legitimate assumption: given two rockets that are identical from the viewpoint of

---

3.   Throughout this book, I operate on the assumption that mental events are mediated, or constituted, by physical events – that "materialism" is correct, in other words. But this assumption plays no substantive role in the forthcoming argumentation, all of which is neutral with respect to whether it is dualism or materialism that is correct. Little more than my phraseology is affected by my assumption that materialism is correct.

There are relatively few philosophical psychologists who are as sympathetic to dualism as I am. That said, there are reasons to accept materialism. For example: Given the fact that the mental affects the physical, and *vice versa*, and given that the exchanges of energy between the mental and physical realms do not perforate or undermine the nomic integrity of the physical world, it follows that the mind is itself physical (in the sense that it's constituted by physical events). But, for reasons that I am currently in the process of stating, I believe that there is an "explanatory gap" – that there is no way to understand the mental *in terms of* the physical. More precisely, letting $P_1 \ldots P_n$ be any physicalistic statements (statements concerning the spatiotemporal realm that involve no concepts such as *perception, shame, hope*, etc.) and letting $M_1 \ldots M_m$ be any mentalistic statements, there is no way to understand why $P_1 \ldots P_n$, given that are true, $M_1 \ldots M_m$ should also be true. So I am an explanatory dualist, if not an ontological dualist.

Why do I accept materialism (of the ontological, not the epistemic variety)? The physical world is causally closed. Whatever affects it is physical, and so is whatever it affects. The mental affects the physical. So the mental must be physical. Smart (1959) puts forth this argument, as does Fodor (1968).

See Kuczynski (1999, 2000, 2004) for attempts on the present author's part to defend dualism. These can be accessed online at: http://philpapers.org/s/John-Michael%20Kuczynski

a NASA engineer, even one shorn of all human limitations, the chances of them being microstructurally identical are nil.) Also, those houses are in qualitatively identical environments. So nothing happens to the one the exact likes of which doesn't happen to the other.

One day, because of an architectural defect, the one house falls, and so, consequently, does the other. Speaking from a mechanical, but *not* a molecular point of view, both houses fell for the same reasons. By hypothesis, each house is composed of molecules and, therefore, is in some sense nothing but an aggregate of molecules. We must therefore conclude that:

(WP[4])   Given either one of those houses, the laws governing that house *qua* macro-entity are different from those governing it *qua* aggregate of micro-entities.

WP entails that:

(WP*)   Given either one of those houses, the *principles* in terms of which its macro-characteristics are to be understood are different from those in terms of which its microcharcteristics are to be understood.

By parallel reasoning, the fact that

(PM[5])   the physiological mediates the mental,

doesn't entail that

(PM*)   the laws governing the physiological are identical with those governing the mental,

A fortiori PM doesn't entail that

(PM#)   the mental is to be understood in terms of the same principles as the physiological.

These points explain and justify the 1st and 2nd contentions put forth in Section 1.2.1, and they establish that, given only that the physiological mediates the psychological,

---

4.   Short for "whole, part." In this book, I will frequently put the viewpoints of actual or, more usually, hypothetical (but representative of actual) interlocutors in indented passages. And I will give each such passage a two-letter label, so as to make it easier to refer to it. In each case, the letters in question are associatively connected with the contents of the indented passage in question. I do not know of any author who does this. But this practice conduces to clarity and brevity. It makes it clear whether or not a given statement expresses the author's position or someone else's. And it makes it unnecessary to use the tedious locutions associated with indirect discourse.

5.   Short for "physiological, mental."

we cannot conclude that psychology is to be studied physiologically. We cannot conclude that some one set of laws governs both domains.[6]

To be sure, the physiological *implements* the psychological; therefore, psychological events *comply* with physiological laws. But that does not mean that physiological laws *govern* psychological events. Nor does it mean that psychological events are to be understood in terms of physiological laws. Your IBM's hardware complies with the laws of physics; its hardware mediates its software, and the events mediated by its software therefore comply with the laws of physics. But you can completely understand your computer's software-mediated events while having only a schematic and low-resolution knowledge of the hardware underlying those events; and you can completely understand the physical events mediating your computer's operations without understanding those operations or even knowing of their existence. Indeed, one could have a completely exhaustive knowledge of your IBM's hardware and not even be in a position to make rational inferences as to the nature of the operations mediated by those events. For those operations are to be understood in terms of concepts (*storage device, input device, random access memory*) that have no place in physics; and physics is therefore blind to propositions involving such concepts and to the events that those propositions describe.

1.2.4   The 3rd and 4th distinctions identified in Section 1.2.1 have an even deeper bearing on the viability of attempts to scientize psychology by physiologicizing it. Science aspires to identify data-transcendent realities. But we have no way of identifying such realities except *by way of* correct models of the data. And when evaluating the fitness of a model, the relevant question cannot be "Does it fit data-transcendent facts?" For we must establish the fitness of a model *in order* to have any reason to believe it to fit the facts. The fitness of a given model is to be determined by comparing it with the data, as opposed to data-transcendent facts.

Explanation is indeed about finding causes and discovering hidden continuities. (Henceforth, take "continuity" to be short for "continuity or cause."[7]) But those continuities must be model-internal. The data-transcendent entities studied by medicine are identical with (a subset of) of those studied by microphysics. But the data modeled by the former discipline is not (a subset of) that modeled by the latter. For the physician, each of the following is a datum:

(1) Jones is alive.

(2) Brown is dead.

(3) Smith can't move his arms.

---

6. Fodor (1974, 1997) makes similar points.

7. In Chapter 8, we'll see that causes are *ipso facto* instances of continuity and also that instances of continuities are *ipso facto* causes.

(4)   Anderson's breathing is labored.

(5)   Walton's halitosis is even worse than before.

None of those truths is a datum for the microphysicist. Indeed, (1)–(5) don't even exist for him: the concepts *life, death, respiration*, etc. are not ones in terms of which physical (physics-related) laws are formulated, and there is no physical characterization of terms such as *respiration, halitosis*. Similarly, the concepts constitutive of microphysical data (*spin, charge*, etc.) are not ones in terms of physiological laws are formulated. This is because two things that are physiologically identical may be non-physiologically different. No matter how physiologically alike two instances of respiration are, there are no limits to much their respective physical implementations may differ.

Explanations are given by propositions. Thus, it isn't *things* that explain *things*. It is *propositions* that explain *propositions*. Therefore,

(XY)   Given only that X is in fact the cause of Y, it doesn't follow that to explain Y is to show that X is its cause.

X doesn't explain anything, and Y isn't explained by anything. Propositions *about* X and about Y can explain or be explained. But since X and Y aren't propositions, neither explains anything or is explained by anything.

Propositions consist of concepts. The proposition: *Smith is taller than Jones, but Jones is more intelligent than Smith* consists of the concepts *tall, intelligent*, etc. The concepts of life, death, respiration, etc. fall within the scope of medicine, and so do the propositions that they compose. So the medical researcher explains why (4) is true. But he doesn't thereby explain why the corresponding microphysical propositions are true, since the concepts *spin, charge*, etc. don't fall within his field of study and neither, therefore, do the propositions they compose.

The fact in virtue of whose existence (4) is true consists of events of precisely the sort that the microphysicist explains (displacements of tiny quanta of energy). The microphysicist is in principle capable of explaining propositions that hold in virtue of those facts. But *those* propositions consist of concepts like *charge* and *wavicle*, none of which are to be found in any physiological statement.

For the physiologist, the truth of the proposition

(6)   Anderson has severe asthma and he just smoked a pack of cigarettes.

accounts for the truth of (4). For the microphysicist, (6) doesn't even exist, and neither does (4).

The explanatory generalizations of a given discipline consist of concepts distinct from those composing the explanatory generalizations of other disciplines. For the physiologist, the proposition

(7)   Smoking causes asthmatics to experience respiratory distress

is an explanatory generalization. It is only *relative* to that generalization, or some other similar generalization, that (6) explains (4). But, for the microphysicist, (7) is quite as non-existent as (4) and (6). Therefore, (7) is useless for the microphysicist. First of all, it doesn't exist as far as he's concerned. But even if it did, the propositions amongst which (7) establishes bearing-relations don't exist for the microphysicist.

(4) holds in virtue of some fact x. (6) holds in virtue of some fact y. Let m and m* be accurate and complete microphysical description of x and y, respectively. (4) holds in virtue of the very same fact as m, and (6) holds in virtue of the very same fact as m*. Even though x and y are the data-transcendent facts in virtue of which (4)/m and (6)/m*, respectively, are true, y isn't to be explained in terms of x. Propositions about y are to be explained in terms of propositions about x. But if the former propositions belong to microphysics and the latter to physiology, the former will have no bearing on the latter. The bearing relation between (4) and (6) is to be found in (7). (7) doesn't establish any such relation between (4) and m*, or between m and (6), or between any two propositions only one of which belongs to physiology. The same thing *mutatis mutandis* is true of m#, where m# is the generalization relative to which m explains m*.

1.2.4.1   Data are given by propositions. Let us refer to such propositions as "data-propositions." Propositions consist of concepts. Let us refer to those composing data-propositions as "data-concepts."

If D is a given discipline, and $C_1...C_n$ are D's data-concepts, $C_1...C_n$ determine the membership of the set of D-distinctive concepts. They determine that set's membership in two ways. First, they are themselves among its members. Second, the theoretical propositions of that discipline must consist of concepts that are so related to $C_1...C_n$ that those propositions bear on the relevant data-propositions.

Since the class of microphysical concepts doesn't overlap with the class of physiological concepts, no proposition belonging to the one discipline can account for the truth of any proposition belonging to the other.

According to David Hume and C. G. Hempel (1966), a natural law is nothing other than a perfect concomitance: given two properties phi and psi, if, for any phi-instance, there is some (immediately posterior, adjacent) psi-instance, phi-instances are the causes of psi-instances, and "phi's cause psi's" expresses a natural law. To explain an event is to identify its cause. Thus, Hume and Hempel believe that to explain an event is to show it to be a constituent of a correlation-instantiating event-sequence: where event-explanations are concerned, laws are concomitances; and to explain is therefore to correlate. Hume was concerned with event-explanations. Such explanations are typically intradisciplinary (concerned with truths that belong to a single discipline), as opposed to interdisciplinary (concerned with truths that belong to different disciplines): biological truths are typically explained in terms of biological truths, and in this respect biology is representative of every other discipline. (This is a tautology. A statement-set that wasn't to some degree explanatorily self-contained wouldn't constitute a discipline.)

Hempel applies Hume's analysis to interdisciplinary explanation, his position being that one discipline D can be "reduced" to another discipline D* (in other words,

D can be shown to be a mere part of D* or, at any rate, to coincide in respect of its explanatory import with such a part), if any given D-property is coextensive with some D*-property. If D- and D*-properties are thus aligned, it follows that, if phi and psi are D-specific properties, there are D*-specific properties phi* and psi* such that "any given phi-instance immediately precedes an immediately posterior psi-instance" must have the same truth-value as "any given phi*-instance immediately precedes an immediately posterior psi*-instance." It follows, more generally, that D-concomitances are all in lockstep with (the members of some subset of the set of) D*-concomitances. Relative to the Hume-Hempel identification of natural laws with correlations, this means that, if these two sets of concomitances are thus aligned, D is a part of D* (or can be absorbed into D*).

In Chapter 8, we will see just how little truth there is in Hempel's analysis, and a certain plausibility will accrue to the otherwise seemingly outlandish position that a malignance-born, wilful deceptiveness may had had a hand in the vigorous, if not feverish, manner in which otherwise estimable thinkers have attempted to legitimate that doctrine.

1.2.5 Everything just said about the relationship between physiology and microphysics holds of the relationship between psychology and physiology. But there is a respect in which in the latter two disciplines are even more remote from each other than the first two.

Physiological data are given to one as holding in virtue of events having certain locations in a certain coordinate system. (Smith has a heart attack in a certain place, at a certain time.) Microphysical data are given to one as holding in virtue of events having certain locations *in that same* coordinate system. There is some one coordinate system CS such that, given any proposition P belonging to either discipline, P represents the facts (if any there be) in virtue of which it is true (supposing it true) as being in that coordinate system. (From now on, I'll leave out the parenthetical qualifiers.) Every proposition of every discipline *other than psychology* represents the facts in virtue of which it is true as being in CS.

But psychological propositions categorically *don't* present the facts in virtue of which they hold as being in CS. The collision of billiard balls A and B is given to you as having a certain location in space-time. But your *perception* of that collision, though given to you as occurring in the same temporal manifold as the collision, isn't given to you as occurring in the same spatial manifold. That perception, if an object of your awareness, is not given to you as having a location in the same coordinate system as that in which your perception represents the collision as occurring. That coordinate system is identical with the one in which the propositions of astronomy, zoology, etc. locate the things they described.

There are two qualifications. First, your perception *does* have a location in CS. But it's not *given* to you as having such a location. And it's the latter fact that matters, not the former, given that disciplines model data.

Second, facts about people's overt behavior are represented to us as having a location in CS. We know of those events through sense-perception; and our senses locate those events in the same coordinate system as the collision between A and B. There is no denying that Smith's shouting and throwing furniture around is a psychology-relevant datum. But should it turn out that Smith is a robot, his behavior *ipso facto* falls outside the scope of psychology. Smith's behavior is psychology-relevant *only* if driven by perceptions, emotions, etc. on Smith's part. Smith's beliefs, perceptions, emotions, etc. are not given to *him* as having a location in CS. So Smith's behavior is psychology-relevant *only* to the extent that the forces driving it, should they become objects of Smith's consideration, will *not* be given to him as being in CS. *Any* instance of overt behavior is relevant to psychology *only* to the extent that the forces driving it, should they become object's of the agent's consideration, are *not* given to him as being in CS. If there is no such subject, those behaviors are not of psychological interest. A psychology-relevant datum isn't a necessarily a psychological datum; and, if F is the fact represented by some psychological datum D, it is never in CS that D locates F.

The sense in which psychology is irreducible to physiology is therefore stronger than the sense in which physiology is irreducible to physics. There is some one coordinate system, namely CS, such that an event is represented as physics-relevant, or physiology-relevant, or astronomy- or zoology-relevant *only* if that event is represented as being in CS. So physiological propositions represent their truth-makers as being in CS, as do zoological propositions, as well as astronomical propositions, etc.

There is thus *a* sense in which a given physiological truth can be explained in terms of microphysical truths. Let TM be the truth-maker of some arbitrary physiological proposition P, and let L be the spatiotemporal location that P represents TM as having. There is some microphysical proposition M such that TM is M's truth-maker and such that M represents TM as being in L. So M represents TM as occupying a certain space-time region that is coincident with that which P represents TM as occupying. Two distinct things can't be in the same place at the same time, and they can't be represented as being in the same place at the same time. So M represents TM as being identical with the thing which P describes, and P represents TM as being identical with the thing which M describes. There is thus *a* sense in which, for any given physiological truth, there is some microphysical truth that accounts for the former.

But even though the truth-makers of psychological events *do* occupy places in the same space-time occupied by the truth-makers of physiological events, psychological propositions don't *represent* their truth-makers occupying same space-time as those which physiological propositions represent *their* truth-makers as occupying. So psychology isn't reducible to physiology *even* in the weak sense in which physiology is reducible to microphysics.

This entails that[8] psychology is *sui generis*: psychological truths are to be explained in terms of other psychological propositions, so far as that is possible. Of course, the

---

8. In direct opposition to what Steven Horst (2007) holds. Horst's argument is this (I paraphrase): "No discipline is reducible to any other. Therefore psychology isn't reducible to any other discipline. But there is nothing specific to psychology that blocks its absorption into other disciplines and there is nothing specific about the way in which it cannot be absorbed." Horst does not consider the argument I have just stated.

psychological realm is open: it affects and is affected by things outside it. So the hedge ("so far as that is possible") in the penultimate sentence is a significant one. Some psychological events (e.g. the shock Smith is now feeling) have non-psychological causes (e.g. he just fell into ice-cold water).

But that hedge is significant in a second, diametrically opposed sense. Given a psychological event that, unlike Smith's shock, isn't obviously at a point of contact between the psychological and the non-psychological, we should seek a psychological explanation for it; and we should do the same for all psychological events that are not at such contact-points.

This does not mean we should deny that such psychological events have purely physiological antecedents – they do. Nor does it mean that such events are not themselves constituted by physiological events – they are. It means that those antecedents should be assumed to mediate psychological events. It also means that, to the extent that such assumptions are wrong, the conclusion to draw is not that the psychological is to be explained in terms of the strictly physiological, but that the psychological is simply not to be explained. This, in its turn, means *not* that psychological events are inherently mysterious, but that (setting aside limiting cases, such as Smith's shock) they should be assumed to be non-mysterious and therefore to have psychological antecedents.

But we will see that empiricism and empiricism-inspired psychological methodologies make it impossible to satisfy this desideratum.

Many a layman and scientist takes it for granted that "scientific" and "empirical" are synonyms, and many a philosopher has attempted to substantiate this position. To be sure, a hypothesis is to be dismissed if it doesn't square with observation. But this doesn't mean that scientific thought is the same thing as empirical thought. Indeed, the term "empirical thought" is an oxymoron. One is an empiricist to the extent that one's beliefs are directly supported by sense-perception and a non-empiricist to the extent that they are not; and to the extent that thought mediates between one's observations and one's beliefs, the latter are not directly supported by observation.

1.3   Most philosophers describe themselves as empiricists; and most really are empiricists, in that they make heavy concessions to empiricism in their work, even when those concessions lack any empiricism-independent justification. For example, it's extremely difficult to find *any* philosopher who concedes that anything makes anything happen. They all accept the following, distinctively empiricist line of thought, first put forth by Hume (1739):

(CN)[9]   We see events. We don't see forces. Nor do we otherwise sense-perceive them. Therefore, we are not entitled to say that anything makes anything happen. Therefore, statements of the form "given x, y had to happen" are categorically false. Smith's pulling the trigger didn't *make* the gun fire. Brown's hitting the

9.   Short for "causation."

ground, after falling out of an airplane, didn't *make* his skeleton shatter. In each case, one event was followed by another, but no event compelled any other to occur.

CN is radically implausible, and it is demonstrably false, as we will see in Chapter 8. Also, even though empiricism demands that one accept CN (for reasons to be discussed in the paragraph following the next one), it also demands that one reject it. (Incoherent doctrines have incompatible consequences.) When you try to lift a heavy object, you observe that it resists your efforts to displace it. In general, sense-perception *does* disclose the existence of forces.

This doesn't mean that forces exist; after all, sense-perceptions aren't always accurate. What it means is that it cannot be on strictly empirical grounds that one denies their existence. Of course, if one concedes the validity of such grounds, one denies the validity of empiricism. Empiricism therefore fails if forces don't exist.

At the same time, empiricism fails if forces do exist. (This is why empiricists accept CN.) Supposing *arguendo* that forces do exist and supposing *arguendo* that we can directly observe them, we can observe them only through one sensory-modality (our so-called "bodily kinesthetic" sense) and therefore, given the nature of that modality, only in very restricted contexts. We see stars, but we can't touch them, let alone push them or drag them. Supposing that we can ever observe the forces governing the objects of scientific inquiry, it is only in very special contexts. In almost all scientific investigations, vision is the dominant sensory-modality; and in many such investigations, it is the *only* operative modality. Vision does not disclose the existence of forces. So to the extent that science is strictly observation-based, it is blind to the forces, if any there be, that govern the objects of its scrutiny. So either

(i) empiricism is wrong

or

(ii) the results of scientific research are null and void *unless* forces don't govern the things it studies.

So the empiricist has no choice but to deny that forces exist.

"But isn't it an open question," it might be asked "whether vision *does* disclose the existence of forces? Couldn't it be argued that we do see forces at work and, moreover, that we see instances of force *as* such instances?"

Each question is to be answered affirmatively. It *is* unclear whether vision apprises of the existence of forces. For reasons that will be stated in Chapter 8, I personally believe that one *does* visually observe forces and, moreover, that one observes instances of forces *as* such instances. (The only other philosopher I know of who advocates this view is C. J. Ducasse (1969).) But the very fact that this is unclear undermines empiricism. It is often unclear how to interpret the deliverances of one's senses. It is often unclear how to be an empiricist. This is not to make the trivial and obvious point that it is often unclear what sort of theoretical superstructure to impose on the raw data of observation. It is to make the non-trivial point that there is often no clear answer to the question "how am I to describe, in a manner that doesn't prejudge any relevant questions, the raw observational data at my disposal?" And this question is *ipso facto* incapable of being answered on empirical grounds. Throughout this book, we will discover many cases where one must resort to *a priori* thought *in order* to know what it is that one's senses have told one.

There is another problem with CN: its conclusion is self-defeating; it's false if true (and it's therefore false). Supposing CN cogent, the mental activity mediating somebody's beginning to put forth CN is not responsible for the mental activity mediating that same person's bringing CN to a close. But in that case, CN hasn't been put forth: a mere sequence of thoughts isn't a thought-process. Thought-processes are thought-sequences whose earlier installments are responsible for their later installments. We'll develop this line of thought in Chapter 9.

In any case, since the time CN was first put forth, an acceptance of it, or at least an unwillingness to reject it wholesale, has infiltrated almost all of the work done concerning causation, probability, and scientific explanation.[10] Evidently, more scholars accept empiricism than reject it, given that nobody would accept CN unless they were committed empiricists.

But even though many accept empiricism, few try to justify it. Quine (1960) and Berkeley (1710, 1713) are exceptions to this. In Chapter 9, we will evaluate their attempts to justify empiricism.

David Hume (1739, 1740) rigorously established that, *if* empiricism is correct, then:

(a)   We cannot know to what degree our sensory experiences are veridical,

and

(b)   The future cannot be known on the basis of the present; more generally, the unknown cannot be known on the basis of the known.

The doctrines expressed by (a) and (b) are, respectively, *skepticism about sense-perception* and *skepticism about inductive inference*.

Hume accepted (a) and (b) on the grounds that they were corollaries of empiricism, instead of rejecting empiricism for that same reason.

---

10. Ernest Nagel's (1962) book *The Structure of Science* assumes the cogency of CN, and this sullies this otherwise magisterial work. Nagel's acceptance of CN forces him to say that to explain why Smith goes to Church every Sunday is to identify some property phi (other than that of going to Church every Sunday) such that Smith has phi and so do all and only those who go to Church on Sunday. Nagel's acceptance of CN prohibits him from saying that Smith goes to Church because he's afraid he'll burn in Hell if he doesn't. The concept of motivation is meaningless within any CN-friendly explanatory framework. These points are substantiated in Chapter 8.

Nobody believes (a) or (b). David Hume himself said this. But he also said, quite rightly, that, given his acceptance of empiricism, he had no choice but to advocate both.

We will see that (a) and (b) can both be refuted, given but two non-empirical assumptions, namely:

(EA[11])   To explain is to eliminate anomalies;

and

(EA*)   To eliminate anomalies is to eliminate discontinuities and is therefore to eliminate *ex nihilo* events.[12]

EA is a definitional truth. EA* is a substantive but eminently defensible truth.

1.3.1   George Berkeley (1710, 1713), another staunch empiricist, saw that empiricism cannot accommodate the presumption that there are mind-independent entities. But Berkeley rejected (a). He chose to reconcile his acceptance of empiricism with his rejection of (a) by saying that our sense-perceptions *were* the very objects they represented and, therefore, that our sense-perceptions *ipso facto* could not misrepresent those objects. "To be is to be perceived," Berkeley said. (*Esse percipi est.*) Berkeley argued that there were independent reasons to accept this.

Berkeley then argued for a more general point, namely: To exist is to be the object of awareness – possibly, but not necessarily, sensory awareness. "To be is to be conceived," Berkeley said. (*Esse concipi est.*)

The doctrine that to be is to be the object of awareness is known as "idealism." (To be is to be an idea – hence "idealism.")

Relative to an acceptance of empiricism, Berkeley's arguments for these contentions are creditable. So even though nobody accepts the conclusions of those arguments, the errors in them must be precisely identified. Those errors are probably corollaries of empiricism; and it is a distinct possibility that they underlie many a viewpoint that, unlike Berkeley's idealism, is not *obviously* false, and is therefore accepted by many, but is indeed false and must be discredited.

2.0   A corollary of empiricism is that nothing exists that isn't spatiotemporal. The essence of empiricism is: "Believe if you have evidence; don't if you don't. In effect, it exists if, and only if, there is evidence of it." For x to be evidence of y is for x and y to be so causally connected that, given x, y's existence may reasonably be assumed. Smoke is evidence of fire. The reason: fire creates smoke, and nothing else does (or so we'll assume to expedite discussion); therefore, where there's smoke, there's fire. Bill's

---

11. "EA" is short for "empirical assumption."

12. Reichenbach (1956, 1957) asserts both EA and EA*.

drunkenness is evidence of a poor performance on his upcoming exam. The reason: drunkenness diminishes one's ability to think clearly, and one must think clearly to do well on exams; therefore, Bill will do poorly on his upcoming exam.

Non-spatiotemporal entities don't affect anything and nothing affects them. Anything that affects anything is *ipso facto* in space-time is and is therefore spatiotemporal. If x causes y, for any y, then x must have some spatiotemporal relation to y; wherefore x must be in space-time. Since non-spatotemporal entities affect nothing and nothing affects them, there can be no evidence of their existence. Wherefore, non-spatiotemporal entities don't exist as far as empiricism is concerned.

This means that, if empiricism is right, properties (as opposed to their instances) don't exist, and neither do possibilities, numbers, meanings or *abstracta* of any other kind.[13]

2.1 In this book, an "argument" is not a verbal altercation, but a sequence of statements $S_1...S_n$ such that $S_1...S_{n-1}$ are intended to establish S_n. An inference is a judgment on somebody's part to the effect that, for some statement-sequence $S_1...S_n$, $S_1...S_{n-1}$ establish S_n.

It obviously seems reasonable to deny that there are non-spatiotemporal entities. The problem is that, unless they exist, even the most rudimentary inferences don't go through, for example:

> Premise: Bill is human.
> Premise: John is human.
> Conclusion: There is something that John and Bill have in common, namely, the property of being human.

This argument explicitly concerns properties. Most do not. But *all* arguments and *all* inferences presuppose the existence of properties and also of non-spatiotemporal entities of other kinds. The reasons for this lie in two facts:

(i)   Propositions, and propositions alone, are the *relata* of logical relations,

and

(ii)   Propositions are not spatiotemporal.

Taken jointly, (i) and (ii) entail that:

(iii)   The spatiotemporal world comprises no instances of any logical relations.

Given two propositions, there are five logical relations that may hold between them. One may entail the other. One may confirm the other. One may disconfirm the other. One may entail the negation of the other. (In other words, the two may be incompatible.) And, finally, each may be neutral with respect to the other. P entails Q if, given

---

13. This is Quine's (1960) reason for denying the existence of non-spatiotemporal entities.

P, it is not even a theoretical possibility that Q should fail to be true. (*x is a triangle* entails *x has 3 sides*.) P confirms Q if, given P, it is *ceteris paribus* more likely than not that Q is true. (*x has an account at J. P. Morgan's* confirms *x is wealthy*.)

Bearing these points in mind, let us examine (i) and (ii). Even though, as we'll presently see, each contention is correct, neither one is self-evidently correct. For example, some people hold that sentences, not propositions, are the *relata* of logical relations; and some people hold that propositions *are* spatiotemporal; and, finally some hold that propositions don't exist. But (i) and (ii) are both true. This will be established in Sections 2.1.1–2.4. (Section 2.3 will establish a tangential point and can be skipped by those only interested the veridicality of (i)–(iii).)

2.1.1 Truths are true propositions; falsehoods are false propositions. Truths are not identical with the facts in virtue of which they hold. Let F be the fact in virtue of which it is true that

(MH[14]) Mozart was happy at t,

for some time t. The (re)distribution of mass-energy in virtue of which MH is true has long since ceased to exist. But MH is still true. Therefore MH is not identical with that (re)distribution of mass-energy or, by analogous reasoning, with any other. By obvious extensions of this line of thought, no truth is identical with any such (re)distribution. And no falsehood is identical with any such (re)distribution: there are no false *facts*. There are false *propositions*.

We have thus established that propositions are not facts. By itself, this doesn't establish (i); nor does it esatablish (ii). But it is a first step towards establishing each. Let us now take the second step.

Given any proposition P, there is some set of properties $p_1...p_n$ such that

(a) P is true exactly if $p_1...p_n$ are jointly instantiated,

and

(b) the set S whose only members are $p_1...p_n$ is structurally identical with P.

Let me explain each point. The proposition that

(JT) John is tall.[15]

is the meaning of the sentence

(JT*[16]) "John is tall."

---

14. Short for "Mozart, happy."

15. JT is flanked by quotation-marks, indicating that it refers to an expression; JT* is not, indicating that it refers to a proposition.

16. Short for "John, tall."

JT and JT* are distinct entities. JT* is an expression; JT is not. JT is what is meant by "Juan es alto"; JT* is not. (We're assuming that "John" has a specific referent.)

JT is a set whose members are properties. More precisely, it is the smallest set K that contains each of the following properties:

c_1:   the property of being identical with John.
c_2:   the property of being tall.
c_3:   the property of being a property p such that John has p.
c_4:   the property of being a a thing x such that x has p, for some property p
c_5:   the property of being a thing x such that x is tall and x is identical with John.

JT is true exactly if all of the members of K are instantiated. Therefore, JT *is* K and for JT to be true is for K's members to be instantiated. In general, propositions are sets of properties, and for a proposition to be true is for the corresponding set's members to be instantiated.

Russell (1903, 1917), Moore (1995), and Salmon (1986, 2005, 2007) say that

(#)   John *himself*, as opposed to some concept of John, is a constituent of JT.

By this reasoning, JT ceases to exist when John does. But it doesn't. So (#) is false. Also, I can grasp John only by grasping concepts or properties individuative of him. So if there is some proposition-like entity of which John is a constituent, it is totally non-operational: nobody could grasp it.[17] But you grasp JT and so do I: another reason to reject (#).

Salmon (1986, 2005, 2007) doesn't address the second point, but he addresses the first. (Russell and Moore do not.) Salmon says that, when John ceases to exist, JT does not cease to exist – *but it becomes non-existent.* Scott Soames (2003) takes the same view, for the same reason.

The Salmon-Soames view is obviously contraindicated. Fortunately, it is easily avoided. We've already seen why: it isn't John *per se* that is a property of JT; it is the property of being John. When John ceases to exist, that property ceases to be instantiated, but it doesn't cease to exist.

2.1.2   "But why the need for $c_1 ... c_4$?", it will be asked. "c_5's being instantiated is necessary and sufficient for JT's being true. So why not identify JT with c_5 and JT's being true with c_5's being instantiated?"[18]

---

17.   Russell (1917) makes this very point and says that, indeed, there is some proposition of which is a constituent and that proposition is non-operational. See the chapter in Russell (1917) titled "Knowledge by acquaintance and knowledge by description."

18.   David Lewis (1984) identifies the proposition *Smith is tall* with the property of being a thing x such that Smith = x and x is tall. Lewis' position is basically correct; but it needs to be augmented, as we're about to see, in order to accommodate the fact that propositions must tend

JT contains a discrete part corresponding to John and another discrete part corresponding to the property of being tall. Those constituents of JT can be detached from it and used in other contexts, e.g. in the propositions meant by such sentences "John is wealthy" and "Sally is tall." By contrast, c_5 cannot be thus decomposed. Propositions must at least *tend* to be structurally similar to the propositions that express them. Let L be a language in which the propositions meant by "John is wealthy," "Sally is tall," "John is tall," and "Sally is wealthy," were expressed by *simple* expressions. (A simple expression is one that cannot decomposed into simpler ones. "Red" is a simple expression. "Socrates has a red house" is not, and it is therefore a "complex" expression.) Let s_1, s_2, s_3, and s_4 be these (simple) sentences. In L, one couldn't produce s_1 by detaching ""John" from s_3 and "is wealthy" from s_4 and then recombining them; and one couldn't produce s_2 by detaching "Sally" from s_4 and "is tall" from s_3 and then recombining them. This shows that, to the extent that the sentences of a language are semantically simple, that language is expressively frozen: either there is an explicit provision made for a given proposition or that proposition is inexpressible. By the same token, it shows that *ceteris paribus* the more granular a given language's sentences are, the more expressively flexible it is.

Also, in L, the logical relations holding among the propositions corresponding to s_1, s_2, s_3, and s_4 would to no degree be reflected in relations holding among those sentences. In *English*, because "John is tall," "Sally is wealthy," etc. can be decomposed into "John," "Sally," "wealthy," etc., sentential structure mirrors logical structure. In English, the validity of the argument "if Sally is tall, and John is tall, then John and Sally have some property in common" can be read off the syntax of those sentences. In L, on the other hand, the relations holding among s_1, s_2, s_3, and s_4 would be worthless in the way of revealing the relations holding among the corresponding propositions (except – and this only proves our point – in so far as L contained some synonymous sentence that decomposed in the same way as the English sentence "John is tall"), and to the extent that the relations borne by s_1, s_2, s_3, and s_4 with respect to the L-translation of "John is tall" were representative the relations borne by the constituents of other L-sentences to those same sentences, intersentential relations holding among L-sentences would provide no information about the corresponding interpropositional relations.

Let us bring these points to bear on the relationship between JT and JT*. JT's meaning is obviously decomposable into parts corresponding to "John," etc. The structure that our analysis ascribes to JT* is identical *mutatis mutandis* with the one it ascribes to each of SW* and ST*, these being the propositions meant by

(SW[19]) "Sally is wealthy,"

---

to "decompose," as Jerrold Katz (1972) puts it, in ways similar to the sentences that express them. It is presently explained why propositions need only *tend* to have such decompositions.

19. Short for "Sally, wealthy."

and

(ST[20]) "Sally is tall,"

respectively. Our analysis thus validates the fact that the relations holding among JT, SW, and ST mirror those holding among the corresponding propositions.

The *raison d'être* for c_3, c_4, and c_5 is to be understood along similar lines. JT *formally* entails:

(ET[21]) Something is tall,

JT also formally entails:

(SS[22]) Something has some property.

JT, ET and SS are propositions, not sentences. The traditional wisdom is that formal entailment holds among expressions, not propositions. But we've just seen that it holds among propositions. In Chapter 2, Section 7.2, we'll find that, in addition to holding among propositions, formal entailment *fails* to hold among sentences or, indeed, expressions of any kind. Statements to the effect that a given sentence is "formally true," or that a given statement-sequence is "formally valid," are either meaningless or is an abbreviated ways of making statements about propositions.

2.1.3   Attempts have been to show that properties are identical with spatiotemporal entities. For example, some hold that a given property is identical with a spatiotemporal entity whose constituents are that property's instances.[23] According to this viewpoint, the property of being made of water is an object whose constituents are bodies of water. This object obviously isn't spatiotemporally cohesive, and it is thus a "scattered object."[24]

This view is false, since it has the obviously false consequence that any two uninstantiated properties (e.g. the property of being an 8-ft tall person and the property of an 50-ft tall giraffe) are identical.

There is another problem. Let S be the scattered object that *ex hypothesi* is identical with property P, this being the property of being made of water. One changes S by destroying or displacing any given body of water. But one does not, by that means or any other, do anything to affect what it is to be made of water; so one doesn't thereby

---

20. Short for "Sally, tall."

21. Short for "existential generalization, tall."

22. Short for "existential generalization, some property."

23. Quine (1960, 1974, 1977).

24. The term "scattered object" is due to Cartwright (1975); so is the corresponding concept.

affect the property of being made of water. Since, therefore, S and P don't have the same properties, they are not identical.

Also, the concept of a scattered object is incoherent. My pencil is an object. The "entity," for lack of a better word, consisting of my pencil and my car is *not* an object. The things composing my pencil cohere in such a way that, taken jointly, they constitute a prediction- and explanation-friendly system. The same is true of my car. The same is *not* true of the just-described pencil-car hybrid. By moving my car I do not *ipso facto* dispose my pencil to move.

Obviously *ad hoc* contrivances could change this: I could attach the pencil to my car. But that only proves our point, since *that* system would have the cohesiveness, and concomitant prediction- and explanation-conduciveness, characteristic of objects *qua* objects.

"But if the pencil is fragile," it will objected, "then you *could* move one part without moving the remaining parts, or even disposing them to move." Yes, but a fragile pencil is *ipso facto* that much less of a unified being than a sturdy one and is therefore that much less of an object.

To be sure, it would unacceptably paradoxical and revisionist to say of a given fragile pencil that it failed *tout court* to qualify as an object. But that is not to the discredit of our position. A given plurality of entities (particles, bricks, people, etc.) may be an object in one respect, but not another. Smith, Jones, and Brown are the only members of a three-person law-firm. *Qua* such members, they jointly form a single object. But *qua* bar-hoppers, they don't form a single group, since no two of them patronize the same bars.

Some have held that any given property P is identical with the set S that includes all and only P's instances.[25] Those who hold this do so believing that they have thereby spatiotemporalized properties.

First of all, sets are not spatiotemporal entities. The set consisting of my pencil, my desk, and my chair is not identical with any spatiotemporal arrangement of those things, since rearranging those objects doesn't change that set.

Also, sets aren't identical with their intensions. (A set's intension is the property common to all and only its members, and its *extension* is its membership. So the extension of the set whose intention is the property of human is the least inclusive set containing Sally, Fred, Ethel, etc.) The property of being a 10-ft tall person is

---

25. Quine (1970) takes this view. That said, he says explicitly that sets are non-spatiotemporal and that it is therefore in what he believes to be an attenuated sense that, by identifying intensions (properties) with the corresponding extensions (sets), he has spatiotemporalized the latter. But intensions are not extensions, and the concept of a *relative* spatiotemporalization of some *prima facie* non-spatiotemporal entity is not a coherent one. In for a penny, in for a pound. If sets are non-spatiotemporal – which Quine, being a master-set-theorist, knew that they were – then there are non-spatiotemporal entities. And once the existence of some such things is granted, there ceases to be any principled reason, we will see, to deny the existence of any other alleged instances of such things.

different from the property of being a 900-ft tall giraffe. But the sets containing those properties' instances are identical, since both sets are identical with the empty set and, therefore, with each other.

We have thus shown that

(a)   propositions consist of properties

and that

(b)   properties are non-spatiotemporal.

We have therefore justified (ii). Let us now justify (i).

2.2   Let a and b be particular inscriptions of the sentences:

(A)   John reads frequently.

and

(B)   John is an animate object.

Of course, a entails b.

Let MA and MB be a's and b's respective meanings. It is obviously in virtue of the fact that a and b have MA and MB for their respective meanings that a entails b. Therefore, it is really MA that entails MB, and it is only in a derivative sense that a entails b. Exactly similar points hold of any instance of entailment, or any other logical relationship, that initially appears to hold between anything other than propositions. Whence the truth of (iii).

But empiricists deny (iii), as they must, since propositions, if they exist, are non-spatiotemporal. Empiricists validate their denial of (iii) by saying that:

(PN[26])   propositions don't exist,

and by then making the correlative point that:

(SR[27])   *sentences*, not propositions, are the *relata* of logical relations.[28]

Their intention in advocating this view is to show that spatiotemporal entities are the relata of logical relations, the assumption being that sentences are spatiotemporal entities.

We've already seen that PN is false. Now let us show that SR is false.

---

26. Short for "proposition, non-existent."

27. Short for "sentences, relata of logical relations."

28. Each of PN and SR is held by Wittgenstein (1922, 1958, 1965), Ayer (1934), Carnap (1937), Quine (1960, 1970), Field (1977), and Brandom (1994, 2000).

First of all, sentences are *not* spatiotemporal. We must distinguish sentences from their occurrences. To use the contemporary argot, we must distinguish sentence-*types* from sentence-*tokens*. Consider the sentence:

(IR)   "It is raining."[29]

This sentence *per se* is neither true nor false. But a given *utterance* of it is true or false, depending on whether or not, in the context of utterance, it is raining. An utterance of a sentence is an instance of that sentence. Anything of which there can be instances is *ipso facto* a property. Therefore, sentences are properties; and for exactly similar reasons, so are all expression-types.

Also, it's only relative to certain conventions that any ink-deposit means anything or, therefore, that any ink-deposit establishes the truth of any other ink-deposit. So supposing that $s_1...s_n$ are the semantic conventions constitutive of the English language [or of whatever the language in question happens to be], the statement that

(ID[30])   ink-deposit x, if true, establishes the truth of ink-deposit y

is an abbreviated way of saying:

(EC[31])   given their respective meanings, $s_1...s_n$ jointly entail that x establishes the truth of y.

The instance of entailment mentioned in EC obviously isn't a relation among expressions.

Also, even though it is a matter of convention what any given simple expression means, it is not a matter solely of convention, but of convention *plus* non-conventional, logical fact what is meant by any given complex expression. There obviously isn't a convention *directly* concerning the meaning of:

(HF[32])   "People fear everyone they hate, but they don't hate everyone they fear."

---

29. Short for "it is raining." This example is borrowed from MacCawley (1981). The point that sentences are typically context-sensitive was first made by Strawson (1950), as was the corresponding point that many supposed axioms of logic (e.g. the law of non-contradiction) are simply false *if interpreted as concerning expresions of natural language or expressions of any symbolic system that bears any meaningful resemblance to natural language*. Given the context-sensitive nature of "he is here," and the fact that a text may change during the time it takes to utter a sentence, "he is here and he is not here" may be true. Barwise and Perry (1983) also make this point, as does Kaplan (1989).

30. Short for "ink deposit."

31. Short for "existence of conventions."

32. Short for "hate, fear."

There are conventions that directly fix the meanings of HF's simple constituents, but there are none that concern HF as a whole. That HF means what it does is a non-conventional, logical consequence of our conventions.[33] Bearing this in mind, let x be an inscription (written-token) of HF and let y be an inscription of:

(NE[34])   "It's only if nobody hates anyone that nobody fears anyone,"

Let P be x's meaning and let P* be y's. That x and y mean P and P*, respectively, is a non-conventional, strictly logical consequence of $s_1...s_n$. That x entails y is a non-conventional, strictly logical consequence of the fact that they have those meanings and it is therefore an indirect, strictly logical consequence of the fact $s_1...s_n$ entail that x and y mean P and P*, respectively.

So "x entails y" is either false or it is an abbreviated way of saying that

(xy)   *Given* the fact that

(i) $s_1...s_n$ entail that x and y have P and P* for their respective meanings,

and given the additional fact that

(ii) x's having P for its meaning, coupled with the fact that y has P* for its meaning, entails that x entails y,

it follows that

(iii) x entails y.

So it is only in a doubly derivative sense that x entails y: it is only relative to non-conventional, strictly logical principles that x and y mean what they do; and it is only relative to similar principles that, given that they mean what they do, x entails y. Thus, x and y *per se* are not the relata of an instance of entailment or, by exactly similar reasoning, any other logical relation, and the same holds for any two linguistic expressions.

2.2.1   The relata of logical relations must be things that are true or false. This does not *by itself* imply that, if such relata are spatiotemporal, they must be identical with expression-tokens; for expression-tokens are not the *only* spatiotemporal entities that are true or false. But, we will now see, it does have that consequence *given* the fact that it is only *intersubjective* entities that can be such relata.

Beliefs are true or false. But the relata of logical relations cannot be the constituents of any given person's mind. I believe that John is literate. I infer, and thus come to believe, that John is animate. My inference is valid. Sally makes the same inference. So does George. We're dealing with three distinct inferences (but only with one kind of

---

33. Quine (1966) elegantly shows this. See the chapters titled "Truth by Convention" and "Carnap on Logical Truth."

34. Short for "negative emotion."

inference) and with three corresponding pairs of beliefs (though only with one kind of belief-pair). Let $<A_1,A_2>$, $<B_1,B_2>$, $<C_1,C_2>$ be these three belief-pairs.

There is obviously some *one* instance of the relation of entailment in virtue of which the first member of each of these pairs warrants the second. What I've figured out is the very same thing that George and Sally have figured out, and what I've figured out is that something x entails something y, for some x and some y. Whatever it is that I have figured out, it doesn't concern George's beliefs or Sally's or anyone else's.

So while it is true that thoughts are true or false, they are not suited to be the relata of logical relations. The relata of such relations must be intersubjective. If they are intersubjective *and* spatiotemporal, they are *ipso facto* linguistic expressions. *Explanation*: Whatever is

(a) spatiotemporal,

(b) true or false,

and

(c) non-mental

is *derivatively* true or false; its truth or falsity is derivative of its meaning, and its meaning is derivative of stipulations or conventions among animate beings.[35] And anything whose meaning is a consequence of such conventions is *ipso facto* a linguistic expression.

Since linguistic expressions are not the relata of logical relations, the relata of such relations are non-spatiotemporal. Since any non-spatiotemporal entity that is true or false is *ipso facto* a proposition, and since the relata of such relations are things that are true or false, propositions are the relata of such relations.

We have thus established (i) and (ii); and we have therefore established (iii).

2.3 Let P be the proposition meant by:

(S) "1 + 3 = 4,"

S's meaning P is a mind-independent relation holding *between* minds and expressions. More precisely, S's meaning P is three-place relation between:

(a) conventions (and therefore minds, given that conventions are agreements among sapient beings),

(b) expressions,

and

(c) logical principles.

---

35. These points are clearly stated and cogently argued by Searle (1983, 1984, 1992).

But empiricists treat S's being true as a *one*-place relation, that is, as a property.[36] This being their view, empiricists cannot accommodate the obvious fact that S's meaning P is indisputably convention-*based* without saying that it is *wholly* a matter of convention.

In this particular case, the empiricist's subjectivism (viz. his conventionalist/subjectivist conception of arithmetical truth) is a reflection of his inability to countenance the existence of non-spatiotemporal entities: since the empiricist denies that there are such entities, he must deny that entities of type (c) are among the *relata* of instances of the relevant sorts of relations. That leaves him with no choice but to conventionalize, and thus subjectivize, arithmetical truth. (Conventionalization is culture-level subjectivization.)

Empiricism often mistakenly treats relations as properties, and it often treats 3-place relations as 2-place relations. (The relation of loving is a property of of ordered pairs <x, y> such that x loves y, and is thus a 2-place relation. The relation of being in-between is a property of ordered triples <x, y, z> such that x is between y and z, and is thus a 3-place relation.) As a result, empiricists are forced to espouse radically implausible views concerning anything relating to affect or emotion.

Colors, for the empiricist, are "purely" subjective, as are tastes and fragrances.[37] Aesthetic and moral reactions are mere sentiments.[38] Empiricists are *ipso facto* blind to certain kinds of relational structures; and this, we will see, is partly to be explained in terms of the fact that empiricists are *ipso facto* incapable of granting the existence of anything non-spatiotemporal. An illustration is in order.

An object's shape is obviously mind-independent, as are its mass, state of motion, charge, and volume. But what about an object's color? Is color inherent in objects? It doesn't seem so. Ocean water is blue when looked at from far away, but transparent when looked at up close. There isn't a single object whose color isn't a function of the observer's relation to that object.

It's often said that to be red or blue or any other given color is to have a certain microstructure. Bearing this in mind, suppose that B is the microstructure common to all and only blue objects. If ocean water has B, then it's blue; and that means that, when I see it as being transparent (as I do when I cup it in my hand and look at it), I'm simply misperceiving its color. On the other hand, if water doesn't have B, then I'm misperceiving it when I see it as being blue. But it's obviously arbitrary to say I'm having a color-correct perception of ocean-water when I cup it in my hand but not when I look at it from an air-plane.

Empiricists have dealt with this by saying that color is "subjective." Water isn't *really* blue. Water arouses certain kinds of visual sensations in us. We project these onto

---

36. Wittgenstein (1922), Hahn (1933), Ayer (1934), Carnap (1937), and Blackburn (1994, 1998).

37. Locke (1690), Hume (1739, 1751), Blackburn (1984, 1994, 1998).

38. Hume (1739), Ayer (1934), Blackburn (1984, 1994, 1998).

the water itself.[39] There are no blue objects. "Objects are colorless," said Wittgenstein, a die-hard empiricist. There are no color-facts. There are sensations that we projectively and delusively experience as such facts. The same thing *mutatis mutandis* is true of tastes and fragrances.

But if our color-experiences are categorically hallucinatory, why are they so informative? I know that green meat is inedible, that gray-haired people are old, and that a person whose finger-tips are blue has poor circulation.

Colors are mind-dependent, but they are not mental. They are relations, but they are not two-place relations. The color of the ocean is not a two-place relation between me and the ocean: if it were, there would be some *one* color that all of my color-accurate perceptions of the ocean represented it as having; and there is clearly is no such color.

Colors are properties of *three*-place relations. The blue of the ocean is really a property of ordered triples whose members consist of:

(a)   the physical composition of a given body of ocean-water,

(b)   a given creature with a visual system of a certain kind,

and

(c)   that creature's physical relationship to that body of water.

I am not misperceiving the ocean when, while looking at it from an airplane, it appears blue to me. And I'm not misperceiving it when, while looking at it up close, it appears gray. Both perceptions are accurate. Color is a property of three-place relations, and in cases of the first kind one such relation is instantiated, whereas a different such relation is instantiated in the case of the second kind.

So color is mind-dependent but objective. It's an objective relation holding between among objects, organisms, and physical objects. Thus, *given* that I bear physical relation R to some (non-putrid) cut of meat M, and *given* that said cut of meat has physical composition C, I am seeing M's color wrongly if I see it as green and rightly if I see it as red. This is compatible with the fact M might arouse a very different color-experience in a Martian bearing that same relation to it. For the redness of the meat is a three-place property; and, assuming (as we may) that the Martian's visual system is different from mine, the color-relation instantiated in the one case is different from its counterpart in the other.

We have considered two cases where empiricists treat relations as properties, or complex relations as simple ones. In Part II, we will consider many more such cases. Each time, we'll find that, because the empiricist is prohibited from conceding the existence of anything non-spatiotemporal, he is blind to relational structure; and we'll find that his blindness to such structure forces him subjectivize the objective; to hold,

---

39. This was Locke's (1690) view, as well as Hume's (1739, 1740, 1751). Wittgenstein (1922) and Blackburn (1994, 1998) also advocate it.

for example, that it's "just a matter of opinion" whether or not Mozart is a better composer than tone-deaf Larry; that it's "just a matter of opinion" whether or not torturing infants for fun is morally wholesome.

A concomitant of the empiricist's acceptance of such revisionisms is a failure on
his part to understand the nature of emotive and affective ideation. We'll find that,

> (a)   Given some minor concessions to rationalism, our aesthetic and moral intu-
> itions are easily compatibilized with a scientific world-view;

and we will therewith find that,

> (b)   Our instinctive beliefs about our emotions and affects are more easily justified
> than the revisionist views with which the empiricist aspires replace them.

(b) needs to be clarified. You instinctively believe that you would be diminished if you
were to cease to have emotional or aesthetic attitudes. You feel that, if you were to stop
caring about the welfare of your recently kidnapped child, your sphere of awareness
would have shrunk in some important respect. But you also believe that your sphere
of awareness would in no way be diminished if you were to stop having the headache
you are currently having. That's why you have no reservations about taking a pill to get
rid of a headache, but you would have reservations about taking a pill to rid yourself
of your concern for your child.

The empiricist puts your headache in the same category as your concern for your
child's welfare. In his view, each is equally non-cognitive; each is just a "sentiment."

But no one really believes this; and it embodies an understanding of what emotions are that, in addition to being extremely crude, is therapeutically and theoretically
sterile. In any case, in Part II, we'll see that *if* empiricism is false, our intuitions about
these matters are correct. And in Part I, we'll see that empiricism is indeed false.

2.4   Empiricists have made many attempts to spatiotemporalize meaning. These attempts fail quite as badly as their attempts to spatiotemporalize properties. (This is
a consequence of the fact that meanings are identical with sets of properties.) For
example, Wittgenstein (1958) held that "meaning is use."[40] For a given expression to
have a given meaning is for it to be used in a certain way; it is *not* for it to be associated with some non-spatiotemporal object. In Chapter 5, we'll consider Wittgenstein's
reasons for saying that meaning is use. But whatever Wittgenstein's reasons were for
saying it, he was wrong to do so.

An expression-token is not just a burst of sound (or ink-deposit or pattern of light
on a monitor…). It is a burst of sound (etc.) that is linked with a certain meaning or,
in any case, is governed by linguistic conventions. If there are no linguistic conventions governing a token of "flurbaticalosis," then such a token is not linguistic. But if

---

40. This is a popular view. Its advocates include Sellars (1963), Field (1977), Brandom (1994,
2001).

there are such conventions, such a token *already* has a meaning; and non-defective usages of it must conform to those conventions and, therefore, to that meaning. So Wittgenstein's point involves the deeply naïve idea that expressions – he doesn't distinguish between types and tokens – are just noises, ink-marks, etc.

Some have held that, contrary to what the just-stated argument assumes, expression-tokens are bursts of noise (or deposits of ink, etc.).[41] But this assumption of ours is easily shown to be correct. If, on some uninhabited planet, there occurred a sound acoustically just like an occurrence of "1 + 1 = 2," that sound wouldn't token a sentence or otherwise be a linguistic entity. A *bona fide* token of that sentence is an instance of *relation* between, on the one hand, an instance of a certain noise-type (or physical type of some kind) and, on the other hand, certain conventions. The corresponding sentence-type is the corresponding relation-type. This line of thought will be clarified and developed in Chapter 5, Section 2.4.

In any case, it's clear that *if* expression-tokens were nothing but bursts of noise (etc.), then there *could* be linguistic activity on planets on which there was no sentient life. Which is absurd and which, being a corollary of Wittgenstein's argumentative starting point, shows that it's absurd to identify meaning with use.

3.0   Because of the previously mentioned tendency to identify "scientific" with "empirical" inquiry, attempts to scientize psychology have typically been attempts to empiricize it.[42] In Part II, we will identify some of the ways that empiricism-based or empiricism-inspired methodologies have damaged psychology, and we will attempt

---

41. Quine (1974).

42. I say "typically," not "always," because Paul Churchland (1984), Noam Chomsky (1959, 1965, 1980, 1988), and Sigmund Freud (1953, 1998) all tried to scientize psychology, even though none of their respective systems is empiricism-compliant. The present author's viewpoint is that Freud and Chomsky succeeded in scientizing certain sub-domains of psychology, but that Churchland has, at most, only partly scientized any such sub-domain.

Churchland's system is the least empiricism-compliant of the three. This is ironic since he self-describes as a "neuropsychologist," that is, as somebody whose position is that neurology can and should replace psychology. This self-description is misleading, since, as we'll now see, theories that Churchland sees as epitomizing how psychology ought *not* to be done are both more easily translated into biological terms than Churchland's and more easily justified in an empiricism-friendly manner.

First of all, terms like "neuron" and "glial cell" never occur in Churchland's work, except vacuously, and the terms that *do* occur (e.g. "vector-space") express highly theoretical concepts that are internal to contentions that are even *more* difficult to understand in neurological terms than the contentions whose legitimacy it is Churchland's intention to undermine.

For example, Churchland takes it for granted that Freud's model of the mind is spurious. But Freud's model is far easier to understand in physicalistic terms than Churchland's. Freud's starting point is the *biological* truism that, while obviously needing a certain amount of energy to survive, organisms are damaged by energy-overload. Freud says that

to undo some of that damage. But Part II does more than excoriate attempts to empiricize psychology, and there are some respects the contents of Part II are constructive in nature.

Some schools of thought in psychology are spectacular successes, and the research-programs constitutive of such schools yield accurate and deep insights with quite as much regularity as physics or any other paradigm-case of a science. But those same branches of psychology make assumptions that, although correct, are hard to justify and that seemingly cogent arguments seem to prove to be incoherent, for example:

- There is unconscious ideation.
- There is ideation that is not only unconscious, but *subpersonal*.
- People can rationalize; people can deceive themselves.
- People can repress knowledge that they wish they didn't have.
- People can be internally conflicted, and an internal conflict is a battle between conscious and unconscious conceits.
- Repressed emotions may be expressed as symptoms: as compulsions, obsessions, unduly rigid belief-systems, a proneness to sudden bouts of fatigue, displacements, etc.

    (i)   an organism's instinctual drives are hewed to *inter alia* its need to discharge surplus energies;

   (ii)   instinctual frustration involves a failure to discharge surplus energies;

  (iii)   mental illness is the result of such frustration;

and, therefore,

  (iv)   mental illness is but a reflection of a failure on the organism's part to discharge *physiological* energies.

To validate these veritable truisms, and do so in a manner consistent with the clinical data at his disposal, Freud had little choice but to say that we repress, rationalize, displace, etc. So Freud's work, which Churchland reviles, is, for better or for worse, much easier to understand in biological terms than Churchland's. And given the relatively non-theoretical nature of the biological conceits underlying Freud's psychological claims, our second assertion follows, namely, that Freud's system, whatever its merits or demerits may be, is easier to justify in an empiricism-compliant manner than Churchland's.

Also, as Churchland explicitly states, Freud's theories are extensions, not revisions, of "folk-psychology," this being the belief-system in terms of which we instinctively evaluate others. Churchland contends that folk-psychology is no more scientific, and deserves no more credence, than folk-physics or folk-medicine; and Churchland explicitly says, sincerely and correctly, that his objective is to oust folk-psychology, along with derivatives thereof, such as Freudian psychology. But – and I must leave it to the reader to verify this for himself – the belief-system with which Churchland wishes to replace folk-psychology does not compare particularly favorably to the latter in respect of its degree of concordance with the data of introspection (however delusive that may be) or with the data of perception.

Psychodynamically oriented branches of psychology assume, as they must, the coherence of the concepts of unconscious ideation, internal conflict, rationalization, etc. For the record, the present author is convinced that those concepts are coherent and accepts each of the just-stated (asterix-marked) contentions.

But seemingly cogent arguments cast doubt on the veracity of those contentions. Consider, for example, the following argument, which is found in Sartre (1956) and Searle (1992):

(RI[43])   What is repressed is unconscious. So if you're conscious of it, it isn't repressed. But to repress it, you must be conscious of it. And to *keep* it repressed, you must be conscious of it. So if you repress a given conceit, or sustain such a repression, you must simultaneously be aware of that conceit and fail to be aware it. Since that is logically impossible, the concept of repression is incoherent; and by obvious extensions of this reasoning, the same is true of the concept of rationalization.

RI is fallacious, and we will demonstrate as much in Chapter 15. But there is nothing *obviously* wrong with RI. So far as one immediately knows RI to be fallacious, it is because he has *ex parte* knowledge to the effect that there is such a thing as repression; it isn't because RI has some obvious argumentative defect. It isn't because, for example, it involves the fallacy of composition (*if every one of x's proper parts has phi, x itself has phi* – so, like each of the atoms composing me, I must weigh less than a billionth of pound) or the quantifier-shift fallacy (*if for any x, there is some y such that x bears R to y, then there is some x such that for any y, x bears R to y* – so, since every finite number has a successor, some finite number must be bigger than every finite number).

That said, RI *is* fallacious and the conclusion of it *is* false. But RI differs from other fallacious arguments in an important respect. One can establish the defectiveness of some putative mathematical proof without proving the negation of what it is meant to prove. But one must demonstrate the coherence of the concept of repression if one is to show that RI fails to demonstrate its incoherence. Thus, it is only on the basis of what lawyers call an "affirmative defense" that one can undermine RI. Ordinarily, a defense-attorney must establish only that the evidence *fails* to establish his client's guilt; he needn't establish his client's innocence. But if the defense is "not guilty by reason of insanity," he has to show that his client is innocent (in the sense that, when he committed the deed in question, he was too insane to know what he was doing or that what he was doing was wrong). Similarly, to undermine RI, we must actually succeed doing what it says cannot be done; we cannot just show that RI *fails* to show that it can be done.

---

43. Short for "repression incoherent."

4.0   In Part II, we will put forth some viewpoints that psychologists, even those who don't make spurious concessions to empiricism, have been reluctant to articulate, despite the fact that they probably either have such viewpoints or would accept them on hearing them stated. These views concern a condition known as "psychopathy" as well as a very similar, but altogether distinct condition, which I'll refer to as "sociopathy."

My use of the term "psychopathy" is orthodox. My use of the term "sociopathy" is to some degree stipulative, but not entirely so. Although many authorities explicitly state that, as they use them, the terms "psychopathy" and "sociopathy" are synonyms[44], there is some tendency, among both laymen and professional psychologists, to use the term "sociopathy" to refer to a condition that such people rightly believe believe to be less severe than psychopathy but wrongly believe to be but a mild form of psychopathy. In any case, the condition that I will refer to as "sociopathy" is distinct from psychopathy, even though it is similar to it in non-trivial ways, and it is much more pervasive than psychopathy.

A psychopath is someone who doesn't have a conscience and never had one to begin with.[45] A sociopath is someone who had a conscience but ceased to have one. To sociopathize is to dismantle or corrupt one's conscience. One cannot execute this task without rationalizing. Indeed, the implementation of a certain sort of rationalization is identical with, or largely constitutive of, sociopathogenesis.

The sociopath was once a non-sociopath. He once had a conscience along with the multifarious characterological concomitants of thereof. The process of becoming a sociopath strips one of many of those concomitants, but leaves intact some of the formal, skeletal properties of one's personality.

To speak colloquially, sociopaths are people who "sell out" and "die inside," becoming empty husks that, being formally but not substantively like their former selves, are but caricatures of the latter. The pre-sociopath has a distinctively human character-architecture. He has values; he is internally conflicted; he can love others; he grasps the concept of non-instrumental goodness. The sociopath has none of these characteristics.

One becomes a sociopath. One ceases to be a psychopath. Psychopathy is a kind of perpetual infantilism. There is more to it than that, as we'll see, but that's the essence of it.

Unlike the sociopath, the psychopath never sold out. He had nothing to sell. One can't sell out unless one has values. Unlike the sociopath, the psychopath never had

---

44. Cleckley uses them interchangeably; he explicitly says that he does so. So does Martha Stoudt (2005). Hyatt (2001) does not use them interchangeably, and his reasons, though not explicitly stated, seem to coincide with mine. Very few authors are aware of the existence of sociopathy (i.e. of what I am referring to as "sociopathy"). Prominent exceptions include Nietzsche (1966, 1967a, 1967b) and Kernberg (1985, 1993). Niezsche's work is, in its entirety, an exposé of the pervasiveness of sociopathy.

45. Cleckley (1941).

values and, unlike the sociopath, he therefore never developed a distinctively human character architecture.

5.0 In Part II, we will identify the ways in which empiricism has corrupted philosophical and psychological views about aesthetics and morality.

For reasons already alluded to but not yet stated, the empiricist has to take very hard and counterintuitive lines about aesthetics and morality, these being:

(AM[46]) No musical work is better than any other; for none has any merit at all. No work of art of any kind is better than any other work of art; for none has any merit at all. No action is morally better than any other; for none has any merit at all. So far as we feel otherwise, it's because we are delusively projecting our sentiments into the external world, seeing as facts about objects what in actuality are facts about purely emotional, non-judicative responses to those objects.[47]

Some people accept AM. For example, psychopaths truly don't grasp the concept of moral value. So they really do believe the morality-related parts of AM. Tone deaf people truly don't grasp the concept of musical value. So they really do believe the music-related parts of AM.

But setting aside such cases, nobody *truly* accepts AM. And such cases *must* be set aside: the fact that a tone-deaf person believes the sound of a jackhammer to equal Mozart's Jupiter Symphony in aesthetic worth is comparable to a mathematical imbecile's belief that it's "a matter of opinion" whether 4 + 5 equals 9 as opposed to 45. The same thing *mutatis mutandis* holds of a psychopath's belief that torturing infants is neither better nor worse, morally speaking, than giving money to charity.

Many a philosopher professes to accept AM. But such a philosopher's affective and behavioral responses to personal circumstances and to artistic works are totally unlike those of somebody who actually has such views.

In Part II, it will be argued that, without advocating any sort of supernaturalism or counter-scientific view, it is possible to accommodate our aesthetic and moral intuitions. And it will be shown that, so far as people believe the contrary, it is because empiricism has a stranglehold on their thinking.

6.0 In Part II, we will outline an answer to the question: In what ways, and in what manner, does linguistic competence enhance cognitive competence? In other words, in what ways does knowing a language make one more intelligent than (*ceteris paribus*) one would otherwise be, and how does it do so?

---

46. Short for "aesthetics, morality."

47. Hume (1739), Ayer (1934), Stevenson (1937), MacDowell (1994), Blackburn (1998).

Some philosophers have said that:

(V[48])   There is nothing to thinking *other* than manipulating symbols.[49]

Others have said that

(V*)   Although symbol-manipulations obviously facilitate ratiocinative operations, anything that one can think with the help of symbols one can think without them.[50]

According to the second view,

(i)   Although linguistic competence helps one deploy one's cognitive competence, the former doesn't constitute the latter. Mastery of a language helps one use one's intelligence; but one's intelligence is one thing, one's mastery of a language is another,

and

(ii)   So far as linguistic competence enhances cognitive competence, it isn't because of anything inherent in the nature of language or thought; it's only because of contingent facts about human psychology.

V is false. A language is a set of semantic rules. A semantic rule is a proposition to the effect that a given expression has a given meaning. So *"4" refers to the number four* is a semantic rule. The semantic rules for *simple* expressions are purely conventional. "4" could refer to anything or nothing; it's just a matter of convention that it refers to the successor of three.

But what a complex expression means is *not* strictly a matter of convention. Supposing that sentence S has meaning M, S's having that meaning is a *logical consequence* of conventions concerning the simple expressions composing M, but it is not itself a convention. Let P be the proposition meant by

(SN[51])   "There are infinitely many prime numbers."

It is not a matter of convention that SN has P for its meaning. It is a logical consequence of the conventions assigning meaning to "prime," "number," etc. So, given only that one knows of these conventions, one doesn't know what SN means: one must figure out what PN means.

---

48. Short for "view (about language)."

49. Wittgenstein (1958, 1965).

50. Katz (1972), Lycan (1984), Chomsky (1988), Kuczynski (2002, 2003, 2004, 2007, 2009).

51. Short for "sentence concerning numbers."

In general, one must always figure out what is meant by a complex expression. This is because the meaning of such an expression cannot be directly determined by convention. If there were a convention to the effect that SN had P for its meaning, then SN would *ipso facto* be a simple symbol. Let SN* be an expression that, by our stipulation, has P for its meaning and is orthographically and acoustically just like SN. Even though, by hypothesis, SN* has the same meaning as SN, the former is semantically different from the latter. The *decompositions* of the two sentences are different. SN decomposes into a number of meaningful parts; SN* does not.

A related point is that, if somebody otherwise ignorant of the English language were told what was meant by sentence-tokens orthographically (acoustically) just like the one to the right of the indented occurrence of "SN," what that person would know would *not* be that SN meant P, but rather that

(SN#)   "Thereareinfinitelymanyprimenumbers."

meant P.

To be precise, such a person wouldn't even know that SN# meant P, since SN#, not being an expression, doesn't mean anything, and there is thus nothing that one could correctly believe it to mean or therefore know it to mean. What one would know is that *some* sentence-type whose tokens were homophones of those of SN# had P for its meaning.

A *bona fide* English-speaker not only knows what SN means, but also knows how it means it: he knows its "derivation-tree"; that is he knows what the conventions are that govern its simple parts as well as why, those conventions being what they, SN has P for its meaning.

What all of this goes to show is that the ability to think is a prerequisite for the ability to know or learn a language. So V is false.

6.1   But V*, though not completely incorrect, isn't completely correct either. It is hard to believe that, without being linguistically competent, a given creature could think *discursively*. Could such a creature have grasped the propositions and arguments embodied in Adam Smith's work *The Wealth of Nations*?

Surely not. This is what intuition tells us, at any rate, and it is the view of the present author and also, I should think, of most people. Intuition also tells us that one's having the cognitive wherewithal to write a treatise is not, at least not merely, an *effect* of one's having a certain degree of linguistic competence; intuition tells us that the two forms of competence are *constitutively*, as opposed to causally, related, and, therefore, that the relevant linguistic competence is a veritable *component* of the relevant cognitive competence, and not merely a precursor of the latter. The relationship borne by Adam Smith's cognitive competence with respect to his linguistic competence is not comparable to the relationship between borne by a person's being tall and healthy as an adult with respect to his having a good diet as a child. It seems that, at least up to a point, Smith's cogitations needed linguistic vehicles.

To make a stronger point, it seems to be a conceptual necessity, not an idiosyncrasy of human psychology, that Smith's cogitations needed linguistic vehicles of some kind. Some people can multiply large numbers in their heads; they don't need to use pencil and paper. Others, like myself, need to use pencil and paper. But this deficit of mine corresponds to an idiosyncratic fact about me, and not to anything inherent in what it is to multiply numbers. But the same doesn't seem to be true of Adam Smith's relationship to the thoughts embodied in his treatise. In other words, it seems a *necessary* fact – not one rooted in peculiarities of Adam Smith's or in those of members of our species in general – that symbolic operations are needed to mediate thought-processes of certain kinds.

Also, the person who multiplies large numbers in his head *is using symbols*. To be sure, the symbol-tokens he is using consist of mental imagery, not lead-deposits; but that is obviously of no significance in this context. So the fact people can have extraordinarily complex thoughts without speaking or writing anything down does not show that those thoughts aren't to some degree mediated by linguistic operations.

6.2   We thus have two, seemingly discrepant facts to work with:

(1)   One must be able to think in order to learn a language or to understand the expressions composing a language,

and

(2)   There are at least certain kinds of thoughts that one couldn't have unless one knew a language.

In Part II, a way of reconciling (1) and (2) is proposed. Our way of reconciling them is not empiricism-friendly, as it involves the (for reasons to be discussed) empiricism-unfriendly assumption that there is subpersonal thought. Subpersonal thought is unconscious thought that *underlies* conscious, pre-conscious, and repressed ideation. The cognitive operations (if any there be) that mediate vision, language-comprehension, musical ability, etc. are subpersonal. *You* don't figure out how to convert disturbances of your sensory surfaces into visual images. *Your mind* figures it out – but not you, i.e. not your *self*.[52]

In fact, it would make no sense to say that *you* figured this out. To do so, you would already need to be able to have sense-perceptions (or at least some way or other of acquiring information in real-time about the physical world), and you would also have to be able to perform extremely sophisticated post-perceptual operations. And to explain the latter, we'd have to posit *sub*-subpersonal cogitations.

So it would be viciously regressive to say that *you* – your self – carried out cognitive operations underlying sense-perception. Such a position, as Searle (1992) points

---

52. This "assumption" has been vigorously and effectively defended by Chomsky, David Marr, and other cognitive scientists. So, while it may be an assumption relative to this work, it is not an assumption *tout court*, but a well-established theory.

out, would embody the "homunculus fallacy": we'd be explaining your perceptions, thoughts, etc. by positing an entity inside you that *itself* had those thoughts and whose ability to have such thoughts would be no less in need of explanation than yours.

7.0   We will make frequent use of the words "consciousness" and "image" in this work, and we must make it clear what we will mean by those terms.

As it is ordinarily used, the word "consciousness" is ambiguous. Sometimes it simply means "awareness." This is how is it used in the sentence: "Franklin's growing consciousness of the complexities of the real number system made him realize that he was not as formidable a mathematician as Gauss." This is not how we will be using the term. We will be using it in the narrow sense that it bears in statements such as "whereas Smith's hatred of his father is unconscious, his awareness of the excruciating pain in his hand *is* conscious."

Relative to this narrow sense of the word, there are two senses in which a mental entity can be "conscious." It can be conscious in the sense that it is a *constituent* of consciousness. Or it can be conscious in the sense that it is *access-conscious*, to use Ned Block's term, meaning that one can readily become conscious of it. Sensations and perceptions are conscious in the first sense. When not repressed, propositional attitudes, as we'll presently seen, are conscious in the second sense.[53]

This last point needs to be justified. Beliefs, values, and propositional attitudes in general are not constituents of consciousness. They are structures. Unlike sensations and other constituents of consciousness, they are neither ephemeral nor phenomenologically pregnant.

It is inherent in certain propositional attitudes, e.g. one's belief that certain acts are deeply evil, that they tend to give rise to certain sorts of phenomenologically pregnant episodes. But given any one such belief, there is no one such episode to which the former necessarily gives rise; and that belief itself obviously doesn't consist of phenomenology, and neither, less obviously, does the onset of that belief. The onset of a belief is *likely* to be marked by surge of affect. But many belief-onsets are not thus phenomenologically marked. Second, when they are, that phenomenology is not constitutive of them.

7.1   As we will use the term "image," not all images are visual. There are acoustical images, tactile images, and possibly other kinds of images. An "image" is a phenomenology-mediated, sensuous, as opposed to conceptual, awareness of some actual or putative object. If an image is perceptual, it covaries in real-time with its object. A *perception* is an image whose (relatively) immediate cause is some present object. (The operative word is "relatively," since there are inevitably various physical, physiological and cognitive intermediaries.) The points just made about the word "image" hold

---

53. Freud (1998, 1915) makes this point very clearly.

mutatis mutandis with respect to related words, such as "imagery," "imagined," and "iconic."

7.2   To the extent that consciousness represents anything, it does so pictorially – through imagery, in other words. Conscious ideation is pictorial.

Concepts are not pictures.[54] Conceptual ideation is not pictorial. It does not consist of sequences of images. So *reasoning* doesn't consist in having sequences of images. One can reason *about* an image, just as one can reason about the consequences of a flat tax. But – with a qualification to be stated in a moment – conceptual ideation no more consists of images than it consists of government policies. Consciousness consists of phenomenology. Phenomenology is the mental analogue of paint or clay, and consciousness *qua* consciousness is no more capable than a deposit of paint or hunk of clay of mediating ratiocination.

But (and this is the aforementioned qualification) it is an empirical fact that, in some way or other, consciousness *becomes* capable of mediating ratiocination. And when it is made clear how this comes to be, it becomes clear what the kernel of truth is in the otherwise false position that thought is identical with manipulations of symbols.

7.3   Here is what I will argue.[55] Subpersonal ideation is not iconic. It is conceptual and, therefore, ratiocinative. Linguistic expressions give us a way of "perceptualizing" our ratiocinations. We can see occurrences of expressions; we can hear them; and we can touch them (if they are in Braille). This gives consciousness, which is hitherto confined to iconic ideation, a way of mediating ratiocinative ideation. Use of language involves the senses. It is through imagery that we grasp expression-tokens; and consciousness *qua* consciousness is capable of generating the requisite perceptual and post-perceptual images.

Images consist of phenomenology.[56] Images of linguistic expressions are images of garden-variety perceptible entities.

---

54. Freud (1998, 1924) very clearly makes both this point and the preceding one. See Chapter VII of Freud (1998) for a particularly deep discussion of the expressive limitations of iconic ideation. See Freud (1924) for a powerful discussion of the way in which consciousness-constitutive thought is conceptualized by being associated with expression-tokens. Freud's (1924) thesis is the starting point of virtually everything that I say about aesthetic, moral, and linguistic ideation, and also the way in which personal mentation comes to mediate rationality and agency.

55. "Posit" might be the right word, since, as I frankly admit in the relevant parts of the book, what I am saying is speculative.

56. This is probably subject to qualifications, relating to the distinct possibility that there is a conceptual dimension to perception. Perception is not mere sensation. Perceptions are articulated sensations, and the articulations correspond to conceptual knowledge or something comparable thereto.

The kind of phenomenology that mediates perceptual awareness of instances of one expression-type differs from the kind that mediates awareness of a different-expression-type: different expressions, different kinds of phenomenology. For reasons to be stated, subpersonal, non-iconic ideation becomes hewed to sequences of expression-images in much the way that, as Descartes discovered, geometrical propositions can be hewed to arithmetical propositions. As a result, different kinds of subpersonal ideation are associated with different kinds of phenomenology. But the mode of association has a very important property: those subpersonal thoughts are so hewed to the relevant image-series that if (in our judgment) those thoughts are correct (or valid or otherwise congenial), the vicissitudes in those image-series tip us off to that fact. (I will henceforth omit the parenthetical qualifiers.) The same thing *mutatis mutandis* holds with respect to incorrect subpersonal thoughts.

Just as pleasant affects alert us to the presence of certain structural features in works of music (or paintings or buildings), and unpleasant affects alert us to their absence, so congenial phenomenology alerts us to the presence of positive properties (e.g. truthfulness and validity) in expression-image series, and unpleasant affects do the same thing *mutatis mutandis*.

7.4   Berkeley (1710) said that "ideas are always of what is particular," his point being that we cannot have ideas of universals; in other words, we cannot grasp them. But he subjects this contention to a heavy qualification. He says that, although we cannot *directly* grasp universals, we can *indirectly* do so, by grasping linguistic expressions that mean them. A corollary of this contention, which Berkeley explicitly endorses, is that, although we cannot directly cannot grasp expression-meanings, we can do so indirectly, by grasping, and understanding, the corresponding expressions.

There is an obvious incoherence in Berkeley's position. To understand a given expression is to know what it means. If one's grasp of a given expression isn't distinct from one's grasp of its meaning, there is no sense in which one can coordinate that expression with its meaning and, therefore, no sense in which one can know what that meaning is.

But there is a certain, important truth in what Berkeley is saying. Consciousness, so far as it is representational, consists of images. Images do not in any non-derivative way have *abstracta* for their objects, and image-sequences do not in any direct way have propositions or proposition-series for their contents. And it *is* through language that *we* – our *selves*, as opposed to our minds – grasp *abstracta*. *Sub*personal ideation is inherently conceptual. Personal ideation is not; it is inherently iconic. (By "personal" I mean "relating to those strata of the mind *other* than the subpersonal stratum.") And the nucleus of one's self – though not of one's mind, which is an organization within one's mind – is consciousness. (I have not yet substantiated this claim.) So after a fashion, Berkeley is right. *We* don't grasp universals, *except* by way of linguistic-symbols. But – and this is where Berkeley is wrong – our *minds* can grasp universals non-linguistically; and they *must* do so if linguistic expressions are to mean anything to us.

7.4.1   Berkeley conflated images with concepts, using the word "idea" to refer to both. So, after a fashion, he was right to say that we couldn't have "ideas" of universals: images are not concepts and it is through conception that we grasp universals.

There are two reasons why Berkeley failed to distinguish images from concepts:

(i)   Since, according to empiricism, all knowledge is observation-based, and since observation consists solely of imagery, empiricism cannot in any obvious way countenance the existence of non-image-mediated thought; and empiricists must therefore identify concepts with images and thought-processes (sequences of concepts) with sequences of images.

(ii)   Concepts are not constituents of consciousness. So far as they are conscious, they are access-conscious, not consciousness-constitutive. Empiricism is not easily reconciled with the idea that there is mentation that isn't consciousness-constitutive; for empiricism is inimical to the idea of *any* invisible structure.

Empiricists are *ipso facto* disposed to make the mistake of identifying concepts with consciousness-constitutive entities, such as images. So, while Berkeley's failure to distinguish images from concepts may to some extent have just been a reflection of the intellectual epoch during which he lived, it also had roots in his empiricism. This is supported by the fact that Hume, Locke, and other empiricists also erroneously identify images with concepts. Also, to the extent that Berkeley's oversights were reflections of the beliefs prevalent during his lifetime, it is probably to some extent because, during that time-period, the just-mentioned empiricism-backed oversights were prevalent.[57]

7.5   The contentions in Part II that concern the relationship between language and thought are highly speculative, and I do not by any means definitively establish those contentions. But those points are much more important than the argumentatively solid parts of this book. I try to provide considerable argumentative support for most of the contentions put forth in the present work; and (so I would like to believe) I sometimes establish them. But the contentions, if any there be, that I establish are far less important than those which I not only fail to establish but for which I can provide only argument-outlines, not arguments-proper. The latter concern

– The relationship between language and thought.
– Selfhood, rationality, and agency: their interrelations and respective natures.

And

– The concepts of sociopathy and psychopathy, which are derivatives of the just-referenced points about selfhood (etc.).

---

57. At least in Britain and its colonies.

Considerable support is given for the contentions put forth concerning:

- The incompatibility of empiricism with certain plausible psychological views.
- The incompatibility of empiricism with certain plausible assumptions as to how best to study the mind.
- Propositional attitudes.
- Causation.
- Scientific explanation.
- The nature of the mentation mediating the making of inferences.
- The nature of meaning, in particular of propositions (the things we affirm, doubt, negate, etc.).

And

- The nature of the logical interrelations holding among propositions: more specifically, the nature of entailment (P entails Q if, supposing P true, not-Q cannot possibly be true), and the nature of confirmation (P confirms Q if, supposing P true, not-Q is *ceteris paribus* more likely than not to be true).

But, so the present author believes, those contentions, and the considerations adduced in their favor, are more or less just run of the mill philosophy; and so far as there is anything of value in the present work, it is to be found in the parts concerning the aforementioned, relatively speculative psychological contentions.

8.0   Let us resume our outline of the contents of Part I. Many a physicist self-describes as an empiricist. "*Hypotheses non fingo*," Newton said: "I don't frame hypotheses," his meaning being that he "stuck to the facts," and abstained from positing "occult forces," to use Newton's own term.

But Newton's work consisted of theoretical distillations of observational data, not mere reportage of such data. If Newton's theories are right, then

(i)   The gravitational attraction between two bodies is directly proportional to their masses and inversely proportional to the square of the distance between them;

(ii)   A given undisturbed body moves in a rectilinear fashion;

(iii)   A given body's gravitational mass coincides with its inertial mass;

and

(iv)   For every action, there is an equal and opposite reaction.

Supposing that (i)–(iv) are correct, we can observe instances of them. But we cannot possibly observe such instances *as* such instances. (Cf. We can see what are *in fact* aggregates of molecules, but we cannot see them *as* such aggregates.) We can observe instances of compliance with the inverse-square law, but we cannot observe such

instances as such instances.[58] It therefore wasn't on the basis of enumerative induction that Newton posited the Inverse-square Law. Certain concomitances of properties are observable, e.g. those given by statements like "it's a raven and it's black." But
such statements are not to be co-categorized with: "it consists of two objects and their
relationship to each other is governed by the inverse-square law." There is nothing
distinctive about the appearance of pairs objects whose positions with respect to each
other change in compliance with the inverse-square law. This is because neighboring
bodies will affect the form that such compliance takes, and there is no way to know
how to factor out the influence of such bodies unless one *already* knows what laws
they are obeying.

8.1   This does not mean that Newton's methodology was defective; it means that his
methodology wasn't strictly empirical. It is a given that his methodology was non-
defective and also that, relative to the observational data available to him, his results
were accurate (descriptively if not dynamically). In saying "hypotheses non fingo,"
Newton was saying that he didn't form *groundless* (non-observation-based) hypotheses, such as those whose only justification lay in scripture. He was not saying that he
abstained *tout court* from framing hypotheses.[59]

Many a physicist professes to accept empiricism, and probably *does* accept it –
when doing epistemology. But when doing physics, his self-ascribed empiricism is almost certain to drop out of sight.

The exceptions to this only confirm it, given how rare they are and of what a singular nature. One such exception was Ernst Mach. Mach was both a great physicist
and a great philosopher. As a philosopher, he was a hardcore empiricist. (See Mach
1976, 1984.) And at certain junctures, in certain respects, his empiricism actually did
affect his work as a physicist. As a result, he denied the existence of molecules; for he
saw that, as an empiricist, he couldn't countenance their existence, since it was only by
many an empiricism-unfriendly inference that their supposed existence could be teth-
ered to raw observation. As a result, Mach (1960, 1960b, 1986) took the characteristically empiricist position that molecules are but useful fictions that expedite research
but whose existence cannot be countenanced by the *results* of legitimate research.

Mach turned out to be very wrong. Einstein (1956) would soon come to show
that Brownian motion was inexplicable except on the assumption that molecules

---

58. Frank (1949) clearly makes this point.

59. In any case, this is what he was saying if he was sincerely and correctly describing his own
methodology. What I actually believe is that Newton wanted to make it as clear as possible that
his work was not of the same ilk as the work of some his scripture-compliant predecessors. Had
Newton correctly described his methodology, many would have dismissed his work on the
grounds that, like the work of many of his predecessors, it was just so much idle speculation.
For had Newton said, correctly, that, although *guided* by the facts, he wasn't *cleaving* to them
and was instead absorbing them into an intricate theoretical structure, he might well have been
criticized for failing to be "scientific."

really did exist. This was one of the few times that, as a physicist, Mach was wrong about anything. It was also one of the few times that he let his epistemological views affect his work as a physicist.

In general, a given physicist's philosophical (meta-scientific, epistemological) views have little or no effect on his work. Consequently, a physicist who has very wrong philosophical views is not for that reason likely to be less successful as a physicist than one whose philosophical views are spot-on. I would presume the same to be true of biologists, physicists, geologists, and practitioners of each of the other paradigmatically scientific disciplines.

8.2   But a psychologist's philosophical views *do* affect his work. Indeed, they determine what his foundational assumptions are.

As a philosopher, B. F. Skinner (1948) was an empiricist, his position being: "It doesn't exist if you don't observe it or have very direct evidence of it." For this reason, Skinner advocated a doctrine known as a "behaviorism." Behaviorism is the doctrine that mental states are identical with the overt behaviors that are ordinarily thought to be their effects.[60] So minds don't exist, except to the extent that they are identical with dispositions to engage in certain forms of overt behavior.

The justification for this doctrine, says the behaviorist, lies in the fact that

(i)   Minds cannot be sense-perceived,

taken in conjunction with the alleged fact that

(ii)   No evidence of them can be sense-perceived.

Being a behaviorist, Skinner held that psychology, *qua* legitimate discipline, studies nothing other than overt behavior.

There is an obvious objection to Skinner's position:

(SV)   One person cannot sense-perceive another person's mind. Skinner was obviously right about that. But isn't one directly, non-inferentially aware of one's own mind? And since, for that reason, one can correlate one's mental states with one's behavior, can't the behavior of another person be taken as evidence of his being in a certain sort of mental state?

The present author agrees with SV. But Skinner was quite aware that arguments such as SV would be used to undermine his view, and he had a response to such arguments:

---

60. The term "behaviorism" is ambiguous, as it sometimes refers to the doctrine that the mind is inherently devoid of cognitive structure and that it is only through operant conditioning and sense-perception that we learn. Skinner advocated both doctrines. This was no accident. Both doctrines collapse into one, as we will see in Chapter 8, Section 16. A corollary is that, if empiricism is right, minds don't exist.

(SR[61])   If they exist, mental states are inherently private. Science deals with what is public and thus with what is *inter*subjective, not subjective. There cannot possibly be independent corroboration for anything a given person says as to what is going on in his own mind. That means that there can't be *any* corroboration for such a statement. ("Independent corroboration" is a pleonasm.) Consequently, things for which uncorroborated testimony is the only evidence are things for which there is *no* evidence; and such things therefore don't exist for science and therefore might as well not exist at all.

SR assumes the very thing it is meant to establish. For if minds exist, there *is* independent corroboration for a given person's testimony as to his mental condition. I do certain things when, and only when, I'm in certain mental states (or so let us assume, to expedite discussion). I see Smith doing one of those things; so I infer that he's in one of those states. This sort of analogical reasoning, I find, makes it astonishingly easy to predict what other people will do, given what is happening to them now, and to figure out, given their current behavior, what happened to them previously.

Further, Smith is biologically just like me; we belong to the same species. And I know on the basis of well-confirmed scientific theories that specimens of a given biological (or chemical or physical) kind won't agree with each other in certain ways without also agreeing with each other in certain other ways. A given instance of some kind of metal won't have a certain coefficient of expansion unless all other such instances have the same such coefficient. For the same reason *mutatis mutandis*, a given creature with certain biological traits won't have certain other traits unless *all* creatures with those biological traits have those other traits. It would be a singularity of unprecedented proportions if, of the billions of people physiologically just like me, I was the only one whose physiology mediated mental activity. The counter-inductiveness inherent in positing any such singularity would be compounded in this case by the fact that other people's behavior is easily explained and predicted if, and only if, my situation isn't such a singularity. As we'll see in Chapter 5, Wittgenstein puts forth an argument similar to SR, which, predictably, fails for the same reasons as SR.

9.0   We must qualify our earlier statement that Skinner was an empiricist. There are two very different kinds of empiricism. One of them is the doctrine that all knowledge is based on *sense-perception*. (By "sense-perception," I mean sight, hearing, touch, etc.) The other is that all knowledge is based on *experience*.

According to the first, we are to take it for granted that *our sense-perceptions are correct and we know nothing that isn't directly or almost directly supported by them.* Skinner was an empiricist of this sort.

According to the other, we are to take it for granted that *experience, as opposed to pure reason, is the sole source of knowledge.* According to this sort of empiricism,

---

61. Short for "Skinner's response."

we cannot take it for granted that our sense-perceptions are accurate. Berkeley was an empiricist of this sort.

Empiricists of the Berkeleyan kind, but *not* of the Skinnerian, *are* skeptics about the veridicality of sense-perception.

The Berkeleyan view is a more authentic form of empiricism than the Skinnerian view. I'm having various experiences. I know *that* much on strictly experiential grounds. But those experiences could be hallucinations; and although it may be possible to establish that a given perception is veridical, it cannot be an experiential *given* that it is so.

Further, in assuming the veridicality of one's sense-perceptions, one is making an assumption for which there is no strictly experiential foundation. All evidence ultimately takes the form of experience. The footprints in the sand are evidence that another person is on the island *only* to the extent that I see or otherwise observe those footprints. It is thus my observations of those footprints, not those footprints *per se*, that are the evidential foundation of my belief that somebody else is on the island. An assumption without a strictly experiential foundation is *ipso facto* without an evidential or, therefore, an empirical foundation.

Unless one avails oneself of empiricism-unfriendly principles, it is impossible to establish the existence of a mind-independent reality of which our sense perceptions are accurate representations. But the existence of such a reality *can* be established *assuming* non-empirical, analytic principles of a rather trivial kind, e.g. "one explanation is better than another if *ceteris paribus* the world would contain more anomalies if the second were truth than if the first were true."

10.0   Even though, as we'll see in Part I, empiricism is not just false, but incoherent, it isn't by virtue of being false or incoherent that it has derailed psychological research. It is by virtue of embodying a certain attitude. The empiricist would rather know nothing and never be wrong than know much and often be wrong. It is therefore inherent in what empiricism is that it inhibit research, not stimulate it. Thus the researcher who accepts empiricism has *ipso facto* rationalized his failure to make progress and has *ipso facto* made virtues out of the deficits of intellect and character underlying that failure. "I'm not intellectually sterile," he says. "I don't lack the boldness necessary to innovate. I stick to the facts. I don't overdraw conclusions."

But the thinkers who make a difference *do* overdraw conclusions and *don't* stick to the facts. They withdraw those conclusions if the facts turn out not to align with them. But they aren't afraid to be wrong and they aren't ashamed of being wrong. A certain conservatism is necessary if hypotheses are to be subjected to proper scrutiny. A certain free spiritedness is necessary if there are to be any hypotheses to scrutinize. The empiricist sensibility has a place in science. But that place is in the verification-phase of the scientific process, not the discovery-phase.

In Part I, we'll discuss the strictly epistemological basis for this viewpoint. In Part II, we'll discuss the psychological basis for it.

CHAPTER 2

A dogmatic statement of the problems
with empiricism

1.0   In Section 1.1 of this chapter, we will make it clear how certain terms (e.g. "empiricism") will be used in the pages to come. In the course of making these terminological points, we will have to make some philosophical points, but none that are not of a generic, uncontroversial kind.

In Section 2, we will state the contentions that it is the purpose of the present work to defend. We will not provide reasons to accept those views. We will provide such reasons in the chapters following this one and, to a lesser extent, in Sections 3 and 4 of the present chapter.

In Section 3, we will outline a defense of one of the contentions stated in Section 2.

In Section 4, we will state and defend a contention concerning empiricism (one not stated in Section 2) whose veridicality will be assumed in the chapters to come.

1.1   According to empiricism, a given creature x knows a given truth T just in case one of the following two conditions is met:

(i)   x knows strictly on the basis of observation that T is the case, i.e. he knows it entirely on the basis of sight, audition, etc.

(ii)   Using no inference-rules other than those of whose validity sensory-observation has apprised him, x infers from what he directly observes that T is the case.

An "inference-rule" (or "rule of inference") is a truth that is given by a proposition of the form *if P, then Q* (e.g. *If x is round, then x is a figure of uniform curvature*).

Evidence can be of what is past, present, or future. The look of fear on Joe's face is evidence that Joe's stepfather is coming to town (evidence of a future occurrence). The look of melancholy on Joe's face is evidence that his stepfather is in town (evidence of a present state of affairs). The look of relief on Joe's face is evidence that his stepfather has left town (evidence of a past occurrence).

There can also be evidence of what is contemporaneous but absent (e.g. I can have evidence that, at this very moment, someone who is not in my presence is reading an article of mine); and there can be evidence of what is contemporaneous, non-absent, but unobservable (e.g. I can have evidence that, right now, there are various microscopic organisms damaging my ear-drum).

There are different kinds of unobservable entities. Some will come to be observed. Some could come to be observed, but won't. And some cannot possibly come to be observed: this is because observing the world involves interacting with it and therefore disturbing it, and in some cases the disturbances cannot even theoretically be diminished to a point where they don't eclipse the phenomenon we are trying to observe.

In this work, directly observing y to be the case is considered a limiting case of having direct evidence of y. Given this last point, empiricism comes to this: If you have evidence, believe; if you don't, don't. This is subject to the qualification that, for empiricism, all evidence is sensory evidence. (For some empiricists, introspective evidence is a kind of sensory evidence. For others it is not.) Logicians and philosophers speak of "logical" or "mathematical" or "conceptual" evidence; empiricists will have none of this.

In ordinary parlance, "observe," "observation," etc. sometimes refer to perception-based judgments (e.g. "Freud observed that repressed emotions are often expressed in consciousness as their opposites"). In the present work, and in philosophical works in general, the word "observe" has a narrower meaning, as it refers only to sight, touch, etc. and to the acquisition of knowledge based *strictly* thereupon. Thus, relative to the operative disambiguation of "observe," the term "direct observation" is a pleonasm – albeit a useful one, since it helps make it clear exactly how we will be using the term "observation" (and its derivatives: "observes," etc.).

2.0   The main problem with empiricism can be put into one sentence:

(MP[62]) Empiricism is inherently incapable of distinguishing between awareness of facts and awareness of truths, and the reason it is guilty of this failing is that it is inherently incapable of granting the existence of anything non-spatiotemporal.

Having condensed all of empiricism's shortcomings into MP, let us uncondense MP, so as to make it clear what those shortcomings are.

–   Empiricism cannot accommodate the fact that non-spatiotemporal entities exist. Since the non-spatiotemporal, were it to exist, would affect nothing, there could not possibly be any sensory evidence of its existence. So from an empiricist's standpoint, it doesn't exist.
–   Propositions are non-spatiotemporal. Therefore, empiricism denies the existence of propositions. Therefore, empiricism is unable to distinguish *objectual* from *propositional* awareness. In other words, it cannot distinguish awareness of truths from awareness of facts.

---

62. Short for "main problem."

- Truths are true propositions; knowledge is knowledge of truths. Therefore, empiricism cannot accommodate the fact that we are aware of truths. Nor, therefore, can it accommodate the fact that we know anything.
- Empiricism cannot accommodate the fact that we are aware of relations of logical dependence (entailment, (dis)confirmation, incompatibility). This is because propositions are the relata of such relations.
- Consequently, empiricists have very wrong views as to the nature of thought.
- Because empiricists don't know what propositional attitudes are, they don't distinguish between access-consciousness and consciousness proper.
- Because empiricists erroneously assimilate access-consciousness to consciousness proper, they have no choice but to deny the coherence of the concept of unconscious ideation and, therewith, the coherence of the concepts of rationalization, self-deception, repression, and displacement.
- Because they deny the existence of unconscious ideation, empiricists must deny that either language-use or language-comprehension is mediated by anything of which the language-user in question is not conscious. Empiricists must therefore deny that linguistic competence is mediated by unconscious or *a fortiori* subpersonal structures, and they must wrongly hold that there is nothing to knowing a language other than being disposed to have the right cognition-free reflexes.
- Given their erroneous views as to what it is to know a language, empiricists are wrong about

  (i)   the ways in which, by virtue of being linguistically competent, one is more intelligent than one would otherwise be,

  as well as

  (ii) the reasons why linguistic competence enhances cognitive competence.

- The structure of a given creature's psyche is causally and constitutively determined by the nature and degree of its cognitive competence. Thus, empiricism is systemically incapable of saying anything about how linguistic and cognitive competence affect character-architecture or, therefore, about what it is to have a distinctively human character-architecture.
- Empiricists cannot distinguish between urges and desires; between desires and intentions; or between intentions and values. This is because each such distinction is to be understood in structural, not phenomenological terms, and empiricists necessarily overvalue what is to be learned about a given mental state from its phenomenology (or, more accurately, from the phenomenologies of its effects on consciousness).
- Desires are judgments: they are judgments as to what will minimize distress or maximize pleasure. An urge is not a judgment; it is a psychological disturbance, whose cause is disruption of one's metabolic equilibrium, that precipitates a course of action that, thanks to evolution, is likely to restore the aforementioned equilibrium and, therefore, to eliminate the aforementioned disturbance.
- Desires therefore aren't urges.

- Intentions are not desires (*pace* Frankfurt (1988)). Like desires, intentions are judgments. But intentions, unlike desires, are system-level judgments; an intention is a judgment as to what one must do, in a given set of circumstances, if one's psychological architecture is not to be undermined. A desire, on the other hand, is a judgment as to what one must do, in given set of circumstances, if one is to maximize pleasure or diminish pain. (In Chapter 11, we will reconcile these contentions with the fact that people intentionally act self-destructively.)
- Values are judgments. A value is a judgment, on the part of a given person, to effect that if he is to retain, or *a fortiori* consolidate, his psychological integrity, he must act in certain ways and refrain from acting in others.
- Intentions are circumstance-specific judgments as to how to implement one's values.
- Empiricism cannot distinguish between *minds* and *selves*. Snakes are animate. Moreover, they are by no means devoid of intelligence. (They are more intelligent than clams; therefore they have at least some intelligence. But snakes don't have selves.)
- All selves are minds, but not all minds are selves. More accurately, any given self is a proper part of some mind; but many a mind has no proper part that is a self.
- The mind is an information-processing organ. The mind's original purpose, and its only purpose where sub-human organisms are concerned, is to ensure the relevant organism's biological well-being. A self is a mind whose host-body exists to serve *it*. Whereas the snake's mind exists to serve the snake's body, your body exists to serve your mind. The snake's mind exists to ensure that the snakes body survives; your body exists to ensure that *you* survive. Obviously your well-being involves your being physically healthy. But you don't identify with your body: you can imagine waking up in someone else's body, but not in someone else's mind. (This doesn't mean that minds are not constituted by physical entities. It means that a given physical structure can be identical with a mind only to the extent that the former mediates mental activity. Software is implemented by hardware; but it is only to the extent that hardware mediates activity of a certain kind that it can constitute a computer.)
- Selves are minds that have values. A mind that simply facilitates the gratification of instincts has no values. A mind *does* have values if it sees the gratification of instincts, and the concomitant maintenance of its physical well-being, as mere means to its own welfare. This is because such a mind sees value in mind-specific properties, such as the ability to have knowledge, to reason, to form intentions, to have the characterological virtues needed to carry out intentions, etc.
- A value is a belief on a given creature's part as to what, in general, it must do to consolidate or augment its agency. (In this context, thinking is a form of doing.) The first value is given by the proposition: x has value for y if y's agency depends on x. In this context, "first" is being used to denote both chronological and functional primacy; and it is being used to denote two different kinds of chronological primacy: ontogenetic and phylogenetic. There are other values, but they are all

derivatives of this one. In cases where a given creature's agency thrives by virtue of that creature's helping others, helping others is valuable to that creature. (That is, it's valuable in a non-instrumental sense.) Such cases exist. In cases where a given creature diminishes itself by helping others, helping others is of no value to that creature, even though, obviously, its deeds are of value to other creatures: such a creature's deeds are of instrumental, not of intrinsic, value – they are good only because they are instrumental in bringing about a state of affairs of which they are not themselves constitutive. A consequence of the truth that "x is good for y" means "x protects (or augments) y's agency" is that x isn't of value to anyone if it undermines everyone's agency. One of the axioms of contemporary ethics is that, if performed for the welfare of others, self-diminishing acts are intrinsically good. This axiom is false, as we have just seen. Self-diminishing acts of altruism are good in that they promote somebody's welfare. But since those acts are not constitutive of the welfare to which they lead, they are but means, not ends unto themselves. That the aforementioned falsehood is one of the axiomatic starting points of contemporary ethics is to be explained in terms of several factors. One of them: ethicists are predisposed for obvious reasons to co-categorize social (as in, not anti-social) acts with good acts. Another is that the just-mentioned axiom is easily conflated with the truth of that an act is good if it redounds to to the benefit of the agent's agency. Another is that a case can be made, and has been, that (in some cases, in some respects) x's welfare is constitutively dependent on x's mates' welfare. (I think this false, but not indefensible.) We must also remember that people expect to be rewarded (by God, or some such force) for their good deeds; and even those who reject this proposition at one level, probably hold onto it at another level. Even the most stout-hearted people simply stop trying to do good if their efforts yield them nothing (unless they're expecting a pay-off in the afterlife). This does not mean that people don't have values. They do: in fact, creatures that don't are, for that are very reason, non-people. And it doesn't mean that all acts are selfish acts. All acts – that is, all intention-driven behaviors – are value-driven. Sometimes those values make provisions for the welfare of others. When driven by such a value, at least one of the relevant agent's objectives is to help others. At the same time, for the reasons just given, any agent necessarily believes (at some level) that his act will benefit him.

– Because empiricists are forced to cram all of the mind's contents into consciousness, they have no choice but to see emotions and values as being mere "sentiments" that lack any objective basis. The reason: they don't strike consciousness as belonging to the same category as one's belief that $1 + 1 = 2$ or any other paradigm-case of an objectively-grounded conceit, and for that very reason they appear not to belong to that category. ("x strikes consciousness as being phi" and "x appears to have phi" are synonyms.)

– Empiricism cannot distinguish between intelligence and rationality. This is because to be rational is to be intelligent in the way of promoting one's *self*'s welfare, and the concept of a self is one that empiricists don't have.

–   Dogs have at least some intelligence, given that they are more intelligent than snakes. And so do snakes, given that they are more intelligent than clams. But dogs and snakes are not *rational*. The reason: their minds exist for the sakes of their bodies, not *vice versa*.

–   Empiricists don't have the option, as rationalists do, of saying that, embodied in the surges of emotion that we experience, are intuitive, unconscious, rationally generated judgments. So they can't say, for example, that the enjoyment you derive from listening to Bach embodies an awareness of the architectural virtues of his music; for it is impossible (not theoretically, but psychologically) to articulate the contents of that awareness, to the extent that one even has conscious access to those contents.

–   Empiricists are therefore forced to advocate radically counterintuitive views about aesthetics and morality. (No work of music is better than any other. No act is morally better than any other.)

–   Because empiricists must deny the existence of unconscious mental activity, the empiricist must downgrade intuitions to lucky guesses. (This viewpoint is radically absurd, given that, but for these "lucky guesses," there would not have occurred a single one of the theoretical innovations that separate us from our hominoid ancestors.)

–   All propositional attitudes are beliefs.

3.0   These are bold claims. The very last one is probably the boldest of all. An outline of our defense of that point will show it to be eminently defensible, the intended implication being that, in the context of the present work, *prima facie* audacious claims are not necessarily to be dismissed out of hand.

One can have different attitudes towards the same proposition. I can hope that Mom will come home; believe that she will come home; or dread that she will come home. "How is my *dreading* mom's coming home a belief?," it will be asked. "The answer is that it isn't. So you're wrong to say that all propositional attitudes are beliefs."

For me to dread that mom will come home to believe of the proposition *that mom will come home* that

(i)   it is likely to be true,

and that

(ii)   if it is true, it is likely to affect my life in undesired ways.

For me to intend to become the President is for the proposition *that I am currently the President* to be represented to me as

(a)   false,

(b)   potentially true with respect to some future time,

and

(c)   such that its being true would do more in the way of optimizing my condition than would any other proposition's being true (setting aside those that stand no chance of being true, either for reasons specific to my life-situation or for other reasons).

x's fearing that y will win consists in the proposition *y will win* being presented to x as being likely to be true and, if true, likely to have adverse consequences for x's existence. z's hoping that y will win consists in the proposition *y will win* as being presented to z as having positive consequences, supposing it true, for z's existence.

In general, different propositional attitudes towards a single proposition are acceptances of distinct propositions that have a common propositional part.

3.1   This argument-outline will be filled out in the pages to come, and arguments for the other (asterix-marked) contentions will be provided. With each new argument, it will become even clearer than before that the sensibility embodied in empiricism is inimical to the creation and cultivation of viable psychological theories.

This is more important than the fact empiricism is false. For epistemologists, empiricism is a doctrine. For others, it's a mentality. Outside of philosophy, few researchers know precisely what empiricism is or what it entails, and those who do have such knowledge are unlikely to modify their viewpoints or methods so as to bring them into alignment with the niceties thereby known.

4.0   Observations are not homogenous dollops of phenomenology: they are conceptually articulated. The empiricist says that all knowledge is observation-based. But embodied in every observation is conceptual knowledge. This holds no less of introspective observations than it does of sensory observations.

This brings to light that an incoherence lies at the center of empiricism. A consequence of this incoherence is that

(a)   it isn't clear in certain contexts what an empiricist *qua* empiricist ought to think;

And a consequence of (a) is that

(b)   empiricists have no choice but to advocate decidedly non-empirical viewpoints.

An example of (a): According to empiricists, we observe events, but not forces. We see sequences of events, but not the ties that link the members of such sequences to their neighbors. So such ties don't exist as far as the empiricist is concerned. Nothing makes anything happen.

There are three problems here. First, we *can* feel forces. This is obvious whenever one tries to lift a heavy object, to arm-wrestle somebody stronger than oneself, or to push one's car out of a ditch.

Second, the concepts of occupancy persistence, and motion are causal. It's absurd to suppose that x should occupy some place p without having the slightest affect on the behavior of would-be p-occupants. It's absurd to suppose that x's position relative to y has changed but that x's causal relations to y have not changed. It's absurd to suppose that some one object x exists from time t to time t* without x's state at t* being a consequence of x's existence at t. And in this context, surely, the word "consequence" doesn't refer to the relation logical consequence, since the latter is a relation that holds between propositions; so it clearly refers to the relation of causal consequence.

Third, given only what our eyes and ears tell us, it's not clear whether or not we observe instances of persistence, etc. *as* instances of causality. The present author believes that we do thus observe them. Embedded in perceiving an instance of persistence *as* such an instance is a conceit to the effect that the observed object's later states are causal consequences of its earlier states. And even if this contention of mine is false, it is not an empirical datum that it's false.

The empiricist's contention that we don't observe instances of causality was a function of

(i)   His focusing on causal processes of a specific kind,

and

(ii)   His failing to see that instances of that kind can be resolved into instances of persistence.

Also, space-time order must be understood in causal terms. e_1 precedes e_2 if and only if there is an actual or possible signal that can be sent from the former to the latter. A signal is a causal process: a series of events $e_1 \dots e_n$ such that, for any i ($1 \leq i < n$), e_i is the cause of e_{i+1}. So e_1 precedes e_2 if, and only if, e_1 affects e_2's condition.

Let us now justify the first of these three claims; the other two are defended in Chapter 8. Feelings of force are not given to us through sight, hearing, touch, sound, taste, or smell. The sense of touch is involved in, but isn't identical with, the modality through which pushes and pulls are perceptually disclosed to us. Touch apprises one of surface textures, not of mass. It is through our "bodily kinesthetic" sense that we sense-perceive facts of a dynamical (force-involving) nature. So there is a sixth sense: the bodily kinesthetic sense.

But let's suppose *arguendo* that we *don't* feel forces. That means that *either*

(i)   bodily kinesthetic perceptions are categorically hallucinatory

or

(ii)   such perceptions are *not* rightly *interpreted* as experiences of forces, but in some other way.

Hume chose (ii); and he was right to do so, given that (i) is obviously a non-starter. Having chosen (ii), Hume had to interpret the disclosures of bodily kinesthetic perception in such a way as to validate his contention that we are not perceptually aware of forces. To do this, he said that any given instance of what we describe as perceptual awarenesses of forces really decomposes into four other awarenesses: first, some kind of mental event on our part (an intention to move on object, or some such); second, a tactile sense-perception; third, an unpleasant feeling, of the sort one has when one is trying to do that last push-up; and fourth, a touch- or vision-mediated perception of the relevant object's state of motion. Thus, Hume's position was that, if I manage to lift an object that is *almost* too heavy for me to lift, what is going on is *not* that I am perceptually aware of some force, but is instead that

(A) I am introspectively (or, in any case, empirically) aware of my intention to lift the object,

(B) I have a tactile perception of the object,

(C) I have a sensation of displeasure, whose intensity is a function of the massiveness of the object I'm trying to move;

and

(D) upon having those three awarenesses, I know, through either sight or touch or both, in what respect, if any, I've managed to displace the object.

This analysis is decidedly artificial, and it is obviously *post hoc*.

More importantly, *even if this contention of Hume's is right,* it is not an empirical datum that he's right. If it were a datum, Hume wouldn't have to *analyze* our bodily kinesthetic experiences in order to reconcile them with his views about force.

Hume's decomposition of my bodily kinesthetic perception (my "BKP") into (A)–(D) is a theory-driven reinterpretation of perceptions that *prima facie* are counterexample his contention that we don't have empirical evidence of the existence of forces.

This doesn't mean that Hume's position is false. Maybe my BKP really *does* decompose in the way Hume says it does. But supposing Hume's position true, it's a theoretical truth, not a datum.

To be sure, given only that Hume's particular views as to how BKP's decompose are wrong, it doesn't follow that BKP's don't decompose in some way or other. And it may be that, if a given BPK is decomposed, it turns out that not a single one of its constituents is even *prima facie* rightly regarded as a force-perception. But if this is true, it is a theoretical truth, not an empirical datum.

Thus, it is often very unclear how to be an empiricist. Sometimes, in order to figure out how to be an empiricist in a given context, one must first resolve conceptual issues. In order to know what sort of stock to put in our bodily kinesthetic perceptions, one must subject the messages borne by such perceptions to theoretical scrutiny. The ratiocinative wherewithal involved in so scrutinizing such perceptions is *ex hypothesi* non-perceptual. Thus, *when confronted with a body of data, it may be a non-empirical question how to be an empiricist vis-à-vis that data.*

The present author would contend that this is *always* true and that, so far as it ever seems not to be, it's because nothing more than rudimentary and (functionally, not chronologically speaking) instantaneous ratiocinations are needed to answer the question "what would an empiricist say about this body of data?"

This brings us to a second, even more stark example of this principle. There are two kinds of empiricists: those who say that all knowledge is *observation*-based and those who say that all knowledge is *experience*-based. Let's refer to the former and the latter as, respectively, Type-1 and Type-2 empiricists. Type-1 empiricists take it as a given that we should accept what our eyes, ears, and finger-tips tell us; they hold that sense-perceptions are the givens on which knowledge is built and to which all contentions are directly or almost directly answerable. Type-2 empiricists deny that we can ever assume the veridicality of our sensory experiences. In their view, the givens on which all knowledge is based are sensations (e.g. aches, tickles) and sensory experiences, some of which, *if* veridical, constitute awarenesses of external objects, but the veridicality of which cannot be presupposed.

Both forms of empiricisms are incoherent. Let's start with Type-1 empiricism. Mental states cannot be sense-perceived. A corollary of Type-1 empiricism is a doctrine known as "behaviorism": the doctrine that mental states are *identical* with the overt body-movements to which they are ordinarily thought to give rise. One's belief that $2 + 2 = 4$ *is* the totality of behaviors of which, it is generally thought, it is the cause.

There are two problems with behaviorism. First, it's false. I touch a hot stove. I feel pain. The resulting overt behaviors are not identical with that pain.

Second, it is incoherent. Behaviorism is obviously not tautologically true. Therefore, behaviorism cannot be the tautology that overt behavior is identical with overt behavior. There must therefore be some x such that behaviorism is the non-tautology that x is identical with overt behavior. Whatever x is, it must be *presented* to people as being distinct from overt-behavior. Unless it is so presented, behaviorism collapses into the just-mentioned tautology. Surely those presentations cannot be overt behaviors. Thus, behaviorism presupposes the existence of mental states (*qua* things that are not overt behaviors), only then to deny their existence. (I'll henceforth leave out the *qua*-qualification.) Therefore, behaviorism is incoherent and so is Type-1 empiricism.

"But, it will be asked, "can't advocates of Type-1 empiricism say that we *are* of mental states, albeit not through one of the standard senses, but through an inwardly directly analogue thereof (through "introspection," in other words)?"

No. If one countenances the existence of perceptions, beliefs, and other mental entities, one can't take it for granted that facts about the external world are one's epistemic starting point. The beauty of Type-1 empiricism is that it allows one to start with external facts. Because it doesn't question the veridicality of our sensory-experiences, those experiences drop out, and all that's left are the facts of which they (were they existent and also veridical) apprise us. Type-1 empiricism presupposes a view rather like Sartre's, according to which minds are nothingnesses to which external facts are just present. [63] But if one countenances the existence of internal duplicates of external facts, the former being our sole source of knowledge of the latter, then one must ask the question: How do we know that the former are true to the latter? And if one asks that question, one's epistemological starting-point is *not* that we can trust our senses. Rather, one's starting point is Type-2 empiricism, which we'll now critique.

I see the chair. I have a visual perception of it. That's how I know of its existence. But I don't sense-perceive my sense-perception. So how do I know of *its* existence? First of all, I *do* know of its existence – that's indisputable. Second, that knowledge is empirical – that too is indisputable. (My knowledge that I'm having a chair-type sensory-experience – viz. a sensory experience that *if veridical* would be a perception of a chair – is not like my (non-empirical) knowledge that there cannot be laws without government.)

At the same time, it isn't by *observing* myself that I know that I'm having such an experience, or that I know that I believe that $1 + 1 = 2$, or indeed *anything* about myself. (I am setting aside facts about my physical body, which aren't facts about my *self* at all. I am also setting aside the things that can be learned about my unconscious by analyzing my behavior.)

This leaves us with a paradox. For Type-2 empiricism, experiences are our epistemic starting point. But it is not through observation that we know of these experiences. (Do you believe that $2 + 2 = 4$? Yes. Did you have to *self-observe* to answer that question? No you did not.) At the same time, that knowledge is empirical. So a consequence of the second sort of empiricism seems to be that we have *non-observational, empirical knowledge*, which is a (veritable) contradiction in terms.

This, however, is not the incoherence that lies at the heart of Type-2 empiricism. (Whether it is even *an* incoherence is a question we'll defer until Chapter 14.[64]) The incoherence is this. Self-observing involves being so mentally configured that one's

---

63. I say "rather like," and not "identical with," because Sartre was no behaviorist: in saying that minds were nothingnesses, he was not saying that they were nothing. Cf. "Space is not *nothing* – if space were *nothing*, then you and I would be separated by nothing and we'd be adjacent, which we're not. But space is a sort of nothingness, that being why things can occupy it." This is not *cogent* reasoning, in my view, but it's not obviously poor reasoning either.

In the present author's view, "space" has to be defined contextually. To speak of the "space," or spatial interval, between two things is to make an encrypted statement about their causal interrelations – about, for example, how many times a light-beam could pass between them during a given number of rotations of the Earth (or some other periodic process that could serve as a benchmark).

64. I will argue that it is indeed through *a* sort of observation that one knows that (e.g.) one believes that $1 + 1 = 2$, albeit one that is *not* derived through "introspection" or through any one sensory or para-sensory modality. It is derived, I will argue, complex amalgamation of empirical and purely conceptual knowledge.

own experiences are objects of one's consideration. The snake *has* perceptions. Those perceptions are awarenesses. But are those perceptions *themselves* objects of awareness? Do sub-human animals have second-order awarenesses?

Whether they do or not, it is clear that having such awarenesses involves a certain amount of conceptual horse-power. Having a perception is one thing; being aware of a perception is another; and being of aware of a given perception as a perception is yet another. No awareness of the first kind is an instance of the second; no perception is an awareness of a perception. (This is obvious: no argument needed.) Only some instances of the second are instances of the third. To have an awareness of the third kind, one must have the *concept* of a perception. The snake has perceptions, but does it know that it has perceptions? No – for it doesn't have the concept of a perception.

The just-made meta-perceptual points have meta-introspectual analogues. Imagine a triangle. If hosted by snake's mind, would a phenomenologically identical image be an image of a triangle? No. It isn't by solely by virtue of its phenomenological properties that your mental image is a triangle-image. You grasp the concept of triangularity, and it's because you've infused that image with that concept that the former represents the latter. But let us set that aside and ask: If the image in question *is* an image of a triangle, would the snake, were it aware of that image, be aware of it *as* a triangle-image? No. Even if the snake has the conceptual wherewithal to *have* an image of a triangle, it surely doesn't have the concept of an image of an image of a triangle.

Thus, introspection-based empirical knowledge is not strictly empirical. Consider my belief that I am now having the sort of sensory experience that, if veridical, is one of a computer-screen. To have such a belief, one must have concepts that one needn't have if one is to be able to have such an experience. One can see a rock without having the concept of vision, but one must have that concept to believe that one is seeing a rock.

Could the conceptual knowledge needed to report one's introspective findings itself be empirical? No. A *precondition* for such introspective knowledge is that one have certain concepts – e.g. *sensory experience, veridicality, external world*. Therefore, those concepts cannot be acquired *through* experience, and neither can the propositional knowledge that necessarily accompanies possession of those concepts.

To sum up, conceptual knowledge pervades perceptual knowledge, even knowledge that is as strictly based as possible on sense-perception; and this results in the paradox that it's often a conceptual, non-empirical question how to characterize a given body of data in a strictly empirical fashion. For this reason, and others, empiricism undermines itself.

CHAPTER 3

Empiricism's blindness
to the non-spatiotemporal

1.0   The non-spatiotemporal is causally inert. Therefore, there can be no evidence of it. For this reason, the empiricist denies its existence. The spatiotemporal world comprises things – rocks, trees, etc. – not truths or falsehoods: not *propositions*, in other words. Nothing besides propositions can be true or false; nothing besides sequences of propositions can be valid or invalid. (In this context, take "valid" and "invalid" to refer both to deductive (in)validity and to their inductive analogues.) A consequence is that bearing-relations – entailment, confirmation, etc. – cannot possibly be instantiated by anything other than ordered n-tuples of propositions. For example,

(T)   Triangles have three sides

entails

(T*)   triangles have more than two sides.

Thus, the ordered pair <T,T*> is an instance of the relation of entailment. n-place Relations are properties of ordered n-tuples. Entailment is a property of ordered pairs, since it's a two-place property. Redness and roundness are one-place relations.[65]

Obvious extensions of this argument show that nothing besides ordered n-tuples of propositions can be instances of (dis)confirmation or (in)compatibility.

To reason is to attempt to identify the bearing-relations among the propositions one believes or assumes to be true. Propositions are non-spatiotemporal. So nothing could reason if everything were spatiotemporal. Nor could anything know anything, since propositions are the objects of knowledge.

2.0   The following argument is valid:

(AR[66])   Bob smokes. So does Jerry. Therefore there is some property that they have in common.

---

65. Technically, this isn't true. We've already seen that redness is a 3-place relation. Roundness is also a 3-place relation: a given object is round relative to a given inertial framework, and to a given objective that is stipulate to be straight. So roundness is a property of ordered triples <x, y, z> such that x is an object (e.g. a basketball), y is an intertial framework (an object that is stipulated to be stationary), and z is an object that is stipulated to be straight.

66. "Short" for argument.

But if properties don't exist, this argument is not valid. (Actually, this argument doesn't even exist if there are no properties, since this argument consists of propositions, as do all arguments, and propositions consists of properties. But for argument's sake we are granting the empiricist's counter-logical assumption to the contrary.)

"But you are assuming," it will be objected, "that properties are non-spatiotemporal. But you may very well be wrong about that. Some hold that properties are identical with 'scattered objects' consisting of their instances – that the property of being made of water consists of a non-cohesive, extremely voluminous object whose parts include everything that is made of water and nothing that isn't."

We've already seen why properties can't be identified with scattered objects or, indeed, with spatiotemporal objects of any kind. Given any spatiotemporal object O and any property P, one can change O without changing P. So properties are not scattered objects or words or, by obvious extensions of this argument, with anything else that is spatiotemporal.

3.0   According to many philosophers (e.g. Wittgenstein 1922; Carnap 1937; Ayer 1934; Van Frassen 1977), it is linguistic conventions that determine whether a given inference goes through or not.

This is false. There are no conventions that directly concern AR. There couldn't be, since (so we may assume) that argument has never previously been stated.

Also, it is incoherent to suppose that an *argument* could be valid by convention. An argument is a sequence of statements $S_1...S_n$ such that, given $S_1...S_{n-1}$, S_n is (supposedly) likely to be true. (There are spurious arguments. Hence the "supposedly.") We can stipulate what S_i means, for each i ($1 \leq i \leq n$). But *given* those stipulations, it's a matter of mind-independent fact whether $S_1...S_{n-1}$ support S_n. This is a consequence of the fact that our conventions don't determine what there is, except to the infinitesimal degree that our conventions are themselves constitutive of what there is. (It isn't a matter of convention whether Jupiter is bigger than Mercury or whether there is drinkable water in Manitoba.) For P to entail Q is for the argument P, *therefore* Q to preserve truth (or, if it's an inductive argument, for it to be more likely than not to preserve truth, other things being equal). It is not a matter of convention whether $S_1...S_{n-1}$ are true, or whether S_n is true. So if S_n is (likely to be) false but $S_1...S_{n-1}$ are true, then $S_1...S_n$ is a bad argument; and no matter what the truth-values are of the statements composing it, $S_1...S_n$ is a bad argument so long as there is *some* statement series $S^*_1...S^*_m$ such that

(i) $S^*_1...S^*_{m-1}$ are true

(ii) S^*_m is false;

and

(iii)   the *relation* of $S^*_1...S^*_{m-1}$ to S^*_m coincides with that of $S_1...S_{n-1}$ to S_n.

Even if *per impossibile* there are conventions regarding similar arguments, it's a matter of mind-independent, non-empirical fact how those conventions are to be applied to AR and thus whether AR is valid.

3.1   It isn't a matter of convention whether the conventions we adopt are consistent with one another. Nor is it a matter of convention what follows from those that we adopt. (These two statements are equivalent.)

It is a matter of convention that "2" refers to the successor of 1; that "3" refers to the successor of 2; that "+" refers to addition; etc. Let $c_1...c_{n-1}$ be these conventions; in other words, let them be our actual arithmetic-related symbolic conventions. If we wish, we can add another convention, c_n, to the effect that "3" is the smallest integer whose square is greater than itself. But $c_1...c_n$ is not a consistent set of conventions, the point being that, while it's up to us what our conventions are, it's not up to us whether they're internally consistent.

Contrary to what one might think, we can't compatibilize $c_1...c_n$ with one another by adding further conventions to them – by, for example, adopting a convention, c_{n+1}, to the effect that "3" is ambiguous between *smallest integer that is smaller than its square* and 3. $c_1...c_{n+1}$ contains a convention to the effect that "3" refers to 3 as well as one to the effect that some distinct, but homophonic expression also refers to 2. More importantly, the very fact that we'd have to modify $c_1...c_n$ to make that set internally consistent only proves that there are non-conventional, strictly logical desiderata that a given body of conventions must satisfy if it is to be internally consistent.

These same points establish that it's not up to us what our conventions entail. If it were up to us what $c_1...c_n$ entailed, then it would be up to us whether they entailed both P and not-P, for some proposition P. Since that isn't up to us, it isn't up to us what the logical consequences are of $c_1...c_n$ or, by parity of reasoning, what the consequences are of any other body of conventions.

3.2   Words themselves are properties. (We saw why in Section 2.1.3.) This constitutes another reason to reject conventionalism.

Logical relations *prima facie* hold in virtue of non-spatiotemporal facts. Conventionalism is meant to show that they *don't* hold in virtue of such facts. Conventionalism is also the view that they hold in virtue of facts about expressions. But expressions are platonic entities. That is, expression-types are platonic entities – expression-tokens are not. But conventions are inherently general; there can't be conventions governing some one occurrence (token) of the word "two." There are conventions concerning the word-*type* "two."

Thus, even if conventionalism is correct, it doesn't have the pro-empiricism, anti-metaphysical consequences it is meant to have: it doesn't show that there is no non-spatiotemporal realm.

Also, if, as conventionalism assumes, there are word-types, then there are properties. If there are properties, then there are truths about them. And at least some of those truths must be non-empirical. It's an empirical truth about the property of being a mansion made of solid gold that nothing instantiates it. It is a non-empirical truth about that property that, if it is instantiated, then there is a domicile of some kind or other made of some one substance. It is an empirical truth about the word-type "two" that many instances of it occur in books by Russell. It is a non-empirical truth about it that, if its instantiated, those instances don't have five syllables. Another such non-empirical truth is that the membership of a set containing the syllables constitutive of any given instance of that word is incapable of being put into a one-one correspondence with the membership of a set whose cardinal number, when squared, yields the successor of 24.

There is no truth to the position that expression-types are bursts of noise or deposits of ink. There is a shred of truth to the position that expression-types are *types* of noise-bursts and ink-deposits – but only a shred. (Henceforth, take "bursts of noise" to refer, not just to bursts of noise, but ink-marks, hand-signals, and anything else that can token a linguistic expression.) Expression-types are instances of *relations* of a certain kind. The relata of those relations are (i) conventions of a certain kind and (ii) meanings. Any given such convention is to the effect that, if x is a burst of noise, etc. that is, in certain respects, physically similar to some noise-burst resembles some paradigm noise-burst, then, in virtue of having the form "...x...," a given sentence has such and such conditions of satisfaction. An expression-token is an *instances* of the sort of relation just described. We'll substantiate these points in Chapter 5, Section 2.

Also, unless properties existed, we couldn't make stipulations as to how words were to be used. Such a stipulation defines a standard to which usage of a given expression is to conform. A standard is nothing other than a property that ought to be instantiated. (For you to meet a given standard is for you to instantiate some property that you should instantiate.) Since our senses apprise us of facts, not of properties, they don't apprise us of standards; wherefore the very concept of justification must be an incoherent one if empiricism is to be correct.

4.0   There are other, subtler reasons to grant the existence of non-spatiotemporal entities.

There are true thoughts and false ones. What are false thoughts false thoughts *of*? What is the object of a false thought?

Given any belief B, there is some proposition P such that B is true iff P is true. Given any proposition P, there are properties $p_1...p_n$ such that P is true iff $p_1...p_n$ are jointly instantiated. (We saw why this is so in 2.1.2) If S is the smallest set containing $p_1...p_n$, then P is identical with S, and P's being true is identical with S's members' being jointly instantiated. If B* is a false belief, then there is some proposition P* such that B* is true iff P* is true and such that P* that is identical with a set S* whose members include properties $p^*_1...p^*_m$ and nothing else, and whose members are *not* jointly instantiated. Those properties exist, even though the fact in virtue of they would be instantiated does not and neither, therefore, does the fact in virtue of which P would be true.

Non-existent facts can't be the object of awareness. Consider the statement "Smith is aware of non-existent fact F." That entails: "there exists some fact F such that F does not exist and Smith is aware of F," which is self-contradictory. We can be aware of existent, but uninstantiated properties, and therefore of existent, but false propositions. So far as there is any in sense in which we are aware of non-existent facts, it is by virtue of knowing a some proposition-constitutive set of properties to be jointly uninstantiated. It follows that, without uninstanaitated properties, there can't be false thoughts.

It also follows that properties are not identical with their instances or indeed anything spatiotemporal. This is because distinct, uninstantiated properties have the same (null) extension, a consequence being that the property of being a briefcase full of money in JM's room is identical with the property of being an empty briefcase in JM's (briefcase-free) room.

4.1   There are some subtleties we must deal with to complete our answer the question "what are false thoughts false thoughts *of*?" First of all, we must distinguish a thought's *content* from its object. (In this context, "thought" is synonymous with "belief.")

The content of a thought T is some proposition P such that T is true exactly if P is true. There are other conditions that P must satisfy. If B is my belief that

(TT)   Tom is tall,

B is true is true exactly if

(AC)   either Tom is tall or arithmetic is complete.

is true. But AC is not B's content. But for our purposes, it's enough to know that the content of a belief is *some* proposition whose truth is necessary and sufficient for that belief's veridicality.

A true belief is an acceptance of a true proposition. There are two kinds of truths: empirical and conceptual (analytic). Let P and Q be any two empirical propositions such that P is true and Q is false. It isn't by virtue of anything *inherent* in either proposition that P is true and Q is false; it is by virtue of their respective relations to the facts. In general, empirical truths are *extrinsically* but not *intrinsically* different from empirical falsehood.

The same thing *mutatis mutandis* holds of empirical beliefs. Smith believes that Mary is wealthy. Jones believes that Mary is poor. Supposing that Smith (Jones) is right (wrong), it isn't because of anything intrinsic to his belief. It's because of something intrinsic to the *relation* borne by his belief with respect to belief-transcendent facts.

Analytically true propositions *are* intrinsically different from analytically false ones. For a proposition to be analytically true (false) is for it to be true (false) in virtue of its constitution, and nothing besides. Analytically true beliefs are therefore intrinsically different from analytically false ones. Given *only* that Smith believes, whereas Jones disbelieves, that there are regular 17-sided polygons, it *can* be determined who is right strictly on the basis of the structures of their respective beliefs.

That said, what is relevant in the present context is that true *empirical* beliefs are not *ipso facto* different from false empirical beliefs. And in this context, when we use the words "thought," "belief," and the like, we'll be referring to *empirical* thoughts and beliefs.

4.2   The contents of this section repeat, but also justify, points made in Section 4.0.

The content of a thought cannot be a fact. Otherwise, false thoughts would have no contents and thus wouldn't be thoughts. Also, if thought-contents were facts, no thoughts would be true or false. This is a consequence of the fact that

(i)   facts are neither true or false

taken in conjunction with the fact that:

(ii)   it is in virtue of the truth or falsity of its content that a given thought is true or false.

(ii) illustrated: It is in virtue of what it means that "snow is white" is true. An analogous point holds of the belief that snow is white. So if thought-contents were thought-objects, the identification of thought-contents with thought-objects would have the consequence that no thoughts were true (or false). Facts cannot be affirmed. Their existence can be affirmed. But affirming x and affirming x's existence are different things, as we're about to see.

False thoughts, presumably, have no *objects*. So the question becomes: what are their *contents*? Given any thought T, there is some set of properties $s_1....s_n$ such that T is true just in case $s_1...s_n$ are jointly instantiated. (From now on, we'll let "S" abbreviate "$s_1....s_n$.") For a content to be *true* is for some property to be instantiated. (The property in question may be conjuntive in nature.) For a content to be *false* is for some property to be uninstantiated. For there to be such a thing as falsehood, it is enough that there be so much as a single uninstantiated property.

Consider the property of being a square. It exists. That's why we can say of certain things that they don't have it. The proposition *there are no squares* is true iff the property of squareness is uninstantiated. That proposition's being true is identical with that property's being uninstantiated.

For there to be such a thing as *error*, however, it is not enough that there be uninstantiated propositions. There must be propositions (properties) that are presented to some creature as being instantiated that are not instantiated.

The same points *mutatis mutandis* hold with respect to truth (as in true propositions) and rightness (the property of being right).

It is an empirical fact that there exist things (thoughts, perceptions) that have contents. It is an empirical fact that some of these are true and others are false. (We'll omit the necessary qualifications relating to the distinction between veridicality and truth.) The following is a truth but is not empirical: Given any thought T, there is some property P such that P's (not) being instantiated is identical with T's being true (false).

5.0   Since our senses don't tell us anything about non-spatiotemporal beings, they don't tell us whether they exist or not. So if there are reasons for denying the existence of the non-spatiotemporal, they cannot be known empirically.

Most people and scholars simply take it for granted that everything that exists is spatiotemporal. (This is subject to obvious and insignificant qualifications relating to religious and mystical views, e.g. that the Almighty is non-spatiotemporal.) And when any given one of these nay-sayers *does* defend his position, he does so thus:

(MR[67])   The non-spatiotemporal cannot affect the spatiotemporal. So there's no need to posit it. Why posit what you don't have to posit? Why posit what, if posited, would do no explanatory work?

The first sentence of MR is correct. Anything that can affect the spatiotemporal is *ipso facto* spatiotemporal itself. Causes must have spatial and temporal relations to their effects and must therefore be spatiotemporal.

But MR involves a major oversight. Right now you are seeing certain ink-marks. The reason is that light-beams reflected by those ink-marks, and whose structures encode those of those ink-marks, strike your eyes, are precipitating a cascade of physiological and cognitive whose end result is a perception. Let R be the just-mentioned series of light-beams. If struck by R, would a *rock* see anything? No. What's the relevant difference between you and the rock? R doesn't transport perceptions into your cranium; it *elicits* perceptions from you. It does this by activating content-bearing neural structures. The contents in question are concepts of the properties that your R-induced visual experience represents the rock as having. You see the rock *as* having shape, color, etc. and thus *as* being an instance of certain properties; wherefore you, or your mind, must grasp these properties. The rock doesn't grasp any properties. Its structure isn't content-bearing.

We learn about the external world by being on the receiving end of causal processes initiated by its constituents. But those causal processes would not elicit perceptions from us, let alone post-perceptual thoughts, unless *already* embedded in our physiological structures were awarenesses of properties. So, contrary to what MR asserts, we *do* need to posit the existence of the non-spatiotemporal. (Properties are non-spatiotemporal, as we've seen time and again, and we have no choice but to grant their existence.) Causal processes would mean nothing to us and, as far as we are concerned, would bear evidence of nothing *unless* we had causal-process-independent knowledge of non-spatiotemporal entities. So MR is simply wrong to say that there is no need to a posit a given thing if there is no "evidence," for it, where x is "evidence" of y if the two are so causally related that y probably exists given that that x does. For a *precondition* for the existence of evidence, in that sense, is knowledge of what is non-spatiotemporal.

---

67. Short for "main reason." Benaceraff (1965) puts forth an argument similar to MR.

These points are not new. Chomsky (1959) made them. So did Leibniz (1704) and Kant (1787).[68] To teach is to elicit knowledge. You can teach somebody with musical talent how to compose, because the structures that mediate compositional ability are already there and merely haven't yet been activated. For the same reason *mutatis mutandis* you cannot teach the art of composition to somebody in whom such structures are absent.

Points similar to those just made about sense-perception hold with respect to theory-formation. A scientific discipline isn't just a heap of data. Disciplines organize data. Empirical data cannot tell you how to organize them. And even if *per impossibile* empirical data *did* come with instructions as to how it ought to be organized, those instructions would be useless to you unless you understood them. But, supposing that all your knowledge were observation-based, how would you decode them? Where would you acquire the knowledge necessary to do so? First of all, such knowledge would itself be knowledge *about* the data of experience. It would be meta-data, and it wouldn't be available to you unless you'd already organized your experiences correctly. And this, by supposition, you could not possibly have done.

Additional experience wouldn't help; it would just leave you with more material that you had to decode but couldn't. Thus, your knowledge as to how to organize data cannot itself be derived from empirical data. Thus, the principles on the basis of which empirical data are organized must be known non-empirically.

6.0   This brings us to an oversight that has done much to make empiricism seem more worthy of credence than it is.

There are two very distinct ways in which sensory-observation leads to knowledge. In some cases, what one learns from a given sense-perception coincides with its content. I see a dog with a bone in its mouth, and on this basis I know that there is a nearby dog with a bone in its mouth. Here my perception is to the effect that there is a dog (or dog-shaped and otherwise dog-similar) object with a bone in its mouth. This is the content of my perception, and it is what I know on the basis of that perception.[69] In this context, the thing learned coincides with the content of my perception; my learning that thing consists in that content's being transferred from my perception into my ken. Let's say that, in this context, my sense-perceptions are functioning in a "content-transferring" manner and that the resulting knowledge is "CT-knowledge."

6.1   Not all observation-initiated knowledge is CT-knowledge. Sometimes the content of a given sense-perception to no degree coincides with the knowledge in which

---

68. Also, Plato made this point in the *Meno*.

69. In this context, we're setting aside irrelevant subtleties relating to the distinction between objectual and propositional awareness and between conceptual and non-conceptual forms of ideation. The nature of those subtleties will be discussed at length in the pages to come.

it eventuates. Sometimes a given sense-perception *triggers*[70] ratiocinative processes that eventuate in knowledge of a non-empirical kind. You see various marks on a chalkboard. Those perceptions trigger mathematical cogitations that eventuate in your knowing the Pythagorean Theorem. Those perceptions *also* give you CT-knowledge: they make you aware of the fact that a certain chalkboard has certain markings on it. But that CT-knowledge is of no importance *except* in so far as it triggers mathematical ratiocinations. Your knowledge of the Pythagorean Theorem is thoroughly non-empirical. But it was *occasioned*, to use Kant's term, by empirical knowledge that you had.

Two short stories will extirpate any lingering doubts as to the non-empirical nature of that knowledge.

First story: You didn't see a chalkboard. You didn't see any markings. It was all a hallucination. But your hallucinations were experientially just like the veridical perceptions that, in the other scenario, precipitated the cogitations that led to your knowing the Pythagorean Theorem.

In this scenario, your sensory experiences *do not* apprise you of anything having to do with a blackboard or with chalk-marks. So those sensory-experiences, unlike their veridical counterparts, fail to give you CT-knowledge. But you still learned the Pythagorean Theorem, it being irrelevant that the relevant thought-processes were instigated by hallucinations, as opposed to veridical perceptions. You are quite as aware of the truth of the Pythagorean Theorem as you would have been if *ceteris paribus* it had been veridical experiences that instigated that process.

Second story: Smith sees various ink-deposits in a book he's reading. This leads to him knowing that there are more real numbers than rational numbers. Jones hears various noises made by somebody giving a lecture. This leads to him knowing the very same thing. Smith's CT-knowledge is totally different from Jones' CT-knowledge. The markings that Smith sees do not, and couldn't possibly, bear any resemblance to the noises that Jones hears. And yet they've acquired the very same mathematical knowledge. This is because, in each case, that knowledge was the end-product of ratiocinative processes that, although triggered by sensory experiences, were themselves purely conceptual.

6.2   Let us use the term "TR-knowledge" (short for "trigger-knowledge") to refer to knowledge acquired through ratiocinations that happened to be instigated by sensory experiences.

Many philosophers fail to distinguish between CT-knowledge and TR-knowledge, simply assuming that *all* post-perceptual knowledge is CT-knowledge. Many greats (e.g. Locke, Mill, and Quine) are among those who don't make this distinction

---

70. This is the term that Fodor uses, in his masterful (1981b) discussion of the two different epistemic roles had by sense-perception. Kant (1787) was extremely aware of this distinction. He deserves credit for being one of the first major philosophers to recognize it. Kant used the term "occasion" instead of "trigger."

and who for, that reason, endorse some very wrong views. (Cf. Locke's argument that, if mathematical knowledge were non-empirical, then newborns would know the Pythagorean Theorem. Cf. Mill's contention that one learns arithmetical truths by observing physical processes, e.g. a balancing pan's suddenly sinking when an extra pebble is placed on it. Cf. Quine's similar contention that a person's mathematical, logical and philosophical beliefs are empirical beliefs that are unusually deeply entrenched in his belief-system and that he therefore cannot give up without making drastic and pragmatically contraindicated changes to his belief-system. Quine (1951) puts forth a rather elaborate argument in support of this contention, which we will evaluate in Section 7.0.) In any case, no sooner does one make this distinction than knows that empiricism, at least in its strictest form, is false.

This is not to deny that *on certain matters*, the empiricist is right and his opponent his wrong. We *do* have empirical knowledge that we wrongly believe to be non-empirical. And we often wrongly believe empirical matters to be resolvable through pure thought, with the result that we have additional wrong beliefs. For example, a given person's knowledge that weight is at least an *approximately* additive property is empirical, even though he is likely to think otherwise. A consequence of Relativity Theory is that an aggregate of two one pound rocks is just slightly *over* two pounds. This means that it is not *incoherent* (though it is false) to hold that the aggregate weight of two one pound objects is five pounds. This in turn means that, if a person knows that weight is at least approximately additive, he knows it on empirical grounds. If it's because one believes that weight is *perfectly* additive that one believes it to be approximately so, then one doesn't *know* that weight is approximately additive: that belief, being only coincidentally correct, doesn't qualify as knowledge. By the same token, if one really *knows* that weight is at least an approximately additive property – and surely many people *do* know this – that knowledge is empirical, even though those who have such knowledge may wrongly think it conceptual, not empirical, in nature.

In the context of the present work, however, what matters is not that people wrongly take empirical matters to be conceptual ones, but that, because they fail to distinguish CT- from TR-knowledge, they wrongly take conceptual matters to be empirical ones.

7.0 Quine (1951) argues that all truths, setting aside *formal* truths, are empirical. Quine says that, if they exist, (informal) analytic truths, hold in virtue of relations of synonymy. So according to Quine, "a bachelor is an unmarried adult male" is an analytic truth, if anything is, because the term on the left side of the verb is synonymous with the term on the right side. To say that two expressions are synonymous is to say that they have the same meaning. To say that two terms are synonymous, says Quine, is to say that whatever analytically follows from a given sentence S containing the one term also follows analytically from a sentence S* that is just like S except that, in the places where S contained the one term, S* contains the other. So analyticity is to be defined in terms of synonymy, which is to be defined in terms of analyticity, which is to be defined in terms of synonymy. There is thus no non-circular definition of "analytic," and the concept of an analytic truth is thus an incoherent one.

Analysis: Only trivial analytic truths hold in virtue of synonymy relations. Non-trivial ones don't hold in virtue of such relations. An example of a non-trivial analytic truth is: *one has no legal obligations under a government that grants one no protections.* Another is: *any being that had complete knowledge of the future could not possibly be an agent.*

Also, "analyticity" *is* non-circularly definable: an analytic truth is one that holds in virtue of facts about the structures of properties. "A given object isn't a circle unless it encloses at least as large an area as any perimeter-equal figure": this is an analytic truth, and it holds entirely in virtue of the structures of the properties composing it (e.g. the property of being a circle). It does not hold in virtue of synonymy-relations.

Quine would be begging the question if he countered by denying the existence of properties. In alleging that all truths are empirical, Quine is *ipso facto* denying the existence of non-spatiotemporal entities and, therefore, of properties.

Further, Quine's position refutes itself. Consider the statements:

(a) If there are no analytic truths, nothing follows from anything.

(b) If nothing follows from anything, then nothing follows from the truth that nothing follows from anything.

(c) If nothing follows from anything, it follows that, given only that grass is green, it doesn't follow that grass has a color.

Each of these statements is analytically true, and the statement "there are no analytic truths" is therefore self-defeating.

Further, if all knowledge is empirical, then it's always an empirical question whether a given proposition is warranted by a given observation. Until we have an answer to that question, we aren't entitled to affirm any propositions. But observations themselves cannot give us the answer to that question.[71] Observation can't give us knowledge as to how to interpret observations. So, in the absence of non-empirical knowledge, we're stuck at the level of objectual-awareness, never making it to propositional-awareness or, therefore, to belief or, therefore, to knowledge.

7.1 A number of logicians have held that all analytic truths were *formal* truths.[72] They sought to show that a truth is analytic in virtue of having, or being capable as being represented as having, the form *P or not-P* or $(x)((y)Ry \rightarrow Rx))$, etc. This belief underlies Quine's view that it's only on the condition that "bachelor" is synonymous with "unmarried adult male" that

---

71. Dummett (1973) and Bonjour (1998) both put forth this argument.

72. Frege (1879, 1884), Russell (1903, 1920), Carnap (1937, 1956), Quine (1970).

(AB[73])   "All bachelors are unmarried,"

is analytic. For it's only if that condition is met that (AB) is synonymous with:

(AB*)   "All unmarried adult males are unmarried."

And it's only if (AB) is synonymous with (AB*) that the former is formally true. For it's only then that (AB) is an instance of a sentence-schema all of whose instances are true, namely:

(AB#)   All things that have phi, psi, and chi have phi."

But there is no formal characterization of analytic truth. Let L be a language in which "and" means or and "or" means and but that is otherwise just like English. "Bob is tall or Bob is not tall" is false in L. So it's *relative* to the rules of English semantics that "Bob is tall or Bob is not tall" is analytically true. In other words,

> (*)   supposing $e_1...e_n$ to be the semantic rules of English, it follows that "Bob is tall or Bob is not tall" is formally true.

(*) is a proposition, not a sentence, and thus cannot be characterized as formally true or formally false.

Of course, one could turn (*) into a sentence by enclosing it (or the corresponding inscription, rather) in quotation marks. But the resulting sentence is not itself formally true, since it has the same form as many a false sentence, e.g. "supposing $e_1...e_n$ to be the semantic rules of English, it follows that 'Bob is tall or Bob is not tall' is necessarily false." Thus, so-called "formal" truths, e.g. "Bob is tall or not tall," are parasitic on informal analytic truths, such as (*).

There are, of course, famous incompleteness theorems to the effect that arithmetical statements are not formally true. (This requires clarification. "2 + 2 = 4" is not formally true, since it has the same form as "2 + 2 = 5", and nothing having the same form as a falsehood is formally true. Attempts were made to show that arithmetical truths could be expressed as formal truths. But for reasons embodied in the aforementioned incompleteness theorems, those attempts failed.) Arithmetical statements are not empirically true. So they are analytically but informally true.

Knowing that arithmetical statements are not formally true, Langford (1949) said that arithmetical truths must be "synthetic *a priori.*" Langford was thereby stipulating that "formal truth" and "analytic truth" are to be used interchangeably. But this stipulation prejudges a substantive question and it does so in the wrong way.

7.2   Also, formal truth isn't a property of expressions at all. (I have said otherwise, but only to expedite discussion.) Formal truth is a property of expression-involving *relations*. In fact, it is a property borne with respect to non-linguistic entities (meanings) by relations borne by expressions with respect to other expressions.

---

73. Short for "all bachelors."

It is said that:

(ES[74])   "either it is snowing or it is not snowing"

is formally true (or "a truth of logic"), whereas

(KB[75])   "if John knows that he's tall, then he believes that he's tall,"

is not.

But ES *per se* isn't formally true. Some general points about logic will make this clear. A system of logic is the least inclusive set containing

   (i)   certain axioms

and

   (ii)   the consequences of those axioms.

In developing a system of logic, a logician's intention is that:

   (a)   it systematize a maximally comprehensive body of inferences;

and

   (b)   it do so on the basis of as few axioms as possible.

Also, those axioms cannot be known to be false. (But they needn't be self-evident, contrary to what used to be thought.)

A system of logic whose axiom-set includes

   (A)   All sentences of the form *either P or not-P* are true

but doesn't include

   (B)   All sentences of the form *if x knows P, then x believes P*

is likely to systematize a more extensive and important class of inferences, and to do so on the basis of fewer axioms, than an otherwise comparable system that includes (B) but doesn't include (A).

This is what it means to say that ES is "formally true." ES is "formally true" in the sense that it is a consequence of relatively comprehensive and relatively axiomatically conservative systematizations of classes of inferences. KB is "not formally true" in the sense that, although it's obviously a consequence of some systematizations of some classes of inferences, those classes are relatively small and the axiom sets of those systematizations are relatively big. (In this context, a "small" class can have infinitely many members. A class is big if it's membership is diverse; otherwise it's small, even if it has infinitely many members. A given class's arithmetical size – its cardinality – is

---

74. Short for "either, snowing."

75. Short for "knows, believes."

important in some contexts, but in most it is not important. It's usually a class's di-
mension-number, not it's cardinal number, that matters.)

But if one's objective is to develop an epistemic logic (viz. a systematization of
inferences relating to knowledge), then (B) *should* be one of one's axioms. (In point
of fact, epistemic logics typically include (B).[76]) If one's objective is to systematize the
logical interrelations of context-sensitive expressions, e.g. "that man is now in pain,"
then (A) should *not* be one of one's axioms, since in any context where there is no
contextually salient man, "that man is now in pain" has no truth-value, and neither
does its negation. [77]

Thus *no* sentence is formally true.[78] Some sentences, e.g. (KB) and (ES), are *analytically* true. But *formal* truth is a property, not of sentences, but of relations between
sentences (or their occurrences) and axiom-sets. It's only relative to a certain body of
linguistic conventions that a given axiom, or a given consequence of a given axiom
set, has any meaning. So formal truth is a property borne by intersentential relations
with respect to linguistic conventions; and supposing it a truth that relative to conventions $c_1...c_n$, the relation between sentence S and axiom-set A is formal, that truth is
not itself formal. Informal analytic truths *ipso facto* hold in virtue of language-tran-
scendent, but necessary facts. Nothing relating to the way in which mass-energy is
(re)distributed is relevant. Necessary truths hold in virtue of facts about the non-spatiotemporal. Much undeserved credence has been given to attempts to conventionalize logic, owing to the wide acceptance of the mistaken notion that an expression *per
se* can be "formally true."

7.3   According to the conventional wisdom, it is expressions, not propositions, that
are "formally" true. We've just seen how wrong the conventional wisdom is on this
matter. Moreover, setting aside all of the points just made, there is clearly *a* sense in

---

76. See Hintikka (1962). See Hintikka (1969) for the same point *mutatis mutandis* in connection with deontic (morality-related) operators, such as "it is obligatory that."

77. Also, in any such context, "that man is now in pain and that man is not now in pain" isn't
logically true, since, in the time it take to utter that sentence, the man in question might cease
to be in pain. Kaplan (1989) makes this point. So any logic concerned with relations holding
among context-sensitive expressions must *deny* the Law of Non-Contradiction, this being the
principle that:

(C)   Nothing is both true and false.

(C) is clearly true. At the same time, practically any sentence of any natural language, or of any
artificial language with non-trivial expressive capabilities, contains at least one context-sensitive component. So we must conclude, not that (C) isn't a law of logic, but that logic doesn't
concern linguistic expressions.

78. In his brilliant (1953) paper "Is mathematics syntax of language?" Kurt Gödel cogently defends this position; his reasons don't coincide with mine and presuppose rather specific results
in mathematics.

which propositions can be formally true and in which propositions can be the relata of instances of "formal" entailment.

Given what we said in Chapter 1, Section 2.1.2, the propositions *John is tall* is identical with a set S whose members are:

c_1: the property of being identical with John.
c_2: the property of being tall.
c_3: the property of being a property p such that John has p.
c_4: the property of being a a thing x such that x has p, for some property p.
c_5: the property of being a thing x such that x is tall and x is identical with John.

Assuming the truth of *John is tall*, each of c_3 and c_4 is *ipso facto* instantiated, meaning that the propositions *John has some property or other* and *something has some property or other* are true. So there is a member of S, and thus a discrete part of *John is tall*, corresponding to the proposition *something has some property or other*; and it is in that sense that *John is tall* formally entails *John has some property or other*.

John is tall entails *John is not a one-dimensional object*. But there is no discrete part of S that corresponds to the latter proposition. So that entailment is informal.

Unfortunately, it's not easy to assign a meaning to the vague term "corresponds to" that validates the claims just made. But we won't try to solve this problem since we don't have to, given what this book is about.

8.0   In this section we'll see that everything non-spatiotemporal is a property.

Many things that aren't typically thought of as properties are in fact properties. Anything of which there can be instances is *ipso facto* a property. It makes no sense to ask: "How many instances of JM are there?" It *does* make sense to ask: "How many people *like* JM are there?" The second question is asking how many people of a certain *kind* there are. So it is asking, of some property of which I am instance, how many instances there are of that property.

8.1   *Numbers* are properties. A pair of shoes is an instance of the number two. The number two is the property of being a pair; it is the property of being a set S such that for some x, and some y, x ≠ y and x and y both belong to S and, for any z that belongs to S, z = x or z = y.

8.2   *Possibilities* are properties.[79] Possibilities are ways things can be. Such ways are properties. For John to perform the *Appassionata* in the same way as Sam is for there to be some property (of a certain kind, whose exact nature needn't trouble us) that both performances have in common.

---

79. This point is made and cogently defended by Armstrong (1989, 1992).

8.2.1   Having said that a property is a "way things can be (done)," what are we to say about the "property" of being a square circle? We can't say that "square circle" is meaningless; nor can we deny that it has the same sort of meaning as "square table-cloth" and "green circle," which express attributions of *bona fide* properties.

David Armstrong (1998) proposed the following solution, with which I agree. There is no such thing as the property of being a square circle. To say "nothing is a square circle" is to say "there is no thing that is both a square and a circle." In general, so-called "properties" that, for reasons of logic, cannot be instantiated decompose into properties that can be instantiated. So if P is a "property" that cannot be instantiated, the statement "there no instances of P" is equivalent with "there is nothing is an instance of P_1 and P_2 and...P_n," where, for each i ($1 \leq i \leq n$), P_i is a property that can be instantiated.

8.3   *Sets* are properties. Many have thought this (e.g. Quine, Russell, Carnap). But they have thought it for the wrong reason. In their view, the property of being an apple is identical with the set of apples. In general, so these authors held, sets are identical with their memberships.

But this isn't so. If S is the set of apples and there are n apples, no set with n + 1 apples is identical with S. But what it is to be an apple doesn't depend on how many apples there are. No intension is identical with the corresponding extension. No property is identical with the corresponding set.

Nonetheless, sets are properties. Let P be some property such that, for anything S, if S is to be the set of apples, it is necessary and sufficient that S have P. P is not the property of being an apple, since apples aren't sets. The right value of P is not "the property of being an apple," but rather:

(PP[80])   The property of being the property of being an apple.

PP has only instance: the property of being an apple ("PA" for short). x falls into S if, and only if, x is an instance of an instance of PP. We may thus identify S with PP and x's falling into S with x's instantiating any one of PP's instances. (There is only one such instance, of course.) Given any property Q, an analogous argument shows that the set of Q's is identical, not with the property of being a Q, but with the property of being the property of being a Q.

8.4   *Musical and artistic works* are properties. It makes no sense to ask of some specific performance of Chopin's ballade in g-minor "how many instances are there of that performance?" But it *does* make sense to ask: "how many times has that work been played? In other words, how many instances of that work are there?" Thus, the ballade in g-minor is a property, not a spatiotemporal entity.

---

80. Short for "the property of being the property of an apple."

This brings us to an important, anti-empiricist point. Let P be some performance of the ballade in g-minor. It is one thing to hear the noises constitutive of that performance; it is quite another to hear the music *in* those noises. Dogs presumably just hear the noises. When listening to the noises mediating a performance of the ballade in g-minor, a non-musical, but otherwise supremely intelligent being could *ceteris paribus* hear the noises as well as Chopin himself; and unlike the latter, he could instantly identify the mathematical interrelations of the various sounds in question. But, unlike Chopin, he would not hear anything *in* the noises.

He hears everything, but he doesn't hear the music. There is no paradox here, since the two occurrences of "hear" in previous sentences different meanings: one refers to sense-perception, the other to post-perceptual ideation of some kind.

Though not sufficient for hearing the music, hearing the relevant noises is obviously a necessary for it. The noises are what make it possible to externalize the post-perceptual, second-order awarenesses constitutive of one's hearing the music.

Why second-order? Because, if the argument put forth in Chapter 13 is cogent, music externalizes one's own thought-processes.

8.4.1   The following objection is likely to be raised:

> But anyone or anything that can hear the noises *can* for that reason hear the music. You are failing to distinguish perception from post-perceptual responses to perception. The geologist and the layman see the same squiggles on the seismograph. Their *perceptions* don't differ. But their *post*-perceptions do differ: those squiggles mean something to the geologist, but not to the layperson. So the geologist, having seen the squiggles, goes on to have all kinds of mental activity that the layperson does not go on to have. The musical person and the non-musical person do indeed hear the same noises; so they hear the same music. (Assume that the non-musical person is utterly and completely non-musical.) They react differently to what they hear. But there is nothing that the one hears that the other doesn't also hear. And, since music is, by definition, something that is heard, if it's sense-perceived at all, they hear the same music.

The musical person is immediately, intuitively aware of structural, formal properties of the stream of noise that he's hearing. The non-musical person could verify that it had those properties, but he couldn't do so in real time. The musical person's judgments as to the structures instantiated by the noises he is hearing are not perceptions. (Judgments are not perceptions. Thoughts are not perceptions.) But the noises that the musical person is hearing cause him to experience his judgments as perceptions.

Any given structure is capable of being realized by different things. Whatever structure a Mozart sonata has, and whatever structures its component parts have, many things other than a series of noises could have those structures. In fact, *any* sufficiently large and heterogeneous plurality could have any one of those structures: a series of numbers; a pattern of ink-drops; a building. The difference between the musical person (MP) and the non-musical person (NM) doesn't lie in what the former hears; it lies in what he hears in what he hears. Both may hear the very same noises. But, supposing that they do, the former hears structures in those noises that the latter doesn't hear.

It would be possible for someone who didn't hear music in the noises mediating the ballade in g-minor to be just as good, and just as quick, as any musician at identifying the structural features instantiated by that noise-series. So hearing music *in* noise involves more than picking up on structural facts about the noise.

MP *perceptualizes* his judgments about the noises he is hearing. NM does not. That is how they differ. MP hears thoughts as sounds. NM does not. The sounds that MP hears don't exist; he is hallucinating them. But those hallucinations embody correct judgments concerning the noise that he is hearing. That fact, coupled with the fact that MP's hallucinations are *mediated* by veridical perceptions, explains why those hallucinations have the firmness, richness, and constancy of *bona fide* perceptions.

Similar remarks can be made about other art-forms. When you look at a painting of a damsel in distress, you don't really see the damsel. You see discolorations on a canvass. Those discolorations bear a formal resemblance to a damsel in distress, and this has two consequences. First, the discolorations cause you to experience a damsel-image. Second, that image, though not itself a perception, is mediated by veridical perceptions and thus experienced as a perception of an external object.[81]

9.0   Embodied in empiricism is a mistaken view as to what it is for, say, a visual image to be correct. Representations have conditions of satisfaction. For your perception of y to be accurate, it is not enough that y be its cause; there is no causal relation R such that y's bearing R to your perception is enough for the latter to be correct. That perception (henceforth p) has to have conditions of satisfaction. The reason why, in order to be correct, p has to be caused by an object having such and such a shape, etc. is precisely that it has certain conditions of satisfaction.

For p to have such and such conditions of satisfaction is for there to some property P such that p is veridical iff P is instantiated. Thus, the fact that there are sense-perceptions means that there are properties and thus non-spatiotemporal entities. Similar points show that there couldn't be beliefs if there weren't properties.

Indeed, the existence of properties follows from the fact that there is *anything* that has *any* content, whether true or false. False beliefs have contents: if they didn't, they wouldn't be false. They'd be neither true nor false. Hallucinations have contents: if they didn't, they wouldn't be inaccurate. They'd be neither accurate nor inaccurate.

For a sensory experience to be a *bona fide* perception, as opposed to a hallucination, it must indeed have a certain provenance. But for it to have these as opposed to those truth-conditions, it is irrelevant what its origins are. A hallucination of a tiger

---

81. Sartre (1940) explicitly makes some of these points and implicitly makes others.

has such and such truth-conditions: there is some property P such that those conditions are satisfied just in case P is instantiated. The very same thing is true of a *bona fide* perception that is experientially just like that perception. The difference between the two is not that they have different satisfaction-conditions. It's that, in the one case, if those conditions are satisfied, the result is an accidentally true perception, whereas in the other case, the result is a non-accidentally, and therefore knowledge-conducively, true perception.

Empiricism is the view that a belief isn't justified, and therefore isn't knowledge, unless it has a certain mode of derivation. But the concept of justification is not one that an empiricist can countenance. For x to be justified is for it to conform to some standard; there must therefore be some property that x instantiates; indeed, there must be some property that x instantiates that, for reasons inherent in its structure, it should instantiate.

Empiricism is undermined by the existence of things such as beliefs and perceptions that are, of their very nature, *supposed* to be justified and correct. For x to be *supposed* to be a certain way is for there be to some property P such that either x instantiates P or x is defective.

9.1   Content-externalists, e.g. Burge (1977), *deny* my assertion that a perception's or belief's origins are irrelevant to what its content is. Here is their reasoning. Let W be some planet exactly like Earth but many light years away; and suppose that every event on Earth has an exact duplicate on W. So if, on Earth, Jim shakes hands with Tim, then, on W, Twin-Jim shakes hands with Twin-Jim. On Earth, Smith sees Jones drinking a beer. According to the content-externalist, the content of Smith's perception is given by the proposition:

(JB[82])   Jones is drinking a beer,

and so is the content of the Smith's perception-subsequent belief. But on W, the externalist says, the contents of Twin-Smith's perception and post-perceptual belief are given by the proposition:

(TJ[83])   *Twin-Jones* is drinking a beer.

JB doesn't entail TJ and TJ doesn't JB. Therefore, says the externalist, Smith's perception differs in content from Twin-Smith's corresponding perception, even though *setting aside their provenances* those perceptions are qualitatively identical. For the very same reason, the externalist says, Smith's post-perceptual belief differs from

---

82. Short for "Jones drinking a beer."

83. Short for "Twin-Jones (drinking a beer)."

Twin-Smith's corresponding belief, even though *setting aside their provenances* those beliefs are qualitatively identical.[84]

Suppose that, holding all other factors constant, Twin-Smith's sensory experience had *not* been the outcome of some causal process whose initial member was a collision of light-rays with Twin-Jones' body. According to the content-externalist, Twin-Smith's experience was *devoid* of content, or at least had a gap in it where Twin-Jones was supposed to be. So according to the content-externalist, Twin-Smith's perceptual experience is neither veridical nor non-veridical, at least to the extent that it is supposed to represent Twin-Jones. If content is determined by provenance, as the content-externalist maintains, then there is no content without the right sort of provenance.

Correlatively, to the extent that *Jones* – the individual, not some concept or property individuative thereof – is a constituent of my Jones-perception, it follows that an experientially identical hallucination whose origins lay in some brain-malfunction of mine would have *no* content.

As we'll now see, it cannot coherently be maintained that hallucinations are devoid of content or even that they are any less content-rich than their veridical counterparts. First of all, it's only to the extent that Twin-Smith's hallucination *has* content that it is *supposed* to be a perception of either Twin-Jones or some Twin-Jones-lookalike; it's only to the extent that it says, so to speak, *there is a person having properties $p_1...p_n$ standing over there* [where $p_1...p_n$ are properties Twin-Jones is presumed to have].

In general, if x sees y, and z has a hallucination qualitatively just like x's y-perception, there is no sense in which there are gaps in the content of z's hallucination (except such as are also present in x's perception). z's sensory experience is non-veridical – but there are no gaps in its content. And for this reason content-externalism is simply false, as we'll now see.

---

84. Putnam (1975a, 1975b, 1996), Burge (1977), Fodor (1981a, 1987, 1987b, 1990, 1994a, 1994b, 1998a), McGinn (1988). Stich (1983) is aware that, if content externalism is correct, then beliefs and mental entities generally are devoid of causally efficacy. For to the extent that the content of my current visual perception, or of any belief derived from that perception, is constitutively dependent on the existence of some star that has long since ceased to exist, that content content is as non-existent, and therefore as devoid of causal efficacy, as that start itself. Instead of taking this to show that externalism is wrong, Stich takes it to show that concepts such as *perception* and *belief* are incoherent; he thus takes it to show that "folk-psychology" is wrong. It is a fact of profound psychoanalytic and sociological significance that somebody as intelligent as Stich could jettison the belief that we have beliefs so as to validate a doctrine, such as content externalism, that is fashionable but clearly askew. In Kuczynski (2007) I make it clear how Kripke's (1980) and Putnam's (1975) semantic insights can be accommodated without taking the desperate view, taken by Burge (1977), Fodor (1981a), Kaplan (1989, 1989b) and other content-externalists, that an external object, such as a planet, could be a veritable constituent of the *content* of a given belief.

10.0   When you see Smith, your eyes don't tell you that *Smith* is standing over there. The conditions that must be met if your perception is to be veridical are general: There must be *a* thing having certain morphological, chromatic (etc.) properties in a certain location. So long as there is such a thing, your perception is accurate, it being irrelevant whether your *post*-perceptual identification of that thing as Smith is correct or not. And so long as there is no such thing, your perception is non-veridical. Smith's non-existence doesn't render your perception in any way indeterminate; nor does it have any effect on the conditions that must be met if that perception (as opposed to its cognitive sequelae) are to be accurate. Those conditions, be it emphasized, are the same for both perceptions; i.e. the Smith-perception has the same conditions of satisfaction as the Smith-hallucination.

The content of any given cognizance is general. The truth-conditions of your visual experience are satisfied if *there is an entity having such and such properties* – the property of having a certain location relative to you, of having a certain morphology, etc. It may be that you are *in fact* seeing Tim. But for your visual experience to be veridical, it isn't necessary that *Tim* be there. What you *see* isn't that *Tim* is standing over there. What you see is that *an* entity with certain features is standing over there; and, those features being what they are, you *conclude* that it's Tim that you are seeing.

So perceptual content is always general. A given perception's content, if propositionalized, is given by a proposition of to the effect that *there exists something x having properties $p_1...p_n$.* There is no *particular* thing that must have those properties if your perception is to be accurate.

So far as the veridicality of *any* ideation on your part depends on its being Tim specifically that has $p_1...p_n$, that ideation is post-perceptual, not perceptual. But even post-perceptual ideation is, ultimately, general in nature. You can't *just* think of Tim. You must think of him as having these or those features. Tim can't be given to you as a featureless nullity; nor can he be given to you but not given to you *as* being this or that sort of thing. In fact, for you to think of Tim *is* for you to think of certain properties as being instantiated. This is a consequence of the obvious fact that your thinking about Tim doesn't even involve, and therefore isn't identical with, your thinking of some featureless substrate to which certain properties are affixed.

So the content of the your post-perceptual belief (viz. that it's Tim you are seeing, as opposed to some Tim-look-alike) is itself general in nature. Your concept of Tim is identical with a belief on your part to the effect that certain properties are instantiated. (Let $c_1...c_m$ be these properties.) As previously stated, your visual experience is veridical exactly if something or other – it doesn't matter who or what – instantiates $p_1...p_n$. Your post-perceptual conclusion that it's *Tim* who you are seeing is identical with your believing that something uniquely has $c_1...c_m$ and, moreover, that anything having those properties also has $p_1...p_n$. Thus, it's only in a relative, and extremely tenuous, sense that the content of your post-perceptual belief is non-general. (Incidentally, the conception of conception that I'm advocating is the one that Russell advocated. Many philosophers hold that, in light of some semantic discoveries made by Saul Kripke, the

Russellian analysis of conception is wrong. Those philosophers are wrong. This will be shown in Section 14.0 of the present chapter.

Thus, the content of *any* given cognizance is *general*. More precisely:

(AG[85]) Given any cognizance C, there are certain properties $k_1...k_o$ such that the truth-conditions of C are satisfied exactly if $k_1...k_o$ are instantiated.

Thus, given any cognizance, there is, ultimately, no *one* entity that must have the properties in question if that cognizance is to be accurate.

AG entails that:

(i)   Embedded within any given cognizance is a presupposition to the effect that (certain) properties exist.

So either

(a)   our cognizances are categorically erroneous

or

(b)   properties exist.

Therefore properties exist, since the contention that we're always wrong, in addition to being totally implausible, is self-defeating. If I rightly believe that I'm always wrong, then I'm not always wrong. If I wrongly believe it, then I'm not always wrong.

There is another reason to accept (b) and reject (a). To believe that properties *don't* exist is to believe there to be certain properties that aren't instantiated. It is to believe that the property of being non-spatiotemporal is not instantiated. So it is self-defeating to deny the existence of properties.

11.0   The objects of knowledge are truths, not things. Truths are true propositions. We are *aware* of things. But it is truths that we *know*. So object-awareness either isn't knowledge or it is knowledge of a very different kind from one's knowledge that $1 + 1 = 2$ or that Paris is in France.

There is *a* sense in which objectual awareness is knowledge: the dog is aware of the ball's roundness, and we must for that reason credit the dog with *some* kind of knowledge. But, for reasons already discussed (in Chapter 1, Section 2.1.1), it is one thing to be aware of the ball's being round and it's a different thing to be aware of the truth *that the ball is round*. The sense in which a dog *sees the ball's roundness* is entirely literal. The sense in which you see *that the ball is round* is non-literal, being the same as the sense in which you see *that the property of spatiotemporal is not itself spatiotemporal.*

---

85. Short for "any given," as in "any given cognizance."

11.1   For reasons already discussed, empiricism is incompatible with our knowing anything, including truths concerning perceptible features of our immediate vicinity. This is the biggest problem with empiricism.

The second biggest problem is a trivial consequence of the first. Given that

(i)   we wouldn't know anything if empiricism were true,

it follows that

(ii)   we wouldn't have knowledge of dependence-relations.

But (i) is a point seldom made: I have yet to hear even a rationalist say that empiricism prohibited us from knowing *anything*. Thus, rationalists have, unnecessarily and incorrectly, granted that empiricism is consistent with our having *some* knowledge.

The debate between rationalists and empiricists has thus focused on (ii). But (ii) is moot, since, given (i), we wouldn't know anything at all if empiricism were true.

11.2   But even if (i) is supposed false, empiricism still fails, as it cannot accommodate the fact that we have knowledge of dependence-relations, e.g.

(T)   if x is a circle, x is not a square (in other words, x's being a circle depends on its not being a square).

One can see x's roundness, but not its non-squareness, let alone the incompatibility of the former with the latter.

Attempting to compatibilize empiricism with the existence of necessary truths, modern empiricists, e.g. Blackburn (1993), take the view that necessary truths, like T, hold entirely in virtue of how we have resolved to used expressions.[86] Pre-modern empiricists, e.g. Mill (1882), would have said that T is an empirical truth, albeit an unusually well-confirmed one.[87]

The first position fails – we've already seen why – and so does the second. If all questions are to be decided on empirical grounds, then, given any possible datum D and any possible hypothesis H, it is an open empirical question what degree of support D gives to H; and it is *ipso facto* an open empirical question what degree of support an arbitrary datum D* gives to the hypothesis that (for some number n) D gives n degree of support to H, and so on *ad infinitum*.

It cannot be known *through* our senses that our senses are correct. So strict empiricism leads either to skepticism (*we cannot know whether our senses are trustworthy*) or idealism (*our senses are trustworthy because our perceptions are their objects*). No one would advocate either view if he had any way of avoiding doing so. And there

---

86. Cf. Van Fraassen (1977).

87. Cf. Mill (1882), Quine (1951).

is a way to avoid doing so. This way involves being a rationalist, as we'll see, since it involves granting that one has knowledge of analytic truths.

12.0   Rock R is round. You know this. On this basis, you know that R is *not* triangular. There is a difference between knowing that R is round, on the one hand, and being aware of its roundness. In the one case, the object of awareness is a proposition and, therefore, a non-spatiotemporal entity. In the other case, the object of awareness is a spatiotemporal entity. You are aware of R's being round: you are object-aware of it. But you can't be object-aware of R's *not being triangular*. But you can know *that R isn't triangular*.

One is object-aware of *facts*. The rock's being spherical is a fact. But R's *not* being a triangle is not. It is a truth that R is not a triangle, but there is no corresponding fact.

Given that there is no such *fact*, how are you aware of the corresponding truth? How, in general, are you aware of negative truths? By being aware of non-existent *facts*? Wrong answer: "Non-existent fact" is a contradiction in terms.

The right answer: The proposition that

(r₁)   R is triangular.

is quite as existent as the proposition that

(r₂)   R is round.

r₁ consists of various properties, all of them existent. Your knowing that the rock is not triangular consists in those properties' being given to you as not being jointly instantiated.

The non-existent doesn't exist. But propositions about the non-existent do exist. False thoughts are instances of some proposition's being presented to somebody as being true, when in fact it is not true, meaning that the properties composing it are not jointly instantiated.

12.1[88]   According to Frege (1918), true propositions are to be identified with the facts in virtue of which they hold. The proposition *the rock weighs 10 lbs* is to be identified with the rock's weighing 10 lbs.

This position is untenable. If the rock is accelerated, so that its weight increases, the rock's weighing 10 lbs will be a non-entity. But the proposition that the rock

---

88. In what follows, *nota bene*, we are focusing, as we have been doing, only on *first-order* propositions: propositions that are not about propositions (or properties or concepts). First-order propositions always concern spatiotemporal entities. So *Smith is tall* is a first-order proposition. *That the proposition that Smith is tall is true is probable* is a second-order prpostion. And *that the proposition that Smith is tall is true is probable is indisputable* is a third-order proposition.

weighs 10 lbs will still exist, that being why, under those circumstances, we could rightly describe that proposition as false.

Also, if true propositions were identical with the facts in virtue of which they held, and thus with (we are setting aside higher-order propositions) constituents of space-time, with what would false propositions be identical? Non-existent constituents of space-time? True propositions are facts only if false propositions don't exist. The latter do exist; so the former aren't facts.

12.2   One could hold that, although *true* propositions are facts, false ones are not. This is untenable. First of all, true propositions are the relata of logical relations. So are false propositions. Facts are not such *relata*.

At the same time, facts *are* the relata of spatiotemporal and, in particular, causal relations. Propositions are not.

Also, if Q (an arbitrary true, empirical proposition) is identical with its truth-maker, not-Q doesn't exist. And, for any P such that P entails Q, there is no not-Q for P to be incompatible with and thus no way for P to entail Q. So entailment is not a relation that holds among the denizens of the spatiotemporal world.

12.3   What about confirmation? A true proposition can confirm a false one. The truth that

(i)   Smith's fingerprints were on the murder weapon

confirms the falsehood that

(ii)   Smith is the killer.

If propositions were identical with their own truth-makers, then (ii), being false, wouldn't exist, and (i) wouldn't confirm it. In general, false propositions wouldn't exist if propositions were their own truth-makers. A consequence is that true propositions couldn't confirm false ones. Another consequence is that one proposition couldn't to any degree probabilify another without giving it a probability of 100%.

Since there are false propositions, as well as non-null degrees of probability less than 100%, propositions are not facts. False propositions aren't facts, and neither are true ones.

Empiricism is wrong about what it is that we know and it is therefore wrong about how we know it. As we will now see, that doctrine has the absurd consequence that our awareness of propositions, and therefore our knowledge of truths, is objectual in nature; and it has the equally absurd consequence that our awareness of objects is propositional in nature.

Observation is objectual-awareness. Strictly observation-based knowledge would be objectual knowledge. Since it is truths that are known, not objects, and since truths are propositions, "objectual knowledge" is a contradiction in terms, and there is thus no strictly observation-based knowledge. Because the empiricist is wrong about *how* we know what we know (he wrongly thinks all knowledge is observation-based) he is wrong about *what* we know (he wrongly thinks that the objects of knowledge are facts, not propositions).

13.0   The empiricist's staunch unwillingness to concede that propositions, *qua* non-fictitious and non-spatiotemporal entities, seems unimportant when we consider the sorts of truths given by so-called "observation-reports," e.g. "there's a red ball."[89] But the operative word here is "seems," since, as we have noted, the connection between

(a)   seeing the roundness of the ball and seeing that the ball is round

is of the same nature as the connection between

(b)   seeing that the ball is round and "seeing" that it is a closed 3-d figure of uniform curvature.

But, for reasons independent of what we've said so far, very little of what we know, if stated exhaustively and perspicuously, would be given by such reports. In describing what you are seeing as a red ball, you are implicitly judging how it *would* act if acted upon in a certain way (*my hand won't pass through it if I try grab it*); what it *will* do when acted in a certain way (*if I throw it against a wall, it will make a noise*); how objects not yet in its vicinity would behave if placed in its vicinity (*if Rover were near it, he'd put it in his mouth*).

Thus, telescoped into the everyday, "strictly observation-based" judgments that we make are judgments as to what *would* happen, *could* happen, *will happen*, and

---

89. Neurath (1932), Carnap (1934), and Hempel (1965) often speak of "observation reports" and "protocol sentences." (These terms are synonymous.) Never do they acknowledge that

(i)   the contents of observations, be they object-awarenesses as opposed to truth-awarenesses, have to be conceptualized if they are to serve as the basis for reports or sentences of any kind;

and never, therefore, do they acknowledge that

(ii)   such reinterpretations would involve non-perceptual knowledge.

One philosopher who *is* aware of (i) is Davidson (2001c). Unfortunately, Davidson doesn't respond to (i) by deducing (ii). Instead, he responds to (i) by saying that our perceptions *cause* our beliefs to come into existence but do not *justify* them. MacDowell (1994) rightly describes Davidson's position as absurd. But instead of holding that perceptions are objectual awareness, whose contents justify our beliefs by way of non-perceptual knowledge, MacDowell holds that perceptual content is propositional: the content of a perception is identical with that of a newspaper article. MacDowell's position is obviously better than Davidson's, but it is still counterintuitive. But it is neither absurd nor counterintuitive to hold both (i) and (ii).

has happened.[90] Object-aware creatures (that aren't also proposition-aware) are aware only of what is. What *could be*, but isn't, is nothing for them. (From now on, if I describe a creature as "object-aware," I mean, unless I indicate otherwise, that it isn't also propositionally aware.)

An illustration: I'm watching and listening to Jerry play the piano. As I do so, I think:

(*)   If Jerry were drunk, his performance at the keyboard, which is flawless, would be comedically bad.

An object-aware creature can be aware of Jerry's drunkenness (supposing it existent); of Jerry's cacophonous piano-playing (same qualification); of Jerry's flawless playing; etc.

But an object-aware creature is aware only of property-instances. Since Jerry's playing is flawless, there is no instance of his playing poorly for an object-aware creature to be aware of. And since Jerry is behaving in a non-drunk manner, there is no instance of Jerry's drunkenness for such a creature to be aware of.

Thus, when we characterize what it is that, by virtue of its hearing and seeing Jerry play the piano, this object-aware creature sees and hears, we must take care not to endow its visual and auditory experiences with sensitivity to what might have been. What might have been, but isn't, is nothing to a creature that can't grasp propositions.

But what might have been, but isn't, is very real to the creature that can grasp propositions. For such a creature, what might have been *does* exist, each possibility being nothing other than a false proposition.

No creature can grasp non-entities such as *Jerry's playing poorly* or *Jerry's being drunk*; for such things do not exist to be grasped. But a proposition-aware creature can grasp the propositions *Jerry is playing poorly* and *Jerry is drunk*. Further, such a creature can determine, in light of what his senses are telling him, that those propositions are false. This is because, for reasons already stated, only proposition-aware creatures can grasp incompatibilities, e.g.

(**)   Jerry's playing well rules out his having had a bottle of scotch just before the recital.

---

90. Clarence Lewis (1922) makes this point.

CHAPTER 4

Wittgenstein on meaning
Part 1 – the picture-theory

1.0   Empiricists have tried to show that meanings don't exist. Some sounds are meaningful, they grant, while others are not; but that is not because some are, whereas others are not, linked in some way with mysterious, non-spatiotemporal entities.

Empiricists have different views as to what the meaning is of (e.g.) "snow is white." Most deny that there is such a thing. The Mona Lisa is beautiful, but there is no such thing as the Mona Lisa's beauty.[91] Similarly, a sound can be meaningful, the empiricist says, without there being such a thing as its meaning.[92]

Other empiricists have argued that propositions exist, but only by virtue of being spatiotemporal entities (or classes thereof): they are identical with classes of sentence-tokens, with patterns of behavior, with thoughts had by individuals, or with facts (that is, with assemblages of spatiotemporal objects).

We will find reason to reject all such views. Empiricism is inherently incapable of saying what propositions are. Therefore, it is incapable of producing a correct analysis of what propositional attitudes are. Therefore it is incapable of producing a correct analysis of human psychology, given that everything that is distinctive about human psychology is to be understood in terms of the fact that, unlike other creatures, we grasp propositions and have propositional attitudes.

We will start by examining Wittgenstein's so-called "picture-theory of meaning," since it is an exceptionally pure example of an empiricist theory of meaning and thus makes it clear why such theories are categorically broken.

2.0   Wittgenstein (1922) said that sentences are, quite literally, pictures of the facts they describe. He was not making the trivial claim that sentences are picture-like, in that they, like pictures, are representational. He was saying that the relationship between a given sentence and the fact it describes is the same as the relationship between a picture and the fact it depicts.

Why advocate such a view? One reason is that it provides a straightforward answer to the question: What is it for a given sentence to have a given meaning? What is it for "the cat is on the mat" to mean that the cat is on the mat? It means, says

---

91. Cf. Stevenson (1937).

92. Cf. Wittgenstein (1958).

Wittgenstein, that the sentence the "cat is on the mat" *depicts* the fact that the cat is on the mat.

What if there is no such fact? This question cannot be answered without making points that undermine Wittgenstein's theory. So, if only for the purpose of stating Wittgenstein's view before we critique it, we'll assume that there is such a fact.

For "the cat is on the mat" to mean what it does, says Wittgenstein, is for it *depict* things as being a certain way. If correct, Wittgenstein's contention reduces the question "what is it for a sentence to have a given meaning?" to the question "what is it for a picture to represent what it does?" And the latter question, Wittgenstein believes, is not hard to answer: x depicts y if x is a likeness of y.

Nelson Goodman (1966) identified one problem with this theory. If x is a likeness of y, y is a likeness of x. But I am not a picture of any picture of myself. But let us assume *arguendo* that Wittgenstein can side-step this problem.

Wittgenstein correctly says that there is no such thing as one thing's *just* being a likeness of another: it is only relative to some "rule of projection" that one thing is a likeness of another. A rule of projection is simply a function: a rule that assigns at most entity to each entity in a given class. The series of natural numbers resembles the series 1, 2, 4, 9... relative to the function $F(x) = x^2$, but not relative to the function $F(x) = x^3$. With respect to the first function, but not the second, the series 1, 2, 4, 9...is a "transformation" of the series 1, 2, 3 4...

Wittgenstein (1922) says that pictures (drawings, photographs) are transformations of the facts they depict, and Wittgenstein duly says that the same is true of sentences. So in Wittgenstein's view, the English language is a set of rules that jointly define a function F such that F transforms the fact that the cat is on the mat into the sentence "the cat is on the mat."

Wittgenstein explicitly denies the existence of propositions and says that his theory shows that there is no need to posit them. Sentences are coordinated with facts, and *vice versa*. A sentence is true just in case there is a fact with which it's coordinated. There is no need for propositions to mediate between sentences and facts.

2.1 The Picture Theory is unacceptable. If there are propositions, the meaningfulness of false sentences is easily explained: sentence-meanings are propositions, and propositions are false, not non-existent, if not counterbalanced by facts of the right sort.

In response to this, Wittgenstein has no choice but to say, correctly, that the semantic rules of a language determine what *sort* of fact must obtain for a given one of its sentences to be true. In other words, he must say that a sentence's meaning is determined by its *truth-conditions*, and not by the fact, if any there be, that it depicts.

This means that there is no way save the Picture Theory without undermining it and, therefore, that there is no way to save it. Truth-conditions are propositions. If o is an occurrence of "Sam is going to the store" o's truth-conditions are satisfied exactly if the proposition that Sam is going is true. If o is an occurrence of "Sam, go to the store," o's truth-conditions are satisfied exactly if, in response to hearing that order, Sam goes to the store. To say that truth-conditions TC have been satisfied is to say to that proposition P is true. If, In granting that sentences have truth-conditions, consequently, Wittgenstein is conceding the existence of propositions. But this means that the picture-theory is wrong; for given the existence of propositions, one can account for the meaningfulness of sentences without taking the view that they are pictures.

The condition that must be met if

(JT)   John is tall

to be true is that c_1–c_5 be instantiated, these being:

c_1:   the property of being identical with John.
c_2:   the property of being tall.
c_3:   the property of being a property p such that John has p.
c_4:   the property of being a a thing x such that x has p, for some property p.
c_5:   the property of being a thing x such that x is tall and x is identical with

There is no way to account for the meaningfulness of false sentence except by assuming the existence of propositions. But given this assumption, the meaningfulness of sentences is to be explained saying that they encode propositions, not by saying that they depict facts.

There is another reason why meaningfulness of a true sentence cannot to any degree lie in its being counterbalanced by some fact: one can fully grasp the meaning of a sentence before knowing whether it's true, and a precondition for knowing what sort of fact would make it true is knowing its meaning. So Wittgenstein's theory has the false consequence that one can't understand a sentence without knowing whether it is true.

There is a related point. Setting aside analytically true and analytically false propositions, a sentence cannot, merely by virtue of being true, have a different structure from one that is false. But, by obvious extensions of the points just made, Wittgenstein's theory has the consequence that true empirical sentences are structurally different from false ones. Wherefore, Wittgenstein's theory is false.

3.0   There are other problems with the Picture Theory. Incompatibilities do not hold in virtue of facts that can be depicted. There is no way to depict the fact, if any there be, in virtue of which x's being round excludes its being square. Since incompatibilities cannot be depicted, neither can dependence-relations. This is because *P entails Q* says the same thing as *P is incompatible with not-Q* and *P confirms Q* says the same thing as *P is unlikely, given not-Q*.

Negative truths, though sometimes logical consequences of truths that hold in virtue of depictable facts, cannot themselves be depicted. John's being outdoors can be depicted, and *John is outdoors* entails *John is not in the barn*. But John's *not* being in the barn cannot be drawn.

Many a truth has a falsehood as a proper part, e.g. "if JM is less than 6 ft, then he is less than 7ft." By obvious extensions of the argument just tendered, no such truth could be depicted.

With the possible exception of conjunctions (propositions of the form *P and Q*), *no* molecular truth is depictable. A molecular truth is one that is given by a sentence that has another sentence as a proper part. John's tallness can be depicted, and so can Mary's shortness. But *either John is tall or Mary is short* cannot be depicted.

The operations expressed by words like "or," "not," and "if" are obviously of the same kind as that expressed by "and." This entails that conjunctive truths cannot be depicted. It is an interesting question, but one we needn't answer, how this is to be reconciled with the fact that one can take a picture of a tall John standing next to a short Mary.

3.1   Wittgenstein is aware that molecular sentences seem not to hold in virtue of anything that can be depicted. To deal with this problem, he says that any given true molecular statement is a *formal consequence* of one or more atomic statements.

P is a formal consequence of Q just in case *if P then Q* is formally true. A sentence is formally true just in case it is an instance of a sentence-schema all of whose instances are true. So "if grass is green and snow is white, then grass is green" is formally true, and "grass is green" is a formal consequence of "grass is green and snow is white."

In Chapter 1, we saw that analytic truth is a property, not of sentences *per se*, but of relations borne thereby with respect to propositions. The same holds of formal truth, since all formal truths are analytic truths. Therefore the Picture Theory is false, given that, according to it, propositions don't exist.

In Chapter 3, we saw that, for reasons additional to the one just cited, formal truth is a relation between sentences and propositions, not a property of sentences. More precisely, we saw that:

(FT[93])   Formal truth is a relation between sentences and sets of axioms. Relative to one axiom-set, "if John knows that snow is white, John believes that snow is white" is formally true. Relative to others, it isn't. Given *any* sentence S, there is *some* axiom-set relative to which it S is formally true. Thus, so far as it isn't false, the statement "S is formally true," is an abbreviated way of making the vague statement that there are relatively comprehensive and explanatorily significant axiom-sets relative to which S is formally true.

The Picture-Theory obviously isn't compatible with FT.

Finally, many a true statement affirms that the thing that makes it true cannot be depicted. The statement "if x isn't round it's square" implies that there can be no depiction of the ball's being both round and square. So that statement is depictable

---

93. Short for "formal truth."

only if it's false. There are many statements like this, for example: "some things cannot be depicted." There are other, less obvious examples, e.g. "some things are invisible," and "the bricks composing that building could be arranged in ways in which they will never be arranged."

4.0   We don't describe paintings, or pictures of any other kind, as "true" or "false"; we describe them as "accurate" or "inaccurate". This is not so much a fact about language as it is a linguistic consequence of a fact about the nature of truth. Object-awarenesses, e.g. visual perceptions, are not true or false. The reason: the object of an object-awareness is a thing, not a proposition. The same is true of paintings and other externalizations of object-awarenesses.

Propositions *are* true or false, and so are sentences, by virtue of their association with propositions. If sentences were pictures, they wouldn't be true or false. Since they are, the picture-theory is false.

5.0   Whether a given picture has this or that content is to no degree a function of convention. But it is to some degree a matter of convention whether a sentence has this or that content.

Pictures cease to function iconically, and thus cease to function as pictures, the moment their use is conventionalized. Let P and Q be two pictures whose respective properties are $p_1...p_n$ and $q_1...q_m$, and let's stipulate that juxtaposing P and Q in manner M results in an object O whose truth-conditions are TC. Neither P nor Q is functioning *as* a picture when functioning as a constituent of O. By supposition, what O means is a function of what each of P and Q means *relative to certain conventions*. So, *qua* linguistic symbol, O's content is convention-based. So even if O *did* depict a mountain lion attacking a gazelle, it wouldn't be as a linguistic symbol that it did so. Maybe O was a picture of a mountain lion attacking a gazelle that somebody tore in half, those two halves being P and Q, and maybe M is a way of juxtaposing P and Q so that they once again form a single picture. Be this as it may, to the extent that O's content is convention-independent, it isn't a linguistic symbol, and to the extent that it isn't, it is.

6.0   The essence of Wittgenstein's semantics is:

(SF[94])   Same fact, same meaning.

In other words,

---

94. Short for "same fact."

(SF*)   Two sentences differ in meaning only if some fact could make the one true, but not the other.

Nothing can make "2 + 2 = 4" false, the same being true of "triangles have three sides"; and nothing can make "2 + 2 = 22" true, the same being true of "triangles have four sides." So, for Wittgenstein, all equivalent sentences have the same meaning, a corollary being that all analytically true sentences are meaning-identical as are all analytically false sentences.

But "2 + 2 = 4" obviously doesn't mean the same thing as "triangles have three sides," and "2 + 2 = 22" obviously doesn't mean the same thing as "triangles have four sides."

In identifying sentential with pictorial representation, Wittgenstein identified propositional with objectual awareness. The essence of Wittgenstein's semantics is a failure to make this distinction, and it is also the essence of empiricism.

7.0   I urge readers not interested in technical minutiae to skip all of the remaining sections of the present chapter, including this one.

We will now substantiate the earlier-stated contention that:

(c)   Statements (indicative utterances) are always to the effect that some property has some other property (or they can always be represented, without loss of content, as being to that effect); and while many a sentence is true in virtue of some spatiotemporal fact, any such sentence directly concerns properties and only indirectly, and only the most tenuous possible way, concerns anything spatiotemporal.

More concisely: S is a meaningful sentence if S says of some object x and some property phi that x has phi. In other words, any sentence S is equivalent one of the form: <x has phi>.

This claim defended: Any given sentence is either (i) non-molecular (e.g. "Smith is tall," "Smith is afraid of Jones," or (ii) a quantified generalization (e.g. "some people smoke") or, finally, (iii) molecular and non-quantified (e.g. "Smith is tall and Jones is short"). We'll now see that any sentence belonging to any given one of these categories can be (re)parsed so as to have the form <x has phi>.

7.1   *Non-quantified non-molecular sentences*: Any such sentence either says of some individual that it has some property or it says of some n-tuple N and of some n-place relation R that N has R. Thus, "Smith is tall" says of some individual that he has a certain property; and "Bob loves Sally" says that one individual (Bob) bears a certain relation (that of loving) with respect to some other individual (Sally), or, equivalently, that the ordered pair <Bob, Sally> has L, where L is a two-place property (a property of ordered pairs, a two-place relation) such that for any x, y, <<x,y> has L> exactly if x loves y.

It's obvious how to extend this procedure to sentences that affirm the existence of relations involving three or more objects. Let R* be a three-place predicate such that <<x,y,z> has R*"> is true just in case x is standing in between x and y. In that case, "Bob is standing in between Sally and Larry" is equivalent with <<Bob, Sally, Larry> has R*," where <<x,y,z> has R*"> is true just in case x is standing in between x and y. <<Bob, Sally> has L> and <<Bob, Sally, Larry> has R*> both have the form <x has phi>, just like "Sally is tall." Given these points, it's clear, for any finite n, how to deal with sentences involving the existence of n-place relations.

7.2   *Molecular, non-quantified sentences*: Let "K" be defined as follows: for any sentences S_1 and S_2, <<S_1, S_2> has K> is true iff the state of affairs described by S_1 is a consequence (of some kind or other) of the state of affairs described by S_2. Thus, "Smith broke his leg because he fell out of a tree" is equivalent with <<Smith broke his leg, Smith fell out of a tree.> has K>, which has the form <x has phi>. "Smith doesn't smoke" is equivalent with "the proposition that Smith smokes is false," which clearly has the form: <x has phi>. Other compound sentences are to be dealt with similarly.

7.3   *Quantified generalizations*: A "quantified generalization" is any statement that says how many members one class of objects has in common with some other class of objects. "Some person smokes" is a quantified generalization, since it says that the class of people has at least one member in common with the class of smokers.

Bearing this in mind, let "E" be defined as follows: for any properties P and Q, <<P, Q> has E> is true iff the class of things having P has a least one member with the class of things having Q. In that case, "some person smokes" is equivalent with <<the property of being a person, the property of being a smoker>, has E>, which obviously has the form <x has phi>. Other quantified generalizations are to be dealt with similarly.

Since any given sentence is either atomic, quantified (and molecular), or non-quantified and molecular, we have thus established that any given sentence S is equivalent to some sentence having the form <x has phi>. Given this fact, there is an obvious answer to the question "what is it for a sentence to be meaningful?" A sentence is meaningful if it attributes some property to some object. A sentence S is meaningful if, for some object x and some property phi, S says that x has phi. In other words, a sentence is meaningful if it says anything about anything.

7.4   The sentence-like expression

(i)   The absolute is one

is presumably supposed to attribute some property to some important object. Since neither that property nor that object is identified, (i) contains undefined terms and therefore says nothing. Once those terms are defined, a meaningful statement results. (If "the absolute" is taken to denote the universe and a thing's being "one" is taken to mean that it's self-identical, then (i) is true and therefore meaningful.)

(i) is comparable to "x is tall." The reason "x is tall" says nothing is that "x" is un-defined – it hasn't been assigned a referent. And no sooner is a referent assigned to "x" than "x is tall" becomes meaningful.

Before "x" is assigned a referent, "x is tall" is neither confirmable nor tautologous. But that's only a symptom of the real problem: *"x" doesn't have a referent*. The same thing *mutatis mutandis* is true of (i) and, indeed, of each of the logical positivists' other paradigms of meaninglessness ("the nothing nothings," "the all is one," etc.).

7.5   Russell (1908), Tarski (1983), and other logicians have held that there are mean-ingless *bona fide* sentences. Their argument is that there are syntactically well-formed sentences (e.g. "this sentence is false") that are true if false and false if true and that, consequently, cannot be meaningful without violating the Law of Non-Contradiction (viz. the principle that *p and not-p is always false*).

Set theorists have taken it for granted that Russell et al. were right about this, and they've gone to extreme lengths to compatibilize set-theory with this alleged truth.

But Russell et al. were quite wrong. The expressions they were thinking of are either false or they are sentence-schemata, not actual sentences.

A sentence-schema is an expression that is just like a sentence except that one of the lexical items in it has been removed and replaced with a variable. So "x is tall" is a sentence-schema.

7.5.1   Let K be the class of all classes that are not members of themselves, i.e. that don't have the property of being self-members. In that case,

(K_1)   "K is a self-member"

entails, and is entailed by,

(K_2)   "K is not a self-member."

By the Law of Excluded Middle (LEM), *at least* one of those statements affirms a truth (a true proposition). By the Law of Non-Contradiction, *at most* one of those affirms a truth. But if the one is true, so is the other, in which case a given proposition is both true and false, which is impossible.

According to Russell (1902, 1903, 1908), the just-stated argument demonstrates the falsity of the Axiom of Comprehension (*for any property P, there is a class C such that C contains every instance of P and nothing else*). This contention of his is widely accepted.[95]

---

95. Graham Priest (2006a, 2006b) takes this to show that there are true contradictions. Priest (correctly) believes that K_1 *is* meaningful and, on that basis, infer (understandably but errone-ously) that it *ipso facto* affirms some proposition. Priest knows that *if* K_1 affirms a proposition, that proposition is both true and false. So Priest holds that some propositions are both true and false. Since, as we'll now see, K_1 affirms nothing, this line of reasoning is spurious. (See Brown (2006) for a helpful discussion of Priest's work.)

7.5.2   The statement:

(S$_1$)   "The class of all spoons has the property of not being member of itself"

is merely an abbreviation for:

(S$_2$)   "The class of spoons isn't a spoon."

And the statement:

(T$_1$)   "The class of non-spatiotemporal entities has the property of being member of itself"

is short for:

(T$_2$)   "The class of non-spatiotemporal entities is non-spatiotemporal."

In general, when used meaningfully, the expression "the property of (not) being a member of itself" is eliminable. Why? Because "itself" isn't to be defined denotatively, i.e. it isn't to be defined by identifying its referent. That expression *per se* no more has a referent than any other pronoun. "He," the expression-type, has no referent; it is *occurrences* of "he" that have referents (cf. "John has a lot money, but *he* doesn't have a car"). Similarly, "the property of (not) being identical with itself" does not have a referent; its *occurrences* have referents. The occurrences of it in S$_1$ and T$_1$ refer, respectively, to the property of being a spoon and the property of being non-spatiotemporal. (S$_2$ is equivalent with "the class of spoons doesn't have the property of being a spoon," the same thing *mutatis mutandis* holding of T$_2$.)

With these points in mind, let's take another look at K$_1$. The property that a thing must have to be a member of the class of spoons is that of being a spoon. What is the property a thing must have to be a member of K? In other words, what does "itself" refer to in K$_1$?

"The answer is clear," it will be said. "It refers to the property of *not* being a member of itself. Since K is the class of all classes that aren't members of themselves, to say that K belongs to itself is to say that K doesn't belong to itself."

But this answer is circular. We wanted to know what "the property of being a member of itself" referred to, and the answer we were given was: "the property of *not* being a member of itself," which leaves us with the same question *mutatis mutandis* as before.

We asked: "What property must a thing must have to belong to K? What does 'the property of being a member of K' refer to?" We were told: "the property of not being a member of itself." We then asked: "What does 'the property of not being a member of itself' refer to?" We were told: "The property of being a member of K." Our questions weren't answered.

Thus, "the property of (not) being a member of itself" *doesn't refer to anything*. It's a free variable; it's like the occurrence of "he" in a token of "he has no friends" that occurs in a context where it is neither assigned a referent (as it would be if, while pointing to John, I said "*he* is a nice person") nor appropriately bound (as in, "if a man envies you, *he* is someone you should fear"). *Therefore "the property of (not) being a member of itself" doesn't have a referent and K$_1$ therefore doesn't express a proposition.* Since K$_1$ doesn't express a proposition, it isn't true or false; and since "the property of not being a member of itself" doesn't pick anything out, we don't have a counterexample to the Axiom of Comprehension on our hands. So to the extent that the motivation for TT lies in the contention that K$_1$ *is* such a counterexample, there is no motivation for TT.

"You are guilty of a serious oversight," it might be said. "Though it doesn't refer to anything, the expression 'the property of not being a member of itself' has a sense, like "the man on the moon," and K$_1$ therefore *does* express a proposition, just like 'the man on the moon plays the violin.'"

First of all, if the expression "the property of not being a member of itself" doesn't refer to anything, then we have made our case: we have shown that we don't have in K$_1$ a proposition-bearing sentence, let alone a true one, and that we therefore don't have in K a counterexample to the Axiom of Comprehension. That said, if that expression has a sense, then (arguably[96]) we were wrong to say that K$_1$ expresses no proposition. But this brings us to the second point: the "the property of not being a member of itself" does not have a sense; it just appears to have a sense, however paradoxical this may sound. Let's suppose for argument's sake that it *does* have a sense. In that case, K$_1$ is equivalent (though not necessarily synonymous) with:

K$_{1S}$:   "There exists something that is uniquely a set of all sets that aren't members of themselves; moreover, that thing is a member of itself."[97]

In K$_1$, we said, the occurrence of "itself" doesn't refer to anything, a consequence being that K$_1$ fails to encode a proposition. To the extent that those arguments were cogent, they also show that the occurrence in K$_{1S}$ fails to refer. The expression "the man whose best friend *that woman* is" does not have a sense *unless the occurrence of "that woman" picks someone out.* If that occurrence is empty, then that expression has no sense; for, under that circumstance, there is no condition that it expresses such that any object, actual or possible or even impossible, could possibly satisfy that condition.

---

96. I say "arguably" in acknowledgement of the fact that Frege (1892) asserts that sentences express no propositions if they contain sense-bearing but non-referring terms. Frege thus holds that "the man on the moon is a violinst" fails to affirm any proposition. But this view of his is inconsistent with the view, which he advocates in the very same paper as the view just mentioned, that "the phi is psi" is equivalent with "there exists something that is uniquely phi and any such thing is psi."

97. Strictly speaking, the correct paraphrase is: "There exists something that is uniquely a set of all sets that aren't members of themselves; and *any* such thing is a member of itself." By replacing the occurrence in K$_{1S}$ of "that thing" with "any such thing," we sidestep the need to answer the question: "to what does the aforementioned occurrence refer?"

The sense of a sense-bearing expression is nothing other than a condition that a thing must satisfy to be picked out by that expression. The sense of "the tallest spy" is the condition of being a spy who is taller than any other. If Smith satisfies that condition, then tokens of "the tallest spy" refer to him; otherwise, they don't. Nothing is picked out by the occurrence of "that woman" in a token, occurring in a woman-free context, of "the man whose best friend *that woman* is." For that reason, in such a context, there is no condition such that, if a thing satisfies that condition, it is the referent of that definite description.

In objection to this, one might say that *there is* such a condition, albeit one that varies depending on whether it is Jane or Sally or Ethel who is picked out by the occurrence of "that woman." But that's the very point we're making: that occurrence is the occurrence of a free-variable, like the occurrence of "x" in "x is even"; and "the man whose best friend *that woman* is" thus no more has a sense than "x is even" expresses a proposition.

Given obvious extensions of this reasoning, the occurrence of "itself" in K_1 lacks a sense, and so does the corresponding occurrence in K_{1S}. So the hypothetical objector's point is doubly misguided: even if it's correct, "the property of being a set of all sets that aren't members of themselves" doesn't pick out a property, and our central thesis still stands. And that point *isn't* correct, so that, just as we said, K_1 doesn't express a proposition, the same being true of K_{1S}, given that latter is equivalent with K_1.

To sum up, "the property of being the set of sets that aren't members of themselves" picks nothing out, and that property, being non-existent, isn't a counter-example to the Axiom of Comprehension or, indeed, to any proposition.

Notice that the rules of English semantics are not at fault here. Those rules are unambiguous as to how anaphoric terms are to be interpreted. Those rules make it clear that, because it contains a free variable, "x is a mad man" affirms no proposition; and those rules make it clear that, for much the same reason, sentence(-tokens) containing free occurrences of pronouns *do not affirm propositions*. So the semantic rules constitutive of the English language assign neither truth *nor* falsity to K_1; so they don't assign *both* truth *and* falsity to K_1. So they *don't* countenance any violation of LCN, at least not to the extent that, relative to them, K_1 violates some logical principle. So those rules do not, at least not to that extent, need to be modified in accordance with TT or otherwise logically reconstructed. So TT is unnecessary.

7.5.3   The fact that occurrences of "itself" are always eliminable is a consequence of a more general principle, namely: the term "self" is *always* eliminable. (I am referring to the term "self" *qua* suffix, as in "himself," not *qua* garden-variety noun, as in "people have selves, whereas lizards do not." All references to "self" are to be thus disambiguated.[98]) In fact, *all* pronouns are eliminable. This point is subject to three qualifications, none of which redounds to the credit of Russell's analysis of K_1.

---

98. Let's start with a purely clarificatory point. The word "self" has two meanings or functions. Sometimes it can function as a garden-variety noun. That's how it's functioning in "Hume

First, when the word "self" occurs in contexts governed by terms denoting propositional attitudes (e.g. "believes," "hopes"), it is not eliminable, at least not in any straightforward way. For example,

(L_1) "Larry believes himself to be a great pianist,"

isn't shorthand for:

(L_2) "Larry believes Larry to be a great pianist."[99]

Larry might have amnesia and not *know* that he's Larry but still believe Larry to be a great pianist. The reason L_1 and L_2 aren't equivalent is that, in L_1, "self" falls within the scope of an expression ("believes") that denotes a propositional attitude. But in K_1 "self" doesn't occur within the scope of "believes" or indeed *any* intensional operator: it is functioning extensionally. So this qualification is irrelevant to our critique of Russell.

Second, when a pronoun functions as a bound-variable, as opposed to a *bona fide* device of reference, it is not eliminable, at least not in any straightforward way. The sentence:

($\$_1$) "If someone gives you \$1,000,000 and asks for nothing in return, that person has a good heart."

is not equivalent with:

($\$_2$) "If someone gives you \$1,000,000 and asks for nothing in return, someone has a good heart."

This is because ($\$_1$)'s meaning is given by a sentence in which "that person" is replaced by a bound variable:

---

denied that he had a self." And sometimes "self" functions as a way of constructing 'terms of laziness,' to adapt an expression of Geach's, viz. expressions that are useful, because conducive to expedience, but technically eliminable. That's how it functions in

(J_1) John punched himself,

which is short for

(J_2) John punched John.

When functioning denotatively (as in "my self – in other words, my soul or psychological essence, or some such – is something that underlies and unifies the various fleeting occurrences and states constitutive of my consciousness") isn't eliminable (at least not in any relevant sense). But (so I am trying to show) when functioning *anaphorically*, it *is* eliminable (cf. J_1 and J_2). Henceforth, all references to the term "self" are to the anaphoric device.

Now the requisite qualifications of our contention (that "self" is always eliminable).

99. Perry (1977) makes this point.

($_3$)   "for any persons x and y, if x gives y $1,000,000 and asks for nothing in return from y, then x has a good heart."

But this is irrelevant to our critique of Russell's point, since the occurrence of "itself" in K_1 clearly doesn't occur as a bound variable. K_1 is a singular statement, not a quantified generalization, since it says of some (putative) object K that K isn't a member of K.

7.5.4   TT says that no meaningful sentence concerns *every* sentence. But TT is given by a sentence that violates that very stricture, and is thus self-defeating, since it's given by the sentence: "All meaningful sentences concern no sentences other than those that belong to orders (or types) lower than those to which they themselves belong."

7.5.5   There are two classes of antinomies: those that are meaningless and, for that reason, neither true nor false and those that that are false. Russell's Paradox is an instance of the first class, and what we've said in connection with it is easily generalized to apply to any other such instance. The so-called " "Liar's Paradox" is instance of the second class. And once we solve it, it will be clear how to deal with at least some other instances of the second class.

Let tf be a token of the sentence-type:

(TF)   "This sentence is false."

According to the conventional wisdom:

(CW)   tf is false if it's true and true if it's false. So if it's either true or false, it's *both* true *and* false. Which is impossible. So it's neither. Therefore there is no proposition that it expresses. Therefore, it is meaningless. But it is a *bona fide* sentence-token.[100]

7.5.6   It is in virtue of what a given sentence-token *affirms* that it is true or false. Describing a sentence-token as "true" ("false") is an abbreviated way of saying that it affirms a true (false) proposition.[101] If it affirms anything, a given token of "this *sentence*

---

100. Advocates of CW (e.g. Russell (1908), Tarski (1930), and Kripke (1975)) take it to be to the discredit of the English language that the rules constitutive of it permit the construction of such a sentence. But, those rules being what they are, it is indeed a *bona fide* sentence-token of English.

101. *A defense of this claim*: No series of noises is a sentence-*type*: an ink-deposit is, at most, a sentence-token. (In this context, "burst of noise" is short-hand for "anything (be it an ink-deposit, a pattern of light on a monitor, etc.) that might token an expression," the same qualification *mutatis mutandis* holding of related terms (e.g. "acoustic"). But, given some ink-deposit, *which* sentence-type it tokens is a function of what it means. A series of noises *acoustically* just like utterances of the English sentence "snow is white" could mean anything. Let L be a

is true (false)" affirms that some *proposition* is true (false). Technicalities aside, "this sentence is true (false)" means "this *proposition* is true (false)."

Suppose that the occurrence of "this sentence" in a token of "this sentence is true" refers to the sentence "snow is white." In that case, what is being said is an abbreviation for:

(TP)   "The *proposition* meant by this sentence is true."

The semantic rule for TP is:

(STF)   If, in context C, there is some uniquely salient sentence S whose meaning is some proposition P, then, in C, a token t of TF is true exactly if P is true; and if, in C, there is no such sentence and therefore no such proposition, then, in C, a token t of TF is neither true nor false, as there is no proposition affirmed by such a token.

The proposition, supposing there to be one, affirmed by a given sentence-token is a function of what its parts refer to. This is a consequence of the "principle of compositionality"[102] namely:

(CM)   What is meant (referred to) by a given expression is determined by what its parts mean (refer to)."[103]

Let O be the occurrence of "the proposition meant by this sentence" in a token t of TP. If O refers to nothing, t is neither true nor false. What t affirms depends on what

---

language such that, for some sentence S that belongs to L, S means chickens can fly" but such that utterances of S are *acoustically* indistinguishable from utterances of the English sentence "snow is white." Obviously utterances of S are not identical with utterances of "snow is white", and tokens of S are not identical with tokens of "snow is white," a corollary being that S and "snow is white" are different sentence-*types*. So sentence-types are not individuated by the physical properties of their tokens; and, what obviously follows, it isn't solely in virtue of a given object's physical (e.g. acoustical or morphological) properties that a given token is an instance of this as opposed to that sentence-type. Given some physical object x, is in virtue, not just of what x's physical properties are, but also of what it means, that x tokens this as opposed to that sentence-type. If a burst of noise acoustically just like a token of "snow is white" were produced a million years ago by some volcano, it would token no expression. Since meaning doesn't supervene on acoustics – since, in other words, two acoustically indistinguishable entities needn't coincide in meaning – no burst of noise *by itself* constitutes an expression-token.

102.   Which was enunciated by Frege (1892). (Some of its more important consequences are clearly drawn in Barwise and Perry (1983).) I don't know whether Frege was the first to state it. (I doubt he was.)

103.   The order in which those parts occur is also relevant, that being why "the man Smith saw standing next to Jones" doesn't have the same referent as "the man Jones saw standing next to Smith."

O refers to. O must have a referent *independently* of what t affirms. Otherwise t won't affirm anything.

This is easily shown. I'm having an exchange with my friend Jerry. I say: "*He* is *her* father." Since the context doesn't supply either one of the italicized terms with a referent, Jerry asks me who "he" refers to. I say "*her* father." Jerry then asks me who "*her*" refers to. I say "*his* daughter." If the answers I've given to Jerry are the only viable ones, then there is *no* viable answer to either question, in which case neither italicized terms refer to anything and I've therefore affirmed nothing.

An adaptation of this story will make its relevance clear. In an email exchange with Jerry, I say: "*the proposition meant by this sentence* is false." Jerry asks: "Which proposition is that?" I say: "The one meant by the underlined sentence." Jerry then asks: "Which proposition is meant by the underlined sentence?" I say: "the one meant by the italicized expression." If the answers I've given are the only viable ones, there is *no* viable answer to either question, in which case neither the underlined term nor the italicized terms refer to anything and I've therefore affirmed nothing.

7.5.7 *Tokens of TP are neither true nor false.* So such tokens are not both true *and* false. So, assuming the correctness of the Strawson-Kaplan view of indexicals, the semantic rules of English *do not* permit the construction of sentences that violate LNC. (Of course, in this context, "English" could just as well refer to any natural language.) For this reason, many a logician-philosopher has argued English (and any other given natural language, given that no other such language is relevantly different from English) was defective. Often, that logician's reasoning is as follows:

> The semantic rules of English are propositions (to the effect that such and such symbols (or symbol-tokens) have thus and such meanings (or satisfaction-conditions)). There exist sentences, such as "K is a self-member" and "this sentence is false," such that (i) relative to those rules those sentences (or their tokens) qualify as meaningful, and such that (ii) the propositions meant by those sentences are, if existent, violations of LCN. Therefore, a logical falsehood is among the logical consequences of those semantic rules. So, if we take the primitive semantic rules (e.g. "Smith" refers to Smith) of English (for example) as axioms, and the derived rules (e.g. "Smith runs fast" is true exactly if Smith runs fast") as theorems – and this is how they are to be taken – then we find there to be violations of LCN, and thus logical falsehoods, among the theorems in question. And no axiom-set can be accepted if it has a logical falsehood as a consequence.
>
> At least one reason for this, be it noted, is that there is nothing that *doesn't* follow from such an axiom-set. So the axiom-set in question (the least inclusive set comprising the primitive semantic rules of English) has the consequence that "Smith runs fast" is true iff Richard Nixon was born on Mars no less than it has the consequence that "Smith runs fast" is true iff Smith

runs fast. This means that, relative to those rules, anything means everything: given any sentence, there is no proposition that it doesn't mean. And this in turn means that, relative to those rules, nothing means anything, given that an infinitely ambiguous expression is meaningless. So until we so revise the semantic rules of English that logical falsehoods are not among their consequences, any given English sentences means everything and therefore rules nothing out and therefore, in effect, means nothing. Thus, until we so revise those rules, there is, in effect, no English language. So we must revise them.[104]

We have seen the semantic rules of English *not* to be guilty of at least two of the violations of the laws of logic of which they have been alleged to be guilty. And there is reason to believe that the considerations on the basis of which we established this cannot be so generalized as to acquit the semantic rules of English of many other, similar charges of non-compliance with the laws of (classical) logic.

---

104. See Russell (1908) and Tarski (1983).

CHAPTER 5

Wittgenstein on meaning

Part 2 – meaning as use[105]

1.0   Like his contemporaries, Wittgenstein soon saw the shortcomings of his first theory. So he came up with a second. His second theory, like his first, was meant to show that there is no need to grant the existence of propositions. But the two theories are otherwise very different.

The second theory comes to this: *meaning is use.* Wittgenstein himself used these very words to summarize his second theory, which, when stated perspicuously, is as follows:

(WA[106]) If, all of a sudden, people did nothing with $20 bills other than wipe their noses, $20 bills would be as worthless as tissue paper. If, all of a sudden, people never used the sentence "it's a glorious day outside" except right before breaking up with a significant other, then that sentence would have a very different meaning from the one it actually has. If you want to know what is meant by a given sentence, know how it is used: once this is known, there's nothing left to know about its meaning. Its meaning, so far as it can be said to have one, *is* its use.

Concepts are word-meanings. The concept of justice is the meaning of the word "justice." So a corollary of the points just made is that, if you want to know about justice or numbers, or abstract objects of any other kind, learn how the corresponding words are used. Once you know exactly how people use the word "justice," you'll *ipso facto* know everything there is to know about its meaning.

And you're on a fool's errant if you try study that concept in any other way: *for there is no such concept.* We talk about words as having meanings, and sometimes as expressing concepts. But such statements, assuming them not thoroughly misguided, are abbreviated ways of talking about the communal role played by 'justice' (or the corresponding word, if you are speaking a different language).

---

105. My interpretations of Wittgenstein's notoriously obscure arguments owes much to Hacker and Baker (1980, 1984a, 1984b, 1985).

106. Short for "Wittgenstein's argument."

Nothing means anything. There are no concepts. There are no properties. There are no propositions. We came up with the concept of a proposition because we wanted a way to distinguish between "snow is white," which is meaningful, and "ikfsdahfsd," which is not, and the most obviously explanation is that there is an entity – a proposition – that is the meaning "snow is white," while there is no such entity corresponding to "ikfsdahfsd."

But the correct answer to the question "why is the one expression meaningful, while the other is not?" has nothing to do with propositions or other such fantasms. The right answer is that, our customs being what they are, "ikfsdahfsd" is useless. Were I to utter it, I wouldn't be commending you, censuring your, asking your opinion about the economy, or, indeed, doing anything (other than behaving oddly). But should that expression be assimilated into our practices, it *would* be meaningful. Meaningfulness *is* assimilatedness into practice.

Meaning is use. Know how it is used, and you know what it means.

Analysis: WA is not tenable. An utterance of "I'm in the room right next to yours" could be used in a variety ways: to threaten; to titillate; to reassure; or just to state a fact. But one must distinguish that sentence's literal meaning from its functional role. Given only what a sentence literally means, nothing follows as to what it can be used to do and nothing follows as to what its occurrences convey. (Given only what sentence's literal meaning is P, it doesn't even follow that S can be used to transmit P. For S might be so long and intricate that nobody understands it.) What a sentence can be used to do is a function only in part of its literal meaning; it is also a function of the context. Supposing T to be a token of some sentence S, what T conveys depends on a number of factors: who produces it; who hears it; what the auditor believes; what T's physical properties are; and the changes undergone by the speaker in the process of producing T. It isn't enough to know what T literally means. Who is saying it? (A mid-level Mafia capo?) Who is he speaking to? (An underlying? Or a superior?) How was it said? (Gravely? Jokingly?) What T conveys is the vector sum of its literal meaning and the facts identified by the answers to these questions.

Similar points hold with respect to any given sentence. Given what is literally meant by "I'm in the room right next door to yours," you'll react one way to my tokening that sentence if you that know that I'm an axe-murderer, and another way if I'm a long lost lover. But what can be inferred from a given token of it obviously depends on the circumstances, and not just on its literal meaning.

On the basis of the fact that any given sentence can be used to convey anything, given the right circumstances, Wittgenstein infers that expressions don't have fixed meanings. That is comparable to a person's some rock to have gotten lighter because X successfully lifted it right after Y tried but failed to do so. Just as the right conclusion to draw is that that X is stronger than Y, not that the rock has gotten lighter, so the right conclusion to draw about "I'm in the room right next door to yours" is that it has a fixed, circumstance-invariant meaning, but that the *meaning of that meaning* is circumstance-dependent.

Meaning cannot be use. One reason is there are meaningful expressions that are never used literally and infinitely many that aren't used at all. Another reason is that, once you know what a given expression means, you won't acquire new knowledge about that meaning by acquiring additional knowledge as to how that word is used.

Also, if meaning were use, what would be meant by highly use-variable sentences, such as "I'm coming over" or "I'm right next door"? Nothing – a sentence whose meaning is so mercurial is one that has no meaning at all, and therefore isn't even a linguistic expression. (In Chapter 3, we established that there cannot possibly be meaningless linguistic expressions.) Given that such sentences obviously are meaningful, and have perfectly stable meanings, this is a problem for Wittgenstein's model.

But it's not a problem for the other model, according to which literal meaning is fixed, it being the variable nature of circumstance that accounts for the variable nature of what a given sentence-token suggests.

1.1   "But Wittgenstein rejects the idea that there are meanings," it will be said. "In the argument you just gave, you question-beggingly assumed that there are such things."

We did indeed make that assumption; let us now show that we were right to do so. How people use an expression is causally determined by what they know its meaning to be. I cut myself badly. I dial 9-1-1. I say "I'm badly hurt." Why didn't I say "send over a cheese pizza" or "Nigeria's economy is now growing faster than ever"? Because those words have the wrong meanings. If meaning *were* use, it couldn't *govern* use.

Two conditions must be met if a given person's noise-making is to qualify as *bona fide* speech. He must know the meanings of the noises he's making, and he must produce them intentionally. If, by some freak accident, a coffee machine were to produce noises homophonic with a token of "I'm badly hurt; please send an ambulance"; it wouldn't be saying anything. If somebody who does know what those words mean but utters them involuntarily, he is not saying anything.

In order for anyone to say anything, words must have meanings, and there must therefore be true propositions saying what those meanings are. Such propositions are nothing other than semantic rules. So in order for anything to mean anything, there must be semantic rules; and in order for a given person to say anything, he must know the relevant rules.

Noise-production that isn't governed by knowledge of such rules is not linguistic, and duly rule-governed usage of an expression is *ipso facto* governed by, and therefore doesn't constitute, its meaning.

2.0   In the upcoming discussion, the word "concept" is being used in the same way it is used in the sentence "anything that falls under the concept *triangle* falls under the concept *closed figure*." It is being used to refer, not to psychological entities, but to the meanings of predicates, e.g. the meaning "x is a closed figure."

Wittgenstein says that to understand the concept of number is to know how "number" (or some equivalent term) is used. But if I am to know that "number" is the word whose usage I am to study, I must be able to grasp the concept of number independently of that word.

Wittgenstein's position concerning concepts is as follows:[107]

> Concepts don't exist. So there is no such thing as the concept of number. But the word "number" is meaningful, and there is a sense in which there exists something that is its meaning. That meaning, if it exists, is not some abstract object. That meaning consists of actions on the part of human beings.
>
> Given that there are no concepts, conceptual analysis is a fruitless task. But there is something that isn't fruitless that resembles conceptual analysis. Much of the knowledge that philosophers hoped to achieve through "conceptual analysis" *are* acquired by doing this other thing. This other thing is the study of word-usage. It is by learning how the word "number" is used that one learns its meaning. That meaning has depths. But those depths are to be plumbed by doing sociology, not conceptual analysis.

Let NM be the concept expressed by the word "number." I obviously had to observe people *in order to* learn that NM was its meaning. But once I learned what "number" meant, any further empirical observations that I had as to how it was used gave me no further information at all about its meaning.

Empirical observations on my part have led (indirectly) to a deepening of my understanding of NM, that is, of the concept of number. Though I've known the meaning of the word "number" since I was three, it wasn't until I was 24 that I found out that integers can be identified with second-order properties and that real numbers can be identified with sets of rationals. But in thus deepening my understanding of NM, I was no more adding to my *semantic* knowledge than physical chemist is adding to his semantic knowledge by learning the chemical composition of a Zip-lock bag. Semantic analysis (what the linguist does) mustn't be confused with conceptual analysis (what the philosopher does) or with objectual analysis (what the chemist does).

2.1 If Wittgenstein were right about meaning, what would it be for two noises to betoken some one word? It is no answer to say: "the speaker's intention to token a certain word, along with the acoustical properties that result from his executing that intention, determine which word has been tokened." Unless there is *already* an answer to the question "when are two different sounds tokens of the same word?" the speaker can't have a non-defective intention to token a given word.

Part of what makes a given token of the word "dog" be a token of that word, as opposed to some other word or no word at all, is what it sounds like. But if words were individuated *strictly* by the acoustical properties of their tokens, language couldn't

---

107. These are my words, not Wittgenstein's.

exist, as we would then be bound by prohibitively rigid standards in regards to how we could token a given word.

My meaning will become clear if we contrast words with musical notes. Two tokens of the same note may have different timbres or volumes; but they must have *exactly* the same frequency. An A tokened by Beethoven had precisely the same frequency as an A tokened today, and neither note has the same frequency as any token of any other note.

But there is no strictly acoustical property that all and only tokens of "bet" have in common. Some tokens of "bet" are acoustically just like tokens of "bit," while others are acoustically just like tokens of "bed."

Two numerically and qualitatively distinct noises, x and y, are both tokens of some one word N by virtue of (*inter alia*) the fact that three conditions are met:

(i)   There is a semantic rule to the effect that a necessary condition for m, this being an arbitrary noise, to be an instance of N is that m bear a certain acoustical relation (one of similarity) to n, where n is some noise (not noise-type);

(ii)   Each of x and y bears the requisite degree of similarity to n;

(iii) Each of x and y is produced by somebody who is aware of each of (i) and (ii), and who produces it with the intention of complying with (i) and (ii).

(i) entails that two (acoustical) tokens of a given word cannot sound entirely different. (ii) entails that each of x and y sounds enough like n that their being tokens of the same word is not ruled out. And (iii) entails that each of x and y is an instance of *bona fide* speech – not of a coffee-machine's or parrot's producing homophones of speech.

While supporting our critique of Wittgenstein's view, our analysis is independently verifiable, and we may consider his view to have been refuted.

3.0   Wittgenstein put forth several arguments to the effect that meanings don't exist and that, consequently, linguistic behavior isn't to be understood in terms of them. Scholars have consolidated these various arguments into two arguments, commonly known as: "the private language" and "the rule following" arguments. But we can't make an informed judgment as to whether scholars were right to consolidate those arguments, or to consolidate them in the way they did, before we state each one individually and evaluate it.[108] So, instead of using the terms "Private Language Argument" and "Rule Following Argument," I'll refer to the arguments in question as "Argument #1," "Argument #2," and so on.

---

108. We'll see that scholars were right to consolidate those arguments in the way that they did.

Argument #1 (A1)

To understand an expression is to know what it means. Some take this to entail that, given any meaningful expression E, there is some object M that is E's meaning. But this is not the right view.

Let s be an arbitrary token of "the cat is on the mat," and let m be s's meaning, supposing for argument's sake that it has one. According to the conventional view, to understand s is to know that m is its meaning: In general, to understand an expression is to couple that expression with the right meaning. The expression is one thing, the meaning another; and one needn't grasp the one to grasp the other.

But you won't find the meaning of "the cat is on the mat" by rummaging through your closet or going on a Safari. Your bowling ball isn't the meaning of s. Neither is the bird on the windowsill. Nor is anything else in the universe.

Supposing that m exists and that I am beholding it, how does my doing that help me understand m? It doesn't. m is just another object; and when attempting to understand s, it's no more useful to examine m than it is to examine my favorite shirt.

"But m is s's meaning," it will be said. "So if properly examined and understood, it will avail you of s's meaning." But in that case, m is just another sign that has to be interpreted. If the just-described view is right, meanings are just more signs; and, like signs, they need to be deciphered. If we look for the meanings of these signs, we're obviously on a fool's errand.

Therefore, Platonic objects, if they exist, are useless. Trying to account for the meaningfulness of "the cat is on the mat" by positing some object that is its meaning is pointless; that object will be as useless as any bowling ball or tennis racket in the way of enabling you to understand the sentence in question.

Analysis: A1 assumes that meanings, were they to exist, would *themselves* have to be interpreted. But meanings aren't interpreted. They're either grasped or they're not grasped. It is *expressions* that are interpreted, not meanings. Contrary to what Wittgenstein assumes, meanings, if existent, are not signs. Signs *bear* meanings. Meanings don't *bear* meanings; they *are* them.

Wittgenstein seems to think that non-spatiotemporal entities, were they to exist, would be similar to spatiotemporal entities. This is not just *a* fallacy; it is *the* fallacy underlying all antagonism towards the non-spatiotemporal. The property of being a man is not a man and it isn't man-like. The property of being spatiotemporal is not itself spatiotemporal and therefore doesn't in any significant way resemble its instances.

Properties are best thought of as "ways of being." (David Armstrong (1998) used this very expression to make this very point.) By virtue of weighing 200 lbs, I am one way; I'd be a different way if I weighed 500 lbs. Given some other 200 lbs person, there is a property that we both have, since there is some way that we both are.

Ways of being must be distinguished from *instances* of such ways. I am not identical with the way one must be to weigh 200 lbs. When I gain or lose weight, that way is unaffected.

Argument #2 (A2)

Consider the function $F(x) = x^2$. Like all functions from numbers to numbers, this can be thought of as a rule that assigns no more than one number to each number falling into some class. So it can be thought of as a rule that assigns 1 to 1, 4 to 2, 9 to 3, and so on. Alternatively, this function can be thought of as the set of ordered pairs generated by the just-mentioned rule, that is, as the least inclusive class containing <1,1>, <2,4>, <3,9>, and so on.

Obviously, you can often identify the number that $F(x)$ assigns to a given number. For example, it doesn't take you long to figure out that $F(13)$ is 169. But there are infinitely many numbers such that, given any one of them, you haven't even considered the question of what the value of $F(x)$ is for that particular number. Thus, in so far as you grasp this function, it cannot be by virtue of your knowing all of the ordered pairs generated by that function. It cannot be by virtue of your knowing that function's "extension," as logicians would put it. It must be by virtue of your knowing how, when given some number n, to apply $F(x)$ to n, i.e. to figure out the identity of the number that $F(x)$ assigns to n.

Surely you can't be said to grasp $F(x)$ if, when evaluating $F(x)$ for a given number n, you apply $F(x)$ to n in haphazard way. Supposing that you grasp this function, it must be in a principled way – a way embodying due sensitivity to the relevant rules – that you determine the value of $F(x)$ for argument n.

So to grasp one rule – namely, $F(x)$ – one must be able to apply that rule to particular cases, and to do so *in a principled* (rule-governed) way. This means that grasping any one rule involves grasping a second rule and, therefore, involves grasping infinitely many rules. To evaluate $F(x)$ for $x = 13$, I must understand the principles – the rules, we could also say – involved in that function's assigning 169 to that number.

At this point a problem arises. My grasp of $F(x)$ is, by itself, worthless: my grasping it means nothing except in so far as I can apply it – except, that is to say, in so far as I can use my grasp of it to figure out which number that function assigns to a given number. But given only that I grasp $F(x)$, I don't necessarily know that $F(13) = 69$. Taken by itself, my concept of that function is quite silent concerning as to the identities of the values of that function for particular arguments. That concept must therefore be supplemented: if my knowledge of $F(x)$ is to be operationalized, I must have knowledge, not just of $F(x)$, but of how to *apply* $F(x)$ to particular cases. I must now how, for a given number n, to *interpret* $F(x)$ for $x = n$.

Knowing how to interpret something involves knowing rules. Knowing how to translate from Spanish to English involves knowing rules, and so does knowing how to interpret a dream or a statue. Similarly, knowing how to interpret F(x), for x = n, for arbitrary n, involves knowing rules of some kind.

But F(x) is itself a rule. And yet when the time came to apply that rule, we found that we had to use other rules. But what was true of F(x) must hold of these new, secondary rules. There's nothing distinctive about F(x); it's a rule just like any other. We found that rule to be useless unless interpreted, and we found that knowledge of rules other than it was necessary to interpret it.

So it is only to the extent that we grasp, and know how to apply, rules other than F(x) that we can evaluate F(x) for any specification of the variable. But for reasons analogous to those just given, these secondary rules don't tell us how they are to be applied; and the same will be true of the tertiary rules on the basis of which we are interpret the secondary rules; and so on *ad infinitum*.

This shows that rules, if considered as platonic objects, are useless. Nothing is explained about Timmy's behavior by supposing that he grasps F(x); for, as we just saw, merely grasping that rule is innocuous: unless Timmy grasps rules other than F(x), he won't be able to mobilize his grasp of F(x). But F(x) was arbitrarily chosen; it is not, in the relevant respect, distinctive among rules: *all* rules are such that, to know how to apply them, one must know rules other than them.

This is not to deny the arithmetical fact that F(13) = 169. Nor is it to deny the anthropological fact that many a person knows that F(13) = 169. It *is* to deny that anything is to be gained by supposing one's grasp of F(x), or of any other rule, to be constituted by one's awareness of some platonic entity. For, as we just saw, even if such entities existed, and even if we grasped them, we *still* wouldn't even have begun to have an explanation of what it is for some to know that (e.g.) F(13) = 169.

This line of thought can be generalized. We believe there to be such a thing as "thinking." And it is a datum, I suppose, that people think. On the basis of this datum, it's assumed that thinking is entirely intra-cranial. But this assumption is quite false.

To a large extent, thinking involves the following of rules. Mental activity is not *ipso facto* ratiocinative. Free-associations are not ratiocinative; neither are dreams. To qualify as ratiocinative, mentation must be rule-governed: it must be controlled by, for example, one's knowledge that if P is one of one's premises, one is not entitled to hold not-P without either rejecting P, or rejecting one of one's other assumptions, or finding fault with some aspect of the way in which one derived not-P from those starting assumptions. So "rule-governed thought" is a pleonasm, and "*non*-rule-governed thought" is a contradiction in terms. But if one tries to mentalize the process of following a rule, one's efforts yield nothing of explanatory value.

This last point must be qualified, as it doesn't hold with respect to *all* rules. In particular, it doesn't hold with respect to *social* rules. Social rules are spatiotemporal entities; and, like all such entities, they are distinguished by their causal properties – by the effects they have on things. The rule being *stay off the grass*, the effect of walking on the grass is that I am ticketed, or some such. Because social rules are spatiotemporal entities, we don't need to mythologize to explain what it is to follow them; we need to posit Platonic hyper-entities or other such chimera. Why don't I walk on the grass? Because I don't want a ticket.

If a rule isn't social, it's not a spatiotemporal entity. There are rules like *keep off the grass*: rules that people create and enforce. These are spatiotemporal. It is generally assumed that, in addition to social rules, there are rules of a non-social kind: rules that don't prescribe or proscribe any specific mode of conduct and which people don't create, at least not in the straightforward sense in which people create rules like *stay off the grass*. Supposing there to be such rules, an example of one would be $F(x) = x^2$. Rules of this second kind, it is said, are not spatiotemporal.

Bearing these points in mind, let's suppose that we try to cognitivize the following of a non-social rule, such as $F(x) = x^2$. Let's suppose, in other words, that we try to find some mental process with which a case of following some non-social rule is to be identified. Since (so we are supposing *arguendo*) non-social rules are non-spatiotemporal, we must regard any given act of rule-following as involving the rule-follower's being aware of, and operating with, Platonic entities; we must regard any case of rule-following as involving, or being, some sort of juggling of Platonic entities.

But we've seen that this conception of thought is an incoherent one. Platonic entities, if they exist, aren't any more self-interpreting than rocks or trees. So given only that we've attributed a grasp of $F(x) = x^2$ to some person, we've explained nothing about him; nothing about his knowledge that F(13) = 169; and nothing about anything else relating either to what he knows or how he acts. And when trying to say what it is for a given person to know that F(13) = 169, it does us no good to credit that person with a grasp of *other* Platonic entities. Everything we just said about $F(x) = x^2$ will hold of these other entities. So in positing them, we're trying to pay with checks drawn from an already over-drawn account.

Rule-following, it must be concluded, *is not a strictly psychological phenomenon*. This must be understood aright. There is a difference between, on the one hand, somebody whose mathematical insight led him to believe

$F(13) = 169$ and, on the other hand, somebody who believes it for some spurious reason: *but the difference is not psychological.*

Let A and B be individuals of the first and second types, respectively. (So A understands why $F(13) = 169$, whereas B does not.) And let m be any mental entity in A's mind (any process, any structure) the likes of which is not in B's mind. The fact that m is in A's mind is not the relevant difference between A and B. To be sure, there is a relevant difference between A and B. (If there weren't, either both of them would understand why F assigns 169 or neither of them would.) But that difference is not of a strictly psychological nature.

The conventional wisdom is that thinking is a psychological process. The conventional system is wrong. Rule-following is not a mental process, and neither is thinking, at least to the extent that thinking is identical with rule-governed ideation.

I do not deny that people think. I deny that people think on their own – *provided that their doing so is parasitic on their being duly acculturated.* For reasons to be stated presently, rule-following is inherently social, and so therefore is thinking. One must be embedded in the practices of a community if one is to be able to think. But what's important for now is the negative component of my claim, namely: rule-following is not a psychological act, and neither, therefore, is thinking, at least to the (considerable) extent that thought is necessarily rule-governed ideation.

Analysis: (A2) assumes that

(a)   one can grasp a principle without knowing how to apply it.

But (a) is false. Consider the principle (or rule) that:

(SR)   Motorists must stop at red lights.

I'm driving and I happen to be approaching a red light. For me to grasp SR *is* for me know that, because I am approaching a red light, I am to stop my vehicle. For me to grasp SR *is* for me to know what to do when approaching a red light. Knowledge of how to apply SR is built into knowledge of SR. Knowledge of secondary principles is no part of the story.

Matters *seem* to be different with other principles. "Surely I grasp the function $F(x) = x^2$," it will be said. "But, just as surely, I have to *figure out* how to apply that function to 1,198,976. A knowledge of that number's square isn't built into my grasp of that function. You're therefore simply wrong to say that, if one grasps a given principle, one *ipso facto* knows how to apply it."

The reason this argument fails is to be understood in terms of Chomsky's (1965) distinction between *competence* and *performance*. Competence is ability. Performance is the ability to deploy ability. Given any sentence that is very long, say 10,000 words long, but otherwise normal, I won't be able to understand it. But it isn't that the part of my mind that mediates language-comprehension isn't up to the job. *That* part of my mind *is* up to the job. It's the other parts that are to blame: my memory isn't good enough; I can't stay focused, or even awake, long enough. *If* I didn't have any issues relating to memory, fatigue, boredom, etc., I'd have no difficulty processing the sentence. If my linguistic competence is to operate at full force, other abilities of mine must be intact: I must be able to hear (or see) the sentence-token in question; I must not be drowsy; the sentence must not be so long that too much is demanded of my patience, powers of concentration, and sheer physical stamina.

Let S be some sentence that is 200 words long, and thus very long, but otherwise ordinary. There is some rule R, this being a rule of English semantics, that assigns a given meaning M to S. Be it noted that R is a function, in the most literal sense of the word. Unlike $F(x) = x^2$, it is not a function from numbers to numbers. But it is still a function: from expressions to meanings.

R is a derived, not a primitive rule. In other words, R is not like the rule that assigns Plato (the person) to "Plato" (the expression). The latter rule cannot be broken down into simpler ones. R, on the other hand, can be broken down into simpler rules, and those simpler rules are probably capable of broken down into still simpler ones. Indeed, we may have to go through several rounds of breaking down complex functions into their components before we arrive at any simple semantic functions.

There is no difference between understanding a simple semantic rule and knowing what is meant by (what one knows to be) a given occurrence of the expression in question; and one cannot know what is meant by a simple combinatory device without *ipso facto* knowing what is meant by its application to a given expression (provided one knows the meaning of that expression); if one knows what is meant by "the father of___" and "Socrates," one *ipso facto* knows what is meant by "the father of Socrates."

But consider the expression:

E: "The cousin of the nephew of the sister of the nemesis of the father of the sole cousin of the favorite relative of Socrates' best friend's best friend's worst enemy, who happens to be identical with Socrates' best friend's best friend."

E is the same sort of expression as "the father of Socrates." But whereas you immediately understand "the father of Socrates," you don't immediately understand (*). You have to compute the latter's meaning; you must figure it out. But this doesn't have to do you with your degree of linguistic competence. It has to do with your linguistic performance, that is, with your ability to deploy your linguistic competence. Given the distinction between competence and performance, there is no gulf between knowing a given principle and knowing how to apply it under a given set of circumstances.

Let us now return to the objector's (correct) point that a given person x can grasp $F(x) = x^2$ without being able to immediately identify the square of 1,198,976. This case is perfectly comparable to the case of a fluent speaker y of English having difficulty understanding a 200-word of his language. In each case there is a function that somebody grasps (in x's case, a function from numbers to numbers; in y's case, a function from words to meanings) and there is therefore a respect in which each of somebody is competent.

To square 1,198,976 is to multiply it by 1,198,976. The rule for multiplication is not hard to grasp ($n0 = 0$, $(a(b + 1) = ab + a)$), and neither is any one of the steps, taken individually, that is involved in multiplying 1,198,976 by itself. Given how many simple steps are involved, however, and given how many iterated operations, problems not specific to one's mathematical competence will blunt the role that one's mathematical competence has on the final result. But it's only to the extent that factors *other than one's mathematical competence* have a hand in one's computations that those computations will go awry.

Argument #3 (A3)[109]
Consider the function:
$G(x) = x^2$ iff $x < 99^{99}$; otherwise, $G(x) = 1$.

---

109. What follows is Kripke's exposition of an argument of Wittgenstein's, which many Wittgenstein scholars claim isn't really Wittgenstein's argument at all, but Kripke's misinterpretation thereof, and to which they thus refer as the "Kripkenstein" Argument.

Many claim that Kripke misunderstood Wittgenstein's argument. In response, I would like to make four points.

(1)   Kripke's analysis *seems* spot-on; and, although it is only meant to hold with respect to the argument put forth in the *Private Investigations*, it holds no less with respect to arguments found in Wittgenstein's *Remarks on the Foundations of Mathematics* and in his *Philosophical Grammar*.

(2)   It's never been clearly stated how exactly Kripke erred. It's simply been asseverated, by professional Wittgensteinians, that he did err. And whereas Kripke's argument is quite clear and (as we will see) capable of being adjudicated, these Wittgensteinians did not replace Kripke's argument with one that was comparably clear; and, as a matter of historical fact, every attempt to rebut Wittgenstein's arguments, as the just-mentioned Wittgensteinians interpreted it, has met with the reply: "you don't understand the argument," a consequence being that substantive issues were delayed (probably permanently) pending the resolution of (unresolvable, from the looks of it) exegetical issues.

(3)   Kripke's argument is of interest in its own right, it being a matter of historical, not philosophical concern, whether Wittgenstein himself advocated it.

(4)   Wittgenstein *did* advocate it. Its similarity to the arguments of his that we've already evaluated, and that we have yet to evaluate it, makes this clear, as do the relevant passages in the *Philosophical Investigations*. Wittgensteinians are aware that, judging by the text of the *Philosophical Investigations*, Kripke appears to be right. Their response is to say that Wittgenstein was being "ironic" and was "saying the opposite of what he meant." The passages during which he was supposedly ironically saying the opposite of what he meant are hundreds of pages long and don't typographically or stylistically or otherwise differ from the rest of Wittgenstein's writings.

Obviously G(x) is not the same function as $F(x) = x^2$.

But, for any $n < 99^{99}$, what determines whether one is applying F(x) or G(x)? John is applying F(x) to 6; Jerry is applying G(x) to 6. Each is doing so properly, and each gets the right result. In virtue of what fact is John applying the one function as opposed to the other? Does John have some *psychological* property that Jerry lacks such that it is by virtue of having that property that John is applying F(x) to 6, as opposed to G(x)? And does Jerry have some *psychological* property that John lacks such that it is by virtue of having that property that Jerry is applying G(x) to 6, as opposed to F(x)?

No. There aren't any relevant psychological differences. John's mind is just like Jerry's *to the extent* that their psychological conditions are determined by their applying, respectively, F(x) and G(x) to six.

Apply some function; follow some rule. Consider the various mental events that occur as you are doing so. None of those accompaniments is essential to, or constitutive of, your applying that function. Let $a_1....a_n$ be the various mental accompaniments of that operation: the various images that pass through your mind as you apply F(x) to 6, along with their various affective and emotional accompaniments. For any i $(1 \leq i \leq n)$, a_i's non-occurrence is perfectly compatible with your applying either F(x) or G(x) to six. In general, given any kind of psychological condition, being in that condition is neither necessary nor sufficient for one's applying any given rule in any given way.

By obvious extensions of this argument, given only a person's psychological condition, it is completely indeterminate what that person is *thinking*. Have the thought: *2 + 2 = 4*. Let $b_1....b_m$ be the various mental accompaniments of that thought. Everything we said about a_i $(1 \leq i \leq n)$ holds of b_i $(1 \leq i \leq m)$. *Thus, thinking is not a psychological process.*

Analysis: Wittgenstein asks: "How do I know that it's F(x) that I'm applying to 6, and not G(x)?" First of all, contrary to what Wittgenstein says, working with the one function is not psychologically the same as working with the other. If I'm working with large numbers, I'll tread very wearily if, for some reason, I'm working with G(x), whereas I'll act with relative abandon if I'm working with F(x).

F(x) and G(x) would not necessarily become more interchangeable, in all the relevant respects, by choosing some number higher than 99^{99} to mark the point of divergence between the two functions. For sometimes what matters is not *at what point* the function becomes bent, but *whether* it is bent. The fact that there is kink *somewhere* in the extension of G(x) may make it unsuitable to describe how two otherwise similar universes are different if one them but not the other, is governed by some law L. And we may need to have such information if we are to figure out whether our world is governed by L.

Mathematics is an *a priori* science. But it is on the basis of empirical considerations that we consider some domains of mathematics worth exploring and others not. If I'm describing the behaviors of physical objects; if I'm trying to determine the amount of energy needed to heat a certain quantity of a certain kind of metal by a certain amount within a certain amount of time; if I'm trying to compute the lifespan of a certain galaxy; if I'm working on *any* problem concerning large numbers that are growing at a continuous rate – if any of these conditions are met, I have no *a priori* assurance that replacing F(x) with G(x) wouldn't lead to the wrong results. Even though mathematics is a non-empirical science, the reason we are interested in some functions, e.g. F(x), as opposed to others, e.g. G(x), is that functions of the second kind, but not the first, are useless when it comes to describing the physical world. It's a theoretical possibility that we might come across objects the changes in whose velocities (or weights or temperatures etc.) were easily described in terms of G(x). But we have yet to come across such objects. And anyone working with F(x), were he told that he *might* be working with G(x) or any other similarly bent function, would stipulate that it was his intention *not* to work with it and that it *was* his intention to work with some non-bent function, like F(x).

The function that, as a civil engineer, it is my intention to apply is monotonic; the rate at which it's growing is always increasing; the rate at which the rate which its growing is constant; and that function is continuous. Any function that doesn't meet these requirements is not the function that it is my intention to apply. G(x) doesn't meet these requirements. Supposing *arguendo* that, when I plug 99^{99} into a given function, I find that I get 1, I'll just replace that function with F(x) or some other well-behaved function; and when asked to describe the rate at which some object is accelerating, or to describe the trajectory of some projectile, I will consciously *not* use G(x) or any other function that fails to satisfy the previously mentioned desiderata.

People who are using a given function aren't always just pairing off numbers with numbers. The physicist needs to know that the function he's working with changes uniformly; and were he forced to use G(x), instead of F(x), he'll have the very nontrivial job of making sure that his results aren't vitiated.

I'm driving. I stop at red lights. How do I know that I'm obeying the rule *stop red lights*? How do I know I'm not obeying the rule *stop at red lights unless you are wearing a flannel shirt*? I know, because I know that, if put on a flannel shirt, I'll still stop at red lights.

How do I know *that*? I know it the same way I know that, if I were drunk right now, I'd either not be typing or I'd be making more typos than I actually am. I know it the same way anyone knows any counterfactual truth.

Wittgenstein says that thinking is not psychological processes. (Rule-following is a kind of thinking.) His argument is that none of the psychological "accompaniments" of a given instance of someone's complying with a given rule are necessary or sufficient for that act of compliance.

When Wittgenstein refers to the "accompaniments" of some act of rule-following or thought, he is referring to the accompanying *phenomenology*. He is referring to pains, itches, and mental images. He is referring to constituents of consciousness. But propositional attitudes are not constituents of consciousness.

Less obviously, the deployment of a propositional attitude (as when one puts one various mathematical beliefs to use in an effort to solve some problem) is not *constitutive* of consciousness. The events that initiate a given such process, or bring it to a close, are often thus constitutive; and *some* process-internal events are consciousness-constitutive. But for the most part consciousness is to thinking what a driver is to the events happening under his car's hood: the driver can initiate those events (by turning the key in the ignition); he can regulate them (by stepping on the gas or the break-pedal); he can pick the destinations to which those processes will transport him (by turning the wheel); and he can end them (by shutting off the ignition). The driver can regulate what happens under the hood. But unless he's an engineer, he has little knowledge of what is going on there and only very indirect control over it.

When I work, I decide *what* to try to solve; I decide whether a solution that occurs to me is any good; and I decide, either because I'm tired or because I've found what I believe to be an acceptable solution, to terminate those ratiocinations. But those decision points are singularities. For the most part, I am just waiting; like a man stranded on a desert island, waiting for message in a bottle; like an undercover agent's handler, waiting for him to surface with new findings.

Also, contrary to what Wittgenstein says, mental imagery sometimes *is* thought-constitutive. To be sure, there is no *one* kind of mental imagery that need accompany an attempt to solve a given math problem. Given only that you are adding 135 to 156, nothing can be inferred as to what sorts of images are passing through your consciousness. Wittgenstein infers from this that mental imagery is not to any degree constitutive of one's ratiocinations. But this inference is spurious. Thought-constitutive mental images are but segments of ratiocinations that for the most part do not consist of imagery. Phenomenologically consecutive images are likely to be *ratiocinatively* disjoint. If one considers those images in isolation of their ratiocinative underpinnings, the occurrence of any given one is likely to make no sense relative to the occurrence of the preceding image. But if one considers them as installments in a thought-process, most of whose installments are not images, the occurrences of the one, given the other, makes perfect sense. Wittgenstein tried to understand mental imagery on its own terms, in isolation of its ratiocinative context. He thus had no choice but to see such images as cognitively empty. Since he didn't distinguish between access-consciousness and phenomenal consciousness, believing all consciousness to be phenomenal consciousness, this left him with no choice but to embrace the tautologically false conclusion that thoughts are not mental.

3.1   Argument #4 (A4)

> Somebody who already speaks some language can invent a private language. For example, you could create a new language L such that the L-translation of a given English word was that word spelled backwards (so L-translation of "snow" would be "wons"), and such that L was otherwise just like English.

So there is clearly *a* sense in which private languages are possible. But this is not the sense I have in mind. My contention is that, setting aside languages that are just transformations of existing languages, there cannot possibly be such a thing as a private language. A creature that does not have a language cannot, acting on its own, create a language for itself; and a creature that does have a language cannot create a language for itself, except by transforming the language it already knows into a new one.

You are on a desert island, let us suppose, and always have been, and thus don't speak English or any other language. One day you decide to name some of the things with which you are familiar. You stipulate that trees, birds, poisonous berries, and edible berries are to be called, respectively, "wobs," "tats," and "riffles, and stuffles." You do the same thing *mutatis mutandis* for everything else to which you wish to refer, and you create the syntactic rules and the connective terms (words like "if" and "only") by which these expressions can be combined into sentences.

Let PL (short for "private language") be this language. Having invented PL, you invent a way of writing down PL-expressions.

Everyday, you keep a diary of the day's events. You firmly resolve to use the words of PL in strict compliance with the stipulations that you made about their meanings on the day you created PL. You will never *intentionally* violate any one of those rules.

One day, while looking at your diary, you think that "wobs" means "poisonous berries." Of course, relative to your initial conventions, you are wrong. But what does that matter? If some one English speaker misuses a word – if, for example, he uses the words "red" and "blue" to mean *blue* and *red*, respectively – others will correct him.

Your situation is comparable to one in which *every* English speaker all of a sudden started using "red" to mean *blue* and "blue" to mean *red*. In such a situation, "red" *would* mean *blue* and "blue" would mean *red*; and in your case, "wobs" *really* does mean *poisonous berries*, and the stipulation you originally made as to that word's meaning would be null and void.

You cannot possibly be wrong as to what an expression of PL means. What such an expressions is what you take it to mean. So there is no wrong way to use an expression of PL. But if there is no wrong way to use an expression, it means nothing. A private language, therefore, is an impossibility. Language is inherently public.

Analysis: Suppose that, while writing your to-do list for the next day, you think that, relative to the rules you laid down, "riffles" means *edible berry* and that "stuffles" means *poisonous* berry. In that case, your mistake will have very real consequences. It isn't always other people who penalize those who misuse words.

Second, Wittgenstein is confusing language-misuse with language-shift. If everybody suddenly using "red" to mean *blue* and *blue* to mean "red," a language-shift would have occurred. The pre-shift and post-shift languages would be genidentical, but not actually identical.

So the private linguist who uses "stuffles" to mean "poisonous berry", in violation of the semantic rules he originally laid down, is responsible for a language-shift. Let's suppose that he invents PL on Monday and, on Tuesday, uses "stuffles" to mean "poisonous berry". In that case, relative to Monday-PL, he is speaking wrongly; relative to Tuesday-PL, he is speaking correctly. He may in due course be the worse for misspeaking relative to Monday-PL. But because nobody besides this person speaks PL or any of its successors, every mistake that makes relative to PL_i is a non-mistake to PL_{i+1}, where i is an arbitrary unit of time during which no language shift occurs and at whose end such a shift does occurs.

"But how does this undermine Wittgenstein's argument?" it may be asked. "If every mistake is *ipso facto* a language-shift, then the language being shifted is useless, for the very reason Wittgenstein cites: Any word of that language (or language-series) means whatever its one speaker takes it to mean."

This brings us to the next problem with Wittgenstein's hypothesis. Any given language is only as useful to its speakers as their memories of its semantic rules are good. In the case of English, but not of PL, if one person misuses a given word, there will be others to remind him. But, at the end of the day, the English speaker has nothing but his memories to rely on. If, because of a memory problem, a person can't remember what "diffident" means, no matter how often others remind him, it is of no consequence that others are there to remind him. By the same token, if I *do* know what "diffident" means, it's only because I remember what it means.

Similarly, if the lone speaker of PL remembers the semantic rules he laid down, he will be able to use PL-expressions properly; and if he forgets them, his inability to use them is no different in kind from the inability on the part of an English speaker with a defective memory to use English words. The difference between PL and English is that in the one case, but not the other, there are multiple back-up copies, as it were, of the relevant semantic rules. But English is not for this reason *more* of a language than PL. A manuscript of which there are many copies is not more of a manuscript than one of which there is only one.

Wittgenstein is a hard-core empiricist. Wittgenstein's subsequent refusal to grant the existence of non-spatiotemporal entities, such as propositions and concepts, forces him identify semantic rules, and indeed *all* rules, with rules in the *social* sense. Since thought is rule-governed ideation, Wittgenstein thus has no choice but to identify thinking with the following of *social* rules. Such rules by definition govern pluralities of people: a man stranded on an island can't be subject to social rules. Wittgenstein must therefore hold thinking is an inherently social process. Thinking, for Wittgenstein, cannot possibly consist of "occult" (private, mental) operations. It constitutively involves others people.

Thus having no choice but to find some interpersonal practice with which to identify thought-processes, Wittgenstein concludes that thought is identical with symbol-manipulation. Relative to his own premises, Wittgenstein has no choice but to come to this conclusion. Wittgenstein's anti-empiricism thus forces him to hold that to think is to engage in overt acts of symbol-manipulation.

This view is untenable. Overt behaviors involving symbol-tokens do not mediate linguistic behavior unless those behaviors are driven by an understanding of the linguistic rules corresponding to those expressions. In denying that there are "occult" mental processes, and in alleging that "the body is the best possible picture of the mind," Wittgenstein is doing more to superficialize the mind than Descartes or Hume. The latter granted the existence of mind, but claimed it to be nothing more than consciousness, so that there couldn't possibly anything more to the mind than meets the eye. Wittgenstein is saying that there's nothing more to mind than overt behaviors. This is empiricism, of the non-Berkeleyan sort, taken to its logical conclusion.

Wittgenstein qualifies his position by saying that the creatures in question must be duly acculturated, lest their behaviors fail to mediate thought or anything mental. But this qualification neither softens his position nor adds to its credibility. Creatures in whom there are no occult processes are zombies, and zombies cannot be acculturated. Further, there is no plausibility to the view, urged by Brandom (1994), that groups of appropriately interrelated zombies *collectively* think. Given that

(a)   Every member of group X is a zombie

it must be inferred that

(b)   Group X itself is without consciousness

Technically, such an inference is an instance of the "fallacy of composition." (What if the members of group X are neurons, as opposed to people? In that case, X *does* mediate thought, even though none of its constituents do.) But, substantively, such an inference is in no way fallacious and is indeed obviously *de rigueur*.

4.0   Empiricists cannot grant the existence of propositions. For this reason, some empiricists deny that there are propositional attitudes; they deny that anyone believes anything or regrets anything. Skinner took this position, and so do some contemporary empiricists, such as Paul Churchland.

But most empiricists grant the existence of propositional attitudes, and such empiricts have no choice but to identify them with relations between people and spatiotemporal entities, such as sentence-tokens. So, for example, according to Quine (1956) and Carnap (1934), to believe the proposition that

(PTO[110])   Smith frequently walks to Toledo, Ohio

---

110.   Short for "proposition, Toledo, Ohio." PTO, *nota bene*, is a proposition, not a sentence.

is to believe that the *sentence*

(STO[111])   "Smith frequently walks to Toledo"

is true.

But what if Smith believes STO to mean that 2 + 2 = 4? In that case, he believes it true but doesn't necessarily believe PTO; and even if he does believe PTO, he doesn't believe it by virtue of accepting STO.

And what about somebody who doesn't speak English but believes, as do many non-English speakers, that snow is white? Carnap and Quine are forced to say that a belief PTO is a belief either that STO *or some translation* thereof is true.

This presupposes that one must speak *some* language or other to believe that snow is white. Even if this is correct, it is sufficiently doubtful that it cannot legitimately be *assumed* to be correct. Further, if, as Quine and Carnap maintain, propositions don't exist, what does it mean to say that some Arabic sentence X is the translation of STO? Quine and Carnap are prohibited from saying that both sentences express the same proposition.

"The right view," Quine and Carnap tell us, "is that those two sentences are *used in the same way*." But it may be that the only respect in which X and STO are used in the same way is that they are used to affirm the same proposition. With this qualification, Arabic speakers obviously *don't* use X in the same way as English speakers, for the same reason that English speakers don't use the sentence "Abdul often walks to Riyadh" in the same that Arabic speakers use the Arabic translation of that sentence.

Having advocated the view just critiqued, and then recanted it for the reason just given, Quine took the desperate measure of saying that no sentence is a translation of any sentence. He justified this position *post hoc* by saying that, when translating from one language to another, one must take into account *only* the overt behavior of the two groups of speakers being studied. One cannot, Quine insists, rely on any beliefs that have any basis in one's knowledge of one's self. Therefore, Quine says, one cannot to any agree rely on one's beliefs about humanity, so far as those are based in one's self-knowledge. Quine then correctly says that, *given only* how people overtly behave, it is "indeterminate" what they mean when they speak or write. Given his premises, Quine has no choice but to conclude that it is indeterminate what people mean when they speak or write – and this is what he does conclude.

Quine isn't making the trivial point that a person's behavior often fails to make it clear what that person is thinking. He isn't saying that, given only how a person behaves, it is *epistemically* indeterminate what he is thinking: he is saying that it is *ontologically* indeterminate. There is no fact of the matter. Am I now thinking that 2 + 2 = 4? Neither a "yes" nor a "no" is correct. Given any proposition P, the question "is X thinking P?" cannot correctly be answered with a "yes" or a "no." This means

---

111.   Short for "sentence, Toledo, Ohio." STO, *nota bena*, is a sentence, not a proposition.

that it can't be answered with a "yes," and this means that nobody is ever thinking anything. Thought doesn't exist. We're just bodies.

The flaw in Quine's argument is obvious. I moved to Peru when I was eight. I had not previously been taught Spanish or exposed to the Spanish language. I quickly learned Spanish. And I learned it in such a way that, when I was finally a Spanish-speaker, I wasn't an English-speaker translating his thoughts into Spanish: I simply thought as a native Spanish-speaker does. When I was learning Spanish, I obviously relied heavily on my intuitions about what other people thought and felt when they spoke, and those intuitions obviously drew heavily from knowledge on my part as to when *I* would say such things. What is equally obvious is that if I hadn't been allowed to draw on my self-knowledge, and if I had regarded the Spanish-speakers before me as so many thought-free bodies, I wouldn't have learned a word of Spanish.

The traditional view, which I accept, is given by the so-called "Argument from Analogy". I know that when I'm in pain, I scream and clutch the wounded part of my body. I see Smith behave in that way. So I believe he's in pain. In general, where I am concerned, I know both the internal (mental) and the external (behavioral) story; where others are concerned, I only know the external story. The external story is the same. Because I am like others, the internal story must also be the same.

Wittgenstein (1958) rejects this argument. In his view, given only that I know how *my* mental states are correlated with *my* behavior, I cannot reasonably make any inferences as to how another person's mental states correlate with his bodily behaviors. I cannot reasonably infer that he even has mental states. For if I make such an inference, Wittgenstein says, I am over-generalizing, just like someone who believes that all birds are black because the one bird he's ever seen was black.

Wittgenstein's reasoning is spurious. We saw why in Chapter 1, Section 8.2. We know on the basis of experience that we sometimes only need experience of one instance of a given kind to make reliable generalizations about every instance of that kind.[112] A given instance of an element won't have a given freezing point unless the same is true of every instance of that element. A given member of a species won't be able to fly unless other members of that species are able to fly. Relative to these facts, it would be a singularity of unheard of proportions were I the only person who had a tendency to raise his voice when angry or to smile nervously when frightened.

If the argument from analogy goes through, then thought *is* private, in which case Wittgenstein's whole system is sunk. Wittgenstein thus had no choice but to look for a flaw in that argument. Wittgenstein knew there to be no such flaw, I suspect, and that he therefore couldn't produce legitimate argumentative grounds for his nihilistic views about the mind. So instead of duly dropping his views, he resorts to shrill sloganeering: "[n]othing [about another person's mind] is hidden"; "there are no depths [to any given person's mind]"; "The best picture of the human mind is the human body." These statements are so implausible that, speaking psychoanalytically, it's more

---

112. Hume (1739) makes this point very clearly.

reasonable to assume that Wittgenstein was stating the opposite of the truth, so as to weaken his readers' hold on it, rather than trying to transmit it to them.

After presenting the arguments that we've considered, Wittgenstein says that the very concept of a philosophical argument is an incoherent one and that any attempt to *defend* a philosophical view is *ipso facto* misconceived. Philosophers should exhort, not argue.

The *Philosophical Investigations* consists of two parts. In the first part, Wittgenstein puts forth arguments, all of which we've examined. In the second part, there are no arguments. There are only bare assertions, one of which is that good philosophical works contain nothing but bare assertions.

Wittgenstein's contention that philosophical argumentation is *ipso facto* misconceived doesn't make an appearance until *after* Wittgenstein had put forth the arguments that we've considered. We may safely conclude that this contention of his was a *post hoc* attempt to legitimate arguments of his that he knew to be wanting.

Operating independently of each other, Wittgenstein and Quine, both staunch empiricists, came to the same, radically counterintuitive conclusion, to wit:

(QW[113]) When trying to figure out what another person means, one must focus *only* on his body movements. No weight at all is to be given to any intuitions one has that have any basis in one's beliefs about oneself, or in one's beliefs about one's similarities to others. All introspection-based data concerning the mind is unconditionally, permanently off-limits.

This is not the view of somebody who goes where the data takes him. But it is a consequence of strict fidelity to at least one kind of empiricism.

---

113. Short for "Quine, Wittgenstein." See Quine (1960).

CHAPTER 6

Some consequences of the empiricism-driven conflation of analytic with introspective knowledge

1.0   There are two forms of knowledge: direct and indirect. In this context, these terms are synonymous with, respectively, "non-inferential" and "inferential." There are two forms of inferential knowledge: deductive and inductive. It is wrongly thought that there are two forms of inductive knowledge: enumerative and explanatory. In actuality, all inductions, if legitimate, are of the explanatory variety, as we will see in Chapter 9.

There are five distinct kinds of direct knowledge:[114]

(i)   Sense-perception (sight, hearing, touch, etc.). Note: "Sensory observation" and "sense-perception" will be used interchangeably in this work.

(ii)   Sensual but non-sensory knowledge: This is the sort of knowledge one has of the fact that one is experiencing physical pain or pleasure.

(iii)   Pseudo-perceptual knowledge: This is the sort of knowledge one has of the fact that one's consciousness is currently hosting *iconic* ideation of some kind, i.e. that there are *images* of this or that sort in one's consciousness.

(iv)   Knowledge of one's access-conscious propositional attitudes and of the concepts constitutive thereof. So my knowledge of the fact that 10 + 11 = 21 is "conscious" in the sense that, even though it is not a *constituent* of my consciousness,

(a)   It is a constituent of my mind

and

---

114.   I have argued that there is no such thing as *perfectly* direct knowledge. In fact, in this very book, we've already found reason to believe that some forms of *prima facie* direct knowledge (e.g. one's knowledge that one is currently imaging a house) are indirect, in that that they embody post-experiential conceptual operations. But little stock is to be put in this: given that raw experience isn't knowledge, all knowledge embodies such operations. But, as I've argued elsewhere (Kuczynski 2009, Chapter 9), there is reason to believe that knowledge acquired directly from the senses (e.g. my knowledge that I'm now typing) is inferential. That said, such knowledge is clearly direct in a relative sense.

(b) I can readily become conscious *of* it.

And the same is true of my concept (my grasp) of the number 10, of addition, etc.

Condition (a) is necessary, because, although I can readily become conscious of the lamp, the resulting instance of knowledge would be of the sort described in (i).

Knowledge of this kind is knowledge of beliefs, emotions, character traits, and other psychological structures that aren't repressed or otherwise access-unconscious.

(v) Awareness of primitive conceptual truths.[115] Philosophers usually describe conceptual truths as "analytic"; I will use the words "conceptual" and "analytic" interchangeably.

For a proposition to be conceptually true is for it to be such that:

(a) It holds no matter what is/was/will be the case in the spatiotemporal world,

and

---

115. Be it noted that all but an infinitesimally small fraction of analytic truths aren't primitive. *There are continuous functions that cannot be differentiated at any point; propositional attitudes are not constitutive of consciousness; analytic truth cannot be formalized; laws are narrow-scope assurances of protections of moral right; supposing that there is no optical test whereby one can determine one's state of motion, and supposing that light travels faster than anything else, it follows that a given event can precede some other event relative to one framework and follow it with respect to another, where a "framework" is a object that is stipulated not to be moving;* etc. There are what Joshua Parsons aptly calls "deep analytic truths."

Also, be it noted that definitions are not analytic. As ordinarily used, the statement "a yard is a distinct of three feet" is but a slovenly way of saying: "the word 'yard' refers to a distance of three feet," which describes an empirical fact about linguistic usage.

One final point: Some hold that whether a given analytic truth is primitive is a function of what one's axiomatic starting points are. According to this line of thought, the truth that orange isn't red may or may not be primitive. (If one thinks of orange as the "sum," with respect to some kind mixing-operation, of red and yellow, then, presumably, then the truth that orange isn't red will not be primitive. If one has a more direct grasp of what it is to be orange, that same truth will (or may) be primitive.) If this is right, primitiveness isn't a property a given truth P, but a relation between P and some other truth(s) Q.

My feeling is that, although there are some analytic truths that, for the reason just given, may or may not be primitive, there are some that simply cannot be primitive and others that simply cannot fail to be primitive. If it is only by virtue of grasping the proposition that orange = yellow + red that one grasps the proposition that orange isn't red, then one does not genuinely grasp the latter: one grasps some other, related proposition. So the truth that orange isn't red is absolutely primitive. A similar line of thought shows that certain analytic truths are absolutely non-primitive.

(b) It holds entirely in virtue of the structures of concepts (in the objective, not the subjective, sense[116]).

So one's knowledge that orange isn't blue, that squares aren't circles, etc. are, arguably, instances of *primitive* analytic knowledge.[117]

2.0   There is a sixth kind of knowledge that we'll often discuss in this chapter, namely: inferential analytic knowledge. We'll describe such knowledge as being of type-(vi). So your knowledge that continuous series needn't contain their own limiting points is an instance of knowledge of type (vi).

The distinction between (i) and (ii) is of little relevance to our present concerns. It is (iii)–(vi) that we must now discuss.

The kind of knowledge described by any given one of (iii), (iv), (v), or (vi) is different in some fundamental respect from the kind of knowledge described by any given one of the other three. A tendency to overlook these distinctions has had ruinous consequences for the more psychologically oriented branches of philosophy and, to some extent, for psychology itself.

Here are three illustrations of this point. KA[118] and KA* are arguments of Kant's; HA[119] is an argument of Hume's.

Kant's (1787) first argument:

(KA) When I think *7 + 5*, I don't necessarily think *12*. The same thing *mutatis mutandis* is true for any ordered triple of numbers $<x, y, z>$ such that $x + y = z$ (setting aside cases, such as *1 + 2 = 3*, where x and y are very small and cases, such as *1,000,000 + 1 = 1,000,001*, where x and y are very close together). Therefore, it isn't a *conceptual* truth that *7 + 5 = 12*. In others word, it is not one that one knows to be true by analyzing the concepts constitutive of it. So it isn't *analytic*.

   At the same time, *7 + 5 = 12* is not an empirical truth; for it is not on the basis of sense-perception that one knows it. It is on the basis of pure

---

116. To clarify the parenthetical qualification: In this context, the word "concept" is being used, not to refer to psychological structures, but to refer to *abstracta* of a certain kind, whose nature we clarified in Chapter 3, Section 8.2.1. So in this context it has the same meaning as the occurrence of the word "idea" in the sentence: "The very idea of an integer smaller than 1 eluded the Romans." This is how the word "concept" will be used throughout the present work. It will be shown that concepts, in this sense of the word, are neither psychological nor spatiotemporal.

117. Locke was, to my knowledge, the first to point out the existence of this sort of knowledge, and some of these examples are his.

118. Short for "Kant's argument."

119. Short for "Hume's argument."

thought. Therefore, it is *a priori*; in other words, it is to be known through pure thought, as opposed to thought involving sense-based beliefs.

Therefore, *7 + 5 = 12* is both synthetic and *a priori*. Synthetic *a priori* truths don't hold in virtue of facts about concepts *or* in virtue of facts about the non-mental world. The only class of facts left are facts about mind. Therefore, arithmetical truths hold in virtue of facts about minds – more specifically, in virtue of facts about our *forms of thought*.

Analysis Kant's belief that arithmetical truths are synthetic and also *a priori* embodies a failure to distinguish between knowledge of type (iv) and knowledge of types (v) and (vi).

Kant is failing to distinguish the two different meanings of the word "concept." (This is a consequence of his failing to make the just-mentioned distinction.) *7 + 5 = 12* holds in virtue of facts about the concepts *7, addition*, etc., and thus holds in virtue of facts about "concepts" *in the objective sense of the word*. But it doesn't hold in virtue of "concepts" *in the subjective sense of the word*, since it doesn't hold in virtue of any-one's *grasp* of anything or, indeed, in virtue of any fact about anyone's mind. Because Kant is conflating these two different types of concepts, he is conflating introspection-based, empirical knowledge with analysis-based, non-empirical knowledge.

Kant seems to be dimly aware of the ludicrousness of saying that *11 + 23 = 34* is a fact about our minds. So, instead of using the term "psychological," he uses the term "transcendental," thereby obfuscating his actual view and giving Kant-scholars a way of rebutting the obviously correct point that Kant was erroneously making mathematics a branch of psychology.

Kant's (1787) second argument:

(KA*)   Geometrical propositions are not empirical. It isn't through sense-perception that one knows that:

(a)   If A is the area of a circle having a perimeter of length n, and A* is the area of any closed, non-circular figure with a perimeter of that same length, then A is larger than A*.

If I discover that what I took to be a circular patch of earth enclosed a smaller area than some perimeter-equal non-circular patch, I'll know that I was wrong about the shapes of at least one of those patches. Since no observation can give one a reason to reject it, (a) is non-empirical.

But (a) is also non-analytic. For I can obviously think:

(b)   A is the area of a circle having a perimeter of length n, and A* is the area of any closed, non-circular, perimeter-equal figure,

without also thinking:

(c)   A is larger than A*.

Therefore, my grasp of (c) isn't constitutive of my grasp of (b). So the latter concept is no part of the former; and analysis of the former cannot provide one with a legitimate reason to accept the latter. So it isn't through conceptual analysis that one knows (a) to be true, and (a) is therefore analytic.

So it isn't through observation that one comes to know (a). Nor is it through conceptual analysis. So how *does* one know it? One knows it by examining one's own mental imagery. One imagines two perimeter-equal closed figures, one a circle, the other not; and, by scrutinizing both images, one finds that the circle image is also an image of a greater area than the non-circle image.

Analysis: Kant is confusing knowledge of types (v) and (vi) with knowledge of type (iii). It isn't in virtue of any fact about any mind that (a) is true. In a world devoid of sentient beings, circles would enclose greater areas than perimeter-equal non-circles. At the same time, Kant is right to say that (a) is not an empirical truth.[120] (We're assuming, as Kant does, that "circle" means "Euclidean circle.")

(a) is known through conceptual analysis. It is not known by studying one's own mental images. In this context, mental images are likely to be *vehicles* for the thoughts on the basis of which one learns (a). In fact, mental imagery is a vehicle for thought of just about *any* kind, and it's obviously particularly likely to be involved in geometrical thought. But it isn't by *introspecting* that one knows (a) or any other truth. It isn't by studying one's circle-images and oval-images. Were (a) to be known in that way, it would be an empirical truth: one to be known through observation – not through the use of the senses, but through observation no less. But that isn't how geometrical truths are known. So Kant is confusing knowledge of type (iii) with knowledge of types (v) and (vi).

But mental images *can* be objects of investigation. Their ratiocinative function isn't *always* to mediate conceptual analysis. If asked "can you imagine a 9-sided figure?", I will respond by having various mental images and scrutinizing them to see if any of them are images of 9-sided figures. But my subsequent knowledge that I can't imagine a 9-sided figure is empirical and *a posteriori*.

Hume's (1739) argument:

(HA)   When I introspect, I come across various sensations, perceptions, and images. But I don't come across a self. Indeed, I don't come across any structure underlying the sensations, etc. that populate my consciousness. I must conclude that there is nothing more to my mind, or my self, than the various fleeting occurrences hosted by my consciousness.

Here are Hume's exact words:

"For my part, when I enter most intimately into what I call *myself*, I always stumble on some particular perception or other, of heat or cold, light or shade,

---

120. We're assuming, as Kant does, that "circle" means "Euclidean circle."

love or hatred, pain or pleasure. I can never catch *myself* at any time without a perception, and never can observe anything but the perception."[121]

Analysis: Hume is conflating type-(iii) knowledge with type-(iv) knowledge. Supposing that Hume *did* have a self, he obviously couldn't know it through sense-perception. He obviously knows this. Being an empiricist, Hume concludes that he must know it through some inwardly-direct analogue of sense-perception.

But that doesn't follow. Hume believes that 1 + 1 = 2, and he knows that he believes it. But it isn't by rummaging through mental imagery that he knows it. It isn't through *any* sort of self-observation that he knows it.

In any case, type-(iv) knowledge isn't a form of type-(iii) knowledge. HA assumes otherwise and therefore fails.[122]

This leaves us with a problem. Like any other instance of type-(iv) knowledge, my knowledge that I believe that 1 + 1 = 2 is empirical. This seems to entail that this knowledge is observation-based. "Observation-based knowledge" and "empirical knowledge" are veritable synonyms. There is no obvious way, other than to assimilate type-(iv) knowledge to type-(iii) knowledge, to validate the presumption that it is in a strictly empirical manner that a given person knows himself to believe that 1 + 1 = 2.

There are defensible views, we will find, as to how to validate this presumption that *don't* involve the grotesquely mistaken assimilation of type-(iv) to type-(iii) knowledge. But, we'll also find, none of those views can be established except on the basis of premises that are incompatible with empiricism.

In any case, given only what we've seen thus far shows, it's already becoming clear just how a sensitive and difficult a task it is to conduct psychological research in genuine accordance with the most banal methodological truisms (e.g. "don't believe if you don't have evidence").

3.0 There is another problem with Hume's analysis. Sense-perception is first-order awareness. In other words, non-mental entities are the objects sense-perception. Introspective awareness is higher-order awareness. In other words, mental entities are the object of such awarenes. This is no less true of one's awareness of one's sensations and conscious mental imagery than it is of one's awareness of one's propositional attitudes.

---

121. Hume (1740: 252).

122. Incidentally, how *do* I know that I believe that 1 + 1 = 2? This knowledge is neither empirical nor, it very much seems, observation-based. But empirical knowledge *is* observation-based knowledge. We will solve this paradox in Chapter 14, where we will see that it is on the basis of observation that one knows oneself to believe that 1 + 1 = 2: if one has such knowledge, we will find, it is only by virtue of one's having correctly modelled multifarious observational data concerning one's own linguistic behavior and mentation.

This entails that introspection is not sensory or para-sensory in nature; it entails that what Hume is tendentiously describing as inwardly directed vision is actually conceptual, not (para)perceptual, in nature.

One's knowledge of one's conscious condition is obviously empirical. It is on experiential, not conceptual, grounds that I know that I feel well-rested. But such knowledge is empirical in that it is a conceptualization of experience, like a scientific theory, not in that it is a direct derivative of experience.

Having a mental image of a house doesn't involving introspecting. Introspecting involves taking note of the fact that one is having such an image. To have a mental image of (what one knows to be) a house, one needs the concept of a house, but not the concept of a mental image of house; but one *does* need the latter concept to know that one is having a mental image of a house.

A concept-free mind can *have* a pain. So it can have pain-awareness. But it can't be aware *of* its pain, at least not *as* a pain. Having the latter sort of awareness involves conceptualizing one's pain-awareness; it involves having the *concept* of pain, which is *not* necessary to *have* pain, and duly applying that concept to one's experience. So even the most low-level reportage of the occurrences in one's mind embodies conceptualizations of one's experiences and, to that extent, is not strictly empirical.

If housed by a snake's mind, an image phenomenologically just like your house-image wouldn't be a house-image. There is no paradox here. When a bat hears Bartok, does it here music? No – but it hears the same noises as any person and, in fact, hears them better. For the same reason *mutatis mutandis* there is no paradox in saying that

(a) your house-image, if transposed into a snake's mind, would cease to mediate a house-image

or, therefore, that

(b) to know what it is you are experiencing, you need to have the concept of an image of a house, in addition to the concept of a house.

4.0 Assuming my reasoning cogent, animals must have concepts, given they obviously have sense-perceptions. But surely your beloved Rover doesn't grasp *abstracta*.

No – *Rover* does not. But his *mind* does. It's obvious that there is *a* sense in which dogs and snakes are incapable of conceptual ideation. It's also obvious they are percipient nonetheless. These two positions are reconciled by taking the Chomskyan view that Rover's brain mediates *deeply* unconscious ideation. The deeply unconscious ideation posited by Chomsky is *impersonal*. In this respect, it is very different from the Freudian unconscious. The contents of the Freudian unconscious are access-unconscious. But they often used to be access-conscious and often will be so again. The constituents of the Freudian unconscious are often numerically identical with (past or future) objects of access-consciousness. Each such stratum comprises propositional attitudes that belong to one's *self* – that proper-part of one's mind's integration with which one identifies, not to the part which mediates language-comprehension and vision (etc.) and with which one no more identifies than with the biochemical processes mediating respiration.

There is no intrinsic difference a propositional attitude that is repressed and one that isn't. There are intrinsic differences between the personal and subpersonal strata of mentation. Rover's subpersonal mind mediates ideation that, although *in* Rover, is not *of* him. The Rover who gleefully wags his tail when he sees you bringing him his dinner is not a concipient being. But Rover's mind is much smarter than Rover. That is why, despite Rover's serious intellectual shortcomings, Rover can have sense-perceptions, can walk, run, and orient himself with respect to other objects, etc. Such functions are mediated, not by Rover (*qua* entity that is happy to see you), but by mental organs that, although constitutive of the same brain that mediates Rover (same qualification), do not themselves do so.

Freud was talking about *your* unconscious; he was about something that belongs to you but that you are not aware of. Chomsky is talking about something that is unconscious because, even though it belongs to your mind, it doesn't belong to *you* at all.

4.1 "But how can it belong to my mind," it will be asked, "without belonging to me?" To say that x belongs to your mind, but not to you, is to say:

(i)   x is either identical with, or mediated by, a structure constitutive of the same brain that comprises the structures that mediate you;

and

(ii)   x is a mental process on which your mental activity constitutively depends.

Let x be some installment in the highly articulated series of cognitive events mediating between your retinas' being stimulated in certain ways and your subsequently seeing the snake in front of you. Obviously *you* know nothing about x, and x isn't the sort of thing of which you could be non-theoretically aware. But x is either a cause, or is constitutive, of your perception of the snake; and the likes of x are constitutive of your visual experiences, even if x is not. Nonetheless, constitution is not identity; and, even though you identify with your visual experiences – even though they are "ego-syntonic," wherefore you see them as belonging to *you* – you no more identify with x than you do with the operations mediated by your pituitary gland.

There is an obvious sense, we have observed, in which dogs, snakes, etc. are non-concipient. But we've also seen that concipience is a *sine qua non* for percipience. And dogs, etc. are obviously percipient.

These facts *can* be reconciled with one another, *but only by distinguishing between self and mind; only, that is, by distinguishing the part of the mind with which one identifies from another, unconscious part with which one does not identify; only, that is, by recognizing two very different kinds of unsconciousness, viz. the personal (Freudian) unconscious and the impersonal (Chomskyan) unconscious.*

So relative to obvious facts and equally obvious principles, Chomsky's position that there is subpersonal mentation is *de rigueur*. Relative to those facts, it is not merely *a* reasonable way of modeling the data: it is the *only* way of modeling the data. In this relativized but non-trivial way, Chomsky's position is *a priori* true.

In light of these points, the roots of the considerable scorn heaped upon Chomsky's views are surely of an emotional, as opposed to scientific nature.

5.0   Edmund Hussserl saw that Hume was loading non-empirical judgments into what he was falsely representing as conceptually uncontaminated, strictly empirical reportage.

Husserl (1977) self-described as a rationalist. Indeed, he claimed that he had direct ("eidetic") intuitions of platonic forms. But as a theoretician of psychology, Husserl (1977, 2004) was an empiricist. So for our purposes, Husserl counts as an empiricist, even though he makes many non-empirical claims in the *Logical Investigations* and other non-metapsychological works of his.

Husserl tried to scientize psychology. He thought that this involved empiricizing psychology.[123] (And *up to a point* he was surely right about that: a purely *a priori* psychology cannot be tenable.) Husserl took it for granted that, if done properly, psychology would be based, *not* on one's perceptions of people's body-movements, but on direct encounters with one's own mental states. (Again, Husserl was right about this, for the reasons given in Chapter 1, Section 2.0.) Thus, in his efforts to scientize psychology, Husserl had to work within the following boundary assumptions:

(A)   Hume's "introspections" were contaminated with non-empirical ideation,

(B)   Introspection (on some disambiguation of the term) is to progress in psychology what sense-perception is to progress in physics;

(C)   A scientific psychology is an empirical psychology.

Given these reasonable assumptions, Husserl came to the conclusion that, before engaging in the introspections on which psychological progress depends, the psychological researcher must suspend (or, to use Husserl's term, "bracket") all of one's assumptions concerning the images, sensations, etc. that one will come across.

To do this, Husserl rightly inferred, one must drain one's introspections of any *ex parte* beliefs concerning their objects. Since, as Husserl saw, such beliefs are embodied in the way in which one conceptualizes those objects, one must deconceptualize one's introspections. One mustn't say that one is experiencing an image of a house. One must describe that image as it would be *if stripped of all of its conceptual articulations*, the idea being that these conceptual articulations are no part of the image itself and are projections thereupon of the investigator's prejudices.

---

123. Husserl was not an empiricist. He believed that we have direct awarenesses of platonic *abstracta*. But, we will now see, Husserl utterly failed to see the bearing of his non-empiricism on his attempts to scientize psychology.

Husserl appropriately described his methodology as the *phenomenological* method; and he used the term "phenomenology" to describe the meta-psychological views embodied in this method, taken in conjunction with the totality of hypotheses resulting from its implementation. (There would be few such hypotheses, for reasons that we'll now discuss.)

Also, Husserl referred to the aforementioned cleansing process as the "phenomenological reduction." So in Husserl's view, one will fail as a psychological researcher unless, prior to introspecting, one so changes one's disposition towards one's own mental states that, when one encounters them, they present themselves to him as conceptually unarticulated phenomenological blobs.

5.1   Not only is the phenomenological method destined to fail: it seems that its very purpose is to cripple psychology and therewith to stymie man's attempt to acquire any insight into himself.

If you are asked to describe your perception of a given object, G. E. Moore observed, all you can do is describe the object. Try to describe your perception of the book in front of you: all you can do is describe the book itself. Perceptions are diaphanous.

Let's look at the phenomenological reduction in light of Moore's insight. If you are asked to "phenomenologically reduce" your perception of the piece of paper, you no longer have a perception. By performing the phenomenological reduction, you destroy the perception. You don't unearth it from the rubble that's hiding it: that rubble *is* the perception.

5.2   Each of (A)–(C) is reasonable. (A) and (B) are unqualifiedly true. And (C) is qualifiedly true: it's true on *some* interpretation of it. But Husserl chose the wrong interpretation. Given his acceptance of (A)–(C), Husserl had a choice between

(i)   Taking the position that, to see them as they are, one must strip the objects of introspection of their (apparent) conceptual articulations

and

(ii)   Taking the view that empiricism is incoherent, in that it requires investigators to strip their observations of the conceptual articulations that distinguish them from meaningless dollops of phenomenology.

Husserl wrongly opted for (i).

5.3   "But you're seriously misrepresenting the nature of the phenomenological reduction," it will be said. "The phenomenological reduction doesn't involve purging ones perceptions and introspections of their contents; it involves abstaining from making the assumptions about those contents that we are accustomed to making."

This rejoinder is to be given no weight. I see a house. I can certainly suspend my belief that my perception is veridical. But that won't affect how I describe the perception. When I describe the perception, I'll do so by describing the house.

I can make sure that, when I describe the house, I don't take into account what I have learned in advanced physics; I can make sure that I don't comment on the coefficient of expansion of the metal composing the gutters. But there are some beliefs of mine I cannot suspend, for example, that:

(i)   there is an external world;

(ii)   certain objects bear certain spatiotemporal relations to others;

(iii)   some objects are larger or more massive than others;

and

(iv)   some objects are transparent whereas others are opaque.

Even if I have suspended my perception-based belief that there is a house yonder, I cannot describe my perceptual experience except on the assumption that it is veridical and, therefore, in terms of its putative object. To describe that perception, I must identify the description embodied in it; so I must say that it is a perception to the effect that there is an object in such and such a place [etc.]. Adherence to Husserl's methodology prohibits me from doing just that.

But supposing *arguendo* that we can study the non-presentational residue with which the phenomenological reduction leaves us, how we are supposed to study it? With what concepts and by what methods? We obviously can't do to those methods and concepts what we did to the perception whose residue we're studying. We can't purge our methodology of all the beliefs embodied in it: a methodology *is* a system of beliefs. When we study this residue, we'll do so using the same framework of which, in performing the phenomenological reduction, it was our intention to purge ourselves. But if that framework is legitimate, we should never have purged ourselves of it; and if it wasn't, we can't use it to study the results of the phenomenological reduction.

5.4   I've described two methodologies that have been referred to as the "phenomenological method" (often by one and the same person, wrongly believing that he was referring to one and the same methodology). One of them involves draining our mental presentations of all content and then describing what is left over. The other involves suspending our belief that our perceptions are veridical as well as our acceptance of what science (and experience generally) has taught as about the putative objects of those perceptions. The first methodology is incoherent. So is the second, as we'll now see.

The justification for perception, we have seen, cannot come from perception and must therefore come from non-empirical, analytic principles. Thus, embedded in our belief that perception is a source of knowledge is the belief that it is not the *only* source of knowledge. If we are empiricists, we reject those principles. But when describing our perceptions, we must grant them. If a given perception is described *as it would be* if an acceptance of those principles weren't embodied in it, all that's left is conceptually unarticulated phenomenology: the most unintelligent form of mental activity conceivable.

So when attempting to describe our perceptions, we must assume that they are veridical and we must therefore countenance at least some non-analytic truths. This does not mean that our perceptions *are* veridical. It means that, *qua* student of the mind, one cannot be a strict empiricist.

It goes without saying that, *qua* student of the external, one cannot be a strict empiricist, given that perception cannot self-justify. None of this means that empiricism is wrong. But it means that an acceptance of empiricism is incompatible with the very existence of any attempt to study anything. It means that, if empiricism is correct, nothing, or next to nothing, can be known: nothing about the external world, and nothing, or almost nothing, about the external world.

5.5   The essence of empiricism is that you shouldn't posit it unless (a) you see it or (b) can infer it from what you see, using only principles learned strictly from observation. Thus, empiricism abjures hidden structure. Given how jagged and gap-ridden consciousness is, there is no way to explain the events constitutive of it without positing hidden structure. Therefore, empiricism is incapable of yielding such explanations.

For this reason, "scientific" psychologists often say that the discontinuities within consciousness are to be filled in by positing unobserved physiological occurrences, with the qualification that those occurrences *don't mediate anything mental*. These researchers are right to hold that unobserved physiological processes mediate both conscious and unconscious mental phenomena. But if, as these researchers contend, nothing other than mentation-free physiology mediates between the events populating consciousness, then the mental *qua* mental is a freak of nature. The mental, according to such scientists, is nothing like the physical (physics-related), the chemical, or the biological. These three domains have spatiotemporal and, therefore, explanatory integrity; non-adjacent biological phenomena are connected by biological phenomena. The connections may not be perfect, and the corresponding gaps must be filled with non-biological, chemical or physical events. But on the whole the biological realm is a cohesive, non-fragmentary one, the same being true to an even higher degree of chemistry and physics. But, if the just-mentioned researchers are correct, the mental is nothing like this: the mental isn't a unified domain at all, being nothing but a series of disjoint *ex nihilo* obtrusions into an otherwise integrated, explanatorily well-behaved world.

This is the legacy of empiricism to psychology. In any case, it is the legacy of a resolution on the part of many a psychologist to be "scientific," which, understandably, is equated with a resolution to "stick to the facts," which in turn, understandably, is equated with a resolution to be empirical. The fallacy in this reasoning is that science is not about *sticking* to the facts. It is about organizing the facts, and it is therefore about positing hidden structures to restore to nature the continuities of which observation strips it. The empiricist's injunction that we "stick to the facts" is either the triviality that correct theories are fact-consistent or it's the absurdity that one can model data without extrapolating.

6.0 Many thinkers are aware of the fact that "introspection" is an act of conceptualization, and not of theoretically innocent reportage. This fact is *prima facie* inconsistent with empiricism. Some empiricists, e.g. Hume, overlook this fact. Others, e.g. Husserl, are aware of it and try to reconcile it with empiricism by empiricizing introspection; that is, by stripping introspection of its conceptual component. (Since introspection *is* conception, this approach is doomed to fail.) There is a third response that we haven't yet considered. Its two main advocates are Daniel Dennett and Paul Churchland:

(DC[124]) So-called "introspection" isn't anything like sense-perception. Introspection is actually a kind of conception. In introspecting, one is forming judgments; one isn't merely beholding. Beholding yields data. Conceptualization does not. This is a matter of definition. *What* is conceptualized is data, not *how* it is conceptualized. For many reasons, the conceptualizations of (so-called) introspective data embodied in folk-psychology are not good ones, and there are other superior conceptualizations of that data. Relative to the latter, the mental doesn't exist. Therefore, the mental doesn't exist.

The conclusion of DC is spurious. (We'll say why in Section 6.1.) But the first premise is correct and important. Like perception, introspection is phenomenology mediated; and, like perception, introspection tracks its objects in real time. This dual similarity obscures the fact that introspection is to be co-classified with conception, not with perception.

There is thus such a thing as "real-time" conception. In fact, real-time conception pervades the cognitive life of any human being. The most obvious instances of this relate to language-comprehension. An Arabic sentence-token is just so much noise to a bat, but a bat hears the sounds mediating such a token better than any Arabic-speaker. A musical work is just so much noise to somebody who doesn't have the requisite musical intelligence. (This is less obvious if one considers pop-music than if one considers modern classical music.) A painting is just so much ink to somebody who doesn't have the requisite visual intelligence. (This is less obvious if one considers representational art than if one considers non-representational art.) But there is obviously *a* sense in which one hears speech or music and in which one sees visual art. One *para*perceives language, music, and art. Paraperception is phenomenology-mediated, real-time conception.

6.1 In any case, DC is not tenable. One problem with it is that perceptual data is no less theory-heavy than psychological data. So, if cogent, DC establishes the non-existence, not just of the mental, but of the non-mental as well. I couldn't begin to describe what I'm seeing right now without assuming the truth of many a theory. This is only partly for the trivial reason that some of the entities I'd be describing (e.g.

---

124. Short for "Dennett, Churchland."

my computer) are by-products of recent theoretical innovations. It is mainly for the reason put forth earlier:

(LV[125])   Just as a hunk of clay must be sculpted if it is to be a work of art, so phenomenology must be articulated if it is to mediate perception. Our perceptions
divide the world up into instances of general categories (*rock, tree, chair*).
Each such category is individuated by the counterfactual properties of its
instances. For an object to be a copper bar is for it to have certain causal
proportion (e.g. a certain degree of conductivity, durability, malleability: *if*
subjected to certain stresses and strains, it bends in a certain way, to a certain
degree; *if* a given part of its surface is electrically charged, the rest of it will
soon have the same charge.) Pure phenomenology tips us off to phenomenal
properties, e.g. color. Phenomenal properties tip us off to non-phenomenal
properties, e.g. degree of viscosity. Certain pairs of non-phenomenal properties logically cohere: viscosity and liquidity, for example. Other such pairs do
not so cohere: viscosity and solidity, for example. Perception is phenomenology articulated in accordance with our knowledge of such cohesion-relations.
Since the phenomenology mediating perception co-varies in real time with its
external causes, so does perception itself. Perception is thus a phenomenology
mediated, real-time tracking of external objects.

It is a datum that there are mental entities, and it's a datum that it's a datum. The data
of introspection are theory-laden. Given one's views as to what it is to be a datum, this
may entail that there are no mental entities. If so, one should jettison those views.

6.2   One question arises. It seems as though, if LV is correct, perceptual awareness is
propositional, not objectual. But we've insisted that it's the other way around.

Nonetheless, our view is easily reconciled with LV. The perception-generative
operations described in LV are subpersonal. The resulting perceptions are personal.
Subpersonal truth-awareness is constitutive of personal object-awareness.

A related point, which it is the purpose of Chapter 13 to establish, is that paraperception is sub-personal truth-awareness embodied in personal object-awareness.
The delight one takes in listening to a Bach fugue embodies subpersonal awareness of
truths about the structural properties of the sounds one is hearing, and those subpersonal awarenesses are expressed at the personal level in the form of phenomenological episodes.

We've made heavy use of the assumption that there is such a thing as subpersonal
mentation. It is now time to discharge this assumption.

---

125.   Short for "Lewis's view." Clarence Lewis (1922) put forth an argument similar to LV.

CHAPTER 7

Subpersonal mentation

1.0   The process of unrepressing knowledge, Freud (1915) argues, consists of two phases. First, an analogue of the repressed knowledge is implanted in the subject's consciousness. That conscious knowledge is numerically distinct from its repressed counterpart, but it is also qualitatively identical with it. Obviously they differ *extrinsically*. This is partly for the trivial reason that, by supposition, one of them is access-conscious and the other is not. But it is also for the non-trivial reason that the one that is access-conscious, unlike the one that is repressed, lacks the appropriate emotional concomitants, since the patient hasn't yet had time to delineate the consequences of what he knows or, therefore, to be aware of those consequences in any but a deracinated, purely intellectual manner.

The second phase consists of the patient's delineating those consequences and *de*-deracinating his knowledge of them. A precondition for his doing this is that he overcome the incentives he previously had to repress that knowledge. Therefore, the repressed analogue of this knowledge is free to become conscious, as the forces that kept it submerged in the unconscious have been withdrawn. Two qualitatively identical bodies of *conscious* knowledge inevitably merge into one such body. So, ultimately, de-repression *does* involve the movement *in propria persona* of the repressed conceit into consciousness.

But subpersonal knowledge is never transferred from one mental stratum to another. By reading Chomsky and Marr, I acquire conscious knowledge of the subpersonal knowledge they describe. But the former is merely an analogue of the latter. Also, whereas the conscious conceit implanted by the psychoanalyst in the mind of the patient is qualitatively identical with the corresponding represed conceit, the subpersonal knowledge described by Chomsky et al. is qualitatively very different from its conscious analogues. That conscious knowledge is not a *bona fide* duplicate, but a conceptualization, of the corresponding subpersonal knowledge. The former is schematic and theoretical, like our knowledge of the nature and behavior of electrons. By contrast, the conceit that the psychoanalyst implants in his patient's consciousness *is* a *bona fide* duplicate of its repressed counterpart. Both conceits consist of the very same concepts (*hatred, father,* etc.), arranged in the very same way. Those conceits differ only in the (numerical, as opposed to qualitative) sense in which my knowledge that $1 + 1 = 2$ differs from your knowledge of that fact.

2.0   Some, e.g. Searle (1992, 1994, 2004), argue that sub-personal processes are strictly physiological; they embody no intelligence; they are purely reflexive.

This view is indefensible. You hear a long sentence of your native tongue. You've never before heard that sentence or one much like it. But you understand it. Let's start with those facts.

The English language is a collection of rules. The simplest ones have the form: x *refers to y*. Most such rules are not so straightforward. But even those that have the form x *refers to y* have a rather complicated form. To say that

"x refers to y"

is to say that

in virtue of having the form "....x...," a given sentence is true just in case...y...

So to say that "Socrates" refers to some object O is to say that, in virtue of having the form "Aristotle admired Socrates," a given sentence means that Aristotle admired O.

In fact, even this definition of what it is for x to refer to y is incomplete, given that not all sentences are in the indicative mood. A more accurate definition would be:

x refers to y exactly if, in virtue of having the form "...x..." a sentence encodes a proposition (not necessarily one that it affirms) to the effect that...y...

Thus semantic rules of the form x *refers to y* are highly complex, and any semantic rule of any other kind is even more complex. Consider the word "because." It won't do to say that "because" picks out a relation of some kind. The statement "John is tall because John ate lots of vegetables as a child" isn't synonymous with "John is tall, the relation that P bears to Q if P is a consequence of Q, John ate lots of vegetables as a child."

"Because" can only be defined indirectly:

Given a sentence S and sentence S*, "S because S*" is true iff either:

(i)   The proposition meant by S* entails, or otherwise confirms, the proposition meant by S (cf. "John has more than 2 cars because he has 3 cars");

or

(ii) The state of affairs described by S* is (partly) responsible for the state of affairs described by S (cf. "John has more than two cars because John made a lot of money on Wall St. and spent much of it on cars").

Similar points hold of any other given sentential connective. For example, the meaning of "or" is give by a rule to the effect that:

Given two sentences S and S*, "S or S*" is true just in case S isn't false and S* isn't false.

Similar points hold of predicates. The meaning of the word "red" isn't given by the rule: "red" refers to the property of redness. That is why "George is wearing a red shirt" is meaningful, whereas "George is wearing a property of redness shirt" is not.

The meaning of "red" is given by a rule similar to the one for "because," but even more complicated.

And yet people absorb and apply these rules without the slightest difficulty. Any given instances of such linguistic competence is naturally characterized as a case of somebody's having a mastery of such and such semantic rules. Supposing such characterizations to be correct, the rules in question are not access-conscious, and they're obviously not access-unconscious in the same way as your antipathy towards your best friend. So either they're access unconscious in some deeper sense or they don't exist. Those who take the latter view have to say that there is a physiological characterization of our linguistic competence. But this is not a viable view, as we're about to see.

2.1   Having heard the sentence, "either Julie will be coming to the party tonight or Mary won't let us go for a boat ride with her," you understand what you have heard, and you do so instantaneously and flawlessly. But if you're like me, you can't give a creditable definition of even one of that sentence's constituents.

Also, were you to have conscious, discursive knowledge of the meanings of "or," etc., that knowledge wouldn't operate quickly enough for it to result in your *hearing* meaning in the noises mediating the relevant occurrence of "either Julie will be coming to the party tonight or Mary won't let us go for a boat ride with her." It would have the very different of resulting in your *judging* those noises to have a certain meaning. Your conscious, discursive knowledge that "or" is an operator such that [etc.] isn't appropriately hewed to the parts of your mind that mediate audition; it doesn't exchange information with those modules in such a way that you will *hear* the noises mediating linguistic expressions differently from the way you'd hear other noises.

There is no shortage of philosophers who insist that the concept of sub-personal mentation is incoherent. For example, according to Searle (1992), your understanding the sounds "Julie will be coming to the party tonight or Mary won't let us go for a boat ride with her" is a purely physiological process. By this Searle means *not* that it is a physiological process that mediates mental activity. He means that it is a physiological process that mediates no such activity at all. It *results* in mental activity; for it affects what happens in consciousness and there is nothing to the mind apart from consciousness. But beyond that there is nothing mental about it.

3.0   In defense of his view, Searle makes two points:

(SV[126]) Mentality is consciousness. This is an analytic truth. "Unconscious mental activity" is a *contradictio in adjecto*. An obvious corollary is that subconscious, let alone subpersonal, mentation doesn't exist.

---

126. Short for "Searle's view."

(SV#)　Linguistic behavior can be described *as though*, mediating between input and output, between hearing and understanding a given sentence-token, our minds were following various rules. But for any act A, on anyone's part, there are infinitely many rules R, such that A accords with R but is not an act of following R. In walking from x to z, I am complying with the rule *for any point in time t during interval, you to are to be x inches away from boulder B*. But I am not in all likelihood following that rule.

　　So given only our linguistic behavior *accords* with various rules, it doesn't follow that, in so behaving, we are *following* them. And there is no reason to suppose that we are following such rules: the fact that our behavior *accords* with them can be explained in strictly physiological, non-psychological terms.

　　So Chomsky's contention that we are *following* such rules is explanatorily inert; and there is no reason to grant it.

3.1　No sooner does one distinguish between access-consciousness and consciousness-proper than one ceases, assuming one rational, to give any credence to Searle's claim that mentality and conscousness are identical.

　　It is inherent in what propositional attitudes are that they cannot be constituents of consciousness and, therefore, that, when they are "conscious," it is in the sense that they are access-conscious. And there is no *a priori* reason why anything that is access-conscious *must* be so. This follows from the fact that there is nothing of which one is conscious of which one *must* be conscious. Any given consciousness must be distinct from its object – the two must not be numerically identical and neither must be a constituent of the other. Distinct objects are *ipso facto* such that the existence of the one is not logically dependent (though it may be *causally* dependent) on the existence of the other.

　　In any case, to make a more modest claim, for which more specific grounds will presently be cited, there is no *a priori* reason why propositional attitudes must be access-conscious. I believe that Greenland is larger than Iceland. I've believed that for years. But it wasn't until a moment ago that my consciousness accessed it.

　　Why is it incoherent to suppose that my consciousness might have trouble accessing a given a propositional attitude? Your IBM sometimes has trouble accessing its own contents. You lose a document. You do a search. You can't find the document. But it's there, that being why the FBI has forensic computer-specialists. Why is it so absurd to assume that, on occasion, your mind is similarly incapable of retrieving information buried within *its* recesses?

　　Also, it often takes considerable intellectual resources to be consciously aware of just what it is one believes. Brown believes that Smith is a liar. Brown believes this because he has other beliefs, e.g. Brown believes (because he knows) that Smith's smiles, and his facial gestures in general, lack the muscular accompaniments that they would have if they were sincere; that Smith is oddly unresponsive to data that, were he telling the truth, would be cause for intense joy or intense distress; etc.

Supposing that none of these beliefs is repressed, will Brown necessarily be *automatically* aware that he has them? It seems that, even if these various beliefs are access-conscious – in other words, even if they aren't repressed or otherwise withdrawn from his consciousness – there's a good chance that Brown doesn't have the wherewithal to conceptualize them properly or, therefore, to know that he has them.

My visual perception of the contents of my room is obviously conscious. It's conscious in every sense of the word. But, because I have no artistic talent, I couldn't produce a visual representation *of* that representation.

It's one thing to have the cognitive wherewithal to have a first-order representation, e.g. a perception, or a belief that doesn't itself concern a belief. It's quite another to have the cognitive wherewithal to correctly conceive of that cognitive wherewithal. And without such meta-cognitive wherewithal, one can't know what one's propositional attitudes are.

Oftentimes, the requisite meta-cognitive resources are minimal: that's why, setting aside repressed propositional attitudes, it seems impossible that one should hate Jerry without knowing it. I say "seems," not "is," because, even in cases, such as this one, where one is certain to have the requisite meta-concepts, it doesn't follow that one deploys those meta-concepts in the requisite ways. One's ability to deploy one's abilities is always imperfect. "Competence always surpasses performance," as Chomsky would put it.

3.1.1   Pains are given to you *as* pains. They couldn't be given to you any other way. (I'm not talking about emotional pain, which, as we'll see in Chapter 14, needn't be given to you as what they are.) Sensations are self-classifying; so are all phenomenology-constituted items.

Paul Churchland holds that one can have wrong beliefs about one's sensations. So far as that is true, it's because wrong beliefs are being superimposed on correct beliefs (or, more precisely, on accurate objectual awarenesses). The marathon runner who is feeling tired can rationalize: he can tell himself that he's feeling good. And maybe he can, after a fashion, sell that falsehood to himself. But even if he makes the sale, the resulting false belief is superimposed on more fundamental, veridical awareness on the runner's part – one not mediated through conceptual ideation – of how he is feeling.

The self-classifying nature of sensations and other constituents of consciousness is a consequence of the fact that they are *themselves* consciousnesses and, therefore, experiences. But propositional attitudes are not experiences. They can be *objects* of experience: one's hatred for Jerry can overwhelm one. But propositional attitudes are enduring structures that underlie consciousness. And less cognitive wherewithal is needed to *have* a given propositional attitude than is needed to conceptualize it correctly or, therefore, to know that one has it. To believe that Rover is furry, I need to have certain concepts at my disposal. To believe that I believe that Rover is furry, it is necessary but not sufficient that I have the aforementioned concepts: I also need the requisite meta-concepts. I need to have concepts of concepts. To believe that Rover is furry, I need to have the concept of furriness, but not the concept of the concept of furriness; but I do need the latter concept to believe (or therefore know) that I believe that Rover is furry.

And not only is there no *a priori* guarantee that, for each belief that I have, I have the meta-concepts requisite to my knowing that I have that belief. There is an *a priori* guarantee that I *lack* at least some such concepts. Otherwise to have a single concept, e.g. the concept of furriness, I'd have to have a concept of that concept, and a concept of *that* concept, and so on *ad infinitum* – which is absurd.

Searle doesn't distinguish between consciousness and access-consciousness. But if he did, and his contentions were otherwise unchanged, his contention that the mind is utterly transparent to itself would entail that a given person was access-conscious of every one of his propositional attitudes. And this, we have just seen, is not logically possible.

3.2   SV is logically false. SV# isn't logically false. But it's false, as we'll now see. Searle's contention that:

(MC[127]) Mentality is identical with consciousness

entails that

(MC#) Whatever is a part of your mind, but not of your consciousness, exists only *qua* disposition on your part to have conscious experiences of a certain kind.

And, taken in conjunction with the fact that

(AD)   Any dispositions that you have are mediated by physiological structures,

MC also entails that:

(MC*)   Any such disposition is identical with, or mediated by, a physiological structure of some kind.

Searle knows that MC entails MC#. So he accepts MC#, and he is thus a *dispositionalist* about non-consciousness-constitutive mental entities. So according to Searle, your belief that $1 + 1 = 2$ is constituted by with your disposition to judge that Jim must have two cars, given that he has one car in Iowa and and one car in Nebraska and no other cars. (More accurately, it is, if Searle is right, constituted by your disposition to have the consciousness-constitutive concomitants of a judgment of the just-mentioned kind.) Of course, that *one* disposition isn't all there is to that belief. But the latter, Searle holds, is identical with that disposition *plus* innumerable other similar ones.

Given his acceptance of MC, Searle has no choice but to take this view, and to take the same view *mutatis mutandis* of each one of a given person's propositional

---

127.   Short for "mentality, consciousness."

attitudes, character traits, memories, etc. And given his acceptance of both MC# and AD, Searle has no choice but to accept MC* – and accept it he does.

3.2.1   But dispositionalism doesn't model the data. You learn that either Smith is living in the barn or that 1 + 1 = 3. Although you know that 1 + 1 ≠ 3, you don't immediately integrate that knowledge with what you've just learned. But after getting a good night's rest, you realize that Smith must be living in the barn.

It's clear what happened. While you were sleeping, you derived new knowledge from old knowledge. This means[128] that the knowledge encoded in one physiological structure was appropriately integrated with the knowledge encoded in some other such structure. (Let PS and PS* be the two physiological structures in question.)

Even though this is obviously the right thing to say, a dispositionalist cannot say it. He must say that it's simply a coincidence that you wake up believing that Smith is in the barn. A dispositionalist is prohibited from saying that, while you were unconscious, PS and PS* were functioning *as* bearers of knowledge. For, were those structures so functioning, there would *ipso facto* be psychological entities that weren't constituents of consciousness or mere dispositions to have such constituents. Prohibited from holding that, while you were unconscious, PS and PS* had any distinctively psychological properties, the dispositionalist is *a fortiori* prohibited from holding that those two bodies of knowledge, operating beneath consciousness, pooled together and begot a third piece of knowledge.

A consequence of dispositionalism is that, upon waking up, you don't *know* that Smith lives in the barn: you believe it but don't know it. If dispositionalism is right, nothing ratiocinative mediated between the belief-system you had just before dozing off and the one had you immediately upon waking up. So none of the information embodied in the pre-sleep belief-system did anything in the way of giving you a legitimate reason to believe that Smith is in the barn. Given obvious extensions of this reasoning, there is many a knowledge-constitutive belief K such that dispositionalism has the false consequence that K is nothing more than an arbitrary opinion.

Given how widely accepted dispositionalism is, and how wrong it is, another illustration of its erroneousness is in order.

I intend to be a Senator, and I'm currently running for that office. To win the election I need a tremendous amount of financial support. One day I hear that Company X, which had been financing my campaign, has decided to finance a rival candidate. I immediately become angry, fret about how to generate the needed revenue, and so on. According to the view in question, my intention to be a Senator is dead *except* upon my being stimulated in certain ways. But if that's so, why would P bolt into action under circumstances like the one just described? Why would my hearing the bad news about Company X result in *P*'s being roused, and not some other physiological structure? How would I, or any part of my mind, know that I ought to respond to this bad news in a way characteristic of somebody who had an intention to be Senator? If,

---

128. Assuming the truth of materialism.

qua such an intention, P is dormant while I'm hearing the bad news, then, during that period, I *don't* have an intention to be Senator, and there is nothing in me that will respond to the news in ways characteristic of such an intention.

One could say that, *upon* hearing the news, P starts acting as such an intention. But if, while I was hearing the news, P *didn't* mediate such an intention, why would the news about Company X prompt to start behaving as such an intention? Unless my intention to run for senator were on the alert, even when it wasn't manifesting itself in overt behavior and conscious states, stimuli such as the bad news about company X would fall on deaf ears. During the stimulation-free intervals, there would, by supposition, be no intention in me to run for Senator. And since, by supposition, P didn't mediate such an intention during those intervals, it would not, when stimulated, have any proclivity at all to react *as* such an intention. And if we suppose that there is some other part of my mind/brain that, when I was duly stimulated, would know to wake P up, so to speak – to prompt it to start behaving as such an intention – then *that* physiological structure (or whatever it is) is always functioning *as* an intention to run for Senate.

Unless the physiological structures mediating propositional attitudes were always functioning *as* such attitudes, we wouldn't have dispositions of the kind that the advocate of the dispositionalist view identifies with such states. The same is obviously true of all non-occurrent mental structures. They are functioning *as* mental entities in between bouts of generating consciousness-constitutive states and overt behaviors.

4.0   Given only that each boy is liked by some girl, it doesn't follow that some girl likes each boy. In other words, given only that, for each boy x, there is some girl y such that y likes x, it doesn't follow that there is some girl y such that, for each boy x, y likes x. To think otherwise is to commit the so-called "quantifier-shift" fallacy. (In this case, the quantifiers in question are "for each boy x" and "there is some girl y.")

SV# is guilty of that fallacy. Suppose that, for each i ($1 \leq i \leq n$), there is some rule R_i such that act A_i accords with R_i. It doesn't follow that there is some one rule R_j, such that, for any i, A_i accords with R_i.

To be sure, if n is finite, we can always contrive some rule, if only a patently artificial one, with respect to which each of $A_1 \ldots A_n$ is complying with R*. But there are infinitely many sentences that you understand. There are infinitely many (derived, not primitive) semantic rules. *Ceteris paribus* two English speakers assign the same meanings to the same sentences of English. So setting aside plainly irrelevant performance-inhibiting factors, such as fatigue, memory loss, and general intelligence, each of two English speakers will, for any finite number n, assign the very same meanings as the other to English sentences $s_1 \ldots s_n$.

According to Chomsky,[129] this means, first, that:

---

129. Chomsky (1965, 1980, 1988).

(i) There is some one body of semantic rules $r_1...r_m$ such that each of x and y accepts $r_1...r_m$ and such that, assuming m_i to be the meaning of s_i ($1 \leq i \leq n$), it is by virtue of his delineating the logical consequences of $r_1...r_m$ that each person takes s_i to have m_i for its meaning;

and, second, that:

(ii) Since, clearly, neither x nor y is consciously performing the just-mentioned logical operations, those operations are unconscious; and since, clearly, they aren't in the same category as constituents of the Freudian (repressed) unconscious, being system-constitutive in nature, as opposed to system-internal; it follows that they are subpersonal.

Searle rejects both (i) and (ii). Searle's position is that, for each i, it is on the basis of a thought-free reflex that each of x and y assigns m_i to s_i. x and y aren't following the same rules, Searle says; for neither is following any rules. Their assigning the same meanings to the same sentences is to be understood in strictly physiological terms.

So Searle's position is that *psychologically* it's a pure coincidence that x's meaning-assignments agree with y's, but that this is no cause for alarm since *physiologically* it's no coincidence.

Searle doesn't distinguish the statement that:

(1) For any number n, it can be a coincidence that, for each i ($1 \leq i \leq n$), each of x and y assigns m_i to s_i.

from the similar-seeming, but very different statement that:

(2) It can be a coincidence that, for any number n, for each i, ($1 \leq i \leq n$) each of x and y assigns m_i to s_i.

(1) is coherent. But (2) is incoherent. The statement:

(3) for any n that you choose, no matter how high, each of x and y assigns meanings $m_1...m_n$ to $s_1...s_n$, respectively,

is equivalent to:

(4) for any i ($1 \leq i \leq n$), it is a foregone conclusion that each of x and y will assign m_i to s_i.

(4) entails that:

(5) should each of x and y assign m_i to s_i, their doing so is *not* a coincidence.

So (2) amounts to this:

(2*)   It can be a coincidence that, for any number n, for each i, $(1 \leq i \leq n)$ it is *not* a coincidence that each of x and y assigns m_i to s_i.

(2*) is self-contradictory.

To be hair-splittingly precise: (2*) is ambiguous, and it is coherent on *one* of its two disambiguations, namely:

(2#)   By some coincidence, given any n, no matter how high, x and y came to be guaranteed to assign the same meaning (namely, m_i) to o_i, for any i $(1 \leq i \leq n)$.

But (2#) isn't compatible with Searle's position. (2#) is compatible with its being the case that, because of some evolutionary fluke:

(i)   there is some one body of semantic rules $r_1...r_m$ such that each of x and y accepts $r_1...r_m$ and such that, assuming m_i to be the meaning of s_i $(1 \leq i \leq n)$, it is by virtue of his delineating the logical consequences of $r_1...r_m$ that each person takes s_i to have m_i for its meaning.

Not only would Chomsky grant (i). He does grant it. For he surely grants that, on some delineation of the term "evolutionary fluke," it *is* an evolutionary fluke that (i) is true.

4.1   "All you've shown," it will be said, "is that x and y are guaranteed to assign the same meanings to the same sentences. I don't see how that conflicts with Searle's view that they are *physiologically* compelled to assign those meanings to those sentences."

This brings us to another confusion on Searle's part: He doesn't distinguish the statement:

(i*)   X complies with the same laws as Y

from the non-equivalent statement that:

(ii*)   X-internal events are to be explained in terms of the same principles as Y-internal events.

Just as Searle believes, cognitive processes are realized by physiological processes. But it doesn't follow, and it's *a priori* improbable, that the psychological relations between physiological events can be understood in physiological terms.

Here we must remember the points made in Chapter 1, Sections 1.2.1–1.2.4. *Qua* punch-card automaton, Babbage's calculator is adding numbers. *Qua* heap of molecules, it's doing something else. *Qua* calculator, your calculator is doing the same thing as Babbage's machine. *Qua* heap of molecules it's doing something else. Considered in *strictly* physical terms, those two computing machines bear no resemblance to each other. Considered in functional terms, they are identical.

This is not to say that calculators think: they do not. But the points just made are easily mapped onto physical structures that do mediate thought. Let M be the part of Mozart's brain that mediated his musical intelligence, and let B be the corresponding part of Beethoven's brain. (We'll speak about them in the present tense, even though they are no more.) For Searle's thesis to go through, each of the following conditions would have to met:

(a) M's cognitive properties would have to be perfectly aligned with its physiological properties; each articulation in the ideation mediated by M would have to correspond to some articulation in M's physiological structure and *vice versa*;

(b) The same would have to hold of B;

(c) The way in which M's physiological and cognitive properties were aligned would have to coincide with the way in which B's physiological and cognitive properties were aligned.

The *a priori* probability of each of these correspondences holding is small. The empirical probability – in other words, the probability *given* what medical research has revealed – is negligible.

These points are easily mapped onto the debate between Searle and Chomsky. For each of x and y to assign the same meanings to the same sentences, no matter how many sentences they are given and no matter how heterogenous those sentence-collections are (relative to the constraints set by the syntactic rules of English), three conditions would have to be met:

(a*) x's cognitive properties would have to be perfectly aligned with his physiological properties;

(b*) The same would have to hold of y;

(c*) The way in which x's physiological and cognitive properties were aligned would have to coincide with the way in which y's physiological and cognitive properties were aligned.

The *a priori* likelihood of their psychologies being so perfectly aligned to their respective physiologies is small, and the actual likelihood is even smaller.

We must also remember that medical science individuates brain-centers on the basis of their presumptive cognitive functions. So brain-physiology is not done innocently: it is done in light of our knowledge of psychophysical concomitances. In keeping with this tradition, we have *defined* M and B as those physiological structures that mediate Mozart's and Beethoven's respective musical competencies. This stacks the deck in Searle's favor. And yet, relative even to these Searle-friendly provisions, M and B differ physiologically much more different than they do cognitively.

These points can be distilled into a three-sentence conclusion: Searle's thesis goes through only if two instances of a given form of mental competence cannot possibly be realized by physiological structures that (*qua* such structures) differ even minutely from each other. But that isn't so. So Chomsky's position prevails, whereas Searle's fails.

Language-comprehension is but one of many involuntary cognitive functions. Other examples of such functions are: sense-perception, aesthetic para-perception (e.g. one's seeing a damsel *in* the discolorations on a given canvass), judgments concerning the trajectories of moving objects, and judgments concerning the emotional meanings of other people's facial expressions. Chomsky's language-related position *mutatis mutandis* holds of any given such function. Therefore, the corresponding version of Searle's view does not so hold.

Initially, Searle's position seems very conservative: "Why posit unconscious entities when we can let physiology do the work? And why do so *especially* when a so-called unconscious entity is a surd, like the Cheshire Cat's grin?"

But Chomsky's position is extraordinarily conservative compared to Searle's, and it is only relative to prejudice-based antipathy towards the notion of unconscious thought that it seems the other way around. For Searle, x's being in agreement in with y consists of an endless series of inexplicable coincidences. For Chomsky, it's evidence of their being driven by a similar mechanism. Given Searle's extraordinary intellectual gifts, nothing but a hypertrophied resolution on his part to "stick to the facts" could be responsible for his believing Chomsky's contentions to be ill-conceived or his work to be methodologically defective.

CHAPTER 8

Empiricist conceptions
of causation and explanation

1.0   Hume holds that we don't observe forces. In his view, we don't see or otherwise sense-perceive, anything *make* anything else happen. Since Hume's time, and because of him, it has been a mainstay of empiricism that *forces are not observed*. Events and sequences thereof are observed, says the empiricist.[130] But forces *per se* cannot be observed. Therefore they don't exist as far as we are concerned. Thus, nothing makes anything happen.[131]

What empirical grounds, asks Hume, do we have for saying that e_1 caused e_2 to occur. Two conditions must be met. e_1 and e_2 must spatiotemporally adjacent; second, they must instantiated a regularity, meaning that, given any event (relevantly) like e_1, it immediately precedes and is adjacent with an event (relevantly) like e_2.

(HC[132]) e_1 is the cause of e_2 iff$_{DF}$

    (i) e_1 immediately precedes and is adjacent with e_2

    and

    (ii)   the sequence of events consisting of e_1 and e_2 instantiates a regularity; more precisely, any event like e_1 immediately precedes and is adjacent with an event like e_2.

Hume grants that sentences like "Bill's throwing water on the Lucy is what caused her to wake up" are sometimes true. But he holds that such a sentence is true only if taken to say of some pair of spatiotemporally adjacent events that it instantiates a regularity. Such a statement is false, according to Hume, if taken to mean that some event disposed some other event to occur.

---

130. Wittgenstein (1922), Ayer (1934), Frank (1949), Hempel (1965), Carnap (1966).

131. Like C. J. Ducasse (1969), I myself do not believe that empiricism is committed to the view that nothing makes anything happen, or therefore to the explanations of explanation to which that doctrine has given rise. But that view is one that view has always been a central component of empiricism. We will set aside the question of whether empiricism really is committed to that view and simply accept that empiricists have accepted that view.

132. Short for "Hume on causality."

2.0   There are many problems with HC. First of all, HC doesn't distinguish actual from epiphenomenal causality.[133] Let e_1 be some event that causes both e_2 and e_3, which are otherwise mutually independent, and suppose that e_2 immediately precedes and is adjacent with e_3. In that case, HC has the false consequence that e_2 causes e_3. E.g. the rotation of the Earth with respect to Sun causes day to follow (and be adjacent with) night, etc. But day doesn't cause night. (Thomas Reid made this very point.) The agitated behavior of the farm animals immediately follows and (we may suppose) is adjacent with the jagged readings on the seismographs. But it's the incipient earthquake that causes both, the animals aren't responding to the seismographs-readings.[134]

But this criticism is far from definitive, some will say:[135]

(DH[136])   Time weeds out cases of pseudo-causation (also known as "epiphenomenal causation"), thereby distinguishing them from cases of *bona fide* causation. Earthquakes aren't always preceded by agitated behaviors on the part of animals or on the part of needles on seismographs. In other cases, where the pseudo-causal process is a *bona fide* concomitant of the actual causal process, the pseudo-causal process can be shown to be part of a more comprehensive *genuinely* causal process.

DH doesn't adequately deal with the night-following-day problem, since, even if HA is supposed true, it has the false consequence that night causes day to follow. But there is a more important fact. We know that, if HA, is right, night causes day and *vice versa*. But we don't for a second let that fool us into thinking that night *does* in fact cause day. Our intuitions as to what causes what are not, evidently, what they would be if HA were correct (and our intuitions were hewed to it).

As for the fact that many a pseudo-causal process (or kind of process) is ephemeral, the same is true of many a genuine causal process. The gun is fired once in place x. All the birds there immediately fly in opposite directions. We know what caused what, even though we're dealing with a one-off incident.

To be sure, we can *ex post facto* look for regularities of which that one is an instance. But so far as we have any incentive to do so, it's because we already know that we're dealing with a casual process. We already know that it was Smith's pulling the trigger that caused the gun to fire, that being why we want to find some regularity of which that event-sequence is an instance. By the same token, we already know that the skittish behavior of Brown's horse was not the cause of the earthquake, that being why we don't want to look for some regularity of which that event-sequence was an instance.

---

133.   Mackie (1977) puts forth this argument.

134.   Mackie (1980) makes this point.

135.   Nagel (1962), Carnap (1966), Mackie (1980).

136.   Short for "Defense of Hume."

If Hume is right, our causal intuitions track adjacencies and regularities. But that isn't what they track. So far as they seem to track such regularities, it is because they track mechanisms that in some cases tend under certain conditions to give rise to them.

We automatically know that the hectic behaviors of the animals, and the agitated behavior of the needle on the seismograph, aren't responsible for the earthquake, even though they immediately precede/are adjacent with it (and their likes immediately precede/are adjacent with other, similar tectonic disturbances). We know this because any given case of pseudo-causation proves, on inspectionion, to involve discontinuities not involved in their real counterparts. constant conjunctions tip off us to continuities, to causal mechanisms. but it's the mechanism, the continuity, that is the sine qua non of causality, that being why there are confluences of events that are not related as cause and effect but that, if HA were right, would be so related.

To the extent that an investigator's methodology is that of an empiricist, he is blind to anything that isn't either depicted or itself a depiction. The invisible is, for him, truly invisible.

For this reason, empiricist philosophers of science, Hume being the first and the greatest such philosopher, deny that anything makes anything happen; and they deny, consequently, that anything disposes anything to happen. (x "disposes" y to happen iff x tends to make y happen.) They deny the existence of causes.

First we know what causes what. Only then do we look for regularities.

3.0   HA analyses causality in terms of space-time: e_1 causes e_2 if e_1 immediately precedes and is adjacent with e_2, and the sequence e_1-e_2 instantiates a regularity. Thus HA presupposes that space and time are not to be understood in causal terms. It presupposes that they are not identical with causal relations among events or with by-products of such relations.

Suppose it were to turn out that "e_1 precedes e_2" actually meant "some causal processes beginning with e_1 could end in e_2"; and suppose it were to turn out that "e_1 and e_2 are simultaneously in different locations" meant "no causal process can start with the one and end with the other." Relative to these suppositions, to say that "e_1 precedes/is simultaneous with e_2" *is* to make a causal statement, a consequence being that space-time is to be understood in terms of causality, not *vice versa*, and HA is viciously circular.

And those suppositions are indeed correct, and spatiotemporal relations therefore *are* causal relations. It makes no sense to say that x has gotten closer to y, or has outlasted y, but has done so without there being a change in x's causal relations to y. If the amount of time it takes a light beam to travel from x to y; if x's magnetic or gravitational pull on hasn't change; if there is no operation such that, if one is to get from x to y, one must perform that operation more times than before: if any one of those conditions is met, then, first of all, x wouldn't even have appeared to have gotten closer to y. Furthermore, there wouldn't be any conceivable grounds for saying otherwise; that is, there wouldn't have been any event that, if known, would warrant our saying that x had gotten closer to y. Even if events ordinarily unknown to us because of interference effects are included in this statement, there would be no event that if (*per impossibile*) known would warrant a reappraisal of x's causal relation to y.

Similar points hold with regard to the time-interval between two events. Let x and y be one pair of non-simultaneous events and let x* and y* be another such pair. If each of the intervals coincides with the other in respect of how many iterations of any given period process can occur during it; if *ceteris paribus* each the intervals coincides with the other in respect of how many how much energy is needed to keep a process going (e.g. a factory assembly line); if *ceteris paribus* in each coincides with the other respect of how much work must be done for an event starting with the first of the two events to have a given effect on the second event: if any of these conditions is met, there will be neither apparent nor actual grounds for supposing there to be a difference in length between the two intervals.

There can be no spatiotemporal changes without causal changes. The reason: spatiotemporal changes are causal changes.

Also, notions such as displacement and occupancy are to be understood in causal terms. To say that A has been moved from one place to another is to say nothing if it isn't to make a statement about how things have changed in respect of what would-be occupants of A's new place must do to occupy that place.

3.0.1 The points just made enable us to a answer a difficult question: What exactly is wrong with Hume's answer to the question: On what basis is one justified in saying that x causes y? Hume's answer to this question, though false, is an extremely plausible one. First of all, it's partly right: just as Hume says, if x and y are disjoint, or y-like events sometimes fail to follow x-like events, then x cannot possibly be y's cause.

But Hume's analysis is false. It's false because it makes a false assumption, and it's plausible because that assumption seems incontestable.

That assumption: Changes consist of events.

The truth: They don't.

There are events, but the spatiotemporal world doesn't consist of them.

More precisely: The spatiotemporal world obviously undergoes change, and any such change is an event; but such events are of a very different kind from those described by the statements in terms of which both scientists and laymen describe the world.

Let us suppose for the time being that the external world consists of events and that those events correspond to the structures of true statements, such as (so we let us suppose) "John punched Fred." Events are discrete, isolable entities. They are to the four-dimensional world what atoms (in the sense of indivisible, basic particles) are to the three-dimensional world.

Let us now drop that supposition and speak the truth. The world consists, not of events, but of seamless energy-flows that are conveniently represented as events; and to the extent that the world has a granular structure, the articulations in it don't correspond to boundaries that that separate events, or event-parts, from one another.

Some have said that the sub-atomic world is discontinuous: given two positions, it is sometimes said, there isn't necessarily a position between them. (Incidentally, this isn't consistent with the empirical data. See Salmon (1984).) Be this as it may, most people, and most scientists, know little or nothing about any such discontinuities; and the discontinuities corresponding to true non-microphysical statements, e.g. "John punched Fred," don't correspond to discontinuities in the external world. If the structure of this sentence corresponded to that of the corresponding reality, the latter would consist of two distinct entities (John and Fred) united by a third (an instance of somebody's punching somebody). But the corresponding redistribution of energy is but a gentle rippling of the quantum, whose constituents, if it has any, can no more be identified with the likes of John and Fred than a cool summer breeze.

This is not to say that events don't exist. They do exist. That is a truism. But the world no more consists of them than it consists of truths. In fact, the supposition that the world consists of events is a corollary of the spurious supposition that it consists of truths. The world consists of facts, not of truths – not, that is to say, of true propositions. Truths hold in virtue of facts, but are not identical with them. Events are nominalizations of truths. The event consisting of Smith's killing Brown is the nominalization of the truth that Smith killed Brown.

A pig is thrown off a rooftop and it splatters upon hitting the ground. This process can't be atomized. It isn't like the whole-number series (0, 1, 2, …). It isn't a sequence of any sort, and it therefore isn't a sequence of events. The redistributions of mass-energy that constitute change do not have a digital structure. The world has an an analogue, not a digital structure. Hume's analysis assumes otherwise, and that is why it's wrong.

Let ME be the the mass-energy displacement mediating the pig's being thrown off the rooftop and subsequently splattering. Observation not only doesn't represent ME as consisting of discrete parts; it represents it as not consisting of such parts; it represents, not as homogenous, but as seamless.

It is only with considerable artifice that ME is represented as consisting of some event x and some adjacent event y such such that y-like events never fail to follow x-like events. But anyone witnessing ME knows that he is witnessing an instance of causation. Such a person knows this because he knows that he is witnessing an instance of continuity.

So why does Hume counter-empirically attribute his having such knowledge to his having mentally decomposed continuities, such as ME, into regularity-instantiating event-sequences?

Because this false contention of Hume's is a distortion of a correct one. (That correct claim is given by the very last sentence of the next paragraph; that sentence is to be understood in terms of those preceding it.) Given somebody who personally observes ME, instead of hearing about it second-hand, that person cannot possibly put the contents of his observations into words, let alone understand them, without conceptualizing them. (Like all sense-perceptions, one's observations of ME must be conceptually articulated if they are to be linguistically articulated.) There is the analogue-world of sense-perception, and there is the digital world of conception. What continuities are to the former, regularity-instantiating event-sequences are to the latter; and the falsehood that instances of causation are to be identified with such adjacencies is the concept-world analogue of the perception-world truth that continuities constitute causation.

"You say that ME doesn't consist of events," it will be said. "But if ME doesn't consist of events, nothing does. So you are saying, absurdly, that there are no events. You are saying, therefore, that nothing happens. Since that's false, you're wrong."

If taken as anything other than an empty truism, the sentence "there are events" is similar to, and absurd in the same way as, the sentence "the world consists of ordered four-tuples of numbers." (I am referring to the four-tuples by which events are located in space-time. Given an event E, each of its three spatial coordinates is given by a number, and so is its one time-coordinate. So E's space-time location is given by some ordered four-tuple of numbers.) Each statement falsely identifies articulations in our beliefs about the world with articulations in the world itself. So far as those beliefs are correct, the former articulations can be mapped onto the latter. But the mapping-relation isn't identical with the identity-relation. We will now justify this last claim; doing so will involve our repeating some points that we made a moment ago and that we justified in Chapter 1, Section 1.2.2.

The world doesn't consist of truths; it consists of facts. Truths hold in virtue of facts, but they aren't identical with facts. Supposing that P were the shortest conjunction consisting of every truth, there would be no event E such that E's occurrence wasn't a logical consequence of P. (In this context, "event" is short for "event or state of affairs.") Given P, there is nothing about the universe that remains unsettled. But it would be a mistake to say, for that reason, that events were constituents of the world; and this mistake would not just resemble the one just cited, but would be a version of it.

Smith has a stroke. Let E be that event; let R be the space-time region occupied by E, and let D be the mass-energy displacement(s) mediating E. Setting aside events that occupy proper sub-regions of R, more than one event has occurred in R. At least one biological, non-psychological event (E*) has occurred; and at least one physical, non-biological event (E#) has occurred. We could say, it will be suggested, that only one event has occurred, namely D, and that D can be described in various ways: biologically (whence E*'s occurrence), physically (whence E#'s), or medically-psychologically (whence E's). But such a suggestions would be false. The reason it would be false is that, given any two of the three events described (E, E*, and E#), the individuation-conditions of the one are different from the individuation-conditions of the other. Let us now discuss why this is so.

Expressions like "Smith's stroke" (and "World War II" and "the sack of Troy") are explanatorily significant: there are truths whose explanations are given by sentences of which "Smith's stroke" is a non-redundant constituent. (Smith taught linguistics; now he can't even read. Explanation: Smith's stroke destroyed the brain-centers mediating his ability to read.) Whatever it is that is explanatorily distinctive about the referent of "Smith's stroke," not everything about D is involved in that expression's referent's being thus distinctive. Therefore, "Smith's stroke" and "D" don't co-refer, and Smith's stroke is therefore distinct from D. Given this fact, if if we insist on saying that Smith's stroke is a constituent of the external world, then we must say that it is distinct from D and also, by obvious extensions of what we've said, from E* and E#; and we must therefore say that distinct events can be spatiotemporally coincident.

But such a view is absurd. (If x constitutes y, in the sense in which the marble constitutes the statue, then x and y aren't distinct, at least not as we are using that word, even if x and y are not identical.) Our only conceivable reason for distinguishing space-time regions R and R* is that one of those regions hosts, or could host, an event not hosted by the other; and our only reason for identifying those two regions is that neither hosts, or could host, an event not also hosted by the other. E's modal properties are different from E*'s. Supposing E and E* to be constituents of the external world, they are, by supposition, spatiotemporally coincident with each other. A consequence of that supposition, therefore, is that some region of space-time isn't self-identical. That supposition being an absurd one, the conclusion to draw is that events aren't constituents of the external world. This is no absurdity. It's a truism. For it is a corollary of the truism that true propositions (truths) are distinct from the facts in virtue of which they hold. We thus see the justification for our earlier claim that events are to be thought of, not as constituents of the external world, but as nominalizations of truths. (In the process of making a point distinct from the one we are currently making, Russell (1903) that the event of Caesar's being killed by Brutus is the nominalization of the truth that Brutus killed Caesar.)

A consequence of our stipulating that 'E' and 'D' co-referred would therefore be that some region space-time wasn't identical with itself. Therefore, it is not a matter of convention that those expressions don't co-refer; it is a matter of substantive, albeit non-empirical fact.

Hume's analysis of causation involves a failure to distinguish facts from truths. This failure is the heart of empiricism. (See the first sentence of Section 2 of Chapter 2.) Thus, empiricism is responsible in a way distinct from those already identified for Hume's very wrong conception of causation. That conception is one that, although not universally accepted, is more widely accepted than any other; indeed, it is the only existing analysis of causation, setting aside the analysis put forth in Section 18.0 of the present Chapter.

3.1 "No spatiotemporal changes without causal changes," we said. That said, there can be causal changes without spatiotemporal changes. I gain weight while remaining stationary with respect to ball B. Thus, my gravitational pull on B increases, even though my spatiotemporal relation to B hasn't changed.

But to say that spatiotemporal changes are causal changes is not to make the absurd claim that nothing other than changes in relative position affect causal relations;

it is to make the demonstrably correct claim such changes necessarily do affect such relations.

Also, it's suggestive that, if I gain weight while remaining stationary with respect to ball B, the latter has a greater *tendency* than it previously did to approach me. Of course, my weight-gain may increase the gravitational pull I exert on B by such a miniscule amount that, given the other forces acting on it, B has but an infinitesimally increased tendency to head in my direction. But causal changes unaccompanied by spatiotemporal changes are oftentimes thwarted by the causal changes associated with other spatiotemporal changes: the ball's movement towards me is thwarted by forces counteracting the changes in myself. We will leave it open whether *all* causal changes that don't involve relative changes in position can be identified with thwarted spatio-temporal changes in relative position.

3.2   Hume assumes that the concepts of precedence in time and adjacency in space can be understood in non-causal terms. In making that assumption, he's assuming that a given event's space-time location isn't constituted by its optical and, more generally, causal relations to other events; and he is therefore assuming that there is some non-relational way of understanding space-time position. But there isn't, and his analysis of causality is therefore defective.[137]

In defense of Hume's position, a device known as the "Hume world" is used.[138] This is a world in which the same events happen that happen in our world, in the same space-time order, but in which nothing makes anything happen. Such a world would be indistinguishable from ours, Humeans say, showing that there is no empiri-cal foundation for the belief that we ourselves don't live in a Hume world or, therefore, that in our world anything makes anything happen.

The problem is that this supposed Hume-world is replete with instances of causa-tion. Any instance of persistence, or indeed of occupancy, is an instance of causation: persistences are causal processes. Your basketball is a causal process because how it was a few seconds ago is determinative of how it is now, and how it now is determina-tive how it'll be a few seconds from now. When Humeans ask to imagine a 'Hume-world,' they are, though they don't know it, asking us to imagine a world exactly like ours except that *some* of the instances of causality constitutive of our world are absent from it.

3.2.1   "In that case," it will be said, "simply replace the verbiage in question with: 'your finger moves; so does the buzzer; but the first thing doesn't make the second happen.'"

---

137.   Reichenbach (1956, 1957). Einstein and Infeld (1961). Einstein (1962).

138.   Carnap (1966).

Once again consider B, the ball that is rolling on the pool table. At any given moment, it is pushing against the table. On each such occasion, the table responds by pushing against B. And it is the latter push that propels B.

"But why believe that anything is pushing anything?" it will be asked. "Why not believe only what our senses tell us, viz. that the ball is moving? Why posit occult forces?"

Because were it not for such forces, the ball wouldn't exist for more than an instant, and it therefore wouldn't exist at all. Suppose that B's state at t (Bt) isn't responsible to any degree for B's state at t* (Bt*). In that case, what grounds have we for saying that Bt and Bt* jointly constitute some one ball? Why not just say that B winked out of existence at t, to be replaced by some other ball at t*?

Of course, given only that, were it not for causal ties, the ball wouldn't persist, it doesn't follow that, were it not for such ties, the ball wouldn't move along the surface of the pool table. But once it's granted that such ties exist, and consequently that it is coherent to posit such ties, it is an empirical question whether the ball's describing a given trajectory is to be explained in terms of them. And, the empirical data being what it is, that question is to be answered affirmatively.

4.0   A *transcendental argument* for a proposition P is one to the effect that, unless P were true, it couldn't even be asked whether P were true.[139] What follows is a transcendental argument for the existence of instances of causation, that is, of things' making other things happen.

Let m be the various events and structures mediating your mind at the instant you started reading this sentence, and let m* be the various events and structures mediating your mind at the instant you start reading the next sentence. m is *genidentical* with m*.[140] That is, m and m*, though not numerically identical, are causally related in such a way that they constitute distinct phases in the existence of one persistent entity.

Unless m* were m's causal successor, there would be no thought-processes linking m to m*. m* wouldn't host any thought process, or cognitive structure, hosted by m. *Nothing* would link m to m*. By the same token, given that m and m* *are* genidentical, it follows that there is at least one instance of causation. No thought happens instantaneously; no two thought-episodes are genidentical unless one of them

---

139. Kant (1787) invented the concept of a transcendental proof. He provides several such proofs. The argument that follows is similar to one put forth by Kant (1787).

140. I believe it was Minkowski who first spoke of "genidentity." The only philosopher I know of who speaks of it is Arthur Pap (1948, 1958). The words "genidentity," "genidentical," etc. are no longer used, and neither are the corresponding concepts. As a result, contemporary analyses of identity tend to be artificial, for reasons discussed in Kuczynski (2009).

is responsible for the other's existence. Thus, given that thought-episodes can link together into thought-processes, it follows that things make things happen.

4.1 "If you are right," it will be said, "then the problem with Hume's analysis of causality is not that it makes undue concessions to empiricism, but that it is a misapplication of empiricism. You say that instances of occupancy and persistence are *ipso facto* instances of causality. You also suggest that one sees instances of occupancy and persistence *as* instances of causation. I don't know whether you are right about this. But assuming for argument's sake that you are, an empirical conception of causality *is* the right one. For, relative to that assumption, we see instances of things making things happen, and we see them *as* such instances; so that, if we stick with what our senses tell us, we'll come to the right verdict – namely, that causality is compulsion, as opposed to regularity-instantiation."

Supposing this true, it follows that empiricism is incoherent. If questions about how to *interpret* our observations have to be settled *before* observational data can be logged, then empirical reportage necessarily embodies non-empirical, meta-observational assumptions, a straightforward corollary being that empiricism is false.

And whether or not the present author's views about persistence and occupancy are correct, empiricism *is* incoherent in the way just mentioned. There is no such thing as a conceptually innocent observation-report. To be sure, some observation-reports are more theoretically committed than others. But if purged of their theoretical commitments, our observation-reports would be stilted and useless. One couldn't talk about "radios" or "telescopes," obviously. One couldn't even talk about "space" and "time," since one doesn't observe such things. One observes events that are so interrelated that it is natural to suppose that space and time exist. But that supposition is just that: a supposition – not a datum, but a way of modelling the data. And that supposition is a false one, at least according to Leibniz (1704), Einstein (1956), Russell (1919, 1928) and Reichenbach (1956).[141] According to these authors, there are time-like and space-like relations, but there are no empty vessels corresponding to the terms "space," "time," and "space-time."

The fact stated in 3.4.2 is yet *another* illustration of the fact that sensitive conceptual issues must be resolved if we are to correctly describe what our senses disclose to us.

5.0   Given any two spatiotemporally adjacent events, e_1 and e_2, e_1 being the first of the two, there exists infinitely many categories K_1 and K_2 such that e_1 and e_2 belong to K_1 and K_2, respectively, and such that e_1 is the only member of K_1. This means that a consequence of Hume's theory is that, given any two spatiotemporally adjacent events, one is the cause of the other. I hug my kitty; it has a stroke. Cause; effect.

---

141.   Leibniz (1966), Russell (1919), Reichenbach (1957), Einstein (1962), and Gardner (1976).

To deal with this problem, Humeans have to start talking about *relevant* similarities: they must say that K_1 must pick out a class of objects that is similar to e_1 not just in *some way or other*, but in some *explanatorily significant* way.

But Hume's analysis is supposed to tell us what it is for e_1 to be related in an explanatorily significant way to e_2. The fact that, in order to acquire this information, we must avail ourselves of *ex parte*, Hume-ulterior knowledge means that Hume's analysis is wrong (or so revisionist as to be presumed wrong, other things being equal).

Further proof of the erroneousness of Hume's analysis, and of the correctness of our positive analysis of explanation, is found in a famous puzzle due to Nelson Goodman.[142] Any given green emerald confirms:

(EG)   All emeralds are green.

Let something be "grue" if it's either examined before t and it's green or it's examined after t and it's blue.

In that case, supposing the present to be t, EG has exactly as much support – no more, no less – than

(EB)   All emeralds examined after t are blue.

But surely something has gone wrong. the last 20 green emeralds I saw didn't provide a whit of support for EB, but they provided plenty of support for EB.

5.1   Goodman's puzzle is easily adapted to show that any body of data can provide any amount of positive support for any hypothesis.

The solution: Explanations aren't found by finding regularities and subsuming events under them. Explanations are found by finding hyper-continuities.

Bearing this in mind, consider the hypothesis that:

(EG)   All emeralds are grue (green/blue if examined before/after t).

Remember what we said earlier: There is no such a thing as strictly enumerative confirmation. So far as my rolling double sixes 100 times in a row confirms that the dice are weighted, it's because it confirms that there are mechanisms that dispose that outcome.

My coming across a green emerald confirms EG *to the extent* that it confirms that there is something about emeralds in virtue of which they are likely to be green. EG is only indirectly confirmed; what is directly confirmed is the existence of the aforementioned posited mechanism. Suppose that, as the data rolls in, hypothesis h gains in support. This means that, as the data rolls in, more anomalies are created by rejecting h than by accepting it. This in turn means that more discontinuities are created by rejecting h than by accepting it.

---

142.   Goodman (1954).

5.2   What if h itself posits a giant discontinuity? And what if there are alternatives to positing that discontinuity? Green emeralds (examined before t) don't confirm EB the way they confirm EG. EB itself posits discontinuities – many objectual discontinuities, and some nomic discontinuities. (And it's hard to calculate all of the objectual and nomic discontinuities involved in those explicitly mentioned in EB.) So far as EB is confirmed, otherwise non-existent anomalies come into existence. But a hypothesis is confirmed in so far as otherwise non-existent anomalies are pushed *out* of existence. EB, if true, is an endless source of anomalies. So anything that confirms EB, and therefore disconfirms its negation, is anomaly-productive. Therefore, EB is such that it cannot be confirmed without being disconfirmed.

Simon Blackburn (1984) says that what counts as continuity is "relative to our linguistic practices." This is not true. First of all, 'grue' and 'bleen' are not colors; they are color-related predicates, as any date-stamped photographs show, and a consequence of EB's being correct is the world is replete with otherwise non-existent discontinuities.

What Goodman's puzzle shows is that explanation isn't about finding regularities and subsuming events under them. What it shows is that certain regularities are broken, explanatorily useless, whereas others are not, and it identifies the broken ones – they are the discontinuity-generators. It therefore tells us which ones are not broken: the ones that destroy more discontinuities than they create. Which means that, even in the case of a non-broken regularity, it's not the regularity *per se* that is explanatorily important; it is the various hyper-continuities constitutive of that regularity. The regularity is a class of hyper-continuities. It's the hyper-continuities that make the regularity a good one, not the regularity that makes the hyper-continuities good. We are interested in regularities only in so far as they are hyper-continuity-conducive, only in so far as, unlike EG, they don't fracture reality, like EB, which means we're interested in continuities, ultimately, the regularities being of interest only in so far as they may help us find the continuities.

5.3   There is change; change in the manner of change; change in the manner of the manner of change; and so on. What we typically refer to as conditions of changelessness are teeming with lower-order changes; they are conditions of (very) high-order changelessness. The apparent exceptions to our analysis of explanation ('to explain is to eliminate discontinuities') vanish when we take into account the different levels of change(lesness). A hypothetical, continuous series of events, linking a and b, may be non-explanatory; but, if so, that's because, while staving off an n-level change, it permits the occurrence of $n+1$-level changes.

Green emeralds (examined before t) provide *no* support for EB. They provide no support for the hypothesis that there exists some property of emeralds in virtue of which they're blue if examined after t. data supports regularity-generating mechanisms; it doesn't directly support regularities.

The idea that green emeralds *directly* support EG is thus an instance of the gambler's fallacy. They support EG only in so far as they support the idea that there is something about emeralds in virtue of which emeralds are disposed to be green.

Green emeralds, examined before t, don't support the hypothesis that there is some-thing about emeralds in virtue of which, if examined after t, they are disposed to be blue.

Let m be any mechanism that would turn green emeralds blue; or let m be any mechanisms that would result in all the emeralds' we've found having been the green ones, and the all the emeralds' we're going to find being the blue ones. We could imag-ine finding evidence that warranted belief in such a mechanism. We could imagine our discovering that all the emeralds we had yet to consider were on some other planet, where, because of the atmosphere, or some such, they were blue. Or we could discover that our own atmosphere was going to change in such a way that hitherto green emeralds would turn blue.

But finding green emeralds would constitute support for such a hypothesis. Find-ing an emerald that is green in xyz (the substance that is currently in our atmosphere) and blue in abc (the substance that is going to be in our atmosphere) would constitute such evidence. and it would constitute such evidence only because, given what we know about emeralds, more anomalies would be created that this emerald, or these emeralds, were singularities than by supposing that they had a garden variety chemi-cal reaction to their environment that involved their turning blue.

To sum up: green emeralds don't support EB; they support EG. Second, although there is evidence that would support EB, it would be very different from that which supports EG. Third, so far as EB were worthy of consideration, supposing it true would have to lead to fewer anomalies than supposing it false.

6.0 In Chapter 5, Section 4.1, we considered Wittgenstein's feeble attempt to show that a given person doesn't have the right to conclude that the mental concomitants of other people's behaviors resemble those of one's own; one doesn't even have the right to hold that other people's behaviors have such concomitants. Wittgenstein's argu-ment: One cannot make an inference about a plurality of objects on the basis of just one instance of that plurality. In Chapter 1, Section 8.2, we saw that B. F. Skinner put forth a similar argument.

The points just made reinforce our earlier critique of Wittgenstein. Wittgenstein's argument assumes that probability is a statistical, not an explanatory notion. We'll see that empiricists have no choice but to make this assumption. But that assumption is false.

You've held over 30,000 first-editions in your own hands. Every single one of them smelled like pipe-tobacco. You knows all of this. Does that knowledge entitle you to believe that first editions always smell like pipe-tobacco, or even that they're prone to? No. Your uncle smokes a pipe. He also collects first-editions, and the first-editions with which you are (odor-)acquainted belonged to him. So it wasn't their be-ing first editions, but their belonging to a pipe-smoker, that was responsible for their smelling like pipe-tobacco.

This reasoning can be inverted. You know that your uncle smokes a pipe. He lends you a single book. It is one he values greatly, and he wants you to return it in the condition in which he lent it do you. It smells like pipe-tobacco. You are probably right to infer that many other objects smell like pipe-tobacco: your uncle's other first editions; his other, less valuable belongings; and so on. Given your knowledge that

(i)   your uncle smokes a pipe

and that

(ii)   that his first edition of *Moby Dick* smells like pipe-tobacco,

you know of causal mechanisms that link instances of one property with instances of some other property. For you know that your pipe-smoking uncle smokes doesn't take precautions to prevent objects that he values, or *a fortiori* ones he doesn't value, from smelling like pipe-tobacco.

Mathematically minded probability theorists often include among their axioms an "axiom of diversity": given two instances of phi that are also instances of psi, the less those instances of phi *otherwise* resemble one anther, the more they confirm *all phi's are psi's*.

This axiom is easily explained and therefore shouldn't be an axiom. To the extent that those phi-instances resemble each other, you have no assurance that it is *by virtue of* their being phi's that they are psi's. Given two cancer-stricken methamphetamine addicts who eat only fatty foods, you don't know whether to blame their cancer on their recreational or their dietary habits.

In any case, it is only relative to a jejune, purely statistical conception of probability that Wittgenstein's argument works. At the same time, the empiricist cannot distinguish between statistical and explanatory probability. This is because explanatory probability is a *causal* notion – Your uncle's pipe smoking *causes* his books to smell like-pipe tobacco, Fred's drug habit *caused* him to get cancer – and empiricists deny that anything makes anything happen.

6.1   Empiricists have tried to statisticalize the explanatory probability, their position being:

(EP[143]) You don't need to posit causal mechanisms to explain why all of your uncle's possessions smell like pipe-tobacco, given only that his copy of *Moby Dick* does. There is some class K_1 such that the only instance of K_1 is that copy of Moby Dick, K_1 being the class of your uncles possessions. But there are many classes K_2 such that you've encountered many instances of K_2, all of them smelling of pipe-tobacco, and such that your uncle's book belongs to K_2. K_2 might be the class of objects owned by smokers, or the class of objects owned by eccentrics who have smelly personal habits, or some such.

---

143. Short for "empiricists on probability."

Yes, your only grounds for choosing one reference class over another is your independent knowledge that, in so choosing, you are grounding a concomitance in a causal mechanism. Given 1,000,000 green emeralds examined before t, you conclude that the next one is green, not blue, even though each of those emeralds was grue (green if examined before t or blue if examined thereafter). Given an arbitrary emerald, the corresponding instance of greenness can be shown to be an installment in a continuous, structure-preserving, causal series (of a complex kind, with the specifics of which we needn't bother). And the existence of each pre-t emerald is itself an instance of a larger, structure preserving continuity. That a given emerald remains green during an arbitrary t-inclusive interval is obviously an instance of system-internal continuity. That all emeralds do so is an instance of systemic continuity. These continuities would be torn asunder were post-t emeralds to be blue. This doesn't mean they won't be blue. It means that, to the extent that they are, the hitherto non-anomalous is anomalous.

The "problem of the priors" – how to pick the right reference-classes when interpreting a formal probability-calculus – cannot be solved on statistical grounds; it has to be solved on grounds of causality and, therewith, of continuity.

7.0   In Section 4.0, we put forth a transcendental argument to the effect that gen-identical thought-episodes are *ipso facto* the relata of *bona fide* instances causation. We can use this point to rebut Hume's two attempts to show that there is no such thing as the self or, what is the same, that selves are identical with the mental activity they mediate.

Hume says that (this is a paraphrase):

(H₁)   When I introspect, he encounters only various tickles, itches, etc. – various qualia – but nothing corresponding to a self. So, since introspection yields no self, there is, I must conclude, no empirical evidence that there is a self. Since "empirical evidence" is a pleonasm, like "unmarried bachelor," it follows that there is *no* evidence support the contention that I have a self (or, more accurately, that I have a self *unless my self is constituted in its entirety* by the various aforementioned tickles, etc.).

Here are Hume's exact words:

> For my part, when I enter most intimately into what I call *myself,* I always stumble on some particular perception or other, of heat or cold, light or shade, love or hatred, pain or pleasure. I can never catch *myself* at any time without a perception, and never can observe anything but the perception.[144]

Hume then provides a very different, and much more powerful argument – this one being conceptual, not empirical in nature (this is a paraphrase):

---

144. Hume (1740: 252).

(H$_2$)   Imagine a mind in which there is no activity, a mind in which neither an idea
nor a feeling or a perception was to be found. That mind is a complete nullity
is thus no mind at all.

Here are Hume's exact words:

> When my perceptions are remov'd for any time, as by sound sleep; so long
> am I insensible of *myself*, and may truly be said not to exist. And were all
> my perceptions remov'd by death, and cou'd I neither think, nor feel, nor
> see, nor love, nor hate after the dissolution of my body, I should be entirely
> annihilated, nor do I conceive what is farther requisite to make me a perfect
> non-entity.[145]

7.1   Let's evaluate these arguments, starting with H$_1$. Notice that, while he's describing his tour of his own psyche, Hume repeatedly uses the term "I." This is not merely
a concession to English grammar. Hume's position is that *he* has taken a tour of *his
psyche* and found no evidence of a self.

But the very fact that *he* found no self despite *his* best efforts shows that *there is*
a self there. It also shows that this self is to be distinguished from the whirlwind of
psychic debris coursing through Hume's mind at any given moment. Perceptions and
tickles and itches come and go; but there is something that endures, which registers
the existence of the various tickles, perceptions etc. and takes note of what, if anything, they have to say.

Let b be the confluence of mental events occurring right when you began reading
the last sentence, and let b* be the corresponding confluence occurring right when
you finished (Let S be the just-mentioned sentence.) Obviously you didn't have to be
reading S for your psyche to endure during that interval. But it was sufficient for b*'s
being identical with b, although it wasn't necessary for it, that the thought-process initiated by b was brought to a close by b*. It isn't because b and b* belonged to the same
mind that b initiated a thought-process that b* concluded. It is because b initiated a
thought-process that b* concluded that b and b* belong to the same mind.

In general, it isn't because two segments of a thought process belong to the same
mind that they constitute one, unbroken thought process. It is because they constitute
one unbroken thought-process that they belong to the same mind.

The self endures by virtue of the relations of cohesion that endure among the par-
ticulars that it hosts. The self has those cohesion-relations to thank for its existence,
not *vice versa*.

7.2   We can thus explain how Hume's mind managed to exist for the duration of his
inward tour. Let H be Hume's mind at the beginning of its tour, and let H* be Hume's
mind at the end of it. It wasn't because H and H* belonged to some one mind that they

---

145.   Hume (1740: 252).

cohered. It was because they cohered that they belonged to some one mind. Of course, that particular thought-process or sequence of ideation wasn't necessary – just as, even though clouds consist of water-molecules and nothing besides, there is no one water molecule whose removal from a given cloud would obliterate that cloud. But, it would seem, there must be *some* coherence between minds separated in time – there must be *some* unbroken stream of ideation, beginning with the one mind and ending with the other – if those two minds are to be a single one.

The last statement must be qualified – and the needed qualification makes it clear H_2 fails. Supposing a given brain to be cryogenically frozen and successfully reactivated, the pre-freeze brain mediates the same mind as the post-freeze brain – even though there was no thought process connecting the two. What connects the two, what makes them one mind, as opposed to two, is that the brain-structures that mediate the mental activity of the first mind are identical with those that mediate the mental activity of the second. Those brain-structures are enduring mental entities.

What unites the pre-freeze brain with the post-freeze brain isn't occurrent ideation. It is the persistence of a single structure that mediates ideation. So the 'self' thus, *pace* Hume; it consists of the awareness-mediating enduring *structures* underlying mental activity. Hume was right that if a mind were stripped of all of its contents, *including the structures it comprises*, it would cease to exist. To that extent, his second argument goes through. But he was wrong, as the case of the cryogenically brain shows, to say that a mind would cease to exist if emptied of all occurrent activity.

But Hume couldn't countenance the idea of an "enduring structure." Hume's world consists of events, nothing more. It doesn't also including underlying structures that govern the events. Supposing that the world were, as Hume believed, structure-free, then a given mind would exist only as it mediated an unbroken sequence of occurrence mental phenomena.

7.3   Hume's analysis of the self *would* have been correct if he hadn't doctored it so as to make it conform to his empiricism.

Hume likens minds to clouds. Clouds are aggregates of molecules. Minds are aggregates of thoughts.

Contrary to what Hume holds, minds aren't comparable to clouds. Whereas clouds are one-tiered, unstructured entities, minds are multi-tiered and otherwise structured entities. Clouds are just molecule-aggregates. Those molecules are not hierarchically organized. Interactions among pairs of such molecules must be understood on their own terms; they cannot be understood in terms of the structure of the cloud. Systems are to be understood from the top down. Aggregates are to be understood from the bottom up. Corporations are systems: the way a corporation is structured determines the way its members interact. Clouds are aggregates: a cloud's constituents interact determine the way it's structured.

Minds are systems, as opposed to aggregates. Minds are hierarchically organized. They consist of enduring structures that mediate mental activity. And there isn't just one layer of structures or one layer of activity. There is a structure that mediates activity that does not itself mediate the creation or dissolution of structures; there is a deeper layer that mediates the creation and dissolution of the just-described first-order structures; and so on. (The "and so on" obviously doesn't mean *ad infinitum.*) Correspondingly, there are different kinds of mental activity: some of it isn't structure-building; some of it creates first-order structures; some of it creates *those* structures; and so on. There is remodeling; remodeling of the structures responsible for remodeling; and so on.

When Hume was conducting his introspective journey, the inner-flame that beheld the various "perception...of heat or cold, light or shade, love or hatred, pain or pleasure" was itself, like the various things it beheld, an occurrent phenomenon. But whereas those pains and pleasures represented the deployment of first-order structures, the inner flame represented the deployment of a second-order structure. The Cartesian Ego that described those "perceptions...of heat [and] cold [etc.]" regulated the activity it beheld: it chose, or was able to choose, whether or not to let that perception of cold to lead to a decision to put a coat on.

"The bottommost constituents of the mind," it is tempting to think, "must respond only to local, as opposed to systemic, pressures; for those constituents *are* the system and therefore fall outside its scope. So to the extent that there are any nuclei of mental activity, they must consist of renegade mental structures, and the mind must *ultimately* be like a swarm of wasps."

This involves a non-sequitur. It is possible for *all* of the constituents of a given system to fall within its scope. The United States is a democracy, and everyone composing that democracy is subject to its laws. There isn't a stratum of people who can do what they want.

There are two ways that a system can be organized: horizontally and vertically. Horizontal organization consists of the separation of activities into different strata. Vertical organization consists in the existence of structures that coordinate those strata. A society governed by an omnipotent dictator would be a better example than a democracy of a horizontal organization: everyone falls under the dictator's dominion, except the dictator himself, and he falls under nobody's dominion. But actual dictatorships are not perfect instances of horizontal organization; for even the dictator himself needs the cooperation of some of the people he governs, and to that extent he falls within the scope of the system he presides over.

There are ways to take what Hume is saying:

(i)   The mind is a whirlwind of activity; it is ultimately just like a swarm of wasps or aggregate of water-molecules.

(ii) The mind is organized. But that doesn't mean that there exists some "transcendental ego." To say that $x_1...x_n$ are organized cannot ultimately be to say that some entity x_{n+1} oversees them. (One commits the homunculus fallacy if one says otherwise.) For $x_1...x_n$ to be organized is precisely for none of them to govern all of them; it is for their interactions to generate power-vortices by which those same interactions are then governed. So *there is* an ego (or maybe more than just one), but this ego is not another constituent of the mind.

I believe that Hume's book contains two conflicting accounts of the nature of the self, corresponding to (i) and (ii), respectively, but that *ultimately* the passages where he affirms (i) – and he does affirm it – are initial attempts to affirm (ii), which, being a point that he was the first to make, was one he had to figure out how to articulate and, therefore, was likely to misstate before stating it correctly. It is on the basis of the following passage in Hume's book that I say this:

> As to causation; we may observe, that the true idea of the human mind, is to consider it as a system of different perceptions or different existences, which are linked together by the relation of cause and effect, and mutually produce, destroy, influence, and modify each other. Our impressions give rise to their correspondent ideas; said these ideas in their turn produce other impressions. One thought chases another, and draws after it a third, by which it is expelled in its turn. In this respect, I cannot compare the soul more properly to any thing than to a republic or commonwealth, in which the several members are united by the reciprocal ties of government and subordination, and give rise to other persons, who propagate the same republic in the incessant changes of its parts. And as the same individual republic may not only change its members, but also its laws and constitutions; in like manner the same person may vary his character and disposition, as well as his impressions and ideas, without losing his identity. Whatever changes he endures, his several parts are still connected by the relation of causation. And in this view our identity with regard to the passions serves to corroborate that with regard to the imagination, by the making our distant perceptions influence each other, and by giving us a present concern for our past or future pains or pleasures.

Notice how liberally Hume liberally talks about causation in this passage. Taken together with the fact that

(a) this passage occurs *after* he puts forth his analysis of causation and *after* he puts forth his introspection-based attempt to show that selves don't exist,

this confirms my view that

(b) Hume's *actual* views about the mind are the ones put forth in the just-quoted passage and, therefore, that, had he not attempted *post hoc* to empiricize the views put forth in that passage, his analysis of selfhood would have been stunningly accurate, instead of embarrassingly inaccurate.

Hume started out with a correct analysis of the self, and then changed it, so that it would conform to

(i)   his *a priori*, empiricist view that all knowledge is observational (and therefore, if concerned with one's self, introspection-based)

and also

(ii)   his empiricism-driven belief nothing makes anything happen.

That Hume's analysis *would* have been right had he not so altered shows that either (i) or (ii) is false, and it suggests that both are false.

Unless things make things happen, nothing can be explained. Hume knew this. He knew it consciously. Cf. Section 22 of Hume (1740): "All reasonings concerning matter of fact seem to be founded on the relation of Cause and Effect." (Consistency is the hobgoblin of mediocre minds.[146]) So why did Hume (1739, 1740) say otherwise? Because he *compartmentalized*. How is compartmentalization possible? How can a person both believe and disbelieve a given proposition? We will answer that question in Chapter 15.

8.0   Nothing makes anything happen.

Let's refer to this four word slogan as "NC," short for "no cause."

NC is Hume's legacy to the philosophy of science.

NC entails either that nothing causes anything to happen. But Hume takes it as a given that there are instances of causation; and for the reasons discussed earlier, he concludes that, supposing NC to be true, the only way to validate statements of the form "e_1 causes e_2 to occur" (i.e. the only way to interpret in such a way that they come out true) is to say:

(HC[147]) e_1 causes e_2 to occur iff e_1 precedes and is spatiotemporally adjacent with e_2 and the sequence consisting of e_1 and e_2, in that order, instantiates a regularity.

Hume is probably right to say that, given NC, EC is the only interpretation of causal statements that validates them.

If correct, HC has far-reaching consequences as to what it is to explain an event.

Let's start with a platitude: To explain is to find causes; to explain an event is to identify its cause.[148] A vase breaks at time t*. Let B be that event. This vase collided with the ground at t, this being right before t. (Let us set aside subtleties relating to the vagueness of the term "right before.") Let C be *that* event. (Mentally infill the relevant

---

146.   This is an old saying. I did not come up with it.

147.   Short for "empiricist analysis of causation."

148.   In any case, this is a necessary condition for explaining an event. But it is not sufficient. We saw why in Chapter 1, Section 1.2.4.

details about the vase's mass, the thinness of its walls, the rate at which it was traveling upon impact, etc.) We want to explain why vase broke at t. It turns out to be a natural law that:

(BV[149]) given any event involving an object x having properties $p_1...p_n$ that collides with a surface having properties $c_1...c_m$, that even is adjacent to, and immediately followed by an consisting of x's being shattered,

It also turns out that

(BV#) At t, the vase had properties $p_1...p_n$ and the floor had properties $c_1...c_m$ and, also at t, the vase collided with the floor.

BV and BV# jointly entail that:

(BV*) The vase broke at t^*.

8.1   Thus, a consequence of the empiricist analysis of causation is the so-called "Deductive-nomological" analysis of explanation:[150]

(DN) To explain an event O is to identify one or more natural laws $L_1...L_n$ such that, given those laws and given a sufficiently precise description of O's immediate antecedents, it logically follows that O occurred.[151]

DN evaluated: If O is any event, there are infinitely many antecedents of O^* such that the sequence consisting of O followed by O^* is an instance of infinitely many universal generalizations. (A universal generalization is a statement of the form "all phi's are psi's.") For example, the fact that

(RP[152]) The pencil on JM's desk is red

is a logical consequence of

(RP#)   Every writing utensil on JM's desk is read

taken in conjunction with

(RP*)   The pencil on JM's desk is a writing utensil on JM's desk.

But RP* and RP#, taken jointly, do not explain why RP is true.

---

149. Short for "broken vase."

150. Advocated by Hempel (1965, 1966) and, in an attenuated form, by Salmon (1984).

151. Hempel (1965, 1966).

152. Short for "red pencil."

8.2   In response, advocates of DN must say that RP# is not a *natural law*. (In this context, "natural law" and "sentence expressing a natural law" will be used interchangeably.) But then the question arises: What sort of universal generalization *does* qualify as a natural law? The only credible answer is the one given by Hempel (1965), namely:

(CF[153]) A universal generalization is a law *if it supports counterfactuals.*

According to this viewpoint, the reason that

(EM[154]) "metal expands when heated"

is a natural law is it's true that:

(EM*) "if that table *were* made of metal, it *would* have expanded when heated"

and the reason RP* is not a natural law is that it's false that

(EM#) "If that green pencil *were* on JM's desk, it *would* have become red."

8.3   This position is unacceptable. The reason we believe EM to support counterfactuals, and thus to qualify as a natural law, is that we have independent knowledge of many an instance of some metal object's being heated and expanding *for that reason*. So *independently* of EM (or of any other natural law, by obvious extensions of what we're saying), we know the cause of many a case of some metal object's expanding; wherefore, we know the *explanation* of each of those events. So a *prerequisite* for our being able to distinguish natural laws from non-nomic universal generalizations is our having explained at least one event, an obvious consequence being that DN is false.

8.3.1   Natural laws may well be counterfactual-supporting generalizations. But advocates of DN cannot say that they are. We've seen one reason for this. Here is another.
   Assume it a truth that:

(CP[155]) *Ceteris paribus*, Kennedy would have been reelected if he hadn't been shot.

What makes CP true? Not events in other realities, obviously: for how could we possibly know CP to be true (or false) if it described such events?
   CP is true because it makes a true statement about the causal laws governing the world. It says that situations relevantly like one in which Kennedy wasn't assassinated cause the occurrence of situations relevantly like one in which he was reelected. So if P is an arbitrary actual situation relevantly similar to one in which Kennedy didn't

---

153.   Short for "Counterfactual."

154.   Short for "expanding metal."

155.   Short for "*ceteris paribus*."

get shot, and Q is an arbitrary actual situation relevantly similar to one in which Kennedy was reelected, CP is to the effect that P is (causally) incompatible with not-Q. As we've noted, our senses cannot apprise us of incompatibilities. So empiricism cannot countenance CP.[156]

All counterfactuals hold in virtue of relations of logical or causal dependence. The statement

(JF[157]) *Ceteris paribus*, if Jim had fallen off of that building, he would now be injured

is equivalent with:

(JF2) *Ceteris paribus*, situations relevantly similar to one in Jim fell off that building are causally incompatible with situations relevantly similar to one in which Jim is not injured.

Given that counterfactuals are causal statements, and given that "x caused y to happen" is (for the appropriate x) the right explanation for y, advocates of DN are prohibited from advocating a counterfactualist analysis of natural law. According to such an analysis, natural laws are given by counterfactuals (or – what comes to the same thing in this context – statements that entail them); counterfactuals are given by causal statements; explanations are causal statements; DN is intended to be an explanation of explanation.

8.4   To show that x is an instance of a regularity is to show that it is but one member of a whole class of events we can't explain. To explain Bill's ability to speak by saying "everybody Bill's age can talk" is to say: "I have no idea why Bill can talk or why Ethel or Larry or anyone else can do so." Regularities sometimes tell us where to look for causes. (If I know that everyone who has entered house X in the last 10 hours has died, even though each was previously healthy, I certainly know where to look for the causes of the those ten people's deaths.) But regularities are but shadows cast by underlying causal mechanisms.

That said,

(a)   on occasion, explaining a given event *seems* to be the same thing as showing it to instantiate some regularity,

and

---

156. Interestingly, Quine and van Fraassen, both distinguished empiricists, hold that counterfactuals categorically fail to be true – either because they are meaningless or because it is indeterminate whether what they're saying is true.

157. Short for "Jim fell."

(b)   *part* of what it is to explain a given event is sometimes to identify some such regularity.

Each of (a) and (b) is a consequence of the following three truths, taken jointly:

(i)   To explain x is to identify its cause.

(ii)   Effects are *ipso facto* continuous with their causes; if x immediately affects y, x and y are *ipso facto* neighbors (relative to at least one form of causation, though perhaps not relative to all).

And

(iii)   Discontinuities are themselves irregularities.

9.0   False though it is, however, DN has at least a semblance of plausibility if taken as an explanation of physical explanation.[158] But DN has no plausibility if taken as an explanation of psychological explanation. Bill believes that he'll burn in Hell if he skips Church. Bill doesn't want to burn in Hell. *That's* why Bill doesn't skip Church.

But advocates of DN deny this, saying that the real explanation is given by (the likes of) the following:

(1)   All pious people go to Church every Sunday.

(2)   Bill is pious.

Therefore

(3)   Bill goes to Church every Sunday.

But it is neither necessary nor helpful to cite some uniformity of which Bill's going to Church is an instance. Not necessary, because if you know that Bill thinks he'll burn in Hell unless he goes to Church, you've got your explanation right there. Not helpful, because even if you know that all and only pious people go to Church, you don't know whether it's Bill's piety that's the cause of his doing so. Maybe it's a concomitant of the actual cause. Maybe pious people are evildoers and rightly feel guilty about that fact; and maybe they go to Church because they know that, thanks to the token acts of expiation they perform there, they can continue their evil ways while being at ease with themselves.

---

158.   It has been said, by *inter alia* some very great physicists and philosophers, that reality comprises nothing but events, and that "forces" are but "mathematical fictions" with the help of which we state in an abbreviated, tractable form truths that would otherwise be hard to express in a way that served the interests of science (or of ordinary communication). Such thinkers have also tended to advocate DN. Hempel himself received an advanced degree in physics.

This is what Freud would say, and it fits the facts. For decades, a high-ranking federal agent by the name of Robert Hanssen sold top-secret information to the Soviets. During this time, he attended Church several times a week, knowing on many such an occasion that, on that very day, he would guarantee the deaths of American agents in the Soviet Union by apprising the Soviets of their identities.

10.0   Astonishingly, most philosophers and many psychologists have simply taken it for granted that DN provides a correct analysis of explanation in the physical sciences.

Such scholars have dealt with the problem of psychological explanation in one of two ways:

(i)   They've advocated the totally false view that DN holds no less of psychological than (so they wrongly believe) it does of physical explanation;

(ii)   They've denied that DN holds of psychological explanation, and on that basis said that psychological explanation is not the same sort of thing as physical explanation.

Such thinkers are not making the trivial point that the body of data modeled by psychology is distinct from the body of data modeled by physics (or any other physical science). They are making the following, decidedly non-trivial point.

(DA[159])   Let $d_1…d_n$ be some body of data that physics (or any other physical science) must model. Let H be a hypothesis that adequately models that body of data; and let R be the relationship that H bears with respect to $d_1…d_n$ such that it is by virtue of bearing R to $d_1…d_n$ that H adequately models that body of data.

Bearing this in mind, let $d^*_1…d^*_n$ be some body of data that *psychology* must model. Let H* be a hypothesis that adequately models that body of data; and let R be the relationship that H* bears with respect to $d^*_1…d^*_n$ such that, it is by virtue of bearing R* to $d^*_1…d^*_n$ that H* adequately models that body of data.

R ≠ R. In other words, what it is to explain a psychological truth is different from what it is to explain a physical truth. In the last sentence, the word "explain" is being used in two different ways.

Wilhelm Dilthey (1883) advocated DA.

10.1   DA is false. Either the term "explanation" is ambiguous or it isn't. And it isn't. So we can't say that the word "explain" means one thing coming from a psychologist's mouth and a different thing coming from a physicist's.

---

159.   Short for "Dilthey's analysis."

Dilthey's justification for thinking otherwise is that psychologists explain by rationalizing, whereas physicists do not. All advocates of DA justify their acceptance of it in this way.

Psychology *does* explain by rationalizing. But the right conclusion to draw is that DN is wrong and that, even though physicists do not explain by rationalizing, nonetheless what psychologists are doing *is* at bottom what physicists are doing. (What they are doing is the same. How they are doing it differs; so does what they are doing it to.)

Even though the physicist doesn't explain by rationalizing, physical explanations are similar in *some* respect to psychological explanations. There is some property P that both types of explanation have in common such that it is by virtue of having P that a given statement-series is a viable data-model.

The commonality is not hard to find. The physicist is looking for causal mechanisms and so is the psychologist. Since the psychologist is dealing with rational actors, causal mechanisms often take the form of rational motivations and explanation therefore often takes the form of rationalization.

11.0   Accrding to Hempel (1965), psychology seldom produces *bona fide* explanations: most of the "explanations" it yields, Hempel says, are but outlines of explanation.

Relative to his acceptance of DN, Hempel is right to say this. Given some psychological event e_2, it is seldom possible find some event e_1 such that the sequence e_1-e_2 is an instance of exceptionless regularity, setting aside those that are obviously contrived or otherwise defunct (e.g. every case of JMK's dawning a striped shirt on June 12, 2012 was immediately followed, in both space and time, by JMK's playing handball).

But this is to the discredit of DN, not of the psychological explanations we are wont to accept:

> Anomalous fact (A): The Menendez brothers killed their parents.
>
> Explanation (E): They knew they were about to be disinherited and they wanted their parents to die before that happened; and because they weren't deeply principled people, they did not have moral reservations about expediting their parents' demise.

If DN is right, E is no explanation at all. Not *every*body who is amoral and wants to avoid being disinherited kills his or her parents.

DN is incompatible with the datum that E, even if incomplete, has explanatory value. If DN is right, E's having explanatory value is contingent on there being some exceptionless generalization of which the relevant sequence of events is an instance. So, according to DN, if $P_1...P_n$ are the properties that E ascribes to the Menendez brother, there are properties $P_{n+1}...P_{n+m}$ such that anyone having $P_1...P_{n+m}$ also kills his parents. By the same token, if DN is right, E has no explanatory value *unless* $P_1...P_n$ is a segment of $P_1...P_{n+m}$.

But the relevant generalization, supposing there to be one, surely doesn't have the form:

(RG[160]) A person inevitably kills his parents if (1) he believes that he's about to be disinherited, (2) he is unscrupulous ... and (85) he had taken to patronizing extremely expensive restaurants.

No matter how much we extend $P_1...P_n$, we'll always be able to produce counterexamples: "What if the person having $P_1...P_{n+m}$ has a billionaire uncle who, he knows, will give him \$10,000,000 the next day *on the condition* that no blood is shed?"

We obviously can't take care of these problems by adding to $P_1...P_{n+m}$ the property of having no properties *other* than $P_1...P_{n+m}$. The property of weighing exactly n lbs isn't on that list; but any given person having $P_1...P_{n+m}$ also weighs exactly n lbs, for some n.

Further, we can't add to $P_1...P_{n+m}$ the property of having no *explanatorily significant* properties *other* than $P_1...P_{n+m}$; for then our explanation would be circular.

Finally, we can't add to $P_1...P_{n+m}$ some property like *is identical with somebody who kills his parents* or *is identical with Eric or Lyle Menendez on Aug. 12, 1993*; for then our explanation would be trivial.

11.1   In an effort to deal with the fact that few explanations satisfy the desiderata embodied in DN, Wesley Salmon (1984) proposed the following watered-down version of DN:

(DN*) To explain an event O is to identify one or more natural laws $L_1...L_n$ such that, given those laws and given a sufficiently precise description of O's immediate antecedents, it logically follows that it is *more likely than not* that O occurred.[161]

But DN* is no better than DN. First of all, it obviously fails for the same reasons as DN to give a feasible account of psychological explanation. Second, there are many truths P and Q such that,

(i)   Given P, it's less than 50% likely that Q is true;

and such that

(ii)   P is the explanation of Q.

E explains A; but surely a given person's being unscrupulous, on the brink of being disinherited, etc. doesn't make it more likely than not that he'll kill his parents.

---

160. Short for "relevant generalization."

161. Hempel (1965, 1966).

Another example: Smith got emphysema because he smokes two packs a day, but less than 50% of people who smoke that much get emphysema.

Everything that we said about DN is easily adapted to hold with regard to DN* or any other DN-derivative. DN is systemically flawed, and it's no use trying to tinker with it.

12.0   The right approach is to accept that E, or some other similarly "incomplete" explanation, is the right one and *also* to accept that there is such a thing as *probabilistic causation*.[162]

According to Leibniz (1704), the two cornerstones of cogent thought are the law of non-contradiction (not both P and not-P) and the "principle of sufficient reason" (nothing is the case unless there is a reason for it to be the case). The principle of sufficient reason (psr) is ambiguous. It can mean either:

(i)   any given event has a cause, meaning that, if E_2 is an event, there is a prior event E_1 such that, given E_1, E_2 *had* to happen;

or

(ii)   there is a *justification* (a *reason*) for the occurrence of any given event.

Be it noted that it is events (or conditions) that have causes, whereas it is propositions that have justifications. So (ii) is more accurately put thus:

(ii*)   There is a justification for any given (sufficiently circumscribed) proposition affirming the occurrence of an event.

Whether (ii) is true is not our concern. It will be argued that (i) is false. In other words, it will be argued that:

(H)   a given event E_1 can cause (or the affirmation of its existence can justify) the occurrence (or affirmation thereof) of an event E_2, even if, given E_1's occurrence, there was only an n% chance (where n is any number greater than 1 and less than 100) of E_2's occurrence.

Our defense of H will involve our repeating and developing some points in Chapter 1, Sections 1.2.1–1.2.4.

Complying with laws is different from being governed by them. Everything complies with the laws of microphysics; and, presumably, all higher level laws hold in virtue of microphysical laws.

But consider this. We have two houses that are architecturally identical, meaning that the way in which their medium sized parts (their constituent bricks, planks,

---

162. What follows is similar to a view put forth (in a lecture that I attended) by Paul Humphreys.

etc.) are interrelated are identical. Despite that fact, the microphysical structure of any component of either house is completely different from the corresponding structure of any component of the other house. However, these differences have no bearing on the dynamic interrelations on the bricks, planks, etc. which those microrealities constitute.

Both houses fall. They both fall for the same reason. That reason has nothing to do with the microstructures of their parts. It has to do with the fact that some plank x in the one house was improperly affixed to some other plank y and that plank x* in the other house was, in the very same way, improperly affixed to plank y*, where x* and y* are x's and y's respective counterparts.

The mechanical (Newtonian, macro-level) laws involved in both cases were the same. At the same time, in both cases, those laws were operative only because of facts about the relevant microconstituents, which, of course, obey a completely different set of laws.

We thus have a choice. We can say:

(a)   The laws compelling the collapse of both houses differed. The reason: the one house was microstructurally different from the other; and, at the end of the day, everything supervenes on micro-reality.

Or we can say:

(b)   In both cases, the same laws were involved; but those laws were *implemented* by different microphysical mechanisms.

(b) is the right option. For, if we go with (a), we make it a mere accident or coincidence that both houses fell, even though it was clearly no accident.

12.1   This brings us to the next fact. Most laws hold only probabilistically. Two situations that are indistinguishable from Newtonian perspective could have different outcomes: in the one case but not the other, there might have occurred some quantum event that happened to ramify outside the normal sphere of influence of such events. (It is possible, given quantum mechanics, and it is therefore consistent with Newton's laws, so far as the latter are consistent with quantum mechanics, that I could walk through a brick wall.)

Given this, we *could* say:

(c)   Since, given initial conditions C_1, Newtonian laws don't provide a 100% guarantee that non-initial conditions C_2 will obtain, we can't *really* say that C_1 brought about C_2. So far as such a thing could correctly be said, it would be shorthand for some unwieldy, but correct, microphysical statement.

But if we went with (c), we'd make it impossible to produce precisely the sort of explanatory meaningful generalization discussed earlier in connection with the two houses. This means that we would make it impossible to produce otherwise easily identified and illuminating explanations.

Here we have a choice. We can say either

(#)   'The structural (non-microphysical) defects in the houses *caused* them to collapse'

or

(##)   Those defects *did* not cause those houses to collapse, since causes operate with 100% efficacy, and such defects don't *always* lead to outcomes such as those described.

If we go with (#), we satisfy the explanatory desiderata described earlier. If we go with (##), we hold onto our *a priori* belief that, if E_2 results from E_1, then, given E_1, E_2 couldn't have failed to occur. This position, though not to be jettisoned lightly, is so inimical to explanation that it must, in fact, be jettisoned.

12.2   Newton's laws, even after recent development in physics are taken into account, hold almost 100% of the time. So let's consider some laws (or 'principles,' if you consider my use of the word 'law' question-begging) that are very obviously probabilistic.

Smoking causes cancer. This would seem to be a law of sorts. (At the very least, it's a principled regularity. And, as we're about to see, if we identify laws with perfect concomitances, as opposed to principled regularities, then principled regularities have all of the explanatory virtues that laws are supposed to have and therefore might as well be identified with laws.) But less than 30% of smokers get lung cancer. Nonetheless, if asked, "why did Jerry get lung cancer?," the right answer (we may reasonably assume) is "because he smoked a pack of cigarettes every day." So here we can say that

(E_1)   Jerry's heavy smoking

is what caused

(E_2)   Jerry's cancer,

even though events relevantly like E_1 are unlikely to bring about events relevantly like E_2.

Let us now suppose that Larry smokes as much as Jerry but doesn't get cancer. In that case, it's hard to see how E_1's being the cause of E_2 could be maintained. "What we must say," it is natural to believe, "is that E_1 did not *by itself* cause E_2 – that there was some other factor."

Surely there *was* some other factor. (To facilitate discussion, let's suppose that other factor to be one that falls totally outside the reach of medicine; let's suppose that it was some quantum-event that over-ramified.)

But biology attempts to provide explanations. It thus attempts to produce propositions that bear on one another in ways that, given data (falling into certain categories), light can be shed on that data's existence. The law (if I may so speak) that smoking causes lung cancer is not an ideal law; too many hidden variables are unaccounted for. But – let us suppose, going on the hypothesis that those hidden variables belong to quantum physics, not biology – there would be no way to include those hidden variables in biologically meaningful generalizations. Let's say that, in Jerry's case, there occurred some quantum event Q, the likes of which did not occur in Larry's case, and that, when combined with Jerry's habits, Q led to his getting cancer. When explaining why *Jerry* got cancer, we can mention Q, and in doing so we'll be providing a much better explanation than we'd otherwise be.

But neither Q nor anything comparable thereto has any place in any *biological generalization*. So, when explaining why *Fred's* smoking led to his lung cancer, the fact that Q played a role in Jerry's case is explanatorily idle. So, though causally operative in Jerry's case, there is a sense – an epistemic, not an ontological sense – in which Q was irrelevant. It was irrelevant in that, *qua* situation capable of being biologically explained, Q did nothing.

That said, it would be absurdly revisionist to say that Jerry's smoking habits didn't cause him to get cancer. Since such habits lead to lung cancer only a fraction of the time, we must say that there can be such a thing as probabilistic causation, meaning that E_1 can be the cause of E_2, even though, given E_1, there is a less than 100% of E_2's occurring.

For the reasons just given, there is no doubt that *epistemically speaking*, i.e. speaking from the viewpoint of explanation, there is such a thing as probabilistic causation. But that's a very different thing from saying that, *ontologically* speaking, there is such a thing as probabilistic causation. The orthodoxy these days is that, ontologically, there is such a thing as probabilistic causation.[163]

12.3   In order to move on, I must make some foundational points. Scientific explanations justify events and must therefore show those events to comply with natural laws.[164]

Justification is a relationship that holds between propositions, not between facts. Facts don't *bear* on anything. (That is, they don't bear on other things in a logical or confirmational sense. They obviously bear on them in a causal sense.)

Propositions consist of concepts. Facts consist of objects and, therefore, of instances of first-order concepts. A (non-analytic) proposition is a conceptualization or, as we might also say, a propositionalization of a given fact. A given fact admits of indefinitely

---

163. Incidentally, John von Neumann's proof that the introduction of hidden variables could not make quantum physics be deterministic was shown, by Bell (1957) and Bohm (1958), to establish that quantum physics could not be made *epistemically* deterministic, it being left open by von Neumann's proof whether it could still ontologically deterministic.

164. I do not believe that this is all that is involved; indeed, I myself hold that our knowledge of laws are based on our knowledge of mini-explanations – we know about the inverse-square law only because we *already* know that my releasing the pencil caused it to drop.

many propositionalizations. I walk across the room. The mass-energy displacements constitutive of that fact are necessary and sufficient for the truth of each of many different kinds of propositions – atomic, chemical, physiological, psychological.

Two propositions, P_1 and P_2, can hold in virtue of the very same fact, and yet be such that neither has the slightest explanatory bearing on the other. It may be that for each psychological truth that holds in virtue of my deliberately walking across the room there is a corresponding biochemical truth. But *chemical reaction xyz occurred* isn't in any obvious way explanatorily relevant to *JMK felt it in his professional interest to stampede in a visibly angry fashion across the room.*

12.4   Scientific disciplines presumably aspire to identify truths. But their first objective must be to model data; for it is only through data that truths can be known. There must therefore be a way of evaluating the fitness of a model without knowing whether it is true; for we cannot know what the truth is without first knowing whether that model is a good one.

Disciplines consist of propositions, not of facts. Those propositions, when true, hold in virtue of facts. But they are not themselves facts. The proposition *the gray rock has a larger mass than the blue* is different from the *fact* that the *ceteris paribus* more energy is needed to displace the first rock by a given amount than the second. As previously stated, propositions consist of concepts, not of (spatiotemporal) objects. A scientific discipline is an attempt to model a certain body of data. Data can be thought of as propositions (truths[165]).

Disciplines are individuated primarily by the *data* that they aspire to model, and only secondarily, if at all, by the truths underlying those data.[166] Dogs and plants are physical objects and no more fall outside the scope of physics than rocks. But biology and botany are not physics. How is this possible? Biological data is not physical (physics-related) data. Strictly speaking, it isn't dogs whose behavior falls within the scope of physical laws: it is the dog-constitutive particle-heaps that do so. Such heaps aren't dogs, since the heap can undergo change (redistributions of its constituents) without the dog's undergoing any (biologically meaningful, dog-relevant) change. Thus, *qua* dog-constituting heaps, those heaps fall within the scope of biology, not of physics. *Qua* mere (non-dog-constituting) heaps, they don't fall within the scope of biology, belonging exclusively to physics.

To model propositions is to systematize them in such a way that their bearing relations on one another are identified and appropriately organized. Propositions about facts are exceedingly crude representations of those facts. Consider the proposition:

---

165. They're truths of a non-conceptual, non-propositional kind. But that subtlety can and should be ignored here, since what matters is that data, unlike non-representations (e.g. rocks), are things to which the concept of accuracy (truthfulness) applies, and data are therefore relevantly proposition-like.

166. See Chapter 21 of Kuczynski (2010).

(*)   JM walked across the room.

(*), though true, tells us nothing about the myriad atomic, chemical, and physiological events in virtue of which (*) is true. Propositions consist of tendentious conceptualizations of bodies of data: of inquiry-driven over-consideration of certain aspects of those data and under-consideration of other aspects of them. So it is inherent in what propositions are that they leave out facts. Those facts are often causally relevant. But they cannot always fit into the system propositions constitutive of a given discipline. The generalizations constitutive of disciplines are constructed of concepts under which those facts may not fall. Therefore, the law (or principles, if you prefer) constituting those disciplines may not acknowledge the existence of those causally efficacious factors. So, explanatorily speaking, those factors may not exist, even though, ontologically speaking, they do exist.

Science, so it is often said, has no interest in what is not operational. Since a particle's momentum and position cannot simultaneously be determined, the concept of simultaneous momentum and position is without scientific significance.[167] Assuming this principle correct, then events that, ontologically speaking, are causally efficacious are, explanatorily speaking, non-existent; a consequence of which, as we've seen, is that, at least from a discipline-internal (explanatory) standpoint, such causes don't exist; which, in its turn, establishes our claim that (epistemically speaking) there is probabilistic causation and that "the principle of sufficient reason" is false. More precisely, it establishes, or suggests, that its false on its epistemic, not its ontological, disambiguation.

13.0   A doctrine known as "behaviorism" is perhaps the ugliest embodiment of the resolution compatibilize psychology with the empiricist belief that to explain a sequence of events is to identify a regularity of which it is an instance.

Behaviorism is the doctrine that mental states are identical with body-movements: a searing pain is identical with the body-movements which we'd ordinarily misidentified as its effects.[168]

Behaviorism is false: surely nobody ever *actually* thought otherwise. But many scholars felt that they had no choice but to advocate behaviorism, their personal reservations about it notwithstanding, since they accepted each of the following propositions:

(1)   Mental states *qua* private entities are not fit objects for scientific research and therefore don't exist as far as science is concerned.

---

167. I am not alone in rejecting this. Kripke (unpublished lecture), Ernest Nagel (1962), and Einstein (1956) himself all reject it. Einstein: "God doesn't roll the dice."

168. Watson (1924), Skinner (1948).

(2)   All sciences are either identical with physics or are watered down versions of physics.

and

(3)   DN is correct.

(1) and (2) are closely related. So far as scholars accepted (2), it was because they didn't see that explanation involves data modeling, and, consequently, because they didn't see that it was *only* to the extent that adequate models apprise us of data-transcendent facts that explanation is identical with the identification of such facts.

Had behaviorists seen that science is in the business of data-modeling, they would have known that they could understand psychological truths on their own terms, and that they were under no scientific obligation to conditionalize their acceptance of a given psychological proposition on its being capable of being absorbed into physics.

By the same token, since behaviorists didn't see these things, they believed that psychology was only as legitimate as it was capable of being absorbed into physics; and they believed, probably rightly, that psychology could be absorbed into physics *only* if psychology identified mental entities with overt behaviors.

As for (3): We've seen time and again how inapplicable DN is to the explanation of propositions composed of psychology-specific concepts (e.g. *desire for money, fear of disinheritance*). Some people (rightly) rejected DN for this reason; others (wrongly) took it to mean that psychological explanation is *sui generis*; and behaviorists took it to mean that psychology should study body-movements, since (so they thought) explanations of body-movements conform to DN and (so they thought) such explanations are genuinely scientific – unlike the, as we saw, inherently open-ended, probabilistic "explanations" of non-behavioristic psychologists.

13.1   The behaviorist rightly says:

(WB[169])   We shouldn't put too much stock uncorroborated testimony of the man wearing the tin-foil hat who claims to have seen flying saucers. That said, if other people make similar allegations, and they do so independently of that man, then perhaps the man was telling the truth and it might be worth it for scientists to investigate these allegations.

But in saying that, absent any corroboration, the eccentric man's testimony deserves no credence, the behaviorist is conceding that this individual's reportage is indicative of mental activity and, consequently, that behaviorism is false.

For the behaviorist, the supreme methodological maxim is: *it exists if the public can know about it and not otherwise*. But the *raison d'être* for this maxim is that, lest we foolishly accept as truth what is in fact the product of delusion or insincerity; lest we let rogues and madmen lead us about by the nose with their fairy tales; we shouldn't

---

169.   Short for "what behaviorism says."

put too much stock in a single, uncorroborated allegation. So the publicity-criterion ("don't believe if it can't be publicized") is meant to be a bulwark against insanity and fraud and thus very much presupposes the existence of the mental.

13.2   Given their acceptance of the claim that:

(SP[170]) *to the extent that mental entities exist*, they are identical with dispositions to engage in certain overt behaviors,

behaviorists had no choice but to hold that:

(LR[171]) For one to have a command of the English language is for one to have various behavioral dispositions, e.g. a disposition to say (produces the noises) "very well, thank you" upon hearing "how are you?"

According to behaviorists, thought cannot mediate between stimulus and response. So these dispositions are purely reflexive, like a knee jerk. Obviously these reflexes are not mediated by inborn mechanisms: people aren't *born* being disposed to say "very well, thank you" upon hearing "how are you?" At the same time, if behaviorism is to be correct, nothing cognitive can be involved in the acquisition of those reflex-mechanisms. So the behaviorist must conclude, and always does, that it is through *operant condition* that one develops the set of reflex-mechanisms that, in the behaviorist's view, constitute one's grasp of a language. In other words, it is through a regimen of the very same kind that Pavlov used to get his dog to salivate upon hearing the sound of a bell.

LR is untenable. There are many reasons for this. First, as Chomsky (1959) points out, one consequence of LR, coupled with the points below it, is that if a suitably conditioned person hears "how are you doing?," one will *reflexively* bark out "very well, thank you." But this isn't so. To use Chomsky's rather more vivid example, when one sees a fire, one doesn't bark out "fire! fire! fire!", even though this is precisely what we must do if LR is right.

And as Chomsky also points out, many of the expressions we use are ones that we've either never heard, or have heard only a few times, but understand instantly and produce without hesitation when necessary. This shows, first, that it isn't through operant conditioning that language is learned and, second, that our responses to linguistic stimuli embody the deployment of mechanisms of a *cognitive* nature that are not acquired through experience. Those mechanisms must be pre-experiential, since they cannot (without rendering LN viciously regressive) be learned. ("Pre-experiential" doesn't mean the same thing as "inborn," since the structures subserving a given cognitive function could obviously come into existence post-utero.) And those

---

170. Short for "scientific psychology."

171. Short for "language, reflex."

mechanisms are *cognitive*, since they mediate behavior that can't be understood in terms of the specificities of one's perceptual experience and is clearly principle-driven.

To illustrate the last point: The syntactic rule governing the word "since" is extremely intricate; but a child has to hear it used but once or twice to use it unerringly. Obviously the child's use of it is hewed, not to the color of the shirt of the person he heard using it, or the timbre of that person's voice, or to any other context-specific "noise" (in the information-theoretic sense of the word). The child's use of it reflects his knowing *a priori*, at the time of his hearing the two or so occurrences of it that he heard before knowing its meaning, just what it was about those occurrences that was relevant to how the word "since" should be used. This means that what the child learns from experience is structured by a pre-experiential knowledge of how situations must be understood if they are to yield useful information.

Our ability to use those expressions that we have heard obviously doesn't result from operant condition. I know how to use the word "law." This is, of course, in part because I've heard that word used. But it isn't because of operant conditioning that I use it correctly. The requisite conditioning-regimen couldn't possibly exist. One can't be operantly conditioned to use an expression correctly unless the circumstances in which it is right to use it are perceptibly different from those in which it is wrong to use it. For me to be operantly conditioned to use the word "law" correctly, there would have to some observable property P such it would be correct to use that word in a given environment just in case that environment had P. But there is no such property. Whether a given usage of the word "law" is correct depends on the discursive, not the physical context. Since there's nothing perceptible that distinguishes contexts where one can, from those where one cannot, use the word "law" appropriately, there is no way to operantly condition a person to use that word correctly.

14.0   There is another problem with behaviorism. How a person reacts to a given physical stimulus is a function, not just of the nature of that stimulus, but also of what is in that person's mind. If I have a $100,000 in Smith's house, whereas you have no money there and also hate Smith, I'll react one way to the sound "Smith's house is burning down" and you'll react differently. So attempts to reduce mental states to overt behaviors end up reducing them to overt behaviors *plus mental states*: thus, what was supposed to be reduced hasn't been.

To remedy this problem, a doctrine known as "functionalism" was put forth. It was wrongly taken for granted that functionalism is not identical with behaviorism.

Functionalism is the doctrine that, for any mental type M, and any entity x, it is solely in virtue of what x's causes and effects are that x falls into M, if it does so fall, or fails to fall into M, if it does so fail.

If your intention is to get into law school, you're likely to do certain things: study for the LSAT, send off applications to various law schools, etc. And your intention is not likely to come out of nowhere: it probably resulted from a high degree of ambition, from your having certain aptitudes, a certain sense of right and wrong, and, importantly, your being raised in a culture in which, given those attributes, the law is a desirable profession. (I stress that I am merely expounding functionalism here, not arguing for it. I don't think an intention to go law school has any one sort of cause, and I think, as I'll explain, that this is a problem for functionalism.)

Functionalism is the doctrine that if *anything* has the requisite causes and the requisite effect, it is *ipso facto* an instance of the mental kind in question. If x is your intention to go law school, it isn't in virtue of anything intrinsic to x, it is in virtue of what x's origins are and what its consequences are; it is, in other words, in virtue of x's "causal role."

14.1   Among the causes of your going to law school are mental entities: ambition, a desire to have a job of a certain type, etc. And mental entities (e.g. happiness at being wealthy, remorse at defending a serial killer) will be among the effects of that intention.

In general, mental entities are among the causes and effects of mental entities. This means that functionalism hasn't in any way eliminated mental entities. But functionalism is meant to explain how the mental arises out of, and can be reduced to, the physiological. The *raison d'être* for functionalism lies in the (supposed) fact that, without denying the obvious fact that mental entities exist, it good a job as behaviorism of reducing the mental to the physical.

David Lewis (1970) saw this problem and proposed a solution:[172]

(LF[173])   Let $M_1 \ldots M_n$ be a list of every type of mental state. And, for each i, let $S_{i1} \ldots S_{im}$, be an exhaustive list of sentences describing the causes and the effects of instances of S_1. Any mental entity will have both physical and purely psychological causes and effects. So being hit on the heat is caused by something physical and leads to various physical things (overt retaliatory behaviors). So if S_1 will contain terms referring to overt physical inputs and outputs as well, probably, terms referring other mental entities. For each one relevant types of causes and effects, produce a sentence saying that its instances are prone to bring about, or be caused by, instances of being hit on the heat. Consolidate all of the resulting sentences into one big passage Z. (Z doesn't have to be a conjunction. It just has to be a single discourse.) Z will say, for any given type of mental entity, what the causes and effects are of its instances.

For reasons previously stated, Z will contain constant terms that refer to mental states, and it will also contain terms that refer to physical states. For sentence S that is a constituent of Z, replace each occurrence of a term referring to (a kind of) mental state with a variable, taking care to use the

---

172.   Lewis (1966, 1970, 1972, 1980). See also Ramsey (1929, 1929b). Also see the chapter titled "the Ramsey Sentence" in Carnap (1966).

173.   Short for "Lewisian functionalism."

same variable for each such kind. The result will be an open sentence or, equivalently, a sentence-form i.e. it will be an expression that contains free variables but is otherwise just like a sentence (e.g. "x + 2 = 5"). Then *bind* the free variables appropriately. In other words, prefix that open sentence with a quantifier (e.g. "for all x," "for some y,"), thereby forming a closed or *bona fide* sentence. (Different quantifiers will have to be used in different cases.) The result will be a sentence S* that contains no terms referring to physical inputs and outputs, but no terms referring to mental entities. The latter will have been replaced with variables. (So instead of "pain causes one to scream," we are left with "there is some x such that x causes one to scream.") Do the same thing *mutatis mutandis* for each sentence occurring in Z. Let Z* be the resulting sentence. Z* will completely describe the human psyche without using a single term that refers to anything mental; every term in Z will refer to physical inputs or outputs. In this way, it is widely held, Lewis has done (i) reduced the mental to the physiological while (ii) doing justice to the fact, to which behaviorism did not do justice, that how one behaves is often times a function of one's mental condition, and not just of one's physical situation. Z* is sometimes referred to as the "Ramsey-Lewis" sentence ("RL" for short). (Frank Ramsey invented the just-described device (*eliminate occurrences of unwanted terms, replace with variables, bind with appropriate quantifiers*) that Lewis used. Ramsey's purpose, however, was to reduce statements about theoretical entities to statements about observables.)

Lewisian functionalism isn't just *a* form of functionalism. It is the only form of functionalism that isn't viciously circular.[174] Functionalism is given by the conjunction of the following contentions:

(i)   x's causal role (what causes it/what it causes), and nothing else, determines to what mental type, if any, x belongs; there is nothing to being a belief that arithmetic is incomplete or an intention to be President besides having certain antecedents and consequents;

(ii)   Among the causes or effects of any instance of any given mental type are physical entities (as in, physical entities of the sort that don't mediate mental activity, e.g. blows to the cranium, overt body movements);

(iii)   Among the causes or effects of any instance of any given mental type are other mental entities;

And

---

174.   Behaviorism is a form of functionalism. But we're setting aside, since we've seen that it's untenable.

(iv)   Given (i)–(iii), the existence of the mental can explained in terms of the existence of the physical *while* doing justice to the fact that mental entities cause
or are caused by other mental entities.

But, as Lewis saw, (iv) does *not* follow from the conjunction of (i)–(iii) *unless* one
"Ramsifies out" all mention of mental entities in one's description of the non-mental
causes and effects of mental entities. So Lewisian functionalism *is* functionalism.

14.2   Question: What sort of circumstances that would prompt one to say:

(GI[175])   "I suppose that's a good idea, but I'll have to think about it first."

Answer: Circumstances in which the speaker has certain beliefs, doubts, preferences,
etc. He wants to accept the invitation just tendered, but is worried about the consequences of doing so. He doesn't want to accept that invitation, but doesn't want to
decline it in an overly-direct fashion. Etc.

In general, those circumstances are ones in which the speaker has certain beliefs,
doubts, desires, etc. (This is a tautology: no matter what they sound like, bursts of
noise aren't speech if they don't have psychological causes.)

There are obviously infinitely many possible reasons why one might utter those
words. Thus, there is no finite list of stimuli that could lead one to utter GI.

If each sentence in Z were of finite length, Lewis's proposal might work. Suppose
that sadness had just (say) 567 causes, that an intention to run for Senate had just 123
causes, and so on. In that case, the lists of possible causes and effects of instances of a
given type of mental state would be finite and could therefore just be listed.

But those lists are not finite and must be identified intensionally, i.e. in terms of
some property peculiar to all the items on that list; and in these intensional definitions, the term being defined is defined in terms of mentalistic concepts. There is no
type of mental entity whose instances are such that *both* their causes *and* their effects
fail to include something mental. It may be that certain kinds of pain only have physical causes. But those kinds of pain have all kinds of mental effects. Similarly, it may
be that certain mental states (e.g. an intention to punch) has only physical effects; but
such states have all kinds of physical causes.

So RL is a surd: there is no such sentence, because the recursive definitions needed
to identify the relevant classes are loaded with the very terms, these being mentalistic
terms, that it is RL's purpose to eliminate.

14.3   There is another problem with RL. If RL is right, mental states do nothing. Let
x be the physiological structure mediating an intention to become a lawyer. And let's
suppose that Lewisian Functionalism (or any other kind, for that matter) is correct. In
that case, it isn't in virtue of being an intention to become a lawyer that x leads its host

---

175.   Short for "good idea."

to take the LSAT, etc. Rather, its simply that x *does* lead that person to take the LSAT and, in virtue of *that* fact (and others like it), qualifies an intention to become a lawyer. So it isn't that, by virtue of being an intention to become a lawyer, x has such and such effects. It's that x happens to have such and such effects and, having had them, *then* qualifies as an intention to become a lawyer. So x, though caually efficacious *qua* physiological entitity, is causally impotent *qua* mental entity.

Functionalists can't say: "It is x's being an intention to be a senator that brings about thus and such." For functionalism, x, *qua* mental thing, must do nothing. For if, *qua* mental thing, x is potent, then for that very reason x's being an intention to run for Senator doesn't consist in x's having a certain causal role. Rather, x's having that causal role merely reflects x's being such that *qua* intention to run for Senator, it has certain causal virtues.

So functionalism strips the mental of efficacy. It doesn't deny that mental entities exist. But it says that the physiological structures with which such entities are identical are not causally potent *as* mental entities. *As* physiological structures, they are causally potent; but *as* mental entities, they are nullities, causally speaking.

But anything spatiotemporal that lacks causal powers *ipso facto* doesn't exist.[176] So functionalism is just behaviorism all over again. This was temporarily obscured by the fact that it was merely supposed, totally implausibly, that, for each mental states, there was some finite list of possible causes and effects of instances of that state. But this isn't true, and given any such list, at least some of the properties that a thing must have to be on the list are psychological.

14.4   In this section, "physical" means "physics-related," except when it the context makes it unambiguous that it is to be taken in its usual, more generic sense. So, with that qualification, atoms are "physical," but hearts and kidneys are not.

The objections to functionalism that we've made thus far are of a technical nature. But there is a substantive, non-technical respect in which functionalism is wrong-headed, which we will now identify.

Functionalism embodies the view that the mind must be reduced to be understood. We've already seen why, in general, disciplines cannot be reduced to other disciplines. But there is a difference in this respect between biology, for example, and psychology. Physicalizing the biological (were it possible) wouldn't involve obliterating it. Physicalizing the psychological *would* involve obliterating it.

Disciplines consist of truths. There are two kinds of truths: data and theoretical truths, the latter being propositions whose acceptance the data warrants. Let B be an arbitrary biological truth, e.g.

(SA[177]) Smith is having an asthma attack.

---

176. Fodor (1968) makes this point.

177. Short for "asthma attack."

Brown is a physician who personally witnesses Smith's attack, let us suppose. So Brown has observations $o_1...o_m$ that SA correctly models, and that is why he accepts SA. But SA isn't the only correct model of $o_1...o_m$. There is some physical proposition that equally adequately models those observations, namely:

(PB[178])   in sub-regions $r_1...r_m$ of R, objects $o_1...o_o$, having masses $m_1...m_o$, are moving with velocities $v_1...v_o$ [etc.]

for the appropriate values of $r_1...r_m$, etc.

Green is a physicist who doesn't know anything about physiology or medicine. Green has observations, $o^*_1...o^*_m$, that are content-identical with Brown's. This means that, if $c_1...c_m$ are the respective contents of $o_1...o_m$, they are also the respective contents of $o^*_1...o^*_m$. SA and PB are models of the same data. (Any perspective-related differences between these two sets of observations are irrelevant, since SA is no less a good a model of $o^*_1...o^*_m$ than PB, and PB is no less a good a model of $o_1...o_m$ than SA).

Disciplines model data. Data are truths. Smith and Green are modeling the same truths. "But that's not true," it will be objected. "Smith is modeling truths involving concepts such as *labored breathing* that are no part of the truths that Green is modeling."

What Smith sees is some object moving about in certain ways, producing certain noises, undergoing chromatic changes of certain kinds, etc. And that is just what Brown sees. The concept of respiration is internal to the lower echelons of Brown's model of the data. Supposing that $d_1...d_m$ are the respective contents of $o^{(*)}_1...o^{(*)}_m$, and $p_1...p_m$ are the respective contents of $d_1...d_m$, $p_1...p_m$ are to the effect that, in a certain place. So there is some one set of truths, namely $p_1...p_m$ such that each of SA and PB models those truths.

Bearing this in mind, let $t_1...t_m$ be any collection of psychological data. t_i, for arbitrary i ($1 \leq i \leq m$), is to the effect that one is in pain, or that one is seeing a giraffe (or, in any case, having a giraffe-type perception), or that one is appalled at Lester for plagiarizing his dissertation. As a materialist, I believe that the *facts* in virtue of which such feelings, etc. exist are in the same space-time as those in virtue of which SA and PB are true. But $t_1...t_m$ do not present those facts *as* being in the same coordinate system as the one that contains R. So $t_1...t_m$ do not coincide with $p_1...p_m$. By obvious generalizations of this line of thought, *no* body of psychological data coincides with *any* body of physical (or physiological or chemical, etc.) data.

Green and Smith model the same truths in different ways. Any two physical scientists model the same truths in different ways. But there are no psychological data $T_1...T_m$ that so much as overlap with any physical (physics-related, chemistry-related, etc.) data $P_1...P_m$.

---

178. Short for "physical basis (of said asthma attack)."

What the practitioner of a discipline knows, he knows only through the data that it is his discipline's purpose to model. Objectively speaking, the facts modeled by psychology are the same as (a subset of) those modeled by physics. But *epistemically* speaking, the one set of facts doesn't even overlap with the other. At the same time, speaking both objectively *and* epistemically, the facts modeled by any one physical science coincide with (or are of the same basic kind as) those modeled by any other such science.

So, in both the epistemic and the objective sense of the word "fact," the physiologist and the physicist are given the same facts to work with, even though they part ways when modeling those facts. But, in the epistemic sense of the word "fact," the facts that the psychologist has to work with don't even overlap with those that the physicist (or physiologist or chemist etc.) has to work with. And it's the epistemic sense of the word "fact" that's the operative one; for facts are science-relevant only to the extent that are knowable or bear on what we know. Unalterably "noumenal," data-transcendent facts do not fall within the scope of science.

Epistemically speaking, physics and physiology model the same facts. So even though neither can be reduced to the other, the two can be *reconciled*. For both are theoretical superstructures that converge on some one set of facts. *What* the two disciplines are studying is the same. *How* they study it is different.

But psychology and physics don't converge on *any* one set of facts. What they're studying is different (except relative to a non-epistemic, science-irrelevant interpretation of the phrase "what they are studying"), and not just how they're studying it. So not only can psychology not be reduced to physics (or physiology, etc.); the two disciplines cannot integrated even in the weakest conceivable way. It's as though the psychologist and the physicist inhabited two different realms. There is an "explanatory gap," to use Joseph Levine's expression.

14.4.1   "But surely you are wrong," it will be said. "The data of astronomy don't overlap with those of zoology."

Yes. But that's not relevant. What's relevant is that the *kind* of data modeled by the one discipline is of the same basic kind as that modeled by the other. There is some one coordinate system CS such that the data modeled by each are to the effect that such and such mass-energy displacements are occurring in CS. To be sure, the *specific* displacements studied by astronomy don't overlap with those studied by zoology. But they study different propositions belonging to different sub-species of some one species. They study the same kinds of truths, though not the same *sub*-kinds.

"But there is another problem with what you've said," it will be said. "For there is likely to be to be some i $(1 \leq i \leq m)$ such that t_i is to the effect that somebody is engaging in overt behavior of some kind, e.g. that Larry is throwing furniture about."

Not true. In Chapter 1, we saw why this must be so. *Prima facie* Larry's throwing furniture about is a psychological datum. But even though it is *a* datum and even though it is psychology-*relevant*, it is not itself a psychological datum. It's a datum for physics, not for psychology; for the latter, it's a significant truth that isn't a datum. This is because the relevance of Larry's behavior to psychology is contingent on its being driven by forces that are correctly described by truths $l_1...l_m$ that are either known (or to be known) introspectively or that model introspectively known/knowable truths. If it turns out that Larry is a zombie or a robot, the fact that he's throwing furniture around (etc.) *ipso facto* ceases to be of any concern to psychology, showing that it is itself one of the data that psychology must model. It corresponds to a *truth* that psychology must model. But that truth is not that:

(LF[179]) Larry is throwing furniture about (etc.)

It is rather that:

(LF*) Larry is throwing furniture around (etc.) and the causes of his behavior are correctly described by truths known directly or indirectly through introspection.

14.5   There are two senses in which psychology is irreducible to physics (or any physical science). It's irreducible to the latter in the generic sense in which biology and every other physical science is irreducible to physics; and it's irreducible in the deeper and more specific sense that, in the epistemic sense of the word "fact," the facts psychology models aren't the facts that physics models.

Functionalism embodies an ignorance of both facts. The reason: it overlooks the model-internal (or, equivalently, the data-relative) nature of explanation. It wrongly assumes that if psychological *facts* (in the objective sense of the word) are shown to be a subset of physical *facts* (same qualification), then psychological truths *ipso facto* fall within the scope of physical theory. Because functionalism fails to take into account the model-internal nature of explanation, it is perforce blind to the very obvious fact that it is propositions, not objects, that are the *relata* of explanations. And because functionalism is blind to this, it is also blind to both of the senses in which the psychological is irreducible to the non-psychological.

Also, functionalism is guilty of a rather ugly hypocrisy. It's supposed to be different from behaviorism, in that, unlike the latter, it acknowledges the existence of the mental. But it's a veritable tautology that functionalism doesn't acknowledge the existence of the mental. Functionalism is by definition the doctrine that the mental is *whatever it is* that mediates between non-mental input and outputs in the right way. This means that, as far as functionalism is concerned, there is nothing distinctively psychological about the psychological: a person's mind might as well be a heap of pork and beans, so long as that heap mediates between input and output in the right way. If the functionalist says that there is more to the mind than this, he is saying it isn't in virtue of a thing's causal role that it is a mind; in which case he is rejecting functionalism. Thus, the functionalist cannot coherently distinguish his position from

---

179. Short for "Larry, furniture."

behaviorism, and we've already seen why the obvious spuriousness of that doctrine redounds to the discredit of empiricism.

15.0   Let us distill the contents of the previous sections into a form that makes their methodological ramifications clear.

It is a datum that there are psychological data. It may be that there are no models of that data that can be assimilated into the data-models yielded by physics. But it's the scientist's job to model the data that he's given. It is *not* his job to prejudge the significance of that data. A scientist's suspicion that there is no physics-friendly way to model psychological data is not a good reason to deny the existence of such data.

Many have thought otherwise. But their position is true only *relative* to the *a priori*, and therefore non-empirical, assumption that physics is the only legitimate discipline.

Ironically, this *a priori* belief is an embodiment of empiricism. To be sure, we *do* have knowledge of our own minds, and that knowledge is empirical. But it is not empirical in a way that validates empiricism: one has direct knowledge of the fact that one is imagining a transistor radio; but that knowledge, though direct, is *theoretical*. It involves having second-order concepts, e.g. the concept of the concept of a radio, the concept of the concept of a perception. The conceptual machinery needed to mediate intelligent awareness of one's conscious mental states cannot ultimately have an empirical basis. *A fortiori* the same holds of one's awareness of the contents of one's pre-conscious, one's personal unconscious, and one's subpersonal unconscious.

Empiricists therefore have no choice but to turn a blind eye to the deliverances of introspection. And that is just what they do; and by their own admission, they do it for the reason just given. Daniel Dennett (1990) denies the existence of consciousness. He defends his position by saying, first, that

(a)   many an *a priori* assumption is embedded in our lay-beliefs about the contents of our own minds

and, on this basis, saying that

(b)   minds don't exist.

(a) is correct. (b) is not. But Dennett is an empiricist; and, relative to an acceptance to empiricism, (b) is *de rigueur*, given (a).

Paul Churchland (1984) accepts this line of thought and thus denies that we have beliefs, intentions, etc.

Of course, it's unempirical to turn a blind eye to empirical data, and psychological data is about is as empirical as data can be. At the same time, Dennett and Churchland are, in a way, being true to empiricism in denying the existence of such data. To their credit, they deny that the things I'm describing as "data" are in fact data, and they thus do as good as a job as possible of compatibilizing empiricism with the distinctively empiricist view that minds don't exist.

The problem is that *all* data is as theory-heavy as psychological data. I couldn't begin to describe what I'm seeing right now without assuming the truth of many a theory. (And this is for the non-trivial reasons given earlier, not for the trivial reason that some of the entities I'd be describing, e.g. my computer, are by-products of theoretical innovations.) A consequence is that, if Dennett and Churchland are right about psychological data, they are also right about perceptual data: the latter aren't really data, they must say, since they are theoretically committed. So Dennett and Churchland are guilty of a doubly-incoherent view: they accept empiricism while denying empirical psychological facts and while also implicitly denying empirical non-psychological facts. And this double-incoherence is the consequence of their views' being truer to empiricism than that of many other empiricists. Because they are empiricists, Dennett and Churchland cannot be coherent without being incoherent.

16.0   Throughout this book, we've insisted that it is only by data-modeling that we acquire theoretical knowledge.

Ironically, this position is one that empiricists are more likely to advocate than rationalists. Rationalists tend to claim that, when properly done, science identifies truths. Empiricists tend to claim that, when properly done, science generates useful suppositions whose correspondence to the truth can never be authenticated. "There really *are* electrons," says the rationalist. "Maybe," responds the empiricist. "But all we're entitled to say is that the data is usefully organized by supposing that there are electrons."

It's generally taken for granted that these two positions cannot be reconciled. But they can be reconciled. To see why, we must sensitize ourselves to a subtle distinction. Consider the following two sentences:

(i)   For any n you choose, it is possible that, by coincidence, Smith throws heads n times in a row

(ii)   It is possible that, by coincidence, for any n you choose, Smith throws heads n times in a row.

(i) and (ii) make different statements. (i) is true. (ii) is incoherent. If it's supposed that, for any n, a coin tossed n times in a row by Smith lands heads all n times, it is *ipso facto* supposed that Smith is a mechanism that guarantees a certain output (a heads-toss) given a certain input (a coin toss). If Smith is such a mechanism, it's not a matter of coincidence that coins tossed by him always land heads; and it's *only* if Smith (or some Smith-involving entity) is such a mechanism that it can justifiably be asserted that, for any n, n consecutive tosses that he makes will be heads-tosses.

Bearing these points in mind, consider the following pair of sentences:

(1) For any n you choose, it is possible that, by coincidence, models M and M*
(M ≠ M*) model data $o_1 \ldots o_n$ equally well.

(2) It is possible that, by coincidence, for any n you choose, models M and M*
(M ≠ M*) model data $o_1 \ldots o_n$ equally well.

(1) is unambiguously true. But (2) is incoherent. For any given n, it can be a coincidence that M and M* both model $o_1 \ldots o_n$. But it can't be a coincidence that, for any n,
M and M* both model $o_1 \ldots o_n$.

It can be a coincidence that two models agree with respect to some frozen body
of data. It cannot be a coincidence that they agree with respect to some ever-growing
body of data. One doesn't need to know of any principled connection between M and
M* to assert that they agree with respect to some pre-existing, finitely large body of
data. One *does* need to know of some such relationship to assert that they agree with
respect to an ever-growing, unbounded body of data.

What would one have to know to be justified in asserting that M and M* agree
with respect to some body of data *and also* with respect to any conceivable future
extensions thereof? Knowing that M is a logical transformation of M* would obviously
suffice. But in that case, M and M* are the same model, contrary to our supposition.

So one's grounds would have to be empirical. The fact that M and M* *have* agreed
thus far is not by itself a good reason to hold that they will always agree: it is a good
reason *only* to the extent that it corresponds to some link between M and M* that
guarantees that they will be in lockstep.[180] Thus, one has no reasonable assurance that
M and M* will remain in lockstep unless one has some *meta*-model M+ such that
(i) M+ saves the phenomena and such that (ii) a consequence of M+ is that M and
M* will indeed remain in lockstep. But if that condition is met, then M and M* are
superfluous: M+ has replaced both.

To sum up: There are only two good reasons to hold that M and M* will agree
with respect to future data:

(MM)   M and M are the same model

and

(MM*) Neither M nor M* is an operational model; some third model is doing what
they are supposed to do, and doing it better.

So (a) is wrong; and so therefore are (b) and (c). Given these points, the following
argument is clearly spurious:

(a) Any given body of data can modeled in a number of different, equally legitimate ways.

(b) We can pick the right model only if we know the truth.

---

180. This point will be clarified in the next chapter.

Therefore,

(c)   We can't pick the right model unless we have model-independent access to the truth.

Only empiricists put forth this argument, and most empiricists accept it.[181] And they must do so, for much the same reason they must be skeptics about sense-perception. (See Chapter 9, Sections 1.0–4.0.)

But (a) is false: we just saw that, unless a body of data is frozen, there is at most one model of it; and we've also seen that the data-bodies science models are not frozen. Since (a) is false, so are (b) and (c).

We're now in a position to show that, even though it's only by data-modeling that we can acquire scientific (theoretical, as opposed to strictly observational) knowledge, there is nothing that, for that reason, we cannot know.[182]

The objects of study are truths. So the objects of study are not facts, but relations between data and facts. When you study a heart (*qua* heart, not *qua* lump of molecules), you are not studying an object, as strange as that may sound; you are studying a relation holding between an object (a heap of molecules) and various data. If the objects of investigation were *things*, as opposed to relations of the sort just described, the objects of a botanist's investigations would form a proper subset of the objects of a microphysicist's investigations. But there is nothing that is the object of both botanical and microphysical scrutiny.

"But botanists *do* study the same things as microphysicists," it will be said. "The microphysicist studies the plant *qua* lump of molecules; the botanist studies the lump of molecules *qua* plant."

These *qua*-qualifications indicate that we don't study objects *simpliciter*, but objects *as understood or described in a certain way*. But this is merely a circuitous way of saying that we study truths *about* objects, truths being identical, not with facts, but with relations borne by data thereto.

Such relations are objective, and although they do not themselves fall within the scope of physics, one of the *relata* of any given instance of such a relation is something that does so fall. So to the extent that the objects of study involve mind-independent

---

181.   Quine (1977) states it a particularly clearly and effective manner. Berkeley (1710) was the first to state it, and since that time many greats have embraced it, e.g. Mill (1882), James (1910), and Pearson (1911).

182.   So far as there are things we cannot know, it isn't because knowledge-acquisition involves data-modeling; it's either because we don't have the intelligence or energy or longevity to model our perceptions or because can't have the requisite perceptions. (So far as we can't have the requisite perceptions, it's either for biological reasons (e.g. our physiological structure doesn't allow us to hear things the a bat does) or for strictly logical reasons (e.g. we can't know what we will in 20 years; since one must interact with the world to study it, the thing one ends up learning about is qualitatively different from the thing one sought out to learn about).

facts, those objects are consistent with the (propositions expressing) the laws of physics. But to the extent that the objects of study are truths, and therefore non-spatio-temporal entities, they are not themselves governed by the laws of physics. So hearts, plants, brains, and thoughts *are not governed by physical laws*. At the same time, they cannot fail to be *consistent* with such laws. This entails that attempts to physicalize psychology, or even biology, are doomed *ab initio*.

17.0   The term "behaviorism" is ambiguous. Sometimes it refers to the doctrine already critiqued. Sometimes it refers to the doctrine that it is solely through perception and operant conditioning that we learn. In this section, we'll use it to refer to the second doctrine.

Behaviorism *is* empiricism. According to empiricism, it's only through sense-perception that one learns. This is tantamount to saying that *ab initio* the mind is a blank slate. (Indeed, "blank slate," or "tabula rasa," is the very term Locke (1690), the first great empiricist, used to describe the mind's initial condition.) This in turn is tantamount to saying that it is only through sense-perception that the mind learns. And this is nothing other than behaviorism.

Not all knowledge is factual knowledge. There is also procedural knowledge (knowledge-how). Behaviorists must say that it is through operant conditioning that we acquire procedural knowledge. For they cannot say, as we'll now see, that it is through any one perception that one learns (for example) how to use the word "fire": and, it will be clear, what is true of one's ability to use that word is true of any any given instance of procedural knowledge.

How do you learn what "fire" means? "Through sense-perception," says the behaviorist; "you see fire while hearing utterances of the word 'fire.'"

Yes, but how do you know that "fire" isn't being used to refer to some accompaniment of the fire, e.g. the fire-place, the logs in the fire-place, or the photograph on the fire-place mantel.

"Because," says the behaviorist, "you hear utterances of "fire" on different occasions, in each of which there is fire but only in some of which there are fire-places or photographs. So you come to *associate* the word 'fire' with fire. In general, to have procedural knowledge is to have the right associative reflexes. The mechanisms subserving these reflexes are purely physiological; there is nothing cognitive about them."

"Is it an option," we might ask, "for the behaviorist to say that one learns the meaning of "fire" by hearing it uttered in the presence of fire *just once?*"

"It is not," the behaviorist rightly answers. "W. V. O. Quine (1960, 1974) made this clear. Even if, on the one occasion when you hear it used, the word 'fire' is in fact being used to refer to fire, you cannot rule out the possibility that it is being used to mean *thing that Skippy is roasting marshmallows with* or *thing that is now consuming Leonard's manuscript*. You can't rule out these possibilities unless you hear 'fire' being used in different contexts, such that, given any one of these alternate meanings of 'fire,' that word perceptibly doesn't bear that meaning in at least some of these contexts."

But can't we say that, because of how your mind is structured, you automatically exclude these alternate interpretations of "fire" and home in on the right one?

"*Given* our assumption that the mind is *ab initio* a blank slate, we cannot say this," the behaviorist correctly says. "To say that we are preternaturally capable of excluding erroneous interpretations of a given word is to say that we have *a priori* knowledge of what it makes sense to identify as the meaning of a given word-token. It can only be through repeated experiences of that word that we know what it means; it can only be through operant conditioning."

The behaviorist assumes that a being devoid of cognitive structure can have sense-perceptions. That is not the case. The photon-induced disturbances that elicit perceptions from you would elicit nothing from a rock. There are no perceptions in the rock to elicit.

"But nothing other than physiology mediates between those disturbances and the perceptions in which they eventuate. There is no reason to posit any intervening cognitive structures."

In Chapter 7, we considered this position and put forth two arguments to the contrary. Given the points made in Section 15.0, we can put forth a new and better version of the second argument.

Henceforth, mentally infill the obvious qualifications, e.g. "other things being equal," "setting aside performance-inhibiting factors," and so on.

Any given person will have only finitely many perceptions during his lifetime. But class of stimuli that would elicit accurate perceptions from him is infinitely large and infinitely varied. Thus, if K is the least inclusive class containing every type of stimulus whose instances would elicit accurate perceptions from a given person, K's membership is infinitely large and infinitely varied. A corollary is that, for any n, no matter how large, two people will have the same perceptual responses to n-many instances of the same perceptual stimuli. Another corollary is that each such perception will be veridical.

Since K is infinitely large, we're not dealing with a coincidence, but with a principled correspondence. In principle, and to at least some extent in actuality, mental types are "multiply realizable" with respect to physiological types. In other words, given any distinctively mental property P (e.g. the property of being a belief that snow is white), there need not be any physiological property P* such that all and only instances of P have P*. So if x and y are instances of some one mental type M, x and y, though both physiological entities, needn't bear any distinctively *physiological* resemblance to each other; and it is therefore possible that it is only *as* instances of M that x and y resemble each other. And given that K is infinitely large, it is impossible that x and y should resemble each other in any other way. Being infinitely large, K cannot be defined extensionally, that is, by listing its members. It must be defined intensionally, that is, by citing some property that all and only its members have; and that property is necessarily psychological, as we have seen.

Let us develop these points. Let K* be the class of perceptions brought about by members of K. K's members are infinitely varied, and so are K*'s; and the differences between any two members of K* are consistent with the differences between any two members of K. K*-differences track K-differences; and if K# is the smallest class whose membership contains every instance of this tracking relationship, K#'s membership is infinitely large and also, more importantly, infinitely diverse. In other words, the number of *types* of psychological differences instantiated by the members by K#'s members is infinite. There is thus no strictly *physiological* characterization of K#'s membership. There isn't *any* mental type all of whose instances are necessarily of the same physiological type. There is no physiological characterization of any mental property or *a fortiori* of the psychological *differences* between instances of any psychological property and instances of any other. There is thus no strictly physiological characterization of the mechanisms that assign members of K* to members of K. Those mechanisms must be understood in psychological terms.

Perception leads to knowledge. So the members of K* are knowledge-conducive. They wouldn't be knowledge-conducive unless their respective K-causes *justified* them. Though physiologically implemented, the mechanisms linking K-causes to their respective K*-effects are psychological in nature and thus operate by mediating ideation. That ideation embodies a sensitivity to relations of justification and is *ipso facto* ratiocinative. Being a precondition for sense-perception, the knowledge embodied in the just-mentioned mechanisms cannot itself be acquired through sense-perception and therefore cannot result from operant conditioning. Therefore behaviorism is false, and so is empiricism, since empiricism *is* behaviorism.

18.0　According to Carl Hempel (1966), the question "can psychology be absorbed into physiology?" is strictly empirical. In Hempel's view, future empirical findings might warrant either an affirmative or a negative answer to that question. This belief of Hempel's is to be understood in terms of his conception of what it is to reduce one discipline to another. Given any disciplines D and D*, Hempel believed, to reduce D to D* is to demonstrate that any given D-concept is co-extensive with some D*-concept; in other words, it is to show that:

(a)　given any D-concept C, there is some D*-concept C* such that C is instantiated just in case C* is instantiated.

Hempel rightly believed (a), assuming it true, to entail that:

(b)　Given any D-proposition P, there is some D*-proposition P* such that P* is true just in case P is true.

Hempel rightly believed (b), assuming it true, to entail that:

(c)   If K is any class of events that it is D's responsibility to explain, there is some class K* of events that it is D*'s responsibility to explain such that K-events are perfectly correlated with K*-events.

Finally, Hempel believed (c), assuming it true, to entail that:

(d)   D has been assimilated into D*, meaning either that, given D*, D's existence is superfluous – there is no reason for D to exist – or that D, though not superfluous, is nothing but a branch of D*.

Contrary to what Hempel believes, (c) does not entail (d), and the reason for this is obvious. If there is anything true that D can say that D* cannot say, D cannot be absorbed into D*; if there is some D-truth that isn't logically equivalent with any D*-truth, D is to that extent incapable of being reduced to D*. So if P is some D-truth to the effect that correlation x exists, and P* is some D*-truth to the effect that correlation y exists, D is incapable of being absorbed into D* unless P is a logical consequence either of P* or of some other D*-proposition. To the extent that P isn't such a consequence, there is something true about the world that D can say that D* cannot, it being of no relevance whether those two correlations can be correlated. Thus, Hempel was wrong to hold that D can be absorbed into D* if any given D-concept is co-extensive with some D*-concept.

Science has but one objective: to produce an accurate and complete description of reality. If there is some truth T that a given discipline is incapable of recognizing, that discipline is to that extent incapable of being replaced by one that does recognize T. Each of the last two statements is a platitude – an empty truism, whose negation is therefore an absurdity – and, given how acute Hempel was, it must be asked why he countenanced an analysis of interdisciplinary reduction is so flagrantly inconsistent with such obvious truths.

It is must therefore be asked why Hempel believed otherwise.

The answer is: Hempel was an empiricist; and because he was an empiricist, he was sometimes forced to deny the obvious, this being one of those times. Being a die-hard Humean variety, Hempel believed that to explain is to correlate. To explain events, Hempel believed, is to find first-order correlations. (To explain event x is to find an event y such that a y-similar event accompanies any given x-similar event.) To explain first-order correlations, Hempel believed, is to find second-order correlations. (To explain a correlation x is to find a correlation y such that an instance of y accompanies any given instance of x.) To explain psychological correlations, according to Hempel, is to correlate them with physiological correlations; therefore, Hempel concluded, psychology is capable of being absorbed into physiology to the extent that such second-order correlations exist.

We have considered Hempel's answer to the question "what is it to reduce one discipline to another?", and we have found that answer to be false. What is the correct answer to that question?

To say that one discipline D can be "reduced" to some other discipline D* is to say that there is nothing that D has to say about the world that D* cannot also say. If there is any reason to reduce D to D* it's because, in addition to being able to say whatever D can say, D* can say it better. For all intents and purposes, therefore, to say that D can be reduced to D* is to say that, if D can say it, D* can say it better; it is say, in other words, that, if P is some D-truth and P* is the corresponding D*-truth, P* is richer in information than P. To say that P* is richer in information than P is to say that, while otherwise coinciding with P in respect of the information it bears, P* is more precise than P and also that P* is a constituent of correct theories that yield more knowledge of the world than any theories of which P is a constituent. (There is a subtlety here. If P* is richer in information than P, then P and P* aren't the same proposition. So when it's said that "D* can say whatever D can say, and can say it better," what is really meant is: "given any D-truth P, there is some D*-truth P* such that P* contains more information about the world than P, and for that reason is qualitatively different from P, but, within the limits set by those facts, is as much like P as a proposition can be.") Thus, to say that psychology can be reduced to physiology is to say that, if psychology can say it, so can physiology, the implication being that physiology can also say it better than psychology. Thus, to the extent that there are psychological propositions that are not equivalent with physiological propositions, psychology cannot be absorbed into physiology; and, given any disciplines D and D*, to the extent that there are D-specific propositions that aren't logically equivalent with D*-specific propositions, D can't be absorbed into D*.

"If one discipline can recognize a truth that the other cannot," we said, "the first is to that extent incapable of being absorbed into the second." This is a truism, not a debatable hypothesis. Hempel might have rejected empiricism on the grounds that it led him to deny this truism, were it not for the fact that there seems to be a cogent, empiricism-independent reason to deny it. Heat is molecular motion. (A given body's temperature is a function of the mean kinetic energy of the molecules composing it.) But when a three-year old discovers that fire is hot, he isn't discovering anything about micro-events; and when a chef says that the pan is too hot to touch, he isn't saying anything about molecules. So far as S has the form "…heat…," it concerns the property to which the chef is referring, and it doesn't concern (or appears not to concern) that property so far as it has the form "…molecular motion…." There are (so let us suppose) laws governing the generation, loss, and redistribution of instances of the aforementioned perceptible property. (That supposition is coherent. In fact, it's approximately true.) Let L be an arbitrary one of those laws, and let P be a proposition to the effect that L holds. It turned out (so let us suppose) out that L holds in virtue of some other law L*, such that L* concerns the behavior of molecules. (This supposition, like the previous one, is approximately correct.) Let P* be a proposition to the effect that L* holds. There is obviously some sense in which somebody affirming P isn't saying the same thing as somebody affirming P*. The first person is talking about macrophenomena; the second is talking about microphenomena. Relative to the suppositions we've made, thermodynamics (the study of the perceptible phenomenon referred to as "heat") is reducible to statistical mechanics (the study of the micro-phe-nomena constituting that perceptible phenomenon). In point of fact, thermodynam-ics can (to a non-trivial extent) be reduced to statistical mechanics.

It used to be thought that thermodynamics was capable of being completely ab-sorbed into statistical mechanics. This turned out to fall short of the truth (see Horst 2006) – but only by a little. And given how close to the truth it is, the idea of assimi-lating thermodynamics into statistical mechanics is obviously a coherent one, and so, therefore, is the more general notion of absorbing one discipline into another. This seems to show that one discipline can be absorbed into another, even if neither says anything said by the other. We have insisted that D can't be absorbed into D* if there is so much as a single D-truth that isn't also a D*-truth. But in light of the points just made, this contention of ours seems positively preposterous, and Hempel probably regarded that contention as preposterous, given that he accepted those points.

Nonetheless, that contention of ours is correct. If it seems false, that's because one has either overlooked, or has failed to draw the consequences of, an important distinction, which was first made by Saul Kripke in 1969: the distinction between, to use Kripke's own terminology, "reference-fixing" and "meaning-giving." Consider the statement that

(1) Assuming there to be one object O such that O has memorized every line of everything of Shakespeare ever wrote, "Brump" refers to O

Compare (1) with the statement that

(2) "Brump" is synonymous with "someone (it doesn't matter who) having the property of being the one and only person to have ever memorized everything Shakespeare ever wrote."

Were it true, (1) would be a semantic rule, and the same is true of (2). Let us assume (2) is in fact a semantic rule, and let us also assume that "Brump" is unambiguous. In that case,

(3) "Brump weighs over 200 lbs"

has the same meaning as

(4) "there exists exactly one person who has memorized everything Shakespeare ever wrote, and that person weighs over 200 lbs."

In that case, therefore, one needn't have any idea as to the identity of the Shakespeare reader in question to know what (3) says about reality: to know what must be the case for (3) to be true, one needn't have any empirical knowledge, other than a knowledge of the semantic rules of the English language.

But now let us suppose that (1) is a semantic rule. (We will continue to suppose that "Brump" is unambiguous.) In that case, the statement:

(5) "To know what must be the case for (3) to be true – to know what (3) means, in other words – one needn't have any empirical knowledge, other than a knowledge of the semantic rules of the English language"

is ambiguous. To understand a sentence is to know what it means. Therefore,

(6) "One needn't have any empirical knowledge, other than a knowledge of the semantic rules of the English language, to understand (3)."

is ambiguous, and so is

(7) "M is the meaning of (3),"

for any value of "M" that validates it. In other words, (7) is ambiguous if M is a meaning that (3) bears. (7) is unambiguously false, but still ambiguous, if M is some meaning that (3) doesn't bear.

In each of the two scenarios we're about to consider, Jerry, and Jerry alone, has memorized everything that Shakespeare ever wrote. (Assume that the name 'Jerry' is unambiguous.)

First scenario: Smith speaks perfect English. (1) is a semantic rule of English. So "Brump" refers to Jerry. But Smith doesn't know that "Brump" refers to Jerry. (3)'s literal meaning is the proposition (henceforth, ""P") that Jerry weighs over 200lbs. Smith doesn't know that P is (3)'s meaning. To understand an expression is to know what it literally means. So there is obviously a sense in which Smith doesn't understand (3), and there is obviously a corresponding sense in which he doesn't know what "Brump" means. But there is obviously a sense in which he does know what "Brump" means, and there is a corresponding sense in which he understands (3). It is in the sense that he knows the identity of the semantic rule for "Brump" that he knows what it means, and it is in an exactly similar sense that he understands (3). It is in the sense that he doesn't know the identity of the object assigned to "Brump" by the former rule that he doesn't know what the expression means, and it is in the sense that he doesn't know the identity of the proposition assigned by the latter semantic rule to (3) that he doesn't understand that sentence. Smith's not knowing that proposition's identity is obviously a consequence of his not knowing that object's identity. (3) "fixes the referent" of "Brump," but it fails to "give the meaning" of that expression. (3) identifies the conditions that no referent of "Brump" can fail to satisfy and that any such referent cannot fail to satisfy. (3) therefore "fixes" the identity of that expression's referent. But (3) doesn't say who that referent is, and it thus fails to "give the meaning" of "Brump."

If someone knows that (3) is the semantic rule for "Brump," let us say that he "RF-knows" that word's meaning and that he "RF-understands" sentences of the form "…Brump…," setting aside sentences of that form that he doesn't understand for some other reason. If P is the proposition meant by a sentence of that form, and a given person knows that P is that sentence's meaning, let us say that "MG-understands" that sentence and that he knows the "MG-meaning" of that sentence as well as, consequently, the "MG-meaning" of the word "heat." ("MG" is short for meaning-giving.") Obviously a person can MG-understand an expression that he RF-understands.

An unambiguous expression has a single MG-meaning. But no expressions has a single RF-meaning. Given any object O, there are infinitely many properties that O uniquely has, and any expression E that refers to O has infinitely many possible RF-meanings. (In any case, supposing E to be an expression of language L, the number of E's RF-meanings is identical with the number of those of propositions that L can express.) But we will that a given unambiguous expression has but one RF-meaning. (This assumption is innocuous, since it is easily corrected for.)

Let X be a person who RF-understands an expression E that he doesn't MG-understand, and suppose that it is by virtue of associating proposition P with E that X understands E. (In other words, suppose that P is E's RF-meaning.) And let Y be someone who MG-understands E; and suppose that it is by associating P* with E that Y understands E. (In other words, suppose that P* is E's MG-meaning and, therefore, its meaning in the strictest possible sense.) P is distinct from the proposition P* that a person associates with E by virtue of MG-understanding it.

It is on the basis of our sensations that we first become aware of heat. We touch hot pans, or otherwise come into contact with hot objects, and we consequently have heat-sensations. Supposing that S is an arbitrary heat-sensation, the statement

(8)   The word "heat" refers to the cause of S-similar sensations (where an "S-similar" sensation is one that resembles S in the relevant respect)

is ambiguous, as it could mean either

(9)   There is some phenomenon O such that O is responsible for the occurrence of S-similar sensations, and "heat" refers to to O

or

(10)   Anything that causes that causes S-similar sensations is, for that very reason, the referent of the word "heat."

(9), not (10), is the correct disambiguation (8). Anything can be the cause of anything. Given some hot object O, there could be some species of creatures that didn't have S-similar sensations when touching O. (Take "hot" to have a precise meaning, a "hot" object being one whose temperature is at least n degrees Fahrenheit, for some value of n.) It obviously wouldn't follow that O was not hot. But that would follow if (10) were the correct disambiguation of (8).

"Heat" therefore refers to molecular motion. But there is more to say. (9) is not the semantic rule for "heat." To know what "heat" refers to, one doesn't have to have S-similar sensations. Gloxo is a Martian. Gloxo's intellect is no less sharp than a person's, and his senses are no less acute. But Gloxo's sensations aren't always qualitatively identical with their human counterparts, even though they are no less knowledge-conducive. When Gloxo touches a hot object, he has a Q-similar sensations. Q-similar sensations are no less distinctive than S-similar sensations, but they are otherwise nothing like them. Gloxo knows that a given object is hot, and (so we may assume) that it is appropriately described as "hot," if he has Q-similar sensations when touching it. There is nothing about that word's meaning that we can know that Gloxo cannot. So even though the semantic rule for "hot" is encoded in the proposition meant by (9), that proposition is not identical with that rule. There is some condition O – namely, that of being constituted by molecular activity of a certain kind – such that the semantic rule for "hot" is given by the proposition:

(11)   A given object is "hot" just in case its condition is O.

(11) is a semantic rule. Not only does it express a definition; it expresses a semantic, as opposed to an analytic or a scientific definition. The sense in which it expresses a definition is the same as the sense in which, for some person O

(12)   "Socrates" refers to O*

expresses a definition.
    It is not in the semantic, but in the analytic sense that

(13)   An object is correctly described as a "circle" if it encloses at least as large an area as any perimeter-equal object,

and it is not in the semantic, but the scientific sense that

(14)   "precedence" (in the chronological sense) refers to the property borne by one event e with respect to another event e* exactly if e's occurrence could initiate a causal process that could create e* or otherwise influence it.

There isn't anything about the semantics of the word "circle" of which a person is ignorant by virtue of not knowing (13), and there isn't anything about the semantics of the word "precedence" of which a person is ignorant by virtue of not knowing (14). Ignorance of either (13) or (14) is substantive, not semantic ignorance. Ignorance of (11) is semantic ignorance (embedded in which is substantive ignorance).
    It is only because of prejudices on our part that this last claim is counterintuitive. Many a known semantic rule assigns some object O to some expression E without anyone's knowing E to be O's referent. We know many a truth T of the form

(15)   something uniquely has such and such characteristics,

even though we have no idea what it is that has the characteristics in question. It's often known that

(16)   There is some condition – some disease – such that all and only people with such and such symptoms have that disease,

even though we haven't the foggiest notion as to the nature of the condition underlying those symptoms – even though, in other words, we don't know from what bodily disfigurement people with those symptoms are suffering. But that doesn't prevent us from naming that disease. Two people suffering from the same disease may have different symptoms, and two people having the same symptoms may not have the same disease. The connection between a given disease and a given symptomatic expression of that disease is almost always circumstantial; but that connection, though usually circumstantial, is often sufficiently tight that we can identify the presence of that disease in a given person on the basis of that person's symptomology, even though we may have no knowledge at all as to the nature of that disease. Neither emphysema, schizophrenia, nor motor-neuron disease is individuated by the symptoms to which it is likely to give rise. (Given any symptom likely to be had by anyone suffering from any given one of these diseases, it is theoretically possible that someone not thus afflicted should have that symptom and that someone thus afflicted should not have that symptom.) But, owing to the tight, albeit circumstantial, associations between instances of any one of those maladies and the presence of certain symtomologies, there have been words that unambiguously referred to those maladies as long as there have been references to anything. So there have been words whose semantic rules assigned them objects as to whose identities everyone using any such word was ignorant. People have therefore uttered sentences of the form "...D...," where "D" is any term referring to such a disease, and have therefore affirmed propositions of the form ...D... as to whose identities those talking and those listening were ignorant.

Similar points hold of the word "heat." Only few savants know what "heat" means, in one sense of the word "means," even though, in another sense of that word, every English-speaker knows what "heat" means; and only a few savants understand any sentence having the form "...heat...," in one sense of the word "understands," even though, in another sense of that word, every English-speaker understands many a sentence of that form.

Let us relate these points to the relationship between thermodynamics and statistical mechanics. Supposing S to be a true sentence of thermodynamics, S's RF-meaning differs from its MG-meaning, and S's MG-meaning coincides with S*'s MG-meaning, where S* is some sentence of statistical mechanics. What S says about the world coincides with its MG-meaning. Thus, if P is the MG meaning of a given true sentence of thermodynamics, P is identical with, and therefore composed of, the same concepts, as some proposition of statistical mechanics. Consequently, there isn't a single concept that is a constituent of a single proposition of thermodynamics that isn't a constituent of some proposition of statistical mechanics.

Examined superficially, the relationship between thermodynamics and statistical mechanics appears to be inconsistent with our claim that D can't be reduced to D* unless D-propositions consist of the same concepts as (the members of some subset of) D*-propositions; and relative to what such an examination suggests, that claim of ours is likely to appear to be too strong – so strong as to be absurd, in fact, not just false. The points just made stave off the objections to our position that such an examination is likely to prompt, and thus provide negative support for that claim; it is now time to provide positive support for it.

Hempel's position, it will be remembered, is that psychology/physiology/… would be reducible to physiology/microphysics/… were it to turn out that any psychological/physiological/… concept C was co-extensive with some physiological/microphysical/…concept C*. Hempel rightly says that it is an empirical question whether this condition is satisfied. It is an empirical fact that it is not satisfied. But let's suppose that it were. Let us suppose that any given physiological concept C is co-extensive with some microphysical concept C*. When it is made clear this supposition entails, it ceases to be an option to accept Hempel's views concerning interdisciplinary reduction and it ceases to be an option to reject the alternatives to those views that we have been advocating. (What we will say about the relationship between physiology and microphysics holds of the relationship between any two distinct disciplines.)

We'll begin by describing a hypothetical universe W that resembles ours in some important respect, but also differs from ours in some important respects. In W, everything that is round is also green and everything that is green is round: the class of round things is co-extensive with the class of green things. But this is just a coincidence. The natural laws operative in W don't require green things to be round; nor do they require round things to be green. In W, there are sapient beings that do not in any relevant respect differ from us; and some of those being speak English. Referring to some object O that is round, and therefore green, English-speaking W-resident Smith says:

(a) "O is round,"

and he then says:

(b) "O is green."

Wishing to showcase his ability grasp counterfactual truths, Smith makes one last statement:

(c) "While remaining round, O could stop being green; some prankster might paint O red, while otherwise leaving O unchanged. "

Question: In W, does (a) mean the same thing as (b)? Answer: No. The reason: In W, (c) is true.

Second question: In our world, does (a) mean the same thing as (b)? Answer: No. The reason: (c) is true. More precisely: Given that (c) is true in W, it follows that, in our world, (a) doesn't mean the same thing as (b).

We're now going to describe another hypothetical universe W*. W* resembles W in many significant respects. In W*, as in W, a given thing is round just in case it's green; and in W*, as in W, there are sapient beings, some of then English-speakers, who do not differ from us in any significant respect. But W* differs from W in some respects, the most important one being that, in W*, it isn't a coincidence that the class of green things is co-extensive with the class of round things: it is a law of nature that a thing cannot be round without also being green or green without also being round. In W*, if somebody dunks a green object in red paint, that object stops being round; and no sooner is a moist, non-green lump of clay squeezed into a sphere than it becomes green. Referring to some object O* that is round, and therefore green, English-speaking W-resident Brown says:

(a*)   "O* is round,"

and he then says:

(b*)   "O* is green."

Wishing to showcase his ability grasp counterfactual truths, Smith makes one last statement:

(c*)   "The laws of nature being what they are, O* will be green as long as it's round, and round as long as it's green; and for that reason, one couldn't correctly affirm (a*) while denying (b*); but one could coherently do so – somebody who did so wouldn't be in the same category as somebody who affirmed (a*) but then denied that O*' was a cube – and what (a*) says about the world is therefore different from what (b*) says about the world.

Question: In W, does (a*) mean the same thing as (b*)? Answer: No. The reason: In W, (c*) is true.

Second question: In our world, does (a*) mean the same thing as (b*)? Answer: No. The reason: In W, (c*) is true. More precisely: Given that (c*) is true in W, it follows that, in our world, (a*) doesn't mean the same thing as (b*).

With these points in mind, consider the statement:

(d)   Any given physiological property is co-extensive with some microphysical property.

(d) could be false. It is false; therefore, it could be false. What is actual is possible. (Suppose that what were actual were not possible. In that case, it would be impossible. But the impossible obviously isn't actual.) Given that, in actuality, (d) is false, it follows that, even if it were true, it would still be capable of being false; it wouldn't be in the same category as:

(e)   A given object could simultaneously be round and triangular.

Thus, supposing, as we are, that every physiological property C is co-extensive with microphysical property C*, it doesn't follow that

(f)   x is an instance of C

says the same thing as

212   Empiricism and the Foundations of Psychology

(f*)   x is an instance of C*.

Not only does it not follow: it's false. It's false if it's mere happenstance that physiological properties are co-extensive with microphysical properties – cf. what we said about (c) – and it's false if there is some law of nature requiring those two bodies of concepts to be so aligned – cf. what we said about (c*).

Thus, supposing (e) and (e*) to be true, and to be identical with truths T and T*, respectively, T isn't the same truth as T*. And the sense in which T and T* are distinct is a particularly robust one. The truth that

(g)   x is a circle just in case x is a closed planar figure of uniform curvature

is obviously distinct from the truth that

(h)   x is a triangle just in case it is the area enclosed by three lines, such that any two intersect, but such that not all three intersect.

And those truths aren't just distinct: they are non-trivially so. A cognitively normal person – nay, an extremely intelligent one – could go his whole life knowing the one but not the other. Nonetheless, each of those truths is a logical consequence of the other. So even though they are distinct, and in a particularly robust way, they are not distinct in a way that is of any significance to empirical science. There is no conceivable empirical datum that could confirm the one but disconfirm the other. Given any two logically equivalent truths, no matter how non-obvious it is that they are logically equivalent, nothing could confirm the one but disconfirm the other; and if the a given datum D (dis)confirmed the one to a given degree, that datum would necessarily (dis)confirm the other to that same degree. So even though (g) and (h) are entirely distinct truths, the differences between those truths are irrelevant to empirical science and, as far as empirical science is concerned, those truths are therefore identical.

Unlike the difference between (g) and (h), the difference between (f) and (f*) is empirically significant, and the second is therefore more robust than the first, robust though the first may be. Given any possible world W#, no matter what the laws of nature in it may be, (g) and (h) are non-interchangeable from the viewpoint of W#-science: (g) and (h) are no less interchangeable in a world in which physiological concepts are perfectly aligned with (some subset of the set of) microphysical concepts than they are in a world, such as ours, in which they are not so aligned This has the consequence, as we'll now see, that, were those two concept-sets so aligned, that fact would make it extremely hard to discover facts about the structure of the universe that would otherwise be relatively easy to discover.

In our world,

(A)   the laws governing the physiological realm are completely different from those governing the microphysical realm.

And in our world,

(B)   there isn't a single physiological concept that is co-extensive with any micro-physical concept.

(B) forced us to become aware of (A). But (A) and (B) are otherwise completely unre-lated. Neither is a logical consequence of the other.

Let W# be a universe such that (a), in W#, each physiological concept is co-extensive with some microphysical concept, and such that (b) W# is otherwise just like our world (or, in any case, is as much like our world as (a)'s being true allows it to be). In W#, the laws of physiology would be distinct from the laws of microphysics. Those two sets of laws would be no less distinct in W# than they are in our world.

This is readily shown. There are three possibilities as to why, in W#, each physi-ological concept is co-extensive with microphysical concept. (i) It's just a coincidence. There is nothing about the laws governing W# that requires those two sets of concepts to align in that way; they just happen to do so. (ii) It's not a coincidence; the laws of logic make it necessary that they so align. (iii) It's not a coincidence; the natural laws operative in W# make it necessary that they so align. There is no third possibility. There is no fourth possibility.

Suppose (i) to be the case. In that case, it's a tautology that "C is instantiated" pro-vides no support for "C* is instantiated," for any concepts C and C* such that one of them – it can be either one – is any given microphysical concept and such that other is any given physiological concept. "It's a coincidence that both P and Q are the case" is synonymous with "neither fact has anything to do with the other."

(ii) can't be the case. The laws of logic don't vary from universe to universe. In our world, it's an empirical fact that physiological concepts aren't co-extensive with micro-physical concepts. Therefore, it's an empirical fact that matters are different in W#.

Suppose (iii) to be the case. There is a metabiological principle that we must ac-cept, and the justification for which we must know, if we are to know what that suppo-sition entails or why it entails it. That principle: There cannot be physiological truths unless there are physiological laws. (The bearing of this principle on (iii) will become clear as soon as we've stated the justification for that principle.) Suppose that there are no physiological laws in W#. A tautologous consequence of this supposition is that, for any physiological concepts C and C*, the proposition that C is instantiated (if supposed true) provides no support for the proposition that C* is instantiated. (All variants of the parenthetical qualification will henceforth be left unstated.) But it is incoherent to suppose that, given any two physiological propositions, neither one's being true is inherently (as opposed to purely circumstantially) dispositive of the other's being true. (In a moment, we will clarify the parenthetical qualification.) An organism is, tautologously, a structure that consists of reliably functioning biological mechanisms that interact with one another in reliable, principled ways. Given that there cannot possibly be physiological mechanisms in a world unless there are organ-isms in that world, it follows that there cannot possibly be organisms in a given world

unless some of that world's occupants were governed by by principled relations holding among physiological entities – unless, in other words, physiological laws were operative in that world. It is incoherent, therefore, to suppose that no physiological laws
are operative in W#, even though some of W#'s occupants are physiological entities.

In W#, any given physiological property is, by supposition, coextensive with
some microphysical property. If there are no physiological facts in W#, and thus no
instances of physiological properties, then that supposition is either false or vacuously
true (and therefore as good as false). So it must be assumed that there are physiological facts in W#. This entails, as we've just seen, that there are physiological laws in W#
(or, if you consider "law" to be too strong a word, there are in W# physiology-specific,
principled relations among distinctively physiological occurrences). This means that
there are physiological properties phi and psi such that, in W#,

(i)   those properties are instantiated;

(ii)   phi's being instantiated is responsible for psi's being instantiated

and

(iii) it is in virtue of the just-mentioned phi-instance's being a physiological phe-
       nomenon that it leads to the aforementioned psi-instances; and it is only to
       the extent that the aforementioned psi-instance is a physiological occurrence
       that it is the result of the just-mentioned phi-instance's being a physiological
       occurrence.

Given two physiological events E and E*, there is a difference between

(a)   E's occurrence being causally responsible for E*'s occurrence

and

(b)   E's occurrence doesn't just lead to E*'s occurrence; E's occurrence has that
       effect in virtue of its being physiological in nature.

Given any physiological property phi, there is no one microphysical property psi such
that instances of phi have to be realized by instances of psi. So far as there are circumstances in which there is some one such microphysical property, that fact is entirely
accidental: it isn't inherent in what it is to be an instance of phi. This means that, so far
instances of phi cannot be realized by instances of any microphysical property other
than psi, those phi-instances aren't physiological occurrences: they are non-physiological occurrences that realize or constitute spatiotemporally coincident physiological occurrences.

Bearing this in mind, consider the statement that:

(PM)   In W#, any given physiological property is co-extensive with some micro-
       physical property.

A consequence of the points made in the paragraph preceding PM is that, strictly speaking, PM cannot possibly be true: supposing phi to be an arbitrary physiological property that, in some universe, is not multiply realizable, it is despite, not because of, phi's being a physiological property that it isn't multiply realizable in that universe. To the extent that phi is a physiological property, it is multiply realizable; and to the extent that phi is not multiply realizable, it is despite its being a physiological property and it is because of circumstance-specific factors that have no basis in phi's being a physiological property. (To the extent that x is a heart, x pumps blood; and to the extent that x doesn't pump blood, it's because of circumstance-specific factors that have no basis in x's being a heart.)

To sum up: Physiological properties are multiply realizable. More precisely, a given property phi is multiply realizable in so far as it is a physiological property; and so far as that property is not multiply realizable, the reason is that factors having no basis in phi's being a physiological property are preventing phi from being multiply realizable. This means that, given any physiological property phi and given any set of circumstances S, phi is multiply realizable in S to the extent that phi's being a physiological property is determinative of what, if anything, instantiates is. It follows that x is capable of instantiating phi only if x is a physiological entity, and it therefore follows that there is no conceivable universe in which PM is true.

But there is an attenuated sense in which there are possible universes in which PM is true. It can be true in the sense that:

(PM*) If x* is any non-physiological entity that constitutes an instance of any given physiological property phi, there is some microphysical property psi such that x* is an instance of psi.

In PM*, the occurrence of the word "constitutes" refers to the relation that the clay composing a statue bears with respect to that statue. That relation is not one of identity. The statue isn't identical with the clay of which it is composed. It is possible to destroy the statue without destroying the clay. Therefore the statue doesn't have the same properties as the clay. Therefore the statue isn't identical with the clay. Constitution isn't identity. Thus, supposing PM* true, it isn't possible for any instance of a microphysical property to be an instance of any physiological property: if x is an instance of some microphysical property, x can constitute some instance of a physiological property, but x cannot be identical with any such instance.

Let us now determine what PM* entails concerning W#. To do this, we must distinguish between two very different reasons why it is that, in W#, any given physiological property phi is (if only in the loose sense just discussed) co-extensive with some microphysical property psi. (From now on, all variants of the parenthetical qualification will be left unstated.)

Reason #1: There is some subset of microphysical properties such that, by sheer happenstance, x is an instance of any given physiological property just in case it is an instance of one of the members of that subset. In other words, in W#, it is not nomi-cally necessary that any given physiological property be co-extensive with a member of that subset; it just so happens that, even though it isn't nomically necessary, x is an instance of any given physiological property just in case it is an instance of one of the members of that subset.

Reason #2: There is some set of microphysical properties such that the natural laws operative in W# – or, in any case, W#-internal laws of some kind or other – make it necessary that x is an instance of any given physiological property just in case x is an instance of some microphysical property.

If Reason #1 is the operative one, then – by supposition, effectively – it is nothing but a coincidence that, in W#, each physiological property is co-extensive with some microphysical property. (In this context, it will be recalled, we are granting Hempel's assumption – false though we have shown it to be – that it is logically possible for any physiological property to be co-extensive with any microphysical property.) Suppos-ing that Reason #1 is the operative one, physiological occurrences of type K that are currently implemented by microphysical occurrences of type K* might cease to be thus implemented; they might at any point come to be implemented by microphysical occurrences of type K# (where, of course, K# and K* are different properties). Thus, supposing Reason #1 to be the operative one, any existing alignment of the physiolog-ical and the microphysical is both fortuitous and fragile. So far as such an alignment is fragile, one isn't justified in correlating physiological with microphysical events, let alone in attempting to explain physiological events in terms of microphysical events, except in so far as one has knowledge of the logically and, moreover, nomically con-tingent fact that physiological events of type K are realized by microphysical events of type K*. Thus, if Reason #1 is the operative one, it isn't possible, and doesn't even appear possible, to reduce the physiological to the microphysical.

Let us thus suppose Reason #2 to be the operative one. In other words, let us suppose that, in W#, given any physiological property K, there is some microphysical property K* such that it is nomically necessary that x is an instance of K just in case x is an instance of K*. One might think that, under these circumstances, there would be at least some sense in which, in W#, physiology can be reduced to microphysics. One would be wrong. Under the circumstances in question, the W#-operative laws of physiology would no more be capable of microphysical interpretations than their counterparts in our world. Let L be the natural law (if that's what it is: this hedge will presently be explained) responsible for the relevant alignment in W# of the micro-physical and the physiological. It isn't by microphysicalizing the laws of physiology that L brings about this alignment; it is by constricting the class of entities that fall within the scope of utterly non-microphysicalized physiological laws.

In W#, the aforementioned alignment is, by supposition, nomically necessary. But it isn't because of anything inherent in the physiological laws operative in W#. There is nothing about those laws themselves that makes any less multiply realizable than their counterparts in our universe. So far as they are less multiply realizable than their real-world counterparts, it is because of idiosyncrasies, none of them constituted by physiological laws, on W#'s part. Let L be the shortest list containing every physiological law operative in W#. Given some physiological property phi, and given some instance x of phi, L doesn't require x to have this as opposed to that microphysical implementation. Given only what we've said about them, the physiological laws operative in W# are no less permissive, and no more deterministic, than their real-world counterparts; and, given only what we've said about W#, it is possible that the the the former laws are identical with the latter laws. (If the former are more deterministic than their real-world counterparts, or they aren't deterministic in the same way as their real-world counterparts, it isn't by virtue of anything that we've said about W#.) What's going on in W# is that factors of a non-physiological kind are diminishing the scope of the class of entities that fall within the scope of physiological law.

In W#, therefore, the laws of physiology are no more capable of being characterized in microphysical terms than their real-world counterparts. This means that, in W#, physiological explanations are no more capable than real-world microphysical explanations of being understood in microphysical terms.

As far as the W#-operative laws of physiology are concerned, it is nothing but an accident that there is but one way that microphysical phenomena can implement physiological phenomena. An analogous point holds with respect to the W#-operative laws of microphysics. It cannot possibly be in virtue of anything inherent in those laws that microphysical phenomena are so limited in respect of their ability to mediate physiological phenomena. There is no possible universe where the laws of microphysics so much as recognize the existence of physiological phenomena; wherefore, there is no possible universe where there is a microphysical law to the effect that, for some physiological property phi, there is some microphysical property psi such that instances of phi must be realized by instances of psi.

By supposition, some law L is operative in W# that prohibits physiological phenomena from being implemented in ways in which they could otherwise be implemented. (In my judgment, the very concept of such a law is incoherent. But for now, let us suppose for argument's sake that this isn't so, and that L is one of the laws governing W#.) And let us continue to suppose that, in W#, there are sapient beings, some of whom speak English, who are in no relevant respects different from us.

The fact that L is operative in W# obscures what would otherwise be relatively transparent facts about W#'s nomic structure. In our world, it's patently obvious that neither physiological phenomena nor physiological laws can be understood in microphysical terms. The reason this is obvious is that, in our world, neither L, nor any L-like law, is operative. But in W# this wouldn't be at all obvious. L's existence would obfuscate important, and otherwise transparent facts about W#'s structure. Because of L, the W#-internal laws of physiology would appear to have less scope than they do have, and they would appear to be deterministic in ways in which they are not in fact deterministic. And in W#, the physiological appears (or would appear to its sapient inhabitants) to converge with the microphysical, even though there is no such convergence.

In W#, microphysics would be no more capable than it would be in our world of generating explanations of physiological occurrences. In W#, one would be more capable than one is in our world of making correct physiological predictions on the basis of microphysical knowledge, and that would foster the belief that physiology could be astrophysical But that belief would be an illusion.

A pair of stories will clarify this last point. On the basis of microphysical data, W#-scientist S makes a correct physiological prediction. Knowing that his prediction came true, S believes that his reasons for making that prediction were the right ones. S is wrong. (The next scenario is similar to one described by Carnap (1966). Carnap was making a point similar to the one we're making, but not coincident with it.) In our world, scientist S* points a gun at Brown and pulls the trigger. A nanosecond later, Brown falls down. S* believes that Brown fell down because he had just been shot. S* is wrong. There were no bullets in S*'s gun, only blanks; and Brown is an actor who, for some acting-related reason, fell down, as though he'd just been shot, right after S* pulled the trigger. S*'s pulling the trigger did indeed cause Brown to fall down. (That is, it was a distal, partial cause of Brown's falling down.) But S* is completely wrong as to the nature of the causal mechanism linking his pulling the trigger with Brown's collapsing. In our world, situations like the one just described are the exception, not the rule. In W#, they are the rule, not the exception. W# is replete with concomitances that mimic principled relations, and W# is therefore replete with instances of pseudo-causal relations that (for the very reason that they are such relations) are easily mistaken for actual causal relations. In our world, there are many concomitances; but they are less likely than those in W# to be mere mimicries of principled relations. Consequently, what appears to be an instance of causality is more likely in our world than it is in W# to be an actual instance of causality. Thus, W#-scientists are, other things being equal, more likely than their real-world counterparts to have false beliefs as to what causes what; and – what is far less innocuous – they are more likely than their real-world counterparts to have false beliefs as to their host-universe. (I will henceforth omit the expression "other things being equal.") W#-scientists would be more inclined than their real-world counterparts to mistake contingencies for nomic necessities. For example, they would be likely to see the limitations of the physiological laws operative in their world as being rooted in those laws – when, in actuality, their roots lie elsewhere. In general, because of the over-abundance of explanatorily empty concomitances in W#, it would be hard for scientists there to distinguish between real causal relations and mere mimicries thereof; and in our world, it would be relatively easy to make such distinctions, owing to the relative scarcity of such concomitances.

Thus, Hempel's analysis isn't just wrong: it's the exact opposite of the truth. The concomitances that, in Hempel's view, make it possible to discover the laws of nature actually make it hard to discover them: the fewer such concomitances, the easier it is to identify the actual nomic structure of the world.

The world is governed by laws. One of the objectives of empirical science is to identify those laws. To the extent that it fails to do so, science has yet to do what it is supposed to do. Given only what we've said about W#, it is possible that the physiological laws operative in it are identical with those that are operative in our world. But a scientist in W# would be much slower to become aware of that fact, other things being equal, than his counterpart in our world. Moreover, the existence of physiological-microphysical concomitances in W# would dispose scientists in W# to have some very wrong metascientific views that, other things being equal, their counterparts in our world would not be disposed to have. In our world, many a philosopher, and many a philosopher-scientist, has argued that high-level explanation-conducive relations, such as the laws of physiology, are necessarily capable of being replaced by low-level (microphysical) laws. But, in our world, that position hasn't been taken seriously: many a scientist professes to believe it; but few scientists, if any, make any attempt to implement it: that supposed belief of theirs does nothing, or next to nothing, in the way of regulating the work of those scientists who profess to believe it. This suggests that, if those scientists do in fact believe it, they also believe its negation: they accept it at one level and reject it another, it being their rejection of it that is operative in their work. And the reason why, for all intents and purposes, scientists don't believe it is, presumably, that the empirical facts are so discrepant with it. If this presumption is correct, it's not unreasonable to infer that the W#-counterparts of these scientists really do believe it; that is to say, their acceptance of it regulates their work.

Let us sum up. According to Hempel, D can be reduced to D* to the extent that D*-phenomena are concomitances of D-phenomena. In our world, there are few, if any, pairs of disciplines, D and D*, such that D*-phenomena are concomitants of D-phenomena. This fact about our world has made it relatively easy for us not to fall prey to some very wrong scientific and metascientific views.

Hempel's analysis has a defect that we have to mention. Let B be the shortest list that contains every biological law and let MP be the shortest list containing every microphysical law; and let's suppose, counterlogically, that the laws composing the one list can be alligned with those composing the other in precisely the way that, according to Hempel, they must be alligned if biology is to microphysicalized. Relative even to these assumptions, Hempel's analysis cannot be implemented until we know everything there is to know about biology that we'll be able to produce a list of every biological law, and an analogous point holds of microphysics. So Hempel's analysis can't explain anything until there is nothing left to be explained.

Let us move on to a seemingly unrelated topic whose intimate connection with the points just made will become apparent.

Can psychology be reduced to physiology? According to Hempel, this is an empirical question. I will now argue that

(1)   It is a logical, non-empirical question,

and I will also argue that:

(2)   The answer to it is "no."

Here is an outline of the argument about to be put forth. (In the present context, "discipline" means "empirical discipline.") Although any given discipline employs principles of logic, such principles are not discipline-specific. Thus, given any discipline-specific proposition P, the question "is P true?" is empirical. But, given some discipline D, the question "does P belong to D?" usually isn't empirical. It is an empirical question, to which the answer is obviously "no," whether it is true that

(EP) envious people are, for that reason, more likely to think objectively than non-envious people

But it is not an empirical question whether EP is a proposition of psychology. Given any discipline-specific proposition P, the question "is P true?" is empirical. But, given an arbitrary discipline D, the question "does P belong to D?" is not empirical. (The second claim must must be justified; given only what we've said, it could be false. Moreover, it is subject to heavy qualifications. At the right time, we will justify it and duly qualify it. But for now it must be treated as an undischarged assumption.) Since discipline-specific propositions are always empirical, discipline-specific truths are empirical, and discipline-specific falsehoods are possible truths. Therefore, given any two disciplines D and D*, D can be absorbed into D* if, and only if, there is no true proposition and no false proposition that D can affirm that D* cannot affirm. (This truism has been rejected, but only because, blind to the distinction between RF-meaning and MG-meaning, thinkers have seen counterexamples to it where there are none.) No psychological propositions is logically equivalent with any phsyiological proposition. Given any proposition P, it is a logical, non-empirical question whether or not P is psychology-specific and also whether or not P is physiology-specific. Given any psychological proposition P, it is a truth of logic that either P or not-P is correct, and it is a truth of logic that neither P nor not-P is logically equivalent, let alone identical, with any physiological proposition. It therefore follows from truths of logic, and is thus itself a truth of logic, that there are psychological truths that are not equivalent, let alone identical, with physiological or otherwise non-psychological truths; and it is therefore a truth of logic that psychology cannot be reduced to physiology.

Let us now state the argument just outlined. (1) and (2) are both consequences of principles that have either been established already or that will presently be established. There are ten such principles:

Principle #1 (already established): Given any two disciplines, D and D*, establishing concomitances between D-phenomena and D*-phenomena does nothing in the way of assimilating either discipline into the other.

Principle #2 (already established): Establishing such concomitances not only does nothing in the way of reducing D to D*: it actually obscures the nomic structure of the world. No physiological property can be co-extensive with any microphysical property.

Principle #3 (already partly, but not completely, established): Given a physi-ological property phi and a microphysical property psi, it is possible for some psi-instance x to be identical with something that constitutes some phi-instance y; but it is not possible for x itself to be identical with y itself.

Principle #4 (already partly, but not completely, established): D can be reduced to D* if, and only if, there neither is, nor can be, any D-truth that isn't equivalent with some D*-truth.

Principle #5 (already partly, but not completely, established): Blind to the distinction between RF-meaning and MG-meaning, philosophers have seen counterexamles to this analysis where there are none, and they have therefore embraced analyses, such as Hempel's, that assume the truth of its negation. Because this analysis is a truism, its negation is an absurdity, and so, conse-quently, are the alternatives to it that philosophers have embraced.

Principle #6 (not yet established): L is a surd; the very idea of such a law is an incoherent one.

Principle #7 (not yet established): One-place physiological expressions – e.g. "liver," "heart" – denote relations, not properties. "x is a liver" doesn't have the same grammatical form as "there is something y such that x bears R to y." But (for the appropriate values of the variables in the latter) both sentences affirm the same proposition and therefore have the same logical form.

Principle #8 (not yet established): " It is a law of nature that such and such is the case" isn't equivalent with "it is a consequence of the laws of nature that such and such is the case."

Principle #9 (not yet established): If S is a psychology-specific sentence – as opposed to a psychology-specific proposition – S's RF-meaning coincides with its MG-meaning.

Principle #10 (not yet established): Given any discipline D, D may be identi-fied with a set of sentences S such that S includes (i) every statement that D accepts, (ii) the negation of every such statement, (iii) every statement D will ever come to accept or whose negation D will come to accept, and (iv) every statement that D could conceivably accept or reject.

Let us start off by establishing Principle #7. "x is a planet" doesn't appear to make a relational statement; it doesn't appear to affirm a proposition of the form "for some object y, x bears relation R to y." But "x is a planet" does affirm such a proposition. An object that is qualitatively just like Jupiter but isn't orbiting around a star isn't a planet. Jupiter wouldn't be a planet if it weren't orbiting around some star or other. (Not everything that orbits around a star is a planet. Asteroids aren't planets. But nothing that doesn't orbit around some star is a planet.) Thus, "Jupiter is a planet" doesn't express a proposition of the form: "x has phi." It expresses one of the form: "there is some some star y such that Jupiter orbits around y." For something to be a planet is (in part) for there to be something having certain properties to which it bears a certain relation.

Like the sentence "x is a planet," the sentence "x is a liver" expresses a relational proposition; it does not express a proposition of the form "x has phi." (The relational proposition affirmed by "x is a liver" is vastly more complex than the one affirmed by "x is a planet.") For something to be a liver isn't for it to be made out of this or that material; it isn't for it to have these or these intrinsic properties; it is for it to be embedde in a certain way in a structure of a certain kind; it is for it to have a certain causal role within such a such a structure. Thus, "liver" is really a relational term; and the same is true, for the same reason, of "heart," "kidney," and every other organ-term.

Of course, a given thing's material composition affects its relations to other things. A human liver couldn't be made of glass; were a glass object to occupy the place currently occupied by your liver, it wouldn't interact with your other body-parts in the right ways, and it would therefore fail to be a liver. But that only proves our point: so far as a thing's being made of glass disqualifies it from being a person's liver, it is because, given any person P, that thing's being made of glass would prevent it from interacting in the right ways with P's other body-parts. Also, given only that a thing's being made of glass makes it unsuitable to be a person's liver, it doesn't follow that there couldn't possibly be some a creature of some kind whose liver it could be.

But, for argument's sake, let's suppose that, the laws governing our universe being what they are, there is no nomically possible creature C such a thing's being made of glass wouldn't disqualify that thing from being C's liver. In that case, a thing's having certain microphysical properties would rule out its being a liver. But given only that there are certain microphysical properties that a liver can't have, it doesn't follow that there is some microphysical property phi that any given liver must have; it doesn't follow that there is a microphysical interpretation of the term "liver." Indeed, it doesn't follow that there aren't infinitely many distinct microstructures that a liver can have.

We can go even further in this direction. Let's suppose that there is no possible universe in which there is any creature C such that C's liver could be made of glass. That supposition entails that there is one type of microstructure that no liver could possibly have. But it leaves open the possibility that there are infintely many different microstructures that a liver could have.

It may safely be assumed that, in our world, no two livers are microstructurally identical; and it may safely be assumed that, in our world, there are infinitely many different microstructures that a functioning liver could have. So given only that there are microphysical properties that livers cannot have, it doesn't folllow that, for some microphysical property phi, a thing is a liver just in case it has phi.

In any case, "liver" is a relational term. "x is a liver" means "x bears R to y," where y is some organized multiplicity of objects.

There are physiological facts only if there are organisms. Thus, physiological properties are instantiated only if there are organisms. There is no conceivable object x such that x's being a functioning part of an organism doesn't consist in x's interacting in certain ways with that organism's other constituents.

These points suffice to establish Principle #7; and, as we're about to see, they constitute a first-step towards establish Principle #8. We've seen that one-place biological predicates denote relations; in other words, if "phi" is any such predicate, "x has phi" says that that x bears some relation R to some object y. This isn't a peculiarity of biological predicates: given any predicate "phi," it is inconceivable that "x has phi" should be a scientifically significant statement and yet fail to say, for some relation R and some object (or plurality of objects) y, that x bears R to y. Consider the term "electron." Supposing for argument's sake that "x is an electron" says nothing about how x interacts with other things, it follows, tautologously, that "x is an electron" hasn't the slightest explanatory value. It's obvious that, given any predicate "phi," if there is nothing to which a given thing need bear any relation of any kind in order to satisfy that predicate, then, tautologously, a world in which "x is a phi" is true is not, for that reason, different from one in which it is false. So microphysical predicates (e.g. "electron," "positively charged") are no less relational than physiological predicates.

Any given natural law L* is given by some proposition P*. P* is a "law-affirming proposition." Moreover, P is the law affirming proposition that "corresponds" to L*. Let PL be a list of all of the physiological laws operative in hypothetical world W, and let ML be a list of the microphysical laws operative in W. For each entry on each list, there is a corresponding law-affirming proposition.

If all of these propositions are conjoined, the result is some proposition P. A logical consequence of P, we will suppose, is that:

(G)   Given any physiological property phi, there is some microphysical property psi such that x instantiates psi just in case (the material constituting) x instantiates phi.

Does the fact P entails G mean that G is itself a law-affirming proposition? No. Indeed, it entails that G is not a law-affirming proposition. The laws listed by PL *by themselves* guarantee G's truth. P *by itself* entails G. By supposition, given any one of the laws governing W, the corresponding law-affirming proposition is one of P's conjuncts. Nothing has to be added to P to make it entail G: P doesn't have to be conjoined with some other proposition; in particular, P doesn't have to conjoined with a law-affirming proposition or, therefore, some law-affirming proposition that isn't one of its own conjuncts. It follows that, without itself being a law of W, G is a consequence of the laws governing W. (To be precise, it follows that, without itself being a law of W, G is a consequence of the law-affirming propositions, taken jointly, that correspond to the laws that govern W.) These points establish Principle #8.

Some notational conventions will help us move forward. Given an object x, let "m(x)" be an abbreviation for "either x or the material constituting x." (Thus, on each of its disambiguations, "x instantiates phi just in case m(x) instantiates psi" is a consequence of "x instantiates phi just in case x instantiates phi," but it is only on one of its disambiguations that the first sentence is a consequence of the second.) And if, for some property phi and some property psi, x instantiates phi just in case either x itself or m(x) instantiates psi, let us say that phi and psi are coextensive*. (Thus, coextensive properties are coextensive, but coextensive* properties aren't necessarily coextensive.)

We have established that

(^)   "it is nomically necessary that any given macro-property phi be coextensive wth some micro-property psi"

is not logically equivalent with

(^^)   it is a law of nature that any given macro-property phi be coextensive wth some micro-property psi.

Supposing it true, (^^) obviously entails (^). But (^) doesn't entail (^^), and Principle #8 is therefore correct.

We will now establish Principle #6. We will do this by proving that (^^) is incoherent.

Let P be the proposition that, in hypothetical universe W, it is nomically impossible in W for there to be a macro-property phi that isn't coextensive* with some micro-property psi. Let P* be a conjunctive proposition such that (a) each of P's conjuncts afffirms one of the laws governing some possible universe W; (b) there is at most one such law that is not affirmed by one of those conjuncts (in other words, there is either no such law or there is exactly one such law); and (c) if there is a law that isn't affirmed by any one of P*'s conjuncts, that law is given by P.

If Principle #6 is false, then

(^^^)   P is compatible with P*.

P is not a microphysical law; nor is it a macrophysical law. There isn't a single microphysical phenomenon x such that x is to be explained in terms of P. There is no microphysical entity y such that x's relationship to y is governed by P.

Nor is P a macroophysical law. To the extent that macro-events are to be understood in terms of micro-events, macro-events are not to be understood in terms of P. To the extent that macro-events are to be understood in terms of other macro-events, macro-events are not to be understood in terms of P.

Two microphysically identical situations (or universes) cannot be macrophysically different. It would be incoherent to say, although Bill's microstructure was just like Jim's, Bill was having a heart-attack and Jim was not. The macrophysical "supervenes" on the microphysical. If (^^^) is true, then the macrophysical doesn't supervene on the microphysical. If (^^^) is true, two situations that were particle-for-particle duplicates of each other could mediate qualitatively different macro-events: one of those situations could involve some volcano's erupting, while the other did not.

But two microphysically identical situations canot be macrophysically different. Therefore (^^^) is false. Therefore, P is not compatible with P*, and Principle #6 is correct. This has the consequence, we will now see, that if any given macro-property is coextensive with some micro-property, that is nothing but an accident, and therefore has no explanatory value. (Supposing this true, it obviously follows that Hempel's anaysis is false, and it also follows – for reasons that aren't obvious but will be made clear soon enough – that seemingly platitudinous mainstay of empiricism is incoherent.)

Supposing for argument's sake that, for some macrophysical property phi, there is some microphysical property psi such that phi is coextensive* with psi, there are seven possible explanations of this fact. (In what follows, the terms "macrophysical" and "microphysical" be replaced with any predicates belonging to any disciplines D and D*, respectively, such that D-facts supervene on D*-facts. The pound-sign ("#") is meant to distinguish (1) and (2) from (1#) and (2#).)

(1#) It is mere happenstance. It isn't a consequence of the laws of logic or of nature.

(2#) It is a truth of logic that, given any macrophysical property phi, there is some microphysical property psi such that phi and psi are coextensive*.

(3#) (2#) is false; but given any macrophysical property phi, there is some microphysical property psi such that it is truth of logic that phi is coextensive* with psi.

(4#) It is a consequence of the laws of nature, but it is not itself a law of nature, that, given any macrophysical property phi, there is some microphysical property psi such that phi and psi are coextensive*.

(5#) (4#) is false; but given any macrophysical property phi, there is some microphysical property psi such it is a consequence of the laws of nature that that phi and psi are coextensive*.

(6#) There is a law of nature that is given by the proposition that, for any property phi, there is some microphysical property psi such that phi is coextensive* with psi.

(7#) (6#) is false; but given any physiological property phi, there is some microphysical property psi such there is a law of nature that is given by the proposition that phi is coextensive* with psi.

(2#)/(4#)/(6#) entails (#3)/(5#)/(7#), but (#3)/(5#)/(7#) does not entail (2#)/(4#)/(6#). The proposition that

(AG) Any given macrophysical truth is logically equivalent with some microphysical truth is a consequence of (2#), and also of (3#). AG entails that D is reducible to D* if D-truths are logically equivalent with D*-truths; and AG therefore entails that, so far as there are concomitances between D-phenomena and D*-phenomena, that fact is irrelevant to whether D* can assimilate D, except to the extent that such concomitances are indications of logical equivalences of the just-mentioned kind.

For argument's sake, suppose (4#) to be true. Let LP be the physiological laws operative in W. In that case, macrophenomena could be correlated with microphenomena. But that fact does more to obscure W's nomic structure than to reveal it. Let W* a world that is governed by the same physiological laws as W, but that isn governed by different microphysical laws. In W*, macrophenomena are multiply realizable with respect to microphenomena: given only that m(x) has macro-property phi, thre are infinitely many distinct microproperties psi that x might have.

In W, macro-phenomena are in lockstep with micro-phenomena. W's microphysical laws i therefore prohibit the occurrence of events that W's macrophysical laws do not prohibit. There is nothing that W-macrophysical laws prohibit that W*-macrophysical laws permit. For, by hypothesis, those two bodies of laws coincide. At the same time, there are physiological occurrences that can occur in W* that cannot occur in W, for the reason that the W-entities constituting macrophysical objects are subject to laws to which their W*-couterparts are not subject. In W, there are physiological occcurrences that cannot occur but whose W*-counterparts can occur. But this isn't because the phsyiological laws in W are any less perimssive than their counterparts in W*. It is because the microphysical laws in W limit the behavior of non-physiological entities that constitute physiological entities in ways that the microphysical laws in W* do not limit the behavior of such entities. The fact that, in W, each physiological property is coextensive* with some microphysical property obscures W's nomic structure; for it prohibits occurrences that are physiologically possible and, were there beings just like us in W, it would dispose those beings to misidentify the laws of physiology in their universe; and to that extent, it would blind them to the nomic structure of their world.

The fact that, in W, the two sets of laws are in lockstep doesn't have the consequence that physiological and microphysical truths converge any more than they would in a universe, such as W*, where those two sets of laws are not in lockstep. Given only that e and e* are physiological events and that e is e*'s cause, it doesn't follow that e's causing e*'s occurrence is itself a physiological event. e's causing e* is a physiological occurrence only to the extent that e's being a physiological event is responsible for e*'s occurrence. e's causing e* to occur is non-physiological to the extent that e*'s occurrence was an effect of e's having some non-physiological property – its having a certain mass or temperature. (e: Smith's burping loudly at time t. e*: Smith's dying of hypothermia at later time t*. Smith is in Brown's house. Brown's house is in Alaska. It is currently winter. Smith's burping offends Brown, and Brown therefore kicks Smith out of his house. Smith has nowhere to go and he isn't wearing winter-proof clothes. Forced to remain outdoors, Smith dies of hypothermia at t*. e and e* are physiological events. But it was e's being an anti-social gesture, not its having any distinctively physiological property, that is responsible for e*'s occurrence. In this context, therefore, two physiological events are related as cause and effect but, relative to the laws of physiology, the connection between e and e* is purely circumstantial – even though, relative to other laws, it is not circumstantial. Thus, e's being e*'s cause isn't an instance of physiological causation and therefore isn't an instance of a physiological law.)

The laws of W being what they are, e couldn't have caused e* to occur unless m(e) caused m(e*) to occur, where "m(x)" denotes the material constituting x, and m(e) couldn't have caused m(e*) to occur. But this doesn't mean that, in W, physiology is any more capable than it is in W* of being microphysicalized. Let us suppose that e's causing e*'s occurrence is indeed an instance of physiological causation. (e: Smith goes into anaphylactic shock at t. e*: Smith's having blue fingertips (in consequence of e's making it hard to Smith to breath) at t*.) In W*, let us suppose, there is an event e# that is physiologically just like e and that, for that reason, brings about the occcurrence of an event e*# that is physiologically just like e*. In W*, m(e#) would not make m(e*#) happen, at least not for the same reason that, in W, e made m(e) happen. In W*, the laws of physiology are obviously distinct from the laws of microphysics; each set of laws makes a contribution to W*'s nomic structure; the one contribution is obviously distinct from the other. By supposition, W*'s physiological laws are identical with W's. Therefore, the contribution made by W*'s physiological laws to W*'s nomic structure coincides with the contribution made by W's physiological laws to W's nomic structure. By supposition, W*'s microphysical laws are different from W's microphysical laws. Therefore, the contribution made by W*'s microphysical laws to W*'s nomic structure is different from the contribution made by W's microphysical laws to W's nomic structure. Therefore, the physiological laws in W are no more capable of reduced to the microphysical laws in W than the physiological laws in W* are capable of being reduced to the microphysical laws in W*. This shows that, even though there is obviously a sense in which, in W, it isn't accident that the physiological tracks the microphysical, there is another, sense in which it is an accident, it being the second sense, not the first, that is relevant to whether a given statement constitutes a correct answer to the question: What is it to reduce one discipline to another?

We have thus established that (#4), were it true, would to no degree enable microphysics to absorbe physiology (or any other discipline that studies objects constituted by those studied by microphysics), and it obviously follows that (#5'), were it true, would just as innocuous in that respect as (#4).

(#6) couldn't possibly be true; it is incoherent. We have already established this. (#7) cannot be true unless, for any given macrophysical property phi, there is a microphysical property psi such that x instantiates psi just in case m(x) instantiates phi. Therefore, (#7) is incoherent, given that (#6) is incoherent.

If D is to be reducible to D*, we must conclude, it is not enough that it be possible to correlate D-phenomena with D*-phenomena; it is necessary that every D-truth be a logical consequence of some D*-truth. So if there is so much as a single psychological truth that isn't equivalent to any physiological (or otherwise non-psychological) truth, then psychology cannot be reduced to physiology (or any other discipline). The sentence

(EV) "suicidal ideation is driven by anger towards the world that one has turned against oneself"

is obviously psychology-specific; and either that sentence or its negation is a psychology-specific truth. There is obviously no physiology-specific sentence PS such that PS entails SV or such that SV entails PS. But this does not by itself show that psychology-specific propositions are never equivalent with physiology-specific propositions. Thermodynamics-specific sentences aren't logically equivalent with statistical mechanics-specific sentences, but thermodynamics is (to a non-trivial extent) capable of reduced to statistical mechanics. Given the distinction between RF-meaning and MG-meaning, we found, this fact is compatible with our contention that a discipline that is blind to a given truth cannot absorb one that isn't thus blind. Thermodynamics can be absorbed into statistical mechanics to the extent, and only to the extent, that the MG-meanings of thermodynamics-specific propostions coimcide with statistic mechanics-specific propositions. To establish that physiology cannot absorb psychology, it is necessary to show that the MG-meanings of psychology-specific truths do not always coincide with physiological truths. This can be established, and we'll establish it right now.

Botanists don't study data; they study plants. They are not interested in data for its own sake; they are interested in it only to the extent that it apprises them of facts about plants.

Let T be an arbitrary tree. Smith knows that T is a tree. He knows this because, events involving T cause Smith to have certain kinds of experiences. (Those events probably involve light bouncing off of T and making its way to Smith's eyes.) Those experiences are awarenesses; they bear information and thus have conditions of satisfaction.

It isn't in virtue of T's causing Smith to have such awarenesses that T is a tree. The connection between T's being a tree and its leading to such experiences is circumstantial. That connection may be extremely tight. But no matter how tight it is, T's being a tree has nothing to do with anyone experiences. There is no perception or thought that anyone could have that would be incompatible, except in a strictly evidential as well as circumstance-specific sense, that would be incompatible with T's being a tree.

A corollary is that it isn't in virtue of how T looks, or is otherwise perceptible, that T is a tree. A non-tree could look and feel exactly like T.Given some object T*, there is some set of causal properties that T* has if, and only if, T* is a tree; and, no matter what T looks like, and no matter what sorts of experiences or thoughts T-involving events cause us to have, T is a tree in virtue of its having those causal properties.

"Tree" is a "natural-kind" term. This means that, in virtue of being a tree, an object has causal properties that it would otherwise like and, consequently, that it is governed by laws that wouldn't otherwise govern it. It is because of its causal properties that T is a tree; it isn't because of its effects on anyone's ideation.

That said, we are able to know that T is a tree only to the extent that its having those causal properties is dispositive of its causing people to have certain kinds of experiences. Let K be an arbitrary natural kind. There is some property P such that, if a given thing is a member of K, it is by virtue of its having P. It is only if a thing's having P disposes people to have experiences the likes of which they wouldn't otherwise have that one can know that thing to have P or, therefore, to be an instance of K. But, if K is any non-psychological natural kind, there can be none but a purely circumstantial correlation between, on the one hand, a given thing's having P and, on the other hand, a given person's having experiences of a certain kind.

It is for this reason and this reason alone that, in virtue of having the form "…tree…", a given sentence's RF-meaning might diverge from its MG-meaning; and it is for an analogues of this reason that the same is true of sentences of the form "…heat…." and of the form "…iron…."

Let P and P* be any two distinct properties. If x's having P is responsible for its belonging to some natural kind K#, and x's having P* is responsible for our being able to know that x belongs to K#, then, in virtue of having the form "…K#…", a sentences RF-meaning is distinct from its MG-meaning.

If K is a psychological natural kind, there may be, and there is likely to be, some property P such that (i) it is in virtue of its having P that a entity is a member of K and (ii) there is a constitutive, non-circumstantial correlation between a given object's being an instance of K and people having experiences of a certain kind. This is because, if K is a psychological natural kind, its members may themselves be experiences, a consequence being that the very properties an object must to be a member of K coincide with the properties it must have if we are to know it to be a member of K.

But the principle just stated is a consequence of a more general principle. Supposing that x is an instance of psychotic ideation, it is in virtue of x's content that it is such an instance. Given any property phi such that phi corresponds to a psychological natural kind and given any instance x of phi, it is in virtue of x's content that x has phi. Supposing x to be an instance of ratiocination, as opposed to free association, x's being such an instance is a consequence of x's content. Supposing x to be a desire (or, therefore, a desire of this or that kind), it is in virtue of x's content that x is a desire (of this or that kind). But given any property chi such that chi corresponds to a non-psychological natural kind, it is not in virtue of x's content that x has chi. Supposing that x is heart and supposing, counterlogically, that x is content-bearing, x's being a heart isn't a consequence of its being content-bearing or, therefore, of its bearing content of this or that sort. Supposing that x is both a physiological entity and a mental entity, it isn't in virtue of x's being content-bearing, let alone its bearing this or that specific kind of content, that x is a physiological entity; and it is in virtue of its being content-bearing that x is a mental entity.

Not one of the statements just made is empirical. Each is analytically true. It would make no sense to say that empirical discoveries might prove that x's being content-bearing might not have the consequence that x was a mental entity; and it would make no sense to say that x's being cntent-bearing had the consequence that it was a heart of a lung. Many hold that mental entities are identical with, or mediated by, physiological entities. But it would either make no sense to say, of some arbitrary entity x, (a) that it was in virtue of x's being a desire for world-peace that x was a frontal lobe, and it would make equally little sense to say (b) that it was in virtue of x's being a frontal lobe that it was a desire for world peace. This does not mean that mental entities are not constituted by physiological entities. What it means is that, for any psychological property phi, x instantiates phi only on the condition that there be some physiological property psi such that m(x) instantiates psi.

Given what we've said, it follows that

(i)   at least one psychology-specific sentence's RF-meaning coincides with its MG-meaning;

(ii)   the MG-meaning of at least one such sentence is a proposition that, for reasons of logic, couldn't be equivalent, let alone identical, with any physiology-specific proposition;

(iii)   for some proposition P, it is a logical, non-empirical truth that P is psychology-specific;

(iv)   for some proposition P*, it is a logical, non-empirical truth that P* is a phsyiology-specific proposition;

and

(v)   there is some psychology-specific propositoin that doesn't entail any physiology-specific proposition and also isn't entailed by such proposition.

(i)–(v) jointly entail:

(A)   Principle (#9) is correct;

(B)   It is a logical, non-empirical question whether psychology can be reduced to physiology;

and

(C)   The answer to that question is "no."

But the points made in this section have a consequence that is more important that any one of (i)–(v), namely: Unless Hempel's views about interdisciplinary reduction are inconsistent with empiricism, and unless the same is true of Hume's analysis of causation, empiricism has an obviously incoherent consequence, namely: To explain is to fail to explain.

Further, those points suggest what the right answer might be to the question: "What is it to explain an event?"

In the forthcoming argument, "discipline" means "empirical discipline."

Given some discipline D, there is a difference between a given proposition's being used by D, on the one hand, and its being D-distinctive, on the other. Psychologists surely use the proposition that a proposition cannot be true if it's negation is true, but that proposition isn't a distinctively psychological proposition, unlike the proposition that people wish to undermine those they envy. The latter proposition is "psychology-specific." In general, a given proposition P is "D-specific" if it belongs to D, for some discipline D. The negation of a D-specific proposition is itself D-specific. (This last statement is a substantive truth, not a stipulation, for reasons that will become clear.)

Given two distinct disciplines D and D* and some proposition P, if D doesn't over-lap with D*, and if D does overlap with with D* but P falls outside the area of overlap, P's being D-specific doesn't necessarily rule out its being D*-specific.(In thus defining "discipline-specific," I am not assuming that P could be both D-specific and D*-spe-cific without, for that very reason, falling into (a possibly otherwise non-existent) area of overlap between the two disciplines: it is not being assumed that the second "if"-clause isn't counterlogical in nature.) In describing a proposition P as D-specific, for some discipline D, one is distinguishing principles that D merely employs, but don't belong to it, from principles that fall into the class of propositions individuative of D. There are obviously contexts where biologists use principles of physics. (Physi-cians not only use, but are aware of using, the principle that unsupported bodies fall. But that principle is not medicine- or biology-specific.) More importantly, there are principles of logic that all disciplines use, but that don't belong to any discipline. So far as a given truth T of logic is being put to physics-specific use, T assumes a physics specific-form. But that doesn't mean that T itself is physics-specific.

Incidentally, there are in fact discipline-specific logical truths. This is a conse-quence of three facts. First, so-called "formal logic" isn't identical with logic-proper. Second, by any reasonable measure, for each explanatorily useful truth of formal logic, there are infinitely many such truths of informal logic. Third, given that there are discipline-specific concepts (e.g. "electron," "kidney," "envy"), there are discipline-specific logical truths. But in this context, we will operate on the assumption that discipline-specific truths are empirical. Though false, this assumption is innocuous in the present context, its sole role being to abbreviate otherwise prohibitively long statements. So, in the argument about to be put forth, a given proposition is "disci-pline-specific" only if it is empirical.

Given any discipline-specific proposition P, the question "is P true?" is always em-pirical. But the question "does P belong to D?" – in other words, "is P D-specific?" – is non-empirical in some cases (but not all, for reasons stated a moment ago).

Let P be the proposition that x's judgments about y are less likely to be based on cogent thought if x has strong feelings about y than if x is emotionally neutral towards y. P is an empirical proposition. But it is a logical, non-empirical proposition that P is psychology-specific. (Let P* be the proposition that P is psychology-specific. P* belongs to metapsychology, not psychology; and the fact that P* is non-empirical is consistent with the (putative) fact that discipline-specific truths are empirical, relative to the (false but, in this context, innocuously so) assumption that there is no disci-pline D such that meta-D is itself an empirical discipline.) Another example: Let P be the proposition that weight is a strictly additive property. The question "is P true?" is empirical. The question "is P physics-specific?" is non-empirical.

Suppose that x's position at t is p and that it's density at t* is d*. Given only that information, there is no sense in which x's having density d* at t* can be understood in terms of its having position p at t. This doesn't mean that its having d* at t* cannot be explained in terms of its having p at t. But it means that, in order for there to be any sense at all in which its x's t*-density can be explained in terms of its t-place, the information already given must be supplemented with the sort of information that can only be given by general propositions – propositions concerning classes of events, as opposed to specific events. ("But that isn't true," it will be said. "Suppose it a law of nature that, if x's position at t is p, then its density at t* is d*." Unless that conditional were known to be a consequence of some general proposition, it couldn't be known to express a law of nature and thus couldn't help explain x's t*-density in terms of its t-place.)

With these points in mind, consider the obvious truth that:

(P₁)   If x's position at time t is p, and x moves continuously from p to p*, this being its position at t*, there is obviously some significant sense (though it may not be obvious what that sense is) in which, given only that information, x's occupying p* at t* can be understood, if not explained, in terms of its occupying p at t.

Appropriately generalized, this platitude yields an answer to the question "what is it to explain one state of affairs in terms of another?" In each of the P₁-derivatives we're about to identity, the parenthetical qualification will be omitted The other qualification – "given only that information" – is too important to be left implicit.

An object's shape is a logical consequence of the positions of its surface-points. So a logical consequence of P₁ is

(P₂)   If x's shapes at t and t* are s and s*, respectively, and during the interval between t and t* each occupant of each of x's surface-points either remained stationary or moved continuously from one place to another, there is a sense in which, given only this information, x's having shape s* at t* can be understood, if not explained, in terms of its having s at t.

In any case, P₂ is an obvious truth, and so is each of the following analogues of P₁:

(P₃)   If x's density at t is d, and its density changes continuously from d to d*, this being its density at t*, there is a sense in which in which, given only this information, x's having density d* at t* can be understood, if not explained, in terms of its having d at t.

(P₄)   If x's temperature at t is h, and its temperature changes continuously from h to h*, this being its temperature at t*, there is a sense in which, given only this information, x's having h* at t* can be understood, if not explained, in terms of its having h at t.

And:

(P$_5$)   If x's color at t is c, and its color changes continuously from c to c*, this being its color at t*, there is a sense in which in which, given only this information, x's having density d* at t* can be understood, if not explained, in terms of its having d at t.

These are, of course, many more true P$_1$-analogues.

An object's shape either stays the same or changes continuously. For this reason, there is a shape-space*. For analogous reasons there is a volume-space*, a temperature-space*, a color-space*, a mass-space*, a position-space, a color-space*. (Shape-space* is a subspace* of position-space*, meaning that an object's position in shape-space* is a logical consequence of the region it occupies in position-space*. (A single point is a limiting case of a region.) Space*s may be subspaces*, but not proper subspaces*, of each other.) Squareness is a property. Shape is a kind of property, of which square-ness is an instance. Shape-space* consists of the totality of specific shape-properties. In general, if p is a property, a p-space* is a kind of property, and a p-space* consists of its own instances.

Though its sometimes synonymous with "space*," the word "parameter" usually refers to expressions referring to space*s, as opposed to such spaces* themselves, and we're thus better off using the unambiguous term "space*." (Other, less tangible reasons will emerge to opt for this term.)

We've seen that, for any space* s, there is some significant sense in which a given thing's having one s-location at one time can be understood in terms of its having any other s-location at a prior time. We've also seen that, given any two distinct spaces* (neither a subspace* of the other), or given any space* and any any non-space*-gener-ating property P, there is no significant sense in which a thing's having a given location in that space at one time can be understood in terms of its having P (to any degree) at any other time.

Bearing this in mind, suppose that, in some possible universe W, all and only round objects are green. Given some round object x, would its being round account for its also being green? Hume and Hempel say "yes." The present author says "no," his position being that x's being both round and green is a mystery and that it isn't less of a mystery for the fact that there are many other mysteries like it.

In our universe, there is no correlation between an object's shape – that is, its macrostructure – and its temperature. But a given object's temperature can be ex-plained in terms of its microstructure; that is, it's position in temperature*-space can be explained in terms of its position in micro-structure-space*. The reason: those spaces* are one and the same.

It is for a similar, but not coincident, reason that, in our universe, an object's color can be explained in terms of its micro-structure. We must (re)state some general truths about empiricism in order to identify this reason.

Two distinct doctrines go by the name of "empiricism": (i) All knowledge is derived from sense-perception (that it, it is so in the content-transmitting sense, not the thought-triggering; (ii) all knowledge is derived (in the content-transmitting sense) from experience.

Unless there were reliable correlations among sensation-kinds – unless, for some values of K and K*, a sensation of kind K would not occur unless, at some coincident or neighboring time, there occurred (in the mind that hosted the just-mentioned sensation) a sensations of kind K* – no sensation would be evidence of anything or, consequently, of the occurrence (past, present, or future) of any other sensation.

Incidental point: This does not by itself show that type-(ii) empiricism is false. But it does show that type-(i) empiricism is false. According to type-(i) empiricism, it is only through perceptions that we know of concomitances. But we've just seen that knowledge of such concomitances is a prerequisite for sense-perception.

Moving on: Sensations are not perceptions. Any given perceptions consists of sensations. But there is more to perception than sensation. Perceptions are conceptually articulated sensations, or sensation-sets. In perception, the world is presented to us as consisting of property-instances. (n-place relations are to be identified with properties of ordered n-tuples – so the relation of being in-between is a property of ordered triples <x, y, z> such that x is in-between y and z – and properties are to be identified with one-place relations.) It is therefore only to the extent that one is, at some cognitive level, aware of properties that one is percipient (perception-capable). Thus, one must have property-concepts before one can have perceptions. Therefore, concipience precedes percipience. Therefore, type-(i) empiricism is false.

Let S be a sensation-kind such that, under circumstances of certain kinds, instances of S mediate perceptions to the effect that a certain shade of pink was instantiated. As any painter knows, there are other sensation-kinds whose instances mediate perceptions of that same shade of pink, that being why a given painter uses paints of different colors to represent different instances of that one shade of pink. (If he intends to depict a given such instance as being far off, or as being overshadowed by a tree, he uses paint one color, and he uses paint of another color if, other things being equal, he intends to depict such an instance as being close-up, or as not being overshadowed by a tree.) In experiencing an instance of S, a creature isn't seeing pink unless it has some understanding of how an object's color depends on his physical relation to that object. Thus, knowledge of secondary-properties is even more concept-heavy than knowledge of primary-properties.

(It follows, incidentally, that one knows an object's secondary properties on the basis of its primary properties, not the other way around. The opposite has always been taken for granted – but only because sensations were being identified with secondary properties. Time to set the record straight: On the basis of one's sensations, one learns what physical relation one bears to a given object, as well as, of course, what that object's physical properties are; and on the basis of those two bodies of knowledge, coupled with a knowledge of one's sensations, one learns what that object's secondary properties are. This is no less true – though I leave it to the reader to excogitate the underlying reasons on the basis of what I've already said – of taste and odor than it is of color and pitch.)

Secondary-properties are properties of relations. (The relata in question are (or, rather, include) the observer and the observed.) Primary properties are properties of objects, not relations. (Technically, both kinds of properties are properties of relations, as we saw in Chapter 1. But, as we also saw, if ordered n-tuples instantiate primary properties, then ordered n+1-tuples instantiate secondary properties.) So if no property of the one kind can possible generate a space* coincident with (any part of) the space* generated by any property of the other kind.

But it is still possible to explain a given object's secondary properties in terms of its primary properties. Suppose that an object x is red to observer y if x bears R to y (that, in other words, it is a property had by the ordered pair <x, y>, by virtue of that pair's instantiating R). If R is held fixed, it is in virtue of x's micro-structure that it bears R to y. (We are also supposing that y's constitution is held fixed. So we are prescinding from the fact that colors are properties of ordered triples <x, y, z>, where the third parameter corresponds to the observer's constitution.) And so long as R is held fixed, redness may for all intents and purposes be identified with micro-structure (or micro-micro-structure, rather), and for that reason being explained in terms of an object's structure in the same way as an object's temperature.

But there is an important meta-explanatory principle that we have yet to identify but that we will identify if we develop the just-made points concerning empiricism.

In perception, the world is presented as comprising instances of solidity, liquidity, redness, and softness; and it is presented as consisting of objects bearing determinate spatiotemporal relations to other objects. It is also – I would suggest, though it is debatable – presented as comprising instances of sentience and sapience; of different organ-types; of different degrees of health and necrosis.

Consider the property of being solid. (What we will say about this property holds with respect to any of the properties that perception represents to us as being instantiated. We will henceforth describe such properties as being "perception-relevant." I don't want to describe such properties as "perceptible" (or "observable"), since properties, being abstract entities, cannot be observed.) If an object is solid, dislocating it involves either breaking it or moving it, shape-unchanged (more or less), to another place; it means that shape-changes on its part tend to have circumstance-specific causes (equivalently, it tends to keep its shape, unless it is subject to differential (as opposed to universal) forces); it means that alterations of the substance composing one part are less likely to lead to similar adulturations than they would otherwise be (one discolors all of the water in a glass if one discolors so much as a single drop of it; one doesn't discolor an entire basketball by discoloring one part of its surface). Similar points hold any perception-relevant property.

So far as there seem to be counterexamples to this, it is because we are conflating the concept of a perception-relevant property with the concept of a property that we know to be instantiated on the basis of theory-light inferences from observational data. Redness is a perception-relevant property: I can observe that there is a red car in the garage. The property of being owned by Jerry is not perception-relevant: there is no observable difference between things that have that property and things that don't. Consequently, I don't *observe* that there is a Jerry-owned car in the garage: I *infer* it. I see that there is an object with certain properties in a certain place. I know that, in that place, nothing other than a Jerry-owned car could possibly have those properties, and I rightly infer that there is a Jerry-owned car in the garage. So far as we are inclined to think that I can just see there to be such a car, it's because the inference in question is theory-light and we have a tendency to conflate "unobservable" with "theoretical." Molecules aren't just unobservable: they are theoretical – it is on the basis of theory-heavy inferences that we know of their existence. Under ordinary circumstances, there isn't anything theoretical about the fact that there is a Jerry-owned car in a given place, and this disposes us to believe that an appropriately situated person can just see there to be such a car.

(Incidentally, content-externalism is nothing but a generalization of the failure to distinguish between what we perceive and what we know on the basis of perception. The property of being identical with Jerry is not perceptible. What is perceptible is the property of having a certain appearance, a certain height, gait, etc. Given that x has a certain height, etc., I know a given object to be Jerry. That is, if I have knowledge of the first kind, I know that I'm seeing Jerry so long as I know that nobody in the world who isn't Jerry looks like Jerry and so long as I have other, similarly ulterior pieces of information at my disposal.)

Supposing S to be the sort of visual sensation that, in actuality, mediate my perceptions of (certain kinds of) solid objects (as seen under certain conditions), S would mediate no such perception if it weren't accompanied by sensations of the kind that, in actuality, mediate perceptions of instances of those properties that are concomitants of solidity. Were S thus unaccompanied on a single occasion, I would have had a perception of a faux-solid object. Were S routinely thus unaccompanied, it would cease to be evidence of anything's having this as opposed shape; to the extent that spatial relations holding among the points on objects' surfaces are indication of spatial relations holding among external objects, my S-sensations would cease to give me knowledge of the mutual spatial relations of the occupants of the external world; and to the extent that the same fate befell each sensations-type S^* that hitherto mediated my perception of instances of solidity (as such instances), I would cease to have such perceptions, as they would all have collapsed into the conceptually unarticulated sensations that mediated them. This shows that, given any perceptible property P, a precondition for P's being such a property is that it be observed – disclosed to sense-pecerception – as having reliable concomitants. This means that a knowledge of real-world concomitances is in some cases a precondition for sense-perception, and thus not a consequence of it. (This seems to undermine type-(i) empiricism; but whether it actually does do so is a delicate question, which we needn't answer, and won't.)

Next step: Given a discipline-specific truth P, it is, as we've pointed out, an empirical question whether P is true. And given a proposition P*, it is an empirical question whether P* is, in actuality, the correct explanation of P. But it is a logical, non-empirical question whether P* could be an explanation of P; in other words, it is a logical, non-empirical question whether P* would explain P, supposing each correct. (The same obviously holds of any proposition of which P* is a conjunct.)

Let phi and psi be two properties such that

(a) "x is a phi" neither entails nor rules out "x is a psi,"

(b) it is known that O is a phi, but it isn't known that O is a psi or that it is a non-psi

and

(c) to our knowledge, phi's are generally also psi's

Empiricists and non-empiricists both agree that

(d) (c) has no bearing on (b) except to the extent that (c) suggests that there is some mechanisms that disposes phi's to be psi's.

Empiricists deny that there could exist a mechanism of the kind that (c) describes. (And we've seen that, as empiricists, they are right to do so, even though, as we've also seen, they are wrong as to why, as empiricists, they must do so. Why they think they must deny it: there is no perceptible evidence of forces. Why must actually deny it: if they grant it, they are thereby implicitly conceding the the truth of the empiricism-incompatible proposition that logical analysis may be needed to determine the content – the pre-theoretic import – of a content-determinate perception.)

Empiricists also deny (or, as empiricists, should deny) that P entails Q, for any statements P and Q. ("P entails Q" means "it is impossible that both P and not-Q should be true." Only the existent can be observed. Even if the impossible – that is, the necessarily non-existent – could be observed, it couldn't be observed as being necessarily non-existent. Empiricism: "It doesn't exist (epistemically, if not ontologically speaking), if it can't be observed.")

In any case, there is only so much about the world that can be understood in terms of strictly logical relations among truths. And little has been done, in this work or anywhere else, to validate our intuition that there could be mechanisms of the sort that (d) describes.

Fortunately, given the points made in this section, it is clear that there exists a hitherto overlooked coherence-relation – an inference-warranting relation that one body of data can bear on another – in terms of which the concept of a distinctively empirical expanation is to be understood. Thus far, attempts to explanain empirical explanation, and to legitimate it, have involved assimiltating it, obviously spuriously, to explanations of the strictly logical kind (of the kind examplified by "x is a circle because x is a planar figure of uniform curvature") or they self-defeatingly involved trying to legitimate them in terms of concomitances that, by their own logic, could ground nothing.

First of all, space – no asterisk – is a combination of many different spaces*. As it is used in terms like "color-space," "temperature-space," and so on, the word "space," corresponds to our use of the word "space*." We tend to regard such usages of "space" as figurative. They are are not. The word "space" has no meaning except to the extent to that it is used as a synonym for one of the various different "spaces*" that exist. Within the narrow horizons defined by everyday life, there is no practical difference between the various different spaces* constitutive of what we call "space." Blind to the differences between those spaces*, we are either altogether blind to any given one of those spaces* or wrongly believe it to be but an analogue of a manifold (namely, "space") of some more fundamental kind.

In most space*s, if not all, position is relative position. (We will sidestep the question whether the concept of absolute position is coherent.) This means that the statement "x's position is p" means nothing, except to the extent that it makes a statement as to the relationship between x's position and y's position, for some body y. (For expository reasons, we may set aside the subtlety that position-space*, being identical with space (no asterisk), is an alloy of a multitude of different spaces*, rather than a space* in its own right.) But "x's position bears R to y" (for suitable values of "x," "y," and "R") is of only limited informational value. (In other words, the range of possible values of R is very restricted.) It can affirm the fact that x's position is distinct from y's. (In this context, we are assuming that statement not to implicitly concern some third body z, or, therefore, some n^{th} body, for any $3 \geq n$.) It can affirm that there are forces operative between x and y that are drawing those two bodies nearer to each other. But it cannot cannot affirm that at it is x, as opposed to y, or *vice versa*, that is thus responsible for their coming together. Nor can it say anything as to how far apart x and y are; as to how long it is taking them for to come into contact, supposing that they are doing so; or as to the nature of the force, supposing there to be one, that is responsible for their doing so.

When a third body z is added, "x bears R to y" is potentially much richer in information than it was before. In other words, the range of possible values of "R" is wider than it was before. For any number n ($n \leq 3$) the amount of information borne by that statement increases as n increases. (It doesn't necessarily increase indefinitely. How much it increases, and how much it improves in quality, is a function of the laws governing the universe hosting the bodies in question.)

Any given space* is defined by its characteristic "metric." A metric is a definition of congruence. Given a property P, x and y are P-congruent if, and only if, they have P to the same degree. x and y are length-congruent if neither is longer than the other; temperature-congruent if neither is hotter than the other; and so on. Thus, given some property P that generates a space*, a metric is a criterion whereby it is determined whether a given object has P to the same degree as some other object and, if not, whether it has it to a greater or a lesser degree.

For illustrative reasons, I will speak of position-space* and time-space*, leaving aside the fact that these are not in actuality distinguishable. Given some one object L, and given two segments of x and y of L, it can obviously be determined whether x is longer than y and also of course whether L is longer x and whether it is longer than y. But statements about position-space* are worthless unless there is a way of determining how distinct objects compare in terms of length. Given any space*, the concept of an an interval must be defined. (Ordinarily, an "interval" is the time-period separating two, non-simtultaneous events. For us, it is the difference, for any property P, between two things in respect of how much they have P.) It must be said what it is for distinct objects in that space to have the same duration, length, temperature, loudness, density, or color; for any p-space*, it must be determinate whether any two occupants x and y of that space* coincide in respect of the degree to which they have p.) It is incoherent to suppose that there should exist a position space* s such that, if s-ccupants $x_1 \ldots x_n$, should not have determinate spatial relations to one another – such that, if there for no i, j, h, k ($1 \leq i \leq j \leq k \leq n$), there should be no truths of the form the distance between x_i and x_j equals (is less/greater than) the distance between x_j and x_k. This does not mean that, given a position-space*, it must be possible to assign determinate numerical values to any of its occupants, let alone all of them. But it must be possible to compare intervals between pairs of its occupants.

(Incidental point: So far as it is ever useful to assign "absolute positions" to the occupants of a space* – to the extent, for example, that it is useful to say that an event happened in 1492 a.d. – it is not because that statement makes a non-relational statement; it is because each of two people can understand such a statement without having both to use the exact same standard of comparison. If I tell you that Bill is taller than Fred, you don't know anything about Bill's height unless you know what Fred's height is. If I tell you that Bill is 6 ft tall, you don't need such context-specific information to understand what I'm saying, the reason being that there is a plurality of available standards of reference: your tape-measure, your own height, etc. In assigning an "absolute" position to a given occupant x of a given space*, one is thereby affirming an entire class of propositions of the form "the interval between x and y equals/is lesser than/greater than the interval between y and z," any given two of which are, in the relevant respect, identical with each other, but not any given two of which are equally useful for distinct auditors of that statement.)

One understands the dynamics of a given space*'s occupants to the extent that one understands the changes in their interrelations. (This is a definitional truth.) One cannot know have the relevant relational information without knowing that space*'s metric.

In what follows, "event" will be short for "event or state of affairs"; and an "anomaly," as we will be using that word, is not an event whose cause us unknown, but one that has no cause. Assuming, as we are, that spatial* position is always relative, it does not follow that it is a matter of convention what the right metric is for space*. m is a better metric for space* S than y if m's being S's metric leads to fewer anomalies than y's being S's metric. An anomaly is a discontinuity. This is because creation *ex nihilo* is anomalous and discontinuities are instances of such creation.

If a consequence of taking m to be the metric for a given space* S is that there are no anomalies in S, then m is an ideal metric for S. m is the best possible metric for S if, given any other metric m*, m's being taken to be such a metric leads to fewer anomalies than m*'s being taken to be such a metric. Hempel (1952) vividly illustrated this point. If we stipulate that the Dalai Lama's heart-beat is constant, thereby taking it to define the metric in terms of which length in time is determined, then events in the furthest corners of the universe immediately change in extreme ways: previously fast moving objects start to move slowly; and any given such object's change in velocity is discontinuous, dropping to a lower speed without assuming each, or even any, of the intermediate velocities. Avoidable anomalies result if we choose this metric, but not if we choose an optical metric (e.g. one given by the proposition that the speed of light is invariant), that being why we use optical, as opposed to cardiological, definitions of spatiotemporal congruence.

A non-anomalous space* is not one that comprises no changes or only uniform change. It is one that comprises only metric-consistent changes. This means that if one event in such a space* is disruptive, it leads to a proportionally counter-disruptive event e*. Instances of uniformity are null changes and are limiting cases of proportionality-restoration. e causes e* to occur if e*'s failing to follow e would invalidate the metric characteristic of the relevant space*. Relative to metric m, car C is moving uniformly at t. At t*, the lead weight on its roof falls off; otherwise C is unchanged. Relative to m, C's state of motion doesn't change. But the distances between cities have suddenly shrunk and every clock on the planet has just slowed down. Relative to any given metric, C's relations to other objects changed when the weight fell off. Relative to an ideal metric m*, but not relative to a substandard metric, such as m, those relational changes can be explained without positing any instances of action at a distance or of any other sort of discontinuity. e is e*'s cause if an otherwise ideal metric's invalidity is a logical consequence e*'s failing to follow e. Explanation is metric-consistent contintuity-restoration, on the condition that the metric in question be an ideal one and to the extent that it is a relatively good one.

Let x be an occupant of our universe and let T be the trajectory that x describes during x's journey from p to p*, these being its locations at times t and t*, respectively. x's journey is a mystery to the extent that x didn't describe some other trajectory T*. Supposing m^ to be the metric we've chosen, if there is no nomically admissible answer to that question, either our universe is anomalous or m is not an ideal metric. But, we will suppose, there is an m^-consistent answer to that question that doesn't explicitly or implicitly posit any discontinuities. At any given instant during its journey from p to p*, x is a constituent of some energy current distinct from, and orthogonal to, that involved in that journey. Those energy-currents being what they are, and m∧ being what it is, x's describing trajectory T is m∧-consistent and its describing any other trajectory, had it done so, would have been m∧-inconsistent.

Our critique of Hempel's analysis of interdisciplinary explanation was but a means to an end, that end being a correct analysis of explanation. Hempel's analysis is a generalization of Hume's analysis of causation. For Hume, to explain events is to correlate event-types. For Hempel, to explain event-types is to correlate correlations among event-types. For Hume, finding an event's cause, and therefore explaining that event, is identical with finding an event such that the resulting event-pair instantiates a correlation. For Hempel, explaining a correlation involves finding a correlative correlation.

For Hume, it is necessarily an accident that phi-phenomena are correlated with psi-phenomena. (It is not necessarily an accident for people who, unlike Hume, deny that to correlate is to explain.) This means that, for Hume, any given instance of a phi-psi correlation is an accident. If any given member of a class has a property, every member has that property. (If any given person plays golf, every person plays golf.) So Hume's view is that to explain an event is to show it to be an accident that is similar to many other accidents. This means that, for Hume, to explain an event is to show it to be an accident. To explain an event is to fail to explain it.

"But your reasoning involves an obvious fallacy," it will be said. "Supposing it an accident that each of x and y weighs 200 lbs, it is no accident, relative to those facts, that their aggregate weight is 400 lbs." This reasoning does less to support than to undermine Hume's analysis. It's because of x's spatiotemporal relation to y that x and y form an object that weighs 400 lbs. There exists many a property phi no two of whose instances are comparably interrelated, even though there exists a property psi whose instances are so correlated with phi's that in Hume's view any given phi-instance is causally responsible for some psi-instance. For Hume, no instance of any property can possibly cause or otherwise bear on any other such instance. For Hume, therefore, no instance of any correlation can possibly cause or otherwise bear on any such other instance. For Hume, therefore, no such instance can be understood in terms of any other such instance or any muliplicity of such instances. Hume's analysis therefore entails that neither of the events constitutive of such an instance can be understood in terms of the other: each such event is an accident relative to the other. In identifying causation with correlation, Hume is therefore claiming that to explain an event is to show that it is an accident: to explain is to show that there is no explanation. This is what Hume's analysis of causation comes to; and it is what Hempel's analysis of interdisciplinary reduction comes to, for much the same reason "To explain is to fail to explain": this is the methodological significance of empiricism, at least to the extent that the meta-explanatory views of these two philosophers are indeed consistent with that doctrine.

CHAPTER 9

Skepticism about induction
and about perception

1.0   If empiricism is true, it cannot be known to be true. According to empiricism, all evidence is perceptual evidence. But it cannot be known through perception that perception is a source of knowledge. Witnesses cannot self-corroborate.

One perception can surely provide support for one another. I can have a tactile perception that confirms a visual perception. While establishing the veridicality of my visual perception *relative to the assumption that my tactile assumption is correct*, this does nothing to justify the presumption that perception is a source of knowledge.

That presumption *can* be justified, but not on strictly empirical grounds. The justification for it is indirect. We must first establish that an operation known as "inductive inference" yields knowledge.

Suggestively, inductive inference is another casualty of empiricism: a source of knowledge that empiricism claims not to be a source of knowledge. The same empiricist strictures that invalidate inductive inference are those that invalidate perception, and the very arguments that *re*-validate the one re-validate the other. The belief that there is an external world is itself known through inductive inference: hence the points just made.

2.0   There are two kinds of induction: enumerative and explanatory. Hume puts forth an argument against 'induction,' without making it clear which of the two kinds of induction is the one being targeted:

HA: How do you know that the future will resemble the past (To generalize this question: setting aside cases of deduction-generated knowledge, how do you know that the unknown will resemble the known? "In the past, things were thus and so" doesn't deductively entail "in the future, they'll be thus and so." So the connection isn't deductive. It's only if we assume that nature is uniform – if we assume the truth of the uniformity principle (UP) – that we can justify 'things will be thus and so' on the basis of 'things thus far have been thus and so.' The uniformity principles bridges the future to the past, and, more generally, the unknown to the known. If it's assumed that nature is synchronically and diachronically uniform (uniform across space and time), then we can legitimately extrapolate from the limited data we have. But how is UP to be justified? It's not analytic; there's no deductive or purely conceptual justification for it. So it must be justified inductively. But it's only *if* induction is justified that UP is justified. So UP is inherently unjustifiable, and so, therefore, is induction.[183]

Up to a point, Hume is right. Given only that, every time you've tossed the coin, it's landed heads, you have no right to infer that it'll do the same thing next time. Hume is right that any instance of purely enumerative induction is an instance of the Gambler's fallacy.

3.0   But here we need to distinguish enumerative from explanatory induction. Enumerative induction, I submit, is an artifact, a creation of epistemologists. People don't make enumerative inductions. Oftentimes, they make explanatory inductions which are easily mistaken for enumerative inductions. But never do they make truly enumerative ones.

You see the same coin land tails, over and over – a 100, a 1000, in a row. If, while holding onto the assumption that the coin isn't weighted, that there's nothing disposing this as opposed to that outcome, you are indeed guilty of an egregious fallacy in assuming, on the basis of its behavior in the past, that it will land heads this time. Your reasoning contradicts itself. By your own hypothesis, nothing disposes the coin to land tails rather than heads; by your own hypothesis, it's a fair coin. So in assuming that, given its past behavior, its must land tails this time, you're either assuming that, contrary to your own assumption,

(a)   something *is* disposing the coin to land tails this time,

or you are assuming, no less irrationally, that

(b)   for absolutely no reason at all, it's going to land tails this time.

3.1   Now let's change the situation. You've seen the coin land tails 10,000 times and never seen it land heads or otherwise known it to do so. On that basis, you posit some mechanism that disposes the coin to land tails. (*One side is heavier than the other. The table is magnetically charged and so is one side of the coin.*) Having posited such a mechanism, you are not guilty of the gambler's fallacy if, on the basis of the coin's past behavior, you infer that it will land tails this time.

In reality, if you were to see a coin land tails over and over again, never landing heads, you would assume that it was a weighted coin (or some such) and *for that reason* infer that it would land tails next time. Supposedly, there are gamblers who know that the dice they're rolling are fare, but who nonetheless make predictions concerning future rolls on the basis of past roll. I suspect that at some level such people believe that the dice aren't fair.

---

183.   Hume (1740, 1748).

A belief that one has as a result of past conditioning is the result of an act of judgment. If it's because of operant conditioning that one expects the dice to roll double-sixes, one's expectation embodies no thought and therefore is not an instance of an inductively-generated belief.

Also, what is often described as 'mere conditioning' is sometimes an instance of inference to the best explanation. Every time you hear the front-door being opened, you expect to see your wife. This is not a case of conditioned reflex. You know that only your wife has the key; that given her sensibility and the nature of her acquaintanceships, there is no chance that she gave a copy of her key to somebody else; and so on.

3.2   Before t, let us suppose, mechanisms $m_1 \ldots m_n$ (henceforth "m") run things. After t, m is defunct. On this side of the line L, m runs things. On the other, it doesn't. The supposedly cautious path of the skeptic requires inexplicable annihilations, which in turn require equally inexplicable *ex nihilo* creations.

It is analytically true that, given two explanations, the one that leaves us with the fewer unexplained explainers is *ceteris paribus* to be preferred to the other. It follows straightaway that IBE is appropriate for explanations of what we already know, since, but for IBE's, we can't avoid violating the continuity maxim. We are therefore justified in holding that those mechanisms will continue to operate. More precisely, we are required, as a matter of logic, to hold that they will continue to hold *to the extent that the world is explicable*. This doesn't mean that we're right to do so, only that we're it's rational to do so.

3.2.1   "But the skeptic isn't saying that m *isn't* operative on the other side of the line," it will be objected. "He's saying that he has no grounds for saying that it is or that it isn't." If m isn't operative on the other side of the line, all manner of otherwise non-existent anomalies pop up. So his saying that he has no grounds for making the aforementioned judgment amounts to his saying that, given only that H eliminates more anomalies than H*, it doesn't follow that H is *ceteris paribus* preferable to H*. But that is an analytically false position.

To sum up, if there is analytic, non-empirical knowledge, we can justify our faith in our sense perceptions and in our predictions about the future. If there is not, we cannot. We have not shown that these beliefs of ours are correct. We've shown that they are correct *if the world is explicable*. Later we'll discharge the assumption that the world is indeed explicable.

3.3   Given the legitimacy of induction, the legitimacy of sense-perception follows. Consciousness is jagged, discontinuous, and gap-ridden. It is analytic that *ceteris paribus* one hypothesis is better than another if the first does a better job than the second of eliminating such discontinuities. Up to a point, we can eliminate them by positing unconscious psychological phenomena. But we must posit enduring structures to house those unconscious thoughts; for it makes no sense to say that nothing *other* than unconscious ideation is consciousness-external. Plus, even if continuous unconscious ideation mediates between the spontaneities of consciousness, the mind as a whole, unless considered as part of a larger reality, comprises innumerably many such spontaneities. So just as we had to posit the unconscious in order to eliminate the gaps in consciousness, so we must posit the extra-mental in order to eliminate the gaps in the mental. And those extra-mental events must on the whole be as our perceptions represent them as being; otherwise, we eliminate no intra-mental discontinuities by positing them.

This means that the skeptic's position is unfeasible and the non-skeptic's is *de rigueur*. However, given only that the non-skeptic's position is *de rigueur*, it doesn't follow that it's right. Given that Smith's finger-prints are all over the murder-weapon, it is *de riguer* to suspect him of the crime, even though he may turn out to be innocent. It is not analytic that there is an external world. It is not analytic that, given the data of consciousness, there is an external world. It is analytic that, given that data, skepticism is less rational than its antithesis.

4.0   *Idealism* is the doctrine that objects are identical with one's perceptions of them. So according to the idealist, there is no difference between the dog and your perceptions of the dog.

If idealism is correct, our "perceptions" have no objects at all, and they're therefore just hallucinations. But many a distinguished empiricist disagrees. Berkeley (1710), Mill (1882), James (1910), Russell (1921), Ayer (1934), and Carnap (1937), among others, hold that not only that idealism (the latter four prefer the term "neutral monism") allows us to have knowledge of objects, but also that no other doctrine has this virtue. Further, some of the authors just mentioned, e.g. Berkeley, go so far as to say that idealism is the view of common sense. They rightly say that common sense identifies objects with perceptible entities, not with unknown, imperceptible quiddities; on this basis, they spuriously conclude that common sense (unwittingly) identifies objects with "bundles of perceptions."

4.1   Like Berkeley (1710), the linguistically oriented idealists of the early 20th century – James (1907), Russell (1928), Ayer (1934), Carnap (1937) – held that the difference between idealism and realism is one of language.

Realism, they held, is a language (call it "RL"); idealism, they held, is another language ("IL"). Any statement of the one language, they believed, can be translated into a statement of other. Let us use one of Berkeley's own examples:

(RE)   "the Earth revolves around the sun"

is the RL translation of the IL-statement

(IE)   "If a percipient being (of a certain kind) were in such and such a location, it would have thus ands such experiences."

4.2   There is no way to translate statements of RL into IE. According to those who hold otherwise, the statement that:

   (i)   the table exists unperceived

is the RL-translation of the IE-statement that:

   (ii)   if I did certain things (e.g. walked into the next room) I'd have such and such experiences.

But how are we to describe the experiences in question. They would have to be described as experiences that *would* be veridical *if* there were a table there. They have to be described as perceptions *to the effect that* there was a table in front of me.

   But in that case, the table isn't a bundle of perceptions; it's a non-entity. Idealism thus collapses into the view that our perceptions are awarenesses of nothing.

   One might try to side step this, as Jackson (1977) did, by adverbializing our descriptions of the contents of our perceptions. Instead of seeing a table, I am having 'tably' perceptions.'

   But there is no way to say what a 'tably' perception is except in terms of what it is to see a table. In trying to translate from RL to IL, we must constantly make surreptitious use of knowledge that idealism says we don't have and that we wouldn't need to have if IL and RL really were languages, as opposed to substantive hypotheses.[184]

   Also, there is no IL-translation of the antecedent of

(IW)   "If I walked into the next room, I'd have such and such perceptions."

For an idealist, there are no rooms, and there is no such thing as walking. But, as we've just seen, in order to describe perceptions of tables and rooms, one must assume that there really are such things and one must therefore assume that idealism is false.

5.0   Idealism is an old doctrine. There were idealists before there were philosophers. Many forms of psychosis are marked by an acceptance of positions similar to idealism, and psychosis predates philosophy. Also, all infants are idealists. It is only when the newborn learns that his caregivers have needs of their own that he acknowledges that they have any existence outside of his own thought-sphere, and it is only when he generalizes this insight of his that he learns that the world as a whole is similarly thought-independent. The rituals employed by primitive peoples – their rain-dances and sacrificial rites – are vestiges of the infant's spurious belief in, to use Freud's term, the "omnipotence of thought," and psychosis is in large part nothing other than a recrudescence in the adult's mind of the infant's idealism.

   Indeed, it is every person's natural wont to be an idealist. That is why we are so quick to project – to see our own sentiments behind the deeds of others – and to see

---

184. Michael Dummett (1978) makes this point.

our own psychical peculiarities writ into the structure of the world. (In primitive man, the world in question comprises both the social and physical worlds. In modern man, it comprises only the social world.) That in turn is why people are drawn to situations that validate their pre-existing world-views. One would think that anxiety-prone people would be be drawn to situations that settled their nerves. They are not. They do not avoid anxiety-triggers; they seek them out. Anxiety-prone people are drawn to situations that give them a legitimate reason to feel anxious. For the same reason, calm people are drawn to calm environments. It's the anxiety-prone person who goes into emergency-room surgery, and the calm-person who goes into library-maintenance.

Further, if an anxiety-prone person is in a calm-environment, he will try to turn it into an anxiety-ridden one. In general, so far it is within a given person's power to change his environment, he turns it into one that validates his pre-existing world-view; and his environment – his world – is thereby assimilated into his psyche.

So it isn't just newborns and psychotics who are idealists: it's everyone. A non-psychotic's idealism operates within a fundamentally non-idealistic belief-system. The anxiety-case who is drawn to high-stress situations does fundamentally see the world as it is. He is a bit quick to see problems where there aren't any. But he doesn't think that the fire-hydrant in front of him is a dog. The psychotic's idealism is not subordinated to a correct world view.

Given that there have been idealists as long as there have been newborns, George Berkeley (1658–1783) obviously wasn't the first idealist. But he was the first idealist with whose work contemporary philosophical thought is meaningfully connected. Berkeley was also the only person, *sans* qualification, to make anything resembling a creditable case for idealism. Russell (1914), Carnap (1967) and other 20th century idealists did nothing to improve Berkeley's arguments; they merely rearticulated those arguments with the help of recent developments in mathematical logic.

These moderns self-described as "neutral monists," not as "idealists"; and they defined "neutral monism" as the position that both mind and matter are built out of perceptions. But perceptions are mental. So this isn't *neutral* monism. It's *mental* monism; it's Berkeleyan idealism. And the 20th century idealists did nothing to substantiate idealism that Berkeley hadn't himself done.

It's obvious that Idealism and Realism are not different languages. Carnap et al. surely knew that, try as they presumably did to believe otherwise. And it's obvious that, despite their asseverations to the contrary, neutral monism is identical with Berkeleyan idealism. Also, Berkeley is seldom mentioned in the works of his 20th century imitators; and when he is mentioned, it's always disdainfully.

Of what relevance are these moral invectives to the present work? Empiricism forces its advocates to believe things they don't believe. To validate these beliefs, they must believe other things that they don't really believe (e.g. that idealism and realism are just different languages). And to make themselves psychologically capable of advocating views they know to be false, they must diminish themselves as human beings (by denying credit to those to whom it is due – a particularly sociopathic form of viciousness). Empiricism directly corrupts belief-systems and indirectly corrupts people.

That said, let us now consider Berkeley's arguments for idealism. There are two.

5.1 Berkeley's first argument:

> Let's set aside the so-called perceptions had by people who are on drugs, who are hallucinating, and who are dreaming.
>
> From the viewpoint of common sense, it's a datum that the remaining perceptions are accurate. So the perception I have from the top of the building, in which people are represented as being no bigger than ants, is accurate; and so is the perception I have when standing at the base of the building, when people are represented as being my size (or, if I'm a child, as being veritable giants). Both (sets of) perceptions can't be right. An object can't both have and not have a quality.
>
> Imagine that you are one tenth your current size. You'd see people as giants. but your perceptions would be accurate (given that you're not on drugs). Now imagine that your 10 times your actual size. Your perceptions would *correctly* represent people as midgets. So one and the same person would be both small and big; and, by similar arguments, one the same car would be moving quickly and slowly; one and the same rock would be both light and heavy.
>
> Since, by supposition, we've excluded deviant perceptual experiences – those induced by sleep, drug-consumption, and psychosis – the ones we're examining are all veridical. (In any case, it's a datum that, for common sense, they're veridical.) Therefore, if we suppose that our perceptions are depictions of transperceptual entities, we must suppose all of them – or all but an arbitrarily selected few – to be falsidical. It being a datum that they're veridical, we can't do that. So instead of saying that perceptions represent transperceptual realities, we say that the perceptions *are* the reality: the rock *is* the perceptions we have of it.

Analysis: Berkeley's argument involves two very basic non-sequiturs. "Big," "fast," and "heavy," are *comparative*, and so are most of the other terms we use to describe external objects. Smith is 1 ft tall. Brown is 6 ft tall. Jones is 60 ft tall. Smith sees Brown as big *compared to him* and Jones sees Brown as small compared to *him*. Smith's perceptions are compatible with Jones'. Jones and Smith would agree that, given some one ft metering rod, it could laid length-wise 60 times next to Jones, 6 times next to Brown, and once next to Smith. The rod would 'look big' in that it would appear to be his own size; and it would appear small to Brown, in that it would appear to 1/60th *his* size. But Smith and Brown would agree as to the size of the stick relative to Smith and to Brown.

Our perceptions *do* apprise us of the actual dimensions, velocities, etc. of objects. (Sometimes we need the help of prosthetics, such as microscopes and telescopes.) But when trying to determine the size of some house, you rightly consider its *relational* properties; you disregard its *phenomenal* properties except to the extent that they help you acquire such relational knowledge. If you are very close to the house, you don't let your subsequent *feeling* that it's overwhelmingly big determine your estimate as to its size; and if you are far from it, you put just as little stock in your *feeling* that it's small. To establish size is to establish comparative size. You determine the house's size by determining how much bigger it is than some other object. The spellbinding phenomenology drops out. All that is left are affectively neutral perceptions of instances of comparative largeness and smallness. All that is left, therefore, are instances of *comparative* properties and, therefore, of *relations*, e.g. the relation borne by x with respect to y iff x is larger than y, or heavier than y.

5.2   Berkeley's second argument:

> Try to conceive of a chicken that isn't conceived. You can't do it – because, if you did it, you would *ipso facto* conceive of the chicken that you were trying to conceive of as unconceived. To be, therefore, is to be conceived.

Analysis: Berkeley's injunction:

(C)   Try to conceive of a chicken that is unconceived.

is "syntactically ambiguous." (In other words, it has two meanings, but not because there is an ambiguous item in it, but rather because it can be parsed in two different ways.) It can mean:

(C_1)   Consider some chicken x: Now try to consider the proposition x isn't being thought of.

Or it can mean:

(C_2)   Consider the proposition: there is some chicken x that isn't being thought of.

If I obey C_1, there is some specific chicken that I'm thinking of. But there is no specific chicken that I need be thinking of to comply with C_2. Berkeley takes the object of "conceive" to be a noun denoting a chicken. He should take it to be a noun denoting a proposition. The proposition *there are chickens that you aren't thinking of* can be thought and accepted without there being any specific hitherto unconceived chicken, or therefore any hitherto unconceived chicken, that I'm thinking. Right now I'm considering (and accepting) the proposition: "there are primes greater than 8,887,777, which I know to be true; but there is no prime number x such that I am thereby thinking of x.

PART II

CHAPTER 10

Emotion as belief

1.0 In this chapter it will be argued that emotions are beliefs. In this chapter, we won't argue that desires are emotions. So should it turn out that they are emotions, insert the phrase "except for desires" in the second to last sentence.

That said, we will find in the next chapter that desires *are* beliefs. And by the end of the book, we will have established that *all* propositional attitudes are beliefs. So far as this strikes us wrong, it is because we have internalized some very wrong, empiricism-based views concerning emotions and other propositional attitudes.

In Sections 2.0–3.2, we will consider the surprisingly popular view that propositional attitudes don't exist – that nobody actually has beliefs, regrets, etc. We will see that the arguments for this view don't go through, and we'll therefore operate henceforth on the assumption that the contrary view is the correct one.

In Sections 4.0–4.1, we'll try to resolve some problems questions relating to the differences, if any there be, between propositional attitudes (e.g. one's belief that Sally is a great composer) and objectual attitudes (e.g. one's love of Sally).

Implicit in our answers to these questions are reasons for believing all emotions to be beliefs, and the rest of this chapter will therefore consist in our delineating the implications of the statements made in these sections.

2.0 A number of philosophers *deny* that we have propositional attitudes. Though radically implausible, this view has no shortage of capable advocates (e.g. Donald Davidson, Daniel Dennett, W. V. O. Quine, Paul Churchland, Gilbert Ryle, Ludwig Wittgenstein, B. F. Skinner). We must establish that these authors are wrong before we try to say what propositional attitudes are, lest we waste our time on a non-question.

Those who deny that we have propositional attitudes all do so for the same reason: they accept an "interpretivist" analysis of the mental. Calculators don't have beliefs, the interpretivist says, but it's useful to interpret their behavior *as though* they did.

It's easy to predict what will show up on the calculator's monitor if you do so on the assumption that the calculator is adding digits. You enter "2," "+," "2," "=," and "ENTER," and you enter them in that order. It is easy to predict that a "4" will appear on the monitor if you pretend that the calculator is a thinker. But one couldn't possibly make such a prediction if one regarded the calculator as just another physical object. There would be too much to learn about the calculator's internal condition and too little time to learn it. What is true of calculator is true of people, the interpretivist says. Just as the *right* way to interpret calculators is to regard them as structures that mediate electrical, so the *right* way to interpret people is to regard them as structures that mediate physiological activity. (Imagine trying to predict a person's behavior no the basis of his physiology.) But the only *feasible* way to interpret calculators is as cogitators, and the same is true of people. But it mustn't be forgotten, says the interpretivist, that human beings don't cogitate and that our assumption to the contrary is just a useful fiction.

Dennett (1989) put forth this very argument.

Interpretivists almost always take it as a given that mental entities don't exist: they are "eliminativists." And they are all eliminativists, and therefore interpretivists, for the same reason: its "unscientific" to believe in mental entities – believing in them is like believing in ghosts. Eliminativists thus have no choice but be interpretivists, given the indisputable fact that it's *useful* (prediction – conducive) to impute propositional attitudes to people.

2.1   Donald Davidson (2001b, 2001c, 2004[185]) is an interpretivist who tries to provide eliminativism-independent grounds for his position. So far as other interpretivists try to provide such grounds, what they say coincides with what Davidson says.

According to Davidson:

(DP[186]) In saying that "Jim believes that Joe stole Mary's boat," one isn't claiming there to be some relationship between Jim, on the one hand, and some abstract entity, on the other. In making such a statement, one is putting Jim on a three-dimensional coordinate system. The coordinates of the x-axis are terms like "believes," "hopes," "regrets," and so on. The coordinates of the y-axis are terms like "that Joe stole Mary's boat," "that inflation is currently skyrocketing," and so on. The coordinates of the z-axis are instants in time. The ordered-triple that determines a person's position on this plenum is determined by his overt behavior.

The word "determined" is ambiguous, as it can refer either to causal or to logical determination. So the last statement of the last paragraph ambiguous, as it could mean either that:

(i) On the basis of a person's overt behavior, we *figure out* what his psychological condition is and, on that basis, where he belongs on this plenum (i.e. a person's behavior is *causally* determined by his behavior, wherefore the former is evidence of the latter);

or that:

---

185. See, in particular, Chapter 6, which is titled "Representation and Interpretation," of Davidson (2004).

186. Short for "Davidson's position."

(ii) A person's behavior *itself* determines where he belongs on that plenum, any concomitant psychological states either being indistinguishable from his behavior or altogether non-existent (i.e. a person's behavior is *logically* determined by his behavior, in that the former *is* the latter).

(ii) is the right disambiguation. For (i) entails either that interpretivism (the position that I, Donald Davidson, am defending) is wrong or that it is nothing more than the truism that, when trying to figure out what another person's propositional attitudes are, we must take his overt behavior into account.

The usefulness of describing people as though they had propositional attitudes lies in the following fact. The function that assigns a position in this plenum to a given person, at a given time, does so on the basis of that person's behavior. (Following Quine (1960), I [Donald Davidson] hold that a person's overt behavior is all we have to go on in the way of understanding him.) As long as that function doesn't assign relatively similar coordinates to people who are behaving in relatively different ways, or relatively different coordinates to people who are behaving in relatively similar ways, that function will, to the extent that a person's behavior is reflected in his overt behavior, perfectly capture how any given person differs, in any given respect, from any other person.

Thus, that function will correctly characterize what any given person is like *compared to* any other person. The fact that we use terms like "believes" and "that Joe stole Mary's boat" to mark the coordinates on the relevant plenum doesn't mean that people's minds are cluttered with representations of propositions or with attitudes thereto, just as the fact that numbers are used to marks positions in space-time doesn't mean that space-time is cluttered with numbers.

Davidson's position evaluated: The position Davidson is defending is false and his defense of it is weak. Trees aren't usefully described *as though* they had beliefs; neither are rocks or sand-dunes. The reason: They don't have propositional attitudes. It's irrelevant that, unlike rocks and trees, calculators *are* usefully described as ratiocinating; for they are by definition artificial ratiocination-simulators. We so design them that they resemble thinkers.

Davidson is saying obliquely what Dennett (1989) says clearly. Calculators don't really calculate, but you'd have a devil of a time predicting a calculator's behavior except on the false assumption that it *is* calculating; and you'd have a devil of a time predicting another person's behavior except on the false assumption that he has propositional attitudes. Being identical with Davidson's position, Dennett's fails for the reason just given.

3.0   Paul Churchland (1984) says that propositional attitudes don't exist. His argument can be represented as consisting of two premises and a conclusion, these being (i), (ii) and (iii), respectively.

(i)   The belief that there are propositional attitudes is part of folk-psychology. We don't put any stock in folk-physics or folk-physiology. So *ceteris paribus* we shouldn't put any stock in folk-psychology.

(ii)   Folk-theories aren't *necessarily* wrong. (Hence the "*ceteris paribus*" in the last sentence.) It's an empirical, not an *a priori* truth, that folk-physics turned out to be wrong, and it's theoretically possible that some species exists whose members are born knowing the Theory of Relativity. But folk-psychology *is* wrong. We know this because it has yielded nothing. No progress of any kind has been made in psychology. The reason: psychology has assumed the veridicality of folk-psychology.

(iii)   Conclusion: Propositional attitudes don't exist. *Explanation*: Folk-psychology is wrong. The essence of folk-psychology is that we have propositional attitudes. We can't believe that we have such things without accepting folk-psychology. Therefore we don't have such things and they don't exist.

3.1   *Churchland's argument evaluated*: Folk psychology is a belief system; so its mere existence guarantees that there are beliefs. To that extent, folk-psychology verifies itself, and to that same extent, Churchland's position undermines itself.

It has often been said that Churchland's position is self-undermining, and when it is said, it's said for the reason just given.[187] Churchland (1984) says that such arguments beg the question (this is a paraphrase, not a quotation):

(CP[188])   Smith believes in witches. One of the things he believes about witches is that they, and they alone, deny that witches exist. Brown says to Smith: "Witches don't exist." In response, Smith says: "Your contention defeats itself and establishes the truth of mine." Obviously Smith's argument is no good.

One day Smith comes up to me, Paul Churchland, and says: "I believe that there are beliefs. Being a counter-example to itself, your belief to the contrary undermines your position and establishes mine." This argument of Smith's fails, and it fails for the same reason as his other argument.

The first part of CP is correct; the second part is not. Smith's first argument *does* fail. Brown's denial of Smith's theory confirms that theory only if there is independent reason to accept that theory. Smith gives Brown no independent reason to accept it; so Smith's retort to Brown rolls foul.

---

187.   Hacker (1996) puts forth the argument just stated.

188.   Short for "Churchland's position."

Smith's theory concerns witches, not theories. Therefore it doesn't concern itself, and it can no more be a confirmatory or a disconfirmatory instance of itself than an object known to contain no metal can confirm or disconfirm the hypothesis that all metal objects expand when heated.

But Churchland's theory *is* a theory about theories. So Churchland's theory is to itself what a heated metal object is to the hypothesis that all heated metal expands. Churchland's theory is to the effect that there are no beliefs and, therefore, no theories. So Churchland's theory *does* counterexample itself, since it is to itself what a heated, non-expanding metal object is to the hypothesis that all heated metal expands.

The presumption that we have beliefs, doubts, etc. is a strong and deeply rooted one. The attempts we've considered to undermine that presumption are artificial and otherwise insufficiently probative to warrant the drastic revision of our belief-system that they would warrant if they were correct. So far as there have been other attempts to uproot that presumption, they were not meaningfully different from the two just considered. So we will henceforth operate on the assumption that there are such things as propositional attitudes.

4.0   Not all attitudes are propositional; some are objectual. Love is an example of an objectual attitude. (One loves Mary or Sally.) So is hate. So is admiration. So indeed is any emotion that one might have towards a person or anything else that isn't a proposition.

Even though there are such things as objectual attitudes, they consist of propositional attitudes. (Objectual *awarenesses* do not so consist; but the former are not *attitudes*.) One's admiration for someone is contingent on one's beliefs about that person: no sooner does one find out that Smith plagiarized his award winning novel than one ceases to admire Smith. The relationship between one's beliefs about Smith and one's level admiration towards him is constitutive, not causal. It isn't that your belief that Smith is a great writer *causes* you to admire Smith. It's that your belief that he is a great writer *is* your admiration of him, or at least a component of it. (To be sure, your believing that Smith is a great writer *may* be what caused you to admire Smith. But if so, that is because it itself became a constituent of that belief or because was causative of some other, similar belief that became such a constituent.)

Contrariwise, when you find out that Smith is a plagiarist and all-around fraud, your admiration *ipso facto* dies. And so far as your admiration lingers, it is only because you haven't really reconciled yourself to the fact that he's a plagiarist. It is not because your belief that he was a greater author was a now-defunct *cause* of your admiration of him. It is because your belief that he was a great writer *was* your admiration of him, or at least a part of it.

It is not even theoretically possible to admire somebody as to whose lack of merit one is completely convinced. Thus, any instance of admiration consists of at least one belief. Exactly similar points hold with regard to any instance of any objectual attitude and thus of any instance of love, hate, envy, or amity.

"But surely that isn't categorically true," it will be said. "Obviously lusting for someone is different from having various beliefs about them. Surely there are pure objectual attitudes: objectual attitudes that don't consist of propositional attitudes."

In the pages to come, we'll see that all emotions are beliefs and that all affects embody beliefs. We'll thus see that lusting for someone *does* consist in having certain beliefs. So far as this seems obviously false, it's because we have internalized erroneous empiricism-based theories concerning emotions. Telescoped into one's having lust for someone, or into one's having any affect of any kind, are all manner of beliefs. Those beliefs are not only unconscious, but subpersonal; and for reasons to be discussed, their entry into consciousness is contingent on their being disguised as ratiocinatively unarticulated dollops of phenomenology.

There are pure objectual *awarenesses*. Perceptions are such awarenesses. But if the argument I've put forth is cogent, there are no pure objectual *attitudes*. To have an attitude towards something, so I am trying to show, is to have a belief about it. To have a negative attitude towards one's job is to believe it to be beneath one, or some such. To have a positive attitude about it is to believe it to be worthy of one, or some such.

4.1   The term "propositional attitude" is misleading, as it suggests that my belief that

(US[189]) I have been unfaithful to my spouse

can be decomposed into two distinct parts, namely:

(i)   an awareness of a proposition (namely, *that I was unfaithful towards my spouse*);

and

(ii)   an acceptance of that proposition.

The conventional wisdom is that this propositional attitude *is* to be decomposed in just this way. The conventional wisdom is not to be accepted. What is it to have "an attitude of acceptance" towards US? Presumably, it is to *believe* US. But in that case, the just-stated analysis of US is viciously circular, since, according to it, to believe US is

(i)   to be aware of it

and

(ii)   to believe it.

Functionalists, such as Jerry Fodor (1976, 1987, 1990), hold that (ii) is identical, not with a belief, but with my awareness of US's having a certain *functional role*. To believe a given proposition P, says Fodor, involves two things:

---

189. Short for "unfaithful towards spouse."

(i*) being aware of P,

and

(ii*) that awareness's having certain causes and effects.

If Fodor is right, the just-presented analysis is not viciously circular, at not least not for the reason given.

But this cannot be the right analysis. Let ph be the physiological structure mediating my awareness that P. ph doesn't cause anything; nor is it caused by anything. For *objects* neither cause, nor are caused, by anything. *Events* and *conditions* (which are systems of events) are what have causes and effects. ph's coming into existence, this being an *event*, has a cause; so does ph's undergoing a change in temperature, this being another event. And ph's having a certain temperature, this being a condition, has certain effects; so does ph's having a certain volume, this being another condition.

Presumably, ph's being an awareness of P has effects. But this presumption is false if ph's being such an awareness *consists* in its having certain effects. To say that content *is* causal role is to say that content isn't causally responsible responsible. But that's obviously wrong: the content of my wish to be a lawyer obviously *is* a cause of my deciding to study for the requisite examinations.

Functionalizing one's awareness of P strips that awareness of causal efficacy, and functionalism is therefore false.

4.2 There is a way to analyze (i) that, unlike the two analyses just considered, doesn't have any obvious demerits. Sense-perception is predicational, as Barry Stroud (2001) says. One can't just see the rock; one must see the rock *as* having this or that shape or location or size or color.[190]

---

190. This is is a corollary of the fact that the spatiotemporal world *consists* of property-instances. There is nothing in which property-instances inhere.

    Locke held that property-instances necessary "inhere" in substances or, as Locke called them, "substrates." Locke's position is that of commonsense, so far as commonsense has any view on the matter. And few philosophers explicitly negate Locke's contention; most tacitly accept it; and, among those who explicitly weigh in on the matter, more affirm it than deny it. And those, such as Hume and Russell, who do explicitly deny it are excoriated for doing so.

    But as Hume and Russell themselves state, Locke's contention is true *only* "substrate" and "inhere" are taken to mean, respectively, "aggregate of property-instances" and "belong to." But in that case, Locke's contention is exactly what we are saying.

    But that isn't Locke's contention. Locke advocates the commonsense-based view that there cannot be free-floating property-instances. Locke's view is incoherent. Nothing can possibly be propertyless, since a propertyless thing wouldn't have a location in time or space and therefore wouldn't exist in the same realm as the property-instances it supposedly underlies. So substrates are surds, and so *a fortiori* are instances of things' "inhering" in them, whatever that means.

An analogue of Stroud's point holds of one's awareness of propositions. Propositions are not *just* presented to one; they are presented as true, false, possible, etc. I submit that for one to believe P is for P to be presented to one as true. One's believing P is P's being presented to one as true, much as one's seeing the rock as gray identical with the rock's being presented to one as gray.

To say that P is presented to one as true is not to say that P *is* true. Just as one can have inaccurate perceptions of rocks, so one can have inaccurate conceptions of propositions.

For me to believe P is not for me to have

(a)   an awareness of P

and

(b)   a mental state or structure, separate from that awareness, consisting of my accepting P.

For me to believe that (e.g.) 2 + 2 = 4 is for that proposition to be given to me as true. For me to believe it probable that George is in Canada is for the proposition that George is in Canada to be presented to me as probable.

An analogous point clearly holds with respect to sense-perception. My seeing the rock as gray is not decomposable into

(i)   My having an awareness of the rock

plus a separate state consisting of

(ii)   My predicating grayness of that rock.

My awareness of the rock *consists* of its being given to me as gray. For any property p that I sense-perceive the rock to have, my sense-perceiving the rock as having p *is* my sense-perception (i.e. sensory experience, not necessarily a veridical one) of the rock, or at any rate is constitutive of it.

Similarly, my believing it probable that George is in Canada consists in my seeing that proposition, not necessarily veridically, as being probable. One's awareness of non-spatiotemporal entities can be predicational. (I say "can be," not "is," because, whereas one obviously cannot see an object without seeing it *as* having these orthose properties, it is *prima facie* possible to be aware of a propositoni without being aware of it *as* true or false or improbable.)

This analysis doesn't have the unfortunate consequence of decomposing propositional attitudes into two distinct parts, which cannot be reunited into the unitary entities that they clearly are. And what we have said about belief is easily extended to every other propositional attitude. For me to disbelieve P is for P to be presented to me as false. For me to disbelieve that 2 + 2 = 5 is for that proposition to be presented to me as false.

5.0   The empiricist view of emotions is that they are cognitively empty. They are nothing but affective reactions, like, supposedly, the revulsion you experience when eating rotten food. Even that feeling of revulsion, I will argue in Sections 6.1.2–6.1.3, is not cognitively empty, contrary to what empiricists assume. (Hence the "supposedly.") Little ideation, if any, is as decorticated as empiricists hold.

Empiricists believe that emotions are antithetical to thought and that, although *caused* by beliefs, they are animalistic, judgment-free effusions.

This is not the right way to think about emotions. Consider your fear that

(ML)   Your mother-in-law is coming to town.

We can't say that this consists of two distinct parts: an awareness of a proposition, on the one hand, and some kind of attitude towards it, on the other. What would that attitude be? We can't say that it would consist of *fear that ML*; for, according to the view in question, that attitude is distinct from your awareness of ML.

It would obviously be viciously regressive to say of that attitude that it embodied awareness of some *other* proposition.

If we decompose propositional attitudes into an attitudinal part and a propositional part, we have a choice. We can take a functionalist view of that attitude, which we've already shown not to be a live option. Or we can say of that attitude it is an *effect* of the relevant person's awareness of the proposition in question, which we'll now see not to be a live option.

Suppose that your awareness of ML causes you to have a migraine, or indigestion, or to be in some other uncomfortable state. That wouldn't mean that you *feared* that your mother-in-law was coming to visit. It could be that you're overjoyed that she's coming to visit but that, when you're overjoyed, your heart-race increases and, because of some physiological quirk of yours, you get a headache whenever your heart-rate increases.

A positive emotion can *cause* distress (my feeling happy causes my heart to race, which in turn causes me to have a painful heart-attack); and a negative emotion can *cause* happiness (my being depressed lowers my blood pressure, thereby alleviating the severity of the headache I am experiencing). So it isn't virtue of a given emotion's *causing* one to feel good (bad) that it is a positive (negative) emotion.

Laughter can set off asthma attacks. Positive emotions lead to physiological changes, which can trigger migraines. Anything can cause anything. Surges of positive emotion have physiological concomitants, and those concomitants could in principle precipitate acute distress.

In high school I knew a talented athlete whose lungs filled up with fluid whenever he did vigorous exercise. He loved playing soccer but couldn't do so without experiencing serious respiratory distress. Of course, it wasn't his enjoyment *per se* that caused his lungs to fill up with fluid. But we could coherently imagine his ailment to be such that his enjoyment *per se* did have that effect. So it is not by virtue of what its effects are that a given emotion is positive or negative.

Supposing that this person were cured of his ailment, his subsequent delight would consist in his recognizing that his life had thereby improved. His delight would be identical with a belief that his being cured would improve his life in some way.

Similarly, your fact that fear that your mother-in-law is coming to visit is identical with the fact that

(DP[191])   you believe it a distinct possibility that she'll visit and that her doing so, were it to happen, would diminish the quality of your life in some way.

Similarly,

(GB[192])   you are angry that George stole your bicycle

is identical with the fact that

(GB*)   you believe that George stole your bicycle and that, in doing so, he was doing you an injustice [or diminishing the quality of your life, or some such].

The fact that

(FV)   you are happy that your father is coming to visit

is identical with

(FV*)   the fact that you believe that your father is coming to visit and that his doing so, were it to happen, would enrich your life.

Other emotions are to be analyzed similarly.

6.0   But can't one *dispassionately* know that one's life is going to improve? When I first discover that in one year's time Smith is going to give me $1,000,000, I am ecstatic. But doesn't that knowledge soon become disaffected? Can't one have emotionally anti-septic knowledge that one's life has changed for the better (or the worse)?

Yes one can. But that doesn't mean that *any* given belief as to one's life-prospects is disaffected. There are two very different kinds of beliefs: discursive and egocentric. Let T be the truth that it is extremely cold in place p at time t. Supposing that I am in p at t, there are two ways that T can be given to me. It can be given to me as the truth that:

(i)   It is cold in p at t

Or it can be given to me as the truth that:

---

191.   Short for "distinct possibility."

192.   Short for "George stole my bicycle."

(ii)   It is now cold in the place where I am.

T's being given to me in the second way consists in my relativizing it to a cognitive map of which I am the point of origin. T's being to me in the first way consists in my relativizing it to a map in which no person, including myself, is given a privileged position. If I grasp T in the second way, I have an "egocentric" grasp of it. If I grasp it in the first way, I have an "discursive" grasp of it.

Let T* be the truth that Smith is going to give me $1,000,000 in one year's time. Since I am the recipient of Smith's generosity, T* can be given to me as the truth that Smith will give *me* $1,000,000; and it can also be given to me in the same way that it is given to you, namely, as the truth that Smith will give JMK $1,000,000. My grasping T in the first way, but not the second, is identical with my having an emotion.

A given individual almost certainly has egocentric beliefs before he has dispassionate, discursive beliefs; and egocentric beliefs are undoubtedly more central to one's psychological architecture than discursive beliefs. The latter are easily modified and displaced; and such displacements tend to have little or no affect on one's character. After decades of believing otherwise, Einstein became convinced that the universe was expanding. Surely his character didn't change much as a result. But if Einstein had come to believe that everyone was trying to kill him, including his wife and relatives, his character *would* have undergone quite dramatic changes.

To have a correct view of what emotions really are, one must countenance the concept of non-introspectible, unconscious ideation. Our minds are many-layered. Our discursive, theoretical beliefs, e.g. our beliefs about real numbers and economics, tend to be phenomenologically sterile. But such beliefs are not representative of all beliefs or even the most fundamental of our beliefs. Discursive beliefs are not egocentric; they don't concern one's own welfare; and one's welfare doesn't depend on their veridicality (except in ways that are obviously derivative as well as tenuous, e.g. a philosopher's professional welfare can be adversely affected by his having erroneous epistemological views).

Many beliefs, however, are of an egocentric nature. Cf. a person's belief that the rattlesnake hissing at him is likely to bite him. I will henceforth describe beliefs of this kind as "egocentric beliefs." So one's fear that one is about to be mugged is an "egocentric belief," as I will be using this term.

A given individual almost certainly has egocentric beliefs before he has dispassionate, discursive ones; and such beliefs are undoubtedly more central to one's psychological architecture than one's theoretical beliefs. The latter are easily modified and displaced; and such displacements tend to have little or no affect on one's character. After decades of believing otherwise, Einstein became convinced that the universe was expanding. Surely his character didn't change much as a result. But if Einstein had come to believe that everyone was trying to kill him, including his wife and relatives, his character *would* have undergone quite dramatic changes.

In Chapter 13, Section 5, we will develop the points just made concerning the distinction between egocentric and discursive beliefs.

6.1 The word "emotion" is ambiguous; this has predisposed laymen and scholars to accept some very wrong views. An "emotion" can be:

(i)   An enduring structure of a certain kind;

(ii) A phenomenological derivative of such a structure;

(iii) The event of some such structure's coming into existence;

or

(iv) A phenomenological accompaniment of such an event.

The word "feeling" is ambiguous in the same way as the word "emotion." Sometimes it refers to consciousness-constitutive states (cf. "I feel awful right now). Sometimes it refers to enduring propositional attitudes (cf. "his feelings about constructivism are ambiguous"). Sometimes it refers to the onset of such attitudes (cf. "although I didn't know it at the time, it was when I discovered that Dana had been slandering me that my feelings for her changed"). And sometimes it refers to the phenomenological derivatives of the onset of such an attitude (cf. "a feeling of helplessness overcame me when I finally realized that my professional future was in the hands of amoral bureaucrats").

Wishing to avoid ambiguity, I will not use the word "feeling" to refer to the occurrent, phenomenology-constituted states to which emotional attitudes tend to give rise. Instead, I will use the artificial term "phenomenological episode." That one must resort to neologisms in order to discourse unambiguously about emotions shows that some very wrong views about emotion are embedded in language, which in turn shows that those same views are deeply embedded in thought.

It is almost certainly constitutive of Smith's fear that Jones will kill him that it *tends* to give rise to certain kinds of phenomenological episodes. In general, given any egocentric belief, it is presumably constitutive of that belief that it tend to have phenomenological manifestations of a certain kind. But there is no specific phenomenological episode, such that *it in particular* is constitutive of Smiths fear. We must distinguish the falsehood that:

(i)   There is some particular feeling F such that it is necessarily the case that your fear give rise to F,

from the truth that:

(ii) It is necessarily the case that, for some feeling F, your fear tends to give rise to F.

This failure is an instance of the "quantifier-shift" fallacy: the tendency to confuse statements of the form *there is some x, such that for any y, x bears R to y* with those of the form *given any y, there is some x, such that x bears R to y.* We've seen many instances of this fallacy. Cf. the failure, discussed in Chapter 8, Section 16.0, to distinguish between

(1)   For any n you choose, it is possible that, by coincidence, models M and M*
      (M ≠ M*) model data $o_1...o_n$ equally well.

and

(2)   It is possible that, by coincidence, for any n you choose, models M and M*
      (M ≠ M*) model data $o_1...o_n$ equally well.

Aware of the distinction between (i) and (ii), and of the distinction between egocentric and discursive beliefs, we can do justice to the fact that emotions involve conscious feelings, without going so far as to say that emotions are nothing but such feelings.

Egocentric beliefs by definition concern one's welfare. It follows that egocentric beliefs necessarily tend to give rise to phenomenological episodes. The reason this follows is that propositional attitudes are not *actionable* except in so far as they give rise to phenomenological episodes. Your belief that the hissing rattlesnake in front of you is a threat won't cause you to take survival-critical measures, such as fleeing, *except* in so far as that belief jolts you with unpleasant, action-inducing phenomenology. For this reason, egocentric beliefs must tend to have certain sorts of phenomenological manifestations. This reinforces the tendency to confuse emotions with their phenomenological manifestations; and since beliefs obviously aren't phenomenological episodes, it reinforces view that emotions are not beliefs.

Because we tend to take discursive beliefs, e.g. beliefs about arithmetic, as paradigm-cases of belief, we take the fact that emotions are actionable as proof that they aren't beliefs. But not all beliefs are discursive. In fact, discursive beliefs are uniquely unfit to serve as paradigm-cases of belief. A discursive belief is by definition a non-egocentric belief. One's belief that arithmetic is incomplete doesn't have anything to do with oneself. And a given person's beliefs about himself are discursive only to the extent that he is able to treat himself as an object – only to the extent he can set aside the fact that *he* is what that belief is about. So the existence of self-relating discursive beliefs confirms our point that discursive beliefs are non-egocentric. It therefore confirms our point that egocentric beliefs are not emotionally anti-septic and are, therefore, action-dispositive. And, though it doesn't do much to establish it, this is consistent with our position that emotions are beliefs.

7.0   In Section 5.0, I said that even affective reactions embody judgments: a judgment is embodied in one's revulsion at the smell of putrid meat. In this section and the next we will justify this statement.

Our senses of smell are not remotely as keen as those of a bear or a dog. (To simplify discussion, let's focus only on olfactory experiences of comestibles.) But olfaction tracks facts about its objects. Spoiled chicken smells different from unspoiled chicken; very spoiled chicken smells different from moderately spoiled chicken; spoiled chicken smells different from spoiled fish; unspoiled chicken smells different from unspoiled fish.

Our olfactory sense is extremely dull by comparison with our visual, auditory, and tactile senses. And yet any given any two objects that differ from each other to all but the slightest degree in respect of the way in which, or the degree to which, they are unfit to eat, our olfactory sensations of the one will differ in ways appropriate to both the nature and the extent of the differences in the objects in question.

Further, the class of comestibles with respect to which these points hold is in some respects unbounded. If scientists were to invent new food-stuffs, our senses of smell would be quite as good at tracking facts relating to how, and to what degree, instances of those foodstuffs would be unfit to eat. In fact, employees of Snickers and other such corporations regularly produce such inventions; and the olfactory acuity that we have in connection with carrots, chicken, and other perennial staples carries over without a hitch to these new foodstuffs. Like anyone else, setting aside people with defective senses of smell, I can tell instantaneously whether the "cool-ranch" corn-chips in bowl A are off, and I can do the same with respect to the "tangy salsa-flavored" chips in bowl B. And if the chips in both bowls are unfit to eat, I know through olfaction *in what way* they are so, and also how they differ from their counterparts in the other bowl in respect of the manner in which, and the degree to which, they are unfit to eat.

These facts don't square with the supposition that olfactory experiences are by nature reflexive and non-judicative. They are *involuntary.* That's incontrovertible. But "involuntary" doesn't mean "reflexive." All reflexive behaviors are involuntary, but not *vice versa.* Reflexive behaviors embody no intelligence at all: to the extent that ideation is implicated in a given behavior, it is, by definition, non-reflexive. But involuntary behaviors can be supremely intelligent. All but an infinitesimally small fraction of our cogitations are involuntary. We can voluntarily initiate a thought-process, and we can voluntarily choose to focus our cognitive energies on this as opposed to that problem. But the resulting cognitive processes *per se* are involuntary. Once initiated, a thought process "follows its own dark-ways," as Reichenbach (1947) put it. The passage in which this phrase occurs is worth quoting *in toto*, since it relates, not just to the position we are currently in the process of substantiating, but also to the thesis that it is the present work's point to establish:

> If we want to say that logic deals with thinking, we had better say that logic teaches us how thinking *should* proceed and not how it *does* proceed.[193] This formulation, however, is susceptible of another misunderstanding. It would be very unreasonable to believe that we could improve our thinking by forcing it into the straightjacket of logically ordered operations. We know very well that thinking follows its own dark ways, and that efficiency cannot be secured by prescriptions controlling the paths from the known to the unknown. It is rather the results of thinking, not the thinking process themselves, that are controlled by logic. Logic is the touchstone of thinking, not its propelling

---

193. The italics are Reichenbach's own.

force, a regulative of thought more than a motive; it formulates the laws by which we judge thought processes to be correct, not laws that we want to impose upon thinking.

What Reichenbach says about logic holds of empiricism. Empiricism doesn't describe how we actually think or how we should think. But it does describe a standard with respect to which it is appropriate to evaluate the thoughts we have had. To paraphrase Reichenbach:

> If we want to say that [empiricism] deals with thinking, we had better say that [empiricism] teaches us how thinking *should* proceed and not how it *does* proceed.[194] This formulation, however, is susceptible of another misunderstanding. It would be very unreasonable to believe that we could improve our thinking by forcing it into the straightjacket of [empiricism-friendly] operations. We know very well that thinking follows its own dark ways, and that efficiency cannot be secured by prescriptions controlling the paths from the known to the unknown. It is rather the results of thinking, not the thinking process themselves, that are controlled by [empiricism]. [Empiricism] is the touchstone of thinking, not its propelling force, a regulative of thought more than a motive; it formulates the laws by which we judge thought processes to be correct, not laws that we want to impose upon thinking.

Empiricism is correctly taken as a "touchstone of thinking." (I say "a," not "the," because empiricism is irrelevant to the adjudication of purely conceptual propositions.) But empiricists see empiricism as describing how we *should* think, if we are to acquire knowledge. Since involuntary ideation falls outside the scope of personal responsibility, empiricists have no choice but to regard such ideation as either spurious or as noncognitive. Thus, empiricists are *ipso facto* predisposed to categorize the involuntary with the purely reflexive.

7.1 Whether your knee jerks is a function only of how hard the doctor's mallet collides with it; every other aspect of the collision is irrelevant. The mechanism underlying your knee's behavior is therefore rigid.

That mechanism is also binary. Either your knee jerks or it doesn't: two sufficiently strong collisions make it jerk by the same amount, even if one of those collisions is much stronger than the other. (I am leaving it open whether the point made in this paragraph is the same as the one made in the previous paragraph.)

In general, the mechanisms underlying reflexive behaviors are both rigid and binary. There is only one sort of thing that prompts such a mechanism to act, and there is only one way such a mechanism acts when prompted.

---

194. The italics are Reichenbach's own.

The structures subserving cognitive reactions are as flexible as those subserving reflexive behaviors are rigid. Where cognitive structure are concerned, response-differentials are proportional to stimulus-differentials, and along certain dimensions the class of stimulus-response pairs that thus co-vary is unbounded.

The structures subserving reflexes are *mechanisms*. But this is not true of the structures subserving involuntary but cognitive reactions. Mechanisms are not principle-driven. So they can make only limited provisions for principled relations, such as that between, on the one hand, a comestible's odor and, on the other hand, the extent to which, or the way in which, it is unfit to eat.

A story will make this clear. You are a renowned inventor. The military contracts you to build and program a robot ("Gloxo"), which either has a sense of smell or some functional analogue thereof. Let GS (short for "Gloxo's sense of smell") be the physical structure mediating Gloxo's (pseudo-)olfactory activity. Inevitably, GS will obey the laws of physics. So it will respond to particle-collisions in ways that are appropriate to the micro-physical properties of those collisions.

But whether GS mediates genuine olfaction depends on whether it has second-order responses of the right kind. If GS responds to its responses to the aforementioned collisions in a way that is appropriate to the olfaction-specific properties (supposing there to be any) mediated by said collisions, *then* GS mediates actual olfaction. It doesn't mediate olfaction if it doesn't thus respond to its responses to those collisions. Further, it doesn't mediate olfaction if it *does* respond to its first-order responses, but fails to do so in a way that tracks the differences in the various olfaction-specific properties mediated by the relevant particle-collisions.

In Chapter 1, Section 1.2.1, we discussed why there is virtually no chance of there being a microphysical characterization of any given biological property. Whether a given object functions as a heart (or a kidney or even a subcellular organelle) depends only on facts about its gross-structure; its microstructure is relevant *only* to the extent that it must implement the requisite gross-structure. Correspondingly, olfaction picks up on biology-relevant (survival- and health-relevant) properties of its objects: rottenness, wholesomeness, and the like.

Thus, for GS to mediate olfaction, it isn't enough that it be pushed and pulled in various ways. Nor is it enough that *in actuality* those pushes and pulls mediate certain olfaction-specific property-instances. It is necessary that, *in* being sensitive to the requisite particle collisions, GS is thereby sensitized to the olfaction-specific property-instances mediated thereby. But since there is no mechanical characterization of those olfactory properties, you cannot endow Gloxo with olfaction, or anything comparable to it, without sensitizing GS to principles that mediate between the micro-physical and the olfactory. You must see to it that, encoded in GS's structure, is a way of generating olfactory awareness out of the aforementioned collision-caused disturbances. And to do that you must endow GS with sensitivity to *principles*.

This is perfectly possible. The position being advocated isn't that we can't build olfactorily-intelligent robots. We can build them, and probably do. The position being advocated is that olfaction in such robots, as in us, is mediated not by first-order mechanical responses to disturbances of its requisite organs, but by responses to those responses, with the qualification that these second-order responses are connected by way of principle-embodying correspondence-rules to those first-order responses.

For suppose that, when programming Gloxo, you don't use the method just-described, choosing instead to use the brute-force method. Suppose, in other words, that you so construct GS that, given physical disturbances $pd_1...pd_n$, it responds by having olfactory-responses $oe_1...oe_n$. n will not be a large number. This has nothing to do with our current technological limitations: no matter how much technology improves, n will always be a relatively small number. (That is, it will be small relative to what it would have to be if *ceteris paribus* GS were to be more than a caricature of an olfactory organ.). If, for each i ($1 \leq i \leq n$), a special olfaction-related provision has to be made *ad hoc* for pd_i, GS will soon run out of storage space. If, for each i and j ($1 \leq i,j \leq n$), the principle by which GS derives oe_i from pd_i is different from that by which it derives oe_j from pd_j, then

(i)   GS can only have a finite number of different olfactory responses.

(i) entails that:

(ii)   GS's olfactory responses won't register continuous (arbitrarily small) changes in the corresponding physical disturbances.

Another consequence is that, speaking realistically,

(iii)   Unless n is an extremely small number, GS's storage capacity, and its RAM (its ability to locate the contents of its memory-banks), must be enormous. There is thus no feasible way of ensuring that there is anything more than a crude correspondence between GS's behavior and the disturbances responsible for it; and there is no way of ensuring that there holds *any* such correspondence, no matter how crude, outside of narrow limits.

A more important consequence is that oe_i and oe_j won't in any meaningful sense be operationalizations of any *one* sensory modality. Supposing that $v_1...v_n$ are your various visual perceptions, part of what makes them all belong to the same modality is that they all come off the same assembly line. It is, of course, *partly* because of qualities inherent in v_i and v_j, ($1 \leq i,j \leq n$), that they are both visual perceptions. But the operative word is "partly." You automatically integrate the contents of two visual perceptions. But you would not do so if they were generated by different mechanisms – if, in other words, different correspondence-rules mediated between v_i and v_j ($1 \leq i,j \leq n$) and their respective causes. For your mind to regard their respective contents as concerning some *single* space, it is not enough that those contents in fact have some principled relationship to each other: it is also necessary that your mind be sensitive to that relationship. But if it is thus sensitive, then embodied in your visual system is precisely the sort of second-order sensitivity that we've been discussing. Obviously these points apply to olfaction, no less than to sight. So for any two members of $oe_1...oe_n$, to so much as qualify as instances of single modality, it is necessary that GS be endowed with knowledge of (or knowledge-like sensitivity to) some *one* principle that assigns olfaction-specific properties to microphysical properties.

Thus endowed, GS is like a computer that is programmed to pair off any number with its square, as opposed to computer that has been programmed to assign 4 to 2, 9 to 3…and n^2 to n, for some finite n. Problems relating to limitations of storage space have been resolved, as have problems relating to the desideratum that GS's olfactory responses vary continuously with continuous changes in the corresponding disturbances.

Unbounded, systematic, continuous co-variation is *ipso facto* evidence of responsiveness of a principle-based, as opposed to purely mechanical kind. This is a point that Strawson and Grice[195] made in their landmark paper about Quine's[196] views on analyticity, and it is one that Chomsky developed and put to good use in his cognitive scientific work.

There's no denying that *less* intelligence is embodied in our olfactory experiences than in, say, our visual experiences. If I simultaneously see A and B, I will see them as differing in respect of shape, color, size, and position (relative to me); further, I will see each one as consisting of parts that differ from each other in respect of its shape, size, location; and I will see the color of each as having internal structure (as having a certain hue, resolution, saturation, etc.). So vision presents objects as being in a 4-dimensional manifold (space-time) *within which* other multi-dimensional manifolds are embedded (a color-space, shape-space, etc.), *within which* yet other manifolds are embedded (e.g. a hue-space, a saturation-space). Thus, vision is multi-multi-multi-dimensional. Olfaction is merely multidimensional. But this doesn't mean that vision is a cognition-heavy matter, whereas olfaction is not; it means that vision is *more* cognition-heavy than olfaction.

The view that feelings are *just* feelings is a non-starter. Feelings are *not* reflexive. Involuntary – yes. Reflexive – no. They embody thought, sometimes extraordinarily sophisticated thought. But if one takes the empiricist view that the mind is transparent to itself, it is *de rigueur* to co-categorize olfaction, vision, etc. with knee-jerks and epileptic seizures.

8.0　I would like to end this chapter by developing our adaptation of Reichenbach's insight into logic. Self-described empiricists say that they don't want to "over-draw conclusions," as though doing so was the ultimate methodological *faux pas*. But over-drawing conclusions is the *via regia* to scientific knowledge, on the condition that one withdraw one's conclusions when one sees, as one does 9 times out of 10, that they don't square with the evidence. But even that 10th hypothesis will itself be overdrawn

---

195.　Grice and Strawson (1957).

196.　Quine (1951, 1960).

at the time it is tendered. If it weren't overdrawn, it wouldn't have to be tested. But all hypotheses must be tested.

Empiricists say that the most important scientific virtue is inferential conservatism: sticking to the facts. That is not true. The most important scientific virtue is flexibility: a willingness to change one's mind when one knows that one is wrong. One can't have the latter virtue if one is afraid of being wrong. One must see being wrong the way soccer players see attempts to score a goal: you score once for every 100 times you try. But that is no cause for dismay; for it isn't how often you fail to score; it's how often you succeed. Successes outweigh failures.

But empiricists believe otherwise. For them, failures have as much weight as successes; so they're afraid to over-draw conclusions. A fear of over-drawing conclusions is probably a part of a more general attitude of fearfulness. To be sure, there are arenas in which inferential conservativism is indicated: if one is in combat, for example, one should probably stick with the tried and true, instead of gambling on a long-shot. But, unlike the combatant, empiricists are operating in a low-stakes arena: What are the consequences of having a wrong idea? None – apart from the censure of one's colleagues. But such censure means nothing unless it's reinforced by morbid self-doubt. The proponent of an erroneous theory won't feel bruised when he's duly corrected. His attitude will be that of John Maynard Keynes, who said: "When I'm given new data, I change my mind." Unless one is afflicted by such self-doubt, collegial censure is meaningful only to the extent that it is a source of information, and then it's meaningful only in the same way as any other such source.

Of course, one's monetary welfare may depend on the sentiments of one's colleagues. We have been operating on the false assumption that this is not so. But we have been justified in thus operating. One's fear of one's colleagues' scorn is surely not always based strictly on monetary considerations. One's need for peer-validation is too large to be chalked up solely to its monetary importance. It's also of the wrong nature. The need for money leads to action; the need for peer-approval inhibits action. The money-maker is confronting the world. The world isn't meeting his needs; so he tries to change it. The approval-seeker is avoiding confronting the world. It is by being meek and passive that one gets approval; it is by being confrontational that one loses it. In any case, we have been trying to obtain a clear view of the other emotional factors at work, and our inquiry hasn't yet come to an end. So we have been obliged, and will continue to be obliged, to set aside the monetary dimension of one's fear of being criticized by one's peers.

It is only if one cannot tolerate being wrong that one cares one way or the other about the emotional validations of one's colleagues. It is only if one is pathologically insecure that one cannot tolerate being wrong. And it is only if one is holding onto the infantile conceit that one is superhuman that one takes being wrong personally. This is because making mistakes is as inseparable from the human condition as breathing; and shame at being wrong, and thus of not being omniscient, is quite as morbid and regressive as shame at needing to breathe.

Pathological insecurity and pathological grandiosity are two sides of the same coin. I know I can't fly. That's why, even though I'm not happy about the fact that I can't fly, I'm not insecure about not being able to do so. It would only be if I hadn't fully internalized that fact that it would be a source of insecurity. It is only if one has the audacity to believe oneself superhuman that one feels justified in feeling insecure about being wrong. Insecurity-driven humility is crypto-narcissism. "Don't be so humble," said Golda Mier. "You're not that great."

Empiricism is insecurity-driven epistemic humility. Given how defective empiricism is and given how obvious its defects are, the roots of its popularity must be emotional, not logical. In light of the points just made, its appeal must lie in the pseudo-humility embodied in it and, therefore, in the grandiosity embodied in such pseudo-humility. Thus, an acceptance of empiricism is not just methodologically contraindicated, but also medically so. For in cleaving to it, one is cleaving to infantile, and therefore character-weakening, self-concepts.

Empiricism is a way of rationalizing insecurity about one's intellectual limitations. Such insecurity is in its turn a way of legitimating a bloated and infantile estimation of one's intellectual abilities.

To be sure, empiricism does have its merits, and it does have a place in the scientific process. But its place is at the end of that process, where the final touches are being put on theories, not at the beginning, where they are being formed. Empiricism doesn't tell scientists what it is reasonable for them to hypothesize. But it does tell them whether it is reasonable for them to continue to hold onto a given hypothesis.

CHAPTER 11

Desires, intentions, and values

1.0   What is a desire? I want to eat that piece of cake. If I believed that cake to be made of chalk-dust or mud, I wouldn't want to eat it. The reason: I'd believe that eating it would not be a source of gratification. By the same token, since I believe that eating that piece of cake would be exquisitely pleasurable, I *do* want to eat it. My desire to eat that piece of cake, I therefore submit, is identical with a judgment on my part: a judgment to the effect that eating it would be pleasurable.

I don't currently want to drink the contents of that bottle of dishwashing detergent. The reason: I believe that it would bring me no joy and much distress. But I *would* want to drink from that bottle if I thought it to contain a non-addictive, side-effect-free elixir that induced a state of euphoria. Conclusion: My desire to abstain from consuming the contents of that battle is a judgment: a judgment to the effect that failing to so abstain would bring me much grief.

One doesn't have to have a belief to be in an unpleasant state. But one does have to have a belief if one is to have a desire to alleviate or otherwise respond to that state. One doesn't have a desire to take a pill unless one has a belief as to what taking that pill will do. And if one has such a belief, one has the corresponding desire desire. So having the belief is necessary and sufficient for having the desire. Thus, a desire is a belief to the effect that doing such and such will bring pleasure or pain.

"A moment ago," it will be said, "you said that one could be in a state that one wished not to be in, and yet not have any idea how to get out of that state. Wouldn't someone in such a state have a desire without having a corresponding belief? And doesn't this show that desires are not beliefs?"

A distinction is to be made between wishes and desires. I *want* to own a Mustang Camaro. I *wish* I could become invisible. It is within my power to own a Mustang Camaro; I know what to do to acquire one, and I know I can do it. So far as I know, it is not within my power to become invisible or to fly. So I only *wish* that I could fly, whereas I *want* to own a Mustang Camaro. One has a wish, not a desire, when one is convinced that there is no real chance of actualizing the longed for alterations to one's condition.

I thus submit that desires are beliefs as to how to obtain gratification or avoid displeasure. I also submit that intentions are judgments as to how to comply with a value that one has. But I have yet to provide any grounds for accepting the latter contention; in fact, I have to say exactly what it means. We will now provide the requisite clarification and argumentation.

2.0   Intentions are not desires. Empiricists think otherwise. (In a moment we'll say why they think this.) For example, Davidson (2001a) holds that what one *intends* to do in a given context C is identical with what one most wants to do in C. One's C-intention is one's strongest C-desire.

This is false. A man sticks a gun in my face and says: "Your money or your life." I have a choice: lose my money and live or keep my money and die (only to lose it a moment later, when, as I'm lying dead, the robber takes it out of my pockets).

Do I *want* to give the robber my money? "Of course, you do," it will be said. "You want to live. And, the circumstances being what they are, you've got to give the man your money if you want to gratify your desire to live. Therefore you want to give him your money."

I want to live. But that doesn't mean I want to do all the things that are involved in staying alive. Somebody may have to get a leg amputated to live. But they don't *want* to lose their leg. What they *want* is to live. They *judge* that, if they are to gratify their desire to live, they must forego gratification of another, weaker desire. Similarly, I don't *want* to give the gunman my money. I *judge* that, given the circumstances, if I am to gratify a relatively strong desire (my desire to live) I must forego gratification of a relatively weak one (my desire to hold on to my money).

But this is very different from *wanting* to give the man my money. Desires don't cease to exist when they are outweighed. I want to continue to be a professor. I also want to have money. My desire to be a professor is more powerful than my desire for money (and exclusive of it). Does that mean that I don't *want* money? No! If somebody showed up with a briefcase full of money, I couldn't be more delighted. And, with respect to the armed-robbery situation, if a stroke of good fortune were to intervene (if, for example, the gunman were to drop dead of a heart-attack), I couldn't be happier. If, while being robbed, I didn't want to *not* give the man my money, I wouldn't respond this way.

"But one can both want to *not* do something and also to do it," it will be objected. "One can be ambivalent. There is no contradiction in this. What's not possible is for it to be the case both that desires, and has no desire, to do X. But one can want both to do and to refrain from X."

Yes, but that isn't what is going on here. I love my mother and thus want to give her a birthday present. But I'm angry at her, since she wrote a negative review of my last book; so I also want to *not* give her a birthday present. *Here* we have a case of ambivalence. But this is not what we have in the robbery-situation. I don't simply have a desire to *not* give the gunman my money. I *don't* have a desire to give him my money. I see giving him my money as a grim concession I must make to circumstances that I wholeheartedly wish I didn't have to make.

My intention to give the gunman my money is not a desire. It is a *judgment*. It is a judgment that I'll be better off if I give the gunman my money than if I don't. Given only what we've said, that judgment in its turn *may* be a judgment to the effect that, on balance, I will experience more desire-gratification if I give the man my money than if I don't. But given what we'll say in a moment, that isn't what it is. What matters now is that, event it concerns desires and is motivated by my wish to gratify certain desires, that judgment is not itself a desire.

2.1   According to Frankfurt (1988), intentions are *higher-order desires* (HOD's); that is, they are desires about desires. I desire to smoke a cigarette. But I desire to abstain from gratifying that desire, since I want to live a healthy life. If I give in into my desire to smoke, I am acting impulsively, like an animal. Therefore I'm not really acting at all; I'm *re*acting: I'm reacting to a desire. And my behavior, though voluntary, falls short of being intentional. Contrariwise, if I resist that desire and act on my desire to refrain from smoking, my conduct is guided by a *bona fide* intention, as opposed to an intention-impostor, such as an animalistic desire.

Frankfurt says that intentional behavior is value-driven behavior. He is right about this, as we'll see. But intentions are not HOD's. To be sure, there are many things that a person does because he values them. If a person values an activity, he's likely to derive pleasure from doing it. A volunteer (unpaid) fireman is likely to derive a certain satisfaction from doing his job well. But he doesn't do it to have a good time. He does it because he values doing it; and because he values doing it, doing it well gratifies him: the gratification it affords him is a by-product of his belief that he's done something valuable.

In order to become a volunteer fireman, one has to pass various physical fitness tests and examinations, and one must therefore exercise a great deal of self-control at various junctures. Frankfurt would say that, by virtue of my thus exercising self-control, an HOD is dictating my behavior, as opposed to a first-order desire. But my behavior isn't desire-driven in any sense; it's judgement-driven.

Many a so-called HOD is really a judgment. I hate my supervisor and want to insult him. My refraining from doing so is judgment-driven, not desire-driven and therefore not HOD-driven. I want to have a cigarette. My refraining from doing so is judgment-driven, not HOD-driven.

This is not to deny that HOD's exist. It is to show that what Frankfurt describes as HOD's are not desires and are in fact judgments, like my judgment to give my money to the stick-up man.

In some cases, what drives an act of self-denial, of foregoing some pleasure, may be a judgment to the effect that, if one doesn't deny oneself this particular instance of this pleasure, one will in due course have to forego other, greater pleasures. But the operative word here is "judgment." The intention is a judgment concerning my desires; it is not itself a desire. Also, the prospect of pleasures greater than one being foregone isn't always what drives an act of self-denial, as we have seen.

3.0   In Chapter 1, we distinguished between object-awareness and truth-awareness. All truth-aware creatures are object-aware, but not all object-aware creatures are truth-aware. We will refer to creatures that are object-aware but not truth-aware (or otherwise proposition-aware) as *MOC's* – short for "merely object-aware creature."

And we will refer to truth-aware creatures as *PAC's* – short for "proposition-aware creatures." In this section, we will discuss how MOC's become PAC's.

A preliminary point: Some animals are driven by instincts to kill themselves (e.g. drones instinctively kill themselves so that the queen bee may live). Such instincts conduce to the survival of the species, not the individual. But most instincts conduce to the survival of the individual, or are supposed to do so. Since it is exclusively on instincts of this kind that we will focus, the word "instinct" is to be taken refer to instincts of the self-centered, survival conducive kind.

For MOC's, survival is *bodily* survival. The same is true for neophyte-PAC's, that is, for PAC's that have only first-order desires. With the installment of second-order desires, there is, for the first time, a cleavage within the organism's mind: there is a conflict between what it wants to do and what it wants to want to do. For neophyte PAC's, desires have the immediate purpose (if we may so speak) of keeping the organism's body alive and well. With each new installment of nth-order desires ($n \geq 2$), desires become less and less *directly* concerned with the survival of the organism's *body*.

As this superstructure grows, the survival of the physical organisms becomes more and more dependent on *its* welfare, on *its* integrity. Functions that were previously carried out by lower-level ideation come to be incapable of being carried out except by higher-level ideation. It is a general principle of biology that, the more sophisticated the creature, the more sophisticated the cognitive machinery needed to carry out a given operation. A human being's ability to digest depends on the intactness of brain-structures far more sophisticated than those involved in a snake's ability to digest, even though the former operation is not in and of itself more complex than the latter. It is my hypothesis that the discharging of first-order desires becomes comparably encephalized. More precisely, it becomes increasingly dependent on the gratification of higher-order desires. The execution of superstructure-internal operations becomes a *sine qua non* for the gratification of first-order desires, even though the latter can be, and used to be, gratified without the help of any such superstructure.

There thus occurs a reversal. Initially this superstructure existed to keep the physical organism alive. But now the physical organism exists in order to keep this superstructure alive. Initially, the gratification of higher-order, superstructure-internal desires was important only to the extent that it conduced to the gratification of first-order desires. But now the gratification of first-order desires is important only to the extent that it conduces to the gratification of higher-level, superstructure-internal desires.

It is at this point that mind ceases to be nothing more than the servant of body. It is at this point that mind becomes differentiated into two parts: those that constitute a *self* and those that do not. It is at this point that minds come to have *values*. And it is at this point that *intentions*, rather than desires, come to govern behavior.

We see eating, drinking, and other basal acts as *necessary*. But we don't see them as *valuable*. More precisely, we see them as instrumentally, but not as intrinsically valuable. They must be done and thus have *instrumental* value; but they don't have *intrinsic* value, since there would be no reason to do them if they didn't have to be done.

We regard the acquisition of knowledge for its own sake as intrinsically valuable, and we so regard the production and enjoyment of certain kinds of music, art, and literature. We regard certain kinds of literature (e.g. *War and Peace*) as more intrinsically valuable than others (e.g. Harlequin Romances), because the latter minister more directly than the former to basal desires and, what is related, because the desires gratified by the production and consumption of the former, but not the latter, are primarily superstructure-internal. We regard system-internal gratification as laudable, whereas we regard the gratification of first-order desires not as laudable, but as necessary, at best, or as contemptible, at worst. (Cf. the contempt we have for the dope-fiend, for the glutton, etc. Cf. the censorious attitude taken by many to acts of sexual congress that occur outside of oftentimes-draconian cultural strictures.) We regard Bach's music as more intrinsically valuable than Mick Jagger's because, whereas the latter appeals relatively directly to sexuality-based desires, the former directly appeals directly to rationality-based desires and only relatively indirectly to sexuality-based desires. We see rationality as intrinsically valuable because a superstructure of the kind we've been discussing is only as voluminous, and has only as much integrity, as its operations are rational. And we see the scope and integrity of a given such superstructure as determinative of its value because we see that superstructure as being identical with the relevant person's *agency* and, therefore, with his very *self*. It is only to the extent that one's behavior is guided by superstructure-specific desires that one is acting, rather than reflexively reacting. Therefore, it is only to that extent that one is an agent.

4.0   To value something, I propose, is to see it as conducive to the consolidation or enlargement of one's agency. We value reading Mill more than we value reading Harlequin romances, because we know that, by reading the former but not the latter, we are honing our minds and thus fortifying our agency. We value listening to Bach more than we value listening to hip-hop for the same reason.

"But what about altruistic values?" it will be asked. "You hold that x values doing y just in case x sees doing y as conducive to the fortification of his agency. But x may value doing y, because he sees it as helpful to others, even though doing y may, as x well knows, be deleterious to his own agency."

First of all, to the extent that helping others has value, it is because it helps preserve and strengthen their agency. No one would regard it as altruistic or socially valuable to lobotomize everyone, while keeping them biologically alive. So value, in the sense of what is *socially* valuable, is to be understood in terms of what is *personally* valuable. When we say that a given person is doing something of "value," we are saying that it protects or consolidates agency. We are leaving it open whether it is the aforementioned person's agency that it benefits or someone else's.

Also, one sees one's agency as being to some degree constitutively dependent on the welfare of the society in which one is embedded; and, I suspect, one has some tendency to see acts that benefit society's welfare as redounding to one's own benefit. I leave it open whether this is the right way to view such acts.

The President of the University of Nevada, at Las Vegas (UNLV) simply obliterated the philosophy department at that institution. This is presumably at least in
part because that department was not cost-effective. My colleagues had distinctively
moral reactions to this fact.[197] They really did see what UNLV's President was doing
as wrong. But I would wager that few members of the physics department had such
a reaction to that fact (supposing that they were even aware of it). This is not to say
that my colleagues were pretending to have moral reactions. It is to say that they really were having moral reactions *and* that those reactions were self-interested. If one's
life is built around a certain of values, self-interested reactions may coincide with
genuinely moral reactions. If, in exchange for money, Mother Teresa were poisoning the orphans in her care, her life would be drained in meaning. Her values being
what they were, it was in her interest to behave altruistically. So there is less cynicism
than is typically thought in the Nietzschean point that morality is an instrument of
self-interest.

But there is *some* cynicism in it. Authentic moral reactions *can* be expressions
of a basal, value-free kind. My colleagues were afraid of losing their jobs; and their
moral outrage at the dissolution of the UNLV philosophy department embodied that
fear. At the same time, their outrage, even to the extent that it embodied nothing
more than a fear of losing a paycheck, embodied genuine morality. We are more in-
dignant at atrocities that occur in our own countries than we are in those that occur
in foreign lands, even in cases where we know that the latter are far more serious than
the former.

This doesn't mean that morality is to any degree fraudulent. Speaking from an
evolutionary perspective, people's senses of right and wrong are enormously important. But for them, our species wouldn't last long, since we'd always be at each other's
throats; and even though we establish legal systems that make it one's interest to comply with the dictates of morality, the world would be a very different place, and a much
worse place, if those judicial institutions were not reinforced by an independently
existing tendency on the part of people to comply with moral codes. People are more
self-interested than moral. So in relative terms morality is a weak force. But in absolute terms it's a strong force, and that is what matters in the present contest. (Gravity is
an extremely weak force, being billions of times weaker than those that hold an atom
together. But gravity is still, in absolute terms, a powerful force, and in many contexts,
what matter's is gravity's absolute, not its relative intensity.)

4.1   Hedonistic pleasure is value-free pleasure. Accomplishment-based pleasure is
not hedonistic pleasure. Hitting a good backhand is a source of accomplishment-
based pleasure, as is solving a tough math-problem. Shooting heroin is a source of
purely hedonistic pleasure, as is watching TV.

---

197. I don't know what the UNLV President's motivations were in dissolving its philosophy
department. But his decision, though surely partly fiscal in nature, may not have been entirely
so. Some departments simply cease to be operative and should cease to exist.

The object of desire is gratification. Not all intentions aim at gratification. My intention to write a treatise isn't a desire. It's a judgment that I must write a treatise if I am to have a life that embodies certain values.

Such judgments become desire-like. It is with excitement and joy that a skilled professional embarks on a new project. For everyday purposes such judgments are appropriately referred to as "desires." But they are not to be co-categorized with a person's desire for a cigarette.

A ship-captain may intend to remain on his sinking vessel until everyone else has safely disembarked. That intention is obviously not a first-order desire; and it's obviously not a desire to abstain from a certain desire, so as to leave open the possibility of experiencing greater desires down the road. It would be very hard to explain the captain's behavior in terms of his wanting to gratify a desire of some kind. The ship-captain's intention is more naturally thought of as a judgment: one to the effect that he must stay aboard the ship during what little time he has left, lest he violate the values that gave his life meaning.

Not all intentions are so noble. Some aren't noble at all. But all intentions are judgments to the effect that one must act a certain way if one is comply with some value that one has. They are all value judgments. (Not all values are moral values, as we're about to see, and not all moral values are good moral values.) Desires are never value-judgments.

4.2   We see our bodies as existing for our minds. We don't *identify* with our bodies. One can imagine waking up in someone else's body, but one cannot imagine waking up in someone else's mind. It's obvious that our minds help us survive, that a mindless creature cannot experience pleasure or happiness, and that intelligence can be put to practical use. But we see our minds as being intrinsically good.

This is no more of true of intellectuals than it is of athletes, dancers, and others who measure their self-worth in terms of what their bodies can do. Michael Jordan rightly sees his athletic ability as a characteristic, not of his body, but of his self; and he sees it as redounding not to his body's credit, but to his own. If Michael Jordan were to wake up in another body, it would trouble him *only* to the extent that his new body might not be as well-suited as his previous one to do the sorts of things that validated his self-concept.

These facts are to be understood in terms of the fact that athletic ability is cognitive, not somatic in nature. Being coordinated consists in one's mind being intelligent and effective in the way it governs one's body, and athletic ability is therefore a virtue of mind, not of body.

To be sure, there's more to being an athlete than being coordinated. But many of the other characteristics of athleticism, though by no means all, are ultimately cognitive in nature. A soccer player's knowing when to pass the ball is comparable to Napoleon's knowing where to position his troops, the same being true of a squash player's knowing where to place the ball. Of course, there are some strictly somatic components to athleticism, e.g. endurance, strength, size. And, of course, an athlete must be physically healthy. But even such things as speed are largely cognitive in nature. Being fast is, to some extent, about being coordinated. (It's also about having certain physical features.) Being a good dead-lifter or line-backer is about being coordinated. Being coordinated consists in being able to know in real time one's body should do, along with being able to deploy that knowledge in real time.

We don't self-identify as bodies. Anyone would regard the prospect of his mind's being extirpated but his body's remaining perfectly healthy as tantamount to death. We self-identify as mental entities.

Let us end this section by neutralizing a possible objection to this last point. "Good-looking people are proud of their looks. This means that people see their looks as reflecting well on their characters. Up to a point, a person's appearance may in fact reflect well on his character. It takes years of hard work to perfect one's physique; so even though a sculpted physique itself is a virtue of body, not of mind, the discipline involved in acquiring such a physique is a virtue of mind, not of body. But people are proud of those aspects of their looks, e.g. their eye-colors, for which they aren't responsible and which therefore do not reflect well on their characters. By the same token, people are deeply ashamed of aspects of their appearance, e.g. their nose-sizes, for which they aren't responsible and which therefore do not reflect badly on their characters. To the extent that people identify with their minds, they cannot possibly be proud or ashamed of anything for which their minds aren't responsible; and to the extent that people are proud of their eye-colors or ashamed of their nose-sizes, people identify with their bodies. So up to a point, people do identify with their bodies, and you are therefore wrong to say otherwise."

People are indeed proud of facts about their appearance for which they aren't responsible, and they're also ashamed of such facts. But that isn't because they don't identify with their minds; it's because they wrongly regard facts about how they look as embodiments of facts about how they are. Even the most rational and evolved person at some level equates beauty with character and ugliness with its absence. Physically attractive movie stars play good people, and unattractive ones play bad ones. Jimmy Stewart was a good-looking man, but "It's a Wonderful Life" is about George Bailey's excellences of character, not his good looks. Peter Lorre was not a handsome man, but "M" is about Hans Beckert's deficits of character, not his bad looks. On the rare occasions when a good-looking actor's character lacks virtue, or a bad looking actor's character has it, it's because the very point of the movie is that what's on the outside isn't necessarily what's on the inside. The very fact that this ever has to be the point of a movie confirms our hypothesis that people equate good looks with character and bad looks with its absence; and this fact, in its turn, confirms our hypothesis that people regard their appearances as embodiments of their character.

5.0   I have argued that intentions are judgments as to how to comply with one's values and, therefore, as to how to expand and consolidate one's agency. But there is a serious problem with this analysis. People intentionally smoke, drink, give into base urges, and otherwise degrade themselves. I must therefore hold that

(i)   The intentions driving debauched acts embody some sort of ignorance.

For, if (i) is wrong, then

(ii)   Such intentions are straightforward counterexamples to my analysis.

But is there any independent reason to accept (i)? Yes. Whenever a person commits an act of debauchery, he *rationalizes*. Typically, when I'm about to light up a cigarette, I tell myself that:

(RA)   Everybody needs to take a break once in a while. And even though smoking is bad for one's health, I'm fairly sure that I don't do it enough to run any real risk of contracting cancer or emphysema. And to the extent that I'm not sure, it's because I have a neurotic proclivity to doubt, even when there is no reason to do so.

Like all rationalizations, RA is largely true. People *do* need to take breaks. People *do* need to cool off.[198] But I'm taking those truths out of context. There are ways of

---

198. Studies have shown that *ceteris paribus* people who work chronically work less effectively than people who routinely take breaks. (I am indebted to Bridget Dempsey Pumphrey for bringing this fact to my attention.) But, like all studies that establish concomitances, these studies don't make it clear what is causing what. Is ineffectiveness the cause of non-stop work? Or is non-stop work the cause of ineffectiveness? Are non-stop workers people inherently disposed to do substandard work? Or is substandard work simply the result of non-stop work? The answer is "yes" to all of these questions.

People need to take breaks. They simply need to recover. An athlete who never lets his body recover won't progress as quickly or extensively as one who does.

Also, work becomes a chore if done non-stop: even the best composer isn't going to be able to put his heart and soul into his work if he never takes a break. Composing will become an obligation. He won't want to surrender to it, and his work will become stale and mechanical.

Finally, there is a difference between working hard and working compulsively. Working hard is about working properly. Working compulsively is about fortifying neurotic defenses; it's about consolidating barriers between one's conscious mind and the very bodies of knowledge and affect on which one is likely to have to draw in order to do good work.

That said, much excellent work *is* done compulsively. I must therefore take one following positions (or both of them, as they are not mutually exclusive):

(i)   Although neurotic work can be of the highest-quality, it is *despite* being done neurotically that it is of high quality. In other words, neurotically done work can be excellent, but it isn't *qua* neurotically done work that it's excellent. Beethoven may have worked compulsively. But it was because he was a good composer, not because he was neurotic, that his compositions were good.

(ii)   My final point was either false or but a fragment of the truth.

I think both are correct; but (ii) is more correct than (i). In some cases, when neurotically done work is good, it is precisely *because* it is done neurotically. Although compulsions *are* about

cooling off that don't involve smoking. I don't really know that I don't smoke enough to get emphysema or cancer. I don't smoke often. But I may be one of those people who can get lung cancer from smoking five cigarettes a week. And while I *do* have an overdeveloped tendency to doubt, my dubiety in this context may well be justified; it's a borderline case.

Plus, after having a cigarette, I feel logy and depleted, and I'm unable to derive pleasure from activities, such as playing the piano, that really do help me recover from a long bout of work. This last fact is fatal to RA, as it makes it clear that, when I smoke, it's out of an addiction-driven compulsion, not a carefree love of pleasure.

There are times when my smoking a cigarette, or even a pack, is *not* an act of debauchery. It isn't *what* you do that makes an act debauched; it's *why* you do it. There are times when having a cigarette really *is* the optimal possible way to cool off. RA applies to those situations. But those are the very occasions when I don't make any attempt to rationalize or justify what I'm doing. It's when I knowingly lapse that I rationalize.[199]

One can rationalize only if one has conflicting beliefs. If I *knew* that RA was spurious, RA wouldn't work. If I *knew* that *this* was the cigarette that would give me cancer, RA probably wouldn't occur to me and, if it did, it would be an operationally inert series of thoughts, not a rationalization.

When a person rationalizes, it is in order to make himself believe that his values validate an act that they do not in fact validate but that he strongly wants to perform. Few rationalizations are complete successes. (When lighting up, do I *really* believe RA? No – if I did, my mind would be at ease. But I'm anxious.) But seldom are they complete failures. (Although I don't fully accept RA, I accept it enough to have the cigarette.)

"But how can a person make himself believe something he doesn't believe?" We will answer this question in Chapter 15. For now let us operate on the plausible assumption that people can in fact rationalize.

There are no cases where one knowingly gives into depravity *and doesn't rationalize doing so*. People often describe what they're doing as "depraved." But in such cases one of two things is likely to be happening:

---

flight, compulsion-mediated flights don't involve one's turning one's back on *everything* that one knows and feels. Being blind to some things is a necessary for seeing others with maximal sharpness. Somebody whose cognitive field of vision is too balanced, and whose acuity is therefore too evenly distributed, is unlikely to be hyper-aware of anything and, consequently, is unlikely to satisfy one of the preconditions for doing work that is not merely good, but great.

199. I can safely assume that I'm representative of all people in this respect. There are some respects in which one's condition clearly *isn't* representative of all people, and there are respects in which one's condition clearly is thus representative. I enjoy reading Freud. It would be foolish of me to assume that same to be true of others. I like not being confined to a windowless room all the time. It would be foolish of me to assume that, setting aside pathology-based exceptions, people were not categorically like me in this respect.

(i)   They don't *really* think that what they're doing is depraved. By "depraved" they mean "what society wrongly regards as depraved."

(ii) They *do* believe that what they're doing is depraved. But the part of them that is doing the talking isn't the part of them that is committing the action.

(i) illustrated: In the book 1984, Winston Smith, who is the soul of decency, says "I hate goodness; I hate purity." He meant that he hated faux-goodness and faux-purity. A person's objective, in self-describing as "twisted" or "perverted," is often to invalidate a moral code that invalidates his behavior. He believes (sometimes rightly) that what he's doing is estimable, even though, so he also believes (usually rightly), society doesn't approve. And he'll embrace the pejorative epithets that would be used to describe him, so as to show how empty they are.

(ii) amplified: To be rendered innocuous, painful knowledge doesn't have to be repressed. It can be intellectualized. Intellectualized knowledge is knowledge that has not itself been repressed but whose emotional concomitants have been repressed. What was previously a painful reality becomes a mere object of consideration. And when delineating the consequences of the hitherto painful truth, one can tell oneself that what one is doing is virtuous: one is honing one's intellect, after all, and thus enlarging one's sphere of awareness and, therefore, one's very self.

So we *do* engage in actions that we believe to undermine our agency – but only because, having rationalized, we also believe those actions *not* to do so and perhaps even to consolidate it. [200]

Incidentally, intellectualization is peculiar among neurotic defenses in that those who engage in it come out ahead, whereas those who engage in other such defenses either break even or lose more than they gain. To be sure, there is a downside to intellectualization: one's emotional acuity is blunted. But what one loses in emotional acuity, one more than gains in theoretical acuity.

Also, the blunting of one's emotional acuity is easily reversed. It isn't by destroying one's emotional acuity that intellectualization blunts it; it is by inhibiting it. Here we must remember Chomsky's (1965) distinction between performance and competence: competence is ability; performance is the ability to deploy ability. It isn't the intellectualizer's empathic competence that is blunted, but his empathic performance; in other words, it isn't his empathic abilities that are blunted, but his ability to use those abilities. And there is nothing to prevent those second-order abilities from

---

200. Such, at any rate, is the present author's attempt to reconcile what he believes to be a creditable analysis of what intentions are with a very significant *prima facie* problem for that analysis.

But my analysis is not entirely *post hoc*. Psychoanalytic theoreticians (e.g. Otto Kernberg) have held similar views, and they had no ulterior motivating for doing so, unlike the present author. But even if my analysis *is* a *post hoc* rationalization, it isn't on that account false. Cf. the points about intellectualization in the previous footnote.

being restored once the emotional conflicts that precipitated the flight into intellectualization are resolved.

An intellectual is somebody who, at some point in his development, dealt with emotional conflict by intellectualizing, and whose tendency to intellectualize ceased to be a momentary defense and came to be an enduring, stable part of his character-structure. Intellectualizers always become intellectuals. In those in whom the cognitive underpinnings of intellectualism are not present, intellectualization is not a very useful emotional defense; and in those in whom it is present, intellectualization activates abilities with which their possessors will rightly be reluctant to part.

There is an oft-overlooked fact about the intellectual. Often he is accused of being blind to other people's feelings. Sometimes he is guilty of this charge. More often than not the charge is spurious. The intellectual is libidinally self-contained. The validations of others have been replaced by the validations of impersonal logical and ethical norms. The intellectual is often hyper-aware of other people's feelings. But he regards such feelings as being significant only to the extent that they align with impersonal logical and ethical standards. When they do not so align, the intellectual will either have no response to them, except to be dispassionately aware of them, or he will have a justly negative response. Whence the bogus charge of obtuseness.

Also, those who are likely to level this charge are enraged at the intellectual for his unwillingness to validate their own pettiness. The purpose of the charge is to turn their lack of merit into his: their viciousness becomes his blindness. And the rage behind the charge is projective. The person who levels the charge is ashamed at his own viciousness. He sees in the intellectual an externalization of the part of himself by whose character-indictments he is so tormented. And instead of copping to his deficits and eliminating them – which is always a difficult task, and is usually an impossible one – he does precisely what Nietzsche says he does: he makes vices out of the virtues he doesn't have, but wishes he did, and virtues out of the vices he does have, but wishes he didn't. He describes his own weakness as "empathy," and he describes the intellectual's strength as the lack of it. When referring to the intellectual, what he is describing as a "lack of empathy," is strength-based non-compliance with mercurial and hollow social norms. When referring to himself, what he is describing as "empathy" is weakness-driven submission to such norms. His stereotype-driven, overuse of the term "empathy" is intended to blind himself to his lack of it and to the superficiality of character that is responsible for that deficit of his. His allegations that others lack empathy are to be explained in the same way.

The man who lacks legitimacy hates the man who has it. This hatred is projective. He hates himself for lacking it. Wishing to undermine the standards relative to which he lacks it, he describes the man who has it as lacking it, and he describes himself, and others like himself, as having it. He hates the legitimate man for making it so hard for him to believe his own lies.

Should a person replace virtue-based norms with approval based norms, his character-structure will, as an inevitable result, undergoes massive, irreversible changes.

The resulting character-structure is that of the so-called sociopath. We will discuss sociopathy in Chapter 15.

In any case, as neurotic defenses go, intellectualization is one of the better ones. All neurotics are *ipso facto* alienated from their emotions. But the intellectualizer, unlike other neurotics, gets something in return for the emotional knowledge he forfeits; and instead of just being an emotional cripple, like other neurotics, he's an emotional cripple with a volcanic intellect.

Also, whether a given psychological structure is neurotic depends on the context. The very structure that mediates one's neurosis-engendering doubts about one's parents' love for him may mediate one's penetrating epistemological inquiries. Some psychoanalysts hold that a certain amount of neurosis is not only an inevitable concomitant of extreme achievement, but a necessary ingredient for it. For the record, the present author concurs.

5.1 Sometimes *prima facie* debauched intentions aren't debauched intentions. Sometimes one's first-order desires must be given free reign; and in duly giving such a desire free reign, one appears to be behaving in a debauched manner, even though one's behavior is integrated and healthy. A person who is incapable of indulging first-order desires is an emotional cripple – a "stiff," a "square" – a consequence being that emotional non-paralytics inevitably seem on occasion to be wantons.

A person who can indulge only his first order desires is a degenerate. A person who cannot indulge such desires is a robot.

First-order desires typically cannot be extinguished; and they *should* not be extinguished, since they are indispensable to one's psychological vitality. Without them, one's higher-order desires are drained of significance, and one regresses to a condition in which one's higher-order desires are impotent, ironically, but in which one no longer has intact first-order desires. When a person's first-order desires are over-marginalized, and eventually replaced by what were previously second-order desires, that person regresses to a pseudo-human condition, coincident with the one previously mentioned, sometimes referred to as "sociopathy." (In Chapter 15, it will be explained why the two seemingly distinct routes to sociopathy that we've identified are in fact one and the same.) A person whose first-order desires are overly-restrained, or have been destroyed, is – there is no better way to put it – somebody who longer has a soul; he is somebody who has been over-acculturated – acculturated out of existence.

CHAPTER 12

Actions vs. reactions, desires vs. urges

1.0 An act of judgment is one of determining whether some *proposition* is true or false. Creatures cannot make judgments unless they are propositionally aware; objectual awareness is not enough.

Because MOC's cannot make judgments, they cannot act; they can only react. Performing an action involves having an objective. An objective is a proposition that one wants to be true. Since objectives are propositions, MOC's can't have them.

Being propositions, objectives are not psychological entities, even though the *having* of an objective *is* such an entity. Two people can have the same objective; e.g. they can both want to bring about world peace. My having that objective is something psychological, and so is your having it. But *the* objective of bringing about world peace is not something psychological, that being why numerically distinct minds can have it. *The* objective of bringing about world peace is the proposition: *that there is world peace*. One's having that objective is one's intending to make that proposition be true. Since MOC's don't grasp propositions and therefore don't have objectives, their behaviors are purely reflexive.

It often *appears* that MOC's have objectives. The dog appears to have the objective of getting to the piece of red meat before the other dog. But in imputing an objective to the dog, we are illegitimately anthropomorphizing. The dog sees the red meat. This excites it; it disrupts its equilibrium. An animal's equilibrium can be disrupted in different ways. The disruption of this dog's equilibrium on this occasion is such that, for reasons lying in the dog's evolutionary past, it sets in motion instinctive behaviors that are likely to restore the lost equilibrium.

If a human being were to see something that he wanted, e.g. a pile of money, and he saw that some other person also had his eye on it, he would *desire* to be the first to get his hands on the loot. This means that he would form a belief to the effect that he must be the first to get to the money lest he forego a source of gratification. Of course, given only that a person desires to get at a pile of money, it doesn't follow that he will act on that desire. If he suspects that the money is part of a trap of some kind, or if he thinks that his sprinting towards the money will make him look unworthy in the eyes of a benefactor who happens to be observing the situation, he will not act on that desire (though he will still have it). It is only if the person in question judges that it is in his interest to go after the money that he will do so. (To echo a point made earlier, this makes it hard to explain why people do things, such as smoking, that are inimical to their interests. I must ask the reader for some leeway here.)

The dog, on the other hand, doesn't even have a desire. It has an uncomfortable feeling, which activates instinctive behavior and which, if successful, eliminates the discomfort. The uncomfortable feeling excites an *urge* to behave in certain ways – to make haste towards the red meat, to rip it from the jaws of the other dog if it doesn't get there first, etc. The intensity of that urge is proportional to the intensity of the afore-mentioned discomfort. So the behavior involved in the dog's going after the red meat *mimics* the behavior of somebody driven by a strong desire. But the dog is driven by a strong *urge*; no desire is operative. A desire is a propositional attitude, and is therefore something a dog cannot have, since dogs don't grasp propositions. More specifically, a desire is, as previously stated, a belief or judgment to the effect that, in order to experi-ence gratification (or avoid pain) of a certain kind, certain actions must be taken.

The justification for this analysis lies in one fact: *animals always react in the same ways to the same stimuli*. On hearing the starter-gun, race-dogs *always* chase the elec-tric bunny, even though never catch it. If such dogs were driven by *desire* to catch the bunny, they'd eventually stop trying to do so. Unlike instincts, believes are not hard-wired; their existence is a function of the relevant individual's experience. If the race-dog's behavior were desire-driven, it would soon stop chasing the bunny, since its experience would invalidate the relevant desire. But this isn't what happens; the dog continues to chase the bunny.

"But can't we say that the dog is just very unintelligent," it will be asked, "and counter-evidentially continues to have the same belief?"

This question likens beliefs to instincts. Instincts persist no matter what; they are experience-insensitive (except in the sense that experience can cause a given creature to instinctually deactivate a given instinct). Beliefs aren't so deeply rooted. New expe-riences create new beliefs which displace old ones. A so-called belief that exists, and that persists regardless of what its host experiences, is no belief at all. Such a "belief" obviously has its basis entirely in the animal's innate constitution, not its own experi-ence, and is thus an instinct.

We could say that the greyhound 'instinctively believes' that it will catch the bun-ny. But in that case, everything we're saying about the difference between instincts and beliefs will simply transfer over to the distinction between 'instinctive beliefs' and 'non-instinctive beliefs.'

When not senile or otherwise cognitively impaired, even the most prejudiced people, if given enough information, will modify their beliefs. With the greyhounds at the racetrack, we see compulsive behaviors that are neither initiated nor justified by experience and that no amount of recalcitrant evidence does anything to modify.

The dog isn't *taught* to roll over. It is *trained* to do so. The purpose of training a given creature is to make it have certain kinds of *reflexes*; it is to create a way of hav-ing control over its behavior that by-passes as much intelligence-mediating menta-tion as possible. So training is antithetical to teaching. Rover is an award-winning dog. There isn't a single dog-show in which he hasn't come in first-place. But to the extent that Rover's training influenced his behavior, it "de-mentalized" it: *qua* trained dog, Rover's intelligence, so far as he had any, ceased to regulate his behavior. Rover's training activated certain reflex-mechanisms and deactivated others. It taught him nothing.

If a dog is electrocuted every time it puts its mouth around red meat, its instinct to seize nearby pieces of red meat will be put out of commission. But such changes don't reflect any *learning* on the dog's part. The dog hasn't learned anything. Because of its experience, one set of reflexes has replaced another. No judgment intervened. Operant conditioning isn't teaching.

Instinct themselves don't change. Whether a given instinct is operative may change. Experience can deactivate an instinct. But an instinct's being deactivated or activated doesn't reflect the acquisition of knowledge; it is itself just another instinctual response to circumstances. So far as instincts embody knowledge, it is of an ancestral (phylogenetic), not a personal (ontogenetic) nature. Instincts are not sensitive to personal experience.

MOC's can be trained, not taught. Teaching involves the transmission of truths. Since truths are true propositions, MOC's don't grasp truths, since they don't grasp propositions, and they are therefore unteachable.

2.0   MOC's react to things. PAC's react to truths.

A shrew sees a badger with bared fangs running towards him. No reasoning intervenes between his awareness of that fact and his reaction to that fact.[201] To reason

---

201. Many philosophers use the term "implicit thought" to describe unconscious, procedural, and intuitive knowledge. The pianist implicitly knows where to put his fingers. Jim implicitly knew that he should act politely towards his boss. If asked "can an MOC grasp TP?", such an author is likely to say: "yes – implicitly."

Freud (1957) and Chomsky (1959, 1965, 1980, 1988) and their followers never talk about implicit thought. Their position is that thoughts either exist or they don't.

The term 'implicit thought' is often used to dodge substantive questions about the nature of knowledge.

> Person A: X implicitly thought Y.
> Person B: Did he think it or not?
> Person A: Yes…implicitly.
> Person B: So you believe all that Freudian claptrap about unconscious thought.
> Person A: No! X didn't *really* think Y. Hence the word "implicitly."
> Person B: I was lying. I'm a die hard Freudian. So did X think Y or not?
> Person A: Of course! Otherwise I wouldn't have said that he *thought* it.

Those authors who use the term "implicit thought" non-equivocally use it to mean "non-thought." Such authors include Dretske (1982, 1995), Dennett (1978, 1989), and Davidson (2001a, 2001b). According to each, an "implicit thought" is one that a given creature did not have but that *would* have justified its behavior if it *had* had it.

Given that "implicit thought" either means nothing or means "non thought," that expression should be extruded from scientific discourse.

is to identify relations of dependence holding among propositions. Obviously the shrew can't do this. So it can't think:

(TP[202])　　What I want is to survive. I won't survive if I fight that animal. To avoid fighting that animal, I must hide behind that rock. Therefore, to get what I want, I must hide behind that rock. Therefore, I will hide behind that rock.

PACs are, both individually and ancestrally, former MOCs. But how does the MOC become a PAC? A story will help us answer this question.

　　Smith isn't yet a PAC but he is destined to become one. Smith doesn't act; he reacts. Stressors prompt compulsive, pre-programmed behaviors. Because he is an MOC, he doesn't make judgments as to the efficacy of these types of behavior. But one day that changes. He realizes that, when he's hungry, he alleviates his hunger if he does X but fails to alleviate it if he does Y. (In Chapter 14, we'll try to explain how it is that such a change is able to take place.)

　　Before had this revelation, Smith's behavior was *urge*-driven. Now it's desire-driven. Smith is at a stage intermediate between that of an urge-driven creature and that of an intention-driven creature.

　　When dealing with neophyte PAC's, *bona fide* desires lead straight to action. Where such beings are concerned, there is no distinction between intentions and desires. This is because intentions are judgments as to what it is one's interest to do (cf. Chapter 11, Sections 6.0–7.0.), and neophyte PAC's don't distinguish between they want to do so and what it is in their interest to do.

3.0　　There are many steps that a neophyte PAC must take before it acquires a distinctively human cognitive and psychological architecture. But, barring death or injury, it will inevitably take these steps, since they are but reiterations of the one it has already taken.

　　Smith now has a belief as to how best to gratify one sort of desire. Smith obviously has many desires. Smith comes to have beliefs about his desires. He comes to believe that, if he is to maximize the quality and quantity of gratification that he experiences, he must organize his desires hierarchically; he must make the gratification of certain desires a precondition for the gratification of others and he must simply forego gratification of certain ones.

　　A desire is a belief as to how to achieve gratification of a certain kind. (Cf. Chapter 11, Section 1.0.) Smith's belief as to how his desires ought to be organized is itself a desire: a desire about desires.[203] It is a tautology that Smith desires to gratify his desires. His belief as to *how* to organize his desires, so as to achieve maximal

---

202.　"TP" is short for "thought process."

203.　My debt to Frankfurt (1988) is obvious, even though, as we'll see, there are some non-trivial differences between my views and his.

gratification, is itself a desire: a second-order desire: a desire to gratify certain desires before others.

"But you said," it will be objected, "that the behavior of the man who gives his wallet to the gunman is acting is *intention*-driven, not *desire*-driven. You seem to be contradicting yourself."

The victim of the gunman, it was assumed, had values. He also had desires, of course, and perhaps had desires about desires. But any second-order desires he might have had are of no relevance to the situation. What *is* relevant is that he had a *judgment* about his desires. That is why he could act intentionally, unlike strictly desire-driven Smith. Let us now clarify and substantiate this last point.

3.1   At this point, desires about desires, as opposed to first-order desires, come to govern Smith's behaviors. This is when Smith first begins to have a distinctively human psychological architecture, viz. the psychological architecture of a human adult who is not cognitively impaired and who is neither a sociopath nor a psychopath. (In Chapter 16, we'll define these two terms.)

But Smith has one more step to take before he can have intentions and, therefore, before he can have such a psychological structure. When second-order desires come to regulate Smith's behavior, there is *ipso facto* an opposition within Smith's mind. There are Smith's first-order desires. And there are other desires, higher-order desires, that often thwart, and always conditionalize, the gratification of first-order desires. When Smith had only first-order desires, there was no Smith. To put it non-paradoxically, the *body* to which we referred as "Smith" did not house a *self* so long as the only desires thereby hosted were of the first-order variety; and it was only when second-order desires developed that anything resembling a self came into existence. This is partly because second-order desires, though not intentions, are the immediate precursors of intentions.

A given person experiments with different ways of hierarchically ordering his desires. Thus, there are changes in respect of what he wants to gratify more than what. At 15, it was more important to me to gratify my desire to go to parties than it was to gratify my desire to play tennis; at 39, it is the other way around. Each person's desire-hierarchy undergoes many permutations. (Up to a point, but not entirely, this is prompted by the acquisition of new desires and the loss of old ones. When I learned how to play the piano, I acquired a desire to play the piano; and that new desire changed my previous desire-ranking. When I improved as a pianist, my desire to play piano intensified, which precipitated another re-ordering of my desires, even though I did not at that juncture gain or lose any desires.) This means that people have 3rd-order desires: desires about their desires about their first-order desires. At age 20, I worked hard on my piano skills and improved a lot as a result. This led to my having more of a desire to gratify my desire to play the piano than I previously had. This did not by itself lead to my having less of a desire to watch movies than I previously had. But I knew that I'd achieve more net-gratification by playing the piano than by watching movies. As a result, I desired to desire to play the piano more than I desired to watch movies. I fulfilled that desire artificially: by playing the piano more frequently than I had before. I did not automatically come to have a greater desire to gratify my desire to play the piano than to watch movies. Here we have some first-order desires (a desire to play the piano and a desire to watch movies); some second order desires (a desire to gratify my desire to watch movies more than to gratify my desire to play the piano); and a third-order desire (a desire to desire to the gratification of one desire more than some other desire).

He is a soulless dullard in whom first-order desires do not rage, and a degenerate in whom they are not controlled.[204] The importance of such desires to one's character is immeasurable. But their importance to one's behavior becomes increasingly marginal. Originally, they are acted on. When second-order desires take-over, it is only *indirectly* that they are acted on. When third-order desires take-over, it is only indirectly that second-order desires are acted on, and therefore only doubly indirectly that first-order desires are acted on. For each n, when desires of level$_n$ cease to be immediately operative, having been displaced by desires of level$_{n+1}$, one identifies that much less with one's first-order desires. One's first-order desires increasingly become things that are *in* one but not *of* one.

3.2   There are two ways that people intentionally self-destruct. One is by indulging desires that, for reasons of health, they should not indulge, e.g. the desire to have that second piece of cake. Given the platitude that rational agents can look at the world both subjectively and objectively, the fact that people self-destruct in this way can be reconciled with our contention that intentions are judgments as to how to augment (or at least preserve) one's agency. But, it would seem, we cannot thus reconcile this contention of ours with the fact that people intentionally kill themselves.

Sometimes suicides can be at least partially explained in terms of a desire to avoid pain. (Private Smith is surrounded by enemy-troops, and he doesn't want to spend the next 40 years being tortured in a POW-camp.) Let us set such cases aside. They are compatible with our analysis, and they seem not to be psychodynamically comparable to the cases that are relevant in this context – cases like Hemmingway's suicide, or Kurt Cobain's.

It is an empirical question why people kill themselves, and it is an empirical question whether there is some one psychodynamic characteristic peculiar to genuinely suicidal people. (Why the word "genuinely"? I believe on empirical grounds that people who unsuccessfully attempt suicide are typically in a very different psychological category from those who actually do commit suicide.) There will thus be an empirical component to my basically speculation-based attempt to compatibilize the fact that people commit suicide with my contention that intentions are judgments as to how

---

204. "If you have second order desires but no first order desires, you don't have a heart. If you have first order desires but no second order desires, you don't have a brain." – An adaptation of the old saying: "If you're a Republican when you're young, you don't have a heart. If you're a democrat when you're old, you don't have a brain."

to self-improve. But to show that the phenomenon of suicide is consistent with my analysis, it is enough that I produce a coherent, and therefore potentially correct, answer to the question "why do people kill themselves?"

First of all, not all suicide-attempts succeed, and there are obvious differences between real suicide-attempts and fake suicide-attempts. (A person probably was trying to kill himself if he threw himself off of a rooftop; he probably wasn't if he took a few too many Prozacs.) Not every survivor of an unsuccessful, but genuine, suicide-attempt is too damaged to discuss the ideation preceding it. For that reason, we have knowledge about such ideation and, therefore, about the similarities between those who unsuccessfully (but genuinely) try to kill themselves and those who succeed in doing so. Given this information, some facts are clear. Suicides are often preceded by psychotic ideation. Successful people are no less likely than failures to commit suicide. Poor people are actually less likely than wealthy ones to commit suicide. Women who aren't loved by their fathers are relatively likely to commit suicide, as are men who weren't loved by their mothers. (Men who are showered with love by their mothers are relatively unlikely to commit suicide, and such men are even less likely to do so if their fathers were emotionally or literally absent. The present author doesn't know if analogous truths hold of women.)

What I am now going to say is pure speculation – that is, it is an (as of yet, to my knowledge) unverified extension of the non-speculative points just made. Also, the point I am about to make is not my own; my colleague Kasis Kahn made it, in the course of a private exchange. (Incidentally, Mr. Khan is as free of mental illness as I've ever known anyone to be.) People who commit suicide at some level think they are returning to the womb. The non-psychotic part of them knows they are soon going to be swallowed up by the earth. The psychotic part of them identifies this (or transfers their awareness of this pseudo-identity from the depths of the psyche to its agency-controlling higher strata) with going back go the womb and thereby being engulfed by the love they didn't receive as infants.

In any case, supposing that psychosis precedes suicide (and there is plenty of empirical evidence to believe that it always does), the fact that people sometimes kill themselves is obviously easier reconciled than it would otherwise be with our views about intentions. If Mr. Khan is right, a person's intention in committing suicide is to fill a hole in his heart and is thus to correct a serious deficit in his character-architecture. And that is such a person's intention even if Mr. Khan is wrong, so long as any hypothesis at all similar to his is correct.

That said, my analysis of what intentions are is wrong if it is even theoretically possible for a delusion-free creature to intend to obliterate itself. I have no choice but to deny that that this is a possibility. But is there no independent corroboration for this position of mine? People who commit suicide often do so believing that they are going to a better place. Suicide bombers believe that, upon dying, they will have unlimited access to carnal pleasures denied them in this realm. Are such religious beliefs relevantly different from those that Mr. Khan (who, incidentally, is non-religious) imputes to people who kill themselves? And if a person truly – at every cognitive stratum – equates death with oblivion, will he kill himself? "No," I say, and while I believe my answer capable of empirical verification, I also believe it analytically correct.

At the end of Dickens' novel "A Tale of Two Cities," the protagonist says, as he lets himself be executed for a crime he didn't commit, "it is a far, far better thing I do than I have ever done." No – so far as this gentleman's suicide isn't an act of sadistic homicide on Dickens' part, and so far as it is psychodynamically comparable to that of his real-life counterpart, it is an act of cowardly submission to a punitive conscience, abetted by the psychotic, or at least infantile, belief that his hitherto draconian conscience will reward him if he submits to it. Mr. Carton's supposedly noble deed redounds to his discredit, in as much as it devalues the distinction between reality and fantasy and (only party for that reason) devalues life, and to Dickens' discredit, in as much as he is responsible for Mr. Carton's craven act and, further, has so masterfully represented this act of authorial misanthropy as its opposite.

CHAPTER 13

Moral and aesthetic nihilism as embodiments of false theories of rationality and selfhood

1.0   Our ultimate objectives in this work are to provide analyses of:

(i)   Personhood;

(ii)   The distinction between minds and selves;

(iii)   The nature of rationality;

(iv)   The difference between intelligence and rationality;

(v)   The nature of linguistic competence;

(vi)   The relation of linguistic to cognitive competence;

(vii)   The role that one's cognitive competence has in one's having a distinctively human psychological architecture depends on one's cognitive;

(viii)   The difference between rational thought and rationalization;

(ix)   How rationalization is possible;

(x)   How repression and, more generally, access-unconscious ideation is possible;

(xi)   The dependence of one's personhood – one's having a distinctively human psychological architecture – on one's having values. (The values in question are not of a moral kind. They are norms, but not moral norms.)

(xii)   The consequences for one's character-architecture of rationalization;

(xiii)   Sociopathy, this being a collapse of psychological architecture precipitated by excessive rationalization; and

(xiv)   Psychopathy, this being a failure to distinguish conequence of excessive rationalization and psychopath;

(xv)   Why it is that, empiricism being what it is, empiricist efforts to discuss (i)–(xiv) are doomed to fail, in the rare cases where an acceptance of empiricism doesn't blind one to the very existence of a given one of those topics.

But in order to discuss (i)–(xv) creditably, we must first discuss two doctrines that, although deeply related to those topics, might seem quite irrelevant to them. Those doctrines are:

Aesthetic nihilism: No work of art is better than any other.
Moral nihilism: No act is better or worse than any other.[205]

Aesthetic nihilism clarified: According to this doctrine, if my compositional efforts yield nothing more than the sound of a jackhammer, my compositions are no better or worse than Mozart's. Nothing has aesthetic value. We have different affective reactions to different musical works, and we project those affects onto those works. But in so doing, we are delusively seeing as mind-independent facts what are in actuality just facts about our own minds, which have no objective basis.

Moral nihilism clarified: According to this doctrine, no act is better or worse than any other. If Smith tortures babies for fun, and Jones volunteers his time and medical services to burn victims, what Smith is doing is neither better nor worse than what Jones is doing. What each is doing has no moral value. Nothing has moral value. We have different emotional reactions to different acts. And we project those emotions onto those acts. But in so doing, we are delusively seeing as mind-independent facts what are in actuality just facts about our own minds, which have no objective basis.

2.0 Anthony Flew said that there is a foolproof test by which it can be determined whether one has an aptitude for philosophy. If one can understand the Euthyphro Dilemma ("is an act good because God says it's good, or does God say it's good because it really is good?"), one has such a knack; if not, not. Having taught several thousand freshman, I believe that Flew is right, and also that there isn't a middle ground between understanding the Dilemma and not understanding it. The people who get it do so right away. The people who don't never do.

There is an equally foolproof way of determining whether one is at bottom an empiricist or a rationalist. One is a rationalist if, when asked,

(WA[206]) Are some works of art better than others?

one answers "yes," and one is an empiricist if one answers "no." Equivalently, one is an empiricist if, when asked,

(WA*) Does one believe that aesthetic ideation is nothing but non-judicative sentiment?

one answers "yes," and a rationalist if one answers "no."

There is a similar, equally foolproof way of determining whether one is an empiricist or a rationalist. One is a rationalist if, when asked,

---

205. Carnap (1932), Ayer (1934), Stevenson (1937), and Blackburn (1984, 1994, 1998) all advocate both aesthetic and moral nihilism.

206. Short for "work of art."

(MA[207]) Are some acts morally better than others?

one answers "yes." And one is an empiricist if one answer "no." Equivalently, one is an empiricist if, when asked,

(MA*) Does one believe that moral ideation is non-judicative sentiment?

one answers "yes," and a rationalist if one answers "no."

Setting aside degenerate cases – psychopaths and musical imbeciles, for example – people's affective and behavioral responses to situations (e.g. seeing a baby be tortured, hearing a Chopin Ballade) indicate that, whatever their discursive views may be, their *real* views are that some acts are wrong and some pieces of music are good.

In this chapter, it will be argued that moral nihilism and aesthetic nihilism are wrong. Our objective in doing this is not to show that empiricism is false, which has already been done, but to pave the way for a solid defense of the positions we'll take in connection with the points made in Section 1.0 of this chapter. For reasons that will emerge, a correct understanding of musical and moral ideation is necessary for a correct understanding of those positions and our arguments for them.

Incidentally, musical nihilism ("no work of music has any merit") is the same doctrine as musical relativism ("all works of music are equally meritorious"). If there is no difference between mere noise, on the one hand, and music, on the other, then all noise is music; and, since mere noise obviously has no musical value, musical relativism entails that no musical work has musical value. On the other hand, if there is a difference between music and mere noise, then some sound-series must have certain virtues to qualify as music; in which case, some series of sounds can be richer in those virtues than others; in which case, some sound-series are musically better than others; in which case musical relativism is false. So musical relativism, if true, entails that Mozart's piano concertos have exactly as much musical value as the sound of a jackhammer, which is none; and musical relativism therefore coincides with musical nihilism.

3.0 Moral nihilism is a consequence of empiricism. Hume (1739) said that "one cannot derive an 'ought' from an 'is'," his meaning being that what is the case does not entail what should be the case. Having said this, Hume puts forth the following argument (this is paraphrase, not a quotation):

(HP[208]) Value judgments never have any empirical foundation. In other words, there is no sensory evidence to the effect that normative statements are ever true. Therefore, moral statements are never true. We wrongly think otherwise

---

207. Short for "moral act."

208. Short for "Hume's position."

because we want to believe that our sentiments have an objective foundation. We want to believe that things that please us do so because of their merits and that things that displease us do so because of their demerits. We don't want to see what are in fact purely emotional reactions for what they are. So one says "x is good," which validates one's emotional reaction to x, instead of saying "x pleases me," which strips that reaction of validity; and for the same reason *mutatis mutandis*, one says "x is bad," instead of "x displeases me." Emotional reactions are *ipso facto* non-cognitive; they embody purely subjective preferences, not judgments, and they are therefore neither true nor false. Moral statements express emotional reactions and therefore express sentiments, not beliefs, and are therefore categorically incapable of being true.

HP is wrong to assume that, if a reaction is emotional, it fails to embody a belief; and HP is therefore wrong to assume that, to the extent that moral statements embody emotions, they are inherently incapable of being true. HP is, I believe, right to assume that, *if* empiricism is correct, then emotions are non-cognitive (i.e. aren't judgments or beliefs). But, of course, it is my contention that empiricism is incorrect. And we've seen some reasons, which up to a point are independent of the alleged falsity of empiricism, to hold that emotions are beliefs. There are, of course, significant differences between normative and non-normative judgments. So although the contention that emotions are non-cognitive is false, there is a truth of which it is a misstatement, namely: emotions, though beliefs, are not *discursive* beliefs. The former are, whereas the latter are not, of a fundamentally egocentric nature.

This position, I would suggest, does a better job of modeling our intuitions than Hume's. No one who isn't a psychopath *truly* believes that torturing infants is neither better nor worse than donating to the poor.

In addition to modeling these Hume-unfriendly data, our analysis adequately models the two correct contentions that lie at the center of Hume's analysis, namely:

(i) Emotions, unlike discursive beliefs, are inherently action-dispositive. By virtue of being angry at Smith, one necessarily has an inclination to act in certain ways (e.g. to do things that, so one believes, will undermine him). But there is nothing that, by virtue of believing arithmetic to be incomplete, one necessarily has any inclination to do. Of course, by virtue of having that belief *along* with a given emotion, there are ways in which one is necessarily inclined to behave. But this only confirms our point.

(ii) Emotions, unlike discursive beliefs, are inherently phenomenology-dispositive. By virtue of hating your father, there are certain kinds of phenomenological episodes that you are necessarily inclined to have.

(i) and (ii) are obviously similar contentions, given that phenomenological episodes tend to be action-dispositive and, indeed, that such episodes are often the proximal causes of action. But it's doubtful whether (i) and (ii) are equivalent, since it's doubtful whether a phenomenological episode is a *necessary* condition for action.

In any case, Hume's moral nihilism is radically at odds with deeply based intuitions of ours; and, as Hume himself says, empiricism, supposing it correct, entails that such nihilism is *de rigueur*.

4.0 "Given only that Hume's meta-ethical views are at odds with our instinctual views," it will be objected, "it doesn't follow that Hume is wrong. To be sure, if we have an intuition to the effect that such and such, that is *prima facie* evidence that such and such. (In other words, *other things being equal*, that intuition is to be regarded as true; but that intuition is defeasible – capable of being overridden – since other things may not be equal.) We have intuitions about the structure of space and time; and those intuitions turned out to be disastrously wrong."[209]

Moral intuitions track biological facts. A man poisons a reservoir, killing and damaging many. We see that man as despicable and his deed as wrong. Another man devises and implements a way to extract said poison from said reservoir, and he refuses to accept any remuneration. We see *that* man as noble and his deed as morally correct.

Let us say that a truth is "descriptive" if it doesn't embody a value-judgment. So "Stalin was short" is a descriptive truth. By contrast, "Stalin was evil" is a non-

---

209. This is what is often said. Following Reichenbach (1956), I reject it. I don't think we have untutored intuitions to the effect that the structure of space is Euclidean, or even to the effect that space-time is decomposable into space and time. I believe that those "intuitions" are quite as much artifacts of culture-specific educational practices as the contrary intuitions had by those matriculating from post-Einsteinian educational traditions. I believe the view that space is Euclidean to be a highly theoretical one, which our consitutions no more bind us to accept than they do other, incompatible views.

In fact, it wasn't until quite recently – the mid-1800's – that it was understood what it even means to say that space is Euclidean. Until then, it wasn't seen that terms like "point" and "straight line" must given physical interpretations – that they must be identified with physical objects and processes (e.g. "straight line" must be taken to mean "line described by a beam of light" or, in any case, otherwise operationally defined), for anything at all to be meant by the statement that space is "Euclidean. (See Reichenbach (1958) for a defense of similar positions.)

We don't *see* space or time, or otherwise sense-perceive them. We see events. We see events as spatially and chronologically ordered. But we are not non-inferentially aware of some empty vessel (space-time) such that ordinal relations among events are to be identified with corresponding relations among vessel-coordinates.

This doesn't mean that there is no such empty vessel. But it means that our belief that there is one is theoretical in nature. It is a theory to which we are instinctively drawn, that being why, so far as I know, no group of people lacks the concepts of space and time. Of course, some authorities, e.g. Leibniz and Einstein, deny that space-time exists independently of events. But they *have* the concept of an event-independent space-time. They merely question its coherence.

descriptive truth. Non-descriptive truths are identical with moral truths. There are no moral differences without descriptive differences. As G. E. Moore (1912) put it, the moral "supervenes" on the descriptive. Stalin was evil. He deliberately caused suffering. Martin Luther King was virtuous. He deliberately alleviated suffering.

We have observed that moral intuitions track descriptive truths. This fact suggests that moral truths hold in virtue of the same *facts* as descriptive truths, but that we can experience those facts either as morally anti-septic truths or we can experience them as moral truths.

An illustration: Smith tortures an infant and Jones does the same. Smith's circumstances don't differ in any meaningful way from Jones'. Since Smith isn't acting under duress, neither is Jones; and since Smith is laboring under a psychotic delusion (to the effect that he's killing a ghoul, as opposed to an infant), neither is Jones.

Under these circumstances, it would be absurd to say that Smith's act was morally better than Jones' act or was otherwise morally different from it.

A closely related fact is that morally good acts are invariably those that conduce to psychological, biological, or psychobiological welfare, the same thing *mutatis mutandis* being true of bad acts. Smith poisons the reservoir from which people get their drinking water. Smith has obviously acted wrongly. The reason: in so acting, Smith is damaging people. (He is damaging them biologically, and given the severity of the biological damage, he is also damaging them psychologically.) Jones, a physical chemist, uses a solution he just invented to extract the poison from the reservoir, thereby purifying it and making it drinkable. Jones has obviously acted commendably. The reason: Jones has prevented psychobiological damage. (In this context, the words "good" and "bad" refer to intrinsic, not instrumental, goodness and badness. Obviously Smith's poisoning the reservoir is *instrumentally* good – in other words, it is to his advantage, given his objectives – if his objective is to harm the people whose drinking water comes from that reservoir.)

These facts suggest, if they do not outright entail, that moral intuitions are awarenesses of descriptive truths (truths of biology, psychology, and possibly other disciplines, such as economics or sociology).

The likes of Freud and Chomsky have no difficulty accounting for our moral intuitions. Their theories permit them to say that one's negative moral sentiment towards Smith's evil act is an encrypted conscious expression of an unconscious, but otherwise garden-variety judgment, viz. one to the effect that, in poisoning the reservoir, Smith is imperiling the welfare of many people.

4.1   Contrary to what Hume says, one *can* derive an "ought" from an "is." I see that Jones is about to mug an old lady. I know that I should intervene or call the police.

"But it's only *if* you know that mugging is wrong," it will be said, "that you can draw that conclusion from what your eyes tell you." Yes but it's only *if* I know that polar bears have white fur that I know that the bear I'm now seeing is a polar bear. Supposing (*per impossibile*) that one knew exactly how mass-energy were distributed in each region of space-time, would one for that reason have any biological knowledge?

No. To have biological knowledge, one needs biological concepts (e.g. *organ, respiration, immune system*). One doesn't need such concepts to know the physical condition of the universe. (By "physical," I mean "relating to physics.") *If* one knows the physical condition of each region of space-time, *and* one knows how to apply to biological concepts to physics-related truths, *then* one can figure out that there is a reptile on a certain rock, at a certain time. But by the same token, *if* one knows the physical condition of each region of space-time, *and* one knows how to apply to moral concepts to perceptual data, *then* one can figure that one should prevent Jones from mugging the elderly woman. There is thus no truth to the Moore-Hume contention that you can't derive an "ought" from an "is."

Those authors thought otherwise because they believed that if P entails Q, there is nothing in Q that isn't in P. We refuted this position in Chapter 3. A brief review of what we said is in order. The proposition that

(1)   x is a circle

entails that:

(2)   x encloses a larger area than any perimeter-equal figure

(3)   x is the area enclosed by the class of all points equidistant from a given point

(4)   x is a closed, 2-dimensional figure of uniform curvature

and that

(5)   x is shape-coincident with the flat part of the surface of a bisected sphere.

The reason that (2)–(5) are logical consequences of (1) obviously isn't that there is nothing in them that isn't in (1). It is that each is a reconceptualization of (1)'s content. In other words, supposing that (1) is true, and that F is the fact in virtue of which it is true, (1) is one way of conceptualizing F, and each of (2)–(5) is a different way of conceptualizing that same fact. The reason that (1) follows from itself is that it is a degenerate case of a reconceptualization of itself, and that is the reason that, unlike one any of (2)–(5), (1) is a trivial consequence of itself.

5.0   Moral sentiments obviously don't always directly concern one's own welfare. One can make dispassionate moral judgments about long-gone dictators. But such sentiments always have an indirect bearing on one's own welfare.[210] When I read about the behavior of Stalin's regime, I know be in terrible trouble if the U.S. government were to act similarly, I'd. To the extent that I see it as possible that the U.S. government

---

210. Ironically, David Hume made this point and powerfully defended it. To my knowledge he was the first to make it or, therefore, defend it.

should behave that way, the behavior of the Stalin regime excites powerful moral, and emotional, responses. (Given that the U.S. is spiraling downwards economically and that poverty leads to panic-driven political extremism, the misdeeds of the Stalin-administration don't register as historical curiosities.)

Hume argued that a moral judgment is the vector sum of the hypothetical thoughts and emotions (egocentric beliefs) thereby awakened. So his position is this:

(HP[211]) I believe that Stalin acted wrongly. What is involved in my having this belief? First, I think to myself. *Suppose that a Stalin-like figure took over.* So I psychologically put myself in the position of somebody being tyrannized by a Stalinist government. This awakens egocentric beliefs [which, so the present author has argued, are nothing other than emotions]. I know that I hate being under the oppressive rule of a Stalin, even though I know I'm not. I know what kind of emotion [egocentric belief] I would have under such circumstances. So I have a belief that is in some ways similar to a discursive belief and in other ways similar to an egocentric belief. I'm considering a situation different from my own; I'm considering the position of *other people*. To that extent, my belief is discursive. But I'm considering what being in those other people's shoes would be like for *me*, for *my* welfare. To *that* extent, my belief is egocentric.

According to Hume, moral judgments are nothing other than these semi-discursive, semi-egocentric judgments.

Like many authors, the present author thinks that Hume is right about this. The present author also thinks that, even though Hume is for the most part an arch-empiricist, his agreement with Hume on this matter confirms the anti-empiricist viewpoint he is defending in this work.

According to empiricists, the unpleasant burst of phenomenology awakened by consideration of Stalin's wickedness is just that: phenomenology; mere sentiment. This position is inconsistent with the fact that the phenomenological expressions of moral reactions are in lockstep with non-normative, indisputably objective facts about the things to which one is reacting. Stalin killed many people; he did so for no good reason. His administrative methods deprived people of life, liberty, and happiness. They had ruinous effects on people's biologies (cf. the famine in the Ukraine in the early '30's) and their psychologies (cf. the psychological effects of said famine). These are facts.

The unpleasant jolt of phenomenology that I have when reading about these atrocities is the expression of an intuitive, non-discursive awareness that I have of the implications that these facts have about human nature. That jolt is an encrypted and condensed awareness of many facts, e.g. that my circumstances are not so different from those of Stalin's victims, political cataclysms often catch their victims by surprise, even those of their victims who are all too aware that people are more responsive to

---

211. Short for "Hume's position."

empty demagoguery than to reason. Those awarenesses take the form of an action-dispositive phenomenological jolt because they place the propositions thereby known in an egocentric cognitive coordinate system, as opposed to an objective one.

A given person is at the center of his own map of the world – of his own "cognitive map," to use Gareth Evans' (1982) term. He is the point of origin. But people can also look at the world objectively – that is, they can locate truths in a map whose viability isn't person-specific. A given truth can be located in an egocentric, self-specific map, or in an objective, person-non-specific map. I can know that

(MD[212]) Marge [my wife] has the means, motive, and opportunity to kill me

in one of two very different ways: a deracinated purely intellectual way or an experientially integrated way. Knowing it in the first way means locating the corresponding truth in a cognitive map of which I am the center. Knowing it in the second way means locating that truth in a cognitive map that holds no less for you than it does for me. Knowing it in the first way doesn't *give rise* to fear; it *is* fear. Supposing that CM is my cognitive map, for me to have CM-relative knowledge of MD *is* for me to be afraid of Marge. Action-dispositive "feelings" *are* beliefs, albeit ones that locate the corresponding propositions in egocentric as opposed to person-non-specific cognitive maps.

The empiricist abhors the very idea of unconscious psychological structure. So he is forced to say of emotion-mediating phenomenology that it is *just* phenomenology, like the positive sentiment I experience when eating chocolate ice cream.

But this is deeply implausible. Subtle changes in the situations one considers are accompanied by equally subtle changes in the phenomenologies of one's conscious reactions to those situations. Also, intuitions are, or are expressed in consciousness by, phenomenological nuances; and if given enough time, I can convert any such nuance into a discursive judgment. One possibility is that I am *ex post facto* reading material into the original intuition that wasn't there. But that is radically implausible, given how much knowledge is intuition-based. If our intuitions were hewed to some finite, frozen body of facts, it could coherently be maintained that intuitions were just sentiments and that, so far as they were accurate, it was by virtue of some sort of (evolutionary-based) pre-established harmony between them and the facts. But since the class of facts tracked by our intuitions is unbounded, along several dimensions, there are *ipso facto* principled connections between those facts and our intuitions; and given how readily our intuitions lend themselves to discursivization, the structures implementing those principles must be psychological.[213]

---

212. Short for "Marge, dangerous."

213. This argument *mutatis mutandis* is stated more explicitly in Chapter 8, Section 15, and Chapter 11, Section 6.1.3. In Section 5.0 of this chapter, some of the gaps in the just-presented argument are filled in.

At least sometimes, I can say why a given situation arouses a given phenomeno-logical response in me, provided I am given enough time to evaluate the situation. I can say *why* Medvedev's biography of Stalin (*Let History Judge*) aroused such un-pleasant feelings in me, and *why* the *Autobiography of Benjamin Franklin* aroused such different feelings in me. (This sentence must be reworded if it is to be accurate. I thoroughly enjoyed Medvedev's book. It wasn't his book *per se* that aroused unpleas-ant feelings in me; what did so was the knowledge of which that book apprised me.) This strongly suggests that the phenomenological components of moral responses are condensed transmissions to consciousness of intricate judgments. Those judgments make it to consciousness in the form of unambiguous and immediately action-dis-positive feelings.

Let us briefly discuss emotional reactions (purely egocentric beliefs), and then map what we say onto moral sentiments (semi-egocentric, semi-discursive beliefs). When I see the snake hissing at me, my conscious response consists of unpleasant, action-dispositive phenomenology. I react, at the level of consciousness, with a *feeling*. That feeling acts immediately; it speaks unambiguously; it urges me in no uncertain terms to take self-protective measures. Suppose that, instead of having such a power-ful and (both temporally and informationally) condensed feeling, my conscious re-sponse was to form a nuanced and intricate discursive judgment of the situation and its implications for my welfare: in that case, I wouldn't act quickly enough. I'd be in the position of someone who, instead of being given an electric cattle prod in the back, was given a state-department report to read. I wouldn't react in real time.

5.1   Not all emotional reactions to a given situation are *moral* reactions. My beloved father, who recently passed away, used to go to car-races with me. Those were happy times. At such races, there are often car crashes. One day, a few months after my father's passing, I witness a car-wreck. It reminds me of the happy times I spent with my father at the track. So the spectacle of the car wreck makes me feel good. This re-action is not a *moral* reaction. It may be that, in addition to this positive, non-moral emotional reaction, I have other, negative reactions that are of a moral nature. But our point stands: not just any emotional reaction to a situation is of a moral nature.

It therefore won't do to say that moral reactions are merely emotional reactions. There is something that distinguishes garden-variety emotional reactions from moral reactions. It's not hard to identify the relevant difference. Why doesn't the positive feeling I have when seeing the car-wreck qualify as a moral reaction? Because it didn't embody a judgment as to the consequences for anyone of that wreck or of events similar to it.

Suppose that, as a result of witnessing that same disaster, I was appalled at one of the drivers, who I knew to be drunk, his drunkenness being the obvious cause of the wreck and of the various fatalities involved. *That* reaction was of a moral nature. The reason: it embodied a judgment to the effect that somebody had certain attitudes (one of cavalier disregard for the welfare of others) and therefore engaged in certain practices (driving drunk) that had ruinous psychobiological consequences for others and, further, that the likes of those attitudes and practices might well have similarly disastrous consequences for me.

This confirms our point that distinctively moral attitudes are not *mere* sentiments, but embody judgments. Those judgments turn out to be cogent, when we take the time to articulate them. But when we initially have them, they are consciously experienced only as homogeneous jolts of phenomenology. We thus have to assume that underlying those phenomenological episodes are cogent ratiocinative processes of which we have at most only an obscure awareness. And, as we've said many times, the concept of unconscious ideation is one that empiricists cannot countenance (or, historically speaking, have believed themselves, as empiricists, to be duty-bound to discountenance).

6.0   Empiricists would say that my gut feeling about Smith is embodies no unconscious assessment of the situation, being nothing more than a pre-programmed, purely reflexive response to it.

But given any two situations that differ in any significant respect, even to the most minute degree, our "instinctive" reactions to them differ: the intuitions we have in response to the one differ from those we have in response to the other – and more often than not, those differences are appropriate. Smith's expression is *almost* exactly like Brown's, but the muscles around Smith's eyes are just a tad more relaxed than those around Brown's eyes. (I'm either not consciously aware of this difference or, while perhaps being thus conscious, I am not conscious of the role that my awareness of it is playing in my cogitations.) I instinctively see Brown's expression as sincere and Smith's as insincere – and I'm (almost) invariably right.

But that judgment is given to my consciousness in the form of a "feeling." (I have a "bad feeling" about Smith. There's "something I don't like" about the looks of the guy.) Such a judgment isn't given to my consciousness *as* a judgment; it is presented to it as an affect. But unless such judgments underlay such affects, there would be no accounting for the extraordinarily high degree of trustworthiness of the latter.

Gut feelings are proverbially better guides to the truth than over-thought, conscious judgments. It is successful pianists, writers, artists, and scientists who learn to go with their gut feelings. The failures are the ones who are hobbled by conscious, discursive judgments and who turn a deaf ear to the inarticulate feelings that guide their successful counterparts. The latter, but not the former, know how to let their muse take the reigns of agency away from the artifices of a crippled, over-educated conscious faculty of judgment. A person's muse speaks to him through intuitions and gut feelings. Intuitions and gut feelings are, by definition, things for which one cannot find any rational basis at the time of their occurrence. (Sometimes a gut feeling's rational basis emerges with the passage of time.) It is the pedants and phonies who don't write anything unless it has gotten clearance from their actual or internal dissertation adviser or high school math teacher. It is these people who perpetually have that nonexistent condition known as "writer's block."

6.1   There is no doubt that we have our evolutionary pasts to thank for our abilities to make such speedy and accurate judgments. But that's because of the cognitive endowments thereby bequeathed to us.

We could say that we "instinctively" exercise these cognitive endowments. But if we say that, we're saying, in direct opposition to the empiricist, that the speedy and typically accurate "feelings" or "intuitions" that we have *do* indeed embody unconscious judgments.

Words like "instinct" and "instinctual" are ambiguous. Sometimes they refer to the psychological underpinnings of rude and basal proclivities, such as are associated with mating or eating. But sometimes they refer to subtle judgments, and such judgments may incorporate an enormous amount of learnedness. Cf. statements like "Beethoven *instinctively* knew that the next section of his sonata should be a fugato." When referring to such judgments, the term "instinct" is a synonym for "cognitive competence" or for "cognitive ability that is so deeply entrenched that it no longer needs the remediation of conscious ideation."

It is the competent mathematician who can solve a problem quickly and intuitively. It is the incompetent one who can't arrive at a solution before he has consciously, oafishly trudged through the algorithms and formulas that his teachers taught him. The empiricist, because of his antagonism towards the very idea of invisible structure, especially invisible *psychological* structure, has to downgrade intuitions to thought-free "feelings." But intuition is responsible for every sentence of every good book, every note of every great musical work, and every scientific insight. So far as non-intuitive ideation is thus responsible, it is by way of leading to the right intuitions. (Sartre (1956) and Kripke (1980) made similar points.) Thus, it is unreasonable to say, as the empiricist does, that intuitions are "mere feelings"; that no thought underlies them; and that there is no more to them than the unarticulated phenomenological episodes by which they are expressed in consciousness.

7.0   Aesthetic nihilism is a consequence of empiricism. According to empiricism, it doesn't exist if it can't be observed. Art cannot be observed. Paintings aren't seen and music isn't heard. Paint is seen and noises are heard. But paintings aren't paint and music isn't noise. A hawk can see the paint mediating Guernica better any person, but a hawk will never see the painting in the paint. If Guernica were a deposit of paint, hawks could see it. They can't; so it isn't. An artistically intelligent person with poor vision is better at seeing the art in the paint than an artistically unintelligent person with good vision. Therefore, one does not in any literal sense see the work of art. For analogous reasons, one doesn't hear music.

Some composers are better than others. Some works of music are better than others. This doesn't mean that, given any two pieces of music, one is better than the other. In many cases, the works of music are incommensurable: there is no yardstick by which both can be measured. But Mozart and Bach were obviously better composers than many other composers. This fact is obvious to anyone who has so much as a single musical bone in his body.

What empiricists say about aesthetic reactions precisely parallels what they say about moral reactions. To say that Bach is a better composer than tone-deaf Smith, says the empiricist, is simply to say that Bach's work arouses certain pleasant feelings in us that Smith's work does not.

Echoing what was said earlier, this view strikes anyone who isn't tone-deaf as being about as wrong as a view can be. To be sure, there are many people who aren't tone-deaf who claim to have this view; indeed, there are many such people who are musically gifted. But the behavior of such people is totally at odds with the nihilism they espouse. Their external and, to our knowledge, their internal reactions make this clear.

7.1   Hume's beliefs about aesthetics exactly parallel his beliefs about morality. As an empiricist, he is right to have such meta-aesthetic views. And as anti-empiricists, we are right to oppose them, and with arguments similar to those with which we opposed Hume's meta-ethical views.

I will speak only about music, since it is the only art form about which I can speak with any confidence. I am not convinced that my points will always carry over to other art forms. But if they hold with respect to music, Hume's artistic nihilism would *ipso facto* be refuted in connection with one art form, and it would then be implausible to hold that his nihilism was correct with regard to other art forms.

First of all, not all affective reactions to a musical work are *musical* reactions. I hate Smith. He is at my house. I know that Smith has a migraine whenever he hears Chopin's Ballade in g-minor. I maliciously blast a performance of that work from my high-tech stereo-system, knowing that soon Smith will be writhing in pain. My reaction to the music, though emotional, is not a musical reaction. (It may also be that, in addition to having this non-musical emotional reaction, I have a distinctively musical reaction. In point of fact, I adore the Ballade in g-minor and, under the circumstances in question, would derive both musical and non-musical delight from the music emanating from my stereo.)

Another illustration: When I met my beloved wife, I happened to be hearing a performance of the Rolling Stones song *Beast of Burden* (which, like most critics and many *Rolling Stones* fans, I believe to be musically mediocre). Since I associate that piece with that happy incident, hearing it always makes me feel good. That emotional reaction is not a musical reaction. It may be that, in addition to making me feel good, hearing that piece arouses negative reactions of a distinctly musical nature. (In actuality, I do have negative aesthetic reactions to that song, the reason being that it's so repetitive and bland.)

7.2   What is the difference between a non-musical emotional (or, more generally, affective) reaction to a piece, on the one hand, and a distinctively musical reaction, on the other? It's not hard to give a correct, but exceedingly vague answer to this question. But it's hard to give a correct and informative answer to this question; and, in my attempt to do this, I will resort to speculations, for which I will provide little substantiation.

First the vague answer: It's obvious that musical reactions to musical works track structural facts about those works. Each one of the preludes and fugues in both books of Bach's *Well-Tempered Clavier* has obvious structural virtues. (I couldn't begin to state what was structurally distinctive about those works; but I intuitively know a work with such a structure when I hear it, and the same is true of every Bach-afficionado.) The same thing holds of the Beethoven Sonatas, the Chopin Ballades (and Preludes, Scherzos, and Nocturnes), Schumann's *Kreisleriana*, etc.

It is radically implausible to hold, as Hume and other empiricists do, that musical reactions are entirely subjective and that somebody who listens with enjoyment to Schumann's work is not thereby picking up on something in those works that a tone-deaf Schumann-listener is failing to pick up on. Aesthetic nihilism is deeply implausible; and, as previously stated, nobody with a musical bone in his body is a musical nihilist.

When an artistically gifted person claims to be an aesthetic relativist or nihilist, either he isn't being honest or his philosophical views are out of alignment with the views embodied in the cognitive faculty of his that mediates his aesthetic ideation. Both factors are probably operative. People who are completely convinced that aesthetic realism is correct tend to say that it's correct, and people who aren't convinced that it's correct usually aren't being honest with themselves. Sometimes the motivation for such dishonesty is a fear of anti-elitist rage. Sometimes it's a refusal to give up a view of which one believes aesthetic nihilism to be a corollary.

Exactly similar points hold of moral nihilism. Setting aside moral imbeciles – psychopaths, in other words – those who advocate moral nihilism are lying either to themselves or to others; and if they're lying to themselves, it's either because they don't want to have a view that will incur the wrath of others or it's because they believe moral nihilism to be a corollary of a view of theirs that they don't want to give up.

Most moral nihilists are non-psychopaths, but all psychopaths are moral nihilists. In fact, psychopaths are the only true moral nihilists. They are the only ones who, in claiming to moral nihilists, aren't lying either to others or to themselves.

So far as they aren't false, the corresponding points about aesthetic nihilism are only qualifiedly true. The less musical intelligence a person has, the more he can accept musical nihilism without lying to himself. At the same time, a person with no musical intelligence might genuinely reject musical nihilism, since he might know that his unresponsiveness to music is a consequence of his not seeing what's there, as opposed to there being nothing there. But a person with no moral intelligence could not possibly accept moral realism. A tone-deaf person may be able to recognize distinctions relevantly similar to the distinction between good and bad music; he may, for example, be able to distinguish between good and bad visual art, and he may therefore know that his failure to respond to music is to be explained in the same way as some other person's failure to respond to visual art. But the only distinction relevantly similar to that between good and bad acts is that distinction itself, and a moral imbecile thus has no choice but to accept moral nihilism.

One would have to have no artistic intelligence of any kind to be in the same position with respect to aesthetic nihilism that the psychopath is in with respect to moral nihilism. But no one sufficiently devoid of artistic intelligence to accept aesthetic nihilism would have the cognitive wherewithal to understand it or, therefore, to accept it. (This is because the rudiments of at least some kinds of artistic intelligence are indistinguishable from generic forms of cognitive competence. For example, one can't speak a language without for that very reason having a modicum of literary intelligence.) But it's an empirical fact that many a moral imbecile is otherwise cognitively normal and thus capable of grasping philosophical principles. Therefore, some people really are moral nihilists, whereas none are aesthetic nihilists.

8.0   Subjectivism about art and morality embodies a failure to distinguish subjectivity from mind-dependence. Let P be the proposition meant by:

(ER[214])   "Mt. Everest is taller than Mt. Rushmore."

Were it not for our conventions, P wouldn't be ER's meaning and neither would anything else. Since conventions are relations among sapient beings and are therefore mind-dependent, ER's having P or anything else for its meaning is mind-dependent.

No convention of ours assigns P to ER or otherwise governs ER as a whole. Our conventions govern ER's simple parts: for each such a part, there is a convention assigning it a meaning. Those conventions being what they are, it logically follows that P is ER's meaning.

Our conventions are mind-dependent. But *given* those conventions, it is a matter of mind-independent, logical fact that P is ER's meaning; it is a logical consequence of those conventions. And the fact that P is true is, of course, a matter of mind-independent, empirical fact.

Some truths hold in virtue of *relations* between minds and non-mental entities. Such truths are mind-dependent, but not subjective. Truths concerning the truth-values (if they have any) and the meanings of complex expressions are in this category.

8.1   One of the standard arguments for subjectivist/nihilist theory of aesthetics is this:

(SN[215])   Let W be a possible world where there are no animate beings. On some planet in that world, there occurs some event that, by sheer coincidence, creates a series of noises acoustically just like those that, in our world, would constitute a performance of Chopin's ballade in g-minor. Is that series of beautiful?

---

214. Short for "Everest, Rushmore."

215. Short for "subjectivism, nihilism."

Surely not. It makes no sense to say that there could be instances of beauty or ugliness in a world devoid of sentient beings.

That may be true. But in W, a series of noises acoustically just like a real-world token of ER, would be meaningless and would therefore neither true nor false. But that doesn't mean that ER isn't intrinsically meaningful. In W, a sound acoustically like a token of ER is not an expression of any kind. Therefore, ER is not identical with a noise or any other physical object. So, given only that any physical object could have any linguistic meaning, it doesn't follow any linguistic symbol could fail to mean what it in fact means.

The reason that certain noises are meaningful in our world, but not in W, is that, in our world, but not in W, there obtain relations between those noises and our conventions. Our conventions being what they are, tokens of ER must be meaningful and they must mean what they in fact mean. ER, *qua* deposit of ink, is not inherently meaningful. But ER, *qua* deposit of ink, is not a linguistic entity, as we just saw.

What is such an entity is ER *qua* relation between conventions and physical entity, the latter being some deposit of ink. And it is inherent in that *relation* that it be meaningful and that its meaning be P.

It is not inherent in that relation that ER be *true*; for the truth of P depends on the relative heights of Mt. Everest and Mt. Rushmore. But there is a *three*-place relation R such that, given their relative heights, it is inherent in R that it constitute a given token of ER's being truth. So a statement's being true can be thought of as three-place relation, one whose terms consists of human linguistic conventions.

Thus, nothing follows from the fact that the noises mentioned in SW wouldn't be beautiful in W. For beauty is a property, not of noises, but of relations between minds and noises, and is in this respect just like meaning and truth (with the qualification that truth isn't a relation *only* between conventions and noises).

But it isn't merely a theoretical possibility that aesthetic beauty is a property of relations between minds and noises. (Take "noises" to be short for "noises or deposits of ink [etc.].") It seems pretty clear that, our cognitive protocols being what they are, it is fixed which sound-series are beautiful and which ones are ugly. So beauty is intrinsic to *relations* between cognitive protocols and noises. So SN is as spurious, and it is spurious in the same way, as the statement that:

(TS[216]) Since Bill doesn't exist in W, the fact that he's heavier than the quarter in his pocket is determined by Bill's opinion on the matter.

9.0   There is an important difference between aesthetic and moral reactions. Moral reactions are identical with, or relatively immediate derivatives of, self-interest-embodying reactions. But this is not true of aesthetic reactions. My delight in Bach's

---

216. Short for "truth, subjective."

fugue in c-minor (the one in his *Toccata and Fugue in c-minor*, BVW 911) has absolutely nothing to do with my believing that piece to have some bearing on my welfare. My enjoyment of that piece is entirely selfless. And, in this respect, my relationship to that piece is representative of any given person's relationship to any given piece, so far as that relationship is distinctively musical, and not generically emotional, in nature.

What is involved in liking a piece of music? What follows is the previously referenced non-vague, but highly speculative position that I can do little to substantiate.

First of all, there is no doubt that an enormous amount of *intelligence* is embodied in the works of Bach, Beethoven, Schubert, etc.[217] This is instantly obvious to musical and semi-musical people. When people deny it, it is often for the reason that:

(MM[218]) There is no literal sense in which musical works say anything. Therefore, they cannot be evaluated in terms of their degree of concordance with the truth. It is only to the extent that a given thing attempts to say how things are that it can be said to be intelligent. True – there are highly intelligent books that advocate erroneous positions. But though the main contentions of such books are false, those contentions are supported by arguments and considerations that are true or that, if not themselves true, are skillful manipulations of ordinarily truth-conducive methods of reasoning; so that, if only indirectly, the truth *is* a yardstick with respect to which such books can be evaluated, and evaluated positively. But nothing comparable can be said of music. A musical work is just a series of non-linguistic, meaningless sounds. How can it be said that Beethoven's 9th is any more veridical than the sound of a jack-hammer? And how, therefore, can it be said that any *intelligence* is embodied in Beethoven's 9th?[219]

Admittedly, there is an objection to this line of reasoning, to wit: Frank Lloyd Wright's buildings do not in any literal sense *say* anything. But surely there intelligence embodied in them. And, it might be alleged, the same thing *mutatis mutandis* could be said of Beethoven's 9th.

---

217. I do not mean to slight great jazz or rock 'n' roll musicians. No value judgment is implicit in my mentioning Schubert, as opposed to David Bowie. It is only because I happen not to be entirely ignorant of classical music that my references are to the classical greats, not to the jazz greats or the rock greats.

218. Short for "music is meaningless."

219. In private exchanges with me, Dr. Bradley Monroe Cooke, a professor of biological psychology, vehemently advocates this viewpoint. "Where do you draw the line?" he rhetorically asks. "Where do you draw the line between a jackhammer, on the one hand, and Beethoven, on the other?" Dr. Cooke's implication is that it's only when sound-series (or whatnot) are true or false that they can be said to embody any intelligence or, therefore, that the degree of intelligence in them can be assigned a (non-null) value.

But this objection doesn't go very far. In so far as they are technically sound, they embody awareness of facts about physics, engineering, and the like, and can therefore be said to implicitly state truths about those subjects. It is in this sense that functioning airplanes and rockets, though true or false *per se*, imply truths about physics (etc.) and, to that extent, are veridical and, for that reason, embodiments of intelligence. Nothing of the sort can be said about a musical work.

We will identify the problem with MM in the final paragraph of Section 10.2. But what we say there cannot be understood except in terms of extensions of already-made points concerning rationality and agency. So let us begin by restating and duly extending those points:

(AR[220]) Originally, one's agency existed to ensure the gratification of one's first-order desires and to ensure one's physical well being. Then one's agency became so developed that its survival and growth became ends unto themselves, and the gratification of one's first-order desires and one's physical welfare became nothing more than means to the preservation, consolidation, and development of one's agency. One's survival instinct was transferred, from one's body to one's *self*, one's self being the rationality-constituted superstructure whose purpose, when it was still relatively undeveloped, was to ensure the organism's physical survival by regulating the order and manner in which first-order desires were gratified but whose purpose, once it was developed, came to be to be to hone itself and to increase the scope of its powers and responsibilities.

The essence of agency is rationality. Things that *react* aren't agents. Reflexive behaviors aren't actions; reflex machines aren't agents; animals are reflex machines; rational agents are not.[221] To be an agent is to be something that acts. Something that *reacts* is, to that extent, sub-agential. We will refer to things that merely react as "reagents."[222]

Being an agent, as opposed to a reagent, involves being proposition-aware, as opposed to merely object-aware. *Things* (rocks, trees, etc. displacements thereof) are the objects of object-awareness. Things don't imply anything;

---

220. Short for "agency and rationality."

221. The term "reflex machine" is borrowed from Cleckley (1941), who rightly used it to describe psychopaths. In Chapter 16, we'll discuss psychopathy, and there we'll see just how right Cleckley was to describe psychopaths in this way. But the term "reflex machine" applies no less to psychopaths than to sub-agential, sub-rational animals; and this (alleged) fact, as we'll see, is consistent with Cleckley's analysis of psychopathy

222. This hyper-extension of the term "reagent" is justified by the fact that there is no word in the English language that is to the expression "thing that reacts" what the term "agent" is to the expression "thing that acts."

they don't stand in relations of dependence with respect to anything; nothing is a *consequence* of a thing.

In this context, it should be made clear, the term "consequence" has a *logical*, not a *causal*, meaning; it refers to the relationships of entailment, confirmation, compatibility, and incompatibility. And it is in virtue of grasping these relationships that a creature is able to *think*; for thinking consists in delineating relations of entailment, etc. And, as just stated, the only things that bear such relations to anything are propositions. So it is proposition-aware creatures (PAC's), and PAC's only, that can see the consequences of anything.

And it is PAC's and PAC's only that can make *decisions*. A decision is a judgment to the effect that one must behave in a given way, given what one's desires are and given what one believes the consequences to be of behaving in that way as opposed to other ways. It follows that only PAC's can have intentions; for intentions are identical with decisions, give or take some irrelevant linguistic nuances. It also follows that only PAC's can deliberate; for deliberation is nothing other than arriving at a decision.

Incidentally, it is often said that not all intentions follow a process of deliberation. This is almost certainly true. (I say "almost certainly" because I don't wish to rule out the possibility, which I see as more than a strictly theoretical one, that even apparently instantaneously occurring intentions are preceded by rapid, sub-personal ratiocinations.) But I'm inclined to believe that, when an intention is *not* preceded by a process of deliberation, that is because the relevant sorts of deliberation have already occurred, making it unnecessary to repeat them in this particular instances.

These are not new points. Aristotle said that agency was "practical rationality" – that decisions were merely the conclusions of non-theoretical thought-processes. Kant said the same thing. So in saying that intentions are judgments, I am affirming a point that, in addition to being defensible on its own terms, has a venerable heritage, notwithstanding its incompatibility with some contemporary views.

Conclusion: Agency *is* rationality. To be more exact, it's applied rationality. There is no *intrinsic* difference between practical rationality (agency) and "theoretical" rationality. The only difference is that practical ratiocinations eventuate in conclusions that bear on the subject's own welfare, whereas so-called theoretical ratiocinations do not, except in derivative or accidental ways. Practical ratiocinations are perhaps more likely to be corrupted by prejudices and other emotional factors. But practical ratiocination, *qua* ratiocination, is indistinguishable, except in the one respect just mentioned, from purely theoretical ratiocination.

10.0   Here's what we didn't say about rationality, or said only obliquely.[223] So far as consciousness is representational, it represents things by depicting them; iconic representation is the only form of representation of which conscious ideation is capable. Consciousness is mediated by phenomenology, and – it is clear, though it is not clear why it is clear – phenomenology can represent a given thing only by resembling it. Consciousness *qua* consciousness – consciousness *qua* phenomenology-constituted medium – is incapable of conception. Obviously we can consciously think conceptually; but consciousness is not *inherently* capable of conception. It is *inherently* capable only of iconic representation. And it is capable of conception only if supplemented in a way that we are now in the process of describing.

The subpersonal, however, *is* inherently capable of conception. Not all percipient beings are capable of conception *at the personal level of ideation*. (Henceforth, I'll use the term "personal" as short for "at the personal level of ideation." So the word "personal" will be used in an entirely artificial way.) But all such beings are capable of subpersonal conception. All perception is predicational; seeing is seeing-as. One doesn't just see a given object; one sees it *as* red, or round, or nearby or far off. Perceiving things involves ascribing properties to them. Indeed, to see *is* to see instances of properties, and it is to see them *as* such instances. The dog sees the ball *as* round, *as* being in the other dog's mouth, *as* fuzzy, etc.

As a matter of logic, nothing could see something, or otherwise observe it, *as* an instance of property P without at some level having a conception of P. Geckos and cats obviously don't *personally* (at the personal level) have concepts of properties. So, since they do have such concepts, they must have them subpersonally.

10.1   Here are two more reasons hold that animal-minds host subpersonal thought.

First: In us, perception and other involuntary functions are mediated by subpersonal thought. It would therefore be theoretical arbitrariness of the worst kind to hold that matters were different where animals were concerned.

Second: A dog's mind is more intelligent than a frog's. Therefore dogs have at least some intelligence, and so, by obvious extensions of this argument, do most other animals. But animals are not rational. This isn't because their minds don't mediate the requisite sort of intellection. It's because, although their minds do mediate it, they don't do so at the right level: they do so at the subpersonal, not the personal level, the result being that, although your beloved Rover's *mind* is replete with intelligence, Rover *per se* – the lovable, dopy entity that wags its tail when it sees you – is not very intelligent at all. Rationality is personal, as opposed to subpersonal, intelligence. More precisely, it is personal intelligence *that is deployed in ways that are to one's advantage.*

The *raison d'être* for the italicized clause lies in the fact that personal ideation can be both intelligent but not rational. Cf. the mad scientist who thinks he'll win the

---

223. Though we didn't say it, we hinted at it, in Chapter 9, Section 5.1, when we were discussing Berkeley's point that, although we can't grasp *abstracta*, we can grasp symbols that have such things for their meanings.

affections of Sally by building a Frankensteinian monster that routinely brings her flowers. In building that monster, that man is acting intelligently but not rationally.

Though dogs aren't rational, they aren't *irrational*. Irrationality is corrupted rationality; so irrationality is a prerogative of rational beings. Dogs are *sub*-rational. Second, their being sub-rational consists, not in their minds' being incapable of *personal* thought, not of thought *tout court*.

10.2   What is it that transfers intelligence from the subpersonal stratum of mentation to the personal stratum? (For reasons that we'll come to, "transfers" isn't quite the right word, but it will do for now.) The nucleus of the personal stratum is consciousness, and the essence of consciousness is phenomenology. Even our own propositional attitudes are knowable to us only to the extent that they are phenomenologized.

I am referring to the so-called 'conscious' propositional attitudes: those that are access-conscious, to use Ned Block's term, or preconscious, to use Freud's. I am setting aside those that are repressed, it being obvious that *those* propositional attitudes are knowable only through their phenomenological (and behavioral) derivatives.

Also, repressed propositional attitudes are not intrinsically different from unrepressed ones. The sorts of beliefs and sentiments that are repressed are just like those that are unrepressed. There is no intrinsic difference between repressed and a preconscious hatred of one's father. The difference lies in where such hatred is located in one's mind, not in what it is. We have direct knowledge of the one, but not of the other. But that means that our epistemic relation to the one is different from our epistemic relation to the other, not that those attitudes *per se* differ from each other.

For ideation to be transferred, so to speak, from the subpersonal to the personal domain, it must be phenomenologized. The word "transfer," be it noted, has to be taken *cum grano salis*. Subpersonal ideation doesn't *desert* the subpersonal stratum. What happens is that there come to occur conscious, phenomenology-constituted events that *track* subpersonal events. Subpersonal ratiocination always remains subpersonal. But it comes to be duplicated, in a weak sense of the word, by phenomenology-constituted mentation.

Descartes arithmetized geometry. That is, Descartes showed that geometrical statements could be "coded into" arithmetical statements (or, equivalently, that statements of the latter kind could "encode" statements of the former kind).[224] Gödel arithmetized formal logic. I submit, as a hypothesis whose merits have yet to be established, that the phenomenology-mediated ideation constitutive of one's listening to a musical work is hewed to subpersonal cognitive operations in much the way that Descartes showed geometry to be hewed to arithmetic. A musical work is not just a series of sounds. It is a series of sounds that instantiates a structure that could be instantiated in other ways. The structures instantiated by musical works represent

---

224. That is, he identified a rule whereby geometrical and arithmetical statements could be paired off in such a way that, given an arbitrary geometrical statement G, there is some one arithmetical statement A such that G is true iff A is true.

the formal properties of subpersonal thought. Musical works externalize our own subpersonal thought-processes; and in listening to such works, we become aware of such processes. This means that music enables us to increase the scope of our self-awareness. So supposing that pre-musical human beings had awarenesses of order-n, but none of any higher order, musical human beings (who are otherwise like their pre-musical counterparts) have awarenesses of order$_{n+1}$. A given work of music is good to the extent that it externalizes the structures mediating subpersonal thought. Ideally, for each articulation in such a structure, there is a corresponding articulation in that work's structure. That work is a good one to the extent that it satisfies that desideratum, and a sub-optimal one to the extent that it doesn't. Thus, in listening to good music one's self-awareness becomes sharper and more comprehensive. Also, by composing or otherwise performing meta-musical operations (e.g. learning a musical composition or improvising on a melody found in a pre-existing musical work), one "agentializes" otherwise non-agential subpersonal processes. In other words, one brings into the scope of one's agency processes that are otherwise inaccessible to it.

10.3   The delight that we take in music has three sources. First of all, it increases the scope of our self-knowledge. Second, it increases the scope of our agency. Third, it enables the personal stratum of mentation to perform logical operations that it couldn't previously perform but that the subpersonal *could* (and can) perform: there occurs a kind of transference of acumen from the one stratum to the other. (This "transference" is really a process of duplication: the subpersonal doesn't *lose* anything; no intelligence deserts it.) We will now clarify these points; and having done that, we will try to say why, if true, they would account for the delight we take in music.

Consciousness is the nucleus of the personal stratum of mentation. Consciousness *qua* consciousness is not intelligent; to the extent that it mediates thought, it mediates picture-thought, which is the lowest form of thought. (In fact, picture-thought isn't thought at all. Thoughts are judgments. Pictures aren't judgments, and neither are sequences of pictures.) The subpersonal, on the other hand, is inherently intelligent, and whatever intelligence is to be found in the personal stratum of awareness is bequeathed to it by the subpersonal. By "musicalizing" subpersonal processes, we make them perceptible: we give them a tangible, consciousness-accessible form, and we thus endow consciousness with a certain acuity that it otherwise lacks.

The delight we take in music is a form of the delight we take in acquiring knowledge. People are identical with their minds. Therefore one is only as big as one's mind. The delight we take in the acquisition of knowledge is therefore a derivative of our survival-instinct. More precisely, it is one of the forms that our survival-instinct takes when it is so remodeled as to fit into our rationality-mediated integrations.

11.0   The points just made are subject to two hefty disclaimers, and so are the ones about to be made. First of all, they are speculative. Whatever truth there might be in them is easily over-stated. It is only in a highly qualified sense that meta-musical operations agentialize sub-personal processes. Further, within the limits set by that qualification, they probably do so only to an extremely limited degree. Subpersonal processes are inherently incapable of being assimilated into one's agency. Let us proceed with our – as of now, duly disclaimed – speculations.

Our subpersonal ratiocinative processes are invisible to us. We cannot introspect them; nor obviously can we perceive them. But they cease to be invisible when they are coded into the phenomenological episodes that mediate consciousness. Musical works code such processes into the phenomenology mediating audition.[225] In consequence of being thus phenomenologized, such otherwise invisible and (from the viewpoint of one's self) uncontrollable processes fall within the scope of *our* control – the control of our *selves*. And by thus becoming *personalized*, they become, not just subject to the control of, but also constitutive of our selves, having previously been subpersonal, and therefore *im*personal, thus falling clean outside the scope of selfhood. The delight we take in music is the delight that we take in thus expanding the scope of our self-knowledge and, therewith, our agency and rationality.

The delight we take in music is dispassionate. In this respect, it is different from the delight we take in neutralizing a threat to our physical well being, such as a hissing rattlesnake. The latter delight is about keeping our bodies alive. The former is about honing our *selves*. Therefore, the former is an instrumental, the latter an intrinsic good. To a creature endowed with a self, its body's well-being is but an instrument for *its* well being, that is, for its *self's* well being. So, for such a creature, neutralizing a threat (e.g. killing a hissing rattlesnake) is but a means to an end, that end being *its* – i.e. its *self's* – welfare. But, for such a creature, it is an intrinsic good to finally be able to see, and absorb into its agency, and therefore its self, hitherto unobservable thought-processes. For in acquiring such self-knowledge, it expands the sphere of its agency.

11.1 Subpersonal mentation is inherently intelligent. Personal mentation is inherently unintelligent. Personal mentation, so far as it represents anything, consists of pictures. Neither pictures nor the things they represent confirm or entail anything; nor, therefore, do they disconfirm or entail the negation of anything. Personal mentation comprises sensations, as well as pictures. But sensations are obviously no more capable than imagery of mediating rational thought.

Personal mentation *becomes* ratiocinative when it becomes rule-governed. But now we have a problem on our hands. We've given two, seemingly different explanations as to what is responsible for the transference to the personal level of subpersonal, ratiocinative ideation. On the one hand, we've said that this transference involves co-ordinating conscious, and therefore personal, phenomenology-mediated mentation with subpersonal, ratiocination-mediating mentation. On the other, we've said that this transference involves our conscious ideation becoming rule-governed. And we've

---

225. Freud made a very similar point in *The Ego and the Id* and in Chapter VII of *The Interpretation of Dreams*.

said that the latter occurs when we develop higher-order customs, the reason being that this development displaces emotional, consensual-validation-seeking mentation with logic-driven mentation. These two positions are two pieces of one picture, as we'll now see.

11.2   When we self-externalize, as when we express our thoughts in audible or visible expression-tokens, we take the first step towards making our own thoughts perceptible. And once our thoughts are perceptualized, we can *evaluate* them; for we can then compare them with the realities to which they are supposed to correspond.

But self-externalization is only the first step towards self-evaluation. There is a second step. It is the purpose of the next chapter to describe this second step; let us summarize what we will find. If our effusions aren't answerable to any standard, other than the faux-standard of one's peers' emotional validations, then they are neither true nor false. So when the psychological forces driving our self-objectifications are governed by custom, which embodies only the emotional vicissitudes of one's peers, our self-objectifications are not answerable to standards and therefore aren't rational. But when those effusions are governed, not by customs, but by meta-customs, they are no longer directly answerable to the good graces of one's peers; they are at that point directly answerable to canons of logic. And it is only at this point that our conscious, icon-mediated ideation *truly* duplicates or shadows our subpersonal mentation. For our subpersonal mentation is rule-governed, that being why it mediates rational thought; and, consequently, our conscious ideation is not governed by any such strictures, and therefore isn't hewed to our subpersonal mentation, *until* it is rule-governed. And, as just stated, it isn't rule-governed until customs give way to meta-customs, which then convert the just-mentioned customs into rules.

CHAPTER 14

The cognitive and characterological consequences of linguistic competence

1.0   In this chapter, we will try to clarify the relationship between language and thought.

Must one know a language to think? Or must one be able to think in order to learn a language?

It is clear that, by virtue of knowing a language, a person is *ceteris paribus* much more intelligent in at least some respects than he would otherwise be. But what are those respects, and why does his linguistic competence enhance his degree of acuity in them?

Does the acquisition of linguistic competence *cause* one to become more intelligent, much as pushing the button causes the bell to ring? Or is the gain in intelligence *constituted by* one's newly possessed linguistic competence?

Also, what is a language? Are there non-linguisic means of communicating? Or is any way of communicating *ipso facto* linguistic?

These are the questions we will try to answer. They cannot be answered, we will now find, without a clear distinction being drawn being *mind* and *self*. And once that distinction is drawn, we will also find, it becomes clear what it is that makes human beings different from animals: it becomes clear what it is to have a distinctively human psychological architecture, and it therewith becomes clear how rationality is different from intelligence and how rationality is *not* different from agency.

The philosophical knowledge we are about to acquire will give us empirical knowledge. It will give us knowledge of the structures of certain widespread and theoretically significant forms of psychopathology. The theoretical importance of these forms of psychopathology is that they target one's psychological architecture itself. Unlike obsessive compulsive disorder, and even schizophrenia, they are not architecture-internal. The obsessive-compulsive's psychological architecture is overly intact, it being its consequent inelasticity that manifests itself as OCD-distinctive obsessions and compulsions. Unlike the obsessive-compulsive's mind, the schizophrenic's *is* in disarray. But he is still the person he was before he had his last episode, and after taking a few halidals he will be that person again. The psychopathologies to which I am referring involve a dismantling of the very structure of the psyche. So whereas even the most severe forms of schizoaffective disorder involve disorganizations of the *contents* of one's psyche, they leave its basic structure intact.

Not so with these other disorders. And yet, whereas it is seldom difficult to spot a schizophrenic for who he is, those afflicted by these other disorders are particularly good at fitting in with others. In fact, one of the primary symptoms of such afflictions is their hypertrophied ability to fit in. But these points are all by way of anticipation.

1.1   What we will say in this chapter will give some credence to the speculations bruited in the last chapter. Maybe the things we said about aesthetic and moral ideation were true; maybe not. In any case, the same points *mutatis mutandis* can be said about *linguistic* ideation. And when those points are transposed from the moral-aesthetic to the linguistic sphere, their virtues are easier to see.

This is partly for the very reason that those points *can* be so transposed: wrong ideas don't travel well, since it's only relative to other, similarly wrong ideas that they seem right. But that's not the main reason. Nobody denies that some sentences are true and that others are false. When evaluating a sentence, therefore, or sentences-series, we have more than inarticulate feelings on which to base our judgments. In the previous section, I said that a person's *gut* tells him that some composers are better than others and that some acts are morally perfidious whereas others are commendable. I then said that one's gut doesn't lie. I tried to substantiate the second statement; but I basically just urged acceptance of it. But in this chapter, we're dealing with things which, unlike a fugue by Bach, incontrovertibly *do* have meanings, and as to whose identities and truth-values people are in agreement. For this reason, the points made in the last chapter, when transposed into this one, will be answerable to unambiguous standards and, supposing that they meet those standards, will cease to be mere speculations and come to be *bona fide* hypotheses.

1.2   It is often said that a person's linguistic competence is both causally responsible for and constitutive of his ability to grasp properties and other non-spatiotemporal entities.

This position is untenable. A language is a set of semantic rules: it is a set of rules $S_1...S_n$ such that, for each i ($1 \leq i \leq n$), there is some expression E_i such that S_i assigns a meaning (a referent, a property or function, or a proposition) to E_i. There are two kinds of semantic rules: those that are primitive and those that are derived. The latter consist of other semantic rules; the former do not. The semantic rule that assigns David Bowie to "David Bowie" is primitive; it cannot be broken down into other rules. This is not true of the semantic rule that assigns a proposition to tokens of "it was with a heavy heart and an empty stomach that Rupert went to sleep that night."

A semantic rule is a proposition. If I am to use a token of "David Bowie" in a distinctively linguistic way, I must grasp the proposition that "David Bowie" refers to David Bowie, this proposition being the relevant semantic rule. It follows that I cannot use that expression without grasping a rather sophisticated proposition. For an expression E to refer to an object O is for it to the be the case that, in virtue of having the form "...E...," a sentence S encodes a proposition to the effect that O is a thing x such that ...x... So my grasping that "David Bowie" refers to David Bowie consists in my grasping the proposition that:

(DB[226]) In virtue of having the form "…David Bowie…," a given sentence S is true exactly if David Bowie is a thing x such that …x…

So a *prerequisite* for linguistic competence is an ability to grasp DB or other propositions that either equal or exceed it in complexity.

Another such prerequisite is that one be able to grasp and understand the logical interrelations holding among multiplicities of such rules. It isn't by virtue of grasping DB or any other one semantic rule that one can speak English. One is an English-speaker by virtue of knowing many semantic rules, and by virtue of being able to combine, iterate, and otherwise intelligently manipulate them in real time. Of course, there is nothing special about English; these points hold of anyone's ability to speak any language.

Thus, to know a language, one must be aware of propositions and, therefore, of proposition-constitutive sets of properties. One must also be rational. Rationality, it will be recalled, is a form of personal, as opposed to subpersonal, intelligence. (To be rational is to be intelligent about what it is to your advantage to do, while simultaneously being emotionally disposed to do it. Rationality is "emotionally integrated" intelligence about one's own welfare.) *You* know what "snow" means and what "snow is white" means. *You* know the semantic consequences of replacing the occurrence of "snow" in that sentence with "grass." In other words, your *self* has this knowledge. Your subpersonal mind also has it. But what matters in this context is that *you* have it as well.

2.0   That said, language-comprehension is mediated by subpersonal processes. Upon hearing a sentence of your native tongue, you understand it automatically. This doesn't mean that thought didn't mediate between your hearing it and your understanding it. It means that the relevant thought-processes were unconscious. Those processes obviously weren't unconscious in the personal, Freudian sense. They were therefore unconscious in the impersonal, Chomskyan sense.

At the same time, anyone who is linguistically competent *ipso facto* knows, not subpersonally but personally, what is meant by each of many simple expressions and also by each member of a finite but unbounded class of complex expressions composed out of those simples ones; and for many a complex expression $\langle x_1 \ldots x_n \rangle$ that he understands, he knows how that n-tuple's meaning would change if, holding everything else constant, x_i $(1 \le i \le n)$ were to be replaced by a grammatically comparable expression j_i, assuming he knows the latter's meaning. You understand the sentence: "Jim loves Mary." You know what "hates" means. Therefore, you understand "Jim hates Mary."

Any 10-year old English-speaker knows that $1 + 1 = 2$. But unless he's a prodigy, he doesn't know what it is that he knows in having that knowledge. He doesn't know

---

226. Short for "David Bowie."

that, in knowing that $1 + 1 = 2$, he knows that K is a dual set if it's the union of two non-overlapping unit sets. Linguistic competence seems to have both personal and subpersonal dimensions; the subpersonal dimension hosts the rapid computations involved in excogitating the meaning of a complex expression. The personal dimension hosts the semantic knowledge (e.g. the knowledge that "David Bowie" refers to a certain rock musician) from which those subpersonal operations draw.

These points suggest that

(i)   rationality is a precondition for linguistic competence,

and that

(ii)   linguistic competence is chronologically and logically posterior to rationality;

and, therefore, that

(iii)   linguistic competence isn't what constitutes rationality (contrary to what Wittgenstein, Davidson, McDowell, and countless others hold).

3.0   Linguistic competence enormously facilitates thought. Indeed, linguistic competence is a *sine qua non* for rationality, as we will now see, except of the most rudimentary kind. An obvious consequence is that linguistic competence is a *sine qua non* for possession of a distinctively human architecture.

But we've just argued that rationality precedes linguistic competence. How are we to reconcile this with the claims just made? And what is the nature of that pre-linguistic rationality? These questions are to be answered in terms of some general facts about language; and those facts about language are, in their turn, to be understood in terms of some points that we've already made but that we'd do well to make again, given that their bearing on the present topic of discussion may not be obvious.

Rationality is personalized intelligence. It is intelligence that has been transferred from the subpersonal to the personal level of mentation. The nucleus of personal mentation is consciousness. The essence of consciousness being phenomenology, consciousness, to the extent that it is representational, represents through depictions: through pictures essentially, provided that the word "picture" is so broadened as to include not just visual, but also included auditory and otherwise sensory images. Ratiocination is not iconic. Iconic awareness is objectual awareness. Objects don't stand in dependence-relations (e.g. relations of entailment, confirmation, and incompatibility) with respect to each other. Propositions do stand in such relations with respect to each other. Indeed, they are the only the only things that bear such relations to anything or to which anything bears such a relation. To ratiocinate is to delineate such relations. Therefore, consciousness *qua* consciousness is incapable of mediating ratiocination. But when subpersonal concepts become associated with the icons populating consciousness, and when series of such icons become hewed to series of such concepts, then consciousness comes to be capable of mediating thought, if only in the indirect sense in which arithmetical thought-processes become capable of mediating geometrical or logical ones.

Icons are pictures. Pictures represents externalities. For concepts to be associated with icons, they must be associated with pictures and thus with externalities. Words are such icons. (Technically, word-tokens are such icons, since words *per se* are properties and properties are non-spatiotemporal and therefore non-depictable. By contrast, word-tokens are spatiotemporal and audible, visible, or tangible.)

Perceptions represent things by depicting them, and perceptions are therefore pictures of the things they represent. So perceptions of expression-tokens are pictures of expression-tokens. But expression-tokens are not themselves pictures. (A given thing may be both a picture and a linguistic expression; but to the extent that it's the one, it isn't the other. See Chapter 5, Section 5.0.) It is indeed by turning our thoughts into pictures that we enable ourselves to control and evaluate them; and it is indeed by associating our thoughts with expressions that we turn them into pictures. But it isn't by associating our thoughts with pictures that we verbalize them: it is by turning our thoughts into pictures of non-pictures, those non-pictures being expressions. So the truth that we pictorialize our thoughts by associating them with expressions must be distinguished from the falsehood, propounded by Wittgenstein, that we verbalize our thoughts by associating them with pictures.

It isn't by virtue of making pictures available to them that languages enable people to express themselves. So far as a given language L provides a given person P with a way of expressing himself, it is because there is a function that assigns distinct L-expressions to content-distinct P-thoughts. Such a function must assign structurally distinct L-expressions to structurally distinct P-thoughts. A function that doesn't satisfy this condition is undefined except for thoughts whose exact contents have been satisfied, and thus fails to assign expressions to content-new thoughts. A function that does satisfy this condition is defined for content-new thoughts, so long as those thought-contents meet relatively non-constrictive, purely formal requirements.

This is not to say that any existing language satisfies this condition, or even that any possible language could satisfy it. It is to say that a language is inadequate to the extent that it doesn't satisfy it, and adequate to the extent that it does.

3.1 The relationship between thoughts and expressions can be compared to the relationship between numbers and points in space. Numbers don't bear any obvious resemblance to points; equations don't bear any obvious resemblance to lines. But because the number-system is sufficiently heterogeneous that numerical statements can be aligned with geometrical statements, the former can encode the latter.

It is to a considerable degree by virtue of being able to externalize one's thoughts in the form of linguistic expressions that one can evaluate them; and it is by virtue of being able to evaluate one's thoughts that one is rational. At the same time, it is by virtue of being rational that one can embody one's thoughts in linguistic expressions. This is a serious problem. To solve it, we must posit the existence of *proto-languages*. Languages are sets of *rules* dictating when certain expressions-types are to be tokened. Proto-languages are *customs*: customs making it socially incumbent on one, though not formally *de rigueur*, that one make certain noises (or engage in certain overt behaviors) in certain contexts. But custom-governed behavior is not rule-governed behavior and therefore isn't linguistic behavior. This is because customs are not rules. Customs are driven by emotion, and they are reinforced by *ad hoc* and unprincipled responses to uncustomary behavior. Rules are emotionally antiseptic, and they are enforced by explicitly laid down penalties. Of course, people make and enforce rules for emotional reasons: they may be driven by sadism, or self-interest, or personal loyalties. But a rule that is made or enforced for that sort of reason is to that extent corrupt and thus fails *as a rule*. By contrast, a *custom* that is comparably emotion-based is not corrupt, at least not for that reason, it being in the nature of customs that their foundations, and the mechanisms that perpetuate them, are emotional.

3.2   Though not genuinely linguistic, proto-linguistic behavior does serve an important function: it externalizes thought. Let us suppose it customary to say "x_1" when, and only when, it's hot outside. (Assume that, for some reason, the auditors of somebody saying this don't know that it's hot outside – they're deep inside a temperature-controlled cave, let's suppose, and the person saying "x_1" is shouting at them from outside the cave.) Before being articulated or otherwise externalized, one's belief that it is hot outside, though itself an awareness, is not an *object* of awareness. But tokens of "x_1" are externalities and are therefore being observable. Further, one can compare them with other externalities. One can remember (or, if one inscribed it, see) the token of "x_1" that one produced, and one can consider it in light of the weather (in light of whether it is hot outside).

Propositional attitudes, as we have pointed out, are inherently unobservable. They are observable only in the indirect way that electrons are observable. But once it is customary to produce a token of a given sound-type (or shape-type) when it is hot outside, then, if one produces such a token (and does so with no intention to mislead), one's belief that it is hot outside becomes an object of one's consciousness. One can sense-perceive the aforementioned symbol-token and one can also sense-perceive the state of weather; and in light of the latter, one can evaluate the degree to which the occurrence of that token was in keeping with customs. That occurrence expresses a belief that one has, and is thus an externalization of that belief. So, by evaluating the custom-friendliness of the occurrence of that token, one is, in effect, evaluating the veridicality of a belief that one has.

So even though beliefs *per se* are unobservable, their symbolic or proto-symbolic expressions are quite observable; and for that reason, beliefs become observable. And once they are observable, they are evaluable; for, whereas they were previously *identical* with awarenesses, they can now be *objects* of awareness.

All beliefs are unobservable, as are all propositional attitudes, be they access-conscious or repressed. Following Freud (1949), I conjecture that it is only because propositional attitudes become associated with expressions, and in due course with mental icons thereof, that they become observable.

We must recall that consciousness consists of phenomenology, through and through; and propositional attitudes to no degree consist of phenomenology. It is only in so far as they are phenomenologized that propositional attitudes are introspectible.

But not just any phenomenological expression of a given type of propositional attitude is recognizable to introspection *as an expression of that particular type of propositional attitude.* A person in the grips of rage is likely to mistake its precipitating cause for its object. Consider the phenomenon of road-rage. A motorist cuts you off. You think that the homicidal fury you subsequently feel is directed towards him. But that can't be right; what you're feeling is grossly out of proportion to what he did. The motorist merely uncorked the rage you rightly feel towards your boss, who has been tormenting you for the last twenty years. You wrongly take the precipitating cause of your rage to be its object.

Although you've displaced your rage towards your boss onto the rude motorist, that displacement need not be (and, so we will assume, is not) rooted in repression. You are all too aware of your hatred for your boss. If you could ruin his life with impunity, you'd do so in a heart-beat; there would be no emotional resistances for you to work through. It is less in terms of who *you* are that this instance of displacement is to be understood than it is in terms of what propositional attitudes are.

Phenomenology consists of affect. Affects are not judgments. Propositional attitudes are judgments. (See Chapter 10.) Judgments are not reactions. One's immediate response to a situation might be to make a judgment. But responses are not reactions. If I get sick, I am reacting if I wallow in grief, and I'm responding if I go to a doctor. Reactions are driven solely by what is immediately present. Responses are driven by beliefs as to how what is present compares with what isn't present. A judgment is a distillation of a body of information at least some of which concerns what is not immediately present. Therefore, one is not reacting to a situation so far as one's immediate response to it is to make a judgment. Thus, propositional attitudes are responses, not reactions.

Affects, by contrast, are reactions, not responses. Changes in one's affective condition, and thus in one's phenomenology, are hewed to changes in one's immediate environment. Changes in one's propositional attitudes are not thus hewed. Changes of the one kind cannot possibly be in lockstep with changes of the other kind. Therefore, a given person's phenomenological condition leaves it open what his propositional attitudes are.

One's affects are effects of one's propositional attitudes, and therefore aren't constitutive of them. Therefore, we cannot possibly have *a priori* knowledge as to how our affects correlate with our propositional attitudes, and, it obviously follows, so far as we have such knowledge, it is a posteriori, like our knowledge that smoke means fire.

Throughout this book, we've argued that, contrary to what empiricists hold, affective reactions are cognitive. In light of this fact, the points just made must be qualified. (Those points would have been unintelligible if they had been duly qualified when first presented.) A given change in one's mental condition can be a response in one respect, and a reaction in another. Your boss is pathologically envious of your musical talent. One day you and your boss are at a party. In the presence of your boss, your host asks you to sight-read a particularly difficult piano-piece. Relative to what you know about your boss, your subsequent masterful performance is a reaction, but relative to what you know about the markings on the score in front of you, it is a response. In one way, your behavior isn't reflexive; it reflects years of study, after all. In another way, it is reflexive. Your musical knowledge is extremely deeply ingrained. The sense in which you know how to interpret the score in front of you is similar to the sense in which you know how to interpret an utterance of your native tongue. When you hear such an utterance, *your mind* interprets it, but *you* do not; and relative to what your mind knows, your subsequent awareness of that utterance's meaning is a response, even though, relative to what you know, it is a reaction.

Relative to what your mind knows, the affective derivatives of your propositional attitudes are responses, not reactions. Relative to what you know, they are reactions, not responses.

When the rude motorist cuts you off, it is on the basis of your conscious affects that you wrongly judge the rage you are feeling to be directed towards him. Relative to what your mind knows, those affects are intelligent and are therefore not reflexive responses to immediate stimuli. But relative to what you know, they are such responses.

3.3   Custom-driven behavior is not rule-governed behavior. The former therefore isn't true or false, or otherwise right or wrong, and it therefore isn't linguistic. *Custom-driven behavior gives way to rule-governed behavior when there come into existence customs that regulate pre-existing customs.* Let's suppose that it's merely a matter of custom that you should wear a shirt when dining at a public eatery, i.e. that it isn't yet a matter of law. But let's suppose that it becomes a matter of custom, not law, that one cannot wear a shirt while eating pheasant-under-glass. What happens if somebody wearing a shirt is eating pheasant under glass at a public eatery? Clearly we have inconsistent customs on our hands. But let's say that it becomes a matter a matter of custom that, when there are two customs that cannot jointly be followed, the one with the smaller "impact-factor," i.e. the one that has the lesser effect on human behavior, is to be jettisoned. In that case, it becomes a logical consequence of our customs that somebody at public eatery who is eating pheasant under glass *should* wear a shirt. (Obviously more people eat at public eateries than eat pheasant-under-glass.) And in that case, if one chooses to comply with the higher-order custom (*given two incompatible customs, abide by the one with the greater impact factor*), it is *logically*, as opposed to emotionally or socially, incumbent on one to flout one custom and abide by another.

In fact, a higher-order custom may make it logically mandatory to behave in a way that is *anti-social* and that thus incurs the antagonism of others. For, depending on the circumstances, one may have to flout some lower-order custom in order to comply with a higher-order custom. It is precisely when higher-order customs are given preference to lower-order customs that one's behavior is driven by logic, and not, except indirectly, by considerations of one's emotional liaisons to others. Compliance with custom then ceases to be about placating others and preserving emotional equilibriums, and it becomes about preserving the logical integrity of a body of customs.

There thus occurs a reversal the likes of which we've encountered in a number of different quarters. Logic becomes so divorced from emotional validation that it becomes an end unto itself. So long as there are only first-order customs, sound reasoning is important only to the extent that correlates with peer-approval. When higher-order customs come into play, peer-approval is important only to the extent it correlates with sound reasoning.

If a so-called custom is to be complied with for reasons of logic, not for reasons of peer-approval, it isn't really a *custom* anymore: it's a rule. When it becomes a matter of *principle* to behave in a certain way, it is no longer a matter of custom. In performing a given act, one isn't following a rule requiring one to perform that act unless one's reason for performing it is that doing so is consistent with the strictures of logic. So far as one's reason for performing it is to please one's peers, one isn't following a rule.

Logic-driven behavior may be driven by the objective, and may have the effect, of consolidating a social order on which people depend for their welfare. But oftentimes the logical connection between one's behavior and the welfare of one's peers is so recondite that one's behavior, though in fact advantageous to one's peers, is perceived by them as undermining and anti-social.

4.0   The points just made about the social sphere hold of the linguistic sphere. It may be customary to say "x_1" when it's hot, and "x_2," when it's cold. Depending on whether one abides with those customs, one either pleases or displeases one's peers, but one hasn't spoken truly or falsely or otherwise behaved correctly or incorrectly. But this changes when *meta*-linguistic expressions come into existence.[227] A "meta-linguistic" expression is one that builds sentences out of other sentences.

"Because" is such an expression, since, when given "Jim is wealthy" and "Jim is smart," it yields "Jim is wealthy because Jim is smart." "It is not the case that" is such an expression, since, when given "Jim is wealthy," it yields "it is not the case that Jim is wealthy."

Meta-linguistic expressions are sometimes referred to as "connectives." But the latter term is misleading, since some so-called connectives, e.g. "it is not the case that," operate on single sentences and therefore don't connect anything.

Meta-linguistic expressions are functors. A functor is an expression, e.g. "$F(x) = 2x$," that expresses a function. (Functions are not themselves expressions; they are rules that assign objects to objects.) "Because" assigns exactly one object to the ordered pair <"Jim is wealthy," "Jim is smart">. (The quotation-marks are meant to indicate that the members of that ordered pair are sentences, not propositions.) That

---

227. Technically, the term "meta-*proto*-linguistic" should be used instead of "meta-linguistic." Since "x_1," "x_2," etc. aren't rule-governed, they aren't genuinely linguistic; they are proto-linguistic. So the expressions that govern the use of "x_1," etc. are meta-proto-linguistic.

object is the sentence "Jim is wealthy because Jim is smart." Therefore, "because" expresses a function that assigns the proposition that Jim is wealthy because Jim is smart to the ordered pair <Jim is wealthy, Jim is smart>. (The absence of quotation-marks is meant to indicate that the members of that ordered pair are propositions, not sentences.) The reason "because" is described as a "meta-linguistic" expression is that it is a functor whose operands are other expressions, and it's obviously for the same reason that "and" and "or" are so described.[228]

When functors come along, it ceases to be a matter of custom, since it comes to be a matter of *principle*, how to use "x_1," "x_2," etc. Let's suppose it a custom that "x_2Dx_3" is to be used if it's *both* cold *and* raining, the same thing *mutatis mutandis* being true of "x_iDx_j," for all i, j ($1 \leq i,j \leq n$). In that case, it's a matter of logic, and only indirectly of custom, that "x_1Dx_2" is never to be used. (A token of "x_1Dx_2" would be custom-compliant only if *per impossibile* it were both hot and cold outside.)

4.1   When expression-usage becomes logic-driven, the appropriateness of a given expression-token is no longer determined by the emotional reactions one's peers have to it. For this reason, the semantic consequences a universal failure to understand a complex expression are different from those of a universal failure to understand a simple one. If everybody took "enervating" to mean "energizing," it would for that very reason come to have that meaning, but the English language would otherwise be relatively unchanged. In general, a universal misunderstanding of a simple expression tends to be neither innocuous nor disastrous. But a universal misunderstanding of a complex expression *is* either innocuous or disastrous. There are many sentences that are too long or too intricate to understand. The fact that nobody understands them doesn't affect what they mean and it doesn't otherwise affect the languages to which they belong. Understanding-failures of this kind are harmless.

But sometimes people change the meaning of a complex expression so as to validate their failure to understand it. They assign it the meaning that they wrongly think it has. In doing this, they assign an incoherent meaning to at least one of that sentence's constituents. (I am counting the syntactic devices involved in a sentence's constructions, including those that are not phonetically realized, as being among its constituents.) Sentences are complex expressions. What a complex expression means is a

---

228. Incidentally, "or," no less than "because," operates on ordered pairs of sentences; and the same is true of "and," and for the same reason. The fact that "P or Q" is equivalent with "Q or P" is a fact of logic, not of semantics; and semantic rules must not, and generally do not, prejudge, issues of logic or any other semantics-transcendent domain. Cantor proved that, if x is a transfinite cardinal, then "1 + x" is larger than "x + 1." We thus want to say that "+," no less than "<," operates on ordered pairs of numbers, even though before Cantor's time, it may have seemed sheer pedantry to say this.

All of the linguistic devices that enable simple expressions to be combined into complex ones, or that enable complex expressions to be combined into even more complex ones, are functors. *All* meta-linguistic devices are functors.

logical consequence of what its parts mean. If S is the sentence "fear is a more powerful motivator than love" The fact that S means P is a logical consequence of the semantic rules for "fear," "love," and so on. Thus, at least one of these rules must be changed if P is to cease to be S's meaning. Suppose that the meaning of "fear" is changed. (What we are about to say about this word can equally be said of any other given one of S's constituents.) If that change involves that word's coming to bear a meaning additional to the one it already has, then a once unambiguous word has become ambiguous (or, if it was already ambiguous, it becomes ambiguous in yet another way). If that change involves that word's losing its old meaning and being a given new one, then every single sentence containing the word "fear" ceases to have its old meaning and comes to have a new and different one. This would be a disaster. But the alternative, though obviously preferable, wouldn't be cost-free. If a word is ambiguous, people are less likely to see it as ambiguous than they are to consolidate its different meanings into one incoherent meaning. If the word "fear" were made ambiguous, or made more ambiguous than it already is, it is unlikely that its new meaning would be completely different from its existing meaning; it is more likely that its new meaning would enough like any given one of its old ones that people wouldn't distinguish the two. Anglophones would thus be disposed to conflate two concepts that they had previously distinguished, and they'd therefore be less able than before to think about either concept coherently.

   To be sure, the sentence "fear is a more powerful motivator than love" is not likely to be misunderstood. So let us consider a sentence that is likely to be misunderstood; let us consider the consider the sentence: "given any person x, there is some person y such that y loves x," and let us suppose, plausibly, that people took that sentence to have the same meaning as "there is some one person who loves everybody." In that case, *either*

(i*)   people would simply remain wrong about what those expressions meant

or, if they warped the meaning of one of those expressions, so as to validate their misinterpretations of them,

(ii*)   they would thereby weaken the English language in some way: unambiguous expressions would become ambiguous; hitherto easily made points would become hard or impossible to make; etc.

Some of my students have trouble seeing how those two sentences, or other comparably related sentences, differ in meaning. Ashamed of their lack of acumen, such students often go on to deny that those sentences have different meanings, and they justify their position by espousing meaning-conventionalism. "Those expressions cannot possibly have different meanings," they say. "Expressions mean what their users want them to mean. What an expression means cannot possibly be a mystery to the people who use it. Therefore, those sentences can't have meanings we don't know them to have."

   Embedded in this superficially plausible line of thought is the negation of an oft-overlooked truth, namely, that a precondition for there being linguistic conventions is that it be possible for the very people bound by those conventions to be wrong about them. On Monday, you stipulate that expression E has meaning M. Let S be that stipulation. On Tuesday, you may have wrong beliefs about S; you may even have forgotten that such a stipulation was ever made. Therefore, to the extent that S has anything to do with E's meaning M, you can be wrong about what E means. By the same token, to the extent that you cannot possibly be wrong about what E means, S isn't giving it meaning. Supposing that S isn't giving it meaning, what is? Some other stipulation? If so, everything we just said about S holds of that other stipulation. Thus, if E is such that you can't possibly be wrong about what it means, then, whatever that meaning is, no stipulation on your part, or anyone else's, is even partly responsible for its having that meaning. It is only if nothing gives E meaning, and it therefore has no meaning, that it can be such that you cannot possibly be ignorant of its meaning. If an expression has meaning, consequently, it is possible for you, and for any other person, not to know what that meaning is.

These points are easily extended. Let G be some group of people. On Monday, G collectively creates some rule R. On Tuesday, the members of G may have wrong beliefs about R and they may therefore have wrong beliefs about what it is to comply with R. To the extent that a person's complying with G's rules depends on his complying with the rule laid down on Monday, G's members can be wrong about what it is to comply with their own rules. Of course, G's members have the option of covering up their wrong views about their own rules by enacting new rules. But everything just said about R will hold with respect to any given one of those new rules. If a group has rules, there is a difference between complying with them and doing what that group's members believe to be complying with them. If a group has rules, it can have wrong beliefs about them and therefore about whether they're being violated.

Given any convention, and therefore any semantic convention, it must be possible for those bound by it to have wrong beliefs about it and must be possible for them not to know that it exists. Semantic conventions are identical with primitive semantic rules, that is, with the semantic rules that assign meaning to simple expressions. Therefore, given any simple expression, it must be possible for speakers of the relevant language to be wrong about what that expression means. It obviously follows that, given any complex expression, it must be possible for speakers of the relevant language not to know what it means.

That said, there is an important respect in which ignorance of the meaning of a complex expression may differ from ignorance of the meaning of a simple one. Given a complex expression, a person's inability to understand it may have nothing to do with his linguistic competence; his failure to understand it may be performance-based, as opposed to competence-based; that is, it may have to do, not with his linguistic ability, but with this ability to exploit that ability. But any failure on somebody's part to know the meaning of a primitive semantic rule constitutes a lack of linguistic competence on his part.

An expression is useless if we don't know its meaning. At the same time, an expression is useless if it is impossible for us not to know its meaning. In fact, there cannot be an expression as to whose meaning it is not possible for one to in error; for nothing assigns meaning to such an expression, as we saw a moment ago, and such an expression therefore cannot possibly exist, since an expression cannot possibly lack meaning, as we saw in Chapter 4, Sections 7.4–7.5.7.

There are, or at least there theoretically could be, writers who use syntax so masterfully that, during their lifetimes, only a few savants know what they are saying.[229] Such writers are putting the resources of their respective languages to new and legitimate use; they are unearthing the hidden capabilities of those languages. And yet to their less enlightened contemporaries, those authors are producing "drivel."

To conclude, it is when meta-customs come into existence that first-order customs become *rules* – and thus cease to be customs. (Let's set aside the technical point that the aforementioned "meta-customs" aren't really meta-*customs* if the so-called "customs" they govern are rules, not customs. It's a difficult, but unimportant, question how to restate the points just made so as to avoid the inconsistencies embodied in our use of the term "meta-custom.")

5.0   In order to begin to substantiate the points just made, we must state some general facts about language. A language is not just a collection of meaningful symbols. Let S be a set that contains exactly three expressions, x_1, x_2, and x_3, whose respective meanings are *it's hot, it's cold*, and *it's raining*. Given that S satisfies this condition, it follows that no two of the expressions in it can combined into a third.

S is not a language. S is just a set that contains three symbols. Those symbols *could* be used by some one person, or by some one group of people. But that is not enough for them to constitute a single language. A given set of symbols qualifies as a single language in virtue of facts inherent in the interrelations of those symbols; such a set does *not* so qualify in virtue of the fact that the members of a culturally or otherwise

---

229. In any case, there theoretically *could* be such writers. The just-made point *mutatis mutandis* is more appropriately made about music: many a composer has been ahead of his time, and when he was alive, people simply didn't know what he was doing. Generally, great writers are understood in their own times. But I think that some writers are undervalued during their lifetimes precisely because they are such masters of the languages they are using. Gibbons may fall into this category, and so may William James. Many would put James Joyce in this category; indeed, many would say that he is a paradigm-case of such a writer. I cannot evaluate this claim, since, although I read little fiction and must speak with diffidence, I didn't understand a word of the few pages of Joyce that I read. It seemed to me that his was the work of a severe schizophrenic. A page worth's of Charles Manson's thoughts would compare favorably with, but would otherwise be comparable to, a randomly chosen page of *Ulysses*. In any case, having quoted a page worth's of material from *Ulysses*, Cleckley (1941) says that it makes no sense and, partly on the basis of the alleged meaninglessness of Joyce's prose, concludes that Joyce was either a fraud or seriously mentally ill or both. The evaluation I just put forth of Joyce's work is really due to Cleckley; it wouldn't have occurred to me had I not read *The Mask of Sanity*; but when I did read it, what he said about Joyce "clicked," to use the vernacular.

unified group of people all use the expressions belonging to that set. The members of such a group could use 18 different languages. This is not to make the trivial point that such a group might be divided into 18 linguistically distinct subgroups. It is to make the non-trivial point that everyone might use 18 different languages to communicate with everyone else in that group. There are communities all of whose members all speak English, Yiddish, and Hebrew, and each of whose members uses all three when speaking to his fellow community-members. Whether a given expression belongs to English as opposed to Hebrew has nothing to do with who uses it; it has to do with what other expressions it can combine with.

English is a *bona fide* language. Any two expressions of English can be combined into a third. This entails that, along at least one dimension, English is infinitely expressively powerful. Moreover, any two complex expressions can be broken down into parts that can be recombined into expressions other than the original two. This entails that English has a certain degree of expressively flexibility; indeed, given what a large primitive lexicon English has, it entails that English has considerable expressive flexibility. Given any natural language L – Arabic, Russian, Mandarin – exactly similar points hold of L.

The difference between English and S is not the difference between a robust language and a feeble one; it is the difference between a language and a non-language. No two of S's symbols have anything to do with each other, except perhaps in the irrelevant (cultural, non-semantic) sense that some one group of people may use all three.

"But why," it will be asked, "must a set of symbols be integrated in the way just-described to qualify as a language?" Because otherwise, as we will now see, no member of such a set will be true or false.

This is subject to a qualification. The meanings of x, y, and z *can* be true or false, or otherwise meaningful, if the semantic rules for them were laid down by people who were using some *pre-existing* language, such as English. But under that circumstance x, y, and z will also be extensions of English, and we're interested in S *qua* language unto itself, not S *qua* artificial extension of some existing language. So we'll henceforth consider S in the first way.

Let G be some group of people who don't already have a language; and let's suppose that the members of G all live in a naturally temperature-controlled cave. Members of G very much want to know what the weather is like outside. It becomes customary for members of G entering the cave to say "x_1," "x_2," or "x_3," depending on whether it's hot, cold, or raining. And it is on the basis of these "reports" that members of G decide what sort of apparel to don before exiting the cave.

One day, upon entering the cave, some prankster named "Smith" says "x_1," even though, as he well knows, it's extremely cold. His cadres put on their summer gear, only to get frost-bite within seconds of exiting the cave. Has Smith spoken *falsely*?

Smith has spoken falsely only if it is a *rule* that one must say "x_1" when, and only when, it's hot outside. But is there such a rule? It is *customary* among members of G to use "x_1" in that way. But customs are not rules. A custom-breaker's peers may look at him askance; they may even kill him – or they may see his behavior as endearingly eccentric. But however they react to him, their reaction will be emotion-based and *ad hoc*.

Rules, by definition, are never implicit. They must either be stated explicitly, or (as with derivative semantic rules) they must be logical consequences of explicitly stated rules. Smith has acted misleadingly, but not falsely, for, although he has acted contrary to people's expectations, he hasn't broken any rule.

Even emotionally deeply entrenched customs are different from rules. By the same token, some rules aren't backed by any emotion: given some *bona fide* rule R, it may be a matter of indifference to us whether to abide by R or not. In fact, one of the very things that distinguish rules from customs is that customs last only as long as we have certain feelings about them, whereas rules may exist even if we detest them and may fail to exist even if we long for them.

5.1   But *the* difference between customs and rules is that

(i)   rules are either explicitly stated or follow from what is explicitly stated *in accordance with explicitly stated rules,*

whereas

(ii)   customs needn't be stated: they arise organically.

It is a consequence of (ii) that customs exist only as long as they have emotional support, and of (i) that the same is not true of rules.

Violations of rules are not dealt with an *ad hoc* manner: it is inherent in what rules are that, when a rule is laid down, so are provisions as to how to deal with violations of that rule. But it is *only* in *ad hoc* ways, as we've discussed, that people respond to counter-customary behavior.

Customs are merely modes of behavior to which people become habituated. Of course, people can come to depend for their welfare on other people's behaving in ways that are consistent with certain customs. But that is neither here nor there. There are *bona fide* rules which people can violate without in any way affecting anyone's welfare.

We must now recall a point we made a few pages back: it is when *second-order customs* come into existence that customs give way to rules. Bearing this in mind, let's suppose that, in addition to having the symbols (or, more accurately, proto-symbols) "x_1," "x_2," "x_3," etc., members of G also have symbols that enable them to form symbols out of other symbols. So it becomes customary to say "nx_1" (pronounced "en ex one") if it's *not* hot, and "nx_2"" if it's *not* cold, and so on. And it becomes customary to say "x_1cx_3" (pronounced "x_1 see x_3") if it's raining *and* cold, etc.

At this point, how one uses x_i ($1 \le i \le n$) is no longer a matter of custom. Once customs such as those regulating the use of "c" and "n," come into existence, it ceases to be a matter of custom how "x_1," "x_2," "x_3," etc. are used. Given the customs regulating "c" and "n," one is not saying, or even suggesting, anything coherent, or therefore anything at all, if one says ""nx_1c_2." Before there came into existence meta-customs, such as those associated with "n" and "c," how one used "x_1," "x_2," etc. was a matter of how one felt like using them.

And so long as it was merely habitual of people to say "x_1" when it was hot, their using that term when it was cold wasn't *wrong*, except in the weak sense in which telling off-color jokes at a wedding is wrong. Merely customary, as opposed to rule-driven, behavior isn't wrong. But deviations from customs *become* wrong, as opposed to merely emotionally disturbing, when the customs in question themselves come to be regulated by customs.

Paradoxically, it is only when complex expressions come into existence that simple ones do as well. Strictly speaking, "x_1" and "x_2" were proto-expressions, not actual expression, since customs, as opposed to rules, determined how they were used. These proto-expressions became *real* expressions when, and only when, there came into existence higher-order symbols, such as "n" and "c". For it isn't until higher-order expressions come into existence that proto-expressions are used in accordance with rules; and, since actual linguistic expressions are used in accordance with rules, it isn't until higher-order expressions come into existence that proto-expressions become real expressions. Higher-order expressions govern sentences. Since there are no genuine expressions until there are higher-order expressions, there are no atomic sentences until there are molecular sentences, and there are thus no subsentential expressions until there are sentences.

"But in that case," it will be asked, "how do languages ever come into existence? There can't be complex expressions unless there are simple ones. That's a matter of logic – a tautology, in fact. Therefore, the first expressions cannot possibly be complex ones. But – so you say and so we'll momentarily assume – there are no simple expressions before there are complex ones. Therefore, the first expressions cannot possibly be simple ones. The first expressions can't be simple and they can't not be simple. Therefore, there cannot be a first expression, and language can't come into existence. Languages do exist. So you're wrong."

The statement "x is a proper part of y" has many different meanings, and the argument just given involves a failure to distinguish between at least two of those meanings.

Your lower intestine is a proper part of your digestive system. Your digestive system is a proper part of your metabolism. But you couldn't have a digestive system unless you had a metabolism, and you couldn't have a lower intestine unless you had a digestive system.

If your lower intestine were removed, it would cease to be a lower intestine. The tissue that realized it would still exist, at least for a while, but that tissue would no longer be functioning as a lower intestine.

The statement:

(A)   Your lower intestine is operating

entails

(B) Your digestive system is operating.

But (B) doesn't entail (A).

The meaning of the statement

(C) your lower intestine is a proper part of your digestive system

is:

(D) A entails B, but B doesn't entail A.

Thus, it is in a functional sense, not a strictly spatial sense, that your lower intestine is a "proper part" of your digestive system.

The statement

(E) You have a lower intestine

entails

(F) You have a digestive system.

The meaning of the statement

(G) You couldn't have a lower intestine if you didn't have a digestive system

is:

(I) E entails F.

D and I are obviously compatible. Thus, when C and G are correctly interpreted – when, that is, the spatial meanings that they seem to bear are replaced with the non-spatial meanings that they actually bear – they no longer even appear incompatible.

Let us now state the relevant analogues of these points. Consider the statement:

(J) "Smith" is a proper part (in other words, a proper semantic constituent) of "Smith is tall."

The meaning of (J) is not:

(K) Given any occurrence of "Smith is tall," the space-time region occupied by the occurrence of "Smith" is a proper part of the space-time region occupied by the occurrence of "Smith is tall."

If (K) were correct, then, given an occurrence of "Smith is tall," the corresponding occurrences of "ith," "mi," and "all" would be proper parts of the occurrence of "Smith is tall." But they aren't; so K is false.

The statement:

(L) "Smith is tall" has been tokened

entails:

(M) "Smith" has been tokened.

But M doesn't entail L. The meaning of J is:

(N)   L entails M, but M doesn't entail L.

The meaning of:

(O)   There can't be complex expressions unless there are primitive ones

is:

(P)   Given some existing language L, if x is a complex L-expression, there is some L-expression y such that "x has been tokened" entails "y has been tokened," but not the other way around.

The statement

(Q)   E is a simple linguistic expression

entails

(R)   E is a linguistic expression.

R entails:

(S)   There is some language L such that E belongs to L.

The statement:

(T)   L is a language

entails that at least one complex expression belongs to L, and T therefore entails:

(U)   There is some L-expression x and some L-expression y such that, for some L-expression z, x and y are semantic constituents of z.

U entails:

(V)   There is at least one complex of L; therefore, there are complex linguistic expressions.

Therefore, Q entails V.
    The meaning of:

(W)   There cannot be simple linguistic expressions unless there are complex ones

is:

(X)   Q entails V.

P and X are compatible. They don't even appear incompatible.

Thus, when O and W are correctly interpreted – when, that is, the chronological meanings that they seem to bear are replaced with the logical meanings that they actually bear – they no longer even appear incompatible.

For reasons put forth in my book Mind, Meaning, and Scientific Explanation (Chapter 7, 6.3.5), "x is a part of y" never means "the space occupied by x is a part of the space occupied by y." So far as that ever seems to be the meaning of that sentence, it is because one thing's being a part, in the functional sense, of another sometimes involves the first thing's occupying a space that is a part of the space occupied by the second.

If you swallow a penny, the space-time region it occupies is a proper part of the space-time region occupied by your metabolism. But that penny isn't a part of your metabolism. Therefore, the sense in which your heart is a part of your metabolism isn't spatial.

It is in virtue of its causal relations to other objects, not its location, that your heart is a part of your body. Its being inside your body is not an accident: if your heart were elsewhere, it would not, holding other factors constant, have the requisite causal relations. But it's only to the extent that

(1) "your heart has the requisite causal relations"

entails

(2) "your heart is inside your body"

that there is any legitimate, spatial interpretation of:

(3) Your heart is a part of your body"

In fact,

(4) "x is a part of y"

isn't to be understood in strictly spatial terms even if y is a cloud and x is one of the molecules constitutive of y. If a penny were, by some miracle, to hover for an extended period of time inside the space-time region occupied by y, it would not be a part of y.

There are no values of "x" and "y" such that, relative to those value-assignments, (4) makes a strictly spatiotemporal statement. "If y is a trash-heap," it will be objected, "then, so long as x is anything occupying a sub-region of the space-time region occupied by y, (4) makes a strictly spatiotemporal statement."

Not true. If a giant heap of rubbish were dumped on the Washington Monument, thereby burying it, the result wouldn't be a trash-heap of which the Washington Monument was a part; it would be a trash-heap on top of, and surrounding, something that wasn't a part of that trash-heap. The Washington Monument is rigidly affixed to the ground below it. The trash-heap in question is not thus affixed. This constitutes a crucial difference between the Washington Monument and any given one of the banana peels or Coke cans making up that trash heap. If the Washington Monument were uprooted, and its subsequent causal relations to the constituents of that heap were similar to those of one of the aforementioned banana peels, then the Washington Monument would be a part of that trash heap. But this only proves our point; for were that to happen, it would be by virtue of its causal properties, not its location, that the Washington was a constituent of that trash-heap.

6.0   Let us summarize this chapter's main points, and then identify some of the more important consequences of those points. The *simple* expressions of a language cannot be universally misunderstood. (More precisely, when they are universally mis-understood, language-shift necessarily occurs. This qualification is not a purely tech-nical one: it compatibilizes the point just made with the points about to be made.) If everyone "misunderstands" the words "red" and "blue," taking the former to mean *blue* and the latter to mean *red*, then "red" and "blue" *ipso facto* mean, respectively, *blue* and *red*. But the complex expressions of a language *can* be misunderstood. But consider the sentence:

(SB[230])   Tropical nations with flourishing economies would in most cases experience permanent economic depressions were their climates to change in such a way that violent snow storms became the meteorological norm, the reason being that a tropical nation with a flourishing economy is almost certain to depend for its economic welfare on the production and exportation of products, such as certain kinds of fruit, which simply couldn't be grown, at least not cost-effectively, in an arctic climate.

The semantic rule that assigns meaning to SB is a *logical consequence* of the primitive semantic rules of that assign meaning to "snow," "arctic," and the other non-decom-posable constituents of SB. Let P be the proposition meant by SB. It makes sense to say that SB is systematically misunderstood and that people take some proposition *other* than P to be its meaning.

Here is a different, and perhaps more forceful, illustration of the same principle. The semantic rules for the terms "class," "member," "one-one function," "1," "2," "+," etc. are primitive. There is some proposition P such that it is a logical consequence of those primitive rules that P is what is affirmed by tokens of:

(AC)   Supposing that, given any class K of classes, there is a class C such that, for any class k that is a member of K, exactly one member of k is a member of C, then, given the assumption that two classes are equally well-populated iff there is a one-one function pairing off the members of the one with the other and that one class c is better populated than a class c* if there is no function

---

230. Short for "snow is bad for the economy." Incidentally, I don't know whether SB is true or not; I doubt that it is.

that assigns every member of c to a member of c* but there is a function that assigns every member of c* to a member of c, it follows the class of real numbers is better populated than the class of integers, even though each class has infinitely many members.

Moreover, in assigning P to AC, those semantic rules not only determine AC's meaning, but also its truth-value; for mathematical propositions are either non-circumstantially true (true in all circumstances) or non-circumstantially false. But one could grasp the semantics of terms such as "function," "class," "number," etc. without either knowing that AC has P for its meaning or *a fortiori* knowing whether AC is true.[231, 232]

---

231.   Incidentally, P is true. Cantor's famous "diagonal argument," whereby he proved that there are more reals than integers, presupposes the truth of the "axiom of choice," which is the contention that, for any class K of classes, there is a class that contains exactly one member of each member of K.

232.   There is another point that warrants inclusion in this book, but not in the main text. Let English* in which sentences could not be combined into compound sentences but was otherwise as much like English as possible. English* could contain the sentence "John is sick" and "John ate a rotten apple," but not "John is sick because John ate a rotten apple." So English* is expressively weaker than English; and the reason is that, unlike English, English* contains no metalinguistic devices – no expressions (or comparable entities, e.g. grammatically significant ways of ordering words or of inflecting one's voice) that token functors, viz. that turn simple expressions into complex ones and that turn complex ones into even more complex ones. *All combinatory devices are meta-linguistic expressions.*

Be it noted that, if English* contains phonetically unrealized substitutes for "because" and for all other connective devices, then English* isn't expressively inferior to English in the requisite way. Suppose, for example, that, in English*, uttering "John ate a rotten apple" in a certain tone of voice, right after uttering "John is sick," has the effect of producing an utterance whose meaning coincides with that of "John is sick because John at a rotten apple."

Supposing this true, English* *does* comprise an analogue of "because," it being irrelevant that, in the one language but the other, that connective is acoustically realized. (The grammatical devices used by Latin speakers to express relations of direct and indirect objecthood, and also of instrumentality or manner – the accusative, dative, and ablative case-endings, respectively – are accomplished in English through word-order. And, as Chomsky was the first, or one of the first, to make clear, we should let considerations of function, not of acoustics and orthography, determine what we believe about language. To be sure, sounds and inscriptions dazzle us, as do all perceptible entities, and imperceptible, or quasi-perceptible, entities such as word-order strike us as non-entities.

CHAPTER 15

Rationality and internal conflict

1.0 Let's start with a brief recapitulation of some foundational points. Minds are not selves. Some minds house selves, but most do not. The essence of selfhood is agency. One is an agent if one's behavior is regulated by *judgments*. One can make judgments only if one is aware of propositions. So proposition-awareness is a *sine qua non* for agency; object-awareness does not suffice.

Consciousness doesn't mediate judgments: judgments aren't images, and the only representations consciousness mediates are images. So far as consciousness can be said to mediate thought, it mediates only picture-thought, which isn't thought at all. Sequences of images are not ratiocinative. Pictures represent objects, not truths or falsehoods. It is among propositions, not among objects, that relations of logical dependence (entailment, confirmation, incompatibility) are to be found. To reason is to delineate such relations. Therefore, only proposition-aware creatures can reason.

But even in proposition-aware creatures, consciousness, *qua* representational medium, is entirely iconic. So how does consciousness come to mediate awareness of propositions and, more generally, of non-spatiotemporal entities?[233] The process consists of two steps:

    (A)   beliefs and other propositional attitudes are perceptualized by discharging themselves as perceptible (audible) phenomena;

---

233. There is a point we must emphasize, both because it is seriously underemphasized in the literature, despite being important, and because it has special relevance to the viewpoint advocated in this book. Subpersonal thought, whether in humans or in subhuman brutes, is intelligent. It isn't *rational*, because rationality is personal, as opposed to subpersonal, intelligence. A dog's mind is replete with intelligence. A great deal of intelligence is needed to generate sense-perceptions, to generate the kinesthetic sensitivities needed to regulate overt-behavior, and to refer the contents of sense-perceptions to the right pre-programmed instincts. Be it noted that, although instinctual behavior is not rational or even intelligent, instinctual behavior is *activated* by sense-perceptions, and the activation process involves intelligence: it is on the basis of intelligent consideration of the contents of perceptions that the right unintelligent, purely reflexive, instinctual responses are activated. The dog sees red meat; it instinctively pounces on it. That instinctive behavior *per se* is not intelligent. But the dog's mind must (subpersonally) understand what it is seeing; it must know that, given what it is seeing, the right instinctual response to have is to pounce on it. The dog doesn't reflexively respond to the sight of red meat in the way it instinctively responds to a lion running towards it. And this can only be because, at some level, the dog's mind appreciates what it is seeing – sees what it is seeing for what it is – and, for that reason, activates the right instinctual mechanisms.

and then

    (B)   those effusions come to be rule-governed.

Because of (A), one can, after a fashion, observe one's own thoughts.

    Because of (B), one's thoughts come to be logic-driven, like one's subpersonal mentation. And, to put forth an altogether new hypothesis, the logical canons embodied in personal mentation, once it becomes intelligent, coincide with those embodied in subpersonal mentation. To echo previous disclaimers, this is just a hypothesis – if, indeed, that contention isn't too speculative to be dignified with the term "hypothesis."

    But there is this much to say in favor of that contention. A given person's knowledge of the logical precepts that regulate conscious, personal-level intelligence must come from somewhere, and this truism entails that they must come from some other part of that person's mind. Observation cannot apprise us of them, since, as Hume pointed out, observation apprises us of descriptive, not normative truths, and therefore not of logical principles, which are normative in nature. So supposing that person's consciousness not yet capable of the conceptual operations needed to acquire knowledge of these precepts, we must suppose that knowledge to originate in a subpersonal stratum of that person's mind. Wherefore, the contention just put forth is not entirely without support.

    Observation, be it noted, is even more innocuous than Hume would have us believe. For observation *per se* doesn't even apprise us of descriptive truths. Truths are true propositions. Observation is object-awareness, not proposition-awareness and therefore not truth-awareness. It's only because we, unlike subhuman brutes, can convert awareness of acts into awareness of truths that observation constitutes – or, rather, leads to – awareness of descriptive truths or of any other kind.

    Propositional attitudes are inherently unobservable. This is a consequence of three facts:

    (i)   Conscious representations are iconic;

    (ii)   What is observable, in any literal sense of the word, is what can be represented phenomenologically and, therefore, iconically;

and

    (iii)   Propositional attitudes, no matter what stratum of the mind they occupy, are not to any degree constituted by phenomenology.

(iii) is a consequence of the fact that propositional attitudes have propositions for their objects, and for this reason couldn't be depicted unless propositions could be depicted – which is obviously impossible, given that propositions are sets of properties and, therefore, are non-spatiotemporal.

2.0 When personal thought becomes norm-driven, it *ipso facto* becomes value-driven. Norms are standards; they are ways things ought to be. To value something is to see it as norm-compliant – as being an instance of how things should be.

Logical norms are not the only norms. Indeed, the term "norm" is typically used to denote *ethical* norms. In fact, the word "norm" is usually used to denote ethical norms of a specific kind, namely *social* ethical norms ('socio-ethical' norms).

But there is a norm that is much more fundamental than any socio-ethical norm. That norm is given by the proposition that what we should value is the extension and consolidation of agency. This particular value is the *ur*-value – the value underlying all values.

Human beings have values. This is what distinguishes us from other sentient beings. One has a distinctively human psychological architecture just in case one has values.

A creature values nothing if it doesn't value its own agency. There are many different values, but all of them are versions of this one value.

"That's not true," it will be said. "Socio-ethical values require one to diminish oneself."

False. Words like "value" and "valuable" are used equivocally. Sometimes "valuable" means "constitutive of a deployment or expansion of one's agency." This corresponds to the way we've been using the term "value," and to the way it's used in the sentence:

(i) "People who never dare to think for themselves don't see the value of doing so."

Sometimes "valuable" means "likely to bring about something that is constitutive of a deployment or expansion of someone's agency (it being irrelevant whose agency it is that benefits)." This corresponds to the way the word "value" is being used in the sentence:

(ii) "In allowing the government to seize his assets, rather than fighting it in court, Smith was putting the needs of others above his own, and was thus doing a thing of great value."

The word "value" thus has two radically different meanings, and other terms of its ilk (e.g. "good," "right," "virtuous") are correspondingly ambiguous. Sometimes "x is good" means "x is itself constitutive of a deployment or expansion of somebody's agency," and sometimes it means "x is likely to precipitate a series of events that eventuates in a deployment or expansion of somebody's agency."

The second kind of goodness is instrumental goodness. The first kind is intrinsic goodness. When self-undermining acts of altruism are described as "good," what is being said, supposing it true, is that such acts are instrumentally good. But such acts are taken to be paradigms of intrinsic goodness. Thus, the ambiguities we're discussing aren't innocuous. They are both the causes, and the effects, of substantive confusions. Let us now attempt to eradicate these confusions.

To be good to another is to help him preserve and, ideally, expand his agency. His physical well-being is only a means to that end. That is why ridding everyone of physical ailments while lobotomizing them would be supremely evil. One would not be living a good life if, in order to help others, one made no allowances for one's own welfare.

To be sure, there are people for whom helping others is the same thing as flourishing. There are people for whom helping others is what composing was to Beethoven. And in helping others, such people are not undermining their own welfare. (Presumably, physicians and nurses often fall into this category: a physician who wanted to hurt others, not help them, would probably not be a very good physician. Social reformers fall into this category, provided that they're of the well-intentioned kind, like Mother Teresa and Martin Luther King, not the ill-intentioned kind, like Stalin.)

But for most people flourishing is at most only partially confluent with altruistic behavior. And even though there is *a* sense in which a would-be Beethoven is living a "good" life if, out of a compulsive sense of duty, he forces himself to help others, there is a deeper sense in which such a person's life is a bad one. It is "good" in the sense that, because of that person's deeds, *other people's* agencies are preserved and fostered. But it's not good for that person; it's not good in and of itself.

That person has made himself into a means for the welfare of others; he has ceased to be an end unto himself. To that extent, his life has instrumental value and lacks intrinsic value. His martyrdom has therefore drained his life of all value, given that it's *only* to the extent that this martyr is tending to the agency of others that his life has any value of any kind.

This shows that the one and only thing of intrinsic value is agency. This in turn shows that socio-ethical goodness is of a derivative, instrumental kind: socio-ethically good acts are good only in so far as they redound to the benefit of somebody's agency.

Consequently, a socio-ethically good act is good only in so far as somebody's agency benefits from it. The altruist doesn't benefit from his own altruism (I am setting aside the comparatively few people – the Mother Teresa's and Martin Luther King's of this world – for whom altruism and self-interest coincide.) So his altruism has no value for him, and it has only instrumental value for the person who benefits from it. So the one thing that has intrinsic moral value is the consolidation and expansion of one's own agency, socio-ethical goodness being but an instrumental form of goodness.[234]

---

234. Nietzsche advocated a similar view, and his arguments for it, so far as I can make them out, are similar to ours. I say this only to give credit where credit is due. Nietzsche advocated ethical egoism. He was one of the few who did so. Spinoza was another, and my arguments are no less Spizonan than they are Nietzschean.

Given that ethical egoism is, by definition, an anti-social ethical system, Nietzsche's ethical views are reviled. But I agree with them and with his arguments for them, and I hope that I've helped make his ethical views seem less absurd than they are typically claimed to be. It is my duty as a scholar to state my biases and therefore to say how very much I admire the work of Nietzsche and Spinoza.

3.0   First there are urges. Those are replaced with first-order desires. This substitution constitutes the advent of reason-driven behavior and the end of instinct-driven behavior. Those first-order desires come to be replaced with higher-order desires. Eventually, the person's mind becomes "top-heavy". The structure composed of these higher-order ceases to have as a primary function the welfare of the relevant organism's body; and its objective thus ceases to be the gratification of instincts or of first-order desires, given how closely hewed such things are to organismic welfare.

The organism's physical well-being comes to be a means to the promotion of the welfare of that superstructure, and so does the gratification of first-order desires as well as fulfillment of the instincts underlying those desires. Since the superstructure can't even exist in a dead body, let alone flourish, physical well-being is always *a* priority. But it's only an *instrumental* priority. It's a priority only in so far as it is a necessary condition for our psychological existence and *a fortiori* psychological welfare.

A moment ago, I said that, when desires replace urges, reason-driven behavior replaces instinct-driven behavior. This may seem preposterous, given what heavy allowances our objectives make for the gratification of instincts, even those that we hold in contempt. (Cf. a judge who, under the pretext of meting out impartial justice, hands down excessively heavy sentences, so as to gratify raw, instinctual sadism.)

But it ceases to seem preposterous once we distinguish between instinct-*influenced* behavior and instinct-*driven* behavior. Each of us almost always acts in instinct-influenced ways. But our instincts are operative only to the extent that our judgment allows them to be. To be sure, our judgments are often faulty. In fact, it's a rare judgment that isn't to some degree corrupted by rationalization, and it's a rare rationalization whose purpose isn't to facilitate the discharging of instincts that one's judgment, if uncorrupted, would suppress. But instinct-influenced, intention-driven behavior is not to be categorized with instinct-driven behavior. Intention-driven behavior is judgment-driven behavior. Instinct-driven behavior is urge-driven behavior. The latter is reflexive. The former is not.

We often *describe* instances of the former as "reactive," "instinctual," "thoughtless," or "reflexive." But when we describe a given act in this way, what we're saying, if true, is that the judgment driving that act was precipitous and therefore made excessive, rationalization- or laziness-based provisions for the gratification of instincts that should have been gratified in some other, more circuitous way.

"It was *thoughtless* of him to punch his dissertation-advisor," I heard it said of one individual: "it was an act of *pure instinct*." No – it was a judgment-driven act, but the judgment in question was corrupted by self-indulgent, instinct-gratification-conducive rationalizations. The individual in question was later diagnosed as schizoaffective. But his act in the same category as your reading this sentence. Both acts were judgment-driven. The difference is that the one judgment, but not the other, was irrational.

A dog's instinctively attacking the mailman is not *irrational*. Irrationality is warped rationality. Only rational creatures, or rationality-capable creatures, can be irrational. Dogs are *sub*-rational, not irrational.[235] A related point is that dogs are not *insane*; they are *sub*-sane.

Rabid dogs are obviously deranged, but it would be misleading to describe them as "insane." A mentally damaged creature isn't "insane" if its condition is strictly organic. People with Alzheimer's aren't "insane." Nor are people who, because of brain-injuries, have been cognitively diminished. A mentally damaged creature is "insane" only if its condition is either rooted in, or mediated by, emotional disturbances. A rabid dog's condition doesn't meet this condition, and such a creature therefore isn't "insane."

In describing a mentally damaged person as "insane," we aren't ruling out the possibility that his disorder was initiated by some purely somatic disturbance. We aren't even ruling out the possibility that it is being perpetuated by such a disturbance. We are saying that, whatever the ultimate causes of his condition might be, his mental states are interrelated in a pathological manner. Should it turn out that Dr. Frankenstein's condition was initiated by a blow to the head, or that it was sustained by a brain-injury, we might still describe him as "insane." We would do so if, in our judgment, it was by virtue of having an under-inhibited and, for that reason, disorganized mind that he was psychologically damaged. We would not do so if, in our judgment, it was by virtue of having an under-active mind that he was thus damaged. One is insane if, in consequence of a relaxing of inhibitory mechanisms and consequent surfeit of mental activity, one's mind is disorganized. One is psychologically impaired, but not insane, if constant suspensions of mental activity thwart one's ability to process information. These points will be clarified and developed in Section 7.2 of the present chapter.

Whether a person becomes schizoaffective as opposed to obsessive-compulsive, or *vice versa*, may be a function of his brain-structure. But that does not necessarily mean that either disorder is organic. It could mean that a non-psychological factor determines the way in which disturbances in one's object-relations, self-concept, etc. become pathologized.

OCD is most definitely to be understood in psychodynamic terms.[236] Of course, it has physiological underpinnings – but so does one's belief that there are no regular 17-sided polygons. Schizoaffective disorder may have a larger purely somatic component than OCD. But soon after a person becomes schizoaffective, his pre-existing internal conflicts and object-relations come to be heavily implicated in his symptomology. So even if the basis of schizoaffective disorder is purely organic, distinctively schizoaffective ideation can and must be understood in psychodynamic terms.

---

235. Donald Davidson (1981b) makes this point clearly and forcefully.

236. See Reich (1945), Stekel (1949), Freud (1963), Kernberg (1985, 1993), and Salzman (1994). OCD was extremely well understood by the theoreticians of the Freudian school. Contemporary work on it is dismal. (Salzman's work is spot-on. But he is the last of dying breed.)

4.0   What is delusive about the schizoaffective's ideation isn't so much *what* he believes as *how he believes it*.[237] Schizoaffective Sally believes that her mother wants to kill her and, to that end, has enlisted the help of extra-terrestrials, who are now posing as Sally's psychiatrists.

But this delusion of Sally's may well be a distortion of the truth. Sally's mother is trying to undermine Sally (so we may suppose without running afoul of the clinical facts) and has always been undermining of her. And Sally's psychiatrists, though not the homicidal ghouls that Sally makes them out to be, are not very good at what they do and therefore blame Sally's lack of therapeutic progress on Sally, instead of on their own incompetence. "She can't learn. She's too locked into her delusions to heed my words of wisdom. She doesn't *want* to get better: that's the real problem."

These being the circumstances, Sally is right to believe that her mother is seditious and that her psychiatrists do more to impede than to expedite her recovery. Sally is turning these painful truths into puerile fictions by experiencing them, not as sober thoughts, but as cartoon-like, externalized dreams, which, because they are "psychotic delusions," she can rationally dismiss in her moments of lucidity.

To be sure, those delusions are unpleasant. But that is part of what makes them so effective as bulwarks against self-knowledge. They're unpleasant *because they're delusions*. The knowledge buried inside those delusions is unpleasant *because its knowledge*. Her delusions turn painful realities, from which one doesn't wake up, into painful nightmares, from which one does.

Brain-damage and organic brain-disorders lead to delusive and otherwise misguided ideation. But such ideation, unlike the schizophrenic's, is not to be understood in psychodynamic terms. For the damage to one's psyche done by brain-damage and brain-disorders is a consequence of interruptions of mental activity. Distinct mental processes are not allowed to converge, and different parts of the mind are therefore unable to exchange information. Distinct mental faculties are under-interrelated. In the psychotic, they are over-interrelated. There is excessive psychological ferment; whence the anarchical quality of the psychotic's mentation. The mentation of somebody with Alzheimer's is pseudo-anarchical. The problem isn't that the corridors within which normal thought occurs are too full and therefore can't accomodate the high-volume of cognitive traffic: it is that those corridors aren't full enough. The erratic nature of the psychotic's mentation is a consequence of mental processes' interrupting, and corrupting, other mental processes. The erratic nature of the Alzheimer's patient's mentation is a consequence of his mental processes petering out before they so much as have a chance to converge with other such processes. So any given case of psychosis is to be understood in psychological terms, even if it was initiated by a purely organic disturbance and even it is being sustained by such a disturbance. This is because it is by virtue of having over-interrelated mental states that the psychotic is mentally. (Since, by contrast, it is by virtue of having under-interrelated mental states

---

237.   See R. D. Laing (1960, 1961) for a similar line of thought. Also see Rosenfeld (1992) and Kernberg (1993).

that the victim of brain-damage is mentally ill, his not a psychological, but a strictly physiological problem.

This doesn't mean that the only way to alleviate psychosis is through psychotherapy. It doesn't even mean that psychotherapy is the primary way to do so. Medication does much to alleviate psychopathology. Speaking practically, medication is often the only viable way to treat mental illness. Psychotherapy is extremely expensive; and even if the would-be patient can pay for it, his character-architecture may make him unresponsive to it.

But there are two very different ways in which medication can improve a sick person's lot. On the one hand, it can cure him: it can lead to a genuine restoration of the integrity of the illness-ravaged part of him. On the other hand, it can alleviate symptoms, without necessarily doing anything to treat the underlying disorder. The so-called rescue inhalers that asthmatics take open up their airways, but do nothing in the way of restoring the integrity of the tissue lining their airways. But sometimes purely functional improvements permit the occurrence of previously inhibited restorative processes; and by mitigating the symptoms of an illness, a medical procedure that doesn't treat the underlying pathology may permit the occurrence of previously inhibited restorative processes.

5.0   We will now discuss rationality and its relation to internal conflict. In so doing, we will have to discuss the nature of value-driven ideation and the latter's relevance to both internal conflict and and psychological stratification.

Being human, in the psychological sense of the word, consists in:

(i)   having agency

and

(ii)   valuing the fortification of one's agency.

There is a tight connection between intellect and agency. (As previously stated, or implied, Aristotle (350 BC) and Kant (1785) held that agency is applied intellect. The present author agrees with them.) Consider the case of a brilliant person who lets his mind atrophy, so that he becomes a dullard whose intellect can no longer grow and is stocked with nothing but clichés and insights generated by his previous self. That person's agency withers as a result. When that person's intellect was elastic, he could respond to situations dynamically. But now that his intellect is defunct, he must respond to them reflexively.

Now consider the case of an imbecile who, because he was hit by a bolt lightning, suddenly becomes a luminary. His previously constricted cognitive search-space is now huge. What it is in his power to decide to do has expanded: it has expanded as much as his intellect has grown sharper. Thus, one's agency extends exactly as far as one's rationality. Therefore, agency is identical with rationality. This is one of two points that must be kept in mind while reading this section.

The other is that a given act or practice can both strengthen *and* weaken one's agency. A course of action that is *necessary* for the preservation or fortification of one's agency may also undermine it. A closely related point is that people have conflicting *legitimate* values. A person may legitimately value x, i.e. he may rightly see doing x as agency-fortifying; and he may legitimately value y; and yet his doing x may be incompatible with his doing y.

An illustration: Smith is a potentially great scholar. But he has yet to realize his potential and, if he is to do so, must do everything in his power over the next ten to twenty years to cultivate his intellect. He is currently in the process of a writing a treatise that, once completed, will be one of the great intellectual achievements of all time. "Insights such as this fall to one's lot but once in a lifetime," Freud wrote in the preface to the Interpretation of Dreams. These words often pass through Smith's mind. But disaster strikes. Smith's mother becomes gravely ill. She'll die unless Smith takes care of her; she has no one else. This wouldn't be a problem if Smith disliked his mother. But he loves her dearly. Nor would it be a problem if she were senile. For then he'd have only a formal or a sentimentality-based obligation to take care of her. But she's as sharp as a tack, and she's as substantial and a decent a person as she ever was. And until recently, she was Smith's mentor: everything he knows he learned from her. He owes everything he has to her. He is therefore appalled at the thought of ditching his mother. But he is no less appalled at the thought of ruining his own life.

If Smith were to abandon his mother, he would thereby undermine his belief in his own legitimacy as a person, and the concomitant sullying of his self-concept would weaken him. He'd come to see himself as a lowlife, which would have the effect that he'd cease to see himself as bound by the stern work-ethic and high-minded values that have been instrumental to the many professional and personal successes he's had thus far in his life.

At the same time, if Smith abandons his writing project, a part of him will die. Smith is in his mid-20's. Given his mother's condition, he's likely to have to take care of her for another 20 years. Smith knows that if he doesn't cultivate his intellect during that time, he won't be able to write groundbreaking treatises when he's in his 40's. He also knows that he *will* be able to do so if he does cultivate his intellect during that time.[238]

---

238. I've heard it said that intellectuals are at their peak in their late 20's and early 30's. I've also heard it said that, if a given intellectual diligently cultivates his mind during those years, he can continue to grow as a thinker. These contentions may seem opposed to each other.

But I think they're both true. I know people who where geniuses in early adulthood but who, because they didn't develop their gifts, stopped being geniuses. And I've known 80 year olds who were still geniuses and who *did* (from what I can determine from their publication records) vigorously cultivate their minds during early adulthood. I've never known anyone who was a genius as a youth but, without doing everything he could to develop his intellect, remained a genius or even went on to be more than a middling thinker.

Smith has conflicting values. Both values are legitimate. But Smith must renounce one of them. Smith is *conflicted*. Internal conflict is essential to the human condition, or at the very least it is a virtually inevitable result of having a distinctively human psychological architecture.

In order to move forward, we must note that there are two ways in which a person can be conflicted:

(i)   He may have two conflicting values.

(ii)   He may have a value that conflicts with a desire that does not correspond to any value of his.

Smith's situation is an illustration of (i). Smith accepts that he is in a lose-lose situation.

This does not mean that he is happy about it. Nor does it mean that he, while accepting it in some purely intellectual sense, some part of him is holding on to the obvious fiction that not all the paths available to him involve a forfeiture of an important part of himself. Type-(i) conflict leads to repression and rationalization *only* if one turns a blind eye to the ugliness of one's situation. If one doesn't do so, type-(i) conflict leads to garden-variety unhappiness. Freud said that the purpose of psychoanalytic therapy was "to turn neurotic unhappiness into non-neurotic unhappiness." Smith is unhappy in a non-neurotic way.

But type-(i) conflict can lead to growth. *An illustration*: Brown is a creditable athlete: with the right training, he could be a professional athlete, albeit a decidedly mediocre one. But there is nothing mediocre about Brown's musicianship: he is a genius; he has the potential to be truly great composer. But he is currently a mediocre composer, because he spends as much time playing tennis as he does composing. Brown is aware of this; and even though he rightly values both sports and music, he needs to shelve his ambition of being a ranking tennis player and dedicate all of his energies to his compositions. He will still play tennis, of course. But 9/10ths of the energy he currently spends on his tennis will be pressed into the service of his musicianship. So his tennis-skills will plummet, but his compositional abilities will soar.

These personal experiences of mine are reinforced by medical research, which has shown that a person's intellect naturally peaks at certain points in his life and, unless he takes measures to prevent it, tends to wither with age. As a professor, I've known many people who, in their dotage, were famous for an article they'd written 40 years earlier, when they were brilliant, but who were no longer brilliant or even of above average intelligence, the reason being, from what I could gather, that their early successes had made them complacent.

But I've also known who had similar early successes but, not having become complacent as a result, were as sharp in their 70's and 80's as the sharpest 33 year old. (In fact, the person who first apprised me of these developmental facts, or hypotheses, was himself an 80 year old specialist in internal medicine whose intellect was still maximally vigorous and who, though renowned in his 20's, remained industrious and intellectually open and whose intellect, presumably as a result, retained its plasticity.)

As a result, he will cease to be a dilettante, and his life will more than gain in meaning what it loses in enjoyment.

Type-(i) conflict probably occurs at various points in the life of every human being.[239] But type-(ii) conflict occurs at least as frequently and is far more pathogenic than the first kind. If Brown continues to pursue his athletic ambitions, he'll still be a fine a composer, though not a great one, and he'll be a fine athlete. He'll have a fine life. If Smith decides to work on his treatise, instead of caretaking his mother, he will feel *bad* about it, but not *guilty* about it. A person feels *guilty* when, out of weakness, he didn't put the resources available to him to good use. This is not what is going on with Smith: he is making the most of his situation, and he knows it. Since the disputants in a case of type-(i) are two two equally worthy parts of oneself, as opposed to one distinctively human part of oneself and one purely basal part, type-(i) conflict isn't inherently dispositive of character-disintegration. But type-(ii) conflict *is* thus dispositive, since the feuding parties are not equally integral to one's agency and a victory on the part of the (relatively) agency-external party constitutes a diminution of one's agency and, consequently, a reduction of one's self.

An illustration of type-(ii) conflict: Jones is a great writer. He knows it. So does anyone who reads his work. But Jones is underproducing. He has yet to complete a novel. He completed two short-stories, which were excellent, and he's 50% completed five novels, each of which would be a masterpiece, were it completed. But he has stalled out. Not because he's lost his creative fire, but because he's become a heroin addict; and shooting heroin is easy, whereas writing books is insidiously difficult. Jones' heroin addiction is incompatible with his aspiration of becoming a great writer.[240]

---

239. I am setting aside infants, victims of brain-damage, etc. Importantly, no psychodynamic conflict of any kind *ever* occurs in the mind of a psychopath or a sociopath. This is because such people don't value anything – though they have desires that mimic values – and *a fortiori* don't have conflicting values and therefore aren't conflicted. Psychopaths and sociopaths are not psychodynamic. Obviously they have minds; and those minds are teeming with activity. But emotional conflict is no part of their psychological integration, which is an exceedingly crude one, as we'll discuss in Chapter 16. *Criminality* is different from sociopathy and from psychopathy. Criminals may have values; they may have a fully developed psychological architecture. This too will be discussed in Chapter 16.

240. I do not know whether heroin-addiction actually *does* have this affect on one's literary or otherwise professional aspirations. I *do* know that many a great thinker and writer has taken to using morphine at certain points in his life. There have been sometime opium-eaters who did good work while using morphine or other opiates. I have read that the Viet Cong, after performing Herculean feats of military prowess (such as marching 100 miles without food), would smoke opium. The officers and the rank-and-file would get together after a difficult mission and companionably smoke opium together.

But I also know some other things of relevance. First of all, the opium-preparations used by the Viet Cong had about one tenth the potency of heroin, and the same is true of preparations used by the Anglo-Austro-German savants of the early 20th century. Further, the latter didn't even begin to use morphine until they were old and, therefore, until they had long since

Jones has a choice: to use or not to use. But there's another choice he must make first: to admit to himself that he must make a choice or to try to have it both ways. He can't make the first choice unless he admits to himself that he can't have it both ways, and he can't be a writer unless he stops using. The emotional forces at work with Jones may be such that he cannot make the right choice. It may be that he's experienced too much pain and therefore needs a heavy duty anodyne, such as heroin; it may be that neither of his parents loved him, and the warmth that spreads through his body after every dose of heroin serves as surrogate for the much needed love he never received. Perhaps he's just lazy. Perhaps it's all of the above, or none.

Let us suppose that Jones chooses to continue using heroin. Question: When making this choice, how likely is Jones to consciously think the following?

(JC^{241}) I had a choice – be a writer or be a junky – and it was one or the other. I chose to be a junky. My sense of self-worth was largely dependent on the quality of my literary output. The quality and quantity of that output is now about to plummet. But I'm going to do heroin anyway, because I like doing it, soul-destroying though it is.

Not likely. If Jones saw his situation with such clarity, he would probably not be so cavalier about choosing to do heroin. And if he chose to use heroin, despite his high level of self-awareness, his usage of it would probably not become a permanent part of his life – *unless* he became deeply entrenched in his own *rationalizations*.

Jones doesn't tell himself: "I'm lazy. I'm a lazy junkie. I'm a failure. I couldn't hack it." No – drawing on the very skills that would have made him a great writer, he tells himself the following:

(JR^{242}) I have always admired Tolstoy and Dostoevsky for their obvious mastery of their craft. And, undoubtedly, that craft is in many respects a valuable one. It is valuable in much the way a musical compositions is valuable, or intricate patterned Persian rug. But it isn't practical. It doesn't put food in anyone's mouth (except mine and my editor's). In fact, it takes food *off* of the common man's table, and it does so in two different ways.

First, I made more money for two published stories than my building superintendent has made in the last 45 years. So were I to be a literary success, I would be redistributing wealth in an unjust manner.

---

mastered their respective crafts. Somebody who uses opium, let alone heroin, before he has mastered his craft is probably less likely to master it than he would otherwise be. That said, unless one is oneself a heroin user, or at least a heroin-specialist, it's very easy to fall prey to medicinally inaccurate propaganda concerning these things.

241. Short for "Jones' choice."

242. Short for "Jones' rationalization."

Second, great novels turn human suffering into a source of amusement. Steinbeck did a very good job of chronicling the plight of Depression-era dirt-farmers. But did that make the well-to-do want to help these paupers? No. It did the opposite. The average Steinbeck reader is a cultured and wealthy Ivy-Leage graduate. He knows that he had the good luck to be born into privilege and he feels guilty about it. He wonders whether, if *he* had been born to a poor family, he could have accomplished whatever it is he has accomplished. When this person reads Steinbeck – and I know this because I'm one of them – he is able to identify with the misfortunates Steinbeck so expertly describes; and during the few hours it takes him to read "the Grapes of Wrath," he is one of those people, so he believes. When one reads a book, one vicariously becomes its protagonist. So Steinbeck's work gives his readers the illusion that they know what it's like to experience the hard-knocks of life as a depression-era dirt farmer. This illusion of knowledge weakens his sense of guilt and therefore weakens his urge to donate money to his needy brothers and sisters.

Further, this Steinbeck-reader comes to find that, in his own life, there are many analogues of the injustices experienced by the misfortunates Steinbeck so expertly describes. He has experienced many slights over the years: from jealous editors, who knew that, whereas his work had merit, theirs had none; from equally jealous teachers who, wanting him to dissipate his gifts instead of cultivating them, tried to convince him that it was his moral duty to work for the sanitation department; from the committee that gave the college literary prize, not to him, but to the attractive young woman who happened to be dating the committee-chair, for her chic and empty, pseudo-heartfelt, pseudo-Steinbeckian descriptions of the travails of her chamber-maid, her butler, her chauffeur, her grounds-keeper, and her various cleaning-personnel.

Given an arbitrary Steinbeck-reader, reading Steinbeck hasn't made that person *ashamed* of his wealth, we have seen, and it hasn't made him want to help the poor. On the contrary, it has made him think that he's experienced what they've experienced and that he therefore deserves every bit of comfort and luxury of which he can avail himself "There are different forms of suffering," he tells himself. "My shackles are made of gold; theirs of wrought iron. But shackles are shackles, are they not?"

I thus choose not to be a writer; I choose not to minister to the self-indulgences of the leisure-class. I don't want to be someone, like Steinbeck, who does evil, while believing that he's doing good. I don't want to be an Uncle Tom, a member of the lumpenproletariat, somebody whose job is to hand out palliatives to people who, because of their wealth and the social injustices of which they are both the causes and the effects, *should* feel the very pain which my lullabies would ease (were I not too high on heroin to write them).

I grant that being a junkie isn't exactly as the most challenging or heroic way to live. But it's more moral than being a novelist. Not only do junkies not invent the fairy tales that pacify the consciences of the murdering members of our leisure-class: junkies directly give money to poor people; for it is generally poor people who purvey heroin. (There are higher-level, wealthy dealers: so-called kingpins. But the vast majority of people who profit from the heroin trade are not well-off.)

So is it with pride and a clean conscience that I plunge the dope-filled syringe in my arm and press the needle down. I am a hero. The writer I would have been is a criminal. True, that would-be person has his good qualities. He works hard. He's witty. His books enliven the imagination. But I'll exchange my Pulitzer Prize for my innocence any day of the week and twice on Sundays.

Jones doesn't really believe a word of this, at least not when he first tries to sell it to himself. What Jones *really* believes is that junkies are degenerates, both by virtue of choosing to be junkies and by virtue of the effects of heroin-use. Moreover, he believes that the choice he's made is a choice to be lazy and to waste his life. He also knows that, in buying heroin, he's providing economic support for drug kingpins and, for that reason, for people who, to a larger degree than the members of any other group, are responsible for the wretched conditions obtaining in poor, urban neighborhoods.

But Jones conveniently forgets all that. And by repeating JR to himself, as though it were a religious mantra, he retains the solace afforded him by his lies and his convenient lapses in memory.

"But how can anyone *make* themselves believe something they don't?" That is a good question, which we will now answer.

6.0 Rationalizing is not the same thing as lying. To lie is to intentionally misrepresent the truth to another person. To rationalize is to suppress one's own knowledge of some truth and to choose to replace it with a belief that one knows to be false (or, if true, is so only by accident) but is more comforting than its predecessor.

Rationalizing involves two things:

(i)   Lying to oneself;

and

(ii)   Inventing a story to make the lie believable.

"No fraud without a fairy tale." That saying goes double for the frauds one perpetrates on oneself.

A man must support the lies he tells himself with rationalizations. Otherwise those lies are not firmly rooted in his belief-system and correct beliefs are likely to displace them. A given belief on somebody's part won't endure unless it is consistent with that person's other beliefs; it must be a part of his belief system.

Let $B_1...B_n$ be my beliefs. For each i, B_i is a belief in the truth of proposition P_i. One day, let us suppose, I try to believe P_{n+1}; so I try to add a new belief namely, B_{n+1}, to the list of beliefs just mentioned $B_1...B_n$ are either true or, at they very least, logically and empirically well-founded. Those beliefs are based on information generated by our best scientists, while also embodying the wisdom of common sense.

But P_{n+1} conflicts with data and the logical considerations embodied in $B_1...B_n$. So I don't have much of a logical or evidential reason to form B_{n+1}. But, given the contents of Section 5.2. I have extremely powerful emotional incentives to do so.

P_{n+1} is the proposition that my beloved fiancée Sally is not the infamous "Riverdale Killer." Sally and I live together in the ordinarily homicide-free town of Riverdale. But starting around two years ago, somebody starting killing good-looking men in their 20's–40's. For many reasons, it is clear that the killer is a female. The killer left notes which we clearly written in a woman's handwriting. The killer forced her hapless victims to perform acts of a carnal nature with her, before she killed them; and random passers-by, who thought they were merely witnessing an instance of indecency, in which a woman was sexually dominating a man. Those witnesses only saw snippets of the events leading up to the murder of the man in question; they didn't witness that murder itself. But that changed. Eventually, one such passer-by video-taped one of these sex-acts, from beginning to end, along with the beginnings of the post-coital homicide. Unfortunately, this amateur filmmakers failed to get any high-resolution footage of the assailant's face. But what he did get made it clear that the assailent was a female.

Sally is the love of my life. And when she is with me, she is extraordinarily decent. She genuinely loves me. (Or so I believe – and I'm right. Even though she's a serial killer, she is capable of love, and I'm somebody she loves.) I have never loved anyone they way I love her. And I've never been with anyone so bright: she knows what I'm going to say before I even say it, and I never have to go through the tedium of explaining the same point, over and over.

I often hear a news report detailing some homicide in Riverdale. The dates of those killings coincide with suggestive activities on Sally's part. She's gone from the apartment well before they occur; she's back only well after they occur. I have found articles in her possession that are exactly like those that the victims were described to have been wearing prior to their disappearances, but of which the killer had divested them. Sometimes she watches the news with me. Ordinarily, her commentary is brilliant and authentic. But she's uncharacteristically quiet when stories about the Riverdale Killer come on, and what little she does say is curiously wooden and commonplace. And there are even more damning pieces of evidence. She's gotten into the habit of pickling dismembered body-parts (hands, heads, etc.), and each of the victim's is missing a body part of which she now has a pickled specimen. She tells me, in an obviously serious manner, that, even though what the Riverdale Killer is doing is illegal, she thinks that she must have "excellent reasons" for doing it. She asks me if

I would divorce her if "by some remote chance" it turned out she had 'perhaps done a few unorthodox things, maybe, on occasion, killed a person or two."

For these reasons and others like them, a part of me suspects that Sally is the killer. If I knew the statements just made to hold of anyone other than Sally, I wouldn't hesitate to identify that person as the killer. But I love Sally as I've never loved another. To learn that Sally was a monster would destroy me. No one has ever understood me, or loved me, the way Sally does. But if she's a serial killer, then I must doubt the authenticity of my relationship with her; I must seriously consider the possibility that her marriage to me was but a front for her real life, the essence of which was serial murder.

But there is hope. I don't *know* that Sally is the killer. In any case, there is *a* delineation of the term "know," albeit one that has few applications outside of philosophical colloquy, relative to which I don't know it. I haven't seen her kill anybody. She has never said that she has. And when I asked her to explain why she taken to pickling human remains, she had an excellent explanation; and she had an equally good explanation as to why those parts were always of the same kind the killer took as trophies from his victims. (Sally is a research doctor; the body parts in question did have some relevance to research that she was doing and that she had started doing before the Riverdale Killer struck his first victim.) Sally has an explanation for everything.

6.1   None of those explanations is definitive evidence that what she's saying is true. But each, take by itself, is modestly credible. None has much credibility when taken in the context of Sally's other explanations.

But that doesn't matter, because the essence of rationalization is decontextualization. The very purpose of rationalizing is to isolate bodies of information that, if allowed to commingle, will lead to an awareness of the very thing one doesn't want to know. If the rationalizer doesn't take things out of context and view them as narrowly as possible, he'll be either be forced to draw unwelcome conclusions from the data that he already has or he'll put himself in situations where the data is rationalization-proof.

There's a severed head in a jar on Sally's desk. Sally gives me an explanation. It isn't a particularly bad one. (It references things I know to be true. She attended medical school for a while. Although she didn't graduate, she retains an interest in pathology and also has contacts in the medical community.) I take that explanation on its own terms. If I were to consider how well it fit in with Sally's other explanations, I'd find that the totality of her explanations was inconsistent with itself and with well-established facts about the external world. (The head bears a striking resemblance to a missing person who, according to the media, the police are certain is one of the Riverside Killer's victims. Although a certain degree pathology insinuates itself into Sally's thinking, she's basically a sane person, not to a mention a decent one (setting aside her homicidal tendencies); and her pathologies wouldn't be severe enough to motivate the decidedly eccentric behavior involved in acquiring a severed head. [Etc.])

But one doesn't automatically see the ramifications of the information one is given. Thinking is hard work. It's hard in that few people can do it properly, and it's hard in that it takes time and energy for those few to deploy their ability to do so.[243]

If I were to *see* Sally butcher a person, I'd have a hard time rationalizing what I saw. Still, I could do it: I could tell myself that the person she was butchering had threatened her. But I'd have a hard time rationalizing her behavior if I knew that he hadn't threatened her. There are limits to how much one rationalize. Let us discuss the significance of this fact.

With a qualification to be stated in a moment, rationalization isn't an option at such junctures. At such a juncture, consequently,

(i)   One must cop to the truth,

or

(ii)   One must forfeit one's sanity, choosing to live in a perpetual reverie, so that despite the obvious data to the contrary, one can believe whatever it is that one wants to believe.

The earlier-referenced qualification is that:

(iii)   There are two kinds of rationalization. One kind is value-system-internal. The other is not. The latter involve changing the very values relative to which the data forced one to rationalize. So if I were to rationalize away my belief that torturing toddlers was bad, I could, without forfeiting my sanity, continue to have a glowing opinion of Sally.

In Chapter 16, we'll see that rationalizations of the second kind are *sociopathogenic*; they tend to precipitate, or to be constitutive of, a process of dismantling one's conscience, the end-result of which is a grim condition known as "sociopathy." It is grim,

---

243.   Bach was as capable a composer as there ever was. But he was a legendarily hard worker. In fact, part of why composing was so labor-intensive for Bach was that he was so good at it: where a mediocre composer sees one way to resolve a passage, Bach sees 20.

There is a saying: "Genius is 10% inspiration, 90% perspiration." Most of the perspiration results from the genius's being willing, unlike his peers, to spend 10 hours rewriting the same sentence, crafting the same four bars of music, staring at the same Petri dish, looking at the same solar system, etc. But part of it comes from the fact that the genius sees many possibilities where the non-genius only sees one, and for this reason the genius works where the non-genius drudges. The mediocre symphony-composer knows but one way to orchestrate a given tune, one way to fill in the bassoon-part, the double-bass part, etc. The genius doesn't have it that easy. He *could* fill in the bassoon-part (etc.) in the standard, conservatory-approved manner. But for him, the act of orchestrating a tune becomes another opportunity to do something new and important. Unlike his less gifted peers, the genius cannot phone it in; there are fewer junctures for him, than for his peers, at which he can simply apply an existing formula.

not so much for those around the sociopath, as it is for the sociopath herself, who, no longer having values, is incapable of happiness.

Happiness is different from pleasure. Happiness isn't a feeling. A happy person feels bad when he stubs his toe, but he doesn't stop being happy. An unhappy person feels good when she's high on heroin, but she doesn't stop being unhappy. Being happy involves having a tendency to feel good. But not all good feelings are happiness-based. Happiness-based good feelings are those that embody a judgment on one's part to the effect that one's life conforms to the desiderata to which, in judgment, it should conform. To be sure, if one is constant pain, one will be unhappy for that reason. A happy person can stub his toe once without being unhappy. But he won't be happy for long if he stubs it every two seconds. But that isn't because happiness is a feeling. It's because, if a person is in constant pain, he will rightly judge that his life no longer satisfies the requisite desiderata. Thus, happiness is a judgment on one's part to the effect that one's life satisfies certain desiderata, and unhappiness is a contrary judgment. In any case, there is no denying that value-judgments are implicated in instances of happiness. Therefore, dogs cannot be happy, since they cannot make such judgments, even though they can feel good.

6.2 Let us resume our discussion of Jones, the heroin-addicted would-be writer.

It's obvious that, were Jones honest with himself, he wouldn't give any credence to JR. At the same time, it's hard to put one's finger on what is wrong with JR. JR consists of one good point after another, and some of those points are positively insightful. So, while it's obvious that there is something wrong with JR, it's not obvious what the problem with it is; and even though Jones would have no difficulty seeing through JR *if* he didn't have an emotional incentive not to do so, JR has enough logical integrity that Jones can accept it without rejecting central principles of logic, or denying obvious facts, or otherwise blunting his intellect.

It may be obvious to some that JR is defective. But so far as that's obvious, it isn't because of its lack of logical integrity. JR has more logical integrity than many a highly esteemed political speech and many a well-regarded journal-article. JR is an attempt to prove that shooting heroin is a better way to live than writing great novels. That point is obviously false; and *that's* what makes it obvious, so far as it is obvious, that the argument in JR is defective. But if we didn't know *ex parte* that JR's conclusion was false, it wouldn't be obvious at all that there was anything wrong with JR itself.

A story will help make this clear. Gloxo is a hyper-intelligent extraterrestrial. He is a master of assimilating, producing, and dissecting arguments. Gloxo knows nothing about human beings: he knows nothing about their history, their practices, their values, or their psychology. He is asked (it doesn't matter by whom) to evaluate the argument in JR.

Will Gloxo be able to find fault with that argument? It may be that, relative to beings whose cultural and economic circumstances differ but slightly from ours, the argument in JR is cogent or readily modified so as to become cogent. We know that JR leads to a false conclusion and must therefore contain an error. But we have inside information about our species; Gloxo does not, and he must therefore evaluate JR on its own terms. Thus evaluated, JR is not a particularly bad line of reasoning, and Gloxo, we may reasonably suppose, deems it cogent.

Some may balk at this: "How hard can it really be to establish that being a Tolstoy is better than being a junky? Surely you're overstating things, so far as you're not just plain wrong." Disagreements are resolvable to the extent that the disputants are otherwise in agreement, and irresolvable to the extent that they're not. No argument can undermine any argument with whose premises its own are incompatible. The most perfect argument can do nothing to undermine the most spurious one, if neither countenances any of the assumptions made by the other. (By a "perfect" argument I mean one that derives a correct conclusion from correct and non-tendentious assumptions by means of valid logical transformations.)

Rationalizations tend to be ineffective so far as they fail to make allowances for relevant facts and so far as they violate canons of good reasoning. The operative word is "tend." Logical people tend not to settle for illogical rationalizations, but illogical people may have no trouble doing so. Brazenly inaccurate rationalizations are unacceptable to people who pride themselves on being sticklers for the facts, but for others such rationalizations may be quite acceptable. But rationalizations cannot be *too* transparent, lest they fail of their purpose, which is to hide or at least distort the truth, in furtherance of the rationalizer's emotional needs.

7.0   It will help us move forward to add a few points about the differences between psychosis and neurosis. Let us begin by defining these terms.[244]

A neurosis is a mental illness that occurs within an intact psychological structure. In fact, neurosis is the result of a mind's being too intact and therefore too rigid. (A mind can be intact in one respect and dilapidated in another, and a neurotic's mind might be rigid in one respect and amorphous in another.) Neurosis is an overdevelopment of the mechanisms that inhibit the flow of information within the mind and, in particular, that inhibit the entry of information into consciousness. In some cases, the purpose of such a mechanism may be to quarantine emotionally sensitive information. But in most cases the purpose of such a mechanism is emotionally antiseptic, being simply to prevent ratiocinative mechanisms from being flooded with information and, for that reason, either doing substandard work or just shutting down. Consciousness is an exceptionally well-guarded part of the mind. There are two reasons for this. (The second reason is a corollary of the first.) First, consciousness serves an integrative function. It is in consciousness, and in no other part of the mind, that otherwise isolated bodies of information can be integrated. Second, consciousness is the point of contact between mind and world; all sensory, and therefore all

---

244. The contents of this section and the next are based on my own experience. But similar points were made, and cogently defended, by Reich (1945), Stekel (1949), Freud (1963), Salzman (1994), and Kernberg (1985, 1993).

survival-critical, information is initially stored in consciousness. That information must be kept pristine and therefore free of unconscious contaminants, lest you confuse imaginary threats to your welfare with real ones; and such information mustn't be allowed to occlude the cognitive pathways tasked with disseminating this information to the rest of the mind, lest you be too slow to see the consequences of such threats. The purpose of the corresponding inhibitory mechanisms isn't pain-avoidance, but information-management.

This isn't because there are two classes of inhibitory mechanisms: the emotional kind and the epistemic kind. It's because the first class is a proper subset of the second. Pain-avoidance is a kind of information-management. Your spouse is cheating on you. You know this. This knowledge is painful; so you repress it. For some reason or other, it makes its way back into your consciousness. You experience pain. The pain represents information-overload. Taken by itself, your knowledge of your spouse's behavior couldn't possibly lead to information-overload; the person your spouse is carrying on with knows about her infidelities and his consciousness obviously isn't overloaded because of it. But that information has consequences for you that it doesn't have for him. That's why you're overwhelmed and he isn't. It isn't your knowledge of your wife's infidelities that overwhelms you; it's your knowledge of the consequences of that knowledge. Your wife is a person of considerable merit. You won't be able to find a worthy replacement for her unless you make money and lose weight. You won't be able to lose weight unless you have that operation. Because that operation is expensive, it might break you financially, further diminishing your prospects of finding romantic happiness. But it might ultimately be cost-effective, since you'll be a more efficient worker. But this increase in efficiency won't redound to your financial benefit unless you get the promotion. You'll get the promotion if, instead of writing a few substantial articles, you write a flurry of relatively inconsequential ones. For you to do the latter without losing your self-respect, the articles in question would have to meet certain, quite specific requirements. And so on, and so forth. It isn't the information that you have about your wife's dalliances that overwhelms you; it is the corresponding meta-information. You know that, if you are to have any chance of recovering from situation, it is by going on a long journey, about which you know nothing except that, it addition to being long, it will be hard and full of unpleasant surprises. You also know that, should you ever learn exactly what that journey entails, it may turn out that you can't complete it and also that, should it turn out that you can complete it, your doing so may only marginally improve your chances of happiness. You know that you won't be able to tolerate these uncertainties unless you change the way you deal with change; and you know that you don't know whether you'll be able to make the requisite changes to yourself or whether, supposing that you do make them, they will appreciably improve your chances of having the kind of life you want to have. It isn't by their knowledge of the external world that people are overwhelmed, but by their knowledge of, or their knowledge of their ignorance of, the changes they must make to themselves to deal with what they know about the external world.

The concept of neurosis is to be understood in terms of this last fact. Neuroses block the entry of powerful, negatively valued impulses into consciousness. This does not prevent such impulses from being transformed into actions. But it does prevent consciousness from knowing that such transformations are taking place. For this reason, the resulting actions, when not experienced as lethargy or otherwise non-agential symptoms, are experienced as accidents or as incidental by-products of the agent's conscious intentions. The subject's inevitable tendency to repeat such actions *ad nauseam* clearly indicates a pathological disturbance. But the reason that, in the neurotic mind, *verboten* impulses must be discharged in such circuitous ways is precisely that the neurotic mind is so intact: its defenses are on red-alert, and it is therefore only through subterfuges, and in a very reduced and usually totally symbolic form, that *verboten* impulses manage to express themselves.

A psychosis is very different sort of mental illness. Whereas neurosis involves an over-strengthening of faculties that keep the mind intact, psychosis involves a massive disorganization of the mind. But psychoses are typically psychodynamic in nature; that is, they are to be understood, at least in part, in terms of the subject's internal conflicts and his relations to other people and to his aspirations. This is not to deny that the existence of a psychosis is to be explained in strictly genetic, organic terms. It is to say that, once in existence, a condition of psychosis is to be understood, to an extent, in psychological terms.

Purely organic disorders, such as are associated with brain damage or Alzheimer's, may bring about psychosis-like conditions. But whereas psychosis, whatever its organic underpinnings may be, *is* a psychological illness, whose symptoms can be understood in psychological terms (as derivatives of wishes, beliefs, etc.), the psychological disruptions that accompany a purely organic disorder are not to be understood in this way. A consequence is that they are not ameliorated by eliminating intrapsychic conflicts or otherwise deepening the patient's insight into himself.

7.1 Neurotic people see external reality as it is. It is their own feelings to which they are blind. Put more precisely: in so far as a person is neurotic, and not also psychotic or otherwise psychologically impaired, he sees the external world for what it is, his blindness being to his own feelings, not to external reality.

When we sleep, we have visions of ghouls and goblins that haven't been a part of our waking lives since infancy. The reason they surface during sleep is that the maturation-based inhibitions that keep such creatures in the basement of the psyche, where they belong, have been relaxed, liberating these bottom-dwellers from the musty confines of the unconscious, letting them roam around the higher strata of consciousness. The reason why one often feels paralyzed in one's dreams is that the channels that convert one's waking thoughts into overt behaviors have been shut off. That is why the dreamer's intention to slay the evil wizard doesn't result in overt behavior.[245]

---

245. Freud (1998). See Chapters VI and VII.

In the psychotic, those inhibitions are relaxed, not just during sleep, but also during wakefulness. Thanks to his excessively relaxed inhibitory mechanisms, the psychotic is slaying dragons when he should be fixing copy-machines.

The neurotic is in the opposite predicament. *His* inhibitory mechanisms are doing too good a job. So he not only keeps monsters and talking pigs out of his waking consciousness: he *also* keeps out his tender feelings towards his office-mate Marge. So far as he is aware of those feelings, he regards them as threats to his psychological integration: he wants to remain hyper-sane and, just to make sure that he's covered every possible contingency, he treats healthy emotions, such as his affection for Marge, as though they were as much of a threat to his sanity as a psychotic's delusions. The neurotic often excels at tasks, such as fixing machines, that don't engage *verboten* emotions. He also may excel at emotionally sterile tasks, such as inventing formal languages. He may even excel at the analysis of emotions – provided that he has so intellectualized his interest in emotions that his analyses of them don't resonate uncomfortably with his own.

The neurotic may thus be a great psychoanalyst. Indeed, a *sine qua non* for extreme psychoanalytic acumen is that one be neurotic or psychotic (though not cripplingly so), since it is only by having such a condition that one has a sufficiently direct encounter with mental illness that one can understand it or see its roots in the structure of the psyche. But supposing one to have had the requisite direct encounters with psychopathology, it is only to the extent that one has intellectualized the knowledge thereby obtained, divesting it of its characteristically analysis-inhibiting emotional resonances, than one can employ it in psychoanalytically productive ways.

Thus, by intellectualizing emotions, beliefs, and propositional attitudes generally, one can draw on them when analyzing people. So, ironically, the person who intellectualizes his feelings may be a *better* analyst than one who doesn't intellectualize them. The latter can't think about a feeling without arousing constellations of insight-blunting affect. But the former can consider a feeling, and extract the information embodied in it, without having an analysis-thwarting emotional reaction. So sometimes the people who best understand emotion are ones who, because they have turned their own emotions into objects of theoretical interest, are accused of not having any.

That said, the intellectualizer is teeming with emotion. But that emotion is hidden beneath a veneer of logic-driven cool-headedness. (Wilhelm Reich (1945) made this point.) Intellectualization is a way of managing emotion. Emotions can just be *had*, and do not have to *managed*, if, in respect of their frequency and individual intensities, they fall within certain limits.

7.1.1   Let us end this section by justifying our contention that, in order to be a competent psychoanalyst, one must oneself have been afflicted by psychopathology.

Where knowledge of the external world is concerned, the question "what do you know?" is never to be answered in the same way as the question "how do you know it?" But where the internal (psychological) world is concerned, those questions are sometimes to be answered in the same way. This fact, coupled with another fact, has the consequence that there is an important epistemological difference between psychological and non-psychological knowledge. (In this context, "knowledge," refers to spatiotemporal, as opposed to purely conceptual knowledge.)

That consequence: where psychological knowledge is concerned, but never where non-psychological knowledge is concerned, second-hand, descriptive knowledge is sometimes no substitute for first hand, experiential knowledge.

That fact: There are two kinds of awareness: object-awareness and proposition-awareness. We've said this many times; but it's worth saying again, given the nature of the argument about to be put forth, and for that same reason it's worth restating why it's true.

Truths are true propositions. Therefore, truth-awareness is a kind of proposition-awareness. Knowledge is truth-awareness. Therefore, object-awareness isn't knowledge, except in so far as it coincides with truth-awareness. (In a moment, we will see that truth-awareness does sometimes coalesce with object-awareness. We will also see that this happens when, and only when, the object in question is a constituent of one's own psyche.) In any case, as far as science is concerned, no instance of knowledge isn't an instance of truth-awareness, given that the purpose of scientific endeavor is to identify and organize truths (true propositions).

Observations are instances of object-awareness. It is by organizing the information borne by our observations that science moves forward. But the scientist is interested in such information only to the extent that it can be propositionalized. Therefore, the fact that scientific knowledge is observation-based is compatible with our contention that, as far as science is concerned, all knowledge is truth-awareness.

Data are states of awareness. The footprint in the sand is not itself a datum. It is a datum only if somebody knows about it. Moreover, the footprint is a datum only to the extent that somebody knows about it. Unknown facts about its microstructure aren't data. Since, therefore, the footprint is a datum only if there is an awareness of it, and only to the extent that there is such an awareness, any given awareness of the footprint is a datum, but the footprint itself is not a datum. In general, all data are states of awareness.

One learns about the external world through states of awareness. Thus, in studying the external world, one is studying the objects of such states. But one isn't studying such states themselves. In studying the internal world, however, one is studying such states. Botanists study trees; they don't study tree-awarenesses. Psychologists study tree-awarenesses; they don't study trees.

If X is any cognitively normal human being, "X has experienced sadness" is equivalent with "X knows what it is like to be sad." To be sure, those two propositions are not logically equivalent. Given only that a creature has experienced sadness, it doesn't follow that it knows what it is like to be sad. There are three reasons for this. First, not all creatures are self-conscious; and, consequently, not all creatures are ever aware of their own states. Second, there is some proposition of the form "being sad is like__" such that one knows what sadness is like exactly if one knows that proposition to be true; therefore, not all creatures that have had an experience of a given kind, such as an experience of sadness, know what it is like to have had such an experience, given that not all creatures are proposition-aware. Third, a creature that has experienced sadness might might simply have forgotten about those experiences.

That said, no cognitively normal human being has any given one of these three deficits. In this context, we are concerned with cognitively normal human beings. In this context, therefore, "X has experienced sadness" is equivalent with "X knows what it is like to be sad."

This point can be generalized. Let E some sort of experience, i.e. let E be some property whose instances are experiences of a certain kind. There is some true proposition T of the form "experiences of type E are like__" such that a given creature C knows T if, and only if, C has experienced E, and such that, if C is a cognitively normal human being, C knows T if C has experienced T.

Any instance of E-awareness is an instance of object-awareness. Any such instance is also an instance of truth-awareness, and therefore of proposition-awareness, provided that the creature whose awareness is being discussed is a cognitively normal human being.

Thus, where the internal world is concerned, object-awareness and truth-awareness sometimes coincide. They do not always coincide, even where the internal world is concerned. A given person can have knowledge of, and thus know truths concerning, experiences that he himself has not had. Further, not all mental entities are experiences, and we can have knowledge of non-experiential mental entities. But it is a fact, of whose importance we will presently become aware, that, where psychological research is concerned, object- and truth-awareness sometimes coincide.

Where the external world is concerned, object-awareness and truth-awareness never coincide. Given any truth T concerning any external object O, there is no one kind of experience E such that one must have E to know T. Let Smith be a creature that is one-thousandth the size of a human being, but is otherwise just like a cognitively normal human being, and let Brown be a cognitively normal, normal-sized human being. There is nothing that the one person can know about any given plant or rock that the other cannot know.

There are some things about the external world that the one creature can know directly that the other can know only indirectly (through inference). But that doesn't mean that there is anything about the external world that the one can know that the other cannot. It means that, given either one of those two creatures, there is something about the internal world that the one can know that the other cannot. Given some plant P, there are facts about P's microstructure that Smith can know directly that Brown can know only indirectly. What follows isn't that Smith can have P-related knowledge that Smith cannot, but rather that Smith can have P-awareness-related knowledge that Smith cannot. What follows, therefore, is that there is some psychological truth that Smith can know that Brown cannot know, not that that there is some non-psychological truth that Smith can know that Brown cannot know.

There are some experiences the likes of which a person doesn't have unless he is mentally ill. Such experiences bear otherwise unobtainable information about the disfigurements of one's psychological structure that constitute psychopathology; and that information, in its turn, bears otherwise unobtainable information about the structure of the psyche.

A person's mind must be distinguished from the activity that it mediates. Let Smith be some person who is cryogenically frozen at time t, and let B be Smith's body. At time t*, B is unfrozen and reactivated. The mental activity mediated by post-freeze B's brain bears the same relationship to the activity mediated by pre-freeze B's brain that your Tuesday-morning (post-sleep) mental activity bears with respect to your Monday-night (pre-sleep) mental activity. (Actually, since no mental activity has occurred in B's brain during the time B was frozen, its activity at t* is a direct continuation – qualitatively, if not chronologically – of its activity at t, whereas your Tuesday-morning mental activity is by no means a direct continuation of your Monday-night mental activity: while you were sleeping, you had dreams; thoughts ripened; information was processed.) If one's mind were identical with the activity it mediated, then, upon being cryogenically frozen, Smith's mind would simply have been obliterated, and the mind occupying B at t* would not have been Smith's mind: it would have been that of somebody qualitatively just like Smith, but numerically distinct from him. Thus, the mind isn't to be identified with the activity it mediates, and is instead to be identified with the enduring, though obviously malleable, structures that mediate such activity. The mind is a collection of such structures; it is a structure consisting of such structures.

But even though minds aren't the activity they mediate, there is no way to know about a given mind except through that activity. (So far as your behavior provides me with information about your mind, it is because it provides me with informaton about the activity that it mediates.) So it is only to the extent that one knows about the mind mediated by a given mind that one knows about that mind.

Whatever a person knows about his own unconscious mental activity, he knows it on the basis of his conscious mental activity. A person's unconscious is knowable to him only to the extent that it has consciousnes-constitutive derivatives. (Another person's behavior can be a source of information about that person's unconscious mental activity. Even though, on most occassions, nobody is better able to identify the contents of a given person's mind than that person, people are sometimes blind to facts about themselves that are obvious to everyone else. Smith may not be conscious of his hatred of Brown, even though Smith's actions may make it clear (to everyone other than Smith) that Smith hates his Brown. But so far as a given person can correctly interpret Smith's behavior, it's because he can associate it with the contents of his own consciousness. So our point stands: it is through consciousness, and consciousness alone, that one knows of the unconscious.)

Most mental activity is unconscious, and most of what there is to know about the psyche's structure is to be learned through unconscious mental activity. (We will henceforth refer to conscious mental activity as "CMA" and to unconscious mental activity as "UMA.")

Psychopathologies are disfigurements of psychological structure. (Such disfigurements of psychological structure are not to be identified with corruptions of psychological structure. It is one thing to have a broken leg; it is a very different thing to have osteoperosis. The fissure in a broken but otherwise healthy bone is a singularity. None of the fissures in an osteoperosis-ridden bone is a singularity. Some psychopathologies are like broken bones; others are like osteoperosis-riddgen bones. We will justify this point in Chapters 14 and 15.) Such disfigurements are necesssarily performance-diminishing. As a result, what the non-disfigured mind does automatically, its disfigured counterpart either doesn't do or does consciously, this being why, in those afflicted by psychopathology, UMA and CMA coalesce.

Non-obsessive-compulsive Parker doesn't want to visit his in-laws. But he feels that he has a moral obligation to visit them; and he does so, believing that he is thereby fulfilling a moral obligation that he could just as well have decided not to fulfill. Given how poorly Parker's in-laws treat him, it's obvious that Parker does not have any moral obligation to visit them, suggesting that his conscious belief to the contrary is not the real force behind his decision to visit his in-laws.

Like Parker, obsessive-compulsive Johnson doesn't want to visit his in-laws. Unlike Parker, Johnson does not believe that he has a moral obligation to visit them. But because of his condition, he feels compelled to visit them – that is, he has an ego-dystonic compulsion to do so – and he gives into this compulsion. Parker's reason – his actual reason – for visiting his in-laws is no more irrational than Johnson's. It is only because Johnson was conscious of the irrational force behind his behavior that we describe it as "compulsive," and it is only because Parker is unconscious of the corresponding force that we describe his behavior as "non-compulsive." Like Parker, Johnson has to rationalize his compulsion in some way. But Johnson must consciously construct that rationalization; Parker's mind automatically and unconsciously constructs the corresponding rationalization. Also, Johnson knows that the justification he constructs is fraudulent. (When an obsessive-compulsive rationalizes compulsive behavior, which he always does, he is always aware of the spuriousness of the rationalization; and for that reason, that rationalization is "ego-dystonic.") Parker does consciously accept his own rationalization. Presumably, the second point (that Johnson, unlike Parker, rejects his justification for his behavior) is a consequence of the first point (that Johnson, unlike Parker, consciously constructs that justification).

Another illustration (one that, unlike the previous illustration, will play a big part in what we will henceforth say): Non-schizophrenic Smith consciously believes that Mary is malicious. When he dreams about her, she is represented as a witch, suggesting that, at some level, he believes her to be a witch. But during his waking hours, Smith does not have this belief. Schizophrenic Brown consciously believes Mary to be a witch. During his waking hours, Brown must consciously tell himself that she is not a witch. In each person's mind, there is a thought-process that, if left uninhibited, will lead from the belief that Mary is malicious to the belief that she is a witch. In Smith's mind, that thought-process is automatically inhibited (or redirected). In Brown's mind, it is not, and Brown must consciously make the necessary corrections.

In general, what the non-schizophrenic consciously sees as a metaphorical truth, and therefore only unconsciously sees as a literal truth, the schizophrenic consciously sees as a literal truth.

By virtue of having such delusions Brown knows much about the psyche that he would not otherwise know (setting aside the obvious fact that knows what it is like to have such a delusion). First of all, Brown is never completely insane. During his worst moments, he is only relatively so; and sometimes he is lucid. And to the extent that Brown's ideation is psychotic, it isn't because he has undergone a complete cognitive regression; it isn't because his thinking has become exactly like an infants. It is because, while still thinking like an adult, he also thinks like an infant.

Infants aren't psychotic, and neither are dreamers. The reason: in such people, infantile thought doesn't commingle with non-infantile thought. Brown is psychotic. The reason: in him, infantile thought *does* commingle with non-infantile thought. It isn't solely because Brown has regressed that his condition is morbid. Were Brown's psyche to undergo wholesale infantalization, he'd obviously be the worse for it: he would be less functional and less intelligent. But his condition wouldn't be morbid – at least not in the way in which, in actuality, it is morbid. His condition is morbid because part of him has regressed and part of him hasn't.

But such a partial regression wouldn't necessarily be morbid: a person who was sometimes an adult and sometimes a baby would be a source of amusement, but his condition, though substandard, wouldn't be morbid, at least not in the same way as a psychotic's. So far as the psychotic's condition is morbid, it is because, in him, infantile and non-infantile modes of thought are commingled. But – so I suspect, though I have no way to back this up – even such commingling by itself, though function-impairing, would not be morbid, or would be a different form of morbidity from psychosis. I suspect – same disclaimer – that it is the proto-psychotic's attempt to rationalize his infantile ideation that results in a distinctively psychotic form of morbidity. By taking LSD, one induces a partial ideational regression: one lifts rationality-constitutive, distinctively non-infantile inhibitions on thought- and affect-mediating brain-structures. (We will assume that the hypothetical LSD-user we're about to discuss isn't psychopathological – except in so far as taking LSD has induced psychopathology.) The LSD user's condition is suboptimal in some ways; it might even be morbid in some ways; and it involves a commingling of adult and infantile thought similar to that characteristic of psychosis. But the LSD-user's condition is not morbid in the same way as that of the man who has schizoaffective-disorder. The reason can only be that that the LSD-user doesn't try reconcile the two spheres of thought. He knows that he is on drug-trip. Also, since it was his taking a pill, as opposed to his emotional conflicts acting up, that caused his thinking to infantalize (to the extent that it did), the LSD-user's attitude towards the infantile elements of ideation will not be marked by intense emotional defenses (except for user-specific reasons), whereas the psychotic's attitude towards his infantilisms will be one of extreme defensiveness. The LSD-user won't try to rationalize: he won't try to find ways to establish (to himself) that his delusions are sane. He knows they're not: he wants to be insane (for a spell); that's why he dosed up in the first place. But the schizoaffective doesn't want to be a "trip." He wants to be sane. This is partly because nobody wants to have a diseased mind. But it's also because important but ugly truths are embodied in his delusions. His delusions – and this is a point we will now develop and is central to our argument – are concretized, infantilized expressions of potentially correct and sane beliefs.

Non-psychotics see the mind as being homogenous. Brown knows that it isn't. He knows it empirically: when his schizophrenia is acting up, the intrapsychic divisions that remaing invisible to others are all visible to him.

"Contrary to what you assume," it will be objected, "what is happening when Brown's condition is acting up is not that pre-existing intrapsychic divisions are become observable. What is happening is that an otherwise homogenous, non-stratified structure becomes divided. And, contrary to what you asume, the reason it becomes divided is that it is flooded with previously non-existent mental entities. You say that these alien invaders must come from some other part of Brown's mind – some part of it that is ordinarily unconscious. But what grounds are there for that assumption? And what grounds are there, consequently, for your assumption that, if indeed Brown's condition is the result of a collision between two mental strata, everyone's mind is correspondingly stratified? Why not stick with the more conservative assumption that Brown's mind, if stratified, is for that reason different from a sane person's mind? Indeed, why not stick with the even more conservative assumption that Brown's mind, like everyone else's, is non-stratified and that, when his condition is acting up, it is because purely physiological mechanisms are generating mental activity that they shouldn't be generating?"

There are several points to make here. First, to have a delusion isn't to have a wrong belief; it is to have a belief that is right in the wrong way. More accurately, it is to have a belief that might be right but the vehicle for which is some infantile, and therefore false, belief. (Even more accurately, it isn't to have such a belief; it is to experience the conscious activity expressive of such a belief. Beliefs themselves, even delusive ones, don't consist of activity, but of activity-mediating structures. And so far as delusions give rise to hallucinations, those hallucinations are distinct from those delusions. Hallucinations, so far as they are rooted in delusions, or in beliefs of any other kind, are phenomenologicizations of beliefs; they are not themselves beliefs.) Brown believes that Mary is malicious. This belief is correct. One way to have this correct belief is to believe that Mary is a witch. But this is the wrong way to have that belief. In believing that Mary is a witch, Brown is having the right belief, but in the wrong way.

But even when he is symptomatic, Brown also has that belief in the right way; he has it in the same antiseptic, discursive way that Smith has it. And when Brown delusively believes that Mary is a witch, he obviously doesn't drop his belief that Mary is malicious. Instead, he simultaneously has that belief in two different ways. Schizophrenics don't cease to be capable of abstract thought when they're conditions are acting up. They continue to have the abstract, discursive thoughts that they have during their lucid moments, but they also have infantilized, concretized versions of those same thoughts.

According to the objector, the schizophrenic's delusions are cognitive garbage. They come out of nowhere, he believes. ("That isn't my position," he is likely to say. "They aren't the products of spontaneous generation. They are the products of psychologically antiseptic physiology." But that this is no different from saying that they come out of nowhere, given that they are psychological entities.) Suppposing the objector correct, they therefore have no meaningful ties to the schizophrenic's other thoughts. In addition, they are wrong. But they aren't just wrong, at least not categorically; they aren't comparable a mathematician's belief that n = 25, when in fact n = 26. A mathematician's incorrect beliefs are of the same ilk as his correct ones. Brown's belief that Mary is a witch is not of the same ilk as Brown's belief that Mary is more than two feet tall. The belief-system embodied in the latter is hewed to the structure of reality; its purpose is to represent things as they are. The belief-system embodied in the former is hewed to infantile wishes and fears; its purpose is to represent things as the subject wants them to be. (This doesn't mean that it always does represent things that way. Brown doesn't want Mary to be a witch. But her being a witch is consistent with the world's being a magical place, whose occupants are governed by wishes, not by impersonal laws.)

But supposing, as we will, that Mary is in fact malicious, Brown's delusion does not come out of nowhere; in any case, it no more comes out of nowhere than the discursive belief corresponding to it. A schizophrenic's delusions track the beliefs that he has when lucid. So far as the latter are incorrect, it is because of ratiocinative failings on the subject's part; it isn't because of mental disease or defect. To be sure, the two sets of beliefs are not – or, and this qualification is important, seem not to be – in perfect lockstep. Supposing D to be some schizophrenic delusion, there often appears to be no sane belief B such that D is the schizophrenic version of B.

To some extent, this lack of synchronicity is merely apparent; and to the extent that it's real, it can be explained by supposing that, when Brown's schizophrenia is acting up, his thought is disinhibited in ways in which it is inhibited when he is lucid. During his episodes, Brown's defenses are withdrawn, and thoughts that ordinarily aren't allowed to rise to the level of consciousness are allowed to do so. When Brown is lucid, let us suppose, his position is that his mother and father are perfect. But they are not perfect; and Brown knows this all too well, having been on the receiving end of their treachery for years. It's precisely because the beliefs Brown has when lucid are so antithetical to the truth that he is schizophrenic. To be schizophrenic is to able to regress to a condition of cognitive infantilism. Such regressions make it possible for Brown to consciously believe what he really believes; and such regressions also enable him to have those beliefs in a form in which, if taken at face value, they are so brazenly wrong that they aren't a threat to anyone. Brown's mother isn't a witch. When Brown tells her that she is a witch, she can laugh it off; and Brown too can laugh it off, once he regains lucidity. If, when lucid, Brown were to tell his mother that she was petty, hypocritical, and undermining, she couldn't laugh it off, and neither could Brown. Brown's consciously having that belief, and making it known to those who whom it concerned, would disrupt and possibly destroy the network of beliefs and values that, when he is lucid, enable him to live with his mother: his consciously having that belief would thus make it internally impossible for him to continue to live with his mother. And his expressing it would make it externally impossible for him to do so: given that Brown's mother has the character-traits that make such a statement correct, she is likely to lack the character-traits would dispose her to take such a comment in stride, and she is likely to react to such a comment with volcanic hostility.

If taken as attempts to assert already established facts, the statements just made beg the question. The objector says: "Brown's delusions have a strictly physiological, as opposed to a psychodynamic basis." The argument put forth presupposes that they do have a psychodynamic basis. (This doesn't mean that they don't have a physiological basis. It means that, so far as they do have such a basis, it is because the physiological mediates the psychological.)

But those statements are not question-begging if taken to express an alternative way of modelling the data. The objector models the data by saying: Brown's delusions come out of nowhere; they are to be understood in strictly physiological terms. We are modelling the data by saying: Smith's delusions express repressed beliefs. Some say that the concept of a repressed belief is incoherent. In Chapters 13 and 14, we will see that it is coherent. Supposing that it is in fact coherent, the debate between the objector and the present author is strictly empirical.

In any case, so far as lucid-Brown's belief-set appears not to be in lockstep with actively schizophrenic-Brown's belief-set, one possible explanation of that fact is to suppose (i) that those two belief-sets really aren't in lockstep, the reason being (ii) that, when Brown descends into schizophrenia, ordinarily operative cognitive inhibitions are withdrawn, and he consciously believes what he otherwise only unconsciously believes, with the qualification that he believes it in an infantilized, travestied form.

Another explanation of that same fact is that, to some extent, (i*) that appearance is misleading, the reason being (ii*) that not all of actively schizophrenic Brown's delusions are as transparent as his belief that Mary is a witch. The step from "Mary is malicious" to "Mary is a witch" is a small one. The second belief isn't so much a distortion as it is a concretization of the first. Speaking theoretically, it is possible that much more distortion is involved in other cases. Speaking empirically, it is a fact that more distortion is involved in other cases.

When Brown regains lucidity, he'll obviously stop believing that Mary is a witch. But he won't necessarily drop the corresponding discursive belief, namely, his belief that Mary is malicious. Everyone has dreams in which acquaintances of theirs are represented as ghouls or monsters. When Jerry (an arbitrary sane person) wakes up, he obviously drops the belief that Harry (an arbitrary acquaintance of his) is a vampire. But he may not drop the corresponding discursive belief, namely, that Harry is a predator, a parasite, and a fraud. He may always have suspected as much about Harry, and that suspicion may well be correct. If it is correct, he will not, upon waking up, just drop his delusive dream-belief. He'll drop the false parts (e.g. he'll stop believing that Harry can turn into a bat) and he'll hold onto the correct ones (e.g. he'll continue to believe that Harry is an amoral opportunist). It is a theoretical possibility that, upon regaining lucidity, Brown has a similar reaction to his delusion about Mary; and it is an empirical fact that this is how, upon regaining lucidity, schizophrenics often respond to the delusions that they just had.

Our objective is to answer the question: "What is that, by virtue of being afflicted by psychopathology, a person knows that he wouldn't otherwise know?" Given what we've said about Brown, we are almost in a position to answer that question. We need only supplement the our Brown-related points with a few point of a general nature concerning psychology and concerning the nature of explanation.

Every cogntively normal person has a psychological need to see the contents of his consciousness as cohering with one another. (In this context, the terms "consciousness" and "contents of consciousness" refer both to what is consciousness-constitutive and to what is access-conscious. So it refers to sensations, perceptions, and other phenomenology mediated mental entities; and it also refers to non-repressed propositional attitudes.) Such a person wants his experiences to make sense. He wants to compatibilize the contents of his consciousness with one another. If, having been ordered under hypnosis to do so, a given person snaps his fingers whenever he hears the word "submarine," that person, no matter how sane or intelligent he might otherwise be, will rationalize his behavior; and, what is more striking, he will be convinced that his rationalization is correct.

Related to the fact that people need to see their experiences as cohering with one another is that people have an extremely strong tendency to regard what are in fact complex mental states as being simple. (We wrongly regard boredom, embarrassment, and feelings of awkwardness as being emotional primitives. Any instance of any given one of these emotions is the phenomenological expression of a rationalization. There can be awkward silences between two 30-year olds who are on a date, but not between a senile 90 year old and his 30-year old caretaker. In the second situation, but not the first, there is no chance that each hoped to like the other and has to deal with the fact that he doesn't. A song can't bore someone who has the power to turn off the radio or change the station as soon as that song comes on, but it can bore someone who lacks that power. In the second situation, but not the first, a person believes himself impotent to close the gap between how things are and how he wants them to be. Nothing embarrasses someone who doesn't believe that other people's affection for him is conditional on his abiding by certain behavior norms; a person can be embarrassed if he does have that belief. In the second situation, but not the first, the agent believes that others will chastise him, by withdrawing their affection for him, if he doesn't chastise himself first. Any given instance of any given one of these three emotions involves somebody's rationalizing his own powerlessness, and any such instance is therefore psychodynamically complex.) A corollary is that people have an equally strong tendency to regard facts about human psychology that are in need of explanation as not being in need of explanation. In fact, it is often the most opaque psychological truths that people regard as being the most transparent.

Folk-psychology makes it possible for a given person to rationalize his conscious states to the extent that he isn't afflicted by psychopatholgy, and it does the same for him to the extent that he is thus afflicted but has erected defenses that condition any given symptomatic derivative of his condition on its appearing not to be such a derivative. (In this context, "folk-psychology" refers to the totality of platitudes about the psyche accepted by the laity. So I am not using that term in the same as Churchland, who uses it to refer to the position that anyone ever has propositional attitudes of any kind.)

Because Brown is schizophrenic, his conscious ideation includes things whose existence folk-psychology altogether denies and it includes things whose existence, though not themselves denied by folk-psychology, make it impossible for him to reconcile his conscious states with one another without positing the existence of things whose existence folk-psychology denies.

When attempting to reconcile his various conscious states, Brown has the option of taking the position that there is no position to be taken: "that's just how things are." This position is equivalent with the position that his conscious abnormalities have a strictly somatic basis. This is the position that Brown's psychiatrists are likely to urge him to take, and it is likely, partly for that reason, to be his "official" position – the one that he tries to take and that he tells himself he's taken. But it isn't Brown's actual position. (Given only that Brown is psychotic, it follows that it ultimately is not Brown's position, even though it is left open how remote from consciousness, and how non-operational, Brown's defenses have made it.) Brown's delusive beliefs, though false by definition, are in some cases (not all) very obviously transformations of non-delusive beliefs; and in some cases (not all) it is obvious to Brown, when he is lucid, that they are such transformations. Mary isn't literally a witch. When Brown is lucid (to the extent that he is ever lucid), Brown is aware of this fact. But when he's lucid, he is (so we may suppose, without running afoul of the clinical data) no less aware of the fact that Mary is an awful person.

Given these two facts, Brown will inevitably regard his Mary-delusion as a transformation of a correct Mary-related belief of his – and he'll be right. As for the idea that this delusion "came out of nowhere," or was just the product of "crossed wires," Brown will rightly regard it as complete non-starter. A person can't have one such delusion without having That one delusion of Brown's is but one of many that Brown has. Some of those delusions can be explained, and Brown probably knows some of those explanations. (When correct, they are sometimes self-explanatory: if you see your abusive step-father as a ghoul – an actual ghoul, not the metaphorical ghoul that he is – you will not, when lucid, have much trouble deciphering that delusion.) If Brown takes the takes the folk-psychology-compatible position that his Mary-delusion "came of out of nowhere," he thereby eschews that explanation; and if he doesn't eschew it, he has no choice, at least to the extent that he aspires to reconcile his consicous states with one another, but to posit a stratum of mentation within himself of which he is not ordinarily aware.

In many cases, Brown's delusions will correspond to emotions that he consciously has, but are only faintly present in his consciousness during his periods of lucidity. Given such a delusion, Brown is likely, when lucid, to see in it a magnification and a distortion of something of which he is typically conscious. When Brown is lucid, he finds Charles slightly irritating; there is something about Charles that he can't put his finger on that bothers him. During one of his episodes, Brown sees Charles as a vampire; and when Brown regains lucidity, the legacy of this delusion is that Brown now firmly believes what he previously only suspected, namely, that Charles is a manipulative parasite. And it's at least as likely as not that this belief of Brown's is correct and is justified. (It isn't justified by his delusion. The delusion merely forced Brown to admit to himself that he had the belief, the justification for which may consist of a multititude of impressions about Charles, none of which is damning if taken by itself, but all of which, if taken collectively, suggest that Charles is indeed a manipulator and a thief. Brown has a ready explanation for his delusion so long as he is willing to believe that he has always unconsciously or semi-consciously had this belief about Charles.) To the extent that he accepts this explanation, his thinking coincides with Freud's and thus parts ways with folk-psychology.

To be sure, setting aside those delusions of Brown's that are just delusions, as opposed to infantilizations of correct beliefs, Brown will have many a delusion that, if recalled during one of his periods of lucidity, he won't instantly recognize as a distortion of a correct (or, at any rate, a sane) belief. But he will eventually come to see some of those delusions as distortions of correct beliefs. To be sure, not all of Brown's delusions are distortions of correct beliefs: some of them are just delusions. But even Brown's purely delusive delusions are not always to be dismissed; for some of them express emotions that Brown always has, even during his lucid moments, but only in a reduced form. By exaggerating what Brown consciously feels, such a delusion appropriately expresses what Brown unconsciously feels. If Brown accepts the idea that he isn't at all times aware of everything that is going on in his mind, he has no trouble providing himself with a viable explanation of the fact that he has such delusions. He cannot do this if he regards his mind as being transparent to itself. So long as he identifies his mind with his consciousness, he has no explanation besides the null explanation endorsed by contemporary psychiatry ("it came out of nowhere – nowhere other than his damaged brain, that is").

Unless one has experienced some sort of psychopathology – and it needn't be as extreme as Brown's – one can attach no meaning to statements like "a person can have diametrically opposed feelings towards a given person," "for reasons having nothing to do with a lack of intelligence, a given person can have mutually opposed beliefs, desires, and even intentions," and "the narrative in terms of which a given person consciously understands himself is not the one in terms of which he actually understands himself; the former is either a distortion or a negation of the latter." But Brown won't have any trouble understanding such statements, except to the extent that he has erected defenses against such truths. (It's a distinct possibility that he has erected such defenses;

for it's a distinct possibility that, where many a delusion of Brown's is concerned, it was only because Brown consciously accept the corresponding discursive belief or desire that the latter had to express itself as a delusion.) Terms like "divided consciousness" and "divided psyche" mean nothing to somebody who hasn't experienced some form of psychopatholgy, and neither do terms like "unconscious desire" or, therefore, "repressed desire" or, therefore, "repression."

Henceforth, we'll use the term "SAP" to refer to a person afflicted by psychopathology, and we'll use the term "SNP to refer to a person not afflicted by psychopathology. (SAP: (s)omeone (a)fflicted by (p)sychopathology. SNP: (s)omeone (n)ot afflicted by (p)sychopathology.)

Also, delusions aren't as nuanced as sane beliefs. Where the sane person sees platonic affection, the insane person sees sexual ardor. Where the sane person sees people with differences of opinion, the delusive person sees two people who want to kill each other. The madman's mind is infantile. The infant's mind paints in black and white; the adult's, in pastels. For the most part, the infant's monochromatic intellectual pallete is a consequence of the fact that his mind hasn't matured. But up to a point, it's a consequence of the fact that, unlike the non-infant, he isn't an arch-rationalizer, who smothers obvious truths in disclamatory balderdash.

Maturation involves the implementation of repressions, and regression therefore involves their removal. The SAP has two sets of propositional attitudes – those belonging to the part of him that hasn't undergone regression, and those belonging to the part of him that has. To outgrow a belief or desire isn't to cease to have it; it is for it to cease to be operational. (We will establish this in Chapter 14.) To that X doesn't want to have sex with his mother is not to say there is no such desire anywhere in X's mind; it is to say that, if there is such a desire, it isn't embedded in X's psychological architecture in such a way that there is any chance that X will act on it. For these reasons, there is a good chance that a given SAP's psychopathologies will sometimes express themselves in his consciousness in a relatively undisguised form.

Let us put these points into a broader context. People aren't disorganized heaps of thought. (In this context, "thought" covers every kind of mentation.) People are organized, non-heaps of thought. (More precisely, they are the structures underlying such non-heaps.) A given person's thoughts are organized in two ways. They are organized vertically. (Some are higher up than others in the person's thought-hiearchy. In other words, some are more likely than others to be acted on or to be seen action-relevant.) And they are also organized horizontally. (Given two thoughts, neither subordinate to the other, it is determined how the one bears on the other.) In SNP's, non-operational thoughts are unconscious. In SAP's, they are sometimes conscious. The legacy of many a non-operational propositional attitude is a muted, nuanced version of itself. At the age of six months, one has physical affection for one's mother. At the age of 30, one's affection for her is purely platonic. At age two, one believes that one's father is superhuman. At age 30, one believes that he is a decent enough fellow, but nothing more. A person isn't conscious of propositional atttitudes that he has superceded; he is conscious of what is operational, not of what isn't, and what a person has superceded is by definition non-operational. A person must therefore regress to be conscious of superceded propositional attitudes; and he must therefore regress to be conscious, at a given time, of a propositional attitude that is currently operative and also of any one of its no longer operative forefathers. By the same token, if one has regressed, one is inevitably conscious of at least some pair of propositional attitudes whose members include one that is currently operational and one that used to be operational but is no longer. Anyone who one has regressed is, tautologously, a SAP. Thus, there are two reasons why SAP's, and SAP's alone understand statements like: "at some level, every body wants to have sexual relations with his mother." SAP's can appropriately contextualize such statements. A SAP can be conscious of a desire within himself that is not of himself – a desire that is within himself, but not his self. Only a SAP, consequently, can appropriately contextualize seemingly barbaric statements like "boys want to have sexual relations with their mothers and to kill their fathers." Only SAP's experience non-operatiional desires. Only SAP's are acquainted, in the Russellian sense of the word, with such desires. We've seen that, where certain kind of mental entities are concerned, knowledge-by-acquaintance sometimes coalesces with knowledge-by-description. Non-operational propositional attitudes define one such class. Statements alleging the existence of non-operational, unconscious propositional attitudes form the core of any psychodynamically oriented theories of the mind; and if such a theory is ever right, i one must be, or have been, an SAP to understand the mind.

To understand the mind, one must understand psychpathology. (We have already explained why this is so.) To understand psychopathology, one must either be or have been a SAP. We have thus justified our claim that one must have experienced psychopathology to be a competent psychoanalyst.

But this claim must be qualified. Nobody is entirely free of psychopathology. Everyone is a SAP. In the argument just present, statements of the form "if a person is entirely free of psychopathology lack characteristic K" must be interpreted as having the form "to the extent that a person is psychopathology-free, he lacks K."

Given the fact that no one is psychopathology-free, there is another, more significant respect in which the just-stated argument must be qualified. If everyone is a SAP, then, it would seem to follow, everyone has had the sorts of pathology-related experiences that one must have to be a competent psychoanalyst. But not everyone has had such experiences. There are two reasons why the last statement (the one preceding this one) is compatible with the second to last statement.

First, even though everyone is a SAP, most people's psychopathologies are sufficiently mild that their conscious derivatives are not recognizable as such derivatives; they blend in too well – or, given a modicum of rationalization, can be made to blend in too well – with non-pathological mentation.

Second, in cases where a person's condition is severe – more severe, indeed, than it has to be for him to have experiences of the relevant kind – that person is likely to have erected defenses against his own pathology that are so heavy-duty that no symptomatic expression of his condition can enter his consciousness except on the condition that it be distorted beyond all recognition.

The first point is self-explanatory. The second is not, and it must be clarified. Where many a pathology is concerned – and the pathology may be either somatic or psychological – the afflicted party suffers more from his defenses against his condition than from the condition itself: sometimes the pathogen is less a source distress than one's response to the pathogen. People with allergies haver overactive immune-systems; their immune-systems over-react to pathogens that, in and of themselves, would be but mild sources of discomfort. Asthma, allergies, lupus, and arthritis are all ailments that result from over-active immune-systems. Indeed, to have any of these ailments is to have an immune-system that is over-active in some respect. Similarly, mental illnesses themselves are often less function-impairing, and are less a source of distress, than are the defenses erected by the subject against their conscious, symptomatic derivatives. In many cases, what we think of as a mental illness is really the patient's response to a mental illness. People often respond in a decompensatory (maladaptive) manner to mental illness, and what we – and by "we" I am referring to psychiatrists, no less than to others – take to be a mental illness is but the subject's way of maladaptive, but not necessarily pathological, response his condition. And what we think of as psychological health is its antithesis: the subject's condition is so pathological as to have severed the pathways connecting his actual and his conscious selves.

We have justified our claim that

(a)   One must have experienced psychopathology to understand psychopathology, and one must understand psychopathology to understand sanity.

Right after first making that claim, we qualified it, saying that:

(b)   One cannot be a competent psychoanalyst if one's psychological condition is excessively pathological.

There are three points – or collections of points, rather – that we must make before we can justify this claim. We will refer to these points, or point-collections, as "(A)," "(B)," and "(C)."

(A) There are two kinds of mental illnesses that are relevant to this context: those that afflict the ideation mediated by one's psychological architecture, and those that afflict that architecture itself. Obsessive-compulsive disorder and schizoaffective disorder are examples of the first category, and psychopathy (to be distinguished at all costs from psychosis) and sociopathy belong to the second. Ironicaly, sociopaths and psychopaths are often taken to paradigms of sanity, and also of moral rectitude, even though sociopaths and psychopaths differ in fundamental respects from mentally healthy people, whereas those suffer from OCD and schizophreniz do not so differ and yet are universally recognized as being mentally ill. The obsessive-compulsive and schizophrenic are ill by virtue of being too human: distinctively human characteristics over-represented in them. (These claims just made will be justified in the present section, and their meanings will be made clear. The claims that are about to be made will neither be justified nor clarified until Chapter 16.) The sociopath and psychopath are ill by virtue not being human enough: the psychological architecture of such a person is, in fact, not that of a human being. (In this context, I will henceforth use the term "psychopath" to refer to psychopaths and to sociopaths.) What is distinctive about human beings – what separates us from animals – is that we have values. We self-evaluate; we understand our actions in terms of ideals. The psychopath has no values, and he therefore doesn't have a distinctively human psychological architecture. The psychopath's intellect is that of a human being, but he still isn't psychologically human. If an otherwise normal shark had the cognitive acumen of a human being, its psychological architecture would be that of a shark; it would not be that of a person. If such a creature's mind were placed in a human body, it would be able to convince most actual humans that it was one of them. But it wouldn't be one of them. Such a creature's psychological architecture would coincide with that of the psychopath.

In any case, in this section we will focus exclusively on system-internal psychopathologies; and for this reason it is of no importance in the present context that we have not as of yet so much as defined the terms "socioopath" and "psychopath," let alone provided any evidence in favor of the bold claims just made. What is of importance in this context is that people suffering from system-internal mental illnesses are structurally identical with mentally healthy people.

This doesn't mean that system-internal psychopathologies, such as OCD, have no effect on the structures of the psyches of those suffering from them. Like all other system-internal ailments, OCD involves a disfigurement of one's psychological structure. But an obsessive-compulsive's psychological structure is to that of a normal person what an ordinarily healthy person with a broken rib is to a healthy person none of whose ribs are broken. The sociopath is to a mentally healthy person what a person whose skeleton has liquefied is to a person whose skeleton is normal, and the psychopath is to a mentally healthy person what a person who never developed a skeleton to begin with is to a normal person.

Thus, in saying, as we often will, that OCD is a "disfigurement of psychological structure," we are not saying anything incompatible with the contention that OCD is a system-internal ailment. A hair-line fracture is a disfigurement of an otherwise healthy skeleton; it is thus "internal" to a healthy skeletal structure and could be described as a "structure-internal" condition. Osteoperosis, on the other hand, is not system-internal. It involves a disintegration of one's skeleton as a whole, as opposed to a localized fissure in an otherwise intact skeleton, and it is therefore a systemic ailment.

(B) (a) and (b) are perfectly compatible. One cannot be healthy if one does no exercise at all, and one cannot be healthy if one exercises 18 hours every day. Similarly, a competent psychoanalyst must himself have experienced some psychopathology, but he must also not be a psychological wreck.

Everyone has witnessed the overt behavior of mentall unwell people. But that means nothing: everyone has witnessed the overt behavior of reptiles; but no one would say for that reason that anyone understands reptile psychology. And to the extent that witnessing the overt behavior of a mentally ill person does apprise a mentally healthy person of the nature of mental illness, it is because their condition differs but minutely from ours. To be sure, those afflicted by mental illness tend for that reason to suffer from gross functional impairments, and they behave in ways that are radically discordant with societal norms. But minute structural differences between objects are often reflected by vast functional differences between them. (If A is the fastest and, in every other respect, best car in the in the world, and B is exactly like A except that one of the wires in B's battery has been severed, B will be as hypo-functional as A is hyper-functional.) Our contempt for the insane is the contempt former addicts have towards those still struggling with addiction.

(C), (a) is ambiguous, and even though one of its disambiguations is a tautology, and therefore needn't be defended or even stated, its other disambiguation is a non-tautology; and since the second disambiguation is both true and counterintuitive, it must be both stated and justified. (a) is a tautology if "excessively pathological" is means "too pathological to be a competent mental illness." But that isn't how that expression is usually taken, and it isn't how it is to be taken here. In this context, it is to be taken in the way that it is ordinarily taken: one is "excessively" mentally ill if one's condition makes one unable to work or have meaningful ties with others.

Psychopathology is extremely widespread. Indeed, no one is entirely free from it (with obvious, and obviously irrelevant, exceptions, e.g. people who are in vegetative comas). Many a person's ignorance of psychopathology, and of the facts about mental health in terms of which pathological deviations from it are to be understood, is a consequence of that person's having blinded himself to his psychopathologies. The reason why a competent psychoanalyst may seem sane is that he really is sane, the only relevant difference between him and his equally sane, psychoanalytically incompetent counterpart being that, whereas the latter has hidden his disturbances from himself, the former has not. Everyone is to some degree afflicted by psychopathology. But a person's psychopathologies must be uncommonly severe if their effects on his conscious ideation and his behavior are to be recognizable as pathological. If a person's psychopathologies fall "within normal limits," their effects on his life are likely to escape his notice, there being two quite distinct reasons for this: first, those effects are insignificant and therefore too small to notice; second, those effects resemble, or are easily made to resemble, their non-pathological counterparts. Folk-psychology enables people to smooth over defect-based discontinuities in their thought and conduct. (Sometimes those defects are based in pathology. Usually, their roots are more ignominious, being rooted in cowardice, hypocrisy, incompetence, or some other form of weakness that, not being pathological, cannot be dissociated from the subject's identity.) It does this by availing him of many a believable falsehood on the basis of which he can construct a belief-system about himself, and about humanity in general, whereby the apparent similarities between the pathological and non-pathological of his life are taken for actual identities.

So much for preliminaries. There are at least two reasons why (b) is true. First, being damaged makes one incompetent; to the extent that a person is psychologically damaged, he isn't good at anything. To be sure, there are very damaged people who are exceptionally competent in some particular area; such a person might be a great composer or mathematician. But to the extent that a mentally ill person is a good composer, it's only because his psychopathologies haven't corrupted his compositional abilities. (I suspect that the experience of having been mentally ill has opened up artistic and intellectual vistas that would otherwise have remained closed. But this doesn't mean that being ill is in any way performance-enhancing. A person who has recovered from a debilitating illness knows much that he wouldn't otherwise know; but his illness, while he had it, didn't enhance his abilities.)

There is another, less obvious reason why a competent psychoanalyst cannot be too mentally ill. One cannot possibly be mentally ill without being blind to one's some aspect or other of one's own psychological condition; and for the very reasons that one must know about one's own psychological condition to know about another person's, one is incapable of knowing about another person's psychological condition if one is blind to one's own. A neurotic is somebody who has blinded himself to his own desires and whose desires, therefore, must be discharged as symptoms, instead of as actions. Thus, it is inherent in what it is to be neurotic that one have blinded oneself oneself to one's own psychological condition. The essence of neurosis is defensiveness about facts about one's self that one doesn't want to know about; and a comcomitant of such defensiveness is a resistance to seeing facts about others that resemble the fact about oneself to which one is turning a blind eye. (This is compatible with our assertion that a certain degree of neurosis may be a prerequisite for psychoanalytic competence. Neurosis blinds a man in some ways, and opens his eyes in another.)

Like neurosis, psychosis blinds one to aspects of oneself, but it doesn't do so for the same reason. The neurotic's erroneous views about the external world are reflections of his erroneous views about himself. The psychotic's erroneous views about himself are reflections of his erroneous views about the external world.

Neurosis isn't a disruption of one's understanding of the external world; it's a disruption of one's understanding of the internal world. Disruptions of the second kind are likely to lead to disruptions of the first kind. But disruptions of the first kind are merely derivatives of neurosis and are by no means essential to it.

Smith hates his mother. His hatred of her is legitimate; she does him much harm. Because he won't admit to himself how much he hates her, his hatred is expressed pathologically. After hugging his mother, he showers for hours on end. (Analysis: After coming into contact with her, he must cleanse himself, as he would if he had just fallen into a septic tank.) He is impotent with women with whom he is emotionally intimate. (Analysis: A given woman reminds Smith of his mother to the extent that he is emotionally intimate with her, and he therefore wants to withhold his love from her.) These are but two of the many symptomatic derivatives of his matricidal fury. But he blinds himself to his hatred of her; and when she undermines him, he rationalizes her behavior in some way. "Mom is easily distracted," Smith tells himself. "That's why she misplaced my heart-medication. It wasn't out of malice that she did so. She isn't a bad person." In this way, Smith's ignorance about himself leads to ignorance about the external world. But Smith's misconceptions about the external world are mere by-products of his condition, and are in no way constitutive of it. A related fact is that Smith's neurosis-based misconceptions about the external world are very circumscribed; it's only where facts relating to his mother are concerned that his condition leads to misconceptions about the external world.

Psychosis isn't a disruption of one's understanding of the internal world; it is a disruption of one's understanding of the external world. A disruption of the second kind inevitably leads to a disruptions of the first kind. But disruptions of the first kind are merely derivatives of psychosis and are by no means essential to it.

Psychosis is the juxtaposition of psychological adulthood and psychological infancy, and there is no way to understand the psychotic's condition except in terms of its similarities to the infant's. The infant doesn't distinguish between subject and object. He makes that distinction, and thus ceases to be an infant, only when he discovers that there is a delay between between his coming to have a given desire and that desire's being gratified. (In this context, we will set aside cases where the infant has no caregivers or only has abusive ones.) Initially, an infant's desires are gratified instantenously: no sooner does he cry than his caregivers feed him or change him. (Their needs are absorbed into his.) As time progresses, the infant's caregivers are increasingly slow to minister to his needs. (His needs are absorbed into theirs.) The gap between desire-onset and desire-gratification widens, and it does so in at least four different respects:

(i)   A strictly chronological sense (it gets longer);

(ii) A causal sense (more effort on the infant's part is required to ensure the gratifation of his desires);

(iii) A psychological sense (what the infant wants becomes increasingly unlike what he is given; the latter falls increasingly short of the former; the real falls increasingly short of the imaginary);

and

(iv) A probabilistic sense (his desires are increasingly less likely to be gratified, in however reduced a form, after however long a wait-period).

In a person's imagination, one's desires are always gratified. In the first phase of infancy, the imaginary and the real coincide: there is no gap between desire-onset and desire-gratification. Psychosis involves a failure distinguish between subject and object; between the imaginary and the real. The psychotic's condition thus resembles the infant's. But the psychotic's condition isn't merely similar to the infant's: it is a continuation of it. The psychological characteristics definitive of infancy are never extirpated; they continue to exist, but have an increasingly subordinate role in one's mental life. In the psychotic, that stratum of mentation has recaptured its lost dominance. But when this happens, the subject's condition doesn't coincide with the infant's. This is because the psychotic's psychological architecture is basically that of an adult.

Even when the psychotic is symptomatizing, his character-architecture is that of an ordinary, healthy adult; psychosis affects the ideation mediated by one's character-architecture, not that architecture itself. And even though, when symptomatizing, a given psychotic's ratiocinative abilities are blunted in some respects, they aren't necessarily blunted in every respect. In fact, it is a possibility that, where at least some artforms are concerned, artistic creation involves mild psychosis. (I say "at least some artforms," as opposed to "all artforms," because I don't believe that what I am about to say is true of musical composition.) If a person can produce literary or visual art, it is by virtue of his having access to strata of mentation that are inaccessible to others; and it is by virtue of his being able to activate a condition of limited psychosis that he has such access.)

In a person who is in the process of becoming psychotic, infantile mentation reaquires its lost dominance. But it doesnt do so cleanly: infantile thought has to compete with non-infantile thought, and mentation of the one kind infiltrates mentation of the other. Someone having a dream isn't for that reason psychotic. The reason: the regression to psychological infancy is too clean; infantile mentation isn't sufficiently commingled with more evolved forms of mentation. Infants aren't psychotic. The reason: infantile mentation isn't to any degree thus commingled. In the psychotic, such commingling has occurred. The fact that psychosis can lead to a loss of self-knowledge is to be understood in terms of this fact, along with three others, these being:

(1)   Infantile thinking is wishful thinking (so far as one's thought is infantile, one sees things as one wants them to be, not as they are);

(2)   Infantile thinking is incompatible with non-infantile thinking (the infant sees his father as superhuman, whereas the adult sees his father as human);

and

(3)   The psychotic, being cognitively mature, has to take special measures to validate his wishful, psychotic thinking, and he must therefore repress those beliefs of his that express the non-infantile part of himself.

To sum up: Neurosis and psychosis both have the consequence that those afflicted by them know less about themselves than they otherwise would. But they have this consequence for different reasons. In the neurotic, ignorance starts on the inside and works its way out: first he is ignorant of himself; as a result, he is ignorant of the world. In the psychotic, ignorance works its way in: first he is ignorant of the world; as a result, he is ignorant of himself.

There is a gap in the argument just put forth, and to make that argument cogent, we must fill in that gap. In doing so, we will draw on points that we will not justify until the next chapter. There are two very different kinds of mental illness. There are those that corrupt the mediated by one's psychological architecture, and there are those that corrupt that architecture itself. We will refer to the former as "system-internal" mental illnesses and to the latter as "systemic" mental illnesses. Neuroses and psychoses are system-internal pathologies. Sociopathy and psychopathy are systemic psychopathologies. The argument just put forth is incomplete, since it hasn't been established that systemic pathologies make one unfit to be a competent psychoanalyst. But it's easy to fill in that gap. Sociopathization is the process whereby one's defenses against self-knowledge rigidify and become impenetrable. The sociopath is therefore somebody whose psychological structure is itself a defense against self-knowledge. (These statements will be clarified and justified in Chapter 15.) It is therefore self-evident why the sociopath cannot be a competent psychoanalyst.

It is for an entirely different reason that the psychopath cannot be a competent psychoanalyst. One doesn't become a psychopath; there is no such thing as "psychopathization." One fails to stop being a psychopath. A psychopath is somebody who never matured past the point where other people existed only as means to his ends. To be a psychopath is to be somebody who sees people as objects, not as subjects. (We will justify this claim in Chapter 15. Given this fact, it is self-evident why a psychopath couldn't possibly be a competent psychoanalyst.

There may be other systemic mental illnesses. (I believe that certain sexual predilections, e.g. pedophilia, fall into this category. Pedophilia isn't reversible. But that isn't because it isn't an illness; it is because it is a systemic, as opposed to a system-internal illness.) But it doesn't have to be determined whether such illnesses exist to know that those afflicted by them couldn't possibly be competent psychoanalysts. Systemic mental illness involves either a wholesale corruption of the structures that mediate thought or a failure for those structures to develop in the first place, and there is thus a sense in which one suffering from such an illness isn't human. Such a person is biologically human, of course. He may also be cognitively human. In other words, his intellect, if measured in any of the customary ways, may be normal or even supernormal. (At the end of this section, I will state what I believe to be the significance of the hedge – "if measured in any of the customary ways.")

There is nothing in the obsessive-compulsive or the schizophrenic that is absent from that of somebody whose psychological condition is one of perfect health. On the contrary, if somebody has OCD or schizophrenia, it's because he has too much of something that present, albeit in smaller amounts, in those who are healthy. In someone afflicted by a systemic mental illness, certain kinds of distinctively human ideation would be altogether absent. Neuroses and psychoses are imbalances, not absences. Systemic-illness are absences, not imbalances. The neurotic is too anxious; that's why he can't leave his room. The psychotic is too in love with her husband; that's why she calls him every two minutes. There is nothing that the psychopath or sociopath feels that others don't; there is nothing that the psychopath or sociopath feels more of than others. But there is much that they don't feel that others do. Those conditions, to the best of our knowledge, marked by curious absences of affect – by gaps in emotional mentation, not by function-impairing surfeits of it.

I would like to clarify previously mentioned hedge ("if measured in any of the customary ways"). The psychopath's intelligence, so far as he has any, has none of the valuative moorings had by a non-psychopath's intelligence, and its ability to function is, in this respect, less conditionalized than is its counterpart in the non-psychopath. For this reason, psychopaths are likely to over-perform on standardized tests, and formalized procedures for assessing intelligence are likely to yield inflated estimations of the psychopath's intellectual capabilities.

What I am going to say borrows heavily from points that won't have been justi-fied, even in outline form, until the end of the book. The statements made in this paragraph are both speculative and dogmatic.

Psychopaths cannot be internally conflicted. To be internally is to have two in-compatible values; psychopaths don't have values and therefore don't have conflicting values. A psychopath may not want to take a given test, but he won't be conflicted about taking it (except in the trivial sense that he may not have made a determination as to whether it is in his practical intererest to take it). The non-psychopath test-taker is capable of internal conflict, and is likely to have mixed feelings about having to take standardized tests. He is likely to question the legitimacy of the institutional forces, and of the values embodied in those forces, responsible for his being obliged to take that test. (In any case, he is more likely to question those forces and values than the psychopath, who, after all, isn't capable of questioning them at all, since he isn't ca-pable of grasping the concept of legitimacy.) The non-psychopath test-taker is likely to be dispirited by the spectacle of the scoliosis-ridden bureaucrat-psychologist who is administering the test and who, long since having submitted to institution-think, as anyone can plainly see, is but a shadow of what he might have been. The psycho-path test-taker cannot possibly have such an involved response to his circumstances. Himself lacking a distinctively human psychological architecture, he has no concep-tion of what it would be to forfeit one's selfhood; and, unlike his non-psychopathic counterpart, he doesn't identify with the gloomy bureaucrat adminstering the test; he doesn't see in that person what he could become. For the psychopath could not be-come that person. That person once had hopes and dreams; he wasn't an amoral "re-flex-machine," to use Cleckley's term. There is nothing a psychopath wants to which he doesn't feel entitled: not having a concept of legitimacy, he can grasp the concept of having a legitimate claim to something – of being entitled to it, in other words – only to the extent that it coincides with the concept of wanting that thing. The depression-case test-administrator clearly doesn't have an unlimited sense of entitlement; he is hobbled by conscience and by a consequent over-deference to rules and regulations.

For reasons discussed in Chapters 10, 14, and 15, emotions embody value-judg-ments. Psychopaths experience rage, greed, and other affect-mediating conditions. Like a bobcat, the psychopath can have intense feelings; but, like a bobcat, he cannot experience emotions. This explains the psychopath's proverbial coldness: the arctic nothingness one sees in the psychopath once his mask of conviviality falls. In any case, the psychopath's ratiocinations, lacking as they do all of the valuative moorings of those of his non-psychopathic counterpart, are likely to be better adapted to the emotionally sterile and artificially circumscribed environments constituted by, re-spectively, the setting in which the test is taken and by the test itself.

7.2 *Neurotics can think, but they can't feel; psychotics can feel, but they can't think.*

This is the essence of the matter. Of course, taken narrowly and literally, it's false. Psychotics are often brilliant. (Newton was probably schizophrenic. Theodore Kaczynski is undoubtedly sczhizophrenic.) And neurotics often have intense emotions. In fact, the essence of neurosis is a surfeit of emotion, albeit unconscious or conscious but inhibited emotion.[246]

But rightly interpreted the italicized statement is true. The psychotic *qua* psychotic sees things as he wants them to be, not as they are, the reason being that, to the extent that he's psychotic, his feelings get the better of his judgment. And the neurotic *qua* neurotic makes excessive provisions for rationality and objectivity and insufficient provisions for emotion and subjectivity. The essence of any neurosis is a conflict between what one values and what one feels; and it's because the subject chooses to give priority to his values that he drives his emotions into the abyss of the unconscious. Those emotions don't go away; they live on, and they need to be discharged. But is it only through a subterfuge that such an emotion can discharge itself; for it cannot do so with the knowledge or consent of consciousness. Therefore, it doesn't have the assistance of one's conscious agency or of the rationality embedded therein. Thus, the discharging of a repressed emotion is unintelligent and non-agential.

Because they fall outside the scope of one's agency, repressed emotions corrupt it. Repressed emotions are typically discharged in the form of conscious ideation or intentional action. Since consciousness won't *knowingly* cooperate with a repressed emotion, the latter must cloak itself in some way if it is to avail itself of the former's assistance. (A repressed emotion is like a non-Marxist government that needs funds and thus pretends to be Marxist, so that the Soviet Union will give it money.) As a result, motivations that are consciously accepted by consciousness become vehicles for ones that are not. Since, under that circumstance, one's conscious intention is subordinate to some unconscious intention, one does a bad job of executing the former. At this point, unless one has a moment of self-discovery, which is unlikely, the person has to rationalize his poor performance. This involves altering his belief-system, his values, and his intentions in a way that validates his failure to carry out his conscious intentions. So repression is by no means innocuous. (That said, a certain amount of repression is *de rigueur*, for reasons that we touched in Section 7.0 of the present chapter and that we will elaborate in Section 15.0.)

Suppose that Smith no longer cares for his wife, and in fact detests her, but desperately wants to believe that he still loves her. His repressed antagonism towards his wife is expressed in his forgetting to pick up milk on the way home, in his giving the shirt she just bought him to a drinking buddy, and so on. If Smith were conscious of his real feelings, he'd discharge them through action – by getting a divorce, or whatnot. But since those feelings are repressed, they are discharged through inaction – through

---

246. See Reich (1945) and Stekel (1949). The best discussions known to me of OCD are found in Freud's case-study "The Rat Man" (Freud (1963)) and in Freud's (1926) book *Inhibitions, Symptoms, and Anxiety.*

failures on Smith's part to do things that he should do. Those failures, in addition to being non-actions, are also unintelligent: by not buying the milk, Smith incurs his wife's wrath, which complicates his life in draining ways. (Now she won't pick him up after his root canal and he'll have to walk home. He would have predicted this, had his rationality not been compromised.)

In giving away the shirt his wife gave him, Smith was driven by two motives: one conscious, the other unconscious. The first: a desire to help out a shirtless friend. The second: a desire to antagonize his wife. So far as the first motive was the operative one, Smith's behavior was agential. So far as the second was the operative one, it was non-agential. So even though it was through an act that Smith discharged his antagonism towards his wife, he did not do so agentially. In giving away his shirt, Smith wasn't expressing his hatred; he was letting it be expressed.

An analogy may help. Brown's dog Fido is exceptionally vicious. Fido mauls somebody every time Brown takes him outside. It is never with the intention of causing someone harm that Brown takes Fido outside. But Brown likes seeing Fido tear chunks of flesh out of hapless pedestrians, and he therefore doesn't adequately restrain Fido. In letting Fido maim people, Brown is gratifying a desire of his. But it isn't through action that Brown is gratifying it. On the contrary, it is by ceding the reigns of agency to another being. Brown represents Smith, and Brown's dog represents Smith's animosity towards his wife. Smith isn't acting on his antagonism towards his wife; he is merely failing to inhibit it.

"Is there really a difference," it will be asked, "between acting on a desire and failing to inhibit it?"

Yes. Intentions are not desires. I know it would be gratifying to punch the police officer who is writing me a ticket; so I desire to do so. I know that it would be contrary to my self-interest to punch him; so I intend not to do so. A desire to do X is a belief that it would be enjoyable to to do X. An intention to do X is a belief that it would be to one's advantage to do it. (In a moment, we will explain why this analysis accommodates the fact people sometimes knowingly act self-destructively.) Smith didn't judge it to be in his self-interest to give away the shirt his wife gave him. But he did know that doing so would be gratifying, and that's why he did it. To the extent that Smith's motivation in giving away his shirt was to antagonize his wife, his behavior was desire-driven, not intention-driven, and it was therefore non agential. He wasn't acting on his desire to antagonize his wife. It would be closer to the truth – but still false – to say that it was acting on him. Nothing was acting. A person's inhibitory mechanisms are like a damn. In Smith's case, there was a hole in the damn, and water passed through it.

It's one thing to say that there are unconscious desires; it's another to say that there are unconscious intentions. Unconscious desires clearly exist. But could there be such a thing as an unconscious intention? Is the concept of such a thing a coherent one? Some would say that, in giving his shirt away, Smith's behavior was driven, or at least could have been driven, by an unconscious intention to antagonize his wife. Supposing that such people aren't simply failing to distinguish between desires and intentions, are they right?

Yes. Situations like the following are commonplace. Under hypnosis, X is told that, after coming to, he must snap his fingers whenever he hears somebody say "happy birthday," and he's also told that, after coming to, he will not consciously remember being given this directive. X does as he's told. When asked to explain his behavior, X doesn't: "I can't." No matter how intellligent or rational X might be, X inevitably rationalizes and is utterly convinced by his own rationalization, even though there is no conceivable way to legitimate such bizarre conduct.

X's finger-snapping is intention-driven; it is a form of action. (This doesn't mean that it is X who is performing the action; it is compatible with the supposition, and with the negation of the supposition, that there are different centers of agency within X's mind.) To the extent that Smith's behavior expresses rancor towards his wife, it's because of a lack of resolve on his part. Smith is simply failing to inhibit a desire. That isn't what's going on in X's case. People have to take measures from preventing their hostile impulses from spilling over into their actions. People don't have to take measures to avoid snapping their fingers when they hear the words "happy birthday."

Thus, some actions are driven by unconscious intentions, just as Freud said, and the concept of such an action is therefore a coherent one.

There is an interesting difference between Smith's behavior and X's. Smith's act is rationalization-driven. It's an act of hate that he is able to perform only because he has convinced himself that it's an act of kindness. X's behavior isn't rationalization-driven. X's explanation for his behavior is a rationalization, and is therefore corrupt, but that behavior itself, though inane, was pure.

These points suggest that, when behavior is corrupt, it isn't by virtue of having unconscious determinants, but by virtue of having non-agential determinants. X's behavior involves a bifurcation of agency, but not a forfeiture of it. Smith's behavior involves a forfeiture of agency. Thus, Smith's behavior is corrupt, whereas X's is not.

We said that an intention to do X is a belief that it is in one's self-interest to do X. "But that is brazenly false," it will be said, "given that people smoke, drink, eat junk food, and otherwise diminish themselves."

In Chapter 11, we saw that there are two kinds of beliefs: egocentric and non-egocentric. A belief of the first kind represents an attempt to understand the world in terms of a cognitive map of which one's own self is the point of origin. A belief of the second kind represents an attempt to understand the world in terms of a cognitive map in which no person or thing occupies a privileged position. Egocentric beliefs have non-egocentric counterparts, and they are likely to conflict with those counterparts. (Up to a point, the purpose of education, of both the epistemic and moral kinds, is to integrate these two bodies of beliefs.) The egocentric part of me believes that I'm entitled to drive drunk, since, relative the corresponding egocentric map, I'm the center of the universe; the corresponding non-egocentric belief is that I am not entitled to drive drunk, since, relative to the corresponding map, I'm just another motorist. All sapient creatures have egocentric cognitive maps. Human beings also have non-egocentric cognitive maps, and in this respect we are unique among terrestrial beings.

Non-egocentric cognitive maps constitute a relatively superficial part of our psychological endowment. It not only makes perfectly good sense to suppose that a person might lack such a map: many people do lack them, and everybody's non-egocentric map tends to collapse into his egocentric map. (People rationalize. They make special exemptions for themselves. To rationalize is to represent an egocentric belief as a non-egocentric belief.) Because a person's egocentric cognitive map is so deeply rooted in who he is, it isn't easily changed, and it is therefore slow to respond to new information. To be sure, people can and invariably do integrate much of the knowledge they acquire into their egocentric cognitive maps. What one learns is often incorporated into the mechanisms mediating one's affective and involuntary ratiocinative ideation. But a person's cognitive map would be a weak reed if it were too responsive to changes in his belief-system. Instincts are beliefs that have stood the test of time. Beliefs that one acquires during one's lifetime are very likely to be false. A person's cognitive map is of no use to him if it isn't stable, and it isn't stable if it's too quick to respond to changes in his belief-system. A person's egocentric cognitive map is rigid and parochial. By the same token, it's stable and reliable. A person's non-egocentric cognitive map is flexible and objective. By the same token, it's mercurial and unreliable. The part of you that wants to eat that 5th piece of cheese cake is the egocentric part of you. That part of you believes that it's in your interest to have that piece of cake. It has that belief because it actually would have been in the interest of your simian ancestors to have it, and your egocentric cognitive map is rooted in ancestral, as opposed to personal knowledge.

Supposing that A is an on act on the part of some person P, A is a weak-willed act (in other words, it is "akratic" or "incontinent") if two conditions are met. First, P has a non-egocentric belief to the effect that doing A is not in his self-interest and an egocentric belief to the opposite effect. Second, the intention driving A is identical with the latter belief.

Let us end this section by tying up some loose ends relating to the distinction between neurosis and psychosis.

Medical authorities no longer use the term "insane," and they are right not to use it. That term refers both to neurosis and psychosis, and its use therefore obscures the distinction between those conditions. But that distinction mustn't be obscured. Neurosis is the antithesis of psychosis. Neurosis is the result of an overdevelopment of the intra-psychic barriers that organize beliefs and affects. The neurotic is hobbled by the fact that the flow of information within his mind isn't sufficiently free. Psychosis is the result of a crumbling of those same barriers, and the psychotic is hobbled by the fact that the flow of information within his mind is too free.

8.0 Sartre, Searle (1992), and many other philosophers and psychologists have held that the concept of rationalization is incoherent. Their argument is simple but powerful:

(NR[247]) Let's suppose for argument's sake that it's possible to rationalize.

Rationalizing involves one's driving a belief that one knows to be true into one's unconscious. There is thus a wall within one's psyche that divides it into a conscious part and an unconscious part. The rejected belief is, by definition, in the unconscious part. So one is not conscious of that belief.

But one *is* conscious of it. That belief is unconscious only because one is actively keeping it out of consciousness; but one couldn't do that unless one were aware of it.

So, for some proposition p, the statement

(a) x rationalizes

entails

(b) x believes p

and also

(c) it is not the case that x believes p.

But (b) and (c) are incompatible. Therefore, (a) is incoherent.
Nota bene: (c) is *not* the proposition that:

(c*) x believes not-p.

(b) and (c*) *are* compatible. It is not incoherent to impute incompatible beliefs to someone. But it is incoherent to affirm and deny that someone has a given belief. Wherefore, (a) is incoherent, since it implies some proposition *and* its negation.

NR is fallacious, and we will now identify the fallacy in it.

8.1   Let's start with a point on which both opponents and advocates of NR will agree. Given a belief of yours, *you can choose what to do with it*. You know that if you drive a certain van from point A to point B, you will be given $10,000. Everybody agrees that it's up to you what you do with that knowledge.

Let's suppose that you are heart-broken because your girlfriend dumped you. It's not up to you whether or not to be heart-broken. But it's up to you whether or not to ruminate about your girl-friend situation. It's up to you whether to spend your days doing hard labor, practicing the piano, writing a book, dating other women or otherwise diverting energy away from thoughts about your ex-girlfriend.

A related point is that you can change your life in such a way that you diminish the *importance* of your heartbreak. You can join the army, enroll in medical school, or do anything in which the consequences of failure are extreme and in which it's therefore not an option to wile away the time ruminating about Jenny. In such a

---

247. Short for "no such thing as rationalization."

context, you will, for purely practical reasons, have to give low priority to your wish to ruminate about Jenny.

But there is a deeper reason why such a reprioritization may occur in you: *you* may change. Once you empower your previously feeble mind by learning about medicine, you may come to value intelligence; you may come to be attracted only to intelligent women and to cease to be attracted to not-so-intelligent women, such as Jenny (so we may assume).

There are, of course, other ways in which your values might change. Your highest priority, let us suppose, used to be to have a successful marriage and a large family. What you did for a living was a matter of indifference, provided you made enough to support your family. And because you so highly valued marriage and family, Jenny's ditching you was particularly devastating. The devastation was compounded by the fact that it isn't easy to establish a proto-marital relationship with somebody who has all the virtues necessary to raise your (not yet existent but desired) 11 children. Her ditching you thus gives you a negative incentive to devalue marriage and family.

But it also gives positive you incentives to do so. Many opportunities are available to somebody who just wants companionship that are closed off to somebody who wants to find a good mother for his 11 children. The former can date people with mental illnesses, criminal records, and drug habits. So long as those people are otherwise desirable, such people may be ideal partners. In fact, it may be that their misdeeds are motivated by a streak of iconoclasticism that makes their companionship particularly exciting.

In general, a quality that makes a person unsuitable as a parent may make him hypersuitable as a companion. Samantha has borderline personality disorder (BPD). Because she has BPD, or because she has the character-traits that pathologicize as BDP, she has a refreshingly spontaneous approach to life and an exceptionally vigorous libido. But even though Samantha is therefore highly desirable as a partner, she is not stable enough to be a competent mother of five.

In any case, the change in your life circumstances may have altered your values in such a way that, whereas Samantha was previously someone to avoid, Samantha is now thoroughly desirable. It is unlikely that just one of a person's value should change: if one changes, others must change so as to validate the first change.

Experience not only changes one's values, but also tends to make them more adaptive: values that cannot be fulfilled are replaced with ones that can be fulfilled. Tautologously, one is better off having values that can be fulfilled than ones that cannot. But there is a non-tautologous reason why it is better to have values of the former kind: values that cannot be fulfilled are likely to be rooted in wish-driven, as opposed to fact-driven, beliefs as to how the world works; and to be mentally ill is to see things, not as they are, but as one wants them to be. A sane person could choose to exchange his grim, actual existence for a pleasant, cyber-existence. But such a person would know what he was doing; he would be all too aware of the difference between fact and fiction. If he weren't, he wouldn't need the help of a virtual reality machine to make life

390 Empiricism and the Foundations of Psychology

bearable: his own mind would be enough; it would mediate the requisite pseudo-realities. It isn't living in a dream-world that's insane. What's insane is living in a dream world that one is trying to believe is not a dream world. What makes it pathological to retreat into fantasy is the self-deception involved: one must tell oneself that the fantasy in question is reality. (The person who lives in cyber-reality isn't lying to himself.) This means that one must devalue the truth and, therefore, that one must ultimately deny that there is such a thing as truth. The inhabitant of virtual reality is all too aware of the distinction between fact and fiction; it is because he is aware of it that he chose to live in virtual-reality. The person who retreats into fantasy is in a different category: his very own mind is the virtual reality machine. So he isn't aware of the difference between fact and fiction. He sees them as interchangeable. This means he no longer has the concept of truth and therefore cannot value the truth. This means that he values nothing. To value X is to believe it a truth that X has some virtue or other. If one doesn't value the truth, one can't see X as inherently better than non-X. A person who has no values does not hold himself to standards. Such a person cannot be an agent; nor can he be rational. Such a person, in other words, cannot be a person. In Chapter 15, it is said why one cannot be a person without holding oneself to standards.

8.2 A story will partly clarify the concept of belief-deoperationalization. You are a defense-attorney: the best in your state, maybe even in the country. You have a client who has been accused of murder. Given the information you have, you know he's guilty. You have no direct evidence of his guilt; all the evidence is circumstantial; and your client insists that he's innocent. But you know that there is no reasonable way to reconcile the information you have with the supposition that your client is innocent, and you know that there is no chance that new data will come in that would warrant reconsideration of your position.

But over the years, you've discovered that a foolproof technique for winning cases: *Believe that your client is innocent; believe it as soon as you take the case; believe it when you're not working; and believe it in the courtroom.*[248] If you don't use this technique, you won't see it as *morally* incumbent on you to get your client acquitted. Of course, you'll have a monetary incentive to acquit your client; lawyers who win are *ceteris paribus* more likely to be hired than lawyers who don't. But that isn't much of an incentive: you've already amassed a fortune; and given your sparkling record, you'll never have any shortage of high-paying clients. But if you believe that your client is innocent, and you don't do everything in your power to get him acquitted, you won't be able to live with yourself.

To be sure, in cases such as this one, where it's clear to you that your client is guilty, you don't *really* believe that your client is innocent. But, as soon as you take the

---

248. I do not know this to be true. I suspect that it's false or, if not false, then subject to heavy qualifications. If a lawyer falsely believes his client to be innocent, he won't take the precautions he'd take, such as not putting his client on the stand, that he *would* take if he knew that his client was guilty.

case, you resolve to look at the world through the eyes of somebody who believes that so and so (the client) is innocent.

You thus deoperationalize your knowledge that he's guilty. You do this by playing a game. That game has one rule:

(R)   Your client is innocent *by definition*. It makes no more sense to think of him as guilty than it makes sense to think of some object as heavier than itself. No conceivable piece of information is incompatible with your client's innocence.

Given any datum that others might take to incriminate your client, find a way to reconcile that datum with your unshakeable assumption that your client is innocent. Incriminating testimony and forensic evidence – all lies and fabrications! Your client's innocence is a fixed point; everything else is variable.

Statements of the form "if so and so (the client) is guilty, then…" are in the same category as statements like "if a person with 10 apples has fewer apples than a person with no apples, then…" In fact, statements of the former kind are in an even lower category than those of the latter kind. It's an interesting theoretical question whether conditionals with false antecedents are true, false, or neither. But statements of the form "if so and so is guilty, then…" don't even exist, as far as you're concerned.

While you're playing this game, you still know that your client is innocent. This point must be made clear, lest it be thought that I'm prejudging the very matters being adjudicated. If God asked you "is your client innocent or guilty?", and promised to send you to Heaven or to Hell for all eternity, depending on whether you answered correctly, you would instantly say: "He's guilty."

Freudians and anti-Freudians may disagree as to the likely psychological effects of your playing this game. But there is no denying that you can play it.

8.3   Let's refer to people who believe in your client's innocence as "B's" (short for "believers").

Your intention, it will be recalled, is to view reality as a B does. Bearing this in mind, consider the following passage:

(#)   I am *supposing* that my client is innocent; I am taking that as an axiomatic truth; and I am deliberately going to model all the data that I have in such a way as to validate this supposition.

Question: Would a B ever have thoughts at all like (#)? No. To the extent that you are conscious of the fact that you are playing a game, you are *not* seeing the world as a B does and are thus failing at that very game. To the extent that you are conscious of the

fact that you are deliberately modeling data in a tendentious and non-truth-condu-
cive manner, you are failing at the game.

It is logically impossible that you should play this game perfectly: if you *became* a
B, there would be no more game. But there is otherwise no limit to well you can play
it, and you want play it as well as possible.

You can't just obliterate your knowledge that you're playing a game. But, while
retaining it, you need to marginalize it, so that it affects your ideation not one iota
more than it has to. To this end, you do to your knowledge that you're playing a game
what you are doing to your knowledge that your client is guilty: you deoperationalize
it. This doesn't mean that you shove it into the unconscious. It means that you resolve
to treat it *as though* it were false, *as though* it were a delusion to which you should
give no credence, even though you can't quite shake it off. (In what follows, the word
"belief" will refer both to beliefs and to belief-contents, it being left to the context how
a given occurrence of that word is to be disambiguated.) Let $B_1...B_n$ be your actual
beliefs *minus* your (knowledge-constitutive) beliefs that

(B_{n+1})   you are playing a game

and that

(B_{n+2})   so and so (the client) client is guilty.

To deoperationalize B_{n+1} and B_{n+2}, and to do so in a way that maximizes how well you
play the game, you must act and think *as if* each of B_{n+1} and B_{n+2} is false, and *as if* you
believed:

(S^{249})   My client is innocent

So suppose that S, when conjoined with $B_1...B_n$, entails that you must reschedule
your tennis game with Fred. And suppose that B_{n+1} and B_{n+2}, when conjoined with
$B_1...B_n$, entail that you *don't* have to reschedule your with Fred. You know the truth;
you know that you don't really have to reschedule your match. But you act as if you
do. Your decisions are based, not $B_1... B_n$, B_{n+1}, B_{n+2}, which is your actual belief-set,
but on $B_1...B_n$, S (meaning: $B_1...B_n$ conjoined with S). If $B_1...B_n$, S entail that space is
metrically amorphous, then you speak and act and, to the best of your ability, ideate
in accordance with the supposition that space is metrically amorphous.

8.3.1   Another story will help us move forward. Your boss detests anyone who thinks
that space is metrically amorphous. Your boss is not a good person, and you don't
like your job, or even approve of it. But this job is your only source of income. If you
lost this job, you'd eventually find another source of income. Nothing catastrophic
would happen: you wouldn't be evicted or jailed. But, to subsidize your living ex-
penses during your job-search, you'd have to have to liquidate some assets and live a

---

249. The "S" stands for "supposition."

more austere manner than you're used to. These being the circumstances, your boss asks you whether you think space is metrically amorphous, and he poses this question in a context where your integrity depends upon your being completely honest right then and there. Even though you may *really* agree with your boss, you do not agree with him *relative to the rules of the game*. Relative to those rules, you think he's wrong. And if you tell him otherwise, you are being a weak, dishonest coward. Even if, upon answering your boss's query with a "yes," you don't quite *feel* like a dishonest coward, the reason being that, relative to your *actual* beliefs, you were being honest, you must add the following proposition to your operative-belief set (namely, $B_1...B_n$, S):

(S*)   I am a dishonest coward who, at the moment of truth, chose to forfeit his integrity rather than imperil a temporary source of income.

So your operative belief-set is now $B_1...B_n$, S, S*.

There is only so much control you have over your mind. Even though your operative belief set is $B_1...B_n$, S, S*, your emotional dynamics and your involuntary thought-processes may be hewed to your *actual* belief-set (namely, $B_1...B_n$, B_{n+1}, B_{n+2}). And to that extent you'll have emotions and beliefs that are based on your actual (non-operative) belief-set. But even though it's not up to a person what he feels or believes, it is up to him what he does with those feelings and beliefs.

8.3.2   A short extension of our lawyer-story will show how these points bear on NR. Your intention, it will be recalled, is to see the world as B's do; and to do that, you must deoperationalize your knowledge of your client's guilt. But you cannot *over*-deoperationalize it. There is a difference between you and actual B's, and it's a difference that you mustn't eliminate. Actual B's needn't care one whit whether your client is innocent; their belief that he is innocent may be strictly evidence-based. But even the most biased B has the option of ceasing to believe in your client's innocence. You do not have that option.[250] You *need* to avoid evidence of your client's guilt. Actual B's do not. At the same time, you cannot operationalize your knowledge of your client's guilt. If you do, you lose. So you need to believe in his innocence, while also deliberately avoiding evidence of his guilt *and* knowing just how to do so.

This can be done. By virtue of believing that your client is guilty, you also believe many weaker, less specific propositions. In general, if you believe a given proposition P, you are likely to believe many a proposition that P entails that is weaker than P*. I know that

(a)   Sam plays golf.

---

250. For a while after it became public knowledge, Ted Bundy's girlfriend refused to believe that he was a killer, even though *before* that fact went public she had a wealth of information that was consistent with his guilt. But, in due course, she changed her mind. She accepted the truth.

On this basis I know that

(b)   Somebody plays golf.

On this basis, I know that

(c)   Somebody does some sport or other.

And on this basis, I know that

(d)   Some animate being does something.

You know that so and so (your client) is guilty of the murder with which he is charged. You know who was murdered, and you know when/where/in what manner that person was murdered. You also know that an operationalized belief in your client's guilt has no place in your current psychological integration, at least in so far as the latter coincides with what is conscious and pre-conscious. You know that, if true, the proposition that your client is guilty invalidates sufficiently many deeply entrenched beliefs and operationalized suppositions of yours that the legitimacy of your belief-system is called into question. Your emotions and values are hewed to that belief-system. If it's misguided, so are they. As you know, if a person is stripped of his beliefs, emotions, and values, not much is left over: nothing, in any case, that would be a person, in the psychological sense; nothing that could mediate a self. So you know that, if true, the proposition

(GC[251]) so and so is guilty

invalidates your very self.

Thus, given your knowledge of the time and place of the murder, you know that

(AE[252])   Any evidence concerning so and so's whereabouts at time t [the time of the murder] would be psychologically

devastating to you.

Given the nature of the murder, we may suppose, the murderer had certain very distinctive, very unusual psychopathologies and personality traits. (Let "M" refer to the totality of these characteristics and pathologies.) So you know that, if so and so should turn out to have M, it's likely that GC is true. On this basis you know that:

(DT)   Any evidence to the effect that so and so has M confirms a proposition that, if true, invalidates my belief-system and, therefore, my very self.

---

251.   Short for "guilty client."

252.   Short for "any evidence."

You can thus know exactly what sorts of evidence are likely to lead to *some truth or other* that would destroy you as a person. (Let "E" denote the totality of these various kinds of evidence.) So you know, or in a position to readily learn, that:

(DE[253]) There is some proposition P such that instances of E make P vastly more credible than its negation and such that my welfare is incompatible with P's truth.

You can know DT, AE, or DE without knowing GC.

You mustn't deoperationalize DT, AE, or DE. Otherwise, you're likely to stumble on information that you simply couldn't handle.

Bearing this in mind, let's suppose that you operationally believe each of DT, AE, and DE; and let's continue to suppose that you've deoperationalized GC. If we set aside your non-operational beliefs, focusing exclusively on those that are operational, here is what we find: You know there to be some proposition P such that

(i)   You don't currently know P's identity

(ii)   Were you to discover its identity, you'd sustain serious psychological damage.

(iii) Any evidence relating to so and so's whereabouts at t would greatly increase my likelihood of discovering P's identity, and so would any instances of M.

Given (i)–(iii), you would be mortally afraid of just the sorts of things that confirm GC, but you wouldn't know that it was GC that they confirmed. You would only know that they confirmed *some* truth that would destroy you, were you to know it. Without having any idea what that truth is, you know that your knowing it would ruin you psychologically, and you know exactly what sorts of situations to avoid if you are to remain ignorant of it.

8.3.3   Let us now consider a game exactly like the one you were playing, but with one qualification: the objective is to see the world as a B does *permanently.*

The things you must do to do well at this game are identical with the things you had to do to do well at the other game. Thus, to do well at this game, you must deoperationalize your knowledge of GC, and you must make sure that you *don't* deoperationalize your knowledge of DT, AE, or DE.

Successfully deoperationalizing your knowledge of GC involved deoperationalizing an entire constellation of beliefs and emotions. It involved deoperationalizing any inferences you might have made on the basis of GC. It also involved deoperationalizing the beliefs underlying GC's emotional concomitants; and to that extent deoperationalizing those concomitants themselves.

---

253. Short for "destructive evidence."

This goes to show that it's never just *one* belief that's deoperationalized, but a constellation of beliefs. For a given belief cannot be deoperationalized unless the beliefs, values, and emotions in which it is implicated are deoperationalized, along with at least some of the beliefs, values, and emotions implicated in it. Any given proposition has infinitely many consequences and is itself a consequence of infinitely other propositions. To grasp a given proposition, one must grasp at least some of its entailment-relations. (It isn't necessary, or possible, to grasp all of them.) One couldn't possibly know that Smith likes to read without believing that Smith is animate, that Smith is literate, etc. Among the concomitants of any given belief are other beliefs, and one cannot deoperationalize the first belief without deoperationalizing those other beliefs. And, of course, one cannot deoperationalize those other beliefs without neutralizing *their* concomitants. So deoperationalization, to the extent that it's carried out successfully, involves systemic changes.

8.3.4 "Deoperationalizing a belief," it will be said, "is different from making it unconscious. You deoperationalized GC; you didn't drive it into your unconscious."

Immediately upon being deoperationalized, a belief is indeed conscious. (Let B be an arbitrary deoperationalized belief.) But with the passage of time, B becomes increasingly alienated from the relevant subject's psychological integration, so far as the latter consists of what is either conscious or preconscious. (A person's psychological integration has (pre)conscious and unconscious components. Let's henceforth refer to the (pre)conscious part of a given person's integration as his "pc-integration.") We've seen that deoperationalizing one belief involves deoperationalizing entire networks of propositional attitudes. Obviously these systemic changes don't occur instantaneously. But over time, the subject's psychological pc-integration undergoes the changes needed to validate the deoperationalization of B.

To clarify this last point: B won't *remain* deoperationalized if all of the beliefs etc. that brought it into existence and that it brought into existence are operational. Supposing that P is the proposition the subject believed-true by virtue of having B, it would rapidly become glaringly obvious to the subject that P was true, or, at any rate, was true *if* various other beliefs of his were true. As a result, B would be reoperationalized. (Or – what would come to the same thing – a belief to the same effect as B (viz. one that constituted acceptance of P) would be generated.) So the subject's psyche must undergo many changes if the deoperationalization of B is to hold. And each one of those changes will increase the degree to which B is estranged from the subject's pc-integration.

8.3.5 After a certain point, even if B is still conscious, the subject won't identify with it. It will be "ego-dystonic." Not only will B not be a part of the subject's preconscious integration: that integration will consist of beliefs, and other propositional attitudes, with which B would not fit. (By one's "preconscious integration," I mean the totality of one's access-conscious propositional attitudes and personality traits.) So B, supposing it still conscious, would be innocuous, at least as far as the subject's preconscious-integration is concerned.

What would B *be*? By supposition, B is a belief to the effect that GC. But, so far as the subject is to be identified with his preconscious integration, B, though *in* the subject, is not *of* him; it's part of his mind, but not of his self. So even if B is still conscious and the subject still has it, his *having* it isn't conscious.

These points *mutatis mutandis* make it clear how it is that you can consciously disbelieve GC, while at the same time doing and thinking exactly what you must if you are to avoid consciously accepting GC.

We have thus refuted NR, and we have thereby shown that the concepts of repression and rationalization are coherent.

9.0   I would like to end by discharging an assumption that I made earlier. I said that "everybody agrees that it's up to you whether or not to ruminate about Jenny [the woman who broke your heart]." But not everybody agrees. Many authorities hold you might have an illness that makes it deterministically necessary that you ruminate about her. According to such authorities, people with OCD *have* to ruminate and engage in their rituals.

I cannot agree with these experts. Smith has OCD. Smith is in deeply in love with Jenny. Jenny dumps Smith. Smith ruminates about Jenny – about how great things were when she was with him, about what he could have done to prevent her love for him from dying, etc. Anyone in Smith's position would ruminate to some extent. But, being afflicted by OCD, Smith's ruminations take up an unusual amount of time and are also unusually emotionally charged.

The objector would say that it's not up to Smith whether or not to engage in these ruminations. That's not true. Obsessive-compulsives do what they do, and think what they think, not because they *have to*, but because they know that they will experience intolerable anxiety if they do otherwise. The neurotic deeds of the obsessive-compulsive are quite as voluntary as his, or anyone else's, non-neurotic deeds. The former are differently incentivized from the latter: therein lies the difference. Were it made clear to Smith that he'd be given $1,000,000 for *not* performing any given one of the OCD-related rituals that he'd otherwise perform, he would abstain from performing it. The ensuing anxiety would give him a strong incentive to perform those rituals. But incentivization is not determination.

A related point is that we don't describe epileptic fits or involuntary muscle spasms as "compulsive." A compulsion, in the relevant sense of the word, is a *belief* – one to the effect that one has an obligation to perform some act. But not just any such belief is a compulsion. For a belief to be a compulsion, it is necessary (but not sufficient, for reasons about to be discussed) that it satisfy three additional conditions:

(i)   it is ego-dystonic,

(ii)   it is opposed to some ego-syntonic belief,

and

(iii)   it is sufficiently powerful that, (i) and (ii) notwithstanding, the subject is disposed to acquiesce to it.

We'll see in the next section that there are two very different kinds of compulsions: those resulting from a conflict between one's ego and one's id, and those resulting from a conflict within one's ego. Addiction-based compulsions are of the first kind. OCD-based compulsions, though involving conflicts of the first kind, are themselves of the second kind.

9.1   Those who claim that the obsessive-compulsive cannot help acting as he does are failing to make three distinctions. They are failing to distinguish involuntary behaviors from compulsively performed acts. They are failing to distinguish compulsively performed acts from acts performed under duress. Finally, they are failing to distinguish mind-internal conflict from self-internal conflict.

Being involuntary, epileptic fits are not intention-driven and therefore aren't acts; for an act is an instance of intention-driven conduct. Whereas the epileptic's agency isn't in any way implicated in the behavior mediating his seizure, the the obsessional's agency is implicated in the behavior mediating his ritualistic and otherwise OCD-specific behaviors, and it is his intention to act as he does. So far as his behavior is compulsive, it's because of the kind of intention that drives it; it isn't because no intention drives it.

Compulsive acts must be distinguished from those committed under duress. Coercion isn't compulsion. A man sticks a gun in your face and asks you for your wallet. If you give him your wallet, you are not acting compulsively. You are non-compulsively taking the one course of action that it is rational for you to take under the circumstances.

There is obviously a sense in which addiction-driven behavior is compulsive. One is addicted to heroin; so one must shoot up. But the sense in which the junkie's heroin-use is compulsion-driven isn't identical with the sense in which the obsessional's rituals are compulsion-driven. Earlier we discussed how weak-willed acts are those driven by egocentric beliefs that are opposed to their non-egocentric counterparts. The junkie's egocentric belief is that it's in his interest to shoot up; his non-egocentric belief is that it is not; the first belief determines what he does if he gives into his addiction, and the second belief determines it if he doesn't. The addict's struggle is of the same kind as that of the person who's trying to lose weight but wants to eat desert. The struggle raging within the obsessive-compulsive is not of this kind. In his case, the war is between two non-egocentric value-systems, each of them legitimate.

Smith, an arbitrary obsessive-compulsive, is an extremely talented xylophone player. He wants to be a professional xylophone player; and were he to become one, he'd wake up every morning happy to go to work. But Smith doesn't just want to have a good time. He wants his life to have meaning. Smith wants to make a contribution to humanity.

To be sure, it's one thing to have a meaningful life, and it's quite another to help humanity's lot. It is by virtue of being true to oneself that one's life is meaningful; it isn't by virtue of helping others – unless, fortuitously, it is by helping others that one is true to oneself. And unless one's life is meaningful, it cannot be principled, except in an empty formal sense: the life of a hollowed out husk is not one of principle. (Altruistic robots don't even have lives, let alone ones of principle.) Being an intelligent authentic person, Smith is (in some way, and at some level) aware of these heterodox truths. But Smith is a young man and hasn't had a chance to mature, either as a thinker or as a person; and, as of yet, he is therefore too limited, both intellectually and characterologically, to understand how he could accept such heterodoxies without either disrupting his own psychological integration or alienating himself from the social institutions on which his livelihood and also his sense of self depend. Smith cannot articulate and justify the heterodox truths underlying these orthodox falsehoods. But has no trouble articulating or justifying those falsehoods themselves, thanks to years of social education. Therefore, his quasi-acceptance of these false orthodoxies has no difficult wresting the reigns of agency from his genuine acceptance of those true heterodoxies.

Thus, even though Smith's intuitions tell him that his life will be meaningful if, and only if, he becomes a xylophonist, he cannot act on those intuitions with a clean conscience. This doesn't mean that he is to no degree able to act on them. But it means that, if he does act on them, there are at least two sense in which those actions won't do justice to those intuitions. First, those actions won't be driven by a firm belief on Smith's part as to the legitimacy of what he is doing, and they will therefore be lacklustre, thus failing to discharge Smith's desire to play the xylophone. Second, the conceit embodied in those actions will be to the effect that Smith's desire to be play the xylophone, being nothing more than an itch that should be scratched, should be defused, not cultivated. So even if Smith acts on that desire of his, it isn't whole-heartedly, and it is therefore in a way that validates the culturally-sanctioned conceit that his playing the xylophone is nothing more than empty self-indulgence. Given that Smith could achieve greatness as a xylophonist, and given also that there is no other way that he could achieve greatness or even find fulfillment, this conceit, though culturally sanctioned and likely to have few opponents, is particularly damaging to Smith.

And because it's damaging to Smith, it's damaging to humanity itself. Even though Smith will be helping humanity by ladling out soup at the homeless shelter, he'll also be hurting it. Indeed, he'll be doing more to hurt it than to help it. Each of the indigents Smith feeds will see in Smith somebody whose dreams died long ago, and so will every other misfortunate who, happening to stare into his Smith's vacant eyes, sees the nothingness behind them. Smith's very existence will therefore send the message that man's lot is to be the walking dead, along with the related message that those who pursue their dreams are stunted and, instead of deserving encouragement, should be stowed away in an asylum, safely kept out of the public eye. Smith's listless soup-kitchen behavior will reinforce commonly held but incoherent and growth-antagonistic notions. (*The only meaningful life is an unhappy one. Only the living dead have meaningful lives. He is a wretch who isn't still-born.*) Smith's listless soup-kitchen benefactions dispirit the people he meets every day, thus throwing cold water on their willingness to work and draining the economy of ten times as much vigor as his acts of charity bequeath to it. So even though, for the reasons earlier stated, there is a difference between between living a meaningful life and living a socially good life, those two sorts of lives tend to converge: for by living meaningfully, one radiates vitality, thus sending the message that this life is a good one and worth making the most of. One sends the opposite message by living altruistically, unless, in so living, one is being true to oneself.

Given Smith's earnest, young man's belief that his parents and teachers have his best interest at heart, and his equally jejune belief that they both know what it is in his interest to do and want him to do it, it is no wonder that Smith has been slow to give due credit to his suspicions as to the veracity and also, more darkly, the sincerity of the orthodoxies propounded by these standard-bearers; and given how much ugliness he'd have to trudge through to do so, it is no wonder that he hasn't yet so conceptualized and otherwise refined those suspicions as to enable them take a firm and uncontested hold of the reigns of agency. Smith is the quintessential obsessive-compulsive. His heart is at war with his head. What his heart believes is true. What his head believes is not. His head prevails for now. But its tenure is insecure: since it's on the wrong side of the Smith's psychological architecture, Smith must be subdued if it is to retain its hegemony. And until Smith is duly subdued, his heart will express itself in counter-hegemonic ways. Smith's actions won't be pure. His conscious intention will be to do one thing; his unconscious intention will be to do the opposite. The result will be a failure to do either properly. Smith's commitment to the aspirations to which he has consciously dedicated himself will be subject to constant disruptions. He doesn't feel like working. Or he does feel like working, but he has writer's block. Or he doesn't have writer's black, but he's too torpid to articulate the thoughts that are coming to him, since half his energy is spent fighting a nagging feeling that what he's doing isn't what he should be doing.

OCD is a war between the head and the heart. The heart has the right beliefs; the head has the wrong ones. The head calls the shots. The heart follows. But the heart, doubtful of the head's legitimacy, takes every available opportunity to stymie the head's intentions. Its legitimacy under constant attack from the heart, the head begins to question its own legitimacy, a likely result being a lack of enthusiasm for its own designs and a consequent failure to execute them properly. The head takes defensive measures. Despite – or because of – the illegitimacy of its own plans, the head becomes maniacally dedicated to carrying out those plans, and it becomes particularly unwilling to question even the slightest detail of its intended way of doing so. For such questioning would activate the head's doubts as to the legitimacy of those plans themselves. Thus, to suppress the constant, deprecatory whisperings of the heart, the head becomes rigid, authoritarian, and fanatical. Hoping to convince itself, and others, that it was right to adopt these traits, the head represents its fanaticism as "discipline" and "integrity." The superficiality of the subject's integration becomes apparent the moment he is meaningfully challenged: he flails like an infant, and there is no pettiness to which he won't resort, and no lie he won't tell to defame his detractors. And the spuriousness of the subject's "fanatical dedication" to his craft is revealed in his complete lack of interest in any information that might actually help him ply his trade competently: he has ears for nothing that warrants any modification of any work that he's done, his interest in the truth long since having given way to a desperate, no-holds-barred attempt to cling to an increasingly splintered, positive self-concept.

But the conflict between the head and the heart needn't end like this; the heart can prevail. It takes time for one's defensive measures to rigidify; and if the subject truly wishes to live meaningfully, he can choose to eschew those defenses and to adopt, in their stead, measures whose purpose is to compatibilize the subject's integration with the truth, instead of insulating it from it. If the head prevails, the subject's fate is the numb, nothingness of neurotic comfort. At some point in every neurotic's development, he is confronted – probably not consciously – with a choice: "to be or not to be?" To live a comfortable lie or an uncomfortable truth? Some choose the latter. Let us return to our story about Smith, so as to clarify and develop these points.

If Smith's head always prevails, Smith's life will be an empty one. Smith is cut off from his own vital energies as long as, instead of expressing his actual, heterodox beliefs, his actions instead express his orthodox, non-beliefs. By the same token, if Smith's head doesn't always prevail, and his heart assumes its rightful place of dominance, he will have a coherent, stable psychological integration and, therefore, a meaningful life. But before either of these destinations is reached – before Smith either becomes the mask that he's donned or cops to who he and shucks off the mask – there will be a long and bitter struggle. Because of this struggle, Smith will neither be a perfect company man nor a full-blown rebel. He will self-identify as a company man, but that identity of his will be subject to constant disturbances. It will not possible for him to subdue these eruptions of his unconscious through will-power alone. Smith is not fighting an external foe. Nor is Smith fighting an internal foe, such as morphine-addiction, that is illegitimate and in his efforts to extirpate which he can and should enlist all of his resources of character. Smith is fighting a legitimate internal foe, and he therefore isn't able to enlist all of those forces. The battle being fought within Smith isn't a battle between Smith's agency and some other thing. The purpose of the battle is to determine the structure of his agency. The contestants are constituents of an agency that isn't yet fully formed. Thus, if one side definitively prevails over the other, it cannot be strictly on the basis of agency-based tactics, and it must therefore be based on such tactics as are available to a pre-agential, or semi-agential mind. This means that, embodied in those tactics, will be the outlook of a mind that hasn't yet reconciled itself to the fact that it is action, not idle fantasizing, that yields results. It means, in other words, that those tactics will embody the infant's belief in the "omnipotence of thought," this being his belief that, to have it, one has but to want it. Among the derivatives of this

outlook is the belief that symbolic operations, such as ritualistic behaviors, can ac-
complish what, in actuality, are to be accomplished only through action. Convinced of
the omnipotence of his thought-processes, the neurotic believes – at some level – that
he can put his rival out of commission by imagining his rival being hit by a bolt of
lightning. (The "at some level" qualifier is crucial. The neurotic is not psychotic. The
higher strata of his mind are quite as aware as the next person's of the causal structure
of the world. The essence of neurosis is conflict; and the conflict involves two parties:
(i) a sphere of mentation, operative only in the unconscious, that is dominated by the
infantile belief in the equivalence of the thought and the deed; and (ii) a sphere of
mentation, operative in the subject's consciousness, that accepts the reality-principle.
In the case of the psychotic, the first sphere of mentation is conscious. The psychotic's
condition is not one of conflict, between regressed and non-regressed spheres of mentation; it is one in which, precisely because there is no internal conflict, his entire
mind has been engulfed in an infantile, and therefore delusional belief-system.)

The obsessive-compulsive does indeed struggle with all his might against violent and sexual impulses. (The obsessive-compulsive absolutely never gives into such
impulses. (Salzman (1994) states this clearly. So do Freud (1926), Reich (1945), and
Stekel (1949).) He is much too scrupulous and intact to do so.) But this struggle is
merely a consequence, and not the essence, of the struggle that constitutes OCD.
Smith wants to be a xylophonist. And though a deracinated, emptily logical faculty of
his judges that he shouldn't become one, he knows deep down that it's what he must
do. It's only because he can't articulate the grounds for these knowledge-constitutive
beliefs of his that they aren't fully conscious and, therefore, that they don't determine what he does with his life. Smith's stodgy and not entirely well-intentioned parents want him to become a lawyer. He recoils at the thought. But he can compatibilize
the thought of his being a lawyer with the part of his mind that makes decisions on
narrowly logical and social grounds. He cannot thus compatibilize the thought of his
being a xylophonist. But since he knows deep down that lawyering is the wrong path,
he is deeply enraged at his parents. But even though his rage is legitimate, he isn't fully
convinced of that fact. (This is only partly because he can't compatibilize with it the
rigid protocols governing his conscious morality-related thoughts. It is also because
that rage is so anathema to his conscious world view that he has no choice but to but
to repress it.) His compulsive behaviors and endless ruminations are bulwarks against
the violent impulses he has towards these people, whom he is supposed to love and
whom, to a considerable extent, he really does love. But the reason he has those violent impulses is that an evolved, legitimate, non-basal part of himself – a part that, if
allowed to develop, would form the core of a strong and coherent identity – is being
denigrated by these loved ones. So Smith's OCD isn't a war between the higher and
the lower; it's a war between the higher and the higher, subordinate to which are some
skirmishes between the higher the lower.

Addiction: Ego vs. id. OCD: Ego vs. ego.

OCD involves two sapient beings. They're both constituents of the same mind, but they're distinct, and the one is trying to undermine the other. The addict's condition involves only one sapient being, and addiction therefore doesn't involve anything's trying to undermine anything. When an addict gives in to her addiction, it isn't because she fought but lost; it is because she didn't fight. There was no battle to begin with. Addiction-based compulsions represent forfeitures of agency. OCD-based compulsions represent surfeits of agency.

The obsessive-compulsive's behavior isn't just voluntary, but hyper-voluntary. This is a consequence of the nature of struggle at the heart of OCD. OCD is a defensive hypertrophication of agency. The obsessional's attitude towards his own impulses is so hostile – for he regards them as such abominations – that he makes too few concessions to them. As a result, his own feelings become alien to him, and he thus has difficulty drawing on them. (This inevitably sterilizes his libidinal and ratiocinative processes. But it is also likely to enhance the latter, by over-focusing and therefore hyper-charging them. Because of this reallocation of energy, a few select cognitive structures become repositories for the all the energy of which the subject's remaining psychical faculties are being deprived.) So it cannot reasonably be maintained that the obsessional "cannot help" doing what he's doing.

In fact, the exquisite distress of the obsessional lies in the very fact that the behaviors characteristic of his condition are voluntary. If they were involuntary, he could just surrender to them; there would be no anxiety or inner turmoil. But inner turmoil is the very essence of OCD. The afflicted subject's obsessions and compulsions are but ways of managing this turmoil.

The obsessive-compulsive asks: "What sort of person should I be?" The junkie asks: "Should I even be a person?" In giving into heroin-addiction, one is making one's personhood a mere means for somatic gratification. The committed junkie has no internal conflicts at all; any struggles she has are with the external world. The reluctant junkie is indeed struggling. But it isn't a struggle between two sets of values or two spheres of agency. It's a struggle between being an agent and being a non-agent. The junkie's compulsions are mind-internal, but not self-internal.

The obsessive-compulsive's struggle is self-internal, and not merely mind-internal. For his is a struggle between two value-systems and, therefore, between two spheres of agency. That is what explains the exquisitely painful nature of his compulsions. When resisting a compulsion, the force against which the obsessive-compulsive is struggling is itself agential. Two agents are battling within him. The junky isn't battling another agent. She's battling a non-agent. Her own agency isn't fully formed, and it's therefore unusually vulnerable to sub-agential urges. One is lured, but not compelled, by such urges. Such urges don't compete for the reigns of agency. They merely bid one to let go of those reigns. "To be or not to be." That's the question for the junkie. Not "who is to have the reigns of agency?", but "is anyone to have them?" For the obsessive-compulsive, it's the other way around. If the obsessive-compulsive gives into a compulsion, it's because one agent overpowered another; it isn't because the obsessive-compulsive forfeited his agency. If the junkie gives into her craving, it's because she forfeited her agency, not because it was overpowered.

The points just made enable us us substantiate some of this book's main contentions and also to adjudicate an age-old dispute between opponents and proponents of Freud's thought; and we are therefore justified in briefly suspending our discussion of ODC. (In what follows, "conscious" is short for "conscious or preconscious.") Supposing that subject S has belief B, there are three senses in which B can be unconscious. (i) S doesn't know how to articulate B. So even though S has no emotional reason not to consciously embrace B, he cannot do so. This robs B of its ability to govern S's conduct. Since S cannot articulate B, he cannot justify it to himself; and B's voluntary ratiocinative processes therefore don't give adequate weight to B. One's conscious decisions are precipitates of one's conscious thoughts. Therefore, B doesn't engage the reigns of agency. (ii) S does not know how to articulate B, and although S accepts B – or wants very much to accept it, since his intuitions urge him to do so – he doesn't consciously know how to justify B. He can't compatibilize an acceptance of B with the canons of reasoning that he consciously accepts. (Those canons may govern either logical or moral reasoning.) Therefore, even though he knows deep down that B is correct, S does not consciously accept it. (iii) B is genuinely unconscious. The problem isn't that S can't articulate B; nor is it that he can't justify it. It's that he isn't aware of B's existence. If B is unconscious in this last sense, let us say, following Freud, that that it is "dynamically" unconscious. If B is conscious in the first sense, let us say that it is "articulation-unconscious," and that it's "justification-unconscious" if it's unconscious in the second sense. (Since the distinction between articulation-unconsciousness and justification-unconsciousness isn't important in the present context, we will sometimes lapse and use the term "articulation-unconsciousness" to refer to both.)

Some authorities hold that all unconsciousness is unconsciousness is articulation-unconsciousness. To be sure, articulation-unconsciousness is an extremely important kind of unconsciousness. We've argued at length that it's what we can articulate, not what we know, that distinguishes us from the brutes. Non-agents become agents, we have argued, by personalizing subpersonal knowledge – that is, by transferring it from the supersonal realm of mentation to the personal realm – and, we have further argued, knowledge is personalized by being articulated. So we can't be faulted for denying the existence articulation-unconscious knowledge, or of underestimating its significance.

But articulation-unconsciousness isn't the only kind of unconsciousness. There is such a thing a dynamic unconsciousness, and it is distinct from articulation-unconsciousness. To be sure, an idea is more likely to be dynamically unconscious if it's articulation-unconscious, and giving a person a way of articulating a belief of his sometimes suffices to make him conscious of it. But the operative word is "sometimes." A person can articulate a belief that he consciously rejects but unconsciously accepts. But not only can a person articulate such a belief: he can justify it, and do so properly – in other words, he can identify the reasons why that idea is correct. (When doing this, he thinks he's making a false idea seem true.)

Also, there are two different senses in which learning how to articulate an idea makes it conscious. Learning how to articulate a given idea may constitute its becoming conscious. In other words, it may be that there was nothing to its being unconscious other than the subject's not knowing how to put it into words. On the other hand, putting it into words may precipitate a series of events that undoes emotional resistances that were subduing it. If articulating a belief is the very same thing as its becoming conscious, it was merely articulation-unconscious. If articulating a belief merely leads to its becoming conscious, it was dynamically unconscious.

Even if the points just made are false, they are not incoherent; wherefore, contrary to what many an anti-Freudian says, it isn't an a priori truth that all unconsciousness is articulation-unconsicousness. And those points are in fact empirically correct. It would be silly to say otherwise; and it would therefore be inauthentic pedantry to say, however correctly, that researchers have established these points.

Let us resume our discussion of OCD.

There are methods of treatment that are based on the conceit that, indeed, the OCD-sufferer can't control his behavior and isn't responsible for it. But should it come as a surprise that, because of such methods, obsessive-compulsives are using their affliction as an excuse to abrogate personal responsibility? And, sadly, so far as such techniques have any effect at all, their effect is indeed to give OCD-sufferers an excuse to succumb to forces that they could control and that ruin their lives unless they control them.

In the process of researching OCD and the methods of used to treat it, I have had occasion to attend many group-therapy sessions for obsessive-compulsives. (Following Freud and Stekel, I will henceforth refer to people with OCD as "obsessive-compulsives.") The therapist running each such sessions urged its participants to view themselves as the passive victims of a purely somatic disorder. In this way, he implicitly urged his patients to relinquish control of their own psychological well-being, and he reinforced this implicitly transmitted message with explicit exhortations to that same effect.

Each such session left me feeling completely appalled, and in each case that reaction of mine had more than one source of justification. First of all, setting aside those session-attendees who didn't talk at all, each attendee made it clear that his condition was mediated by emotional conflict, and and seldom left much doubt as to the nature of that conflict. Each said that his life-situation made it impossible for him to discharge sexual or aggressive urges that that he had; and each said that the ideation accompanying his ritualistic behaviors consisted of fantasies in which he gratified those urges. Many an attendee reported that similar fantasies mediated his obsessions.

In some cases, one of the attendees would describe ideation that didn't manifestly consist of a sexual or violent fantasy on his part; and in some cases, consequently, the ideation in question had to be decrypted. But was usually obvious how to do so. Two examples come to mind. One attendee talked about how, while at the funeral of somebody he loved, or supposedly loved, he was stricken by the belief that not enough blood was flowing into his foot and that, unless he repeatedly jumped up and down, thereby improving his circulation, his foot would have to be amputated. (Interpretation: He was glad about the death whose funeral he was attending, that being why, at the moment the casket was being lowered into the ground, he had an express glee, by jumping up and down.) Another talked about how, while listening to his best friend exchange wedding vows with a woman whom he coveted, he was tormented by a sudden need to scratch his genitals. (Interpretation: He wanted to manipulate his genitals, so as to experience sexual gratification and so as to sully the wedding-ceremony by performing a vulgar and hostile act.)

Sometimes a session-attendee would describe OCD-characteristic behavior on his part that wasn't accompanied by any conscious, OCD-specific ideation. But in practically each such case, the behavior in question was itself one of gratifying, albeit in a distorted and symbolic form, some sexual or aggressive urge. (Often the urge was both sexual and aggressive.) That behavior might consist of the subject's practicing his serve for hours on end (this being an act of violently striking a spherical object with a phallic object), or it might consist of his bathing himself for hours on end (and thus doubly stimulating himself by submerging his person in warm liquid while scrubbing body-parts of his).

Each session-attendee explicitly stated that his life-circumstances made it impossible for him to discharge violent or sexual urges that he had. His dissertation-adviser plagiarized a proof of his and then failed his dissertation – but he couldn't do anything about it, since, the academic world being what it is, he would have been black-listed had he so much as made a peep. His girlfriend refused to have intercourse with him, but didn't have any such reservations when it came to his best friend. His boss gave the account to a nephew, instead of to him, even though the nephew was an incompetent drunkard, whereas he had made a fortune for the firm.

And yet the therapist running the session said that this person's obsessions and compulsions were the results of "defective brain-circuitry." His condition didn't have an emotional basis: one mustn't buy in to that all pre-scientific, Freudian claptrap. No – his anterior cingulate cortex was over-active, and that was the end of it. (The therapist didn't acknowledge the fact that every psychological occurrence has a somatic basis and that, although the obsessive-compulsive's anterior cingulate cortex is indeed over-active, that means only that distinctive psychological facts have distinctive physiological implementations. Do you think that Gauss's brain would have exhibited no peculiarities? What about Shakespeare's? Would none of their brain-centers have been over-active? What about their anterior cingulate cortexes? How sure are we that they wouldn't have as active as those of the session-attendees?)

The subject shouldn't analyze himself, the therapist said, or (though the therapist didn't put it this way) he should do so only to the extent that platitudinizing about his condition counts as self-analysis. In fact, the therapist said, the subject shouldn't change his life-circumstances at all, except in so far as they involved his symptomatizing. He shouldn't blame his homicidal girlfriend for his condition. (When the subject pointed out that she was now in Federal lock-up, having been convicted of aggravated assault and battery, the group-leader knowingly smiled and said: "Let's not play the blame-game, shall we?") Nor should he cast aspersions on his kindly dissertation advisor, whose act of 'plagiarism,' if you want to call it, was really a way of disseminating the subject's insights to the scientific community, and who, in failing the latter's dissertation, was really trying to help him, by challenging him to write a better dissertation (even though the first one couldn't have been all that bad, given that the dissertation-advisor considered it worth copying verbatim and publishing under his own name). Instead of tilting at windmills, the group-leader advised, the patient should recondition himself. Instead of spending his days washing his hands, he should spend them shaking hands with homeless people. And to solidify the gains made through his self-conditioning, the group-leader added, the patient should take up meditation or otherwise auto-hypnotically induce an extirpation of conscious thought.

Each such therapist used the term "cognitive-behavioral therapy" to describe his method of treatment. The presence of the term "cognitive" does less to describe, than to obfuscate, the actual nature of the technique being implemented, whose behavioristic, anti-cognitive bent could not have been more obvious. To be sure, the methods of treatment involved did sometimes require the patient to make direct, as opposed to behavior-mediated, changes to his habits of thoughts. But the cognitive changes subjects were asked to make were, despite being cognition-mediated, of a reflexive, non-cognitive nature. They were asked to take "time-outs," during which they were to count or visualize a situation that tranquilized them.

In any case, so far as that technique did anything to change its supposed beneficiaries, it was to make them replace one compulsion with another. Instead of compulsively washing their hands, they compulsively shook hands with homeless people.

These therapists could not possibly have been completely blind to the spuriousness of what they were saying. Surely an element of dishonesty was involved, this being one of the reasons these sessions appalled me.

But there was another, darker reason. The ailing individuals who attended these meetings were, without exception, people of considerable intelligence and personal merit. And yet, with only a few exceptions, each such person accepted the inanities espoused by the group-leader and conceded the legitimacy of the latter's injunction that recovery from OCD was to be achieved by forfeiting one's agency, not by exercising it.

It is inherent in what OCD is that those suffering from it are of above-average intelligence and morality. Any given such person's condition involves his taking a draconian, moralistic position with respect to impulses of his that a less scrupulous person would allow to vent themselves. Wrongly seeing such impulses as abominations, the obsessive-compulsive denies them all gratification. Bottled up, they assume gargantuan proportions and grotesque forms. They thus become as abominable as their host believed them to be, and now he really is under a moral imperative to suppress them. But they have become inordinately strong, and his consequently Sisyphusian efforts to suppress them are expressed as OCD-distinctive compulsions.

In a person whose conscience is lax, such urges are capable of being discharged through socially permissible forms of conduct. Consequently, such a person's compliance with the dictates of morality isn't contingent on his engaging in the interminable rituals and obsessions on which such compliance depends in the case of the obsessive-compulsive.

These facts about OCD are well known. In any case, my knowledge of them isn't based on what I witnessed at the meetings in question. But what I witnessed confirmed these facts, and my high estimation of the moral level of their attendees is therefore doubly justified.

So is my high opinion of their intellectual levels. It was obvious from what they were saying that they were bright. And, it is well known, it is inherent in what OCD is that it is a thinking man's way of decompensating. Freud said that "civilization began when someone hurled an insult, instead of a rock"; and he made the equivalent point that, in the civilized person, the thought replaces the deed, whereas in his primitive counterpart, "the deed, as it were, replaces the thought." Having OCD involves being to the ordinary civilized person what the latter is to the primitive person: it involves a continuation of the cognitivization of action constitutive of a person's becoming sufficiently evolved that he can be a member of a society, as opposed to a pre-tribal gang. (The "pre-"prefix is important. Tribe-membership involves compliance with exceedingly strict rules and therefore isn't relevantly different from society-membership.) One must hyper-value thought to have OCD. Unintelligent people don't hyper-value thought. Therefore, a certain acuity is a prerequisite for full-blown OCD. Also, unless a given person is able to perceive recondite equivalences, his mental activity won't carry out the symbolic distortions and logical transformations characteristic of the obsessive-compulsive's mentation.

The occurrence of the term "full-blown" in the second to last sentence was not gratuitous. Unintelligent people, and indeed all organisms, have OCD-like conditions that aren't true OCD. The compulsion to repeat, Freud observed, is a pervasive feature of biological existence. The reason for this, Freud rightly said, is that life-forms necessarily have instincts and instincts are "conservative" in nature: instinct-driven behavior begins with equilibrium-disruption and ends with equilibrium-restoration. Thus, all living creatures have a compulsion to repeat. (If a living creature had no such compulsion, as Freud also said, it couldn't respond to new situations by deploying pre-existing mechanisms; it would have to deal with each new situation on its own terms, and its acting appropriately would thus involve its figuring out how to act. This wouldn't be feasible; it would take too long and, setting that aside, it would involve too great an expenditure of energy. A given creature simply wouldn't live long unless most of its behaviors were compulsive, as opposed to cognition-heavy; and any creature that does survive is, for that very reason, dominated by repetition-dispositive compulsions.)

Contemporary psychiatric theory and practice make insufficient provisions for these points (the ones in the second to last paragraph), and they are therefore worth developing.

OCD tends to afflict people who are both scrupulous and intellectual. It afflicts scrupulous people because hyper-morality is a defense against criminal impulses, and OCD is in large part a bulwark against unconscious aggression. It afflicts cerebral people because the ruminations and obsessions characteristic of the obsessive-compulsive mind are intensifications of thought, and it is only if one is intellectual that one's conflicts, when pathologized, are expressed by such intensifications.[254]

Because an overly punitive conscience is a *sine qua non* for OCD, sociopaths and psychopaths cannot have OCD. Many a sociopath says she has OCD. So far as that isn't simply a lie, it's because purely narcissism-driven behaviors – e.g. spending 2 hours on one's nails – mimic OCD behaviors to a degree and are *in a sense* compulsive. But with the sociopath, the compulsion is vanity-based. With the obsessive-compulsive, it is conflict-based. The OCD-sufferer is plagued by thoughts and urges of a sexual or aggressive nature. He sees these as wrong; and although his proximal intention in performing a given OCD-based act is to avoid anxiety, his ultimate intention is to keep these thoughts in abeyance. Underneath his intention to avoid anxiety is to keep the aforementioned impulses from being converted into action. You also intend is to keep those impulses from entering consciousness; that intention is subordinate to his intention to refrain from acting on them: a conscious desire is one step away from being acted on; an unconscious desire is two steps away. The obsessive-compulsive's intention to avoid anxiety is a smokescreen: what he *really* wants is to avoid acting on his basal desires. His psychological integration being what it is, the obsessive-compulsive's struggle against those desires has been transformed into a struggle against compulsions that he knows to be inane and that are relatively innocuous for that very reason.

As previously stated, the OCD-sufferer's violent thoughts are *never* translated into action.[255] So his rituals succeed to that extent. But his consciousness is perpetually plagued by the very violence- and sexuality-laden thoughts and images he wishes to keep out of it, and to that extent his rituals fail.

9.2 Programs of the just-described sort have a success-rate of 0%. There is no way they could possibly succeed. Such programs demand that those in them forfeit their agency. Since forfeiture of agency is the worse kind of failure, such programs fail if they succeed and must therefore fail.

It's a theoretical possibility that by forfeiting one's agency for a time, one brings about the dismantling of the physiological or psychological underpinnings of OCD. Speaking empirically, however, this is not the case, and giving into OCD doesn't make it go away.

OCD never goes away. Its more obvious behavioral and phenomenological manifestations may do so. But ruminations and odd rituals aren't OCD's only effects, or

---

254. See Reich (1945), Stekel (1949), Freud (1963), and Salzman (1994).

255. Salzman (1994) makes this point. So do Freud, Reich, and Stekel.

even its most deleterious ones: they are *manifestations* of underlying inhibitions that cripple thought, skew emotional reactions, and corrupt intentions. Though debilitating, the obsessive-compulsive's tendency to ruminate and engage in rituatlistic behaviors does not constitute his condition.

Clinicians who identify OCD with a tendency to obsess and to ritualize are for that very reason disposed to do nothing about the lasting, structural damage that OCD does to those afflicted by it. One can be conditioned not to obsess and to have no desire to engage in ritualistic behaviors. An obsessive-compulsive who washes his hands too often can be conditioned to shake hands with homeless people and not even desire to wash his hands. But such conditioning no more eliminates OCD than the use of bronchodilators eliminates asthma.

To be sure, such conditioning is enormously important. But its importance is *pre*therapeutic. If an obsessive-compulsive's tendency to ritualize makes it hard for him to leave his room, let alone make it to appointments on time, he won't be able to begin therapy unless he has been duly conditioned. But the elimination of some one, circumstance-specific functional impairment does not constitute the elimination of the underlying condition; and an obsessive-compulsive stands to lose a great deal if his therapist doesn't see this.

This brings us to a larger point: Disorders are not identical with dispositions to have certain symptoms. They are no more identical with such dispositions than a belief that snow is white is identical with a disposition to engage in certain overt behaviors. The distinction between a symptom and the disorder underlying it is to be understood in terms Chomsky's (1965) distinction between performance and competence. A disorder is a corruption of competence; a symptom is a performance-diminishing expression of a disorder. The elimination of a disorder-based functional impairment does not constitute the elimination of the disorder. Symptoms tend to be circumstance-specific; the intensity of an obsessive-compulsive's compulsion to wash his hands waxes and wanes with changes in circumstances. When he's with Sally, with whom he feels at ease, it wanes. When he's with Jerry, by whom he feels threatened, it waxes. Disorders, by contrast, are circumstance-invariant.

A disorder may have relatively circumstance-invariant symptoms, but such disorders only confirm our position. Respiratory distress is a symptom of emphysema. It might seem to be a circumstance-invariant one. But it is only *relatively* circumstance-invariant. Relative to the methods of treatment available 500 years ago, it was perfectly circumstance-invariant. Relative to today's methods of treatment, it is still relatively circumstance-invariant: given an arbitrarily chosen symptom S of an arbitrarily chosen disorder D, the likelihood of a person's experiencing respiratory distress if he has emphysema probably exceeds the likelihood a person's experiencing S if he has D: the first likelihood is large relative to the second.

But the operative word is "relatively." In theory, if not in actuality, there are ways of alleviating the emphysemic's respiratory distress, and even eliminating it, that do nothing in the way of eliminating the emphysema itself. Emphysema *per se* is the condition of having heavily remodeled airways. Since such remodeling involves the replacement of healthy elastic tissue with inelastic scar tissue, a consequence of such remodeling is airway inelasticity, and a consequence of such inelasticity is respiratory distress. But if the emphysemic took a medication that caused his otherwise unchanged airways to regain their former elasticity, he would still have emphysema. And speaking purely theoretically, a restoration of pulmonary elasticity isn't a necessary condition for a restoration of pulmonary efficiency. There could in principle exist a medication that dilated to the airways of the emphysemic to such an extent that, functionally speaking, the inelasticity of the tissue lining them ceased to matter. While under the influence of such a medication, an emphysemic's lung-tissue would be as elastic as a non-emphysemic's. So technically the emphysemic's respiratory distress is a circumstantial expression of his condition.

Theoretically, an emphysemic's airways could be re-*re*modeled in such a way that they had their previous structure and *for that reason* had their previous degree of elasticity. Such a person would cease to have emphysema: but he might still have respiratory distress. He might have vocal chord dysfunction, which narrows major airways, or allergy-mediated asthma, which temporarily narrows intra-pulmonary airways.

Let us discuss the bearing of these points on the nature of psychopathology. The obsessive-compulsive is indeed hobbled by his compulsions. But those are easily eliminated: if he doesn't give in to them, they become latent and eventually disappear without a trace. The same holds of the obsessive-compulsive's obsessions: if he doesn't actively work out their ramifications or otherwise indulge them, they become latent and eventually altogether vanish. But those obsessions and compulsions are but momentary expressions of the obsessive-compulsive's condition. The real damage done by that condition lies in the corruption of the obsessive-compulsive's self-concept: he self-conceptualizes as weak, vulnerable, and prone to misfortune. The obsessive-compulsive sometimes makes valiant efforts to self-conceptualize as strong and capable, and such efforts often lead to enormous functional improvements. But the old self-conceptualizations are ineradicable, their continued existence being evidenced by the insecurity-driven, counterphobic manner in which the obsessive-compulsive attempts to affirm his strength. Thanks to his self-reconceptualizations, the obsessive-compulsive may become genuinely valiant and hardy. In fact, given how maniacally dedicated he is to extirpating every last vestige of cowardice within himself and given how strictly his punitive conscience disposes him to interpret cultural definitions of virtue, he may well become maximally valiant – more valiant than the very people he took as paradigms as valor. But this bold, brash iconoclast has to struggle with all his might not to lapse back into the cautious conservatism that lies at the center of his character-architecture.

An obsession- and compulsion-free person may have the psychological integration constitutive of OCD. Such a person's being asymptomatic is ambiguous. It could correspond *either* to a genuine restoration of functionality *or* to its exact opposite. It could be that the disease is attacking the core the afflicted person's character, instead of discharging itself in symptoms that, although temporarily debilitating, leave his character intact.

412 Empiricism and the Foundations of Psychology

The essence of OCD is "impotent rage," as Dr. Norman Atkins said. Strictly speaking, however, impotent rage is the pathogen, not the pathology *per se*. The obsessive-compulsive remodels his character in such a way as to legitimate his feelings of impotent rage. The end-result of such remodeling is a person who sees himself as a failure-bound, perpetual victim. The sensibility mediating such self-defeatism is the true essence of OCD.

But today's OCD-specialists spurn the idea that there is anything underlying one's obsessions and compulsions. Their view is that scientific thought is empirical thought. This being their axiomatic starting point, they are incapable of distinguishing the symptoms from the disease. Today's scientific OCD-experts hold that, so far as it isn't to be identified with a disposition to have obsessions and compulsions, OCD is to be understood in strictly physiological terms. They give no credence to the possibility, whose very existence they do not acknowledge, that OCD, though obviously mediated by physiology, is to be understood in characterological terms. Being empiricists, today's psychiatrists see psychopathological conditions as being individuated by their respective sympomalogies, not by their effects on, or their roots in, one's personality-architecture.

Empiricists don't theorize; they taxonomize. And today's psychiatrists produce taxonomies, not theories. This is exactly what pre-Freudian psychologists did; and modern psychology (or what used to be modern psychology) began when Freud distinguished between structural and purely descriptive diagnostic methods, thereby refuting the theoretical underpinnings of taxonomy-oriented psychological research-programs. The discipline of cognitive science began when Chomsky replaced Skinnerian descriptivism with Freudian structuralism. Chomsky himself says that it was by generalizing Freud's structuralism that he was able to make his epoch-making discoveries.[256.]

And yet all this progress is being undone under the banner of "science." It isn't "scientific" to posit unconscious psychological structure. (In other words, doing so is contraindicated, relative to an acceptance of empiricism.) Where Freud spoke of the unconscious, we are told, real scientists speak of pure physiology. We have seen why it is illogical, and therefore unscientific, to physiologicize the unconscious.

People with OCD tend to be highly intelligent. If such a person questions a given proposition, he probably has a good reason for doing so. The OCD-sufferer's intellectual deficits may only be apparent if one considers the totality of his intellectual work-product. It may be that any two-page article that he writes is creditable. But a thousand two-page articles don't necessarily embody a cogent system of thought, and the intellectual attrition induced by OCD is typically apparent only if one looks at patterns of statements (or articles or egg-timers, etc.).[257] The rigid diagnostic criteria

---

256. Chomsky (1980, 1988).

257. See Salzman (1994) for points similar to those just made.

countenanced by empiricism dispose their users to focus on situation-internal data and to ignore larger patterns.

OCD is the pathologicization of a certain kind of mind: a mind that, to the extent that it's not pathological, is likely to be a very powerful one. Beethoven had OCD, as did Einstein.[258] OCD isn't to be eliminated; it isn't like a gangrenous leg that must be amputated. OCD is like a powerful army that is fighting an unnecessary war. Such an army is not to be dismantled but redeployed, the same being true of the obsessive-compulsive's psychological architecture.

Also, neurosis, though debilitating, is a sign of psychological health. Only conflicted people are neurotic; only people with values are conflicted; only people with values have a distinctively human psychological architecture; and a mind's having certain degree of structural integrity is both a precondition for, and a consequence of, its mediating value-driven activity. If ceasing to be neurotic involves jettisoning one's values and therefore one's psychological architecture, then one is better off staying neurotic. The upcoming chapter is intended to substantiate this point.

To be sure, a neurosis is, by definition, an illness. But neurosis is a healthy person's way of pathologizing. A precondition for neurosis is a structurally intact mind. The neurotic mind is like a car with an improperly installed battery. Structurally, such a car differs only infinitesimally from an otherwise identical car with a properly installed batter. But, as Freud (1926) observed, tiny structural differences translate into vast functional differences. The other side of the coin is that vast gains in functionality can be achieved, and achieved rapidly, by those whose functional impairments express minor structural problems. Where neuroses are concerned, the diminution of performance is grossly disproportionate to the disturbances that give rise to them. This bodes well for the neurotic: it means that, even though his condition is crippling while it lasts, he stands to make a relatively speedy recovery. (The operative word is "relatively": it takes years, as Freud said and as every analyst knows, to loosen the resistances that sustain a neurosis.) A neurosis is like a severe case of pneumonia had by somebody who is basically healthy: he's completely non-operational while ill, but he isn't ill for long, and his recovery is complete. A healthy person's pneumonia is system-internal: it inhibits his metabolism's ability to function, but it doesn't corrupt his metabolism itself. It's only because his metabolism is intact that he can recover; a broken metabolism can't fix itself. So far as pneumonia affects one's metabolism, it is by affecting one's lungs. Pneumonia is primarily a pulmonary disorder, and only secondarily, if at all, a metabolic disorder.

AIDS is a metabolic disorder. It is an affliction of one's immune system and thus of one's body's ability to regulate its own processes. AIDS often leads to pneumonia. But AIDS is primarily a metabolic disorder, and only secondarily, if at all, a pulmonary disorder.

A neurosis is like a case of pneumonia. It is an affliction, not of one's psychological architecture, but of the activity mediated thereby. It isn't by virtue of having a

---

258. See Davies (2001a, 2001b).

damaged mind that one is neurotic; it is by virtue of having one that misdeploys the resources at its disposal. To be sure, neuroses can bring about severe, and sometimes irreversible, damage to one's psychological structure. Neuroses corrupt the activity mediated by one's psychological architecture. Corruptions of such activity may lead to psychological remodelling and thus to systemic, as opposed to system-internal, changes. But neuroses, though capable of leading to such changes, do not themselves constitute such changes, and neurosis is therefore a system-internal, not a systemic psychological ailment. Sociopathy and psychopathy are systemic, not system-internal, ailments. In a word: the sociopath is what is left over when a person's values – and all of his concomitant beliefs, desires, intentions, and affectivities – have been stripped of him. A psychopath is a sociopath who was never not a sociopath. (These points will be soon be clarified.) This means that, where sociopathy and psychopathy are concerned, the affliction cannot be distinguished from the afflicted. This in turn means that the likelihood of recovery is nil; for it means that the concept of recovery no longer has any meaning.

Even severe forms of psychosis are system-internal and in this respect differ from sociopathy and psychopathy and are less serious than they are. To be sure, sufficiently grave system-internal condition can lead to system-remodeling. That said, psychosis, even in its more severe forms, is a disturbance of what, ultimately, is a feasible integration, whereas sociopathy and psychopthy are not disturbances of integrations, but are themselves integrations, whose very presence means that that the person has, as it were, become the disease and, consequently, the concept of recovery ceases to have any meaning. The distinction between systemic and system-internal psychopathologies is one that has made little or no appearance in the literature, despite its obvious theoretical and psychotherapeutic significance.

The elimination of anxiety should not be an objective of psychotherapeutic treatment. The ability to *tolerate* anxiety should be such an objective. There are two ways of extirpating anxiety. One is by improving one's life in such a way that the anxiety in question is no longer appropriate. The other is to self-remodel, so as to blind oneself to the source of the anxiety. This self-remodelling is identical with sociopathogenesis, as we will now see.

CHAPTER 16

Sociopathy, psychopathy, and criminality

1.0   Everybody rationalizes. Everybody represses. Rationalization and repression are not inherently pathological. They can become pathologized; they can be overused. But the same is true of one's immune system. (Many diseases, the stock example being asthma, are the result of an over-active immune system.) And no one would say that people would be better off if they didn't have immune systems.

In fact, the faculties that enable a person to rationalize and repress are a part of his immune system. Their purpose and, when all goes well, their effect is to sequester knowledge that *should* be sequestered: knowledge that, if allowed to interact with the beliefs constitutive of one's current integration, would destabilize and possibly undermine the latter. Just as a mediocre car is better than no car, a mediocre belief-system is better than no belief-system. But, whereas one can upgrade car-wise by trading in one's economy car for a sports car, it is only through piecemeal improvements of one's existing belief-system that one can upgrade belief-system-wise.

1.1   There are two senses of the word "rationalize." Relative to one of those two senses, to "rationalize" data is to provide a coherent model for it; it is to posit unobservables to account for observables. It is by successfully modeling data that science advances and apprises us of truths about the world of which we'd be ignorant, were our spheres of knowledge limited to what commonsense can reveal to us.

Relative to the other sense of the word, to "rationalize" data is to model it with the intention of seeing things as one wants them to be, not as they are. A rationalization is a model that one produces and accepts because one *wants* to believe it to be true, not because one really does believe it to be true.

Relative to both senses of the word, to "rationalize" is to model data.

It might be thought that emotion-driven rationalizations are *ipso facto* pathological, and that the distinction between healthy and pathological rationalizations is that the former are intended to unveil the truth whereas the latter are intended to bury it.

This is not correct. Although all pathological cases of rationalization are attempts to bury the truth, not all attempts to bury the truth are pathological. The mind has limited resources at its disposal. It has limited energy, storage space, and intelligence. Mentation would grind to a halt if *all* of one's beliefs were operational. Some of one's beliefs must therefore be sequestered. Since access-conscious beliefs are *ipso facto* operational, the requisite belief-sequestration involves rendering some of one's beliefs access-unconscious; it involves repressing them, in other words. Repression of this kind is indispensable to one's psychological well-being and is obviously not pathological.

There is another reason why some instances of repression are non-pathological. One's knowledge doesn't self-deploy. For this reason, there must be an agency within one's mind that searches through the latter's data-banks for circumstance-relevant knowledge. Because this agency couldn't function if its search space comprised the entirety of one's knowledge, that search space has to be limited to what is access-conscious; and some of one's beliefs must therefore be rendered access-*un*conscious: they must be repressed, in other words. Instances of this sort of repression are obviously non-pathological.

Even though such reallocations of data are emotionally antiseptic, they are sometimes carried out by the same agencies that are responsible for conflict-based repression; and since the primary function of such agencies is to resolve emotional conflict, conflict-based ideation is needed to activate them. In such cases, repression of the emotionally charged kind is but a vehicle for repression of the innocent kind involved in emotionally sterile, entirely cognition-related data-reallocation. One's conflicts end up becoming implicated in innocuous acts of system-maintenance, and so do one's methods of resolving such conflicts. Thus, rationalizations, displacements, and other such defenses end up being involved in operations of a strictly cognitive and therefore non-psychodynamic nature.

A similar, but non-coincident, line of thought concerns the mobilization of one's ratiocinative abilities. Intelligence doesn't self-deploy. Meta-intelligence is required to deploy it. One has only a finite amount of meta-intelligence. Therefore, much of one's intelligence cannot be deployed. Access-conscious ratiocinative abilities are *ipso facto* deployable. So in some cases the reason that a given ratiocinative ability is access-unconscious is simply that one's meta-intelligence is limited.

1.1.1   The points just made are corollaries of obvious truths concerning the biological role of mental activity.

The mind's primary function is to ensure the welfare of the organism. Therefore, the mind's powers of knowledge-acquisition are ultimately but a means to that end. That is one of the more important reasons why the mind is so limited in its ability to deploy its own ratiocinative capabilities.

There are two senses in which the mind is limited by the fact that its existence depends on the welfare of the physical organism that hosts it. It is limited in the obvious sense that its existence ceases the moment the organism dies. But it is also limited in the sense that, since its prime directive is to keep the physical organism alive, it corrupts purely theoretical ideation by pressing it into the service of that directive.

There are two senses in which it is the mind's "primary" function to ensure the welfare of the body that hosts it:

(a)   It is the mind's *first* function, speaking chronologically;

and

(b)   It is the mind's most important function.

And there are three senses in which, chronologically speaking, the maintenance of the body's welfare is the mind's first function. It is its first function in:

(i)   The development of any given individual;

(ii) That of the species to which any given individual belongs;

and

(iii) That of living beings *tout court*: obviously the first instances of sentience mediated ideation of the survival-oriented kind, not the theoretical kind.

1.2   Many of us self-identify as thinkers. But it's only up to a point that intelligence and knowledge conduce to a given person's physical well being. Past that point, they are useless in the way of ensuring one's bodily well being. For reasons to be disclosed, we are right to self-identify as mental beings. But since the physical survival of its host is the mind's fundamental concern, our cogitations are pervaded by emotional derivatives of our purely survival-oriented instincts, and it is only at quite singular junctures that our thoughts have the theoretical purity we like to ascribe to them.

A related point is that the mind is a biological entity; it is a part of the human organism. A damaged psyche is less likely than a healthy one to make survival-conducive decisions. A damaged mind is like a damaged heart: it has a job to do and, because it's damaged, it can't do it as well as it should. Other things being equal, psychologically damaged people are more likely to make survival-*non*-conducive decisions than psychologically undamaged people.

1.2.1   Readers may skip to Section 1.3.

One of the shibboleths of empiricism is that hearts *don't* have jobs to do. Empiricists regard all teleological statements (e.g. "it is the heart's purpose to pump blood") as veiled non-teleological statements. But, by their own admission, they haven't yet succeeded in de-teleologicizing such statements.[259]

To be sure, that fact is not very significant. Given only that the exact number of pennies in the world hasn't been established and never will be, it doesn't follow that there is no such number. To take a less trivial example: while it's obviously on the basis of a musical work's structural features that we like it, there is little chance that we'll ever produce a general characterization of the relevant structural virtues of so much as a single piece of music.

---

259. The best such attempt is found in Nagel (1962). I know that other philosophers, most of them empiricists, have rejected it. But I do not personally know that it fails; and when reading it, I didn't notice any logical errors. My reservations about it had to do with the fact that Nagel was clearly producing this analysis *post hoc*, so as to validate his empiricism. It is a very intricate analysis, which no one would think of unless they had an ulterior motive.

That said, deteleologicizing our world-view would vitiate it. A blind person's eyes are defective. Eyes are supposed to see. That's their job. This is a datum. So far as philosophers deny it, they're victims of their own artifices.

In some contexts, an organ's job is to help its owner carry out an intention of his. In a context where my intention is to play the piano, my hands exist to help me carry out that intention. But what a given organ is supposed to do isn't always determined what its owner's objectives are. Even in a context where a person's intention is to blind himself, his eyes exist to give him sight.

A person who intends to blind himself is mentally ill. His eyes have a job to do. It's not for him to say what that job is, and he'll prevent them from doing that job if he carries out his intention. People who mutilate themselves are preventing their organs from doing what they are supposed to be doing, and those people are sick for that very reason. In self-lobotomizing, a person is acting wrongly, even if his intention is to be a happy imbecile. The brain-module that was removed had a job to do. That job was to mediate thought. Given that the self-lobotomizer wanted to destroy that module, so as to put an end to the cognitive activity mediated thereby, the conclusion to draw is "that person is a very sick one," not "so far as that module had a job to do, its purpose was derivative of its owner's objectives."

"The man who blinds himself is indeed sick," it will be said. "But this doesn't prove your point. Even though his intention at that particular instant was to deprive himself of sight, he will surely have a million contrary intentions at later junctures; and what made his act sick was failure on his part to give due weight to these other intentions. Thus, so far an eye's job is to see, it's because of its owners intentions – not any one intention, but the totality of those intentions."

If a man who wilfully blinded himself did not later intend to use his eyes to see, our judgment would not be: "In that case, it wasn't their job to see." Instead it would be: "That man was exceptionally deranged." If a man self-lobotomized and, in doing so, didn't frustrate any intentions he would otherwise have come to have, our judgment wouldn't be: "evidently, it wasn't that brain-module's job to think." It would be: "That man was maximally deranged."

A shovel's job is to help people dig. In and of themselves, shovels are purposeless. Empiricists say that eyes are like shovels – useful only in the sense that they help their owner carry out their intentions. "So far as anything in nature has a job to do," empiricists says, "it's because some sapient creature needs it to do that job."

This line of thinking inverts the correct order of explanation. What we intend to do is a function of what believe our organs are supposed to do. It isn't my intention to use my eyes to see that makes it their jot to see. It's their job to see, and that makes it my intention to use them to see.

"You just happen to know that you can use your eyes to see," an objector is likely to say. "That makes it natural for you to believe that, setting aside your intentions, their purpose is to enable you to see."

When we judge a given organ to have a certain function, our reasons for doing so are not as narrow as the objector suggests; nor are those reasons as tightly connected to our own practical interests.

The biological integrity of an organ can be, and often is, established independently of what its owner wants from it: whether a liver is healthy or not doesn't depend on how it fits into its owner's future plans. (According to Aristotle, the heart, not the brain, is the seat of thought: people think with their hearts, Aristotle believed, not their brains. (In this context, the word "heart" is being used literally.) If somebody of Aristotle's intelligence could be so egregiously wrong as to such obvious organ-related facts, can it with any plausibility be supposed that, so far as one's gall-bladder has a purpose, or one's endocrinal gland, it is only derivatively of its owner's objectives?) Equivalently, what an organ is supposed to be doing can be, and often is, figured out independently of what it is actually doing. A given organ O that isn't doing X may clearly be responsible for doing X. Given (i) O's internal structure; (ii) O's relations to other organs; and (iii) the metabolic consequences of O's not doing X; it may be clear that (iv) O's job is to do X. O's host-organism is a well-organized part of nature; it is not possible to understand nature without understanding that organism or, if not that specific organism, others of its kind. O's failing to do X would discontinue that organism's existence, thereby increasing entropy and degrading the explanatory structure of the universe. So "O is supposed to do X" isn't a veiled way of saying "O usually does X," or "organs like O usually do X," or "O's owner wants it to do X." Rather, "O is supposed to do X" means: "If O does X, the universe is more intelligible, other things being equal, than if O does not do X."

Thus, when we talk about what eyes "should" do, we aren't referring to the intentions of creatures with eyes. We aren't talking about what anybody wants. We are talking about the structural integrity of the universe. A world of sick creatures is more entropic than a world of healthy creatures; a world of no biological creatures is more entropic than a world of sick biological creatures; and so on. Everything always complies with the laws of microphysics. But a body of laws can be limited scope; an individual law can be broken. Inviolable and all-encompassing though the laws of microphysics are, their having those properties is an accident with respect to their being laws (though not with respect to their being microphysical laws). Given two properties phi and psi, if a given thing's having phi is non-circumstantially dispositive, no matter how weakly, of its having psi, then it is a law of nature that phi's cause psi's. If this condition is met, it is irrelevant how few phi's are psi's.

I've read a number of recent sociology-papers in which the author tried to establish inviolable connections between properties. ("All people with a certain type of tattoo carry guns." "All people with long index fingers have certain proclivities.") There are usually counterexamples to such hypotheses, and also to the duly hedged hypotheses that replace them.

This approach to science is ridiculous. Sometimes explanatory relationships are expressed by perfect concomitances; usually they aren't. The idea that they are is based on the mistaken idea that laws are structural facts about the universe that determine how its occupants behave.

A thing's having phi, let us suppose, is dispositive of its having psi. Arbitrary object O has psi. Its having psi is a consequence of its having phi. O's having phi must be locally operative. No structural fact about the universe can have to do with the matter, except in so far as it has duly local consequences. It is understandable that people should have thought otherwise: "The universe is like a pinball machine; its occupants are like the ball," it is thought. "The laws governing it are like the bumpers and rivulets that govern the ball's motion." Not great thinking, but not obviously ludicrous.

Hume and Peirce deny that anything makes anything happen. One would think them innocent of the pinball-machine conception of natural law. One couldn't be more wrong. In saying that nothing makes anything happen, they were saying that, if anything made anything happen, it would be in consequence of structural facts about the universe: the Great Pinball-Machine would be running the show. And it was because they were empiricists that they adopted the no-cause view (NCV); it wasn't because they had misgivings concerning the Pinball-Machine view (PMV). On the contrary, it was precisely because they accepted PMV that they embraced NCV. By itself, empiricism doesn't demand acceptance of NCV. On the contrary, it demands its rejection. We feel forces; we feel them all the time; not a moment passes when we don't feel them. (A psychoanalytically minded author might say that NCV was an attempt to negate the obvious, and obviously unpleasant, fact that we are at all times under the dominion of forces of which we'd like nothing more than to be free. NCV's lack of merit supports this view, as does its intuition-unfriendliness.) Outside of physics, correlations don't correlate with laws, and non-physicists who believe otherwise are doing their respective disciplines a disservice.

In any case, the points made a moment ago enable us answer the age-old question: Setting aside sapience- and sentience-related cases, is there purposiveness in the world? Do the organelles of a plant have purposes? Yes. They have them in the very sense in which a person's eyes have them, even if, because of some psychological disturbance, his intentions involve putting them to countersystemic use.

Let us end by restating some key ideas. The statement:

(MC[260]) "most creatures with eyes are blind"

is an empirical, not an analytic falsehood. It isn't analytic that most eyes see; and it is by virtue of what it is supposed to do, namely see, not what it actually does, that a given thing is an eye. Since, consequently, no teleological statement has a strictly sensory basis, a consequence of empiricism is that all such statements are wrong. But

---

260. Short for "most creatures."

not all such statements are wrong. Some take this to show that God exists.[261] I take it to show that empiricism is overly constrictive.

1.3 Knowing too much damages a person emotionally. To survive, you need to know certain things, but you need to *not* know certain other things. Suppose that you are four years old. You know that your mother and father provide you with food, protection, etc. But your having that knowledge isn't enough. Knowledge by itself isn't action-conducive. *Emotions* are more immediate causes of action than knowledge. (Put more precisely: egocentric beliefs (emotions) are more action-dispositive than non-egocentric beliefs.) So a positive emotion concerning your parents must mediate between what you know (namely, that you depend on them) and what you do.

Given these points, there are two ways in which it may behoove you to be ignorant of a given fact. The second way is the more important one in this context. First, it behooves you not to discover anything about your parents that would lead to your not loving them. Should you stop loving them, they'll pick up on that fact and they'll withdraw much needed support.

Second, your love is so integral to your psychological architecture that, even if it is based on false beliefs, uprooting your love for them would do you more damage than holding onto those beliefs. Like all beliefs, those beliefs are supported by others. But the beliefs underlying your feelings towards your parents are more likely than other beliefs of yours to be rooted in, and indeed to coincide with, beliefs that that constitute the nucleus of your personality. Your belief that Hondas get better mileage than Toyotas has roots in other beliefs of yours: beliefs concerning the reliability of the reports you've read, the accuracy of the odometer in your Toyota, and so on. You'll have to revise at least one of these beliefs if you find out that Toyotas get better mileage than Hondas. But you won't be any the worse for it. The same cannot be said, so we may legitimately suppose, of the beliefs underlying your belief that your father is a legitimate businessman. If it turns out he isn't, then he was lying to you every time he talked to you about his work. Given how often he talked about work, that means that he was lying every day, for hours on end. That means that his character is defective – but not just defective: profusely so. Not a single statement he has made, with a few trivial exceptions, has so much as a shred of credibility, unless you have independent reason to accept it. His lies drain his fatherly teachings of meaning, and they invalidate your very character, to the extent that it embodies an attempt on your part to internalize those teachings.

So supposing that you find out that your parents are spineless or evil or otherwise demeritorious, that discovery will destabilize your belief-system. This is not to say that all such destabilizations are harmful: minor ones are not only harmless, but

---

261. Aristotle and Aquinas take this view. So do contemporary authors, such as Frank Turek (2004). It should be pointed out that Dr. Turek is a theologian first, and a philosopher second; so the fact that he has teleological views should not be taken as evidence of anti-empiricism on the part of philosophers.

necessary for the acquisition of knowledge and for personal growth. But if excessively disrupted, one's belief-system may become insufficiently operative. So emotional damage may lead to crippling disruptions of your belief-system and, therefore, of your ability to acquire knowledge and to make practical decisions based thereupon. And for a youngster, discoveries about the nooks and crannies of his parents' psyches could well bring about such damage.

Children idealize their parents. This does a great deal in the way of their maintaining useful and emotionally positive relations with them. Most children's parents are not great people. In most cases, they are not captains of industry or musical geniuses.

And even if a child's father or mother is a captain of industry or a musical genius, there is inevitably much that is ugly about that person. Nobody's psyche is pristine. There is no one who isn't often selfish, spiteful, prejudiced, malicious, or otherwise contemptible. But what good would it do a five year old to know everything about his father's psyche? He would lose respect for his father. The father would pick up on that fact and would be a worse father for it.

We love and depend on other people. Those people have their merits. But they are only human, and there is inevitably much that is ugly within them. Knowing too much about a friend, lover, or parent would weaken a helpful tie to that person.

Too much knowledge about oneself destroys the psychological underpinnings of accomplishment. During my adolescence and early adulthood, I had a grossly inflated view of my intellectual abilities. I thus believed it incumbent on myself to do everything in my power to develop my mind. When I was 15, I was incapable of saying anything of any merit. 24 years later, thanks to the efforts prompted by my bloated self-concept, I am capable of making points that have a non-null, if only a miniscule, amount of merit, and I have thus made progress that I wouldn't otherwise have made.

I have had the good fortune to have relationships with women who had tremendous merit as people and who were also physically attractive. I fell in love with these women because I idealized them, and I idealized them for the wrong reasons. But if I hadn't idealized them, no relationship would have ensued and I wouldn't have been the beneficiary of the considerable merits that they actually had.

2.0   When is rationalization counterproductive? When it leads to a diminishment of oneself; when the knowledge one forfeits by rationalizing would have enhanced one. (Note: "Counterproductive" doesn't necessarily mean "pathological.") A short (entirely fictitious) story will clarify this point:

(LT[262]) I am out of shape. This leaves me with a choice. On the one hand, I can regularly go for five mile jogs (or engage in some other, comparably fitness-promoting activity). On the other hand, I can do nothing to improve my

---

262. Short for "lazy, tennis."

endurance; I can just lounge around. If I do the first, I'll fulfill my lifelong desire to be a good tennis player. (I have the racket-skills. All I lack is endurance.) If I don't, I won't.

I have two talents: one for mathematics, the other for music. Considerable though my musical abilities are, I have much more mathematical talent than I do musical talent. That is why I am a professional mathematician, as opposed to a professional violinist.

I deeply value being a good mathematician. I also deeply value being a good violinist. I do not deeply value being a good athlete. Being a good athlete would improve my life: How could it not? But it has no relevance to what I'm passionate about.

I choose not to jog (or to do anything comparable thereto). I make this choice because, even though I'm disciplined when it comes to things that are deeply important to me, I'm weak-willed and lazy when it comes to things of middling importance.

Even such contextual laziness and lack of will power are serious defects of character. Aware of this fact, and not wanting to see myself for the wretch that I am, I rationalize:

(MR[263]) I live in a rather dangerous neighborhood. So I might get mugged. Plus, the roads and adjacent walkways are full of potholes and I might break my ankle. [Etc.]

I made the wrong choice. Being a good athlete would make me a better person. I would be able to exercise my agency and rationality in new ways. Plus, by virtue of doing the things, such as getting in shape, that I have to do to become a good tennis player, I'd rectify not entirely insignificant defects of character (viz. my sports-related laziness, which probably has roots in some general weakness of character).

That said, there is a sense in which, even though my choice was based on self-deception, it might have been the right one. One would have to be a maniac to resolve, and to implement one's resolution, to *never* rationalize. And one's implementation of that resolution would *itself* involve many a rationalization! Extreme positions – e.g. a hatred of *all* people who drive fancy cars, a resolution to *never* do anything silly – are themselves rationalizations of one's avoidance of some psychological disturbance. (See Kernberg 1985, 1993.) So there is no way not to rationalize. That doesn't mean that one is in a lose-lose situation. It means that one shouldn't *voluntarily* rationalize and also that, if one finds that some aspect of one's life is completely rationalization-based, one should at the very least re-examine it. (I say "re-examine," not "extirpate," because rationalizations can be commingled with legitimate motivations, and also because, even if a rationalization *initiated* one's becoming (e.g.) an actor, one's *being*

---

263. Short for "my rationalization."

an actor may have become an independent variable, so to speak, to be evaluated on its own terms. "Rationalization-caused" ≠ "Rationalization-constituted.")

2.1 Here we have an instance of a rationalization that is counterproductive. But is it pathological? Not necessarily, as an extension of our story shows. It isn't part of a larger pattern. It isn't part of a general failure to be honest with myself. I generally do my best to see things as they are, as opposed to how I want them to be.

I obviously fail from time to time. Instead of admitting that person X is simply a better mathematician than I am, and that it was fitting that he, not I, should win the such and such prize, I tell myself that he's the beneficiary of a corrupt system.

But I don't deny the legitimacy of the other mathematician's findings. I don't ignore their relevance to my own work, and when I'm reading his work, any thoughts about him or the prize melt away: I am completely absorbed in the formulas before me.

If my bitterness affected my work as a mathematician, *then* we'd be dealing with a very different and much less innocuous sort of rationalization: one that was not only counterproductive but pathological, and not only pathological but *sociopathogenic*. A sociopathenic rationalization is that turns one into a sociopath. It does this by corrupting one's conscience, eroding one's values, and thereby undermining one's agency, rationality (not to be confused with intelligence), and therefore one's very self. Let us now discuss *sociopathy*.

3.0 Some authors use the terms "sociopathy" and "psychopathy" interchangeably. Other authors use the term "sociopathy" to refer to what I will describe as "psychopathy." So my use of the term "sociopathy" is to some extent stipulative. My use of the term "psychopathy" is orthodox.

Psychologists have conflated two very different disorders. A person afflicted by either disorder does not value anything and he therefore doesn't value the truth, except for practical purposes; he cannot love another person, the reason being that loving someone involves valuing them; and, most importantly, he is, to use Cleckley's term, a "reflex machine," not a *bona fide* agent. Both the sociopath and the psychopath are pseudo-agents.

But there are important differences between the two disorders, and they should therefore have different names. One of them is already referred to as "psychopathy"; hence my orthodox usage of that term. The other affliction has no name; and, with two exceptions, no authorities so much as acknowledge its existenece. (Those authorities are Nietzsche (1966, 1967a, 1967b) and Kernberg (1985, 1993).) But that condition afflicts far more people than psychopathy or, indeed, practically any other mental illness.

That affliction obviously deserves a name; I've decided to call it "sociopathy." There is a reason I chose this term. I have noticed that, in so far as the terms "sociopathy" and "psychopathy" are not used interchangeably, there is *some* tendency to use those terms as I will use them.[264] But, so far as I've researched the matter, those who currently use them as I will categorically hold that what they call "psychopathy" is merely a more severe form of what they call "sociopathy." The sociopath's behavior is indeed far less deviant from the psychopath's. But what they are calling "sociopathy" is a different affliction from what they call "psychopathy." Sociopathy is not a mild form of psychopathy; they are distinct disorders, albeit ones that are identical in certain key respects.

3.1 The nature of sociopathization is best understood in terms of the answer to the question: Why do people rationalize in counterproductive ways? Two reasons. First, it's easier to fantasize than to act. It's easier to have a billion imaginary dollars than it is to have 10,000 actual dollars.[265]

Second, a rationalization may be counterproductive in one way but productive in another: it may guarantee survival but prohibit growth. The boot-licker keeps his job, but only by diminishing himself; and in rationalizing his toadyism, he exchanges the uncertainties of a life of meaning for the certainties of one devoid of it.

An illustration: Sally is is a young and attractive woman. She is also a literary genius. She has the potential to be the greatest novelist of all time. But she has yet to cultivate her genius; and her works, though clearly the works of a genius, are not themselves works of genius. As she knows, if she cultivates her abilities, then in around ten years' time she will have surpassed many of the greats: Dickens, Hemmingway, maybe even Tolstoy.

Sally is a very "real" person. She is sincere and greatly values the truth. She detests pretenses of any but the most insignificant kind. And her stories and novels, though only the work of a *potential* master, are brilliant and subtle exposés of the lies people tell others and themselves, and of the pervasiveness of mendacity and the stealth with which it draws people its clutches.

Right now, two men are in love with Sally. Each has proposed marriage. One of them is poor; the other is a billionaire. Bill is the poor one; Tim is the rich one. Sally loves Bill with all her heart. Sally and Bill complement each other perfectly. She's a great novelist. He's a great logician. So they're sufficiently different that neither bores the other and neither can project his own self-loathing onto the other. But they're sufficiently alike that neither alienates the other. They have the same values. To that extent they're similar to each other and therefore agreeable to each other. They implement those values in different ways. To that extent they're different from each other and, therefore, intrigue each other.

---

264. Cf. Hyatt (1994).

265. Given how much one is diminished by taking flight in fantasy, it must be asked: Why do we have this tendency? What evolutionary *raison d'être* could it possibly have? Obviously such flights *per se* have no evolutionary *raison d'être*. But the ability to take refuge in fantasy is a concomitant of a hypertrophied intellect, and the latter obviously does have survival value.

Tim has merit. He's supremely intelligent, in fact, in the commerce-related ways one must be to make a $1,000,000,000. But Sally doesn't love Tim. She just doesn't. Her dreams are not his. What she finds funny leaves Tim cold, and *vice versa*. Also, Tim is extremely controlling. If Sally married him, she wouldn't have the sort of lifestyle that would allow her to continue with her writing. Sally would have to self-lobotomize in order to tolerate being married to him. Sally is dimly aware of these characteristics of Tim's and of their consequences for her, should she marry him. But the operative word is "dimly." It takes time to distinguish between a strong, decisive person and a controlling person; and since Tim *is* strong, as well as controlling, it's easy to see controlling behaviors on his part as signs of strength.

Also, Tim is reasonably physically attractive. And he is principled. He is not a *nice* person, but he made his money in an honest manner and is scrupulous in his transactions with others. Also, Tim routinely treats Sally to fun activities, like hang-gliding, which Bill doesn't have the money for. So even though Sally wouldn't dump Bill for Tim unless Tim had money, Tim would still have some allure for her, and she'd definitely date him if Bill weren't in the picture. Given that Tim has unlimited funds, whereas Bill has none, the situation is decidedly ambiguous.

Sally has a choice. She can augment her agency and imperil her physical well-being, or she can guarantee her physical well-being and diminish her agency.

Sally chooses to marry Tim. Therefore Sally now has *another* choice. On the one hand, she can she be honest with herself. This would involve her consciously believing the following:

(FC[266])   I married for money. My integrity is gone. So is my chance to do anything meaningful with my life. Every night, I am physically intimate with a man I never loved and who is now my jailer, and who I therefore detest more than I've ever detested anyone. I have not only commodified my sexuality, but have done so in a way that constitutes a surrender to the forces of darkness I've been fighting my whole life.

On the other hand, Sally can rationalize. Different rationalizations are available to her. Here is one of the better ones:

(SC[267])   Being a mature an adult is about being responsible. It's about putting practical considerations ahead of one's whims. Sure – I liked to write. And good novels are indeed sources of amusement. But adulthood – nay, true personhood – isn't about amusement. It's about responsibility.

---

266. Short for "first choice."

267. Short for "second choice."

Being married to Bill would have *felt* good. But my relationship with Bill was childish; it was as boy and girl that we loved each other. Bill and I love each other as man and woman.[268]

And Tim and I *do* love each other. My love for Tim doesn't *feel* like my former love for Bill. And perhaps it's not as *pleasurable*. But it's *real*. What Bill and I had was a fantasy. Being with Bill was like playing Monopoly: it was amusing. Marrying Bill would have been like trying to use Monopoly money to buy a car: it would have been unfeasible.

I admire Tim. Tim is a real man. He knows how the world works. He knows that it's a dog-eat-dog world out there. Tim has strength to see things as they are.

Bill was a wimp. He thought his arcane books actually meant something. Bill was clever. He had raw intelligence. But to what use did he put his intelligence? To splitting hairs and dialecticizing about useless subjects. None of his activities were remunerative. While that fact did not by itself drain those activities of meaning, it corresponded to a fact about them that did do so. Bill's failure to make money was a reflection of a failure to go out into the world and stake his claim. It was also a reflection of his inability to have meaningful relations with other human beings. So it wasn't Bill's having no money that bothered me; it was what it showed me about his character. It showed me that he never grew up. He intellectualized so that he could forever remain a child. Instead of ditching his imaginary childhood friends, he just gave them new names. "Captain Crunch" became "Russell's Paradox" and "Miss Piggie" became "The Problem of Induction."

Bill's self-centered infantilism corrupted every aspect of our relationship. Bill made a grand show of caring about my welfare. But did he *really* do so? True – he didn't micromanage my life. In fact, he was positively helpful in some ways. For example, he edited my manuscripts. In fact, he made intelligent and affirming comments about them, which did much to improve them. He also paid my medical bills, which cut into his diminutive financial reserves.

---

268. This paragraph is very similar to one that occurs in a story by Hemingway, titled "A very short story." I deliberately modeled this paragraph on Hemingway's. That story is about a man and a woman who fall in love. The man is a private in the army; the woman is nurse in the hospital where he is recovering from an injury. They plan to get married. After the man is discharged, he receives a letter from the woman. She tells him that she is now married to a General. Marriage with the general, she says, isn't the fun-filled affair that her time with private was. But, she says, "it is as man and woman that [the General] and I love each other, [whereas] it was as boy and girl that you and I loved each other." The woman sociopathized. Hemmingway's work often deals with sociopathy, and so does Tolstoy's. Cf. the latter's *The Death of Ivan Illyich*.

But Bill's supposed helpfulness was a way of undermining me. His kind deeds were helpful *only* relative to my childish, self-destructive whims. Bill was an enabler. His "help" was stunting me and preventing me from becoming a person of *gravitas* and bearing. He wanted me to remain a child, like him, reading and writing arcane books, self-indulgently telling ourselves, in our cold-water flat, that we were somehow superior to people who had actually gone out into the world and staked their claim. Had I stayed with Bill, I would be the worm that he is to this very day.

Thank Heaven that Tim saved me from such a wretched fate!

3.2   Before marrying Tim, Sally *valued* writing. Though exquisitely pleasurable, it wasn't a form of recreation. She was on a mission. There were great books that *had* to be written, which, in actuality, she would write (barring some disaster), just as for the young Beethoven, there were great musical works that *had* to be written, and which, in actuality, he would write.

Sally's relationship to Bill was like her relationship to her writing: it wasn't just a source of gratification; it was something she valued. And the positive feelings she had towards Bill were authentic expressions of her high regard for Bill, which was not misplaced. Bill really was a good person and great scholar. (Of course, her love for Bill was not *solely* based on her high estimation of him. Love has many roots, not all of them intellectual.) What she had with Bill was authentic: it was in line with her values, her aspirations and also – because she found Bill physically attractive – her biological drives.

So SC is *not* something Sally can really believe – at least not the Sally that Bill knew, or the Sally who wrote those brilliant novels. The things that SC describes as "whims," "amusements," etc., were rooted in Sally's values; and if Sally had fulfilled the demands imposed on her by those values, the result would have been an expansion of her sphere of awareness, of both herself and the world, and also of the jurisdiction of her agency. The more one knows about the world, the more one can control it. The more one knows about oneself, the more one can control oneself.

Even if SC is something that *somebody* could genuinely accept, Sally was not such a person at the time Tim proposed to her. By then, she was an extremely developed, mature, multifaceted human being. She had a powerful vision for herself, and a coherent set of values. Her emotions, aspirations, desires, and objectives were all hewed to that vision and those values. Sally had spent years working on a manuscript which, she rightly believed, would set a new standard in Proust scholarship. She was on her way to writing the next *War and Peace*. To the extent that she succeeds in operationalizing SC, all of skills involved in those endeavors are meaningless, as are the values underlying them.

Whether Sally's pre-Tim values were good or bad is irrelevant. What is relevant is that they were *her* values. They were the nucleus of her agency. She had to stay true to them, lest her personality-structure collapse and she effectively cease to exist, it being irrelevant that, if judged by some external standard, they might compare unfavorably to some other person's values.

Tigers must be tigers, Mao said. He was right. Tigers mustn't try to be lambs.[269] So far as tigers *should* value being lambs, it is in the socio-ethical sense of "should," not the agency-relevant sense. Since tigers obviously *shouldn't* be want to be lambs, this confirms the present author's earlier-stated view that socio-ethical values are derivative of the agency-relevant kind.

Ethicists distinguish between "the duty of aspiration" and "the duty of obligation." The duty of aspiration corresponds to my usage of the word "value," and "the duty of obligation" corresponds to my use of the term "socio-ethical value."[270]

Sally's pre-Tim values were integral to her psychological architecture. They had a hand in what she wanted to do and decided to do. They even affected what she believed: Her dedication to the truth, discovering it and apprising others of it, surely resulted in her having beliefs that she wouldn't otherwise have had.

Sally accepts SC, let us suppose, and she has deoperationalized her pre-Tim beliefs with same the acumen and determination with which she hitherto wrote novels. She uses her pre-Tim virtues to destroy her pre-Tim virtues. In this respect, she is like an intellectual genius, who, despite being shackled to a bed in a mental hospital while under suicide-watch, figures out a way to carry out his intention to kill himself and therefore obliterate his mind.[271]

3.3   The consequences of Sally's self-remodeling are ruinous. There are two reasons for this. First, she effectively voided her mind of everything she previously knew, as she cast all such knowledge outside the sphere of agency and her consciousness. What

---

269. I am liberally paraphrasing. Mao's physician informed him that he had halitosis, serious gingivitis, as well as at least one venereal disease. The physician told Mao that his halitosis would repulse his lady-friends and that also, unless he took precautions, he would transmit his venereal diseases to them. Referring to his halitosis and suppurating gums, Mao said: "Does a tiger brush its teeth?" He made a similar comment about his venereal problems. He meant: "I'm a tiger; tigers must be tigers, not lambs."

   I do not know how many venereal diseases Mao had, or which ones. My source, Li Zhisui (1996), Mao's personal physician for thirty years, withholds that information. The author wrote a voluminous work about his time with Mao, which is remarkably candid and oftentimes deeply critical of Mao's character. But there were some things the author simply was not at liberty to disclose.

270. I say all of this only to make it clear what I believe; for those beliefs presumably infiltrate the arguments set forth in the present work and the reader will be better able to evaluate those arguments if he knows about those beliefs, however misguided they may be.

271. Be it noted that the author that the story just told, though fiction, is but a few trivial alterations away from being fact. In this context, the author is speaking largely from personal experience. To much a lesser extent, he is speaking from second-hand knowledge acquired through scholarship, there being an astonishing paucity of relevant literature on this topic.

she did to her beliefs she did to their concomitants. This means that she effectively got rid of her intentions, along with the cognitive underpinnings of her emotions and, therefore, her very sensibility.

Second, Sally is trying to replace one personality with another; and that cannot be done. What can be done is to render one's current personality defunct. Sally has done that. So she is left with no personality. She is a mimicry of a person.

Sally's overhaul of her psychological integration will not change Sally's primal instincts and urges; it will not dismantle the mechanisms that mediate animalistic reflexes. And it obviously won't affect the structures that mediate sense-perception, ambulation, etc. But it will damage everything in her that is distinctively human. Humans are agents; humans are rational; animals are neither. Sally's agency and rationality will be but imitations of their former selves. Be it noted that *intelligence* is different from rationality. Sally's IQ won't change. But rationality isn't IQ. Rationality is intelligence that is applied in accordance with one's values to problems relating to the preservation, diminution, or augmentation of one's agency.

Sally is committing psychological suicide. She is trying to change *who* she is, not *how* she is. But one can't change who one is. One's identity is predetermined. Experience doesn't determine *who* one is; it determines *how* one is who one is.

There have been studies of identical twins who were raised in different environments. One twin would be raised in a mansion, the other in a hovel.[272] One would go to an elite boarding school, the other to the local public school. Such twins were identical in respect of their IQs, degree of spirituality, and to what degree, and in what manner, they were social or anti-social. A person can change himself, but he cannot change *his self.* Changes to oneself, if they are not to render one's self defunct, must occur within limits set by one's inborn biological structure. In internalizing SC, so far as she could do so, Sally was not operating within those limits. This means that, *qua* SC-believer, she doesn't have the support of her own native endowment.

Initially, she had its support. That is why she could still draw on her intellect and determination in carrying out her deoperationalization of it. But having carried it out, she no longer has it.

4.0   Only value-based psychological architectures can undergo sociopathization. To be a sociopath is to have a personality-structure that once embodied values but no longer does so. The pre-sociopath values the truth for its own sake; and she values other people's welfare, the future of the human race, and forms of success other than the acquisition of wealth, glamour, or power. The sociopath esteems the writer who won the book award, even if he plagiarized the award-winning book. Fame and fortune: nothing else matters. In the sociopath's book, a penniless Tolstoy, scribbling away in his dungeon, is no better than a janitor, and he can't hold a candle to a monetarily successful plagiarist.

---

272. For a discussion of such studies go to: http://en.wikipedia.org/wiki/Twin_study

However, the pre-sociopath has values, and sociopath's personality is the skeleton of the pre-sociopath's. For this reason, sociopaths are *formally* very much like (non-psychopathic) non-sociopaths.

This is because sociopathy is the result of rationalization. Rationalizations are attempts to legitimate oneself. They must therefore make formal concessions to values. Consider SC. Because the contentions in SC constitute the sociopathized Sally's marching orders, so to speak, Sally has to *act* like an adult. Her rationalization would be blown to pieces were she to become a serial killer or mobster. Those life-paths are about flouting what is "adult," "correct," and "moral." Her rationalization being what it is, she must *not* act in ways that deviate from social norms.

Rationalizations are not, and cannot be, anything like the following:

(AR[273]) I am going to become a lazy, self-indulgent slob. I will do whatever I want to do, no matter how immoral or otherwise repellant. I will not act like a mature person. I will not act like somebody who, developmentally, never made it past pre-adolescence. I will act in ways that will draw the legitimate censure of others.

AR is the opposite of a rationalization. This doesn't mean that it couldn't be somebody's intention or that, if it were, it couldn't be carried out. It means only that, in so intending, one wouldn't be rationalizing. Somebody with such an intention would be giving up; their conscious intention would be to commit a kind of suicide; and if they carried out their intention, they'd do so consciously knowing as much

Sociopaths don't have moral convictions. But their rationalizations make heavy allowances for moral convictions. This is because rationalizations are moralizations: attempts to make the immoral seem moral. So sociopathy-conducive rationalizations are dispositive of correct, if not hyper-correct, conduct and speech. A person who is genuinely moral will inevitably say and do things that others describe as immoral, even though they're hyper-moral. The employee of an institution who tries to change its iniquitous (but lucrative) practices will be described as "upstart," as "not being a team-player," as "having no respect for authority." Although propriety and morality overlap, the degree of overlap is not 100%. Also, what qualifies as proper varies from context to context. What it was proper for a Nazi (*qua* Nazi) to do is not what is "proper" for a member of the ACLU (*qua* such member) to do.

Consequently, to those who are discerning, sociopaths are off-puttingly fake, and the views they espouse are off-puttingly constrictive.

5.0 Repression and rationalization lie at the root of sociopathy. Sociopathy is the result of a confluence of rationalizations and concomitant acts of repression that are internal to a master-rationalization. But even though the sociopath's condition is the

---

273. Short for "antithesis of rationalization."

result of repression, the sociopath cannot himself repress and has no need to do so. Repression is the result of a conflict between what one knows and what one values. I rationalize my getting drunk by saying that I had to do so in order to fit in with my buddies. I value strength of character and therefore repress my knowledge of the lack of it embodied in my getting drunk.

Sociopaths value nothing. Therefore knowledge and values cannot come into conflict in the mind of a sociopath. There are no values for anything to conflict with.

Internal conflict is the prerogative of creatures with values. The objects of repression are not painful memories. They are memories that are painful *because they conflict with one's values*. If one represses being molested by an otherwise decent parent whom one loves and on whom one is dependent, it is because

(a)   one values the parent and one's relationship to that person

and

(b)   those value-mediating structures conflict with knowledge of facts that undermine their legitimacy.

One can have a deeply painful experience and not repress it. This is because repression doesn't target just any painful memory. It targets memories that are painful for the reason that they constitute knowledge of truths that conflict with one's values.

An illustration: You are being tortured. The person torturing you lacks merit. You've always known that. So, much as you hate him, you are not *disappointed* in him. You also know that it's because of heroism, not cowardice, that you're in this unfortunate position. So you are not disappointed in yourself. You are not disillusioned by anything that anyone did that led to your being in this situation. Either the people involved acted rightly or you already had a duly low opinion of them. In this situation, you have nothing to rationalize.

No disillusionment, no rationalization. But disillusionment isn't *sufficient* for rationalization. One can be disillusioned and cop to the facts. One's friend turns out to be a Nazi and, in due course, one's torturer at Auschwitz. One reconciles oneself to the ugly facts about one's friend, and about people in general, instead of rationalizing them away.

That said, ultimately it's always disillusionment with oneself that one rationalizes. So far as one rationalizes the behavior of one's former friend, it is by virtue of rationalizing one's cowardly acceptance of his behavior.

Most rationalizations don't lead to sociopathy. Most don't even *tend* to do so. There are two kinds of rationalizations: those that target one's knowledge that one has failed to live up to one's values, and those that target those values themselves. Rationalizations of the second kind are sociopathogenic. Rationalizations of the first kind are sociopathogenic only to the extent that they lead to rationalizations of the second kind.

5.1   There is a nuance. Oftentimes people who are in car crashes, or are otherwise traumatized, cannot remember the event or anything immediately preceding it. It obviously isn't because people are ashamed of experiencing such traumas, or are otherwise conflicted about them, that their memories of the latter succumb to amnesia. Nevertheless, I believe that amnesia of this kind is consistent with our model. Traumatic incidents make one aware of one's vulnerability. Or rather, they make one aware of it in a direct, first, experiential manner, as opposed to the deracinated, intellectual manner in which people are typically consciously aware of it.

I suspect that *unconsciously* we are always aware of just how fragile we are. But were such knowledge conscious, except in some intellectualized form, the resulting fear-driven inhibitions would be crippling. This would make one *more* vulnerable than one was previously. Too much fear leads to a speedy death. Kurt Gödel starved to death because he was so afraid of others that he wouldn't eat, for fear of being poisoned. Howard Hughes died of an infection because he was so afraid of germs that he wouldn't leave his room, for fear contracting another infection. A person's consciously remembering an extreme trauma would invalidate any rationalization on his part to the effect that he was *not* always on the brink of obliteration; and such rationalizations are necessary for one's health.

5.2   Readers may skip this section, since its contents play no part in what follows it.

Our antipathy towards the theory of evolution is to be explained along similar lines. First of all, setting aside children and other cognitively underdeveloped people, *everyone* has an attitude of antipathy towards that theory. This antipathy leads some people to repress their knowledge of its truth. In those in whom it does not have this effect, that antipathy is outweighed by other forces, e.g. their admiration for the scientific virtues of that particular theory. Even the evolutionary biologist is unhappy about the fact that he is descended from amoebas. But he is more interested in it than unhappy about it.

I suspect that *everyone has always known that the theory of evolution is correct.* Children see animals as para-people. Children play with stuffed animals, watch shows in which the characters are people-like animals, and have disputes with their pet dogs. Evidently, children aren't troubled by the idea of seeing animals as being cut from the same cloth as themselves. The members of pre-Judeo-Christian religions *explicitly* claim they are descended from animals. A tribe's "totem" is the animal (or animal-kind, rather) from which the tribesmen profess themselves to be descendants. *Home Sapiens* has been in existence for at least 100,000 years, during all but the last 2,000 of which its members saw animals as being of their ilk and as their forefathers.

Whereas it's a complement to be described as a "tiger" or a "stallion," it's an insult to be described as a "monkey" or a "baboon," *even though* the members of the latter two species are exponentially more intelligent than the members of the former two. When contemplating tigers and stallions, we can focus on their virtues, but we cannot do so when contemplating simians; for when doing so, we are reminded of our ignominious simian origins and therewith of our ignominious quasi-simian current selves.

Having stated these conjectures, let us return to the topic of sociopathy.

6.0   Sociopathogenesis is psychological suicide. At some level, Sociopaths are aware of what they've lost, and they resent those who haven't lost it.

An illustration: In some countries, females undergo ritual circumcision. Female circumcision is not comparable to male circumcision. The former is the medically contraindicated removal of the clitoris for cultural, social, or religious reasons. Its analogue for a male would be the removal of the glans. The process doesn't take place in a female's infancy, but rather when she is in her mid-teens, at which time she has at least some awareness of the importance of the clitoris.

The operation *is performed by other women*. Although I do not know this for a fact, I would presume that only psychologically damaged women would freely submit to circumcision.

The procedure seldom involves anasthetic and is seldom performed with sterile surgical instruments. Sometimes it is performed with pieces of broken glass.

Oftentimes, despite the overwhelming cultural pressure to submit to the procedure, females about to undergo it have to be physically restrained. This too is done by females who have themselves undergone the operation.

Analysis: Nobody wants others to have what they have given up. Those who perform the procedure don't want others to have what they gave up. That is why they do so enthusiastically, making no attempt to hide their glee. Human nature being what it is, their enthusiasm is driven by a wish to deprive another person of what one has lost. Misery loves company.

Sociopaths make a show of being friendly. But they don't have friends; for they don't have values, and a friend is somebody one values. To the extent that sociopaths behave authentically towards others, they are unremittingly undermining. But it is always under a moralistic pretext that the sociopath undermines others. This is not primarily because the sociopath wants her amorality to remain a secret from others; it's because she wants to keep it a secret from herself. The sociopath can't act in obviously amoral ways while still abiding by the terms of the rationalization that inaugurated her descent into sociopathy.

7.0   The sociopath: somebody who once had values but no longer has any.

The psychopath: someobody who never had values.

In these statements, the word "values" can be replaced with the expression "a conscience."

The sociopath is somebody with a corrupt and now defunct set of values. The psychopath is somebody who *never* had values. So the psychopath *never* had the character-architecture of a person with values, and their current character-architecture, so far as they have one, is *not* the skeleton of a once value-based character-achitecture.

Hare's (1999) "Psychopathy Checklist" is generally taken to identify the distinguishing characteristics of the psychopath. What follows is a direct quotation:[274]

Factor 1: Personality "Aggressive narcissism"
- Glibness/superficial charm s/
- Grandiose sense of self-worth
- Pathological lying
- Cunning/manipulative
- Lack of remorse or guilt
- Shallow affect (genuine emotion is short-lived and egocentric)
- Callousness; lack of empathy.
- Failure to accept responsibility for own actions

Factor 2: Case history "Socially deviant lifestyle".
- Need for stimulation/proneness to boredom
- Parasitic lifestyle
- Poor behavioral control
- Lack of realistic long-term goals
- Impulsivity
- Irresponsibility
- Juvenile delinquency
- Early behavior problems
- Revocation of conditional release

Traits not correlated with either factor
- Promiscuous sexual behavior
- Many short-term marital relationships
- Criminal versatility
- Acquired behavioural sociopathy/sociological conditioning (Item 21: a newly identified trait i.e. a person relying on sociological strategies and tricks to deceive)

According to Hare and other psychopathy-specialists, a psychopath needn't have all of the characteristic on this list and a non-psychopath may have some of them. All authorities agree that this list has to be applied with at least some discretion. Like Otto Kernberg (1985, 1993), the present authors believes that, although fundamentally accurate, it has to be applied with *extreme* discretion. The reasons for this will become evident in the very last section of the book, in which we discuss criminality, which is radically different from both sociopathy and psychopathy.

There is another problem with Hare's checklist and with Hare's (1999) book on psychopathy, *Without Conscience*, which is considered authoritative. Neither that

---

274. Hare's checklist should really be called "Cleckley's Checklist," since it is found in Cleckley (1941).

book nor that checklist say what it is to be a psychopath. But Cleckley says it clearly on several occasions. Each of the following quotations is one such occasion (the italics are mine):

> Logical thought processes may be seen in perfect operation... All judgments of value and emotional appraisals are sane and appropriate when the psychopath is tested in verbal examinations. Only very slowly and by a complex of multitudinous small impressions does the conviction come upon us that, despite these intact rational processes, these normal emotional affirmations, and their consistent application in all directions, *we are dealing here not with a complete man at all but with something that suggests a subtly constructed reflex machine which can mimic the human personality perfectly.* This smoothly operating psychic apparatus reproduces consistently not only specimens of good human reasoning but also appropriate simulations of normal human emotion in response to nearly all the varied stimuli of life.[275]

> Attempts to interpret the [psychopath's] disorder do not, of course, furnish evidence that he has a disorder or that it is serious. For reliable evidence of this we must examine his behavior. Only here, not in psychopathologic formulations, can we apply our judgment to what is objective and demonstrable. *Functionally and structurally* all is intact *on the outside.* Good function (healthy reactivity) will be demonstrated in all theoretical truths. Judgment as well as sound reasoning will appear *at verbal levels.* Ethical as well as practical considerations will be recognized in the abstract. A *brilliant mimicry* of sound, social reactions will occur in every test except the test of life itself. In the psychopath, we confront a personality neither broken nor outwardly distorted but of *a substance that lacks ingredients without which normal function in major life issues is impossible.*[276]

> The [psychopath's] out functional aspect masks or disguises something quite different within, concealing behind *a perfect mimicry of normal emotion, fine intelligence, and social responsibility* a grossly disabled and irresponsible personality.[277]

To be a psychopath is to be a fraud. It is to be a nobody disguised as a somebody. The essence of psychopathy is phoniness. Cleckley states that clearly. Hare seems to hold that the essence of psychopathy is criminality. Criminality is a frequent by-product of psychopathy, nothing more. In Section 11.0, it will be made clear why criminality isn't the same thing as psychopathy.

---

275. Cleckley (1941:406).

276. Cleckey (1941:420).

277. Cleckey (1941:420).

A complete fraud can't be an agent, or *vice versa*. A complete fraud can't be rational, or *vice versa*. Of course, completely non-agential, sub-rational beings, such as plants, aren't psychopaths, psychopathy being the prerogative of the pseudo-rational pseudo-agent. Indeed, to be a psychopath *is* to be a pseudo-rational pseudo-agent.

Both psychopathy and sociopathy involve being a nobody disguised as a somebody. But those conditions differ in ways corresponding to the differences in their respective modes of origination. Every instance of sociopathy is the result of some rationalization, and the sociopath is bound by the terms of that rationalization. Psychopathy is *not* the result of rationalization. Psychopathy is a *failure to acquire values to begin with*. For this reason, the psychopath's psychological architecture, so far as he has one, isn't even formally similar to that of someone with an intact, mature personality architecture. The psychopath's personality architecture, unlike the sociopath's, isn't the skeletal remains of a normal personality architecture; it isn't even the skeleton of a personality of a personality-architecture whose development was cut off at the time it was no more than a skeleton that hadn't yet been fleshed out.

7.1   Before moving on, let us restate some key points. Psychopathy is not the result of rationalization, and the psychopath doesn't operate within the limits set by some master-rationalization. In this respect, the psychopath differs from the sociopath.

The psychopath often operates within context-specific rationalizations; but no master-rationalizations regulates his ideation or conduct. A consequence is that, whereas the sociopath is, in respect of his behavior, an arch-conformist, the psychopath tends to behave in decidedly abnormal ways. Since the psychopath, unlike the sociopath, doesn't have to operate within some master-rationalization, there are no rules – even empty, purely formal ones – by which he has to abide. The sociopath, it will be recalled, wants to believe himself to be legitimate. His descent into sociopathy was inaugurated by a master-rationalization, and that rationalization defines the structure of his current sociopathic integration. Since that rationalization is an attempt to legitimate who he now is, the sociopath is bound, not by actual morality, but by some mimicry of it.

By contrast, psychopathy is neither initiated nor constituted by some master-rationalization. Consequently, the psychopath doesn't care about being legitimate. He doesn't even know what legitimacy is. He knows what sorts of *behavior* are associated with words like "legitimate," "good," "bad," etc. But he doesn't grasp the corresponding concepts. So he is free to rob and kill. The psychopath isn't bound by *any* code of honor, not even of the wooden, formal sort binding the sociopath.

A consequence is that psychopath's conduct and personality differ dramatically from the sociopath's.

7.2   What is the psychopath like? Psychopaths bear no resemblance to fictitious arch-villains, such as Hannibal Lecter and Dr. No. Those people are psychologically developed and intact. They're just evil. And being evil is very different from having no values. Tigers are predators, but they aren't *evil*. Being evil means grasping values and deliberately flouting them. Psychopaths act like evil people; but that's because a failure to grasp norms can have the same behavioral manifestations as a willful violation of them. (In Section 15.0, where we discuss the nature of criminality, more will be said as to why psychopathy and evil are not to be equated.)

Psychopaths are fraudsters, swindlers, and con-artists. They are "slick." They are expert-manipulators: they know just which emotional buttons to push and when to push them. They are notoriously good at seducing members of the opposite sex. They are often cult leaders and gurus. Psychopaths believe in nothing; so they are never genuinely right-wing or left-wing or otherwise ideological. But the psychopath may be the leader of a left-wing group, a right-wing group, or any group belonging to any political or religious affiliation. The psychopath pretends to be whatever he has to be to defraud others.

Psychopaths have a curiously "vinyl" quality. They hit all the right notes. But there is something distinctively synthetic about them. They can discourse intelligently about virtually any topic – for a few moments. But if asked to show more knowledge of a subject than can be acquired from a magazine, they cannot do so.

Psychopaths are evasive. They can't be pinned down. When asked a question, the psychopath tends to respond with a lecture or a dramatic performance. He thereby avoids answering the question, while making onlookers think that he knows the answer.

This last point must be qualified. When a psychopath knows the answer to a question, he answers it in the same way as a non-psychopath who knows the answer to it. It's when the non-psychopath doesn't know the answer that he differs from his non-psychopathic counterpart. The latter either cops to his ignorance or inadvertently betrays a lack of confidence in what he's saying: he smiles nervously; his gaze wanders; he fidgets. If the psychopath is asked a question to which he doesn't know the answer, he either responds in the way in which he responds to questions to which he does know the answer or he responds with overblown self-confidence.

The psychopath's question-prompted lectures are meant to seem spontaneous, and that is just how they strike people who don't know much about the topic being lectured about. But others see that those lectures are but montages of empty clichés and plagiarized apercus, accompanied by arm-flapping histrionics and confident gesticulations.

7.3 Psychopaths are genuinely developed in one way: they know how to con people. Ironically, it's because the human condition is so alien to them that they are so expert at manipulating people. The psychopath is interested in others only to the extent that he can manipulate them. Because the psychopath's interest in others ends there, every exchange he has with anyone is, for him, an exercise in honing his skills as a manipulator. Because he himself is unlike the people he is manipulating, and also so indifferent to them, he has a major advantage over his non-psychopathic counterpart when trying to figure out just how to manipulate a given person: the psychopath does not have to "tune out" a flood of projective, *a priori* beliefs, and empathy-related (though not necessarily themselves empathic) preconceptions as to his mark's nature. A non-psychopath, even a very evil one, sees his mark as a human being and thus as being like himself. He thus has some incentive *not* to see his mark for who he really is: for he knows that, since he's cut from the same basic cloth as the mark, what he sees in his mark is probably present in himself. Also, even though the predator is evil, he may have an involuntary streak of tenderness in him. In fact, given that he is a non-socopathic, non-psychopath, it's inevitable that he'll have some degree of empathy for others. This blunts his ability to predate; for, in his attempts to override his tenderness, he is likely to become *overly* resolute about being evil towards his target; and such counterphobic extremism leads to tunnel vision, since, by supposition, it involves a desensitization to one's own affects and, therefore, to the intuitions mediated thereby. As a result, the non-psychopathic predator may have an overly emotional, and therefore blinkered, understanding of his mark. The psychopath is incapable of being thus blinkered, and to that extent is more functional than his non-psychopathic counterpart.

One psychopath I know is a professor at a prestigious law school. He teaches legal philosophy. One day, while he and I were attending the wedding of a common friend, he apprised me of his expertise on U.S. foreign policy during the 50's and 60's. I responded by asking a question to which I did not (and still do not) know the answer: "Given how much Korea's situation in the early 50's paralleled Vietnam's situation in the '60's, why is America's intervention in Korea seen as moral, whereas its intervention in Vietnam is seen as an abomination?"

His clearly pre-rehearsed answer was an incoherent, but rhetorically impeccable, concatenation of sophomoric platitudes and two-liners taken verbatim, but without acknowledgement of their respective sources, from the works of Norman Malcolm, Stephen Toulmin, and other neo-Wittgensteinians. (He was under the mistaken impression that I had doctored in mathematics, not philosophy, and would therefore fail to recognize his plagiarized apercus for what they were.) He spoke for 20 minutes, without interruption, with the smooth confidence of a *bona fide* authority. During his soliloquy, a crowd gathered round, all of them awed by this man's brilliance. He finally paused long enough for me to ask him a few questions. His answers made it clear that he no idea who Robert MacNamara was, or General Giap, or Le Duc Tho. But the grandiloquent manner in which he dodged my questions only bolstered the crowd's confidence in him.

7.4   There are only a few things psychopaths enjoy for their own sake:

  (i)   manipulating and defrauding others;

  (ii) having power;

  (iii) having money;

  (iv) being famous or glamorous;

and

(v)   diminishing others and making them suffer.

Why does the psychopath enjoy these particular things? Money and power are things that one needn't have values to enjoy. Many animals are instinctively predatory and acquisitive. We are such animals. In social contexts, these instincts are expressed as desires for wealth and power. Also, all animals instinctively wish to survive. *Ceteris paribus* the more money and power one has, the better one's chances of surviving.

Since being liked by others is more survival-conducive than being disliked (or simply not being liked), it might be thought that the psychopath's love of fame and glamour is to explained along the same lines as his desire for wealth. Such an explanation, however, would be incomplete, if not false.

Psychopaths value nothing and therefore take pleasure in next to nothing. They enjoy mating and predating, since one doesn't have to have values to enjoy such acts. For the same reason, they enjoy strictly instinctual forms of affection-giving. So, for example, the psychopath may enjoy cuddling with his new puppy. (But he can't value his puppy and he therefore can't be concerned for its welfare: for all he cares, his puppy can drown after it stops being cute and fun to cuddle with.) Finally, psychopaths, like all creatures, can experience pleasures of a strictly sensual nature. So, for example, the psychopath can enjoy a good meal. But the psychopath can experience no pleasures other than those of a strictly instinctual or sensual nature.

The psychopath's desire to have money, it must be remembered, is merely a socialized version of an animalistic instinct of some kind – e.g. to survive or to make oneself to desirable to prospective mates. *Cognitively* the psychopath is normal. He knows what causes what. He knows that he is embedded in a context consisting of a plurality people, whose interrelations are subject to certain rules. This knowledge is obviously partly determinative of the nature of the actions to which his purely instinctual urges dispose him. (A dog's urge to mate or flee from danger is similarly affected by what it is aware of. Whether the dog goes in this direction or that is obviously determined by its awareness of the location of the threat or prospective mate.)

7.5   The psychopath's love of fame and its trappings is to be explained in terms of two facts. For the psychopath, there is no distinction between actual merit and the mere appearance thereof. The psychopath is a sensual creature, in the most literal sense of the word "sensual": he is aware of colors, sounds, fragrances, etc. If something is brightly colored, he knows it. If it has some intangible virtue, he doesn't know it. So, for the psychopath, the difference between success and failure is marked by what is visible: by what kind of car a man drives and what sort clothes he wears.

Success and failure may reasonably be seen as social analogues of life and death, survival and obliteration. If this is right, then the unusually intense allure for the psychopath of fine clothes, richly appointed domiciles, and the like, can be understood in terms of the fact that he is a creature who, blind to value, sees nothing *behind* what his senses reveal to him. Success is to be understood strictly in terms of what is perceptible. In the psychopath's eyes, one is only as successful as one's success is perceptible.

The more perceptible – the bigger the house, the flashier the clothes, etc. – the greater the degree of success.

But there is another, subtler reason for the psychopath's intense desire to have the perceptible concomitants of success (fame, wealth, etc.), as opposed to success *per se*. Many so-called "sensual" delights aren't of a strictly sensual nature. One must have values to experience aesthetic pleasure, as we saw. The music itself must be distinguished from the noises mediating it; Rembrandt's masterpieces must be distinguished from the deposits of paint that constitute them. Though mediated by noise and paint, the work of art *per se* is not identical with a series of noises or a discolored canvass. And aesthetic enjoyment, though mediated by audition and vision, is no more identical with such things than one's joy at discovering how to solve Russell's Paradox. It isn't the noises *per se* that one enjoys, but what one hears *in* them. What one hears in them are instances of intricate structures, and musical pleasure is a concomitant of one's awareness of the presence of those structures in the noise that one hears. So one's enjoyment of a piece of music isn't really sensual pleasure at all. It is intellectual enjoyment that is mediated by sense-perception.

Part of the enjoyment, we hypothesized, that one takes in listening to the *Hammerklavier* is the joy, not just of discovery, but of *self*-discovery, the structures instantiated by relevant sounds being externalizations of those instantiated by one's otherwise undetectable subpersonal cogitations. I did next to nothing to substantiate this hypothesis, but it still seems worth stating, if only to reject after being considered.

But the larger point stands: much so-called "sensual" pleasure is replete with valuative mentation. One enjoys acts of intimacy with someone whom one cherishes much more than with someone towards whom one is indifferent, let alone someone whom one dislikes. In fact, acts of the latter two types may be repellent, even if the other party involved fulfills the requisite, purely physical desiderata. This suggests that the pleasure attendant to acts of intimacy with a loved one are not of a strictly sensual nature: such pleasure expresses one's high regard for one's partner.

Other things being equal, the more fully one's partner satisfies the requisite physical desiderata, the greater the pleasure brought by acts of physical intimacy with that person. But this can be reconciled with our position. Noises must meet certain purely physical requirements if they are to be adequate *vehicles* for the ratiocinations in which musical delight actually consists. The same thing *mutatis mutandis* can be said of the corporeal dimension of one's romantic partner's being. If one's partner is hideously disfigured, covered in weeping sores, etc., physical intimacy with that person won't establish the non-corporeal connection that it is its purpose to establish.

Of course, there is a significant purely sensual dimension to one's enjoyment of physical intimacy with a loved one. But what is relevant is that there is also another, non-sensual dimension to it *and to that extent the psychopath cannot experience the joys of such intimacy.* Whatever joy such acts bring to the psychopath, they come entirely from the *strictly* sensual component of such acts. Beyond that, such acts do nothing for the psychopath.

This point holds, not just with respect to carnal activity, but with respect to *every* form of activity in which sense-perception is to any degree a vehicle for mentation of a valuative kind. The psychopath is thus in an unfortunate position. There are many sources of enjoyment for the non-psychopath. There are few for the psychopath. Further, there are no psychopath-specific forms of enjoyment: the non-psychopath can experience all of the strictly visceral and sensual forms of enjoyment available to the psychopath, but the psychopath's sources of enjoyment are but a small subset of the non-psychopath's.

The psychopath must cleave to what is perceptible. Nothing else brings him enjoyment, except for the discharging of basal urges, which will often take rarefied, socialized forms, making it hard to see it for what it is.[278]

8.0   Only an infinitesimally small percentage of psychopaths are serial killers. But, it is generally held, most if not all serial killers are are psychopaths.

The hedge ("it is generally held") is not idle throat-clearing: some authors – I am thinking in particular of Helen Morrison (2005) – hold that serial killers have an even *more* rudimentary psychological integration than psychopaths. They hold that, whereas the psychpath's emotional development stops at around six months, this being the age at which a person first acquires object-relations, the serial killer's stops even earlier. An "object-relation" is a relation to another human being

(a)   That involves an awareness of the distinction between oneself and that other person, and also an awareness of the distinction between that other person and other people,

and

---

278. As previously stated, Cleckley uses the terms "sociopath" and "psychopath" interchangeably, and he himself explicitly states this. But there is one striking passage in his book (1941: 199) where, although he does not know it, he is describing sociopathy:

> It becomes difficult to imagine how much of the sham and hollowness which cynical commentators have immemorially pointed out in life may come from contact in serious issues with persons affected in some degree by the disorder [namely psychopathy] we are trying to describe. The fake poet who really feels little; the painter who, despite his loftiness, had his eye chiefly on the lucrative fad of his day; the fashionable clergyman who, despite his burning eloquence or his lively castigation of the devil, is primarily concerned with his advancement; the flirt who can readily awaken love but cannot feel love or recognize its absence; parents who, despite smooth convictions that they have only the child's welfare at heart, actually reject him except as it suits their own petty or selfish aims: all these types, so familiar in literature and in anybody's experience, may be as they are because of a slight affliction with the personality disorder now under discussion. I believe probable that many persons outwardly imposing yet actually of insignificant import really are so affected.

(b)   That is of an emotional, as opposed to strictly pragmatic nature.

So, Morrison's theory goes, psychopaths *do* make it to the stage at which they have object-relations. But those object-relations are sources of pain. The other party is somebody on whom the youngster depends. But that person is insufficiently attentive or she's positively sadistic. As a result, the youngster in question so parameterizes his emotional disposition to that person, and to people in general, that he can benefit from them to that they extent that they can benefit him while also being insulated from their treachery. So (if this theory is correct) the psychopath *does* have object-relations: but they are selfish and one-dimensional. At the same time, according to this theory, the serial killer's development often stops *before* he has formed object-relations.

8.1   There very clearly are serial killers who are psychopaths (e.g. John Wayne Gacy, Ted Bundy, Jack Unterweger).[279] But with that qualification, the present author agrees with the just-stated theory, his reason being that it is empirically well supported.

For example, Gary Ridgeway, the so-called "Green River killer," was one of the most prolific serial killers ever. But he wasn't manipulative. (Nor was he honest.) He wasn't a con-man, a charismatic manipulator, a seductive man-about-town. He was a blank. During his four decade stint as a serial killer, he held the same minimum wage job, as a box boy at a warehouse.[280]

Jeffrey Dahmer was a blank.[281] During his time as a serial killer, he held a mini-mum-wage job at a candy-factory. He was not a fast-talker; he was not quick or sly in the way that psychopaths are. He was an emptiness. Apart from being a serial killer, the only noteworthy thing about him was how much he drank. He sold his blood for alcohol. He was dishonorably discharged from the army for being drunk *all the time.* When he was interviewed, after being caught and convicted, he flatly said: "Society is not to blame. My parents are not to blame. I did these things because I wanted to do them."

John Wayne Gacy, on the other hand, was a true psychopath. Eventually convicted of raping, torturing, and murdering 33 adolescent boys, he had everyone convinced, prior to being caught, that he was an excellent fellow. He was a senior member of the local Chamber of Commerce and the local chapter of his Political Party. (At one point, the President's wife came to the suburb of Chicago where he lived. Since the president was a member of the same party as Gacy, that party's local chapter was required to greet her. Gacy's fellow party-members unanimously and enthusiastically asked Gacy to meet and greet the First Lady on the party's behalf. He did so. She found him utterly

---

279. See Moss (1999), Rule (2008), Leake (2009) for extensive and subtle descriptions of, re-spectively, Gacy, Bundy, and Unterweger. Moss personally knew Gacy, and Rule personally knew Bundy.

280. See Rule (2006).

281. See Davis (1991).

charming.) Gacy was a clown at children's birthday parties. He did not receive compensation for this. He volunteered his services, he said, because he "loved children." The revelers to whom his clownery brought such delight were only slightly younger than the dozens of youngsters whom he raped, tortured, butchered, and whose bodies he kept as trophies in his basement.

After being apprehended, Gacy always had a story. "I'm innocent. I never killed anybody." "Sure I killed them – but it was in self-defense." "Yes I killed them. And, no, it wasn't in self-defense. But they deserved it; they were trash; by killing them I was cleansing the world and doing humanity a favor."

Ted Bundy was a psychopath-serial killer. Before being caught, he worked on a volunteer basis for a telephone hotline for people on the brink of suicide. Like Gacy, he was a political operative and a rising star in the local chapter of his political party. Although his grades and entrance-exam scores were mediocre, Bundy got into a reputable law-school – but only because the governor of his state, for whom Bundy had successfully campaigned, personally wrote him a glowing recommendation. After three months, Bundy flunked out of law school, because his days' long killing sprees took too much time away from his school-work. Soon after being ejected, he was arrested for possession of burglary tools and a rape kit. He was eventually convicted and executed for the murder of a 13 year old girl.

Unlike Dahmer, Bundy never simply said: "I did it. I did it because I wanted to." Bundy denied everything; then he hinted at his guilt without admitting it. Then he admitted it. Then he retracted his confession. Then he retracted his retraction. Then he blamed society, pornography, the media – all the standard scapegoats.

Unlike Ridgeway, Bundy *while on death row* had a huge female fan club, and many a woman proposed to him while he was on death row. While he stood accused of murder, but before he was convicted, Bundy's own girlfriend paid Bundy conjugal visits, Bundy's relationship with this person began before she or anyone else knew what he was. Like many others, she simply couldn't believe that Bundy was a killer, let alone a serial killer. Later she changed her mind.

8.2 But Bundy and Gacy are representatives of only one subclass of the class of serial killers; and Ridgeway is representative of another subclass. And some authorities believe that the latter subclass is both the better populated of the two and also that its members are better, more pure representations than members of the other class of what it is to be serial killer.

The idea is that, in cases such as Ridgeway's, serial murder is the expression of a unitary pathological deviation, whereas, in cases such as Bundy's, it is the expression of a confluence of many different forces. So what we have in Ridgeway is an isolated, specific deviation. By contrast, what we have in Bundy is such a deviation *plus* various psychodynamic factors. To be sure, Bundy had the requisite serial-killer-specific integration. But in Bundy that integration may to an extent have been a vehicle for ideation that, although obviously pathological, was not serial-killer-specific. In Ridgeway, that integration was operating on its own.[282]

This position is consistent with the available data. Given publicly known facts, it's clear that some serial killers are just blanks, who lack the distinguishing characteristics of the psychopath: the glibness, the charm, the charisma, the faux-empathy, and so on. At the same time, there are some things they do have in common with psychopaths that they don't have in common with non-psychopaths: they don't have meaningful life-plans; they don't care about others; and they lack values, that being why they can kill, and kill prodigiously, without feeling so much as a twinge of remorse. But the existence of those commonalities is consistent with the hypothesis that serial killers, of the Ridgeway-type, are blanks, whose development was arrested before they could form any object-relations. Blanks don't have values, meaningful life plans, etc.

But psychopaths aren't blanks. On the contrary, they're consummate showmen. They are hollow; there is nothing behind the image. But there is an image – of a concerned hotline-operator, a potential head of state, etc.

With those in the other category, there is no image. There's no fraud where there's no image: no appearance of legitimacy; no apparent reason to entrust this person with your life-savings. And there's no psychopathy where there's no fraud. Ridgeway, Dahmer, et al. weren't fraudsters, except to the extent that they had to cover their tracks to conceal their murders; they weren't charmers, swindlers, or dandies. They were sub-psychopathic, not psychopathic. Bundy, Gacy, Unterweger, and Mudgett were arch-fraudsters: they never passed up an opportunity to cheat; to stiff their employees; to plagiarize a term-paper; to pretend to be of royal descent; etc. Serial killing was what got them in trouble, and it was probably what they enjoyed the most. But they were fraudsters first and serial killers second. Ridgeway, Dahmer, and Arthur Shawcross[283] were just serial killers.

8.3   Earlier it was said that psychopaths are notoriously good at seducing others. They are also unusually *prone* to do so. But they derive little pleasure from intercourse *per se*.

So why are so many seducers and seductresses among their ranks? They enjoy the acts deception that led to intercourse, as well as those that such act help to perpetrate. In some cases, the psychopath regards the sexual act as one of pure aggression – as rape. Rapists, in fact, are categorically psychopaths. (But not all psychopaths are rapists.)

Presumably, it's typically male psychopaths who, when having concensual sex, see what they are doing as rape. And setting aside the possibility of one female's raping

---

282. This conjecture of mine, though in keeping with the theory in question, is my own personal addition to that theory; I have not heard other proponents of the theory put forth a similar conjecture.

283. See Norris (1992).

another, it is exclusively male psychopaths for whom it really is rape. But psychopathy being what it is, the female psychopath is likely in some cases to see the sexual act as being one of defiling or diminishing her partner.

Psychopaths derive little pleasure from intercourse. This is because much pleasure that is thought to be of a purely sensual nature actually embodies values. (We discussed this earlier.) Would you enjoy hugging somebody you detested? What about somebody towards whom you were indifferent? You like hugging Sally because you love and cherish her. The same is true of other activities that you perform with her.

Of course, there are people whom one doesn't love with whom acts of this sort may be enjoyable. But in such cases, the act in question is a kind of externalized fantasy. One may know (or believe) that one's partner lacks such and such virtues. But, for the purposes of the act, one pretends that he or she has them. If one were to engage in such acts with somebody who, at every level of one's being, one *knew* to lack all such virtues, acts of a carnal nature with that person would not be very enjoyable, at least not for people of a certain psychological configuration. None of this is meant to deny obvious fact that there is a significant, purely sensual dimension to such activities.

What psychopaths enjoy are the manipulations of which the act of seduction is the culmination and of which it is itself a component. The psychopath enjoys the initial conquest; and the psychopath enjoys making their mark fall in love with them, which is obviously facilitated by engaging in "tender and loving" intercourse with them. But the psychopath derives little pleasure from intercourse *per se*, with the qualifications stated earlier.

Incidentally, the fact the human beings are the only creatures that have "off-season" sexual intercourse is to be explained in terms of the fact that we have values: because we infuse carnal acts with those values, they are enjoyable for us in a way they cannot possibly be enjoyable for value-free creatures.

8.4   These points relate to the famously amorphous sexuality of the psychopath. Psychopaths lack a well-defined sexual identity. (Cleckley (1941) states this clearly, and Hare (1999) duly notes it on his checklist.) They can have sex with anybody: male, female, young, and old. It's all the same to them. For them, physical intimacy has none of the valuative concomitants that it has in ordinary cases. For a non-psychopath, physical characteristics are infused with meaning. It isn't the skin-texture *per se* of an 80 year-old woman that makes her undesirable to a 20 year old. It is her skin-texture *plus* its various meanings. For the psychopath, nothing means anything. So for a 20 year old male psychopath, being intimate with a octagenarian billionaress is like having a meal one doesn't much care for, and being intimate with a stunning 30-year old beauty is like having a dish one does quite fancy.

The psychopath's sexual amorphousness, which is an expression of his generally infantile psychological condition, is often seen as evidence of his open-mindedness, his high-minded disdain for culturally rooted bigotries, and the expansiveness of his ken.

I've heard more than one psychopath described as having a "spacious consciousness." In each case, the psychopath's sexual elasticity was cited as evidence of his great spiritual and intellectual gifts. And in each case, reference's to the psychopath's "spacious consciousness" came to be replaced by less laudatory epithet, in consequence of the passage of time and the unreciprocated transmission of large funds.

For the non-psychopath intercourse is not merely a physical act; it is fraught with emotion. And many of the aesthetic, intercourse-related preferences of the non-psychopath, while seemingly superficial, are associatively connected to object-relations with loved and valued people. At time t, Fred loves Sally, who has blond hair. Sally dumps Fred. Fred recovers emotionally; but his love for Sally embodied a legitimately high estimation of her merits, which disposes him, via the standard associative channels, to idealize, and thence to fall in love with, people who physically resemble Sally.

With males, it is said, love starts on the outside and makes its way to the inside. This statement is ambiguous. On one disambiguation it comes to this: A man initially likes a woman for her appearance and for her appearance *only*. Later, after he comes to know her, he likes her for her. There is some truth in this line of thought, but less than is ordinarily thought.

The other disambiguation gives a better description than the first of the relevant psychodynamics. Men are indeed drawn to women for their looks, but largely (not solely) because those men unconsciously associate certain desired character traits with those looks. Moreover, a woman's having the requisite physical features is not *by itself* enough to sustain his interest in her. Should those features remind a given man of Ethel, who was a luminary, an inspired poet, a subtle visionary, etc. that man may *initially* be drawn to Gertrude, given the latter's physical resemblance to Ethel. But as soon as it becomes clear that Gertrude lacks Ethel's virtues, and has qualities antithetical to them, that man will probably lose interest in Gertrude. I thus suspect that, in some cases, the man is initially drawn to a woman because of her appearance; her appearance prompts a quick examination of her *self*; and if that examination establishes the presence of the requisite psychological properties, attraction ensues.

There are of course many reasons why people fall with in love, and why men fall in love with women. It is my purpose to show that sometimes what is regarded as attraction of a strictly "prurient" kind is a foil for value-laden, positive characterizations of the desired female. That said, there is no shortage of strictly prurient ideation in the human psyche.

8.5   Not all psychopaths are professional swindlers. Some are physicians, law-professors, or engineers. In fact, there are few professions in which they are not to be found.

But the psychopath's professional successes tend to be more apparent than real. This doesn't hold in professions such as football or emergency room surgery, where there is a clear difference between success and failure. But in any profession where fraud is possible, the psychopath's successes in that field are likely to be fraudulent. The psychopath may be a "brilliant" Marxist law professor, who is supposedly showing that classical logic is a machination on the part of haves to oppress the have-nots. But he is probably just blowing hot air. You'd see emptiness in grand claims if you were to read what he's saying instead of witnessing it in person and thus being pied-piped by his histrionics – his dramatic arm-movements, his melodic vocal modulations, his magisterially throwing a copy of *The Wealth of Nations* in the trashcan. Sometimes the psychopath professor may say truly brilliant things, but they are likely to be plagiarized.

These points must be qualified. Psychopaths can be genuinely brilliant. But this qualification must itself be qualified! The qualification is aptly put by Lindner:

> In the literature on [psychopathy] frequent mention is made of the "high" intelligence of psychopaths ... However derived, these notions are misleading or at least insufficient to serve either as diagnostic aids or explanatory propositions ... So far as intelligence *per se* is concerned ... what is outstanding about psychopathy is not its arithmetic proportions but is its peculiar variety and design ... The intelligence of the psychopath can be described only adjectivally and in terms of the [psychopath's] whole personality. Perfectly adapted to his needs in the same way as protective coloring is suited to the preservation of the life of an animal, all those psychological functions (thinking, understanding, imagining, remembering, etc.) which are held to be components of "intelligence" have in the psychopath superimposed on them an aura of shrewdness and secretive cunning, of calculating canniness. These elements not only serve psychopathic ends but effectively distort and divert all known measuring instruments, the rigid designs of which prevent their divinatory use with such individuals ... A further striking feature of the intelligence of the psychopath, and one which appears only after long time acquaintance with such individuals, is concerned with the amazing excess-cargo of uncoordinated and useless information they possess. Frequently one is misled by their typically encyclopaedic range into considering them persons of high intellect, even of culture. Penetration with time, however, discloses that, like the veneer of mahogany applied to inferior wood, this mass of "knowledge" is superficial and undigested; that it is free-floating, lacking the requisite elements of cohesiveness and relativity.[284]

I would like to propose an explanation of the fact that Lindner describes. The psychopath is more interested in seeming smart than in being smart. He *is* interested in being smart, but only because it is hard to seem smart without being smart. For this reason, the psychopath chooses to develop his intellect in ways that lend themselves to meretricious display. The psychopath won't choose to write obscure treatises, whose merits will go unrecognized for centuries, or great novels, which, for decades, only the

---

284. Lindner (1944: 5–6).

critics like. The psychopath wants to dazzle people. He wants whatever gifts he has to be capable of being put on display at a moment's notice.

The non-psychopath has a very different relationship to his talents. He'll inevitably spend time developing skills and acquiring knowledge that have intrinsic value but no display-value. The non-psychopath's talents are like a computer: the visible operations on one's desktop are but hints of the vastly more complex operations underlying them. The psychopath's talents are like a cubist painting: everything is pressed into a two-dimensional manifold. Everything is on the surface.[285]

8.6 That said, there is one respect in which psychopathy can facilitate the *legitimate* development of intelligence. The non-psychopath's cogitations make conscience-based concessions to standards of rigor and evidence. This tends to make him timid and unwilling to speculate. This leads to a fear of asserting things he can't substantiate, which leads to a fear of *thinking* such things: he is likely to be reluctant to embark on trains of thought that don't follow tried and truth pathways.

Also, the non-psychopath, having as he does legitimate concern for others' well being, doesn't want to denigrate another person's viewpoint without having a legitimate reason to do so. This gives the non-psychopath another incentive to be timid about stating, and subsequently about even thinking, anything for which he can't cite solid grounds.[286]

The psychopath isn't thus hobbled. So if the psychopath has intellectual talent, he isn't thus inhibited from working with ideas his confidence in which is based on nothing more than an obscure intuition. His willingness to countenance such ideas may lead to a willingness to *have* such ideas to begin with, the result being a loosening up of his creative powers that leads to ideas that sometimes have merit and that aren't likely to occur to others.

So whereas the non-psychopath's intellectual search-space tends to be limited by considerations of plausibility and feasibility, the psychopath's search-space is limited by nothing other than his own brain-power. The result is that, if a given psychopath is intellectually gifted, he is likely to have some spectacular insights, albeit ones which, for the very reasons that he had them, he probably won't adequately substantiate and

---

285. Cf. Wittgenstein (1958): "There are no depths. Nothing is hidden." He was speaking about philosophy. I propose that he was also speaking about himself.

286. I am not referring to the mercenary intellectual conformism of the pre-tenure professor or the pre-dissertation graduate student. I am referring to a conscience-based wish not to take credit away from those who deserve it.

Of course, non-psychopaths *do* denigrate viewpoints they know to have merit; they *do* bruit many a viewpoint which has nothing to commend itself to them other than its conformity to the bigotries of their auditors. I am speaking about tendencies, not absolutes.

which, for those same reasons, are probably grossly outnumbered by unfounded speculations.[287]

8.7   Like sociopaths, psychopaths are arch-rationalizers. In fact, setting aside directly perception-based beliefs and others of a comparably rudimentary kind, the psychopath's "beliefs" consists for the most part of rationalizations. This is subject to an important qualification. The psychopath can be a competent mathematician, philosopher, musician, or physician, and he can therefore have the beliefs necessary for such competence. But the psychopath's beliefs *about himself* are categorically in the nature of rationalizations; and the psychopath's beliefs about situations relating to his own welfare are unusually likely to be rationalizations, and oftentimes deeply implausible ones.

The psychopath's having these characteristics is the result of the convergence of a few different forces. The psychopath sees nothing as having non-instrumental value

---

287. The word "probably" occurs twice in the last sentence. This is because sometimes psychopaths not only have deep insights but develop them. Perhaps it is never *as* a psychopath that a psychopath has and duly develops an insight; perhaps the psychopaths in question aren't pure psychopaths and it is the non-psychopathic part of them that is responsible for their legitimate accomplishments. This hypothesis, if correct, is easier than its negation to integrate into the model of psychopathy being proposed.

But I think it's false. First of all, the people I'm thinking of are quite "pure" instances of psychopathy. Many people are diagnosed as psychopaths who aren't. But the people I'm thinking of were psychopaths. Second, given how much of a psychopath's intelligence is bound up with his psychopathy and given, therefore, how inaccessible a psychopath's intelligence is to the part of him that isn't psychopathic, it seems probable that, when a given psychopath has and duly develops a great idea, it is *as* a psychopath.

Despite first appearances, this fact is consistent with what we've been saying. The psychopath is characterologically, not cognitively, different from others. Cognitively, the psychopath is no less competent than the non-psychopath: he is as good at adding numbers, playing the piano, and building bird-houses. It is emotionally, not cognitively, that the psychopathic innovator differs from his non-psychopathic counterpart. The non-psychopath who proves the continuum hypothesis does so because he sees doing so as a good unto itself. The psychopath who does so does it to hone and expand the range of his psychopathy.

Psychopaths are as likely to vary in respect of intellectual acumen as the members of the top 45% of the non-psychopathic. (People not in the top 45% don't become psychopaths (or so it is alleged – doubtfully, in my view). See Cleckley 1941; Hare 1999.) It's hard to seem smart without being smart. And seeming smart to people who are themselves smart is typically more fruitful than seeming smart to intellectually deficient people: the former are more likely to be in positions of power. The more intelligent psychopaths know this, and they know that to *seem* smart to their highly intelligent superiors, they must actually *be* smart: in such cases, appearance and reality coalesce. So even though the psychopath cares only about appearance, not substance, there are cases where the two coincide. So if a psychopath solves the continuum problem, it isn't because he's only part-psychopath; it's because he knows he's at a juncture where there's no way to look a certain way without being that way, and it's his intention to look that way.

and therefore sees the truth has having no non-instrumental value. So should he have a wish to distort the truth, he won't be at all resistant to doing so.

Psychopaths are obviously more likely to rationalize about their level of merit – about, for example, whether they are great thinkers – than they are likely to rationalize about circumstances relating to their own well being. But they *do* sometimes rationalize conduct on their part that is obviously likely to have adverse consequences for them. Why is this? Is it because the psychopath doesn't care whether he lives or dies, whether he's in a jail-cell or in his own home? No. He cares about those things. He has animalistic instincts; and the instinct to survive is not just another one of an animal's instincts: it is *the* instinct underlying all others. (This is subject to qualifications relating to the fact that sometimes animals instinctively self-destruct.) So what's the answer to our question?

It is often very hard to know which truths will be of practical value. To be sure, it's obvious in some cases, e.g.

- There is a guy with a gun who is now trying to kill me.
- My heart-medication is underneath my bed.
- In the woods, in a place where I can go with no chance of being detected, there is an unguarded briefcase with $50,000 dollars in it.

But these are extreme cases. Company X just merged with Company Y. You know this. Because of a monsoon in East Asia, this merger will cause Company X/Y's stock to soar. For this reason, if were you now to invest $1,000 in that Company, you'd be a billionaire in ten years' time. But given the available data, there is no way you or anyone else could know this.

It is logically impossible to predict what one will come to know; and, to the not inconsiderable extent that one's actions affect the world, it is therefore logically impossible to predict the future state of the universe. The forthcoming argument was put forth by Karl Popper (this is not a quotation):

(KP[288]) You cannot possibly know exactly what you will know in 20 years. (We are setting aside obvious and trivial qualifications, e.g. if you know you'll be dead in 20 years, you know you'll know nothing.) Let $k_1 \ldots k_n$ be the pieces of knowledge of you'll have in 20 years; suppose that list to be complete. Suppose that you know now that in 20 years you'll know $k_1 \ldots k_n$. In that case, you'll now know $k_1 \ldots k_n$. You'll inevitably acquire new knowledge over the next 20 years. So $k_1 \ldots k_n$ won't be the entirety of what you'll then know, contrary to our hypothesis.

There is a corollary: What one knows affects what one does and therefore affects the world. Therefore, one can't know what one will do in 20 years or, therefore, exactly how the world will be then or later.

---

288. Short for "Karl Popper." This argument is stated in the preface to Popper (2002).

You couldn't possibly know precisely what is relevant to the state of the world in 20 years without knowing the state of the world in 20 years. So you can't know exactly which of the things you currently know are worth remembering and which ones are not.

The psychopath is concerned with the truth only to the extent that he believes it to have practical value. Given KP, he can't possibly know exactly which truths have practical value, or therefore what kind, or how much, practical value they'll have. Having no interest in knowledge for its own sake, the psychopath's ken won't include much of the knowledge that a non-psychopath would have, simply because he values knowledge for its own sake, and that turns out to have tremendous practical value.

9.0   *One becomes a sociopath; one ceases to be a psychopath.*

Though in need of qualification, the second part of the last sentence contains an important truth. Because psychopathy embodies a failure to have developed the ability to have values, it is a kind of permanent infantilism. The psychopath is somebody whose development was arrested in certain ways.

The sociopath is not; the sociopath is somebody who was once fully developed (in so far as anybody is), but forfeited key components of his personality architecture, the likes of these components being precisely what the psychopath never had to begin with.

Why does the second part of the italicized statement need to be qualified? The psychopath is not just a giant infant, and infants aren't psychopaths. A giant infant would be innocent. Psychopaths are not innocent. First of all, the cognitive development of the psychopath may be normal, except in so far it's stunted by his lack of characterological development. In fact, with the qualification just made, the psychopath's cognitive development is usually normal or often hyper-normal. Many a (so-called) child-prodigy turns out to be a psychopath, as is many a (so-called) adult savant.

Why "so called"? The supposedly Herculean intellect of a given psychopath turns out to lack something integral to a genuinely Herculean intellect, or even a modestly sized one. The intellect of a psychopath-savant *is* extremely developed in some ways. But a psychopath's expertise in a given area tends to contain strange gaps, and these gaps are not of the sort found in any expert's prowess at his field: they are foundational gaps. The brilliant-psychopath economist really does have a lot to say; but his performance as an economist is extremely jagged, dazzling highs followed by inexplicable lows.

And the highs are usually internal to failures. If the psychopath-economist is tasked with solving a problem that, like any problem of substance, consists of several sub-problems, he is likely to solve several of the sub-problems brilliantly, but very unlikely to solve all of them, or a sufficient number of them. And the ones he solves may be no more difficult than the others.

Why is this? The psychopath's selective and self-defeating relationship to the truth may infiltrate his relationship to discipline-internal truths. Also, the psychopath has an easier time than others convincing himself that he's solved a problem when he hasn't. This is both a cause and an effect of his lack of interest in the truth for its own sake.

These points must be qualified. *Within limits* the psychopath *is* likely to delight in knowledge for its own sake. First of all, there are contexts where appearing to have knowledge entails actually having it. Second, the psychopath, though incapable of *valuing* the truth for its own sake, can be *interested* in it for its own sake. Acquiring knowledge is often pleasurable. As Aristotle says, we delight in seeing things, and otherwise observing them, even when we know that doing so is useless; and, he then says, this shows that the delight we take in knowledge for its own sake is a basic fact about us. Given how our brains are structured, and given how much energy is allotted to those parts of our brain that mediate knowledge-acquisitive mental activity, it's inevitable that there be energies within us that we can discharge, and therefore urges that we can gratify, only by acquiring knowledge.

10.0   The sociopath is brittle. Although he doesn't have a conscience, he has to function within the strictures of a conscience-born rationalization.

Sociopaths are thus unusually likely *not* to commit the sorts and of infractions that, in society's eyes, would criminalize them. Sociopaths need to believe their own rationalizations, and they couldn't do so if they committed brazenly, non-rationalizably anti-social acts. Sociopaths *live* lies: they don't *tell* them.

Sociopaths often make heavy weather of how "honest" they are and of how they never break their word. And *technically* they are right. Technically, they *are* honest. It's only when you look at the pattern formed by their various acts of honesty that it becomes clear that, collectively, they are a giant lie. Looked at in a formal, legalistic manner, the sociopath is in the right by strictly complying with such and such regulations, and calling the police to report so and so for smoking marijuana, and so on. Looked at more closely, those deeds prove to embody malice, not morality.

Sociopaths lie by taking truths out of context. They're capable of honesty, but not of sincerity. More generally, they're capable of *formal*, but not of *substantive*, compliance with the dictates of morality. For the sociopath, small-scale honesty is a means to large-scale deception, and small-scale morality is a means to large-scale immorality.

Sociopaths lie by telling the truth. They destroy goodness by being good. A non-sociopath's lies distort the facts. The sociopath's non-lies distort the nature of truthfulness itself. By being honest in furtherance of large-scale deceptions, the sociopath drains truthfulness of all value; and by being moral in furtherance of large-scale injustices, the sociopath drains morality of all meaning. The non-sociopathic liar-predator is merely saving his own skin; he isn't trying to undermine virtue itself. But that *is* what the sociopath is doing.

An illustration: Jerry and Tricia work at a pharmacy. The pharmacy throws out medications that have reached their expiration-date, even though in most cases such medications are still effective. It's against the rules for employees to keep expired medications for themselves, even though they're going to be disposed of. Jerry's eight children all have strep throat. They need Cipro (a very strong antibiotic) or they'll die. Cipro retains its potency long after it has officially expired. Jerry keeps some expired Cipro for himself, intending to use it to save his children. Sally knows about this, and knows about his familial situation. She notifies the management as well as law-enforcement, knowing that Jerry will be fired, that his children will die, and that he'll serve a long jail-sentence for possession with intent to distribute.

This is a textbook case of sociopathic pseudo-honesty. The distinctive nature of sociopathic treachery is to be understood in terms of three facts.

(i)   There is a gulf between official and actual morality, and between official and actual truth.

(ii) There are, tautologously, social incentives to endorse official morality and truth, and equally strong disincentives to endorse actual truth and morality, except when they coincide with their institutional counterparts.

(iii) Institutional truth and morality are as obvious and unambiguous as their authentic counterparts are subtle and equivocal.

Given (i), the sociopath and lie and predate while remaining on the right side of institutional truth and morality. Given (ii), the sociopath is rewarded, not penalized, for such lies and predations. Given (iii), the sociopath has no trouble convincing herself her lies and predations are acts of truthfulness and benevolence; and such rationalizations are made even easier by the just-mentioned fact that her chicanery is socially and consensually validated.

It cannot be stressed that, when Tricia reports Jerry to the authorities, she doesn't fully know that what she is doing is malice-driven. She half-knows, but she also half-believes her own propaganda. Only a person with values can maintain a sharp mental distinction between actual truth and its surrogates – social truth (the fictions that reconcile people to the frustrations of having to live with others), emotional truth (the fictions that favorably disambiguate ambiguous and, properly disambiguated, intolerable facts about one's own person), and institutional truth (the fictions embodied in an institution's practices). Sociopaths and psychopaths are as good as others at distinguishing between true and false observation-reports (e.g. "that's red," "he's not wearing a shirt"). But their psychodynamic needs corrupt their meta-observational beliefs.

Let's speak first about the sociopath and then about the psychopath. In what follows, we are setting aside strictly perception-based beliefs, and we are also setting aside truths of the sort that can be known strictly on the basis of observation (e.g. "the light is now green").

The non-psychopathic non-sociopath reads between the lines; he puts statements into context, automatically infilling elided material. The sociopath is a pedant. This is partly, but *only* partly, because the sociopath is being deliberately obstreperous. If the sociopath were able to retain the sensitivities he previously had to unstated truths and to unarticulated, non-codified nuances, he wouldn't believe his own rationalizations. The sociopath has to have a very wooden, formalistic belief-system on whose behalf he can cite ready made slogans (e.g. "good scientists stick to the facts," "good people tell the truth"). The result is that sociopaths are pedants. They have no choice but to be pedants, since they must operate within the boundary-conditions set by their master-rationalizations. And they have boundless hate, since they've given up everything dear to them, including the ability to cherish anything, Consequently, their pedantry *ex post facto* becomes a vehicle by which they can discharge the toxins inside them. But they half-believe their own half-truths. They half-believe that they love working as clerks at Rite-Aid. They half-believe that they were right to have so and so jailed (for stealing an extra paper clip) and then deported back to his native country (where he was executed, as was predicted).

There are many reasons why the sociopath doesn't really believe or disbelieve anything. We've already identified one: they have to strip their minds of the sensitivities on the basis of which all but but the most truths are known. But there are two other reasons. One is that sociopaths *must* believe that the truth is malleable. Even sociopaths (e.g. those who are "reborn" as members of cults with rigid belief-systems) have to believe that the facts conform to their wishes. Sociopaths *have* to believe that truth, morality, and merit are "relative" and a "matter of opinion." By countenancing the idea of a belief- and desire-transcendent reality, one is robbing one's rationalizations of their credibility. And that is not an option for someone, such as the sociopath, for whom there is no distinction between thought and rationalization.

Sociopaths are seldom drawn to authors who advocate views that are well defined and unequivocal while at the same time *not* making concessions to people's emotional needs. They are drawn to authors who make clear contentions *so long as those contentions work for them emotionally.* ("The theory of evolution is a lie." "Your drug-dependence isn't your fault; it's a disease, like bone-cancer, and you are no more responsible for your condition than a cancer-patient is for his.") But setting aside such authors, they are drawn to those who waft spongiform, sentiment-drenched, contention-like non-contentions that any given reader can compatibilize with his own personal emotional needs.

Like the sociopath, the psychopath doesn't really have beliefs. This is because he doesn't understand the concept of truth and to believe a proposition is to see it as true. He grasps the concept of operational truth, not of truth *simpliciter*, and he has operational beliefs, not actual beliefs.

The reason psychopaths are proverbially good at fooling lie-detector machines is not that they are good liars; it is that they don't have to lie. What isn't before their eyes has long since been engulfed in self-serving rationalizations. Psychopaths don't have a zen-like control over their own mental processes on the basis of which they can, while knowing the truth, profess to believe its opposite.

Psychopaths have an extremely rudimentary psychological architecture. Their minds are gelatinous. For them, it's not a question of disassembling true beliefs; it's a question of never assembling true ones to begin with.

This is subject to a qualification. Psychopaths are operators, and they have a clear understanding of the distinction between truth and falsehood so far as that distinction relates to their machinations. And if their machinations have the infliction of pain as their objective, which they often do, they know it, and are morally responsible for it and thus cannot plead "not guilty by reason of insanity."

10.1 Most mental illnesses are system-internal. They afflict the ideation mediated by one's psychological structure, not that structure itself. Sociopathy and psychopathy afflict that structure itself.

The obsessive-compulsive's rituals comply with rigid regulations, and those rigid regulations correspond to rigid, intact psychodynamic walls. The problem with the obsessive-compulsive is not that there has been a meltdown of a systemic or even an intra-systemic kind; it's that, owing to a conflict-based over-bureaucratization of intra-systemic structure, intra-psychical communications don't happen with due alacrity.

The schizoaffective's mind *has* undergone a meltdown. But it is the *contents* of his mind that have become disorganized, not the substructures mediating said content. The schizoaffective's condition is a serious one. But there are different ways in which one can be ill, and it's important to distinguish among these ways. There is a difference between somebody whose skeleton is intact but whose organs have partially liquefied and one whose skeleton has liquefied. The schizoaffective's affliction affects structure-internal ideation. Deviant structure-internal ideation can lead to structural remodeling. But the schizoaffective *qua* schizoaffective has an intact psychical structure.

In my experience, sociopathization is immediately preceded by a brief but extremely intense period of psychosis, which in turn is preceded by years of pretending that things were fine when they obviously weren't. Supposing *arguendo* that I was not dealing with singularities, these facts suggest that there is an element of psychosis in the sociopathy. There is a fact we haven't stated that confirms this suggestion. Even though, relative to the current state of science, schizoaffective disorder is not eliminable, the ingestion of a few pills – a few haldols or risperdals – leads to a speedy, if temporary, restoration of lucidity. Even during these brief intervals, lucidity isn't completely restored. But restoration is often sufficiently complete that there are few or no overt symptoms of their malady, provided that certain triggers are avoided. (Those triggers include sensitive topics of conversation and situations reminiscent of past traumas.) So there is a significant sense in which even the most severe psychoses are reversible; and they wouldn't be reversible if they were structural, as opposed to intra-structural.

But sociopathy is *never reversible*. So assuming *arguendo* that I was not dealing with singularities, the pre-sociopath's psychosis comes to be *embedded in the very structure of his psyche*. Sociopathy is *systemic psychosis*, not *system-internal* psychosis.

So far as the sociopath seems to be getting better, it's because he is getting worse: it's because he's absorbing into the swath of his sociopathy corrupted analogues of the aptitudes from which socopathogenesis alienated him. For example, one of my patients was a gifted writer who sociopathized. For a few years after sociopathizing, she did little writing, and what she did was poor and rolled foul with both critics and erstwhile fans. After some time had past, she was able to reconstitute her literary talent within the confines of her sociopathy. But her literary talent, in its sociopathized form, was a travesty. Whereas she had previously written subtle and devastatingly accurate exposés of popular icons, her line of goods now consisted of nothing but glib, made-to-order celebrity-hagiography-pieces. So she went from being a good writer in a multi-dimensional way, to being non-writer, to being a bad writer, to being a good writer in a one-dimensional way. There was of course *a* sense in which there had been a restoration of functionality; *a* sense in which she had recovered a lost ability by virtue of her becoming able to write very low-grade, but formally good, hagiography-pieces. But that restoration of functionality was ultimately a diminishment of it. During the period when this person didn't write, and also during the period when she wrote poorly, it was because her actual literary ability hadn't yet been infiltrated by her sociopathy. Her inability to write well during those periods was a performance-, not a competence-based problem: she had trouble accessing a still intact ability, the way an oldster has trouble accessing a memory (whose continued existence is verified by the fact that, two minutes later, he recalls it *in toto*). But when this previously fine writer once again became able to write, it was because her literary *competence* had been sociopathized. The apparent restoration of ability was really a diminution of it: her performance-related improvement reflected a competence-related deterioration. There is nothing that one loses upon sociopathizing that one will ever regain, except in the degraded form in which this individual regained her literary ability.[289]

---

289. Curiously, I've known several gifted writers who sociopathized. Most of them wrote non-fiction; two of them wrote fiction. Before sociopathizing, each one came to be a popular success, at which point it became lucrative for him to lie, and each one did. None would admit that he had sold out; each believed his own lies, thereby inaugurating his descent into sociopathy.

Novel writing is no less of a sociopathogen than journalism, since novels are quite as capable as articles of being lies. Be it noted that there is a difference between a story and a lie. Stories are not *ipso facto* lies. Works of fiction are not necessarily lies. *Crime and Punishment* not a lie, even though it's fiction. Lying isn't just about what one is saying; it's also about how one is saying it. What the novelist is saying is different from how he is saying it; and, given how the two differ, the novelist is not lying, at least not solely by virtue of novelizing, even though he is deliberately transmitting non-truths. How he is saying it involves his asking the reader to entertain a hypothetical proposition. ("Suppose *arguendo* that there lived a man whose sole ambition was to build his own commercial shipping vessel…" Novels aren't preceded by the word "suppose," since the injunction to make the relevant sort of supposition is understood.) *What* he is saying consists in what that hypothetical is intended to illustrate. If the fiction-writer knows that he is illustrating a false principle, he is lying; and he begins to sociopathize as soon as he chooses to believe his lie.

I suspect, but cannot say authoritatively, that it is easier for writers to sociopathize than it is for composers. I have not known any who did. But it may well be that composers do sociopathize and, more importantly, that they do so by virtue of adulterating their craft.

That said, I faintly suspect that writers are, whereas composers are not, disposed by their respective crafts to sociopathize. Supposing this true, it is because the professional writer differs from his lay-brethren only to the extent that he does a better job of articulating his thoughts

Psychopathy and sociopathy are *systemic* psychoses. Sociopathization is system-level psychoticization.

11.0 "Psychopath," "sociopath," "criminal."

Relative to how we've been using the words "sociopath" and "psychopath," the corresponding categories are mutually exclusive. Relative to how we will be using the word "criminal," any given two of these three categories are mutually exclusive.

As it is currently used, the word "criminal" is simply ambiguous. Sometimes it means *lawbreaker*. Sometimes it means *career-criminal*. Legal categories are of no scientific importance. So we'll use the word "criminal" to mean "career criminal."

A criminal is not somebody who slips up once. He is somebody for whom crime is a way of life.

The class of career-criminals comprises both psychopaths and non-psychopaths. But non-psychopathic criminals are psychodynamically much more like you and me than they are like psychopaths or sociopaths. So it will expedite discussion if we use the term "criminal" to denote the class of career criminals *minus* the psychopaths in that group. This way, the word "criminal" will denote an explanatorily unified category.

A criminal is someone whose psychological architecture is intact, but whose object-relations with his fellow citizens is like a soldier's object-relations to enemy troops. The pilots responsible for detonating nuclear warheads over Hiroshima and Nagasaki were law-abiding and moral individuals. But their object-relations to the Japanese people had, in that context, been suspended: they saw the Japanese people, not as people, but as blips on a radar screen.

Unlike the sociopath and psychopath, the criminal can and does have meaningful object-relations with others. The criminal really loves his wife; he has a best friend who he cares about; he's distressed by Junior's recent troubles at school. But when he

---

than they do theirs. Everyone is a writer. (To speak is to write: Were Socrates and Homer not writers?) Nobody wants his thoughts to be invalidated. But the professional writer has an extra incentive: by virtue of his career-choice, he is only as worthy as his thoughts. Therefore, the professional writer has an extra incentive to say things he doesn't believe, and he therefore has an incentive to believe such things, since he won't state them convincingly if he doesn't. But compositions can't undermine one another; the composer *qua* composer cannot step on anyone's toes. Composers *can* sell out: the erstwhile composers of string-quarters can write rock 'n' roll. But popular songs are not lies. It cannot be by lying that a composer popularizes his work, whereas it can be, and often is, by lying that a writer popularizes *his* work.

Any practitioner of any craft can sociopathize and, more importantly, can do so by adulterating the way he plies his trade. But the craft of writing seems to be exceptionally sociopathogenic, because the very rationalizations that mediate sociopathization can be identical with one's work-product, whereas one's work-product as a composer or mathematician or food-purveyor, though certainly capable of precipitating sociopathogenesis, cannot themselves *be* the rationalizations involved in one's sociopathizing.

transacts with people, he sees them in much the way a soldier sees the enemy. They are simply marks.

A Mafioso who accidentally bumps into you and apologizes is very possibly being sincere. He may feel bad about bumping into you; he isn't necessarily putting on an act. But if you do business with him, you cease to be human. You become a blip on his radar screen.

11.1 It's tempting to say that the line between criminality and psychopathy is a blurry one.

It is not. The criminal is indeed a fraud. He isn't the banker he is pretending to be. But he isn't a fraud *as* a fraud. As a criminal, he has responsibilities to other people, e.g. other members of his crime family, and he is no less likely discharge his work-related obligations than any other professional. He is obliged to give his capo 30% of what he makes as a pretend-banker, and he is no less likely to comply with that obligation than you are to comply with your obligation to pay your taxes.

A prostitute who knows that she is a prostitute is not a whore; she's just a prostitute. A criminal who knows that he's a criminal is not a fraud; he's just a criminal. So who *is* a fraud? The social worker who, claiming that she is only being "fair," applies regulations so narrowly and inflexibly that they hurt those they would otherwise help; the psychiatrist who undermines his patient by represent the latter's rugged individualism as a pathological lack of "empathy"; the faux-savant who describes his sterility-driven pedantry as "rigor"; the junior employee who describes his toadyism as "respect for his superiors."

The criminal is not such a person. This does not mean that the criminal is a good person. It means that he is an agent, unlike the sorts of people just described. The criminal's functioning as a criminal does involve his dehumanizing other people; it does involve him failing to have meaningful object-relations with people with whom a non-criminal (who wasn't either a sociopath or psychopath) would have such relations. To that extent, the criminal is like the psychopath.

But there is a difference. The criminal *can* have meaningful object-relations. The psychopath cannot. The criminal must *suspend* his object-relations in order to ply his trade. The psychopath has none to suspend. The criminal is meaningfully connected to *some* people; and the ability to have such a connection presupposes the ability to have values; and it thus presupposes that one values the truth, since one must value the truth to value anything. So even if the criminal is meaningfully connected to but one other human being, his being able to have that connection means that he has values and thus has the psychological architecture needed to mediate value-driven ideation. This, in turn, means that he is an agent.

Contrariwise, the fact that the psychopath can't value anyone or anything means that he is a pseudo-agent. He can't act; he can only react, like a dog or a tiger. His reactions don't take the same forms as a tiger's, because his reactions, unlike a tiger's, are mediated through a human being's intellect. But the psychopath is no more of an agent than a tiger.

Recall the earlier cited passage from Cleckley (1941:406):

> Logical thought processes [in the psychopath's mind] may be seen in perfect operation … All judgments of value and emotional appraisals are sane and appropriate when the psychopath is tested in verbal examinations. Only very slowly and by a complex of multitudinous small impressions does the conviction come upon us that, despite these intact rational processes, these normal emotional affirmations, and their consistent application in all directions, we are dealing here not with a complete man at all but with something that suggests a subtly constructed reflex machine which can mimic the human personality perfectly. This smoothly operating psychic apparatus reproduces consistently not only specimens of good human reasoning but also appropriate simulations of normal human emotion in response to nearly all the varied stimuli of life.

The criminal, by contrast, *is* an agent, even in his capacity as a criminal. His context-specific nullification of object-relations is internal to an intact psychological architecture. The criminal is as reliable as any other entrepreneur.

Obviously, the criminal's trustworthiness extends only as far as his self-interest. But the psychopath's doesn't even extend that far. His relationship to the truth is so flexible, his belief-system so corrupted by rationalizations, that he doesn't have a steady, unwavering grasp of what it is in his practical interest to do.

A criminal *can* have meaningful object-relations, and therefore has a distinctively human psychological architecture. A psychopath cannot have meaningful object-relations, and therefore does not have such an architecture.

This makes the criminal *more* dangerous than the psychopath. The psychopath doesn't fully grasp the distinction between fact and fiction. There isn't a well-developed identity underneath the psychopath's pretenses. So he can't defraud others without defrauding himself. He is thus too steeped in his own lies to succeed in an arena, such as politics, where one cannot succeed without clearly distinguishing between fact and fiction.

The psychopath is the consummate empiricist: what isn't in plane view is no more than a useful fiction. The psychopath thus lives in a perpetual present and is therefore doomed to small-timism. The criminal *does* distinguish between fact and fiction. As a result, the criminal, unlike the psychopath, can do harm on an epoch scale. Stalin and Hitler were criminals, not psychopaths.

Stalin and Hitler were evil.[290] They were not sociopaths or psychopaths: their psychological structures were intact. Each had to sidestep many landmines to acquire

---

290. Hitler was also schizoaffective. Stalin was not. Hitler's schizoaffectiveness was implicated in his wickedness. But his wickedness was the dominant force in his personality. His schizophrenia was but a vehicle for his wickedness; and I suspect that he became adept at tapping into it at will.

as much power as he did. Each had to exercise self-control and judgment. Each had to be an agent. Psychopaths are much too reactive to survive, let alone flourish, in highly contested arenas such as those in which those potentates operated. Criminals, however, *do* have the characterological prerequisites to do what they did.

Clearly, Stalin and Hitler were criminals. But this isn't all they were. For criminals *qua* criminals aren't nearly as *evil* as Stalin, Hitler, or Mao. So *evil* cannot be the same thing as criminality. And, as we just saw, it isn't the same thing as psychopathy or sociopathy, given that the evil-doer is an agent, unlike the sociopath and psychopath.[291] It was Hitler's deliberate intention to undermine morality. (The Swastika is the Sanskrit symbol for peace *facing the wrong way*. The original symbol faces to the right; the Swastika faces to the left.) The same is true of Stalin. Neither was trying to do good but failed. They were not incompetent statesmen. They were competent *anti*-statesmen. Each was trying to do what he did do: torture, kill, and destroy. I make these points only to show that psychological theory must make some provisions for the phenomenon of evil separate from those that it makes – or doesn't make, but should – for criminality, sociopathy, and psychopathy.

Evil must be distinguished from hate. Everyone hates someone, but not everyone is evil. But the concept of evil must be understood in terms of that of hate. Evil is generalized, rigidified hate. So whereas your hatred is person-specific, its target being Jerry, Stalin's was not, *its* target being humanity itself.

Wickedness and criminality are not mutually exclusive: only agents can be evil and only agents can be criminals, and a given agent can be both.

Granting that the points just made about wickedness were not argued for, it is hoped that in this chapter we have shown that what was thought to be a single group – that of the "anti-social" individual – consists of 5 distinct groups whose respective extensions are: psychopaths, sociopaths, criminals, people who are evil, and people who hate. And we have made some case that any given two of the first three categories are not just distinct, but mutually exclusive; which, if correct, warrants a considerable rethinking of many a shibboleth of contemporary psychology and criminology.

---

291. Criminality is pragmatically driven selectivity in regards to object relations. Psychopathy is the withdrawl of object-relations at an early age. Sociopathy is the withdrawal of object relations after adulthood has been reached. (The "blanks" who I discussed earlier did not read the developmental stage where they even had object-relations. So they were sub- or pre-psychopathic. This point was clearly stated and cogently defended by Morrison (2005), whose book, I feel, is undervalued.)

Criminality is usually about economics: people deal drugs because they want to make money, not because they want to corrupt civilization. Of course, the life-styles they've chosen are more hospitable to the discharging of ill-will than are most non-criminal life-styles. So considerable wickedness comes to be implicated in the way that criminality is expressed. But criminality *per se* is different from wickedness.

Conclusion

There are two kinds of empiricism. There is the kind that restricts knowledge to sense-based knowledge, and there is the kind that restricts it to *experience*-based knowledge. The latter leads to idealism and thus to pan-mentalism. The former leads to behaviorism and thus to pan-*non*-mentalism.

Both kinds demand the acceptance of constricted views of the mind. The one kind demands an infinitely constricted such conception: *minds don't exist.* The other grants the existence of consciousness but denies that there is anything to the mind besides consciousness.

Behaviorism is just an aberration, which deserves no consideration. The other view, though less aberrant, is misconceived and erroneous. Misconceived, in that it fails to distinguish between access-consciousness and consciousness-proper. Erroneous, in that nothing other than content-transmitting ideation can constitute the genidentity of your pre- and post-sleep minds or can account for their qualitative similarities.

There is no way to understand the concept of repression in strictly empiricist terms, the same being true of the concept of rationalization. These are definitional truths. Repressed ideation is by definition unconscious, and rationalizations by definition involve a bifurcation of mental activity into conscious and unconscious strata. What is unconscious is by definition what is unintrospectible. The unconscious, by definition, can be known only through inference, so far as it can be known at all.

The hypothesis that there is unconscious mental activity is the ultimate deviation from the strictures of empiricism. But there is no way to explain conscious mental activity except on the assumption that there is unconscious mental activity. Hence the sterility of attempts to empiricize psychology and the erroneousness of attempts to identify the empiricization of psychology with the scientization of it.

While making due allowances for the fact that psychological processes are brain-dependent, we have also established the coherence of the concepts forming the nucleus of at least one therapeutically and theoretically fecund attempt to understand the psychological realm on its own terms. To the extent that the points made in this work are not misguided, we have helped psychology begin to undo the damage that empiricism has done to it.

References

Aristotle. (350 B.C.). *Nichomachean ethics.* Retrieved from http://www.constitution.org/ari/ethic_00.htm

Armstrong, D. (1989). *Universals: An opinionated introduction.* Boulder, CO: Westview Press.

Armstrong, D. (1992). Properties. In Steven M. Cahn (Ed.), *Philosophy for the 21st Century* (pp. 181–193). New York: Oxford University Press.

Ayer, A. J. (1952). *Language, truth, and logic.* New York: Dover Publications.

Ayer, A. J. (1954). Can there be a private language? In A. P. Martinich (Ed.), *The Philosophy of Language* (pp. 449–456). Oxford: Oxford University Press.

Barwise, J. (1989). *The situation in logic.* Palo Alto, CA: CSLI Publications.

Barwise, J., & Perry, J. (1983). *Situations and attitudes.* Palo Alto, CA: CSLI Publications.

Bell, J. S. (1987). *Speakable and unspeakable in quantum mechanics.* Cambridge: Cambridge University Press.

Benacerraf, P. (1965). What numbers could not be. *Philosophical Review, 74,* 47–73.

Berkeley, G. (1710). *A treatise concerning the principles of human knowledge.* Retrieved from http://www.earlymoderntexts.com/

Berkeley, G. (1713). *Three dialogues between Hylans and Philonous.* Retrieved from http://www.sparknotes.com/philosophy/3dialogues/facts.html

Berkeley, G. (1934). *An essay towards a new theory of vision.* Oxford: Clarendon Press.

Bertrand, R. (1918). The philosophy of logical atomism. In R. C. Marsh (Ed.), *Logic and Knowledge* (pp. 175–282).

Blackburn, S. (1984). *Spreading the word.* Oxford: Clarendon.

Blackburn, S. (1993). *Essays in quasi-realism.* New York: Oxford University Press.

Blackburn, S. (1998). *Ruling passions: A theory of practical reasoning.* New York: Oxford University Press.

Block, N. J. (1995). On a confusion about the function of consciousness. *Behavioral and Brain Sciences, 18,* 227–247.

Boghossian, P. A. (1997). Analyticity in Hale and Wright.

Bohm, D. (1957). *Causality and chance in modern physics.* Philadelphia: University of Pennsylvania Press.

Bonjour, L. (1985). *The structure of empirical knowledge.* Cambridge, MA: Harvard University Press.

Bonjour, L. (1998). *In defense of pure reason.* Cambridge, U.K.: Cambridge University Press.

Brandom, R. (1994). *Making it explicit.* Cambridge, MA: Harvard University Press.

Brandom, R. (2000). *Articulating reasons: An introduction to inferentialism.* Cambridge, MA: Harvard University Press.

Brown, B. (2006). On paraconsistency. In D. Jacquette (Ed.), *A Companion to Philosophical Logic* (pp. 628–650). New York: Blackwell.

Burge, T. (1979). Individualism and the mental. In A. Pessin & S. Goldberg (Eds.), *The Twin-Earth Chronicles* (pp. 125–141). Armonk, NY: M. E. Sharpe.

Burge, T. (1980). Computer proof and a priori knowledge. *Journal of Philosophy, 77*, 797–803.

Burge, T. (1982). Other bodies. In A. Pessin & S. Goldberg (Eds.), *The Twin-Earth Chronicles* (pp. 142–160). Armonk, NY: M. E. Sharpe.

Burge, T. (1986). Individualism and self-knowledge. In A. Pessin & S. Goldberg (Eds.), *The Twin-Earth Chronicles* (pp. 342–354). Armonk, NY: M. E. Sharpe.

Cain, M. J. (2002). *Fodor: Language, mind and philosophy.* Cambridge, MA: Polity Press.

Cappelen, H., & Lepore, E. (2005). *Insensitive semantics: A defense of speech act pluralism and semantic minimalism.* Oxford: Blackwell.

Cargile, J. (1980). *Paradoxes.* Cambridge: Cambridge University Press.

Carnap, R. (1932). The elimination of metaphysics through logical analysis of language. In A. J. Ayer (Ed.), *Logical Positivism* (pp. 60–81). New York: The Free Press.

Carnap, R. (1933). Psychology in physical language. In A. J. Ayer (Ed.), *Logical Positivism* (pp. 165–198). New York: The Free Press.

Carnap, R. (1934). *The unity of science.* London: K. Paul, Trench, Kubner & Co, Ltd.

Carnap, R. (1937). *The logical syntax of language.* London: Routledge & Kegan Paul.

Carnap, R. (1956). *Introduction to symbolic logic.* New York: Dover.

Carnap, R. (1966). *Introduction to the philosophy of science.* New York: Dover.

Carnap, R. (1967). *The logical structure of the world. Pseudoproblems in philosophy.* Los Angeles: University of California Press

Carroll, L. (2010). *Through the looking glass and what Alice found there.* New York: Create Space Publications.

Cartwright, R. (1975). Scattered objects. In K. Lehrer (Ed.), *Analysis and Metaphysics* (pp. 153–171). Dordrecht: Reidel.

Chalmers, D. (1996). *The conscious mind.* New York: Oxford University Press.

Chomsky, N. (1959). Reivew of B. F. Skinner's *Verbal behavior.* Retrieved from http://www.chomsky.info/articles/1967----.htm

Chomsky, N. (1965). *Aspects of the theory of syntax.* Cambridge, MA: The MIT Press.

Chomsky, N. (1980). *Rules and representations.* New York: Columbia University Press.

Chomsky, N. (1988). Language and the problems of knowledge. In A. P. Martinich (Ed.), *The Philosophy of Language* (pp. 509–527). New York: Oxford University Press.

Church, A. (1958). *The ontological status of women and abstract entities.* Lecture delivered at Harvard. Retrieved from http://www.cs.nyu.edu/pipermail/fom/2005-September/009079.html

Churchland, P. (1984). *Matter and consciousness.* Cambridge, MA: The MIT Press.

Cleckley, H. (1941). *The mask of sanity.* Retrieved from http://www.cassiopaea.org/cass/sanity_1.PdF

Davidson, D. (2001a). *Essays on actions and events.* Oxford: Clarendon Press.

Davidson, D. (2001b). *Inquiries into truth and interpretation.* Oxford: Clarendon Press.

Davidson, D. (2001c). *Subjective, intersubjective, objective.* Oxford: Clarendon Press.

Davidson, D. (2004). *Problems of rationality.* Oxford: Clarendon Press.

Davies, P. J. (2001a). *The character of a genius: Beethoven in perspective.* Westport, CT: Greenwood Press.

Davies, P. J. (2001b). *Beethoven in person: His deafness, illness, and death.* Westport, CT: Greenwood Press.

Davis, D. (1991). *The Jeffrey Dahmer story.* New York: St. Martin's Press.

Dennett, D. (1975). Eliminative materialism and the propositional attitudes. In D. Rosenthal (Ed.), *The Nature of Mind* (pp. 502–507). New York: Oxford University Press.

Dennett, D. (1978). *Brainstorms.* Cambridge, MA: The MIT press.

Dennett, D. (1989). *The intentional stance.* Cambridge, MA: The MIT press.

Dennett, D. (1990). *Consciousness explained.* Cambridge, MA: The MIT press.

Dilthey, W. (1883). *Introduction to the human sciences.* Retrieved from http://www.marxists.org/reference/subject/philosophy/works/ge/dilthey1.htm

Donnellan, K. (1966). Reference and definite descriptions. In A. P. Martinich (Ed.), *The Philosophy of Language* (pp. 235–257). Oxford: Oxford University Press.

Donnellan, K. (1974). Speaking of nothing. *The Philosophical Review, 74,* 3–31.

Dretske, F. (1982). *Knowledge and the flow of information.* Cambridge, MA: The MIT Press.

Dretske, F. (1995). *Naturalizing the mind.* Cambridge, MA: The MIT Press.

Ducasse, C. J. (1969). *Truth, knowledge, and causation.* London: Routledge & Kegan Paul.

Dummett, M. (1973). *Frege: Philosophy of language.* Cambridge, MA: Harvard University Press.

Dummett, M. (1978). *Truth and other enigmas.* Cambridge, MA: Harvard University Press.

Eddington, A. (1928). *The nature of the physical world.* London: MacMillan.

Einstein, A. (1956). *Collected papers*, Vol. 2, 170–182.

Einstein, A. (1956b). *Collected papers*, Vol. 2, 206–222.

Einstein, A. (1962). *The principles of relativity.* New York: Dover.

Einstein, A., & Infeld, L. (1961). *The evolution of physics.* New York: Simon & Schuster.

Evans, G. (1982). *The varieties of reference.* Oxford: Clarendon Press.

Evans, G. (1985). *Collected papers.* Oxford: Clarendon Press.

Falvey, K. (1994). *Externalism, self-knowledge, and skepticism.* Unpublished Dissertation. Department of Philosophy. University of Minnesota.

Falvey, K., & Owens, J. (1994). Externalism, self-knowledge, and skepticism. *Philosophical Review, 103,* 107–137.

Field, H. (1977). Logic, meaning, and conceptual role. *Journal of Philosophy,* Volume LXXIV, Number 7, July 1977.

Fodor, J. (1968). *Psychological explanation.* New York: Random House.

Fodor, J. (1975). *The language of thought.* New York: Thomas Y. Crowell.

Fodor, J. (1981a). Methodological solipsism considered as a research strategy in cognitive psychology. In D. Rosenthal (Ed.), *The Nature of Mind* (pp. 485–498). New York: Oxford University Press.

Fodor, J. (1974). Special sciences: or the disunity of science as a working hypothesis. *Synthese, 28,* 97–115.

Fodor, J. (1975). *The language of thought.* New York: Thomas.

Fodor, J. (1981b). *Representations.* Cambridge, MA: The MIT Press.

Fodor, J. (1987). *Psychosemantics.* Cambridge, MA: The MIT Press.

Fodor, J. (1987b). Individualism and supervenience. In A. Pessin & S. Goldberg (Eds.), *The Twin-Earth Chronicles* (pp. 192–218). Armonk, NY: M. E. Sharpe.

Fodor, J. (1990). *A theory of content and other essays.* Cambridge, MA: The MIT Press.

Fodor, J. (1994a). Fodor. In S. Guttenplan (Ed.), *A Companion to the Philosophy of Mind* (pp. 292–300). Oxford: Blackwell.

Fodor, J. (1994b). *The elm and the expert: Mentalese and its semantics.* Cambridge, MA: The MIT Press.

Fodor, J. (1998a). *Concepts.* Oxford: Clarendon Press.

Fodor, J. (1998b). *In critical condition*. Cambridge, MA: The MIT Press.

Fodor, J., & Lepore, E. (2002). *The compositionality papers*. New York: Oxford University Press.

Fodor, J., & Pylyshin, Z. (1988). Connectionism and cognitive architecture: A critical analysis. In S. Pinker (Ed.), *Connections and Symbols* (pp. 3–72). Amsterdam: Elsevier.

Frank, P. (1949). *Philosophy of science: The link between philosophy and science*. New York: Dover.

Frankfurt, H. (1988). *The importance of what we care about*. Cambridge, U.K.: Cambridge University Press.

Frege, G. (1879). Concept writing. In M. Beaney (Ed.), *The Frege Reader* (pp. 181–193). Oxford: Blackwell.

Frege, G. (1953). *The foundations of arithmetic*. Translated by J. L. Austin. Oxford: Basil Blackwell.

Frege, G. (1891). Function and concept. In M. Beaney (Ed.), *The Frege Reader* (pp. 130–148). Oxford: Blackwell.

Frege, G. (1892a). On *Sinn* and *Bedeutung*. In M. Beaney (Ed.), *The Frege Reader* (pp. 151–171). Oxford: Blackwell.

Frege, G. (1892b). On concept and object. In M. Beaney (Ed.), *The Frege Reader* (pp. 181–193). Oxford: Blackwell.

Frege, G. (1918). Thought. In M. Beaney (Ed.), *The Frege Reader* (pp. 325–345). Oxford: Blackwell.

Freud, S. (1915). The unconscious. In P. Rieff (Ed.), *General Psychological Theory* (pp. 116–150). New York: Macmillan Publishing Co.

Freud, S. (1953). *Project for a scientific psychology*. The Hogarth Press Ltd.

Freud, S. (1949). *The ego and the id*. London: The Hogarth Press Ltd.

Freud, S. (1963). *Three case histories*. New York: Collier.

Freud, S. (1965). *New introductory lectures on psychoanalysis*. London: W.W. Norton and Co.

Freud, S. (1989a). *An outline of psychoanalysis*. New York: W. W. Norton and Co.

Freud, S. (1989b). *Civilization and its discontents*. London: W. W. Norton and Co.

Freud, S. (1998). *The interpretation of dreams*. New York: Basic Books.

Fuller, L. (1964). *The morality of law*. New Haven, CT: Yale University Press.

Gardner, M. (1976). *The relativity explosion*. New York: Vintage Books.

Gettier, E. (1963). Is knowledge justified true belief. *Analysis, 23*, 121–123.

Gödel, K. (1953). Is mathematics syntax of language? In S. Feferman (Ed.), *Kurt Gödel: Collected works*, Volume III (pp. 334–356). New York: Oxford.

Goodman, N. (1954). *Fact, fiction, and forecast*. Cambridge, MA: Harvard University Press.

Goodman, N. (1976). *The languages of art*. Indianapolis, IN: Hackett.

Grice, H. P. (1957). Meaning. In A. P. Martinich (Ed.), *The Philosophy of Language* (pp. 72–78). Oxford: Oxford University Press.

Grice, H. P., & Strawson, P. (1957). In defence of a dogma. *Philosophical Review, 65*, 141–158.

Hacker, P. M. S. (1999). *Wittgenstein on human nature*. New York: Routledge.

Hacker, P. M. S. (1996). *Wittgenstein: Mind and will*. Oxford: Blackwell.

Hacker, P. M. S., & Baker, G. (1980). *Wittgenstein: Understanding and meaning*. Oxford: Blackwell.

Hacker, P. M. S., & Baker, G. (1984a). *Scepticism, rules, and language*. Oxford: Blackwell.

Hacker, P. M. S., & Baker, G. (1984b). *Language, sense, and nonsense*. Oxford: Blackwell.

Hacker, P. M. S., & Baker, G. (1985). *Wittgenstein: Rules, grammar, and necessity*. Oxford: Blackwell.

Hahn, H. (1933). Logic, mathematics, and knowledge of nature. In A. J. Ayer (Ed.), *Logical Positivism* (pp. 137–163). New York: The Free Press.

Hare, R. (1999). *Without conscience.* New York: The Guilford Press.

Hempel, C. G. (1945a). Studies in logic and confirmation. I. *Mind, 54,* 1–26.

Hempel, C. G. (1945b). Studies in logic and confirmation. II. *Mind, 54,* 97–121.

Hempel, C. G. (1950). The empiricist criterion of meaning. In A. J. Ayer (Ed.), *Logical Positivism* (pp. 108–129). New York: The Free Press.

Hempel, C. G. (1952). *Fundamentals of concept formation in empirical science.* Chicago: University of Chicago Press.

Hempel, C. G. (1965). *Aspects of scientific explanation.* New York: The Free Press.

Hempel, C. G. (1966). *Philosophy of natural science.* Englewood Cliffs: Prentice Hall.

Hintikka, J. (1962). *Knowledge and belief: An introduction to the logic of the two notions.* Ithaca, New York: Cornell University Press.

Hintikka, J. (1969). *Models for modalities.* Dordrecht, Holland: D. Reidel Publishing Company.

Hintikka, J. (1969). Deontic logic and its philosophical morals. In *Models for Modalities.* Dordrecht, Holland: D. Reidel Publishing Company.

Horst, S. (2007). *Beyond reduction.* New York: Oxford University Press.

Hume, D. (1739). *A treatise of human nature.* Retrieved from http://www.earlymoderntexts.com/f_hume.html

Hume, D. (1740). *An enquiry concerning human understanding.* Retrieved from http://www.sparknotes.com/philosophy/understanding

Hume, D. (1751). *An enquiry concerning the principles of morals.* Retrieved from http://www.sparknotes.com/philosophy/hume/section5.rhtml

Husserl, E. (1977). *Phenomenological psychology.* Berlin: Springer.

Husserl, E. (2004). *Ideas.* London: Routledge.

Hyatt, C. (1994). *The psychopath's bible.* Tempe, AZ: New Falcon Publications.

Jackson, F. (1977). *Perception: A representative theory.* Cambridge: Cambridge University Press.

James, W. (1890). *The principles of psychology.* Cambridge, MA: Harvard University Press.

James, W. (1907). *Pragmatism.* Cambridge, MA: Harvard University Press.

Jeans, J. (1981). *Physics and philosophy.* Mineoloa, New York: Dover.

Kant, I. (1785). *Critique of practical reason.* Retrieved from http://oll.libertyfund.org/?option=com_staticxt&staticfile=show.php%3Ftitle=360&Itemid=27

Kant, I. (1787). *Critique of pure reason.* Retrieved from http://www2.hn.psu.edu/faculty/jmanis/kant/Critique-Pure-Reason.pdf

Kaplan, D. (1968). Trans-world Heir-lines. In M. Loux (Ed.), *The Actual and the Possible.* Ithaca, New York: Cornell University Press.

Kaplan, D. (1975). Dthat. In A. P. Martinich (Ed.), *The Philosophy of Language* (pp. 316–329). New York: Oxford University Press.

Kaplan, D. (1979). On the logic of demonstratives. *Journal of Philosophical Logic, 8,* 71–98.

Kaplan, D. (1989a). Demonstratives. In J. Almog, et al. (Eds.), *Themes from Kaplan* (pp. 481–563). New York: Oxford University Press.

Kaplan, D. (1989b). Afterthoughts. In J. Almog, et al. (Eds.), *Themes from Kaplan* (pp. 565–614). New York: Oxford University Press.

Katz, J. (1972). *Semantic theory.* New York: Harper and Row.

Kennedy, D. (2004). *Legal education and the reproduction of hierarchy: A polemic against the System.* New York: New York University Press.

Kernberg, O. (1985). *Aggression in personality disorders and perversions*. New Haven, CT: Yale University Press.

Kernberg, O. (1993). *Severe personality disorders*. New Haven, CT: Yale University Press.

Kim, J. (1993). *Supervenience and mind*. Cambridge, U.K.: Cambridge University Press.

King, J. C. (1995). Structured propositions and complex predicates. *Nous, 29*(4), 516–535.

Kripke, S. (1963). Semantical considerations on modal logic. In *Reference and Modality*.

Kripke, S. (1980). *Naming and necessity*. Cambridge, MA: Harvard University Press.

Kripke, S. (1982). *Wittgenstein on rules and private language*. Cambridge, MA: Harvard University Press.

Kuczynski, J.-M. (1999). Is mind an emergent property? *Cogito, 13*(2), 117–119.

Kuczynski, J.-M. (2000). Two objections to materialism. *Journal of Theoretical and Philosophical Psychology, 20*(2), 122–139.

Kuczynski, J.-M. (2002). Does the idea of a 'language of thought' make sense? *Communication and Cognition, 35*(4), 173–192.

Kuczynski, J.-M. (2004). *Kriterion, 45*(109), 81–135.

Kuczynski, J.-M. (2005). The concept of a symbol and the vacuousness of the symbolic conception of thought. *Semiotica, 154*(4), 243–264.

Kuczynski, J.-M. (2005b). Must one know a language to grasp propositions? *Teorema, 24*(2), 43–65.

Kuczynski, J.-M. (2007). *Conceptual atomism and the computational theory of mind: A defense of content-internalism and semantic externalism*. Amsterdam: John Benjamins.

Kuczynski, J.-M. (2009). *Analytic philosophy*. Dubuque, IN: Kendall Hunt.

Laing, R. D. (1960). *The divided self: An existential study in sanity and madness*. Harmondsworth: Penguin.

Laing, R. D. (1961). *The self and others*. London: Tavistock Publications.

Langford, C. H. (1942). The notion of analysis in Moore's philosophy. In P. A. Schilpp (Ed.), *The Philosophy of G. E. Moore* (pp. 321–342). LaSalle: Open Court.

Langford, H. (1949). A proof that synthetic *a priori* propositions exist. *Journal of Philosophy, 46*, 20–24.

Leake, J. (2009). *Entering hades*. New York: Sarah Crichton Books.

Leibniz, G. W. (1704). *New essays concerning human understanding*. Retrieved from http://www.earlymoderntexts.com/f_leibniz.html

Lewicki, P., Hill, T., & Czyzewska, M. (1992). Nonconscious acquisition of information. *American Psychologist, 47*(6), 796–801.

Lewis, C. I. (1946). *An analysis of knowledge and valuation*. Cambridge, MA: Harvard University Press.

Lewis, C. I. (1952). The modes of meaning. In L. Linsky (Ed.), *Semantics and the Philosophy of Language* (pp. 50–66). Chicago: University of Illinois Press.

Lewis, D. (1966). An argument for the identity theory. *Journal of Philosophy, 63*, 17–25.

Lewis, D. (1968). Counterpart theory and quantified modal logic. *Journal of Philosophy, 65*, 113–126.

Lewis, D. (1969). Policing the Aufbau. *Philosophical Studies, 20*, 13–17.

Lewis, D. (1970). How to define theoretical terms. *Journal of Philosophy, 67*, 427–446.

Lewis, D. (1972). Psychophysical and theoretical identifications. *Australasian Journal of Philosophy, 50*, 249–258.

Lewis, D. (1973). *Counterfactuals*. Oxford: Basil Blackwell.

Lewis, D. (1973b). Causation. *Journal of Philosophy, 70*, 556–567.

Lewis, D. (1975). Language and languages. In A. P. Martinich (Ed.), *The Philosophy of Language*, (pp. 489–508). New York: Oxford University Press.

Lewis, D. (1980). Mad pain and Martian pain. In Ned Block (Ed.), *Readings in Philosophy of Psychology*, Volume I (pp. 216–232). Cambridge: Harvard University Press.

Lewis, D. (1984). *On the plurality of worlds*. Oxford: Blackwell.

Lewis, D. (1988). Desire as belief. *Mind, 97*, 323–332.

Locke, J. (1690). *An essay concerning human understanding*. Retrieved from http://www.sparknotes.com/philosophy/johnlocke/section1.html

Long, P. (2001). *Logical form and grammar*. New York: Routledge.

Lowe, C. (2007). *The everything guide to OCD*. Chicago: Adams Press.

Lycan, W. (1984). *Logical form in natural language*. Cambridge, MA: The MIT Press.

Lyons, J. (1977). *Semantics*. Cambridge, U.K.: Cambridge University Press.

Mach, E. (1960a). *Space and geometry in the light of physiological, psychological and physical inquiry*. Trans. by T. J. McCormack. La Salle: Open Court.

Mach, E. (1960b). *The science of mechanics: A critical and historical account of its development*. Trans. by T. J. McCormack. La Salle: Open Court.

Mach, E. (1976). *Knowledge and error – Sketches on the psychology of enquiry*. Trans. by T. J. McCormack & P. Fouldes. Dordrecht: D. Reidel.

Mach, E. (1984). *The analysis of sensations and the relation of the physical to the psychical*.

Mach, E. (1986). *Popular scientific lectures*. Trans. by T. J. McCormack. La Salle: Open Court.

Mackie, J. L. (1980). *The cement of the universe*. Oxford: Clarendon.

Martin, R. (Ed.). (1984). *Recent essays on truth and the liar paradox*. Oxford: Clarendon.

McCawley, J. D. (1981). *Everything that linguists have always wanted to know about logic*. Chicago: University of Chicago Press.

McGinn, C. (1988). *Mental content*. Oxford: Oxford University Press.

McWilliams, N. (1994a). *Psychoanalytic diagnosis: Understanding personality structure in the clinical process*. New York: The Guilford Press.

McWilliams, N. (1994b). *Psychoanalytic psychotherapy: A practitioner's guide*. New York: The Guilford Press.

Merleau-Ponty, M. (1962). *The phenomenology of perception*. In R. C. Solomon (Ed.), *Phenomenology and Existentialism* (pp. 460–465). Boulder, CO: Rowman and Littlefield.

Mill, J. S. (1882). *A system of logic*. Retrieved from http://www.gutenberg.org/ebooks/27942

Morrison, H. (2005). *My life among the serial killers*. Hauppauge, NY: Avon Press.

Moore, G. E. (1912). *Ethics*. Retrieved from http://fair-use.org/g-e-moore/ethics/

Moore, R. C. (1995). *Logic and representation*. Palo Alto, CA: CSLI Publications.

Moss, J. (1999). *The last victim*. New York: Grand Central Publishing.

Nagel, E. (1962). *The structure of science*. Indianapolis, IN: Hackett.

Nagel, E., & Newman, J. (2001). *Gödel's proof*. New York: New York University Press.

Neurath, O. (1932). Protocol sentences. In A. J. Ayer (Ed.), *Logical Positivism* (pp. 199–208). New York: The Free Press.

Nietzsche, F. (1966). *Beyond good and evil*. New York: Vintage.

Nietzsche, F. (1967a). *Genealogy of morals*. New York: Vintage.

Nietzsche, F. (1967b). *The will to power*. New York: Vintage.

Nietzsche, F. (2000). *The basic writings of Niezsche*. New York: Random House.

Nolan, D. (2005). *David Lewis*. Montreal & Kingston: McGill-Queen's University Press.

Norris, J. (1992). *Arthur Shawcross: The genesee River killer*. Wellington, New Zealand: Pinnacle Books.

Olson, K. (1987). *An essay on facts.* Palo Alto: CSLI Publications.

Pap, A. (1949). *Elements of analytic philosophy.* New York: Macmillan.

Pap, A. (1958). *Semantics and necessary truth.* New Haven, CT: Yale University Press.

Pearson, K. (1911). *The grammar of science.* London: Adam & Charles Black.

Plantinga, A. (1974). *The nature of necessity.* Oxford: Clarendon.

Pap, A. (1962). *Introduction to the philosophy of science.* New Haven, CT: Yale University Press.

Perry, J. (1977). The problem of the essential indexical. *Nous, 13*(1), 3–21.

Popper, K. (2002). *The poverty of historicism.* London: Routledge.

Priest, G. (2006a). *Doubt truth to be a liar.* Oxford, New York.

Priest, G. (2006b). Logicians setting together contradictories: A perspective on relevance, para-consistency, and dialetheism. In D. Jacquette (Ed.), *A Companion to Philosophical Logic* (pp. 651–664). New York: Blackwell.

Putnam, H. (1975). The meaning of "meaning." In A. Pessin & S. Goldberg (Eds.), *The Twin-Earth Chronicles* (pp. 1–52). Armonk, NY: M. E. Sharpe.

Putnam, H. (1975b). The nature of mental states. In *Collected papers,* Volume II. Cambridge: Harvard University Press.

Putnam, H. (1996). Introduction to *The Twin-Earth Chronicles.* In A. Pessin & S. Goldberg (Eds.), *The Twin-Earth Chronicles* (pp. xv–xxii). Armonk, NY: M. E. Sharpe.

Quine, W. van Orman. (1951). Two dogmas of empiricism. In A. P. Martinich (Ed.), *The Philosophy of Language* (pp. 26–39). Oxford: Oxford University Press.

Quine, W. van Orman. (1960). *Word and object.* Cambridge, MA: The MIT Press.

Quine, W. van Orman. (1966). *The ways of paradox and other essays.* Cambridge, MA: Harvard University Press.

Quine, W. van Orman. (1970). *Philosophy of logic.* Cambridge, MA: Harvard University Press.

Quine, W. van Orman. (1974). *The roots of reference.* LaSalle, IN: Open Court Publishing

Quine, W. van Orman. (1977). *Ontological relativity and other essays.* New York: Columbia University Press.

Quine, W. van Orman. (1981). *Theories and things.* Cambridge, MA: Harvard University Press.

Ramsey, F. P. (1990). The foundations of mathematics. In D. H. Mellor (Ed.), *Philosophical Papers.* Cambridge: Cambridge University Press.

Ramsey, F. P. (1929a). General propositions and causality. In D. H. Mellor (Ed.), *Philosophical Papers.* Cambridge: Cambridge University Press, 1990.

Ramsey, F. P. (1929b). Theories. In R. B. Braithwaite (Ed.), *The Foundations of Mathematics and Other Logical Essays* (pp. 212–236). Paterson, NJ: Littlefield and Adams.

Recanati, F. (1993). *Direct reference: From language to thought.* Oxford: Blackwell.

Recanati, F. (2004). *Literal meaning.* Cambridge: Cambridge University Press.

Reich, W. (1945). *Character analysis.* Retrieved from http://www.wilhelmreichtrust.org/character_analysis.pdf

Reichenbach, H. (1947). *Elements of symbolic logic.* New York: Macmillan.

Reichenbach, H. (1956). *The direction of time.* University of California Press.

Reichenbach, H. (1957). *The philosophy of space and time.* New York: Dover.

Richard, M. (1991). *Propositional attitudes.* Cambridge, U.K.: Cambridge University Press.

Rule, A. (2005). *Green River running red.* New York: Simon & Schuster.

Rule, A. (2008). *The stranger beside me.* New York: Simon & Schuster.

Russell, B. (1902). Letter to Frege. In J. van Heijenoort (Ed.), 124–125.

Russell, B. (1903). *Principles of mathematics.* Cambridge, U.K.: Cambridge University Press.

Russell, B. (1905). On denoting. In A. P. Martinich (Ed.), *The Philosophy of Language* (pp. 203–211). Oxford: Oxford University Press.

Russell, B. (1908). Mathematical logic as based on the theory of types. *American Journal of Mathematics, 30*, 222.

Russell, B. (1914). *Our knowledge of the external world.* London: George Allen Unwin.

Russell, B. (1917). *Mysticism and logic.* London: George Allen Unwin.

Russell, B. (1919). *The ABC of relativity.* London: George Allen Unwin.

Russell, B. (1920). *Introduction to mathematical philosophy.* London: George Allen Unwin.

Russell, B. (1921). *The analysis of mind.* London: George Allen Unwin.

Russell, B. (1927). *An outline of philosophy.* London: George Allen Unwin.

Russell, B. (1928). *The analysis of matter.* London: George Allen Unwin.

Russell, B. (1948). *Human knowledge: Its scope and limits.* London: George Allen Unwin.

Russell, B. (1950). Logical positivism. In R. C. Marsh (Ed.), *Logic and Knowledge* (pp. 367–382).

Salmon, N. (1986). *Frege's puzzle.* Cambridge, MA: The MIT Press.

Salmon, N. (2005). *Metaphysics, mathematics, and meaning: Philosophical papers II.* New York: Oxford University Press.

Salmon, N. (2007). *Content, cognition, and communication: Philosophical papers II.* New York: Oxford University Press.

Salmon, W. (1984). *Scientific explanation and the causal structure of the world.* Princeton, NJ: Princeton University Press.

Salzman, L. (1994). *Treatment of obsessive and compulsive disorders.* Northvale, New Jersey: Jason Aronson, Inc.

Sartre, J. P. (1956). *Being and nothingness.* Retrieved from http://www.mediafire.com/?gntecjzmze0

Sartre, J. P. (1940). *The imaginary.* Retrieved from http://pvspade.com/Sartre/pdf/sartre1.pdf

Saussure, F. de. (1966). *Course in general linguistics.* New York: McGraw-Hill Book Company.

Schechter, H. (2008). *Depraved.* New York: Simon and Schuster.

Smart, J. J. C. (1959). Sensations and brain processes. *Philosophical Review, 68*, 141–156.

Searle, J. (1969). *Speech acts.* Cambridge, U.K.: Cambridge University Press.

Searle, J. (1979). *Expression and meaning.* Cambridge, U.K.: Cambridge University Press.

Searle, J. (1983). *Intentionality: An essay on the philosophy of mind.* Cambridge, U.K.: Cambridge University Press.

Searle, J. (1984). *Minds, brains, and science.* Cambridge, U.K.: Harvard University Press.

Searle, J. (1992). *The rediscovery of the mind.* Cambridge, MA: The MIT Press.

Sellars, W. (1963). *Science, perception and reality.* New York: Routledge & Kegan Paul.

Scheffler, I. (1981). *The anatomy of inquiry.* Indianapolis, IN: Hackett.

Schlick, M. (1932). Positivism and realism. In A. J. Ayer (Ed.), *Logical Positivism* (pp. 82–107). New York: The Free Press.

Schlick, M. (1934). The foundation of knowledge. In A. J. Ayer (Ed.), *Logical Positivism* (pp. 208–227). New York: The Free Press.

Skinner, B. F. (1948). *Verbal behavior.* Retrieved from http://www.bfskinner.org/BFSkinner/WJamesHefferline_files/William%20James%20Lectures.pdf

Sklar, L. (1974). *Space, time, and spacetime.* Berkeley, CA: University of California Press.

Smullyan, R. (2001). Gödel's incompleteness theorems. In L. Goble (Ed.), *Philosophical Logic* (pp. 72–90). Malden, MA: Blackwell.

Soames, S. (2003). *Philosophical analysis in the 20th century.* Volumes 1 and 2. Princeton, NJ: Princeton University Press.

Stalnaker, R. (1991). Propositions. In J. Garfield & M. Kiteley (Eds.), *Meaning and Truth*. St. Paul, MN: Paragon House.

Stekel, W. (1949). *Compulsion and doubt*. New York: Liveright.

Stevenson, C. L. (1937). The emotive meaning of ethical terms. In A. J. Ayer (Ed.), *Logical Positivism* (pp. 264–281). New York: The Free Press.

Stich, S. (1978). Scientific versus folk psychology. In D. Rosenthal (Ed.), *The Nature of Mind* (pp. 591–600). New York: Oxford University Press.

Stich, S. P. (1983). *From folk psychology to cognitive science: A case against belief*. Cambridge, MA. The MIT Press.

Stoudt, M. (2005). *The sociopath next door*. Retrieved from http://www.translibri.com/pdf/Sociopath_Sample.pdf

Strawson, P. (1950). On referring. In A. P. Martinich (Ed.), *The Philosophy of Language* (pp. 219–234). New York: Oxford University Press.

Taylor, K. (1998). *Truth & meaning*. Oxford: Blackwell.

Turek, F., & Geisler, N. (2004). *I don't have enough faith to be an atheist*. Front Royal, VA: Crossway Publications.

Van Fraassen, B. (1977). The only necessity is verbal necessity. *Journal of Philosophy, 74*, 71–85.

Van Fraassen, B. (1980). *The scientific image*. New York: Oxford.

Van Heijenoort, J. (Ed.). (1967). *From Frege to Godel: A source book in mathematical logic, 1879-1931*. Cambridge, MA: Harvard University Press.

Watson, J. B. (1924). *Behaviorism*. New York: Norton.

Wittgenstein, L. (1922). *Tractatus logico-philosophic us*. London: Routledge, Kegan & Paul.

Wittgenstein, L. (1958). *The philosophical investigations*. Oxford: Blackwell.

Wittgenstein, L. (1965). *The blue and the brown books*. New York: Harper Torchbooks.

Zhisui, L. (1996). *The private life of chairman Mao*. New York: Random House.

Index